US Army Corps of Engineers

FOREST SERVICE U.S. DEPARTMENT OF AGRICULTURE

U.S. FISH & WILDLIFE SERVICE / DEPARTMENT OF THE INTERIOR

NATIONAL PARK SERVICE / Department of the Interior

U.S. DEPARTMENT OF THE INTERIOR / BUREAU OF RECLAMATION

U.S. DEPARTMENT OF THE INTERIOR / BUREAU OF LAND MANAGEMENT

TVA

ALABAMA GAME & FISH

Arkansas Game & Fish Commission

VERMONT FORESTS · PARKS · RECREATION

WEST VIRGINIA DIVISION OF TOURISM AND PARKS / STATE PARKS

WASHINGTON DEPARTMENT OF WILDLIFE

KENTUCKY STATE NATURE PRESERVES COMMISSION

MICHIGAN AUDUBON SOCIETY / working for improved tomorrows

Confederated Salish & Kootenai Tribes   *A People of Vision*

The agency and organization symbols on this page are reproduced with permission. Their use does not imply an endorsement of this Guide by an agency or organization. Symbol accent colors match the *U.S. Outdoor Atlas & Recreation Guide* color codes and are not the official agency or organization colors.

U.S. OUTDOOR ATLAS & RECREATION GUIDE SECOND EDITION

D0887221

Houghton Mifflin Company

Boston   New York

1994

This Guide is dedicated to my son John Bruce the free spirit adventurer wherever he may be—
Praha, Budapest, Varna, Saint Petersburg, Beijing, Hangzhou, Ulaanbaatar, Vladivostok, or Hamilton.

Thanks to all who encouraged and assisted me in preparing this second edition of the *U.S. Outdoor Atlas & Recreation Guide.*

DATABASE DEVELOPMENT, DATA ENTRY, COMPOSITION, TYPESETTING and PAGE MASTERING - Stephen Goheen and Nick Hallett at Top Down Computer Consultants; Bobbi Dye; Peg Hampton at Ibid, Northwest; Lynne Dukelow, Ravalli Republic; DiAna Overlander and Glen Marlett at Parkwood Composition.
CARTOGRAPHY, PHOTOGRAPHY, MAP REPRODUCTION and COPY EDITING - Stewart D. Kirkpatrick, Janice Kirkpatrick, Ken Loucks and Patrice Loucks; Steve Slocomb; and Jack Dukleth at Missoula Blue Print Co.

HOUGHTON MIFFLIN COMPANY in Boston and New York - Marc Jaffe, my Editor; Chris Coffin, Managing Editor; Steve Lewers, Publisher.
PROTEUS INC. - David M. Rorvik, my agent.

AGENCIES, ORGANIZATIONS, their PERSONNEL, and OTHERS - The U.S. Forest Service, Marty Longan, Bob Earl, and Jean Szymanski. The U.S. Army Corps of Engineers, Judy Rice, George Tabb, Allison Smith, Debra Taylor, Billy Bridges, and Penny Schmitt. The National Park Service, Duncan Morrow, Merle Van Horne, and Rick Lewis. The U.S. Fish & Wildlife Service, Jan Carroll, Nancy Marx, and Mary Jo Collins. The Bureau of Land Management, Carol MacDonald, Bob Snyder, and Hugh Wolfe. The Bureau of Reclamation, Dick Crysdale. The Bureau of Indian Affairs, Gary Rankel. The Tennessee Valley Authority, Ellen K. Bean, Jack L. Dodd, and Hope W. Fine. The Nature Conservancy, their Field and Chapter Office personnel. The National Audubon Society, their sanctuary and nature center personnel. The Audubon Alliance member organizations and their personnel. The Association of Nature Center Administrators, Dr. Robert A. Thomas. The State Agencies, their headquarters, branch, bureau, department, district, division, region, and local office personnel. Suggestions from readers: Joan Kappel and Donald Lasher.

The following agency and organization professionals completed one or more of my Atlas questionnaires and agreed to my acknowledging their assistance. Their names are grouped by state and listed without a title or agency affiliation due to space limitations. My thanks also, to the hundreds of men and women who completed questionnaires and chose to remain anonymous.

ALABAMA - Doug Baumgartner, Linda Watters, Monica Moats, Steve Jenkins, Harry Stone. **ALASKA** - John Morris, Ronald E. Hood, C. Fred Zeillemaker, Evan V. Klett, Ted Heuer, Jr., Jay R. Bellinger, Dave Stearns, Paul Schaefer, Michael Rearden, John Carey, Paul McIntosh, Heather Johnson. **ARIZONA** - Max King, James H. Shores, Jr., Owen Martin, Stephanie Dubois, Milton Haderlie, Carrie Templin, Andy Loranger, Roger Castillo, Pete Weinel, Bob Dyson, Lofgne Guffey, Walt Scott, Barbara Alberti, Tom Danton, L. Greer Price. **ARKANSAS** - Elaine Sharp, Jeff Pawelczak, Martin D. Perry, Dennis Widner, Ernesto Reyes, Jr., Marvin T. Hurdle, Clark A. Dixon, Jr., Gary Hawkins, Roger Giddings, Robert J. Bridges, John M. Archer, Karen Hartman. **CALIFORNIA** - Nathan Caldwell, Gary Hathaway, Bonnie Petitt, Joan Wynn, Ernie Martinson, Gary Pingel, Jim Lipke, Fran Colwell, Greg Gnesios, Jean Hawthorne, Duane Siex, Sue Ellen Duree, Ray L. McCray, Mike Mitchell, R. Brian Kermeen, Bob Clopine, Dave Menke, Thomas J. Charmley, Marc W. Weitzel, Kevin Foerster, Denise Dachner, Carol Peterson, Gary R. Zahm, Sue Titchenell. **COLORADO** - Phil Zichterman, Eugene Patten, Jerre L. Gamble, Jackie G. Jones, James E. Jacobson. **CONNECTICUT** - Milan G. Bull, Judy Harpor. **DELAWARE** - Paul D. Daly. **DISTRICT OF COLUMBIA** - Lori E. McKenzie. **FLORIDA** - John Stiner, Mary D. Jones, Scott R. Eckert, Robin Will, Don J. Kosin, Ken Edwards, Yvonne Schutt, Kathy Whaley, Jim Bell. **GEORGIA** - Kent E. Evans, Jim Kidd, Louise Edwards, James Ogden, III, Rachel G. Schneider, Kent Cave, Patricia E. Metz, Skippy Reeves. **HAWAII** - Linda Moore, Richard C. Wass. **IDAHO** - Mel Fowlkes, Linda Strain, David Clark, District Ranger, Larry D. Napier, Richard Sjostrom, Brian Vachowski, Duane Annis, Jack Coyner, Carol Bond, Robert S. Gardner, Tom Geouge, Earl Baumgarton, James W. Simpson. **ILLINOIS** - Larry Wargowsky, Karen L. Drews, James N. Vincent, Al Novara, Andrew C. French. **IOWA** - Barry Christenson, Bruce Weber, Dave Aplin. **KANSAS** - Dave Hilley. **KENTUCKY** - Wesley D. Leishman. **LOUISIANA** - James E. Mic'ulka', Kelby Ouchley, M. Miller, Howard Poitevint, Mike Esters, Diane L. Borden, Kenneth L. Merritt, Eric Sipco. **MAINE** - Douglas M. Mullen, Raymond N. Varney. **MARYLAND** - Kenneth Nicholls, Larry G. Points, Maggie Briggs, Adam G. Karalius, Thomas Jones. **MASSACHUSETTS** - Michael F. Bradford, Thomas R. Comish. **MICHIGAN** - Michael Tansy, Joe Hart, Lynne Landon, Ed DeVries, Don Palmer, Neal Bullington, Anne Okonek, Jim Klus, Dick Anderson. **MINNESOTA** - Gary Tischer, Rick Yates, Thomas J. Larson, Sammy Waldstein, Steven W. Kallin, Dave Tucci, Betty Mc Swain, Mike Murphy, Ralph Lloyd. **MISSISSIPPI** - Randy Breland, Gail Bishop, Tom Prusa, Linda Gaumer, Daniel W. Brown, Gene S. Jackson. **MISSOURI** - Beatrix Treiterer, Ronald L. Bell, Ray Portwood, John Guthrie. **MONTANA** - Pat Gonzales, Bill Haglan, Jim McCollum, Cheryl Clemmensen, John Greer, Gerald Nelson, Jan Halverson, Judson N. Moore. **NEBRASKA** - Jon D. Kauffeld, Bradley W. McKinney, Warren Bielenberg, Mark Lindvall, Jerry Schumacher. **NEVADA** - Terry Baldino, Gary Schaffer, Hugh H. Null, Suzanne Coltman, Refuge Manager, Bruce L. Zeller, Chris Schoneman. **NEW HAMPSHIRE** - Steve Breeser, Jim Halpin, Gregory C. Schwarz. **NEW JERSEY** - Kelly Wolcott, Sylvia R. Pelizza. **NEW MEXICO** - Josie Salas, Lawrence A. Belli, Dwight Devereaux, Michael D. Wirtz, Allan Hinds, John Bruin, Dennis Trujillo, Bill Britton, Tom Smylie, Dan Lentz, Erin Connelly, Bill Moehn, Theodore M. Stans, Gary M. Stocz, John Mangimeli. **NEW YORK** - Kathryn A. Jahn, Don V. Tiller, Manny Strumpf. **NORTH CAROLINA** - Holly Jenkins, Larry Klimek, Marshall McClung, Charles Miller, Bill Lea, Lee Thompson, Donald E. Temple, Jim Savery, Dan Kincaid, Bonnie Strawser, James C. Ryan. **NORTH DAKOTA** - Michael Blenden, Tim Kessler, Brad McCord, Fred G. Giese, Donald Bozovsky, Dean F. Knauer, Mike McEnroe, Bruce M. Kaye, Paul C. Van Ningen, Harris J. Hoistad. **OKLAHOMA** - Berlin A. Heck, Rhonda S. Stewart, Marti Vigil, Bob Peters, James Smith, David Stanbrough, Rodney F. Krey. **OREGON** - Leigh Juve, Daniel M. Alonso, Forrest W. Cameron, Ester Clemence, Greg Stahl, Liz Rayno, Carrie Driskell, Donna Gress, Ray W. Frost, Kent G. Taylor, Henry M. Tanski, Jr., Richard J. Guadagno. **PENNSYLVANIA** - Janeal Hedman, Bob Dodson, Dick Nugent, Janet Mawin, Chuck Smith. **RHODE ISLAND** - Patrick M. Dorcus. **SOUTH CAROLINA** - Kay W. McCutcheon, Glenn W. Bond, Jr., Robert S. McDaniel, Jim Anderson, Patricia A. Ruff, Bill Craig. **SOUTH DAKOTA** - Terry Reetz, Kathryn Steichen, Mark Heisinger, Richard Gilbert, Joseph W. Zarki, David L. Gilbert, Bill Wilson, Thomas Casey. **TENNESSEE** - Reese Scull, Jim Wigginton, Ellen K. Bean, Bryan D. Schultz, Mike Ielmini, Lee Ellison. **TEXAS** - Melvin G. Maxwell, Allan, Deborah Nordeen, James M. Williams, Dom Ciccone. **UTAH** - Max Molyneux, Jay Banta, Diane Allen, Al Trout, Loyal Clark. **VERMONT** - Tony Bland. **VIRGINIA** - Lloyd A. Culp, Jr., John D. Schroer, Yvonne M. Schultz, Bart Truesdell, Buddie Chandler, Cynthia D. Snow, Stephen Chapman, Kathryn R. Hall. **WASHINGTON** - R. Bruce Wiseman, Anne M. Sittauer, Joni Quarnstrom, Penny Falknor, Maydene J. Ewer, James Lillie, Robert Edens, Jr., Bill Hesselbart, David E. Goeke, William Gleason, Mike McMinn, Tim Bertram, Harold E. Cole Jr. **WEST VIRGINIA** - Jerry Wilson, RM, Donald W. Campbell. **WISCONSIN** - Neil Hawk, Nancy L. Haugen, Mike Paremski, John Wilson, Niles Eilertsen, Roy Hitchcock, Brad Knudsen, Patti Meyers. **WYOMING** - Rick Schuler, Jane Gyhra, Earl O'Driscoll, Pat Thrasher, Greg Siekaniec, Mick Barrus, Fred A. Kingwill.

Book Design by John Oliver Jones

Library of Congress Cataloging-in-Publication Data

Jones, John Oliver.
  The U.S. outdoor atlas & recreation guide : a state-by-state guide
to over 5,000 wildlife and outdoor recreation areas / John Oliver
Jones. — Rev. ed.
     p. cm.
  Shows location of recreation areas on state road maps keyed to
information chart with directory.
  Includes bibliographical references and index.
  ISBN 0-395-66329-6
  1. Recreation areas — United States — Maps. 2. Recreation areas —
United States — Directories. 3. Natural areas — United States — Maps.
4. Natural areas — United States — Directories. 5. Outdoor recreation
— United States — Directories. I. Title. II. Title: U.S. outdoor atlas and
recreation guide. III. Title: United States outdoor atlas & recreation guide.
IV. Title: United States outdoor atlas and recreation guide.
G1201.E63J6 1994 <G&M>
338.78'0973'022 — dc20   93-46935
                                              CIP
                                              MAP

Printed in the United States of America

RMT 10 9 8 7 6 5 4 3 2 1

A Marc Jaffe Book

OUTDOOR ACCESS

The *U.S. Outdoor Atlas & Recreation Guide* gives you quick and comprehensive access to America's outdoors. It indicates popular outdoor leisure and recreation opportunities, and provides basic facts you need to make informed decisions about places you might visit. In some ways it is like a baseball or racing program, the ones you use to tell who the players are and their position or to judge and then wager on a horse.

My Access Definition

Access is having a way to visualize locations in relation to one another and the cities they are in or near. It is combining the outdoor recreation details from state and federal agencies and unique private and nonprofit organizations. It is quick access to the local telephone number, street address or post office box, and some location details or directions. It is basic facts organized and easy to find or compare.

The Access Solution!

The *U.S. Outdoor Atlas & Recreation Guide* answers your who, what, where, and when questions about outdoor recreation and wildlife viewing on public lands and selected private areas. It puts that information at your fingertips, giving you access to the professionals in charge of any part of America's outdoors in a minute or less—as quickly as you can dial a telephone number.

The special state road maps are your bird's-eye view of thousands of managed area and/or agency office locations. They are identified with distinctive color-coded and numbered symbols. The numbers are your key to condensed details about locations as provided in the Information Chart pages adjacent to the maps. The chart details are color-coded to match the map symbol colors.

Asking the Right Questions

With this Guide at hand, you will know what questions to ask when you telephone ahead. If you happen to be interested in nature study programs (1,164 locations in this Guide offer them) you will want to ask about program dates, hours, cost if any, and request a free program descriptive brochure if available.

Do you wish to observe or photograph wildlife? This Guide features 1,655 locations with wildlife viewing sites, blinds, or platforms.

You may want to inquire about observable species and ask if there is a free map showing site or blind locations. An agency professional can tell you the best season and time of day to view wildlife and if species are often within camera range.

Answers to your questions will often prompt you to ask other less obvious questions you would not have thought to ask in a letter. One significant advantage of this Guide is that it informs you about nature programs, guided tours, concessionaire services...so you will know if you should bother to call or visit.

Have you ever made a spur-of-the-moment weekend trip decision? Is an agency Information Office or Visitor Center open Saturday or Sunday? A total of 1,397 locations answered yes to this Guide question. The people on weekend duty can tell you about current conditions, unusual recreation opportunities, direct you to a choice campsite, a trail suitable for hiking when younger children are with you, or suggest a productive fishing stream.

New Guide Features

Are you interested in lakeside recreation and boating? This edition features U.S. Army Corps of Engineers, Bureau of Reclamation, and Tennessee Valley Authority offices and recreation areas across the United States. More than 800 of these locations have been added to the state maps and are listed in the Information Chart pages or chapter notes.

Chapter notes compliment the maps and charts. They summarize chapter coverage, give details on special opportunities and the agencies, and now incorporate the special city/agency and outdoor map indexes, and feature a new wilderness and wild river index.

Have you ever wondered who is in charge of America's federal wilderness areas and wild and scenic rivers? Larger rivers and wilderness areas have been added to the maps and 602 are indexed in the state chapter notes with a cross-reference to appropriate federal agency offices. If you desire a wilderness or wild river experience anywhere in the United States, now the people in charge of access and who issue public use permits are only a phone call away.

Do you have a growing concern about the environment, perhaps want to add to your knowledge or stimulate the interest of your school age children or grandchildren? Almost

300 selected local non-profit sanctuaries and nature centers have been added to the chapter notes. They may offer seasonal or year-round daytime or evening education programs, and weekend tours or outings for children and adults.

Are you interested in Native American culture and tribal land recreation opportunities? More than 100 new areas with permitted outdoor activities have been added to the chapter notes.

Is your travel and recreation budget limited and are you trying to stretch your hard earned dollars? A new Information Chart heading (question) is used to signify places with "no charge" campgrounds or campsites available either year-round or seasonally, another indicates if there is any entry fee.

One new heading is used to show whether or not "free" literature is available. A quick inexpensive phone request will usually put the details in your mailbox in just a few days.

Do you want current information about the national scenic and historic trails or national marine sanctuaries? Agency offices and private organization information sources are featured in the Agency Profiles and chapter notes.

Disability Provisions

A special new symbol in the Information Chart pages augments the Americans With Disabilities Act of 1992 by helping to identify outdoor recreation opportunities and facilities. This symbol is employed to indicate drinking water, restrooms, and concessionaire services availability. It also identifies recreation opportunities including accessible interpretive trails, wildlife viewing sites or blinds, agency tours, picnic and camping areas, fishing sites, boating facilities, and more.

When the new symbol appears beside a charted telephone number it indicates a TDD device (a telephone device for the deaf) is available or that you can have someone call for the direct TDD-line phone number. The internationally recognized TDD designation for teletypewriters is TTY.

A Few Words of Caution

Changes in recreation opportunities are continuous. They may be caused by natural disasters such as floods, hurricanes, earthquakes, tornados, and fires, which can destroy access roads and visitor facilities. Agency budget considerations and visitor numbers (crowding) may limit permitted activities and visitor hours or bring about temporary closure of an area. Reinventing government may result in closing or adding new office locations, and higher fees.

Although there are hundreds of thousands of questions and answers provided in this Guide, every possible area of interest to a recreationist could not be included. If you want to take a pet along (as I do my dog Augie, photo), ask about pet rules and regulations or if pets are permitted.

It is always a good idea to contact or visit the local agency or organization office for the latest visitor information, free literature, and rules and regulations before your trip, or visit the local office and talk with the agency personnel in person. You will be glad you did.

John Oliver Jones

JIM WILLIAMS PHOTO COURTESY DESIGN TEC

HOW TO USE THIS GUIDE

The best way to learn to use this guide is to read these highlights pages and examine the illustrations. They illuminate guide content and coverage, map and information chart features, the importance of the chapter notes, and the special indexes. Agency Profiles follow the highlights pages. They profile the agencies that manage America's outdoor recreation lands—fully one third of the United States.

All the question headings on the Information Chart pages and the map and charted answer symbols are explained here. Some question and answer variables are described and comments by local professionals featured. They are included to help clarify the scope of the opportunities available and enable you to communicate more effectively with agency personnel about your specific interests.

Communicating can make a difference. Did you know the descriptive terms used by agencies and nonprofit organizations do not always mean the same thing? Definitions and meaning vary depending on who is using a term, or on your own interpretation, or common sense.

For example, primitive camping may be defined by one agency as a campsite without a picnic table, barbecue grill, or running water. Another agency may describe primitive camping as pitching a tent in the wilderness or in some clearing within an area or park that has no campground or amenities.

Swimming is high on the list of favorite recreation activities. If you choose to swim, common sense should be your guide. Swimming is permitted at many places where there are no lifeguards, and in Alaska if you really want to swim there.

The American Heritage Dictionary defines "backcountry" as a sparsely inhabited rural area. Many agency people and writers use the term backcountry when referring to a federal wilderness, or when writing about hiking in remote or roadless areas where there are no inhabitants for miles around.

Free "backcountry byway" leaflets are available from some agency offices. A backcountry byway may be a trail, an unimproved road passable with four-wheel drive during good weather, an improved gravel road, or a combination of the three, meandering for miles through an uninhabited area, a ghost town, or a remote community.

Sample map and Information Chart page segments featuring descriptive call-outs are illustrated in these highlights pages.

MAP SYMBOLS & COLOR CODES AGENCIES & INITIALS

Agency map symbol and color code and the chart symbol and letter code legends in the illustrated chart segment on page 6 are repeated on all chart page spreads for quick reference.

Numbered symbols on the maps and the symbol numbers in the chart pages or chapter notes are color-coded to indicate a specific agency or organization. Agency initials are sometimes used in the guide to save space in the charts or special indexes.

Federal Agency Coverage
U.S. Forest Service (USFS)
National Forests & Other Areas (Light Green)

The triangle symbol and color code indicates National Forest Offices including forest Supervisors (NFS), Ranger Districts (RD) and the forests or parts of forests they manage. National Grasslands, Monuments, and Recreation Areas managed by the USFS and major Visitor Centers are included. Most symbol (office) locations are situated within or near the land area under their jurisdiction. Some offices manage USFS land areas in an adjacent state.

In this Guide a special color-coded official USFS map titled *Guide to Your National Forests* (pages 18-19) shows the USFS locations, including forests and grasslands. The USFS regional boundaries and headquarters locations are indicated, and the national scenic and historic trails are also featured.

U.S. Army Corps of Engineers (COE) Lakeside Recreation Project, District Offices & Areas (Pink or Light Red)

This COE logo symbol and color code identifies COE District and Project Offices and Lakeside Recreation Areas (LRAs). Most LRAs contain more than one recreation site. The sites within an LRA, or all of the area, may be managed by the COE or another local, state, or federal agency through a cooperative agreement. COE Project Offices function under a COE District Office that may be located in an adjacent state.

U.S. Fish & Wildlife Service (USFWS) Refuge Division National Wildlife Refuges & Offices (Medium Blue)

The National Wildlife Refuges (NWR), Refuge Complex (RC), Wetland Management District (WMD), and Waterfowl Production Area (WPA) offices, are identified with this shield symbol and color code. A few locations that are new or closed are not in this Guide because they are not set up to handle visitors or inquiries at this time.

Map call-outs: STATE WILDLIFE AGENCY OFFICES & WMA'S; MAJOR LANDMARKS; PRIVATE PRESERVES, SANCTUARIES, & NATIVE LANDS; USFWS NATIONAL WILDLIFE REFUGES; MAP COORDINATES & GRID LINES; STATE PARKS; RIVERS & LAKES; WILD RIVERS; U.S. ARMY COE SITES; COUNTY, STATE, & INTERSTATE HIGHWAYS; WILDERNESS AREAS; ADJACENT STATE; MAP SCALE SHOWN IN MILES & KILOMETERS; NATIONAL PARK SERVICE LOCATIONS; NATIONAL FOREST SERVICE LOCATIONS - FOREST SUPERVISORS & RANGER DISTRICTS; BLM OFFICES & SPECIAL RECREATION AREAS

National Park Service (NPS) Parks & Other NPS Locations
(Pink or Light Red)

The square symbol and color code is used to identify the twenty different types of locations managed by NPS. They range from battlefields to parks to a few of the many wild and scenic rivers, and one location category called "parks other." NPS category abbreviations are featured in the "yellow abbreviations block" on these pages and are often used in the Information Charts as part of NPS location names.

Larger, more accessible NPS locations may have several visitor centers, thirty different telephone numbers, and millions of visitors each year. Park literature and maps cover these details. The name, address and telephone number for NPS locations with limited or no "outdoor" recreation opportunities are given in the chapter notes. *Note:* The NPS color code is the same as the color used for U.S. Army Corps of Engineers Lakeside Recreation Areas.

Bureau of Land Management (BLM) Areas & Offices (Tan or Light Brown)

The BLM State, District, and Resource Area (RA) Offices that administer BLM lands are identified with this BLM logo symbol and light brown color code. Special Recreation Management Areas (SRMAs) or Special Recreation Areas (SRAs) are locations with unique or improved recreation opportunities.

SRAs or SRMAs are symbolized on the maps and listed in the Information Chart pages under the managing office. The BLM Wild Horse Adoption Centers in the eastern U.S. are symbolized on the appropriate state maps and listed in the respective charts.

In this Guide a special color-coded *Bureau of Land Management Resource Map* of the western U.S. (page 22) shows the location of BLM lands and District and Resource Area boundaries. The BLM State and District office locations are indicated.

Bureau of Reclamation (BR) Recreation Areas and Tennessee Valley Authority (TVA) Recreation Areas & Offices
(Medium Blue)

This oval symbol and color code identifies both Bureau of Reclamation and TVA recreation areas and offices. The same symbol and color code is used because the areas administered by these two agencies are not in the same states. *Note:* USFWS locations (shield symbol) also utilize the medium blue color code.

TVA sites (lakeshores) are located in the southeast in Alabama, Georgia, Kentucky, Mississippi, and Tennessee. The numerous privately managed areas and facilities along TVA lakeshores in those states and in North Carolina and Virginia are not listed in the Guide.

Bureau of Reclamation recreation areas are found in the western states (Arizona, California, Colorado, Idaho, Kansas, Montana, Nebraska, Nevada, New Mexico, North Dakota, Oklahoma, Oregon, South Dakota, Texas, Utah, Washington, and Wyoming). A number of them overlap state lines. The recreation areas are symbolized on the maps and listed in the chapter notes. Regional Office details appear in the notes.

Federal Wilderness Areas (shaded areas on the maps)

Wilderness areas are located in most states and are named and symbolized on the state maps space permitting. Some comprise separate land areas and may overlay state lines. A wilderness area may be under the jurisdiction of several different agencies. They are listed in the wilderness index in the chapter notes and are cross-referenced to appropriate agency offices.

Wild Rivers (bold blue river line on the maps)

Wild rivers are featured in many states. A few flow through tribal lands. Like wilderness areas, a wild river may be under the jurisdiction of several agencies. Wild rivers are listed in the wild river index in the chapter notes and are cross-referenced to appropriate agency offices. Several are managed by National Park Service offices featured in the Information Chart pages.

Other Federal Agencies

Some federal agencies have nontypical outdoor recreation areas and/or information offices. They are listed in appropriate state chapter notes and include: National Marine Sanctuaries managed by the National Oceanic and Atmospheric Administration of the U.S. Department of Commerce (USDC); the main U.S. Geological Survey offices and Earth Sciences Information Centers. These agencies, and the Department of Defense military base recreation opportunities (fishing, hunting, and wildlife observation) are described in the Agency Profiles pages that follow.

National Trails

National trails are managed by the Bureau of Land Management, U.S. Forest Service, and National Park Service. Trail locations are indicated on the USFS map (pages 18-19) and Alaska, Florida and Wisconsin maps. Access and descriptive information is included under the "National Trails" heading in the Agency Profiles (page 24) or the chapter notes. The names and locations of private organizations active in national trail related activities are provided.

Note: Puerto Rico, U.S. Virgin Islands, and other United States possessions or protectorates outdoor recreation areas managed by various federal agencies are not covered in the Guide.

State Agency Coverage

Some states use separate agencies to manage parks, forests, inland and marine fisheries, wildlife, nature preserves, or heritage areas. Others combine two or more areas of responsibility under a single agency. The agency name usually indicates this. Examples are: Kansas Wildlife & Parks, Massachusetts Division of Parks & Forests, and Montana Department of Fish, Wildlife & Parks.

Agency management responsibilities are covered in the state chapter notes when necessary for clarity. Variations are described in these highlights pages under "State Chapter Notes," and in the Agency Profiles. Guide coverage of state lands is typically of selected sites or offices due to space limitations.

State Parks (SP) & Offices
(Lavender or Purple)

This hexagon symbol and color code identifies state parks. Most are managed by on-site rangers or conservation officers. State park locations may be called by other names such as State Recreation Areas (SRA), Historical Parks (SHP), Marine Parks (SMP), or Resorts (SR).

State Fish & Wildlife Areas & Offices (Orange)

This exaggerated "D" shape symbol and orange color code identifies the Headquarters (HQ) and Region or District Offices, selected Wildlife Management Areas (WMA), Game Management Areas (GMA), Heritage Areas (HA), and sometimes areas with other designations. Depending on the state, areas may be managed from headquarters, region, or district offices, or by an on site field office. In Pennsylvania different agencies manage wildlife and freshwater fisheries (see below).

Special State Agency Coverage
(Medium Blue)

The round symbol and medium blue color code (color code also used for NWR, BOR, and TVA locations) identify the following lands and agency offices. The Florida Aquatic Preserves, Hawaii Natural Area Reserves, Pennsylvania Fish Commission Offices and Fish Culture Stations with visitor facilities, and Kentucky Nature Preserves. The chapter notes have the details.

Other State Agencies

Some states bordering the Atlantic or Pacific oceans or the Gulf of Mexico have a separate agency or division responsible for marine fishery resources. A state may have an agency that manages preserves, sanctuaries, or natural areas. The headquarters offices are listed in appropriate state chapter notes.

Private & Nonprofit Organizations

The organizations selected for listing in this Guide have large land holdings or play a significant role in nature education and/or in preserving the environment and endangered species for future generations.

Preserves, Sanctuaries, Nature Centers & Tribal Lands (Yellow)

This diamond symbol identifies Native American Tribal Land Areas (TLA), The Nature Conservancy Preserves (TNC), National Audubon Sanctuaries (NAS), Independent Audubon Sanctuaries (IAS), and Independent Nature Centers (INA).

Before continuing, take a minute now to examine the illustrated map segment on the facing page. The highlights continue on the next few pages where the Guide information charts are explained and illustrated.

USING THE INFORMATION CHARTS, CHAPTER NOTES & INDEXES

The information charts, chapter notes, and indexes contain a wealth of information to help you plan trips and enjoy America's outdoors. The illustrations, photos, and comments by agency professionals complement the information presented in these highlights.

Symbol Numbers & Map Coordinates

Use the symbol shapes, numbers, and color codes on the maps to locate agency or nonprofit organization areas or office names on the Information Chart pages. The numbers appear under the S# column in the charts. In reverse, the map coordinates in the MAP column enable you to find a numbered symbol on a map.

A few locations in the charts or chapter notes do not have a symbol on the map due to space limitations. This is usually when two or more offices for one agency (typically U.S. Forest Service or BLM offices) are located in the same city. Their symbol numbers in the chart pages always have a star ★ next to them.

The purpose of this star ★ convention is apparent as you view the area around Missoula (map illustration on page 4 bottom left). There is no USFS triangular symbol with the number 49 on the map to indicate the Missoula Ranger District of the Lolo National Forest (symbol 48). Here you would use the map coordinates B1 appearing next to symbol ★49 in the chart segment below to locate Missoula.

In the charts, locations are grouped by agency as shown in the Information Chart illustration on this page. Color codes on the charts match symbol colors on the maps. As an aid to those who have difficulty identifying different colors, the symbol shape is featured with the first number listed in each agency group in the chart.

Note: There is a note in the Information Chart heading on each chart page spread. It reminds you to use the map coordinates instead of the symbol number to locate an area whenever a symbol number has a star ★. The note also reminds you to refer to the yellow abbreviation block on page seven (top right) for common sense location name and address abbreviations.

Location Name

The first location name for an agency group in the chart pages is always **in bold print**. For example the first U.S. Forest Service National Forest or Regional Office, or the first U.S. Army Corps of Engineers Lakeside Recreation Area or District Office listing. *Note:* When state abbreviations appear in parentheses after a federal agency location name the area managed overlaps state lines.

Indented Names

In the Information Chart segment illustration, notice how the Beaverhead Forest and Dillon Ranger District office names are indented or offset under the USFS Northern Region (see S# 1). This feature is used to indicate jurisdiction or management levels in the charts. Offices or land areas under a senior or administrative office are indented under the appropriate location name. In the illustration they show three USFS management levels, region, forest supervisor, and ranger district.

The indents or offsets let you know who a secondary contact might be if a district (or refuge, etc.) you want to contact has moved and the mail forwarding order is expired, or the telephone number changed and calls are no longer being transferred to a new number. Simply contact the parent office.

How do you know if there is no one to assist you at a location listed in the Guide? There will be no mailing address or zip code listed, and the space in the chart column under the angled heading "Info Office (IO) / Visitor Center (VC)" will be blank. The blank space indicates "no" if there is no information office or visitor center.

A number of the locations featured in the Guide do not have an office or visitor center. In the chart illustration (USFWS National Wildlife Refuge medium blue color code) the Hailstone and Lake Mason NWR locations are described (no street address). In the chart illustration both refuges are indented under Charles M. Russell NWR, the parent agency office you would contact for details about visiting either refuge.

Address Data & Location Details

This information appears after the location name in the Information Chart. For many offices, as well as remote sites like the USFWS Hailstone NWR, location details or directions have been provided by the agency. These details may be stated as part of the address, or appear in brackets after the city name or zip code.

Area Codes & Telephone Numbers

Note the **telephone** number for Hailstone and Lake Mason NWRs is the number for C.M. Russell NWR, the office with management responsibility for these two smaller unmanned NWRs. A remote refuge, wildlife area, or preserve may be a few or more than 100 miles from the local agency office with jurisdiction.

The telephone numbers listed in this Guide are usually for the local agency information office. Some locations asked to have their visitor center telephone number listed instead of the office number.

When the disability provisions symbol appears to the left of the telephone area code it

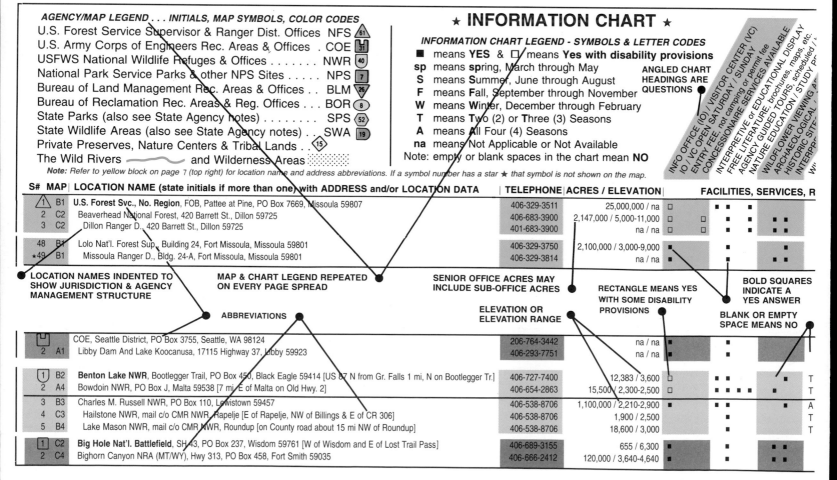

means there is a TDD (TTY) device available for callers. In many cases the TDD telephone number is the same as the office number and in others a dedicated line is available. Due to space limitations dedicated TDD lines are not included in this Guide and you need to call and request the dedicated line number.

Calling For Information

When is the best time to call most places for information? Early in the day is best, or between 9:00 a.m. and 3:15 p.m. in the local time zone. Some agency offices do not open until 9:00 a.m. Others close as early as 3:30 p.m. Summer hours may be longer at busy locations like parks. During the weekend if an information office of visitor center is open the business hours may be shorter than weekday hours. The privately managed nature centers are usually open on weekends and may be closed on Monday and/or Tuesday.

In the next few years there are likely to be a great many changes in area code numbers. There are now about 150 different area codes in use in the U.S. and 640 new ones may be added to the telephone system by the end of 1995.

Acres / Elevation

These figures provided by the agency offices are subject to change as land is acquired, traded, or sold. Some acre figures combine scattered parcels or districts under a senior office. Examples are National Forest (Supervisor) listings, USFWS Waterfowl Production Areas, and BLM state and district office jurisdictions.

A **na** in place of any acreage or elevation details in the chart indicates the information was not provided by the agency or is not significant.

Some locations provided information on elevation range. For example, the Beaverhead National Forest elevation range is 5,000–11,000 feet. High elevation figures are an indication of lower air density, temperature variation, and a potential rapid change in the weather.

Facilities, Services, Recreation Opportunities & Conveniences

The angled headings at the top of each chart page spread represent 34 questions. Vertical color-coded bars and horizontal lines are used to guide your eyes to answers to those questions for each location listed in the chart pages in the Guide.

Answers are condensed in the charts using the answer codes and symbols defined in the legend repeated at the top center of every chart page spread. Together with the location details, telephone number, and acres/elevation data, the charts contain over a quarter of a million answers.

Some answers are given using a season code. Most simply indicate a yes or no answer while others also indicate if there are disability provisions. An answer may prompt you to call ahead or stop and ask other obvious questions. For example, what types handicapped-access facilities are available? Is there a cross-country ski trail brochure? Are there horsepower limits for motorized watercraft, and what are they? Is an off-road-vehicle-use area map available?

ABBREVIATIONS
Abbreviations covered elsewhere in the text are not repeated here.

A.	Area	Nat'l	National	Rec.	Recreation
Assn.	Association	NB	Nat'l Battlefield	Reg.	Region
Ave.	Avenue	NF	Nat'l Forest	Reqd.	Required
Bldg.	Building	NFS	Nat'l Forest Supervisor	R or Rt.	Route
Blvd.	Boulevard		or Nat'l Forest Service	RMA	Recreation Mgt. Area
cm	centimeters	NG	Nat'l Grassland	RR	Rural Route
Cr. and CR	Creek and County Road	NHP	Nat'l Historic Park	RV	Recreational Vehicle
D. or Dist.	District	NHS	Nat'l Historic Site	S	South
Dr.	Drive	NL	Nat'l Lakeshore	San.	Sanctuary
E	East	NM	Nat'l Monument / Memorial	Sat.	Saturday
Fed.	Federal	NMP	Nat'l Military Park	SRA	Special Rec. Area (small)
FO	Field Office	no veh.	no vehicles	SRMA	Special Rec. Management
FOB	Federal Office Bldg.	NP	Nat'l Preserve or Park		Area (large)
Geo.	Geological	NPS	Nat'l Park Service	St.	Street
GMA	Game Management Area	NRA	Nat'l Recreation Area	Sup.	Supervisor (Forest)
Gr.	Grassland	NS	Nat'l Seashore	Svc.	Service
HA	Heritage Area	NWSR	Nat'l Wild and Scenic River	U.S.	United States
HQ	Headquarters	Off.	Office	USFS	U.S. Forest Service
Hwy.	Highway	PO	Post Office	USFWS	U.S. Fish & Wildlife Service
km	kilometers	Pre.	Preserve	USGS	U.S. Geological Survey
L.	Lake	R.	River	VC	Visitor Center
Mgt.	Management	RA or Resource A.	Resource Area	W	West
mi.	mile(s)	RC	Refuge Complex	WMA	Wildlife Management Area
N	North	RD or Ranger D.	Ranger District	WMD	Wetland Mgt. District
Nat.	Natural	RS	Ranger Station	WPA	Waterfowl Production Area

Condensed Chart Answers & Season Codes

In the charts, the yes symbol ■ (a solid black square) means **YES**. Fifteen questions (angled headings) may be answered using the disability provisions symbol □ (a rectangle) meaning the answer is yes; and yes there also are *some* disability provisions. Empty spaces in the chart pages represent a **NO** answer. An **na** in the charts means "not applicable" or information was not provided by the agency or organization.

Disability Provisions Symbol

The rectangle symbol □ indicates one or more persons, facilities, or some special equipment is available to assist those with one or another type of physical disability. The TDD equipment described earlier is one example. Providing access to those with disabilities is an ongoing process and you always need to call ahead or stop at the office or visitor center for current disability provisions (access) information.

Disability provisions are too diverse and numerous to list. Some examples are boardwalks, trails, observation decks or portions of same with wheelchair access, Braille trails, guided tours, concessionaire-operated facilities, equipment, etc.

Season Codes

Six of the questions (angled chart headings) may have a season answer. Season codes are used when "yes" or "no" is not the appropriate answers to a question. The letter codes used to indicate seasons are shown and described in the chart legend at the top center of each chart page spread and in the illustration at left. Keep in mind the season code letters and months they represent are an imprecise guide to seasons. Local climate, elevation, and other considerations will affect "real time" season duration.

For example, wildflowers may bloom in two seasons, spring and summer, but only during the last two months of spring (April and May), and the first month of summer (June). In this case a **T** code would appear indicating two seasons. The question **no-charge campgrounds/sites** might be answered **T** for spring, summer and fall (March through November), but in fact apply from May first through the end of September,

---

the actual period when a no-charge campground is open for public use.

For outdoor recreation answers a season may be obvious, or the best or only season to do something. Personal preference, rules and regulations (fishing and hunting are examples), or your vacation or holiday time may determine the season when you visit.

Angled Chart Headings

Each angled heading (question) in the illustrated information chart segment shown on the next page is numbered for easy reference to the 34 corresponding numbered question and answer explanations (pages 7-15). Question interpretation and rules and regulations can vary among the agencies and at individual sites. Explanations differ in length and are sometimes augmented with quotes by agency professionals.

1. **Information Office (IO) / Visitor Center (VC)?** The main local official source of current recreation information, usually with some disability provisions. A place to secure local maps and directions. Most information offices are not open on weekends and are closed on federal or state holidays. Visitor centers are usually open year-round except on major holidays.

   In the Guide, information office is used in a generic sense. Agency and nonprofit organization offices often serve multiple purposes: they may be administration and information offices; have a visitor center and a bookstore, and may feature displays or audiovisual presentations.

   Most locations in this Guide are offices. A receptionist is usually able to answer your questions and provide and explain literature, maps, and rules and regulations. They may refer you to a recreation specialist or another local office if they are unable to help you.

   Comments from professionals at these information offices indicate how contacting an office for current information can add to your recreation opportunities and enrich your visit. Some quotes show the scope of recreation possibilities, while others include tips on access or note local rules and regulations.

From Arthur L. Seamans, Assistant Area Ranger, USFS, Hells Canyon National Recreation Area, Clarkston, Washington: *"The Hells Canyon National Recreation Area is very large with many diverse opportunities, from RV camping at developed sites to wilderness and wild and scenic rivers. It contains 652,488 acres, of which 214,000 acres are wilderness; 67 1/2 miles of wild and scenic river with segments of the Imnaha, Snake, and Rapid rivers; several developed campgrounds; portions of two states (Idaho and Oregon) with offices in three (Idaho, Oregon, and Washington); and numerous historic and prehistoric sites, lifezones from subalpine to semidesert over very short horizontal distances containing all of the plant and animal communities found in each. No one answer can describe the area or its opportunities."*

From Terry Lewis, Chief, Public Affairs, Bureau of Land Management Eastern States Office, Alexandria, Virginia: *"We have responsibility for very little surface acreage in comparison to the western BLM offices, and none of the lands we administer are developed for recreation use. However, our offices gladly provide information about BLM opportunities in the west. Most weekends, we hold wild horse and burro adoption center programs at different locations in the eastern states."*

The following quote shows the breadth of outdoor recreation opportunities in two USFS Ranger Districts, and how change is continuous. The quote is contained in a letter from Rhonda Stewart, a recreation specialist at the USFS Choctaw Ranger District office, part of the Ouachita National Forest in Oklahoma. The office is one mile south of Heavener, Oklahoma (west side of Highway 259).

The Visitor Center will be open on weekends from May through November. However, the main office will normally be closed on weekends. Our new staff has considered keeping the office open on the following weekends: Memorial Day; Labor Day; opening of major hunting seasons, including both weekends of the deer-gun season; and the weekends before and after the fourth of July. This will be done on a trial basis and continuation will be dependent upon (the number of) visitors using this service.

We have an office/information center at the Cedar Lake Camping Area that will be open weekdays and weekends from May through September.

There are two newly designated wilderness areas—Black Fork Mountain Wilderness (4,583 acres) and Upper Kiamichi River Wilderness (9,691 acres). These are signed for nonmechanized access. We also have two walk-in turkey areas (one is 2,500 acres, the other 1,500 acres), which are also signed. We also have a major roadless area, which is not signed, but happens to have no other access available except on foot or by horse or mule.

A large portion of the area (forest) is accessible by vehicles. The general forest area does not require any permit, fee, or permission for use or access. However, fees are required in our three established camping areas. A special permit is also required for hang-gliding, any activity in which the organizers are charging a fee, and many competitive rides.

There are three major highways, and a scenic drive within the forest boundaries which can be driven in any type of vehicle. However, we also have 150 miles of unimproved dirt roads. On these, we recommend four-wheel-drive, high-clearance vehicles for most of the year.

We have comfort stations and water fountains available at our three camping areas, and at the nature center, which is on Skyline Drive. There are none available in the general forest area.

There are two designated Day Use Only areas in Cedar Lake Campground. One is for equestrian access, the other for swimming, picnicking, and hikers. These are closed between the hours of 10:00 p.m. and 6:00 a.m. The general forest area is open 24 hours.

A note from the District 5 Office of the Ohio Division of Wildlife concerning Paint Creek State Park and Wildlife Area provides an example of several recreation areas located contiguous to one another: a state park and wildlife area, and the Lakeside Recreation Area, managed by the COE. *"There is no state-run information office or VC. The U.S. Army Corps of Engineers (COE) operates a VC at Paint Creek Lake."*

2. **IO / VC Open Saturday / Sunday?** An important bit of seasonal information for spur-of-the-moment trips or weekend travelers. Being open weekends depends on the area, the agency, and often the season. Be sure to call ahead and ask about the weekend hours that may be short during the off- season and long in season, usually summer.

Offices or visitor centers at private preserves or sanctuaries may be open on weekends and closed Mondays and/or Tuesdays. When an agency office is open on Saturday/Sunday, it usually means there are a lot of visitors to the area or seasonal visitation is substantial, for example, during the hunting season, the summer, or the winter season in the southern part of the United States.

Season answers may not be indicative of exact months a VC or office is open. Weekend hours vary depending on the agency or organization and the season. There may be different or extended office or VC hours, typically when there are more daylight hours. Here are a few answers and comments on the weekend question by agency personnel.
"Our office is open Saturday only."
—Vicki C. Grafe, Cross Creeks NWR, Dover, Tennessee.
"One visitor center is open from Memorial Day through October, seven days a week. Another visitor center is open yearlong, seven days a week."—Rachel G. Schneider, Public Affairs Assistant, Chattahoochee-Oconee National Forests, Gainesville, Georgia.
"In 1992 we constructed a new visitor center, two new interpretive trails (one handicapped access), observation towers, auto (tour) route displays, and made major modifications in our program for the visiting public."—Dave Hilley, Quivira NWR, Stafford, Kansas.

3. **Entry Fee, not camping or permit fee?** The fee collected as you enter an area. May be a per person, per family group, or per car fee and may only be collected during the summer season. *"Entrance fees (good for seven days) are collected at various locations within the park from May through September."*—Maurie

---

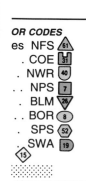

OR CODES
es NFS 61
. COE 31
. NWR 40
.. NPS 7
. BLM 26
.. BOR 8
. SPS 52
.SWA 19
15

★ **INFORMATION CHART** ★

INFORMATION CHART LEGEND - SYMBOLS & LETTER CODES
■ means **YES** & □ means **Yes with disability provisions**
sp means **sp**ring, March through May
S means **S**ummer, June through August
F means **F**all, September through November
W means **W**inter, December through February
T means **T**wo (2) or **T**hree (3) Seasons
A means **A**ll Four (4) Seasons
na means **N**ot **A**pplicable or **N**ot Available
Note: empty or blank spaces in the chart mean **NO**

ddress abbreviations. If a symbol number has a star ★ that symbol is not shown on the map.

th ADDRESS and/or LOCATION DATA | TELEPHONE|ACRES / ELEVATION| FACILITIES, SERVICES, RECREATION OPPORTUNITIES & CONVENIENCES   S#

Sprague, Information Specialist, Olympic
National Park

4. **Concessionaire Services Available?**
Concessionaires are private contractors
who provide various services under an
agreement with a federal or state agency.
Concessionaires may offer rooms, meals,
guided tours, raft or pack trips, or other
recreation related services or facilities.
Concessionaire, facilities, programs, and
guided activities may include provisions
for those with disabilities. Ask for details.

At certain locations there are a variety
of concessionaire services available to
visitors. In addition to hotels, restaurants,
laundry services, and rental equipment,
and horses, some provide guide services
for all types of recreation—fishing,
hunting, hiking, trail rides, overnight
camping trips, and other programs.

Concessionaires are under contract with
the agency at each location and contracts
are reviewed and renewed, sometimes
every year. Often concessionaire services
are only available during part of a year or
season. White-water raft trips, for
example, are only available when water
conditions are safe.

The following comment on
concessionaire service availability is from
Bruce M. Kaye at Theodore Roosevelt
National Park, Medora, North Dakota.
*"The only concessionaire services we offer
are horseback rides and pack trips, which
are available from May through
September."*

5. **Interpretive or Educational Display?**
Indicates one or more unmanned displays
may be enjoyed by visitors. Most are
found inside or near the entrance to an
information office or visitor center.
Displays may be part of a kiosk and
located in the field at a trailhead,
campground, or picnic area.

6. **Free Literature, brochures, maps, etc.?**
Descriptive recreation or educational
literature that may or may not include a
local map and directions. A national park
or forest may provide numerous brochures
totaling more than a hundred pages of
recreation details. These items may consist
of typed pages, a quarterly newspaper, or
a bound book or booklet. There are
hundreds of thousands of pages of free
recreation information available to the
public. Pictured in the photo (top right) is
a selection of joint agency literature,
which is developed when two or more
agencies join forces to combine and
publish recreation information and/or
maps.

When asking about literature, be sure
to explain your specific interests and
needs. The amount of published
information and its content and coverage
is extraordinary. Literature comes in all
shapes and sizes and there may be a small
charge for some items. There is a great
variation in the amount of local
information literature may contain, within

the same agency and among different
agencies.

A national park might send you a
quarterly newspaper containing a schedule
of events, a foldout map, and leaflets on
fishing, seashells, flowers, and various
concessionaire services. However, they
would not include any trail guides,
wildlife checklists, or USGS Park or
Quadrangle maps sold at the Visitor
Center. As a cost recovery measure many
agencies charge a fee for some literature
that used to be available without charge,
and they have increased the prices on
maps and books.

Within state agencies, one region or
district may have comprehensive
recreation literature or maps that are not
available or have not been prepared for
every region or district. The same is true
for National Forest, BLM, and National
Wildlife Refuge offices. The amount of
literature available in a given office varies
according to the number of visitors each
year, special features or facilities in an
area, budget constraints, and other factors.
One response to the Guide questionnaire
included a cover letter with the following
comments concerning literature and
visitation from Penelope J. Falknor,
Recreation Information Specialist, Mt.
Baker-Snoqualmie National Forest. *"I am
sending you a copy of our forest visitor's
map, forest recreation report, information
about the Forest Service/National Park
Service Outdoor Recreation Information
Center, and a brochure listing our
developed campgrounds. We will soon
have a TDD hookup in the Information
Center."*

7. **Agency Guided Tours, scheduled / by
reservation?** These are not the
concessionaire-operated tours. Park rangers
often conduct regularly scheduled tours in

season. Guided tours may only be
seasonally available, require reservations,
be limited to tour groups, and there may
be a fee, or a donation suggested. At some
locations tours may be limited to student
groups, and may take place outdoors,
underground, and/or indoors depending on
the type of location or agency. Ask about
disability provisions.

8. **Nature Education / Study Programs?**
Educational programs available to
individuals or groups, students and/or
adults, usually seasonal and requiring a
reservation. May be conducted indoors
and/or outdoors. Some may be weeklong
or evening programs. There may be a
program fee to cover materials or to
provide a stipend for the program leader.
Some programs and related facilities have
disability provisions. *"We do have agency
guided tours and nature education / study
programs, respectively, but they are not by
reservation."*—Larry G. Points, Chief of
Interpretation, Assateague Island National
Seashore

9. **Wildflower Viewing Area or Drive?**
Specific area or route where abundant
wildflowers may be seen when walking,
hiking, or touring by car in season.

Most areas are not signed, indicated on
a local map, or in a brochure. Ask about
their location, for directions, the best roads
or trails you may take to reach them.
Those with a serious interest in
wildflowers or other plant species should
inquire about flower and plant species
lists.

Wildflower seasons are noted in the
chart. In areas where there is a significant
variation in altitude, the season may begin
early in the spring at lower elevations. As
the weather grows warmer wildflower
viewing opportunities will be found at
higher elevations.

At locations with a temperate climate, wildflowers may be common all year. It is best to view or photograph flowers so that other visitors can also enjoy them. Many areas do not permit picking wildflowers. Some may be endangered species while others could be toxic.

Be sure to ask if picking flowers is permitted before doing so, and for your own protection do not pick flowers you are not familiar with. An early appreciation of nature's beauty and bounty often starts with wildflowers, as shown in the photo taken in western Montana.

10. **Archaeological / Geological Sites?** A dinosaur dig, prehistoric ruin, earthquake or volcanic area, etc. Some sites may combine both. There could be two or more sites managed from one office. Ask about literature, guided tours, and educational programs. For the larger areas, as in a forest, ask for maps, directions, and specifics about disability provisions.

11. **Historic Sites?** One or more buildings, outdoor areas, or both. Be sure to ask about descriptive literature, guided tours, educational programs, or disability provisions.

12. **Interpretive Trails?** Marked trails with descriptive or numbered, and sometimes color-coded signs. An interpretive guidebook, booklet, or leaflet may be available that describes stops along the trail, viewing highlights, and time required to walk the full trail length, portions of same, or shortcuts. There may be disability provisions.

13. **Wildlife is Abundant or Common?** Wildlife is considered abundant or common when in the judgment of local professionals you have a better-than-average chance of observing species in their natural environment. Positive

seasonal answers mean a local professional indicated wildlife species are abundant or common during part or all of the season or seasons indicated.

Keep in mind a wildlife professional has years of outdoor experience and a practiced eye. They know where and when to look for wildlife. Some agency offices maintain a daily log of species sighted by the staff or reported by visitors. Ask about current sightings and the best times and areas to see specific species.

At some federal and most state agency wildlife office locations, mounted wildlife specimens are on display. Why call ahead about wildlife abundance and access? Marvin T. Hurdle, refuge manager at White River National Wildlife Refuge, commented: *"Wildlife is common year-round. However, the refuge is subject to annual flooding and much of it may be inaccessible. We recommend that visitors call ahead about current water conditions."*

14. **Endangered Species are Common?** A positive seasonal answer means endangered species are abundant or common and may be observed without endangering them. At some locations, usually preserves, a positive answer to this question may apply to endangered plants.

Want to know which wildlife species are endangered or threatened? The U.S. Fish & Wildlife Service publishes the book *Endangered & Threatened Wildlife and Plants* (see USFWS literature photo on page 20). It is revised every year or two; the last edition was published in 1992. Species are listed with their common and scientific names, historic range, and where and whether they are threatened or endangered.

The following comments emphasize the

importance of asking local agency personnel for information about protected species. *"We have bald eagles in the spring."*—Harold E. Cole, Jr., Conboy Lake NWR, Glenwood, Washington. *"At LeFleur's Bluff State Park, you may observe protected species any season."*—Dianne Manton, Louisiana State Parks, Baton Rogue, Louisiana. *"Endangered species are present but not abundant."*—Robert Shank, Mount Saint Helens National Volcanic Monument, Amboy, Oregon.

Here is a comment by Kimberly A. Johnson at the Parker River National Wildlife Refuge about permitted visitor activities during the shorebird nesting period. *"The beach is closed from April first to approximately July first to protect threatened shorebird species (piping plover and least tern nesting). Visitors may still walk or bicycle on the road, walk the nature trails, and observe wildlife in other parts of the refuge during that period."*

15. **Wildlife Viewing Sites, blinds, signs, etc.?** A yes answer means there are one or more specific locations or areas with better than average wildlife viewing opportunities.

Sites or viewing routes may be signed. There may be photography or hunting blinds or viewing platforms. Locations include seaside overlooks where whales might be observed during their migration, a spot beside a roadway that overlooks an area where eagles congregate during the spawning season to feed on salmon, or at higher elevations in the western United States, a place where mountain goats or sheep have been observed regularly during summer months.

A number of Audubon Society Education Centers and sanctuaries, Nature Conservancy Preserves and National Wildlife Refuges have special viewing areas, platforms, blinds, and feeding areas where wildlife may be seen in abundance during periods of a day, season, or year. Ask the local professionals about special viewing sites and opportunities when you visit. The photo of visitors on an observation platform with abundant waterfowl in the background (page 11) was taken at the DeSoto National Wildlife Refuge near Missouri Valley, Iowa. Of course, not all viewing areas have signs. Ask about wildlife viewing opportunities and locations, literature describing viewing opportunities, wildlife checklists, and disability provisions.

Wildlife checklists are used by visitors to learn what specific species to look for. A checklist may feature season abundance codes and have habitat codes as well. A National Forest bird species checklist might contain information on woodland habitat for each species. Others include birds, amphibians, reptiles, and other species in one list. Bird lists are the most common, followed by plant lists.

Checklists are based on accumulated information provided by wildlife professionals and amateurs who contribute sighting reports and survey information. These data become part of the general body of knowledge about wildlife abundance in an area. Lists may be published by the agency, a local nature group, or a cooperating association. Sometimes a small fee is charged to cover printing cost.

You can use a checklist to record your observations of wildlife species and then return your marked list to the office. It will be used to contribute to the collective knowledge concerning species abundance or population swings, and also in revising checklist information.

JIM FRATES PHOTO COURTESY USFWS

16. **Developed Picnic Areas / Sites?** Locations with one or more tables, perhaps barbecue grills, running water, restrooms, trash receptacles, or shelters. Inquire about disability provisions. Picnicking may only be allowed at designated sites. A number of preserves and sanctuaries in the Guide do not have picnic facilities or may not permit picnicking. You need to know if it is okay to stop and eat while you are enjoying an outdoor adventure. Always ask about rules that may apply: there may be special rules. For example, at a private preserve or sanctuary guests may only be allowed to picnic if they are accompanied by a member.

If you wish to picnic, ask if it is a permitted activity. This comment is by Frank Drauszewski at the Chassahowitzka NWR in Florida: *"Picnicking is seasonal at our Passage Key NWR."* When you plan a picnic, don't forget to carry out what you carry in.

17. **Developed Campgrounds / Sites?** More than half of all agency campgrounds are not listed in commercial campground directories. The larger areas listed in this Guide often have several campgrounds. When the answer is yes to this question, ask about campground literature and site maps, fees, restrictions, rules, and permits; check on disability provision specifics if necessary.

You may need to reserve a campsite at a popular campground, especially during the busy season. A campground may be partially restricted to tent camping. Sites may have hookups and most agency people who answered yes to this question

indicated they had some sites with water and/or electrical hookups. Sites may not accommodate larger RVs (recreational vehicles).

At some campgrounds sites are available without reservations. At others camping is only available to organized groups with reservations. Chickamauga and Chattanooga National Military Park at Fort Oglethorpe, Georgia, is an example. Most campgrounds with reserved campsites also have amenities like comfort stations and water fountains.

18. **No-charge Campgrounds / Sites?** A campground may have a limited number of "no fee" unreserved sites available seasonally or year round. There may be an exclusively no-fee campground. Ask about the rules, how long you can camp if you wish to stay for several days or longer. No charge may mean primitive camping outside a campground area or within one.

The term primitive camping is used in various ways. It may be a campsite without amenities or a place to roll out your sleeping bag or pitch a tent beneath a tree. Here are some comments by agency personnel about camping in Florida. *"Primitive and tent camping is allowed during hunting season only at our Apalachicola WMA."* —Lieutenant Stan Kirkland, Florida Game & Fresh Water Fish Commission, Northwest Region, Panama City.

"Primitive camping is allowed on park islands and permits are required. The only island access is by private boat." —Lisa Garvin, Public Information Officer, Biscayne National Park, Homestead.

In the photo a primitive camp is being set up among the trees in the Bitterroot-Selway Wilderness in western Montana. *Note:* There may be a charge for a permit

ROY LOWE PHOTO COURTESY USFWS

at some locations or during peak visitor periods. The permit rules are made for our collective long-term benefit. Some of the reasons for permits are to control the number of people in an ecologically sensitive area, to keep track of people entering difficult or dangerous terrain, or to limit the use or consumption of natural resources.

19. Wilderness Areas / Wild Rivers? Federal wilderness areas and wild and scenic rivers are designated by Congress. Vehicles are not allowed and other use restrictions apply. The wilderness and wild and scenic river index in the state chapter notes features local information sources.

An area or river may be under the jurisdiction of more than one local agency office. A few wild rivers have their own National Park Service office and are listed in the Information Charts. Wilderness areas are typically unimproved land and roadless but there may be old abandoned roads. Wilderness access is restricted to foot traffic and horseback. Special rules may apply to boat use on wild and scenic rivers. Contact the appropriate local office for details. The number of visitors may be strictly limited in some areas.

People with health problems or who are not in good physical condition should keep in mind rescue vehicles have little or no access to wilderness areas. Helicopter access could be limited due to local weather conditions or rough terrain.

Be sure to secure a topographic map of the wilderness area you plan to explore. Let others know the date and time you plan to go and return, and your route of travel. Leave a copy of your route map behind with a friend or the authorities. If a permit is required to enter an area, report your return promptly to the local permit

issuing authority.

These two comments from agency professionals concern the wilderness/wild river question in the Guide. *"We would like to clarify our NO answer to the Wilderness Area question. Though we do have a primitive backcountry area, including the 42-mile Lakeshore Trail component of the North Country National Scenic Trail, it is not a Congress-designated wilderness area."*—Brenda J. St. Martin, Public Affairs Officer, Pictured Rocks National Lakeshore, Munsing, Michigan

Michael D. Wirtz with the Santa Fe National Forest Supervisors Office in Santa Fe, New Mexico, said, *"All of our forest districts have a wilderness area located partially on them; on the Santa Fe National Forest the four designated wilderness areas are over nineteen percent of the forest acreage. We also have three of New Mexico's four Wild & Scenic Rivers and a scenic byway."*

20. Walking / Hiking Trails? Walking and hiking (photo, top left) are the most popular outdoor recreation activities. The difference in hiking is distance traveled when walking (a hike takes longer). Some consider foot travel a hike if the trail is difficult.

You may want to carry a daypack or backpack. In a wilderness area or in rough terrain you should carry basic survival and first aid gear in your pack. Some of the areas in this Guide are small and level, ideal for a leisurely walk and there is no need to carry extra gear.

At some locations reservations are required, as this comment by Richard C. Wass, the refuge manager at Hakalau Forest NWR in Hawaii, indicates. *"Visitors should call for reservations to*

hike or hunt. It is important for them to close the gate securely when they enter or leave. A four-wheel drive is needed on the roads inside the refuge."

21. Swimming Permitted, at one's own risk? At most locations swimming is at your own risk, and often restricted to designated (posted) areas. Swimming may be permitted in northern (cold) waters but is not recommended by some of the agency personnel who answered yes to this question. A lifeguard is more likely to be on duty at swimming sites in parks during the busy season. In answering this question, Stephen L. Dyer at the New York State Office of Parks, Recreation and Historic Preservation, had this comment: *"Swimming permitted **only** while guards are on duty at Moreau Lake State Park, near Ganservoort."*

22. Bicycling Opportunities, areas, trails? Some people consider an old logging or back road a trail. Mountain Bike trails are also covered by this question. Be sure to ask if bicycle trails are marked, about trail guides or brochures, and if mountain bike use is permitted and where.

23. Horseback Riding? Yes means bring your own horse. This question does not apply to concessionaire services which may include rental horses or those organized trips on horseback that some concessionaires offer to visitors.

Personnel at many locations where horseback riding is allowed were concerned about readers thinking a yes answer meant you could rent a horse. When the answer to horseback riding is yes in an information chart, be sure to ask at the office or visitor center about trailhead locations, camping facilities, marked trails, and if horses are available locally through a guide, outfitter, or concessionaire.

Hikers should learn about right-of-way rules if they encounter horseback riders on a trail, especially trails with a dangerous dropoff. Some parts of a trail may only accommodate one-way traffic; it is a good idea to inquire about this possibility.

In the western states there are a number of volunteer horsemen and horsewomen who ride with search-and-rescue teams. People on horseback can cover about five times as much ground as a person on foot. They have often helped save people who are lost, especially in wilderness areas.

24. OFF-ROAD Motorized Vehicle Area / Use OK? If you want to use an ORV (or All Terrain Vehicle, ATV) or are concerned about motor noise, inquire about ORV use areas, snowmobile or dune-buggy trails, signs, vehicle types permitted, horsepower use restrictions, special maps or trail guides. Some geographic areas or time periods may be set aside for ORV use, while other areas may be especially designated for year-round use. If you are not an enthusiast you may wish to avoid areas where their use is permitted. *Note:* A new term in use is "off-highway vehicle." Many dunebuggies are licensed for street and off-highway use.

Here are some examples of ORV use restrictions mentioned by agency personnel. Robert Shank at the Mt. Saint Helens National Volcanic Monument in Amboy, Oregon, said the monument is restricted to snowmobile use only. At the Santa Monica Mountains National Recreation Area in Agoura Hills, California, only mountain bikes are permitted. And at Delaware Seashore State Park, between Rehoboth and Bethany in Delaware, the park superintendent, Kurt Ruether, indicated ORVs were only permitted on the beach to facilitate surf fishing access.

Of course some people who own them use their four-wheel- drive trucks off-road as ORVs. In northern locations, agency roads may not be passable in a four-wheel-drive truck during winter months and periods of heavy or drifting snow, especially at higher elevations.

Note: A four-wheel- or all-wheel-drive passenger car drive system is not the same as that used to equip trucks or ORVs. Passenger car systems are designed for highway use in bad weather. Trucks typically have different gear ratios to facilitate travel on rough dirt roads and for off-road use (cross-country or beach), and also higher ground clearance to facilitate back road and off-road travel.

25. **Fishing Allowed in Season, license / permit required?** If fishing is permitted, you must comply with licensing requirements and size and catch limits. If the yes symbol indicates disability provisions, ask for details about lake or streamside access and facilities.

Today, a number of states have a free fishing day during which a fishing license is not required. Some agencies and organizations may require purchase of a special license or permit to fish at a specific location. This fee may be in addition to the state fishing license requirements.

Size and catch limits that are unique to an area, and different than those in the published state regulations could be in effect. At some locations at times of the year, or for certain species, a state or local guide or concessionaire may restrict anglers to catch-and-release fishing.

Note: Local sporting goods stores do not usually have all state agency—published fishing information, and rules and regulations may not be available late in the season. State agency offices are the best sources for fish hatchery, lake and river stocking data, current regulations, and mid-season changes. Be sure to ask about local conditions. There may temporary catch limits due to low water or other problems.

Here is a comment on new fishing opportunities by John Stasko, chief at the Branch of Facility Management, USDI, Fish and Wildlife Service, Patuxent Wildlife Research Center (Patuxent NWR) in Laurel, Maryland: *"We recently built a fishing pier at Cash Lake, which has not been fished since 1957. We issue limited number of fishing permits a day during the season. Permits are issued to those who apply using a lottery system."*

In the fishing photo, a boy and his grandfather team up to land "the big one" on Hurricane Lake in central Florida.

26. **Boating Facilities, ramps, marinas, etc?** Ask for specific information about facilities and the current water level where you plan to use your boat before you travel any distance to a put-in site. A raft or canoe launch area may not have a ramp that will accommodate a boat trailer. Check on specific disability provisions if needed. The chart yes answer may indicate their availability.

In response to the Guide questionnaire, the following comment was received from the Obed Wild & Scenic River office in Wartburg, Tennessee. *"We have a launch area for canoes only."*

27. **Motorized Watercraft OK, check limits?** Ask about horsepower restrictions, boat licensing, use and equipment regulations. Some locations may only allow the use of electric motors, or jet boats.

Motorized watercraft may be permitted where there is no boat ramp or launch area (facility) at a listed location. When boating facilities is answered no and motorized watercraft yes in an information chart, it indicates a launch area may be found at another federal or state agency location or a public marina. The following comments about motorized watercraft indicate the importance of asking about motorized watercraft use and restrictions.

"We answered no on boating facilities, yes on motorized

watercraft because only outboard jet units of limited horsepower can be used on our waters. Few people travel with this type of vessel."—Arthur L. Sullivan, Superintendent, Ozark National Scenic River in Missouri.

"Personal watercraft, hovercraft, airboats, and floatplanes are prohibited in refuge waters."—Jim Bell, National Key Dear NWR

"Jet-skiing is not allowed in the park."—Pat Tolle, Everglades National Park

"Some areas of the refuge are limited to 25 horsepower motors." —Vicki C. Grafe, Lacassine NWR

"Motorized boats are only allowed on the larger lakes located in our forests. Smaller lakes are limited to electric trolling motors, rowboats, or canoes."—Rachel G. Schneider, Chattahoochee-Oconee National Forests, Gainesville, Georgia

"Boat use is limited to hunting season only. This also applies to the use of boat launch areas."—W.C. Kent, Outdoor Recreation Planner, Klamath Basin Refuges for the Tule Lake NWR in Tulelake, California

28. **Non-Motorized Watercraft OK?** Includes canoe, kayak, raft, row, and sail craft. Inquire about seasonal

considerations, hazards, and river classification. It may not be possible to sail, canoe, or raft at some locations.

Water classification on rivers may vary a great deal within a few miles, be safe for the novice along one area, and very dangerous for beginners at another. The use of one or more types of watercraft may be permitted, or could be restricted as indicated by these comments by local professionals.

"All watercraft use is restricted to the period between March first and November first only. This also applies to fishing."—Cheryl Buckingham, Mattamuskett NWR, Swanquarter, North Carolina

"You can canoe, raft, and row, but not sail. Motorized watercraft are restricted to less than 51 horsepower."—Dean F. Knauer, Upper Souris NWR, Foxholm, North Dakota

29. Hunting Allowed in Season, license / permit required? You must comply with state and federal gaming laws, licensing, local permit, and check station requirements.

There are many different hunting situations, special rules and regulations, types of permits, and permit drawings. When hunting is permitted on National Wildlife Refuges, there is usually a limit to the number of people, weapon types, hunting days, and hours. These considerations and restrictions are in addition to state agency game or hunting regulations.

Game and nongame species populations may be at an all-time high in some areas, may be cyclical, and in decline at others, often within the same state. There are many uncontrollable circumstances and continuous changes in the field of wildlife

management. When hunting is allowed, be sure to secure the current rules and regulations, and fulfill all applicable licensing and permit requirements.

30. Winter Sports Opportunities? This includes cross-country and downhill skiing, snowboarding, ice skating, snowmobiling, sleigh rides, and other winter sports. Inquire about activities, facilities, and any special interests you may have, including dogsledding (mushing).

In mountainous areas, ask about avalanche conditions and dangerous areas near or along designated trails. Some snowmobile trails cross or share a part of a cross-country ski trail. Be sure to ask about trail guides and off-road vehicle use on or across ski trails.

31. Park & Walk-In Only Area? Typically a small area where you must leave your vehicle in a parking lot or off the road and walk in. Some areas have disability provisions or may be larger areas with no road access at all. It is a good idea to inquire about parking, signs, etc.

This question does not apply to federally designated wilderness or backcountry areas where vehicles are prohibited, nor to signed areas within a park, refuge, or forest, recreation area where access may be temporarily, seasonally, or permanently closed to all but official vehicles.

Some of the larger areas featured in this Guide have no road access. According to Gene S. Jackson at the National Forests in Mississippi office in Jackson, Mississippi, there are a number of locations with developed recreation sites that are located in a walk-in only area of a forest. In some cases an area may be closed to ORVs, except on designated

trails. Seasonal access can be a consideration as indicated by the following comments.

"The Quincy Lakes Wildlife Area near George is walk-in only during the winter," according to Robert D. Kent, a manager with the Washington Department of Wildlife. Bob Ratcliffe with the BLM Salem District Office in Salem, Oregon, said, *"The Wildwood Special Recreation Area near Welches is walk-in only from October first to April fifteenth."*

32. Day-Use Only? A yes answer to this question means day-use is the only use permitted anywhere within the area. This typically applies to National Wildlife Refuges, private sites, to parks or wildlife management areas where camping is not allowed, and to agency offices. A day may be defined as sunup to sundown or during specific hours. At some sites this could be as late as midnight.

There are a number of outdoor locations where visitors may use specific campgrounds and/or parking areas all night while other parts of the area are closed to public use after dark or at a specific time.

Here are some comments on day-use only and some exceptions. R. Terry Virgin, a member of the recreation staff at Deschutes National Forest in Bend, Oregon, said, *"There are some developed sites in the forest that are day-use only and spending a night in one of them could result in a violation notice."* James Smith, the manager at Wichita Mountains Wildlife Refuge in Indiahoma, Oklahoma, commented, *"This refuge is primarily for day-use only. The permitted activities after dark are camping in a designated campground, fishing, and driving through on a main roadway with no stopping to view wildlife."* Karen May McKinlay-Jones at the Natural Bridges National Monument at Lake Powell, Utah, described their rules on day-use as follows: *"Day-Use Only means there is no use in this park after dark except the campground. Basically, that means our bridge-view drive is closed."* Finally, Jerry Y. Shimoda at the 182-acre Pu'uhonua o Honaunau National Historical Park at Honaunau, Kona, on the island of Hawaii, had this comment: *"This park is open from 6 a.m. to midnight."*

33. Drinking Water? A positive answer means drinking water is available in the field, along a trail, at a campground or recreation area. The photo shows an older type water fountain being used by a young camper. If disability provisions are indicated please ask for details. Some water fountains may be accessible and others not.

Fountain water may be pumped from a well by hand, have a pressurized electric pump, or come from a free-flowing spring. Drinking water may be available in a campground area, at a scenic overlook or along a trail or roadway. If you do not

carry water with you, ask where fountains are located and note those locations on your map.

In colder climates when frozen water could cause damage to a pump or fountain, the water is shut off except during warmer weather. Some places have year-round free-flowing thermal spring water available.

Drinking water availability in the chart pages does not usually apply to agency offices or visitor centers. However, there are some agency offices with visitor exhibits or outdoor recreation facilities that have drinking water.

34. Restrooms? Toilet facilities at recreation or camping areas, a trailhead, rest area, or along an auto tour route. May be portable facilities and only available seasonally. Most locations have some facilities with disability provisions but some do not.

STATE CHAPTER NOTES AND SPECIAL INDEXES

The state chapter notes complement the state maps and Information Chart details. State note contents are described here in these highlights pages. The notes cover a great many important access and information details. They begin with a summary of agency locations in a state followed by the "**City/Agency Index.**"

The city/agency index lists cities alphabetically with the agency offices or areas situated in or close to each city, and with their symbol numbers and map coordinates. Because it is not technically possible to color-code agency locations in the index, the listings are coded with the agency initials used in the "agency legend" located at the top of the chart pages. Use the initials to determine the parent agency (and color code). Example, the NFS initials indicate a National Forest Service location (refer to the top of the chart illustration on page 6).

Federal Agencies

The City/Agency Index information in the chapter notes is followed by "Federal Agencies" information and comments that does not fit the pattern used in the Information Chart listings. Often the notes clarify administrative responsibilities and list or describe useful literature or unique recreation and education facilities and visitor information centers.

U.S. Forest Service Regional Office jurisdictions are noted because those offices are usually your only source for every forest or wilderness map for all forest areas in a region.

U.S. Army Corps of Engineers division and Bureau of Reclamation regional office locations are in the notes. They are sources for recreation area literature and special maps.

National Wildlife Refuge and Refuge Complex Offices may administer separate or contiguous lands extending for hundreds of miles in several states. The notes tell about the Upper Mississippi River National Wildlife & Fish Refuge headquarters in Wisconsin and their Refuge District offices in Illinois, Iowa, Minnesota, and Wisconsin. The twelve river-area "Pool Maps" are mentioned; they are very

helpful for local access along the upper Mississippi River.

More than 160 National Park Service sites are listed in the notes under "Additional NPS Locations." They are typically memorial, monument, or historical locations that offer mostly indoor or limited outdoor facilities.

The National Oceanic and Atmospheric Administration National Marine Sanctuaries are listed under "USDC, Natl. Oceanic & Atmospheric Admin. (NOAA)." Some of the federal agency and private trail association offices for the National Scenic and Historic Trails are listed under "National Trails."

Wilderness & Wild River Index

This index follows Federal Agencies' details. It ties wilderness and wild river names to appropriate agency offices listed in this Guide. The office names are followed by a map symbol number and coordinates in parenthesis. You can use the symbol number to find the office name, address, and telephone number in the charts, and the map coordinates to locate it on the state map.

A larger wilderness may be located within the geographic jurisdiction of several offices while several may be within the area managed by a single office. More than one agency may manage parts of a longer wild river. Some of these listings refer you to an agency or private organization listed only in the chapter notes, or to an office in another state.

Outdoor Map Index

The "Outdoor Map Index" lists official outdoor maps published by the U.S. Geological Survey (USGS) for selected national parks, plus the U.S. Forest Service maps. The Bureau of Land Management recreation maps are described and "intermediate scale" maps are shown graphically and the map names printed within the blocks of a grid overlay on state outlines.

These maps have topographic details, land

ownership and recreation information, and are available at low cost from relevant local agency offices. They may be purchased by mail and most local offices will send you a map order form covering maps they have on hand. You will need to specify the map name and type of map to secure the correct map.

The BLM and USFS maps come in various sizes and shapes. The photo on this page shows several USFS forest maps, a Ranger District map, and a typical map order form. The top photo on page 16 shows representative BLM intermediate scale, resource, recreation maps.

Map prices range from $1 to $6, are subject to change at any time, and have been increasing. Most of the more expensive maps are made of waterproof materials. USFS maps are $2 or $3 while the USGS National Park and BLM maps are currently $4 each. There is no space in this index to list every map, especially the USGS maps.

USGS information: For those who are not familiar with the USGS or their mapping activities and map availability, a brief description is provided here. The USGS produces and sells a larger selection of maps in more sizes and styles than any agency or private organization in the world. They prepare special maps for more than twenty federal agencies. Two types of USGS maps most useful for outdoor recreation are 7.5- and 15-minute quad maps, and 55 the national park maps listed in the Outdoor Map Index.

The USGS recently estimated the replacement cost of cartography for their 57,000 7.5- and 15-minute quad maps at $2.5 billion dollars. Their quad maps are available for 95 percent of the land area in the United States. Each 7.5-minute quad map covers an area ranging from 31,360 to 44,800 acres.

The quad maps cover a set number of degrees and inches of latitude and longitude (lines) on the curved surface of the United States. You can see how the lines move closer together on a

globe as you look from the equator toward the North Pole and the area between the lines gets smaller. Thus quad maps for portions of the southern United States cover more acres than northern quads.

If you were to spread all of the USGS quad maps on a flat surface edge to edge, they would cover almost six football fields. A third of them, roughly 20,000 maps, provide a close-up view of parts or all of the locations listed in this Guide.

In the USGS related photo below there is a fourteen-inch-high stack of free USGS state indexes and catalogs. The state of Alabama index, catalog, and the map grid are in the right side of the photo. The pictured guide to "Topographic Map Symbols" is your key to understanding USGS quad map symbols. Each index lists about a thousand or more quad maps, and other special USGS maps like the national park maps. Smaller states that are adjacent to one another are grouped in a single index. New Hampshire and Vermont are examples.

How do you find out which quad map you need? By using the appropriate state index. Simply call 1-800-USA-MAPS and ask them to mail you a free state index and catalog. Catalogs include map ordering information and a list of local USGS map dealers. Most quad maps cost $2.50. Be sure to ask for the Topographic Map Symbols Guide, for quad maps do not contain a comprehensive legend. These and other USGS maps are available at USGS offices and Earth Science Information Centers (ESIC) listed in the chapter notes.

State Agencies

Following the outdoor maps index details the chapter notes feature "State Agencies" information and comments. States differ in management structure and

the authorities and responsibilities assigned to their various agencies. Many states manage outdoor and wildlife resources under a parent conservation or natural resource agency or both (Missouri). Others have stand alone agencies or commissions in charge of certain public recreation lands, facilities, and resources, such as the separate Pennsylvania Fish Commission and Pennsylvania Wildlife Commission.

Some states combine what could be considered dissimilar responsibilities under one agency, for example, the Montana Department of Fish, Wildlife, and Parks, and the Maryland Department of Forests, Parks, and Natural Heritage. The chapter notes clarify obscure management variations that are not obvious from the agency name. They feature the name,

address, and telephone number of the other important agency offices not covered in the information chart pages. They are included in the notes to enable you to secure information about other state owned or managed outdoor recreation locations, and a states marine resources.

The chapter notes may describe site or area lists and booklets or special maps. One example is the special five map series ($10) covering outdoor recreation opportunities in Utah.

A few state agencies have more than a dozen local (regional or district) offices while others have professionals with local jurisdiction who work from their homes. These facts are provided in the chapter notes.

For state agencies that have them, the agency magazine title, cover and subscription prices, and publication frequency is given. The magazines are available at the agency offices listed in this Guide. Subscription and cover prices are subject to change.

The name, address, and telephone numbers of state tourism agencies or visitors bureaus are listed in the chapter notes. Do you want the latest state tourism agency vacation package? In most states the package is revised every year and it usually includes a large foldout map of the state. The maps provide more local detail than you will find on a typical road atlas map and they are a necessity when exploring out-of-the-way places and finding shortcuts or scenic routes to your ultimate destination.

State forest agency headquarters offices are listed in the notes with a comment about recreation programs.

Private Organizations

The state chamber of commerce and appropriate conservation organization listings complete the notes. You will find more than 100 tribal land areas and almost 300 Nature centers featured. The centers offer free or low-cost nature observation and education opportunities and most are in or near metropolitan areas.

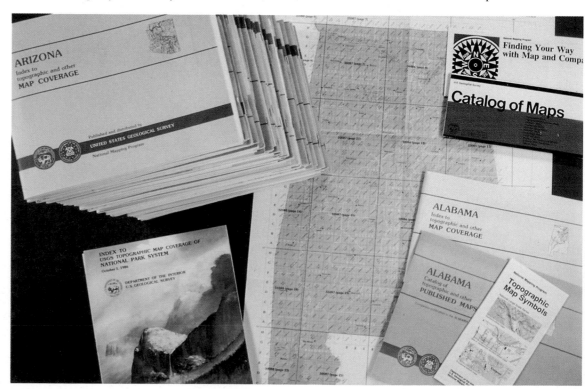

The agency profiles give you a thumbnail sketch of federal agencies and private organizations featured in the Guide. State agencies are covered under state park, forest, and wildlife management agency headings.

FEDERAL AGENCIES
U.S. Forest Service (USFS)

This branch of the U.S. Department of Agriculture is the largest provider of outdoor recreation opportunities on federal land in the United States. The U.S. Forest Service administers more than 191 million acres of national forests, grasslands, and a few recreation areas and monuments. The National Forest System Map on pages 18-19 provides a visual perspective of USFS lands.

The agency cooperates and works with state and local governments, private landowners, the forest industry, and foreign governments (international forestry) in forest management and a other activities, including wildlife management and enforcement of game laws. Research activities focus on the entire field of forestry and wildlife management.

The national forests and other USFS areas are managed locally from Ranger Districts or Ranger Station offices under the supervision of the Forest Supervisor's offices. All are covered in this Guide along with about fifty significant visitor centers (see the chapter notes) and the nine regional USFS offices.

A national forest may consist of separate land areas. One example is the Custer National Forest. The Supervisor's office in Billings, Montana, manages forest land areas and three grassland areas in three states out of seven local Ranger District offices. Geographically, the land segments extend from east-to-west for 650 miles. The elevation low point is under 1,000 feet at Sheyenne National Grassland in North Dakota, and Granite Peak at 12,799 feet is the highest point in Montana.

The local offices are your best source of current information about recreation opportunities and facilities, and road and fire conditions on or adjacent to USFS land. Most office location signs along a highway feature the Forest Supervisor or Ranger District name. However, the ranger station name may be the featured or prominent one on a sign. Stations often serve as the headquarters for a Ranger District.

Ranger District/Ranger Station offices are usually responsible for part of a forest and/or all of a grassland. In the eastern states a Ranger District may manage all of a forest and a Forest Supervisor office may administer a number of national forests in a state or a multi-state area through the local district offices.

One or more USFS offices are within a day's drive from wherever you live within the lower 48 states; local personnel are glad to help visitors. They issue various types of use permits and answer questions about access to lakes, rivers, streams, new campground facilities and trails, and open or closed forest roads. Incidently, foot traffic is usually permitted on closed forest roads.

National forest maps and brochures describing recreation opportunities and facilities in a forest or district are available at the offices. There are thousands of pages of free literature available. In the top photo a visitor is using one of six massive volumes that comprise the Lolo National Forest *Recreation Opportunities Guide* (ROG).

ROG's contain specific site and trail use information and may have hundreds of small maps of trails or showing camping or fishing site access within a forest. Many of our national forests have ROG's. The receptionist can copy a page or two for you and help you plan access to a site or trail using the large local forest Visitor or Travel Map. The Visitor Maps are listed under Outdoor Map Index in state chapters.

Most USFS campgrounds are not listed in typical campground directories available at newsstands or book stores. Neither are cabins and lookout towers that may be rented for a day or up to a week or two. The bottom photo shows the diversity of USFS literature, including a variety of trail guides, directories to cabins and campgrounds, cross-country ski trails, and hunting areas.

One unique USFS facility is the Aerial Fire Depot (ARD) and Visitor Center located in Montana. It is just north of Missoula adjacent to the Missoula County Airport. Guided tours of this world-renowned smokejumper headquarters and training center are conducted during the summer months. The ARD address and telephone number are given in the Montana chapter notes under U.S. Forest Service.

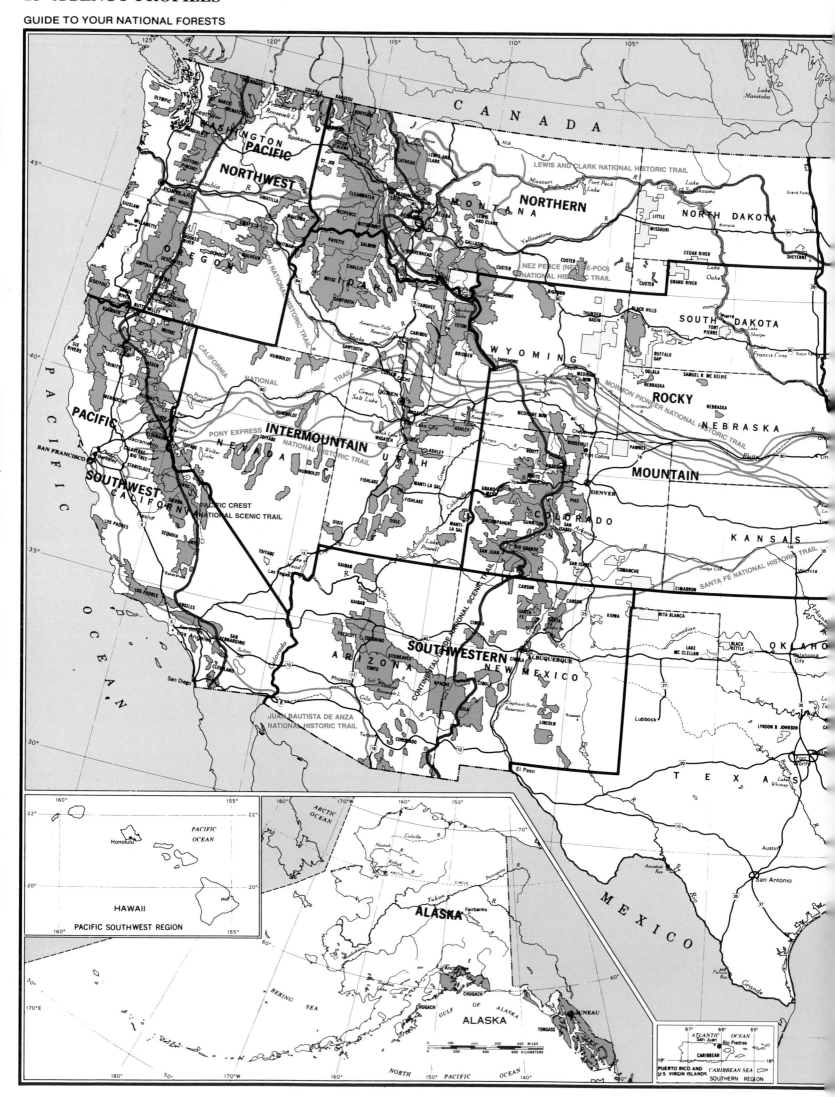

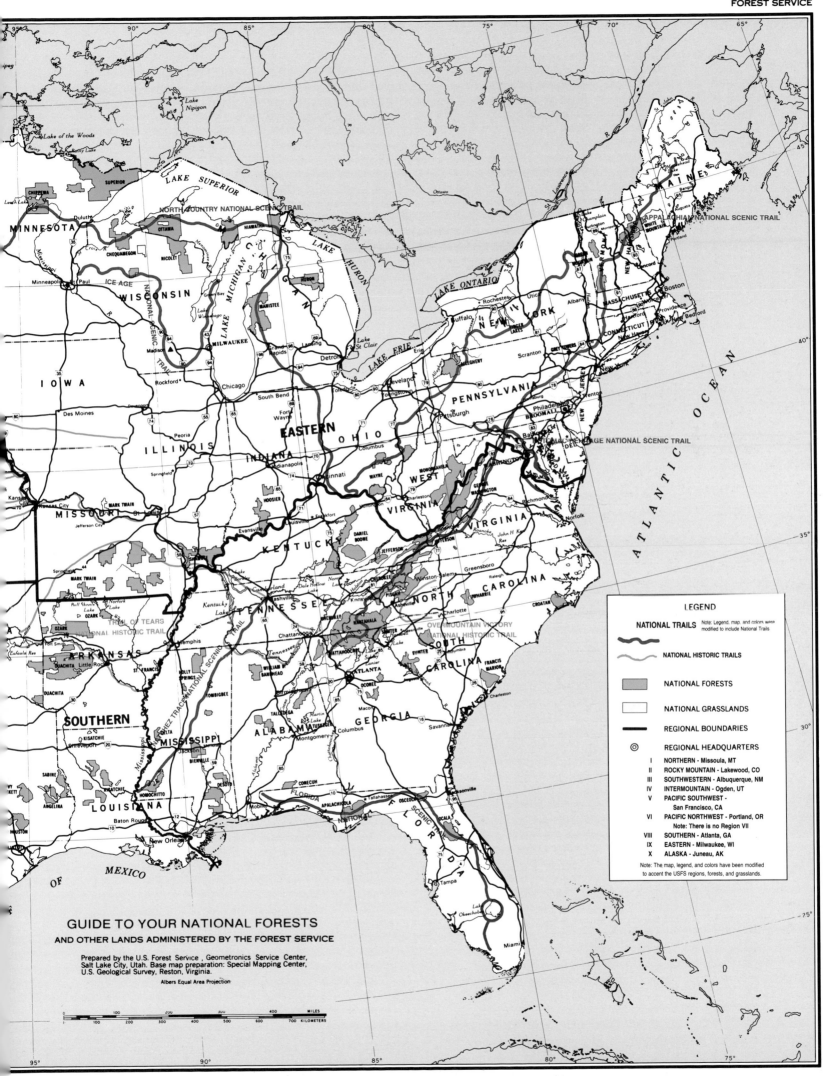

LEGEND

NATIONAL TRAILS — Note: Legend, map, and colors were modified to include National Trails

NATIONAL HISTORIC TRAILS

NATIONAL FORESTS

NATIONAL GRASSLANDS

REGIONAL BOUNDARIES

REGIONAL HEADQUARTERS

I   NORTHERN - Missoula, MT
II   ROCKY MOUNTAIN - Lakewood, CO
III   SOUTHWESTERN - Albuquerque, NM
IV   INTERMOUNTAIN - Ogden, UT
V   PACIFIC SOUTHWEST -
         San Francisco, CA
VI   PACIFIC NORTHWEST - Portland, OR
         Note: There is no Region VII
VIII   SOUTHERN - Atlanta, GA
IX   EASTERN - Milwaukee, WI
X   ALASKA - Juneau, AK

Note: The map, legend, and colors have been modified to accent the USFS regions, forests, and grasslands.

GUIDE TO YOUR NATIONAL FORESTS

AND OTHER LANDS ADMINISTERED BY THE FOREST SERVICE

Prepared by the U.S. Forest Service, Geometronics Service Center,
Salt Lake City, Utah. Base map preparation: Special Mapping Center,
U.S. Geological Survey, Reston, Virginia.

Albers Equal Area Projection

U.S. Army Corps of Engineers

The Corps of Engineers is the second largest provider of outdoor recreation opportunities on federal lands in the United States at more than four hundred "Lakeside Recreation Areas." Corps responsibilities include flood control, hydropower generation, shoreline protection and restoration, water supply, disaster assistance, and fish and wildlife management, on 11.7 million federal acres.

Lakeside Recreation Areas (LRAs or projects) are administered by Corps Divisions and/or in cooperation with state or local agencies. COE LRAs are shown on the Guide maps and described in the Information Charts. Recreation data is also published in ten special full-color COE regional brochures that feature regional maps, recreation charts, and directions. They are available from the COE regional, district, and project offices listed in this Guide.

The aerial view photo shows the U.S. Army Corps of Engineers Waterways Experiment Station (WES), a designated military reservation located in Vicksburg, Mississippi. The 685-acre WES complex includes six major laboratories and specialized facilities.

A free WES Complex brochure describes each of the six laboratories: Information Technology, Structures, Hydraulics, Environmental, Geotechnical, and the Coastal Engineering Research Center (CERC). It also depicts the two self-guided tours available to visitors and the tour stops, and includes a map of the complex. Mississippi chapter notes include visitation hours and driving directions to this unique in the World facility.

U.S. Fish & Wildlife Service (USFWS) National Wildlife Refuges (NWRs)

The USFWS Refuge Division National Wildlife Refuge System traces its beginnings to Florida's tiny Pelican Island. It was established by President Theodore Roosevelt in 1903 as the nation's first refuge.

Today the USFWS, under the U.S. Department of the Interior, manages more than 90 million acres of land and water. Their refuges, waterfowl production and wetland management areas, are critical habitat for endangered species, migratory birds, mammals, fishes, and other wildlife.

There are almost 500 USFWS refuges and other USFWS locations. New areas are being acquired and protected every year. *Refuges are open to the public typically for wildlife-oriented recreation.* Some sites are managed but not open to public visit, or are temporarily closed or not accessible. The laws in Alaska, where 85 percent of USFWS land is located, are different. Special access and usage laws affect visitation rights and privileges.

Local refuge offices publish a variety of free brochures and the photo (right) shows a selection. Many of these feature a small refuge map and give an overview of habitat,

PHOTO COURTESY WES PUBLIC AFFAIRS US ARMY COE - VICKSBURG MISSISSIPPI

management practices, history of the refuge site, and list local and migrating wildlife species. Recreation opportunities and visitor regulations may be included, or featured in separate brochures.

Call the local office to inquire about any special conditions or regulations, hunting permits, group tour information, and to request refuge literature and wildlife species abundance details. There are two unique USFWS locations in major metropolitan areas: the John Heinz NWR at Tinicum National Environmental Center in Philadelphia, Pennsylvania; and the San Francisco Bay Environmental Education Center near San Jose, California.

The state chapter notes provide information on significant refuge areas and literature. Examples are the pool maps available from the Upper Mississippi River National Wildlife & Fish Refuge office and its district offices in Minnesota, Wisconsin, Iowa, and Illinois; and the Klamath Basin Refuges combined wildlife checklist covering six refuge areas in northern California and southern Oregon.

National Park Service (NPS)

The National Park Service manages 80 million acres of federal land in 49 states and the District of Columbia. It is part of the U.S. Department of the Interior. Yellowstone National Park, our first national park, was established by an act of Congress in 1872.

A few major National Park Service parks receive a seemingly endless stream of visitors, and feature a greater number of facilities and services. These sites receive more publicity in the media than the vast majority of park service managed locations, and most other federal or state agency locations. That is the main reason they are so crowded in season.

Arizona boasts the largest number of NPS sites. New sites are added to the system, and site name changes occur most every year. Sometimes sites are combined. A recent addition is the Brown vs. Board of Education National Historic Site in Topeka, Kansas. The latest name change was Fort Jefferson National Monument located 70 air miles west of Key West, Florida, in the Gulf of Mexico. It is now called Dry Tortugas National Park and is not shown on your typical road atlas. This park is only accessible by seaplane or boat. The Lower St. Croix National Scenic River, in Minnesota and Wisconsin, was recently combined with the St. Croix National Scenic Riverway.

Today, there are 367 National Park Service locations including 51 national parks, 10 national seashores, 14 national preserves, 4 national lakeshores, 36 national historic parks, 11 national battlefields, 18 national recreation areas, 72 national historic sites, 76 national monuments, 9 national scenic rivers, and 75 other locations including the White House and Washington Monument. In addition, there are 10 regional offices.

In this new Guide all NPS locations are covered, along with the regional offices. The majority are shown on the maps and listed in the Information Charts. Most NPS locations where outdoor recreation opportunities and facilities are limited are listed in the state chapter notes with their address and telephone number.

There are tens of thousands of free or low cost park brochures, leaflets, maps, and publications available from NPS offices and

Visitor Centers. A few are pictured here (top photo). The foldout park brochures (note Delaware Water Gap brochure) typically show main roadways and visitor centers, and describe recreation opportunities, habitat, and history. Special United States Geological Survey (USGS) maps of larger National Parks are listed in the Outdoor Map Index in the state chapter notes.

Bureau of Land Management (BLM)

The Bureau of Land Management is part of the Department of the Interior, as are the National Park Service and U.S. Fish & Wildlife Service. The BLM manages more than 270 million acres, over 40 percent of all federal land. Most of it is in the more open plains and desert

areas of the western United States. Management considerations and objectives include outdoor recreation, fish and wildlife production, livestock grazing, timber, industrial development, watershed protection, and onshore mineral production.

BLM recreation areas and facilities include more than 460 developed and 1,830 undeveloped recreation areas, 2,260 miles of interpretive and hiking trails, more than 430 boating access sites, plus myriad interpretive wayside exhibits and wildlife viewing routes (see photo).

All BLM state, district, and resource area offices, and selected special recreation management areas are shown on the Guide maps and described in the Information Charts. The special BLM Resource Area Map on page 22 features BLM state, district, and resource area boundaries relative to state boundary lines in the western states. A color overprint delineates BLM land areas and gives you a visual perspective of where the 270 million acres are located.

BLM land is scattered in separate large and small parcels. Much of it is not marked with signs. Some areas are only accessible by crossing private land and may be under grazing or mineral lease. BLM Surface, Public Land Use, and Recreation Maps (see photo, top of page 16) for all areas in a district may be purchased at local BLM offices or by mail. Legitimate access to the vast BLM lands is difficult without having the appropriate map and knowing how to read it.

Since it is your responsibility to secure permission to cross private land to access public land, a visit to the local BLM office and knowledge of those maps can be very helpful.

BLM state offices usually have a "public room" where free recreation area literature and all the BLM maps for a state are available. The lobbies of the local District and Resource Area offices are also sources for BLM maps and literature. Local BLM personnel in the western states can point out BLM land areas to you,

Note: The map color has been modified to accent the BLM State, District, and Resource Area boundaries.

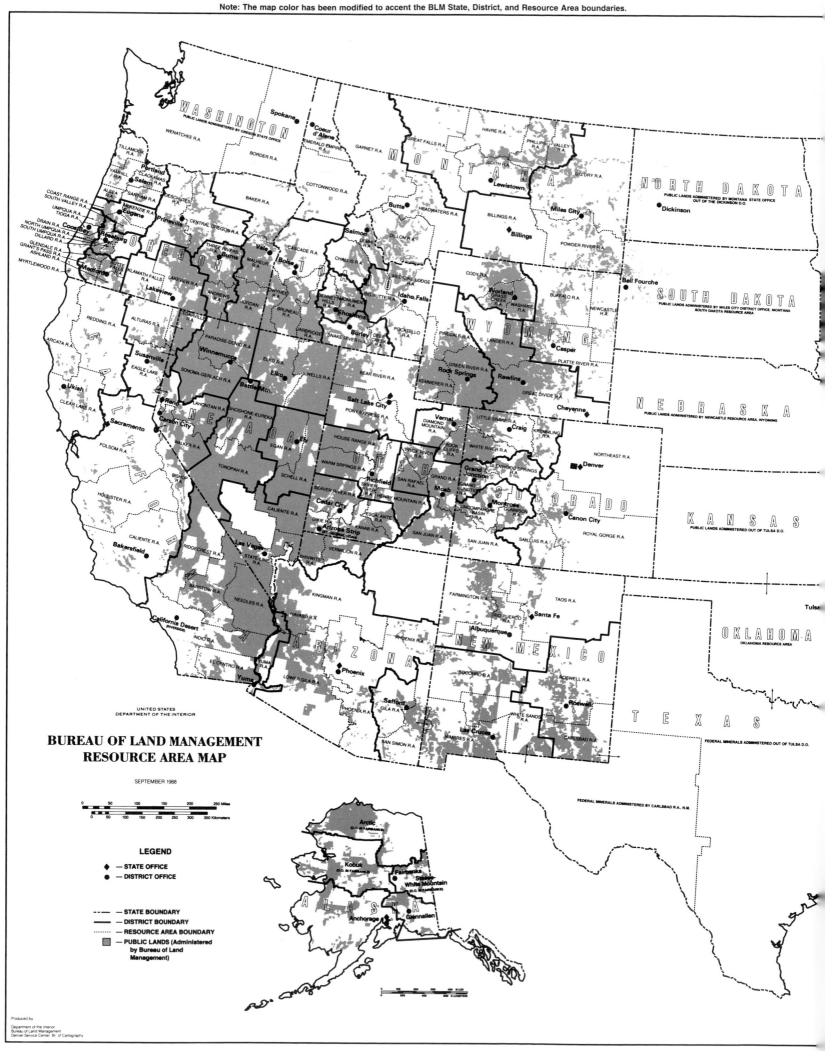

BUREAU OF LAND MANAGEMENT
RESOURCE AREA MAP

SEPTEMBER 1988

UNITED STATES
DEPARTMENT OF THE INTERIOR

LEGEND
◆ — STATE OFFICE
● — DISTRICT OFFICE

— · — · — STATE BOUNDARY
———— DISTRICT BOUNDARY
· · · · · · RESOURCE AREA BOUNDARY
▨ PUBLIC LANDS (Administered by Bureau of Land Management)

Produced by
Department of the Interior
Bureau of Land Management
Denver Service Center Br of Cartography

describe significant features, and indicate the location of special recreation management areas and facilities. Be sure to ask about scenic byways, backways, and recreation area literature. The top photo shows a selection of BLM published recreation literature including the Upper Missouri Wild & Scenic River maps. These maps are printed on waterproof paper and are very useful if you plan a raft or canoe the Upper Missouri in Montana along the actual route of the Lewis & Clark Expedition of 1806. See page 24 for information about the Lewis & Clark National Historic Trail.

The BLM Eastern States headquarters is in Virginia. Other eastern states offices and the temporary Wild Horse and Burro Adoption centers are located in Mississippi, Wisconsin, and Ohio and Pennsylvania. Those offices can furnish information about selected recreation opportunities in the west, and the current schedule for and locations of weekend Wild Horse & Burro Adoption sites that change every weekend during the summer months. The location changes are to give as many people as possible the opportunity to adopt an animal.

Tennessee Valley Authority (TVA)

The offices, outdoor recreation areas and facilities, and projects of the Tennessee Valley Authority are featured in the Alabama, Georgia, Kentucky, Mississippi, and Tennessee chapters The state maps have been modified to show TVA recreation sites. Commercial sites are located in these five states and in North Carolina and Virginia. Local recreation is an important benefit of the TVA system which was designed for flood control and hydropower generation.

TVA manages more than 1,000 square miles of water surface and more than 11,000 miles of shoreline, comprising 1 million acres of federal lands and waterways. One or more TVA recreation areas are within a day's drive of one half of the U.S. population.

Probably the best known TVA recreation area is the Land Between the Lakes or LBL, 170,000 acres located between Kentucky Lake and Lake Barkley in western Kentucky and Tennessee. The LBL office is listed in the chapter notes in both states. Daily programs, camping, a nature center, and one of the largest buffalo herds east of the Mississippi River are a few of the attractions.

TVA works cooperatively with other federal, state, and local agencies, and private interests to preserve the environment and accommodate varied recreational activities and facilities. TVA small wild areas preserve and protect areas of scenic or scientific value and afford opportunities for public use and enjoyment.

A free brochure and map titled *Recreation on TVA Lakes* is available from the agency offices. The brochure covers hundreds of commercial facilities and recreation sites and indicates who manages them. It also features TVA dam and boat docks or ramp/launch locations. TVA will be decentralizing site administration by opening new local offices over the next several years.

Bureau of Reclamation (BOR)

The Bureau of Reclamation manages projects in the 17 western states from five regional offices. The 6.4 million acres of agency lands and waterways consist of an infrastructure of dams, hydroelectric power plants, and water conveyance facilities. These provide flood protection, fish and wildlife habitat, river regulation, water quality protection and improvement, and recreation opportunities.

The Bureau of Reclamation Hydraulics Laboratory facility in Lakewood, Colorado, offers guided tours. The photo shows a tour group viewing a model of the Glen Canyon Dam on the Colorado River in Arizona. People come from all over the world to visit the laboratory and develop an understanding about our most precious resource—water. The Colorado chapter notes have information about tours.

The laboratory is used to test water development concepts and solve engineering and environmental problems of existing water developments. These provide for irrigation, municipal industrial needs, hydroelectric power, recreation, fish, and wildlife. The models are water-activated.

BOR recreation area details are available in a foldout map and chart published by the bureau and available at their five regional offices listed in the chapter notes. They are the Pacific Northwest region in Idaho, the Mid-Pacific region in California, the Lower Colorado region in Nevada, the Upper Colorado region in Utah, and the Great Plains region in Montana.

More than 300 recreation areas are an

PHOTO COURTESY BUREAU OF RECLAMATION DENVER OFFICE - DENVER COLORADO

important part of the BOR reclamation projects. Recreation possibilities includes picnicking, swimming, primitive and developed campsites, boating, fishing, hunting, winter sports, and interpretive opportunities. Facilities may include drinking water, restrooms, boat ramps, trails, and have various disability provisions.

Projects and joint recreation facilities were developed with nearby irrigation districts, county, state, and other federal government agencies or departments. Most areas are identified on the state maps with a distinctive numbered symbol and 279 are listed in the chapter notes. Those that are actually duplications of other federal or state agency locations are not included in the Guide. Examples are the Lake Mead National Recreation Area and Imperial National Wildlife Refuge sites. These are National Park Service and USFWS managed areas with offices in Nevada and Arizona respectively.

National Scenic and Historic Trails

National Trails are designated by the U.S. Congress. Scenic trails are continuously protected scenic corridors for outdoor recreation. Historic trails recognize past routes of explorers, migrations, or military action. These trails are managed, often jointly, by the National Park Service and U.S. Forest Service. Alaska trails are managed by the Bureau of Land Management. Private conservation and outdoor recreation organizations assist in trail development and also provide access information. Approximate routes of seventeen major trails are identified on the U.S. Forest Service Map on pages 18-19.

Three trails, the Iditarod National Historic Trail in Alaska, the Florida National Scenic Trail in Florida, and the Ice Age National Scenic Trail in Wisconsin, are described in the chapter notes for those states under a "National Trails" heading.

Each of the fourteen other national trails cross three to thirteen states. Brief descriptions of the trails are included here along with agency and private organization information sources. The symbol numbers and map coordinates for federal agency offices are indicated in parenthesis as a reference to the appropriate state chapter information chart for other recreation details.

Appalachian National Scenic Trail

Located in the following states: ME/NH/VT/MA CT/NY/PA/MD/WV/VA/NC/TN/GA

The Appalachian National Scenic Trail covers 2,144 miles (3,452 km) stretching from Maine to Georgia. The Appalachian Trail conference maintains the trail through 32 affiliated volunteer trail clubs.

Each year almost 200 people hike the full trail length and millions use portions of the trail. For current hiking information contact:

Appalachian Trail Conference (NPS S# 1, B4)
PO Box 807
Harpers Ferry, WV 25425   304-535-6331
or
National Park Service
Appalachian Trail Project Office
c/o Harpers Ferry Center
Harpers Ferry, WV 25425   304-535-6278

Continental Divide National Scenic Trail

Located in the following states:
MT/ID/WY/CO/NM

The Continental Divide National Scenic Trail covers 3,200 rugged miles (5,150 km), the length of the Rocky Mountains from Canada to Mexico. The 795 developed trail miles extend from Glacier National Park in Montana to Yellowstone National Park in northwest Wyoming.

There are segments of the trail that are open in other states. Hiking and the use of saddle and pack animals is permitted, and off-road motorized vehicles may be used in some places. For ID/MT information contact:

U.S. Forest Service, Northern Region
(S# 1, map B1)
Federal Bldg.
PO Box 7669
Missoula, MT 59807   406-329-3150
and for ID/WY/CO/NM information contact:
U.S. Forest Service, Rocky Mountain Region
(S# 1, map B3)
11177 West 8th Ave.
Box 25127
Lakewood, CO 80225   303-236-9501
alternate contact:
Continental Divide Trail Society
PO Box 30002
Bethesda, MD 20814

Juan Bautista de Anza Natl. Historic Trail

Located in the following states: CA/AZ

The Juan Bautista de Anza Natl. Historic Trail covers 1,200 miles (1,930 km) in California and Arizona from San Francisco to Nogales. The trail was established in 1990 and development is not complete. For information contact:

National Park Service, Western Region
Planning, Grants, and Environmental Quality
600 Harrison St., Suite 600
San Francisco, CA 94107-1372 415-744-3975

Lewis and Clark National Historic Trail

Located in the following states:
MO/KS/IA/NE/SD/ND/MT/ID/WA/OR

The Lewis and Clark National Historic Trail covers 3,700 miles (5,960 km). It extends from Wood River, Illinois, at the confluence of the Mississippi and Missouri rivers, up the Missouri and eventually down the Columbia river to the Pacific Ocean west of Portland, Oregon.

The route follows roads and trails in Montana and Idaho where federal, state, local, and private interests have established motor routes, roadside markers, campgrounds, and museums and exhibits telling about the Lewis and Clark story. For current information contact the offices listed below.

Lewis and Clark Heritage Foundation, Inc.
PO Box 3434
Great Falls, MT 59403
or
National Park Service (S# 3, map D3)
Lewis and Clark National Historic Trail
700 Rayovac Drive, Suite 100
Madison, WI 53711   608-264-5610

Mormon Pioneer National Historic Trail

Located in the following states:
IL/IA/NE/WY/UT

The Mormon Pioneer National Historic Trail covers 1,300 miles (2,095 km). This east-west trail extends through five states from Nauvoo, Illinois, through Iowa, Nebraska, Wyoming, and ending at Salt Lake City, Utah. There is a 1,624-mile long auto tour route that closely follows the trail and is generally marked with the trail logo (sign). For information consult applicable official state highway maps or the national park regional office noted here.

National Park Service, Rocky Mtn. Region
Planning and Compliance Division
12795 West Alameda Parkway
Lakewood, CO 80225   303-969-2380

Natchez Trace National Scenic Trail

Located in the following states: MS/AL/TN

The Natchez Trace National Scenic Trail covers four segments along 110 miles (180 km) of the Natchez Trace Parkway that extends from Natchez, Mississippi to Nashville, Tennessee for a distance of 450 miles. These segments are under development near Nashville and Natchez, and also Jackson, Mississippi. For current information contact:

National Park Service
Natchez Trace Parkway (S# 2, map A3)
RR 1, NT-143
Tupelo, MS 38801   601-842-1572
or
Natchez Trace Trail Conference
PO Box 6579
Jackson, MS 39282   601-373-1447

Nez Perce (Nee-Me-Poo) Natl. Historic Trail

Located in the following states: OR/ID/MT

The Nez Perce National Historic Trail covers 1,170 miles (1,885 km) from eastern Oregon through Idaho to the Bearpaw Mountains in north central Montana. The trail commemorates the historic attempt by the Nez Perce Indians to escape the U.S. Army and avoid moving to a reservation.

It is not a developed trail although some areas are marked. One of these is the Bighole National Battlefield (S# 1, map C2) near Wisdom, Montana. An interpretive program and displays are featured at the battlefield visitor center. For further information about this trail contact:

U.S. Forest Service, Northern Region
(S# 1, map B1)
Federal Bldg.
PO Box 7669
Missoula, MT 59807   406-329-3582

North Country National Scenic Trail

Located in the following states:
VT/NY/PA/OH/MI/WI/MN/ND

The North Country National Scenic Trail covers 3,200 miles (5,150 km) and extends from the Vermont border in the Adirondak Mountains through New York and five other states, ending in North Dakota at the Missouri river. About half the trail route is open for public use and segments cross nine national forests and two national parks. For current information contact:

North Country Tails Association
PO Box 311
White Cloud, MI 49349   616-689-1912
or

National Park Service
North Country National Scenic Trail
(S# 4, map D3)
700 Rayovac Drive, Suite 100
Madison, WI 53711   608-264-5610

Oregon National Historic Trail

Located in the following states:
MO/KS/NE/WY/ID/OR

The Oregon National Historic Trail covers 2,170 miles (3,495 km) extends from Kansas City, Missouri, to near Portland, Oregon. Within the trail corridor there are about 300 miles of visible ruts and 125 historic sites. Roads along the approximate route are marked with trail signs and there are opportunities to travel trail segments by foot, horse, or mountain bike. Contact one of the following offices for information.

Oregon-California Trails Association
PO Box 1019
Independence, MO 64051-0519 816-252-2276
or
Natl. Park Service, Pacific Northwest Region
Oregon National Historic Trail
83 South King St., Suite 212
Seattle, WA 98104   206-553-5366

Overmountain Victory National Historic Trail

Located in the following states: NC/SC/TN/VA

The Overmountain Victory National Historic Trail covers 300 miles (485 km) from Abingdon, Virginia, through eastern Tennessee and western North Carolina, ending at Kings Mountain National Military Park in South Carolina.

Most of this trail is now either road or highway and roadside signs identify many segments. A guidebook is available for seven walking sections and a 20 mile section remains as a trail across the mountains. For current information contact:

Overmountain Victory Trail Association
c/o Sycamore Shoals State Historic Area
1651 West Elk Ave.
Elizabethton, TN 37643   615-543-5808
or
National Park Service, Southeast Region
Planning and Compliance Division
75 Spring St., SW
Atlanta, GA 30303   404-331-5465

Pacific Crest National Scenic Trail

Located in the following states: CA/OR/WA

This trail covers 2,638 miles (4,247 km) from Canada to Mexico running through Washington, Oregon, and California, along the shoulder of the Cascade and Sierra Nevada mountain ranges. It passes through 25 national forests and seven national parks. For current hiking information contact:

U.S. Forest Service, Pacific SW Region
(S# 1, map A4)
630 Sansome St.
San Francisco, CA 94111   415-705-2889
or
U.S. Forest Service, Pacific NW Region
(S# 1, map A2)
PO Box 3623
Portland, OR 97208   503-326-3644

Potomac Heritage National Scenic Trail

Located in the following states:
PA/WV/MD/DC/VA

The Potomac Heritage National Scenic Trail covers 700 miles (1,130 km) extends from western Pennsylvania through West Virginia, Maryland, to Washington, DC, where it splits and follows the north and south sides of the Potomac river to the Chesapeake Bay in Virginia. A number of trail segments are open to public use. For details contact:

Potomac Heritage Trail Association
5229 Benson Ave.
Baltimore, MD 21227
or
Natl. Park Service, National Capital Region
(S# 1, map D1)
Land Use Coordination
1100 Ohio Drive, SW
Washington, DC 20242   202-619-7027

Santa Fe National Historic Trail

Located in the following states:
MO/KS/CO/OK/NM

The Santa Fe National Historic Trail covers 1,203 miles (1,937 km) between Old Franklin, Missouri, and Santa Fe, New Mexico. The trail was largely abandoned when the railroad was built. About 200 miles of trail ruts and traces are still visible in places. For information contact:

Santa Fe Trail Association
Santa Fe Trail Center
Route 3
Larned, KS 67550   316-285-2054
or
National Park Service, Southwest Region
(S# 1, map B2)
Branch of Long Distance Trails
PO Box 728
Santa Fe, NM 87504-0728   505-988-6888

Trail of Tears National Historic Trail

Located in the following states:
TN/AL/KY/MO/AR/OK

The Trail of Tears National Historic Trail covers 2,052 miles (3,304 km) from Tennessee to Oklahoma. The trail commemorates the Cherokee Indians who were moved from the southeast to what was then the Oklahoma Territory in the 1830's.

There are two main routes. Along the Tennessee, Ohio, Mississippi, and Arkansas rivers (1,226 miles). The overland route from Chattanooga, Tennessee to Tahlequah, Oklahoma (826 miles). For information contact:

National Park Service, Southwest Region
(S# 1, map B2)
Branch of Long Distance Trails
PO Box 728
Santa Fe, NM 87504-0728   505-988-6888

Other Federal Agencies

Two federal agencies have nontypical outdoor recreation areas and/or information offices. The Marine and Estuarine Management Division of the **National Oceanic and Atmospheric Administration** (NOAA) coordinate management of the National Marine Sanctuaries. NOAA is a branch of the U.S. Department of Commerce (USDC). The Sanctuaries Program was created by the United States Congress in 1972 to protect areas that have recreational, historical, research, educational, ecological, or aesthetic qualities of national significance.

Sanctuary protection means an area is defined and preserved for research and education. They are also recreational spots for sportsfishing and diving, and support commercial activities such as kelp harvesting and fishing. Thus they are multiple use areas.

Ten sanctuaries have been designated since the program began and other areas are under consideration. They include open ocean and near offshore areas, and they are featured in the California, Florida, Georgia, Louisiana, Massachusetts, and Texas chapter notes. Access details and literature is available from offices listed in the chapter notes.

Limited outdoor recreation opportunities may be available to the general public and/or active and retired military personnel and their guests on local military lands of the **U.S. Department of Defense** (DOD). Budget changes and military base closures are resulting in many changes. The way to check on current opportunities that may be available is to telephone a local base and ask for the outdoor recreation, game or natural resource manager, or the public affairs or Provost Marshal's office. They can advise you about recreation opportunities available to the public and answer specific questions concerning civilian access, and current rules and regulations.

STATE AGENCIES

State agency responsibilities and lines of authority vary. Wildlife, Parks, and Forest management may be under a Department of Conservation (DC), Environmental Protection (DEP), or Natural Resources (DNR). A parent state agency may combine or split the management of natural, wildlife, forest, park, recreation, historical, or other state lands under one or several divisions or bureaus. States like Maryland, Mississippi, Nebraska, South Dakota, Texas, and a few others, combine wildlife and parks and sometimes other resource management like forests or tourism.

State agency variables are covered in the state chapter notes. The agency headquarters and regional or district offices are listed in the charts or chapter notes and their locations indicated on the maps with colored symbols.

The states manage many more recreation areas compared to the number of federally managed areas. Conversely, the actual 61.8 million acres of land managed by the states represents only about ten percent of the total recreation lands managed by the federal government. From more than 16,000 state managed locations, about 2,800 have been selected for this Guide—as there are far too many to include in a single book.

For example, Minnesota has over 900 and South Dakota more than 350 wildlife areas. California and Alaska each have more than 200 parks. A park, forest, or wildlife area may be composed of two or more separate sections. In some states with a limited number of sites, all the wildlife management areas (WMAs) or all the state parks (SPs) are listed in the Guide.

The listed state agency locations usually represent varied outdoor recreation opportunities or they were selected for geographic diversity.

A few unique state agencies and areas are featured. These nontypical state agencies and areas include: 42 aquatic preserves managed by the Florida Division of State Lands; 22 Nature Preserves Commission preserves in Kentucky; 13 Pennsylvania Fish Commission offices and Fish Culture Stations with visitor centers; and Hawaii's 18 Natural Areas Reserves. South Carolina's Heritage Areas (HAs) are combined with their wildlife areas.

Some very large and significant state areas are the Adirondak and Catskill parks in New York and the Pinelands in New Jersey. They are managed by special commissions. Visitor information is included in the chapter notes.

Every state tries to manage outdoor recreation resources based on the amount of public land available, climate and terrain, and local conditions like population density. Some make a special effort to encourage nonresident outdoor recreation while others focus more on the needs of residents. This may be reflected in the amount of information available from an agency, or in some states, higher fees charged nonresident visitors for licenses, permits, or the use of certain facilities.

In the Information Chart pages answers about state-managed areas were furnished by agency personnel using the Guide questionnaire. If an agency did not complete questionnaires, or agency furnished literature did not meet Guide information needs, the charts feature the agency headquarters and regional or division office location information.

Free brochures, booklets, campground guides, new fishing, boating, and hunting regulations, maps, and youth education program support materials, are available at state agency offices. The photo shows an assortment of state agency-published literature.

State tourism departments are listed in the chapter notes and are a good source of free recreation information. Most publish or revise visitor travel guides every year. This free literature typically contains information on historic sites, describes commercial recreation opportunities, and features all the state parks, state forests, recreation areas and campgrounds.

Incidentally, state wildlife management agency offices and wildlife or game management areas are seldom covered in the tourist literature or travel guides. For this reason more game and wildlife management areas and fewer state parks are covered in this Guide.

State Park Management

There are 50 state park agencies, bureaus, divisions, or departments with 14,900 full- and

26,000 part-time employees managing 10 million acres. Recreationists are usually familiar with their home state parks. Many parks have visitor centers and a full-time staff, offer diverse outdoor recreation opportunities and facilities, and attract more visitors than state WMAs, game management and natural areas.

Most official state highway maps feature a recreation chart detailing some or all state park and recreation area locations, and selected facilities. These free highway maps often provide park or campground telephone numbers and the park map location coordinates.

There are more than 800 state parks, recreation areas, and management offices listed in this Guide. State parks and recreation areas

may have developed campgrounds, and offer a variety of outdoor recreation opportunities not available at state wildlife areas. Resort parks encourage group visitation, feature overnight accommodations, meeting rooms, swimming pools, tennis courts, and golf courses.

State Wildlife Management

There are 51 state wildlife management agencies, bureaus, departments, or divisions, with about 32,000 full-time employees. They manage about 23 million acres as wildlife, game or waterfowl management, heritage, preserve, natural, or other areas. Pennsylvania has separate fish and game agencies.

One purpose of this Guide is to emphasize

wildlife related activities and areas that are less likely to attract crowds. Thus more than 1,900 wildlife or natural area locations, agency headquarters and field offices are listed. Most areas do not have on-site managers and few people visit them except during fishing or hunting seasons.

Note: With some exceptions these state-owned lands are open to off-season public use by hikers, birders, nature photographers, campers, fishermen, and other outdoor enthusiasts. They may be closed to visitors at times to protect wildlife during breeding, nesting, or calving seasons. Leased lands are usually restricted to hunting use, but not always.

Typical Guide-listed state wildlife areas are state-owned, but some states lease a few, and sometimes almost all, of their areas from private land owners. Changes in land ownership status and lease arrangements are continuous.

Most state wildlife agencies publish quarterly magazines or newspapers about wildlife and outdoor recreation. The recreation literature availability from local sporting goods dealers is usually limited to fishing or hunting regulations, licenses, and permit applications. Check with the local agency offices for the most current literature, wildlife survey statistics, information on guides and outfitters, changes in regulations, state sponsored tournament dates, records and awards, and current news releases.

Forty-five of these agencies manage habitat for endangered species. All 50 states have nongame or watchable wildlife programs complimenting their game management efforts. Today 31 states receive funds from state income tax checkoffs (donations) for nongame or watchable wildlife programs.

State Forest Management

The state forest agencies, bureaus, divisions, or departments manage 20 million acres within 721 state forests in 39 states. Almost half of the states do not have a forest recreation program (no developed recreation areas or facilities). In states without a program forest land may be open to public use for some outdoor recreation like fishing or hunting.

A forest agency headquarters name, address, telephone number and a recreation program comment, appear in the state chapter notes. Access details or public use rules and regulations are available from those offices. Free state tourism agency travel guides are often a good alternate source for forest recreation facilities information.

Note: When forests are managed by the state park or wildlife agency the forest listings may be combined with park or wildlife area coverage in the Chart. In those cases the symbol and color code used for the state forests will be the same as that used for the parks or wildlife areas.

PRIVATE ORGANIZATIONS

Large and small nonprofit conservation organizations and nature centers number in the thousands. Their diverse interests, agendas, and activities range from full support of federal and state agency activities and objectives, to public education, to speaking out on resource management policy, practices, and issues they promote or disagree with. The land areas they own or protect range from less than an acre in size to huge tracts numbering in the hundreds of thousands of acres.

This Guide includes more than 800 private areas and offices, representing millions of acres. The Private-Organization-published material in the photo is representative of the literature available free or for a small charge. Those who own these areas offer members and visitors unique nature and conservation education and recreation opportunities.

Most state and federal agency offices can direct you to one or more current members of local conservation groups like the Audubon Society chapters and other local outdoor groups. Check with a local member about scheduled activities, meeting dates and locations.

Another information source you can use to reach local groups is the *Conservation Directory* published by the National Wildlife Federation. It is revised every year, published in January, and sells for about $25. You can call 1-800-432-6564 and order the book direct using a credit card. The reference section of larger public or university libraries may have a current copy.

The Nature Conservancy (TNC)

The Nature Conservancy, with more than 700,000 members, is the leading conservation organization in locating and protecting natural communities and rare species. To date they have protected more than 5.5 million acres in North America, and manage over 1,100 preserves. TNC Chapter and Field Office managers authorized Guide coverage of 274 offices and preserves where members and visitors are permitted.

The offices have current information on guided tours and visiting preserves. There is usually a small tour fee, and most tours take place on weekends and are limited to small groups. You may visit some locations on your own with permission. A few are open to drop-in visits, have visitor centers, resident managers, and offer scheduled tours, morning bird walks, and other programs. Guide chapter notes describe published books available from some Field or Chapter offices that cover their preserves.

National Audubon Society (NAS)

The National Audubon Society, with 550,000

members, owns or manages more than 80 reserves and wildlife sanctuaries. Society management objectives include the long-term protection of plants and animals, especially those that are endangered or threatened.

Fifteen sanctuaries were authorized for listing in this Guide, including seven which feature education centers with ongoing recreation and nature education programs for members and the general public.

There are more than 500 active local Audubon chapters in the U.S. Most hold weekday evening meetings monthly (except in the summer). Projects and field trips are planned and nature programs presented at the meetings. Visitors are welcome.

Other Audubon Societies (IAS)

Some of the twelve independent state and regional Audubon organizations provided information on 83 wildlife sanctuaries and nature centers for this Guide. Most are members of the Audubon Alliance and are not affiliated with the National Audubon Society. The Michigan Audubon Society is an Alliance member and is affiliated with NAS.

Their sanctuary locations protect habitat and wildlife diversity. The visitor centers, nature trails, and observation points serve as instruments for local nature education. Members hold monthly society or chapter meetings, and visitors are welcome.

Association of Nature Center Administrators (ANCA)

This Association works to improve the management and use of nature and environmental centers throughout the United States. Some centers are private nonprofit sites and others are under municipal, county, or state government agencies.

The name and address of almost 300 selected nature and environmental centers with membership in ANCA are listed in the chapter notes under "ANCA Locations." Call ahead for information about descriptive literature, visitor hours, fees or donations, and education programs or field trips that may be available.

Native American Tribal Lands (TLA)

According to the USDI, Bureau of Indian Affairs (BIA), Office of Trust and Economic Development, there are about 90 million acres held in trust for or owned by Native Americans. Outdoor recreation on tribal (reservation) land is under the jurisdiction of tribal confederations, councils, wildlife, and business departments.

The chapter notes include management offices for more than 100 tribal land areas in 26 states. The notes indicate if fishing, hunting, camping, biking, boating, hiking, or touring is permitted on those lands. Tribal Offices are your best source for current access details, permits, hunting or fishing licenses, maps, recreation literature, and information about tribal wilderness areas.

ALABAMA NOTES

Summary

There are 28 federal, 57 state, and 5 private recreation areas or local administrative offices covered in this state chapter. Of these, 60 appear in the Information Chart and 30 are covered in the notes. The special indexes feature 2 federally designated wilderness areas, a wild river, and 9 agency published outdoor maps.

Federal Agencies

U.S. Forest Service

Alabama is in the Southern Region (see Georgia chapter - U.S. Forest Svc., Southern Region listing).

National Park Service

The 445 mile long **Natchez Trace Parkway** extends northeast from Natchez, Mississippi, through the northwest corner of Alabama and into central Tennessee where it ends just southwest of Nashville. See Mississippi chapter for Parkway details.

Additional NPS Locations in Alabama

Tuskegee Institute Natl. Historic Site & George Washington Carver Museum & VC (see S# 3, map C3)
PO Drawer 10
Tuskegee Institute (Tuskegee), AL 36088   205-727-3200

Little River Canyon National Preserve (not on map) (57 acres)
No office, new NPS site approved October 21, 1992.

Wilderness/Wild River Index

Wilderness Areas

Cheaha Wilderness (map B2) - 6,780 acres		
Talladega National Forest & RD (S# 5, map B2)		
Sipsey Wilderness (map A1) - 12,646 acres		
Bankhead National Forest & RD (S# 2, map A2)		

Wild River

Sipsey Fork, West Fork River (map A 2)
Bankhead National Forest & RD (S# 2, map A2)

Outdoor Map Index

U.S. Forest Service Maps

Map	Year
Bankhead National Forest	[1986]
Bartram Trail, Tuskegee NF	[1981]
Cheaha Wilderness, Talladega NF	[1987]
Conecuh National Forest	[1983]
Sipsey Wilderness, Bankhead NF	[1987]
Talladega NF, Oakmulgee Ranger District	[1983]
Talladega NF-Talladega & Shoal Creek Districts	[1981]
Tuskegee National Forest	[1985]

State Agencies

Alabama Department of Conservation & Natural Resources (DCNR)   205-242-3486
64 N. Union St.
Montgomery, AL 36130
Parent agency for Alabama divisions including Parks & Recreation, Game & Fish, and Marine Resources.

Division of State Parks & Recreation (S# 1, map C2)
Fifteen of Alabama's Parks accept reservations for campsites. Some have resort motel and cabin facilities

ALABAMA - CITY / AGENCY INDEX

City	Agency Office / Area Name	Code	S#	Map
Alexander City	Wind Creek SP	SPS	21	B2
Andalusia	Conecuh National Forest & RD	NFS	3	C2
	Blue Springs WMA	SWA	5	D3
Atmore	Claude D. Kelley SP	SPS	8	D2
	Escambia Cr. Comm. Hunt Area	SWA	13	D2
Auburn	Chewacla SP	SPS	6	C3
Birmingham	TNC Alabama Field Office	TNC		
Bridgeport	Russell Cave Natl. Monument	NPS	2	A2
Camden	Roland Cooper SP	SPS	20	C2
Centre	Talladega NF & Oakmulgee RD	NFS	6	C2
Centreville	Little River SP	SWA	19	A3
Chapman	Oakmulgee WMA	SWA	6	B2
Cherokee	Butler County WMA	SWA	23	B2
	Wilson Dam Res.	TVA	6	A1
	Muscle Shoals Res.	TVA	7	A1
Citronelle	Thomas WMA	SWA	30	A1
	Frank W & Rob M Boykin WMA	SWA	14	D1
Clayton	Barbour County WMA	SWA	3	C3
Clio	Blue Springs SP	SPS	5	C3
Coffeeville	Scotch WMA	SWA	25	C1
Columbus (MS)	TN-Tombigbee Gainesville Off	COE	6	B1
	Dauphin Island Bird Sanctuary	NAS	1	D1
Daviston	Horseshoe Bend NMP	NPS	1	B3
Decatur	Wheeler NWR	NWR	4	A2
	Mallard Creek Rec. Area	TVA	5	A2
Demopolis	Frank W & Rob M Boykin WMA	SWA	20	A2
	Mallard-Fox Creek WMA	SWA	29	A2
	Black Warrior & Tombigbee WMA	COE	3	C1
	Demopolis WMA	SWA	12	C1
Dothan	Chattahoochee SP	SPS	4	D3
Double Springs	Bankhead Natl. Forest & RD	NFS	2	A2
Eufaula	Eufaula NWR (AL-GA)	NWR	3	C3
	Lakepoint Resort SP	SPS	15	C3
Florala	Florala SP	SPS	9	D2
Florence	Covington WMA	SWA	9	A3
Fort Payne	Seven Mile Island WMA	SWA	26	A1
Guin	DeSoto SP	SPS	7	A1
Gulf Shores	Lamarion WMA	SWA	17	A1
	Bon Secour NWR (5 units)	NWR	1	D1
	Gulf Resort SP	SPS	11	D1
Guntersville	Buck's Pocket SP	SPS	13	A2
	Lake Guntersville Resort SP	SPS	1	C2
Guntersville	Guntersville Dam Res.	TVA	2	A2
	Seibold Creek Rec. Area	TVA	3	A2
Heflin	Talladega NF/Shoal Creek RD	NFS	4	A2
Hollins	William L Holland MA	SWA	7	B3
Huntsville	Monte Sano SP	SPS	15	B2
Jackson	Choctaw NWR	NWR	2	C1
Linden	Chickasaw SP	SPS	7	C1
Lowndesboro	AL River Lakes (Claiborne L.)	COE	3	C2
	AL River Lakes (Dannelly L.)	COE	4	C2
Mobile	AL River Lakes (L. Woodruff)	COE	1	D1
	COE, Mobile District	COE		
MONTGOMERY	Natl. Forests in AL, Super.	NFS	31	D1
	DCNR, State Parks Div.	SPS	1	C2
	DCNR, Game & Fish, Wildlife S.	SWA	4	A2
	TVA - Southern District	TVA	1	A1
Moulton	Black Warrior WMA	SWA	15	B3
Muscle Shoals	Oak Mountain SP	SPS	17	B2
Oxford	St. Clair Community Hunting A.	SWA	28	B2
Pelham	Coosa WMA	SWA	8	B2
Pell City	Wheeler Dam Res.	TVA	4	A2
Rockford	Joe Wheeler Resort SP	SPS	12	A2
Rogersville	Mud Creek WMA	SWA	21	A2
Scottsboro	North Sauty Refuge	SWA	22	A2
Selma	Paul M. Gris SP	SPS	18	C2
Stevenson	Crow Creek Refuge	SWA	10	A2
	Crow Creek WMA	SWA	11	A2
Talladega	Raccoon Creek WMA	SWA	24	A3
	Skyline WMA	SWA	27	A2
Townley	Talladega NF & Ranger D.	NFS	5	B2
Tuscaloosa	Wolf Creek WMA	SWA	32	B2
Tuskegee	Lake Lurleen SP	SPS	14	B1
	Tuskegee NF & Ranger D.	NFS	7	C3
Warrior	Rickwood Caverns SP	SPS	19	B2
Waterloo	Lauderdale WMA	SWA	18	A1
White City	Autauga WMA	SWA	2	A2
York	Kinterbish WMA	SWA	16	C1

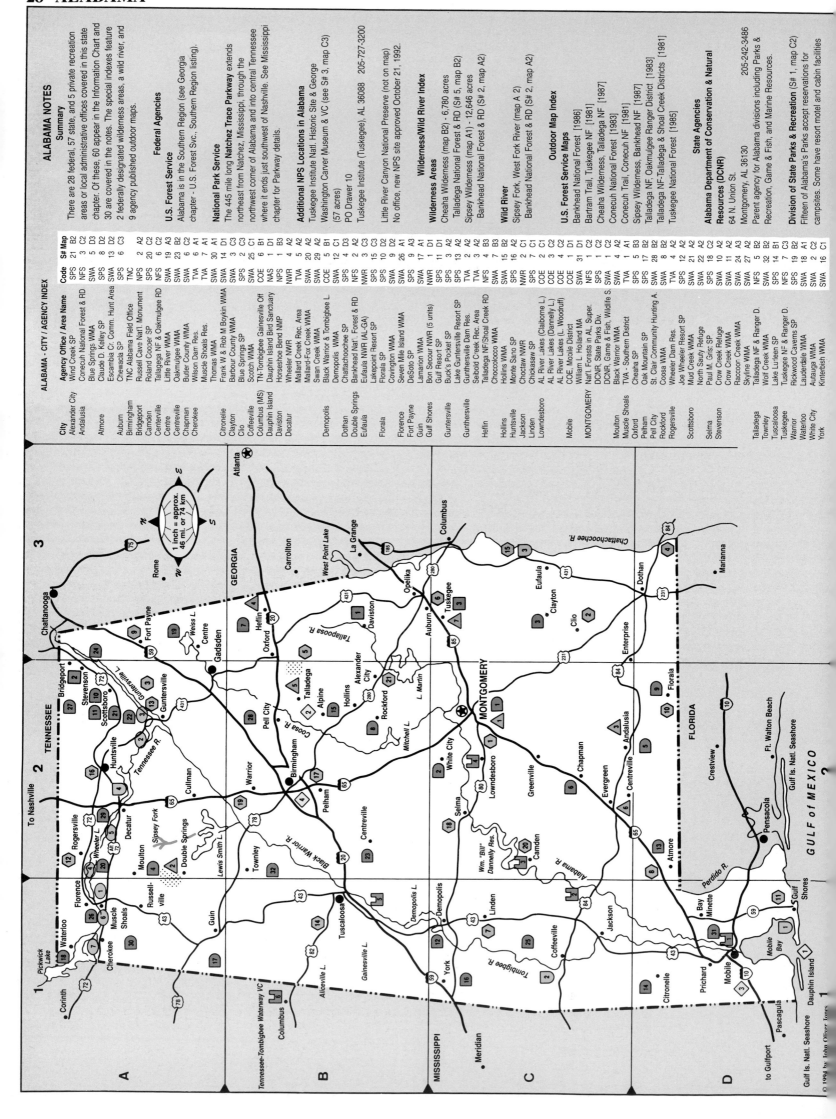

© 1994 by John Oliver Jones.

and golf courses. A park brochure with facility, rate, and recreational activity information is available.

Individual Park brochures are free. They feature small park locator maps and describe facilities and recreation opportunities. Park fees include day use at some locations, and campground use fees except at the four parks where there is primitive camping only. Off-season rates and discounts are available for groups, clubs, senior citizens, and disabled persons.

Alabama State Park map symbol numbers, map coordinates, park name and city are listed below.

S#	MAP	PARK NAME & LOCATION
1	C2	DCNR, State Parks Div. HQ (see chart)
2	C3	Blue Springs SP, 6 mi. SE of Clio
3	A2	Buck's Pocket SP, NE of Guntersville
4	D3	Chattahoochee SP, SE of Dothan

S#	MAP	PARK NAME & LOCATION
5	B3	Cheaha SP, near Oxford
6	C3	Chewacla SP, I-85 exit 51 near Auburn
7	C1	Chickasaw SP, Linden
8	D2	Claude D. Kelley SP, N of Atmore
9	A3	DeSoto SP, NE of Fort Payne
10	D2	Florala SP, NE of Florala
11	D1	Gulf Resort SP, Gulf Shores
12	A2	Joe Wheeler Resort SP, Rogersville
13	A2	L. Guntersville Resort SP, Guntersville
14	B1	Lake Lurleen SP, Hwy. 82 W of Tuscaloosa
15	C3	Lakepoint Resort SP, Eufaula
16	A2	Monte Sano SP, Huntsville
17	B2	Oak Mountain SP, I-65 exit 246 near Pelham
18	C2	Paul M. Grist SP, N of Selma
19	B2	Rickwood Caverns SP, near Warrior
20	C2	Roland Cooper SP, NE of Camden
21	B2	Wind Creek SP, near Alexander City

Game and Fish Division (GFD)

Wildlife Section (S# 1, map C2)

A brochure listing and describing public hunting and wildlife management areas is available from the GFD office in Montgomery. There is no outfitter and guide licensing requirement in Alabama. Hunting guides are required to have a permit from the GFD.

A full color, bi-monthly magazine, Alabama Conservation, covers hunting, fishing, and boating. It is available by subscription for $8 a year. Call 205-242-3151 for an order form.

Alabama Division of Marine Resources
PO Box 89
Dauphin Island, AL 36528
Contact this office for marine fisheries information.

Alabama Forestry Commission
513 Madison Ave.
Montgomery, AL 36130   205-240-9300
Contact the Commission for forest recreation literature.

The Alabama Bureau of Tourism and Travel
532 S. Perry St.
Montgomery, AL 36104
from out-of-state   1-800-392-8096
          1-800-252-2262
Current travel information and free travel guides and maps are available from this office.

A free comprehensive Official Alabama Transportation Department highway map is available from this office and at other state agency offices. State park locations are identified by a green triangle. Light green shaded areas indicate state and national forest land. There are also symbols showing welcome centers, museums, resorts, and covered bridges.

Private Organizations

ANCA Locations in Alabama

Camp Crosby Environmental Education Center
(see S# 2, map B2)
Box 81-A, Rt. #2
Alpine, AL 35014   205-252-3191

Environmental Studies Center (see S# 3, map D1)
PO Box 1327
Mobile, AL 36633   205-661-0998

Ruffner Mountain Nature Center (see S# 4, map B2)
1414 S. 81st Street
Birmingham, AL 35206   205-833-8112

Business Council of Alabama
(State Chamber of Commerce)
468 South Perry St.
PO Box 76
Montgomery, AL 36195
Phone 205-834-6000
Fax 205-262-7371

★ INFORMATION CHART ★

INFORMATION CHART LEGEND - SYMBOLS & LETTER CODES

- ■ means YES & □ means Yes with disability provisions
- sp means spring, March through May
- S means Summer, June through August
- F means Fall, September through November
- W means Winter, December through February
- T means Two (2) or Three (3) Seasons
- A means All Four (4) Seasons
- na means Not Applicable or Not Available

Note: empty or blank spaces in the chart mean NO

Note: Refer to yellow block on page 7 (top right) for location name and address abbreviations. If a symbol number has a star ★ that symbol is not shown on the map.

AGENCY/MAP LEGEND . . . INITIALS, MAP SYMBOLS, COLOR CODES

- U.S. Forest Service Supervisor & Ranger Dist. Offices . . NFS (61)
- U.S. Army Corps of Engineers Rec. Areas & Offices . . COE (31)
- USFWS National Wildlife Refuges & Offices . . . . . . NWR (40)
- National Park Service Parks & other NPS Sites . . . . . NPS (7)
- Bureau of Land Management Rec. Areas & Offices . . . BLM (26)
- Tennessee Valley Authority Offices & Sites . . . . TVA (8)
- State Parks (also see State Agency notes) . . . . SPS (52)
- State Wildlife Areas (also see State Agency notes) . . . SWA (19)
- Private Preserves, Nature Centers & Tribal Lands (15)
- and Wilderness Areas
- The Wild Rivers

FACILITIES, SERVICES, RECREATION OPPORTUNITIES & CONVENIENCES

S#	MAP	LOCATION NAME (state initials if more than one) with ADDRESS and/or LOCATION DATA	TELEPHONE	ACRES / ELEVATION	S#
1	C2	National Forests In Alabama, Supervisor, 1765 Highland Ave., Montgomery 36107	205-832-4470	651,000 / 150-2,400	1
2	A2	Bankhead National Forest & Ranger D., PO Box 278, Double Springs 35553	205-489-5111	179,840 / 400-800	2
3	D2	Conecuh National Forest & Ranger D., Rt. #5, Box 157, Andalusia 36420	205-222-2555	83,000 / 150-300	3
4	B3	Talladega Nat'l. Forest & Shoal Cre, 450 Hwy, 46, Heflin 36264	205-463-2272	115,000 / 600-2,000	4
5	B2	Talladega National Forest & Ranger , 1001 North Street, Hwy, 21 North, Talladega 35160	205-362-2909	105,000 / 600-2,400	5
6	C2	Talladega National Forest & Oakmulg, PO Box 67, Centerville 35042	205-926-9765	na / na	6
7	C3	Tuskegee National Forest & Ranger D., Rt. #1, Box 457, Tuskegee 36083	205-727-2652	11,000 / 300-500	7
1	D1	COE, Mobile District, 109 St. Joseph St., PO Box 2288, Mobile 36628	205-694-3720	na / na	1
2	C1	Alabama River Lakes (Claiborne L.), 1450 Jones Bluff Road, Lowndesboro 36726 [NE of Jackson]	205-872-9554	na / na	2
3	C1	Alabama River Lakes (Dannelly L.), 1450 Jones Bluff Road, Lowndesboro 36752 [at Camden]	205-872-9554	na / na	3
4	B1	Alabama River Lakes (L. Woodruff), 1450 Jones Bluff Road, Lowndesboro 36752	205-872-9554	na / na	4
5	B1	Black Warrior And Tombigbee Lakes, PO Box 520, Demopolis 36732 [S of Tuscaloosa]	205-289-3540	na / na	5
6	B1	Tennessee-Tombigbee Gainesville, 3606 West Plymouth Rd., Columbus, MS 39701 [Aliceville / Gainesville Lakes in W AL]	601-327-2142	4,500 / na	6
1	D1	Bon Secour NWR (5 units), PO Box 1650, Gulf Shores 36547 [from SH 59 at mile marker 13 take SH 180 west]	205-968-8623	na / na	1
2	C1	Choctaw NWR, 1310 College Ave., PO Box 808, Jackson 36545 [from Coffeeville N of Jackson go W on US 84 to CR 21]	205-246-3583	4,220 / 30-100	2
3	C3	Eufaula NWR (AL-GA), Rt. #2, Box 97B, Eufaula 36027 [6 mi N of Eufaula, take Hwy 431 to Old Hwy 165]	205-687-4065	11,184 / 200	3
4	A2	Wheeler NWR, Rt. #4, Box 250, Decatur 35603 [exit I-65 at SH 67, go 3 mi W to NWR, office at refuge]	205-350-6639	34,500 / 565	4
1	B3	Horseshoe Bend NMP, Rt. 1, Box 103, Daviston 36256 [AL Hwy. 49 at Tallapoosa River, 5 mi S of New Site]	205-234-7111	2,040 / 600	1
2	A1	Russell Cave National Monument, Rt. #1, Box 175, Bridgeport 35740 [take CR 91 W & turn on CR 98]	205-495-2672	310 / 630-1,600	2
1	A1	TVA - Southern District, 170 Office Service Warehouse Annex, Muscle Shoals 35660 [below Florence on US 43]	205-386-2221	na / na	1
2	A2	Guntersville Dam Res., NW of Guntersville [AL Hwy. 69]	205-386-2223	na / na	2
3	A2	Seibold Creek Rec. Area, N of Guntersville [AL Hwy. 79]	205-386-2223	na / na	3
4	A2	Wheeler Dam Res., SW of Rogersville [AL Hwy. 101]	205-386-2223	na / na	4
5	A2	Mallard Creek Rec. Area, NW of Decatur [US Hwy. 72 Alt.]	205-386-2223	na / na	5
6	A1	Wilson Dam Res., near Cherokee [AL Hwy. 133]	205-386-2223	na / na	6
7	A1	Muscle Shoals Res., near Cherokee [AL Hwy. 133]	800-252-7275	na / na	7
1	C2	Alabama DCNR, State Parks Div., 64 N. Union St., Montgomery 36130 (see Alabama Notes for details)	205-242-3469	na / na	1
2	C2	DCNR, Div. of Game & Fish, Wildlife Section, 64 N. Union St., Montgomery 36130	205-242-3469	na / na	2
2	C2	Autauga WMA, near White City		7,100 / 400-500	2
3	C3	Barbour County WMA, near Clayton		26,383 / 350-450	3

AGENCY/MAP LEGEND . . . INITIALS, MAP SYMBOLS, COLOR CODES

U.S. Forest Service Supervisor & Ranger Dist. Offices NFS [61]
U.S. Army Corps of Engineers Rec. Areas & Offices . COE [31]
USFWS National Wildlife Refuges & Offices . . . . NWR [40]
National Park Service Parks & other NPS Sites . . . . . NPS [7]
Bureau of Land Management Rec. Areas & Offices . . BLM [26]
Tennessee Valley Authority Offices & Sites . . . . TVA [8]
State Parks (also see State Agency notes) . . . . SPS [52]
State Wildlife Areas (also see State Agency notes) . . SWA [19]
Private Preserves, Nature Centers & Tribal Lands . .
The Wild Rivers —— and Wilderness Areas
Note: Refer to yellow block on page 7 (top right) for location name and address abbreviations.

★ INFORMATION CHART ★

INFORMATION CHART LEGEND — SYMBOLS & LETTER CODES

■ means YES & □ means Yes with disability provisions
sp means spring, March through May
S means Summer, June through August
F means Fall, September through November
W means Winter, December through February
T means Two (2) or Three (3) Seasons
A means All Four (4) Seasons
na means Not Applicable or Not Available
Note: empty or blank spaces in the chart mean NO
Note: Refer to yellow block on page 7 (top right) for location name and address abbreviations. If a symbol number has a star ★ that symbol is not shown on the map.

FACILITIES, SERVICES, RECREATION OPPORTUNITIES & CONVENIENCES

(column headers, top to bottom): INFO OFFICE (IO) / VISITOR CENTER (VC); IO / VC OPEN SATURDAY / SUNDAY; ENTRY FEE not camping or permit fee; INTERPRETIVE or EDUCATIONAL SERVICES AVAILABLE; FREE LITERATURE / brochures, maps, etc.; AGENCY GUIDED TOURS / STUDY PROGRAMS; NATURE EDUCATION / STUDY PROGRAMS; WILDFLOWER VIEWING AREA / DRIVE; ARCHAEOLOGICAL / GEOLOGICAL SITES; HISTORIC SITES / INTERPRETIVE TRAILS; WILDLIFE VIEWING SITES, blinds, signs, etc.; ENDANGERED SPECIES ARE COMMON; DEVELOPED PICNIC SITES; NO-CHARGE CAMPGROUNDS / CAMPSITES; WALKING / HIKING TRAILS; BICYCLING OPPORTUNITIES; HORSEBACK RIDING / at one's own risk; OFF-ROAD MOTORIZED areas, trails; FISHING in season, license / by res.; NON-MOTORIZED WATERCRAFT OK / Use OK; BOATING FACILITIES / ramps, marinas, etc.; WINTER SPORTS OPPORTUNITIES; HUNTING IN SEASON, license / permit reqd.; PARK & WALK-IN ONLY AREA; DAY USE ONLY / no overnight; DRINKING WATER; RESTROOMS

S#	MAP	LOCATION NAME (state initials if more than one) with ADDRESS and/or LOCATION DATA	TELEPHONE	ACRES / ELEVATION	S#
4	A2	Black Warrior WMA, near Moulton	205-242-3469	95,850 / 550-900	4
5	D3	Blue Springs WMA, SW of Andalusia	205-242-3469	23,370 / 100-250	5
6	C2	Butler County WMA, near Chapman	205-242-3469	25,000 / 250-400	6
7	B3	Choccolocco WMA, near Heflin	205-242-3469	45,130 / 900-1,450	7
8	B2	Coosa WMA, near Rockford	205-242-3469	38,000 / 500-800	8
9	D2	Covington WMA, near Florala	205-242-3469	22,490 / 100-270	9
10	A2	Crow Creek Refuge, near Stevenson	205-242-3469	2,496 / 600-620	10
11	A2	Crow Creek WMA, near Stevenson	205-242-3469	2,161 / 600-620	11
12	C1	Demopolis WMA, near Demopolis	205-242-3469	3,587 / 60-90	12
13	D2	Escambia Creek Community Hunting Ar, near Atmore	205-242-3469	4,577 / 150-280	13
14	D1	Frank W. & Rob M. Boykin WMA, near Citronelle	205-242-3469	18,025 / 150-250	14
15	B2	Hollins WMA, near Hollins	205-242-3469	31,600 / 800-1,400	15
16	C1	Kinterbish WMA, near York	205-242-3469	10,400 / 180-300	16
17	A1	Lamarion WMA, near Guin	205-242-3469	24,350 / 450-620	17
18	A1	Lauderdale WMA, near Waterloo	205-242-3469	15,766 / 500-800	18
19	A3	Little River WMA, near Centre	205-242-3469	16,200 / 750-1,300	19
20	A2	Mallard-Fox Creek WMA, near Decatur	205-242-3469	1,500 / 560-660	20
21	A2	Mud Creek WMA, near Scottsboro	205-242-3469	8,193 / 600-620	21
22	A2	North Sauty Refuge, near Scottsboro	205-242-3469	5,200 / 600-620	22
23	B2	Oakmulgee WMA, near Centreville	205-242-3469	44,500 / 260-520	23
24	A3	Raccoon Creek WMA, SE of Stevenson	205-242-3469	7,080 / 600-620	24
25	C1	Scotch WMA, near Coffeeville	205-242-3469	20,000 / 100-330	25
26	A1	Seven Mile Island WMA, near Florence	205-242-3469	4,685 / 410-520	26
27	A2	Skyline WMA, NW of Stevenson	205-242-3469	22,842 / 650-1,800	27
28	B2	St. Clair Community Hunting Area, near Pell City	205-242-3469	5,700 / 560-800	28
29	A2	Swan Creek WMA, near Decatur	205-242-3469	8,870 / 560-660	29
30	A1	Thomas WMA, near Cherokee	205-242-3469	9,160 / 480-850	30
31	D1	William L. Holland MA, near Mobile	205-242-3469	24,000 / 0-10	31
32	B2	Wolf Creek WMA, near Townley	205-242-3469	30,100 / 340-720	32
D1		Dauphin Island Bird Sanctuary, PO Box 189, Dauphin Island 36528 [off Hwy. 193 at E end of Dauphine Is.]	205-861-2882	168 / 10	1

ALASKA - CITY / AGENCY INDEX

City	Agency Office / Area Name	Code	S#	Map
Fairbanks	Arctic NWR	NWR	3	D2
	Kanuti NWR	NFS	1	C2
	Yukon Flats NWR	NWR	1	C2
	Gates of the Arctic NP&P	NPS	13	C2
	Arctic District Office	NPS	1	C2
	Kobuk District Office	BLM	1	C2
	Steese/White Mtn. Dist.	BLM	*2	C2
	White Mountains NRA	BLM	*3	C2
	Northern Region Office	SPS	23	C3
	Chena River SRA (6 areas)	SPS	23	C3
	Harding Lake SRA	SWA	3	C3
Galena	Koyukuk/Nowitna NWR	NFS	16	B1
Girdwood	Glacier Ranger D. (VC)	NWR	8	C1
Glennallen	Wrangell-St. Elias NP&P	NFS	3	C3
	Glennallen District Office	NPS	13	D4
Gustavus	Dry Creek SRS	NFS	6	B2
	Glacier Bay NP&P	NWR	15	C1
Haines	Chilkat SP	SPS	24	C1
	Chilkoot Lake SRS	SWA	2	D4
Homer	Alaska Maritime NWR	NPS	17	B3
Hoonah	Kachemak Bay SP/WP			
	Hoonah Ranger D.	BLM	16	B2

City	Agency Office / Area Name	Code	S#	Map
JUNEAU	U.S. Forest Svc., Alaska R.	NFS	1	D4
	Admiralty Is. NM &			
	Kootznoowoo Wilderness A.	NFS	7	D4
	Juneau Ranger D. (VC)	NFS	9	D4
	Southeast Island Office	SPS	19	D4
	Shelter Island SMP	SPS	22	D4
	Div. of Wildlife Cons.	SWA	1	D4
Kenai	Captain Cook SRA (7 areas)	SPS	4	C2
	Kenai River Spl.Mgt. Area	SPS	6	C2
Ketchikan	Tongass NF, Ketchikan Area	NFS	12	D4
	Ketchikan Ranger D.	NFS	14	D4
	Misty Fjords Nat'l. Mon.	NFS	15	D4
King Salmon	Alaska Peninsula NWR	NWR	4	C2
	Bechard NWR	NWR	5	C2
	Alagnak Wild River	NPS	10	C2
	Aniakchak Nat'l. Mon. & Pre.	NPS	6	D4
	Katmai Nat'l. Park & Pre.	NPS	11	C4
Kodiak	Kodiak NWR	NWR	5	D4
	Kodiak Region Office	SPS	8	C2
	Buskin River SRS	SPS	7	C2
	Shuyak Island SP	SPS	9	C2
Kotzebue	ADWC - Region 4	SWA	13	A2
	Cape Krusenstern Nat'l. Mon.	NPS	5	A2

City	Agency Office / Area Name	Code	S#	Map
	Kobuk Valley National Park	NPS	12	A2
	Noatak National Preserve	NPS	14	A2
	Kotzebue Field Station	BLM	8	A2
McGrath	Innoko NWR	NWR	7	B2
Nome	Bering Land Bridge NP	NPS	4	A1
	Nome Field Station	BLM	9	B1
	Kigluaik Mountains	BLM	10	B1
	ADWC - Region 5	SWA	6	B1
North Pole	Captain Cook SRA (7 areas)	SPS	5	C2
Paxton	COE, Alaska District	COE	6	C3
Petersburg	Denali-Clearwater SRA	BLM	12	D4
	Tongass NF, Stikine Area	NFS	14	D4
	Petersburg Ranger D.	NFS	18	D4
Seward	Seward Ranger D.	NFS	5	C2
	Kenai Fjords National Park	NPS	10	C2
	Caines Head SRA	SPS	3	C2
Sitka	Tongass NF, Chatham Area	NFS	6	D4
	Sitka Ranger D.	NFS	10	D4
	Sitka National Hist. Park	NPS	11	C4
Skagway	Klondike Gold Rush NHP	NPS	10	C2
Soldotna	Kenai NWR	NWR	10	C2
Talkeetna	Kenai Peninsula Reg. Office	SPS	13	C2
	Montana Creek SRS	SPS	2	C2
Thorne Bay	Thorne Bay Ranger D.	NWR	13	A2
Tok	Teltin NWR	NFS	16	D4
		NWR	14	C3
	Tok Field Station	BLM	14	C3
	Fortymile SRA	BLM	15	B3
	Eagle Trail SRS	SPS	17	C3
Trapper Creek	Denali SP (6 areas)	SPS	10	C2
Wasilla	Mat-Su/Valdez/Copper Basin RO	SPS	14	C2
Willow	Nancy Lake SRA (4 areas)	SPS	14	C2
Wrangell	Wrangell Ranger D.	NFS	19	D4
Yakutat	Yakutat Ranger D.	NFS	11	C3

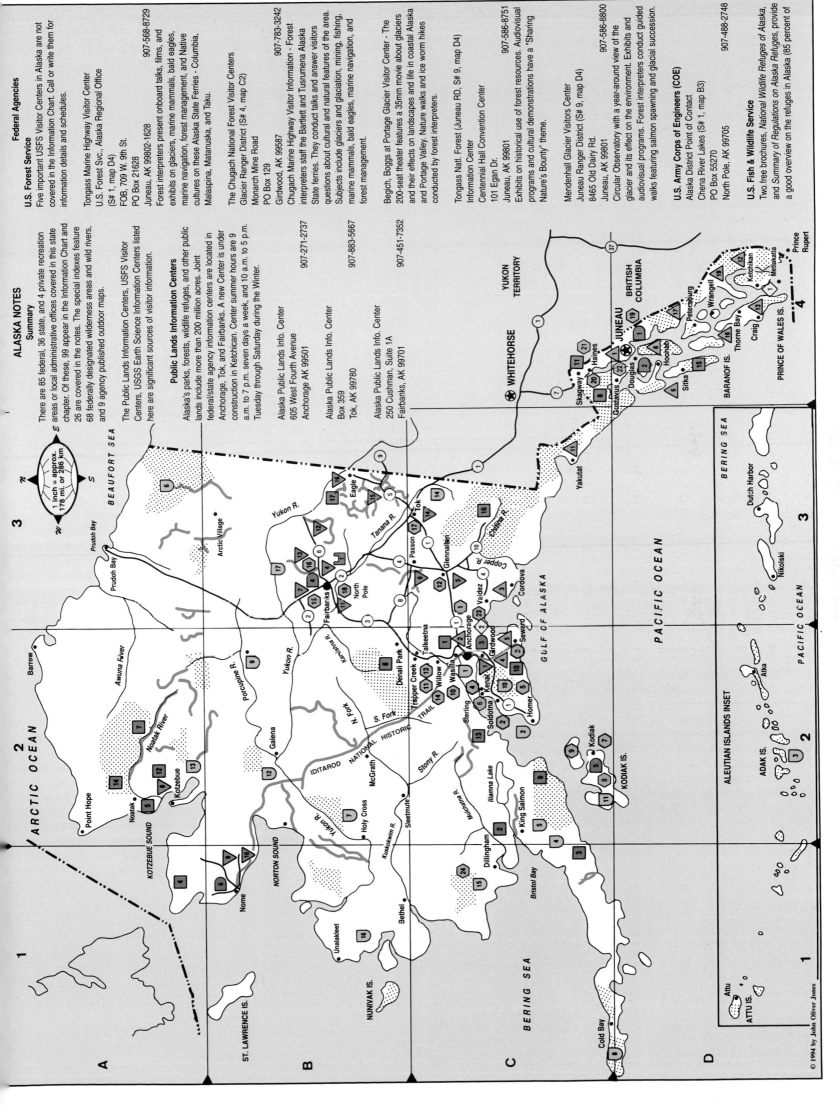

Federal Agencies

U.S. Forest Service

Five important USFS Visitor Centers in Alaska are not covered in the Information Chart. Call or write them for information details and schedules.

Tongass Marine Highway Visitor Center
U.S. Forest Svc., Alaska Regional Office
(S# 1, map D4)
FOB, 709 W. 9th St.
PO Box 21628
Juneau, AK 99802-1628   907-568-8729
Forest interpreters present onboard talks, films, and exhibits on glaciers, marine mammals, bald eagles, marine navigation, forest management, and Native cultures on these Alaska State Ferries - Columbia, Malaspina, Matanuska, and Taku.

The Chugach National Forest Visitor Centers
Glacier Ranger District (S# 4, map C2)
Monarch Mine Road
PO Box 129
Girdwood, AK 99587   907-783-3242
Chugach Marine Highway Visitor Information - Forest interpreters staff the Bartlett and Tusrumena Alaska State ferries. They conduct talks and answer visitors questions about cultural and natural features of the area. Subjects include glaciers and glaciation, mining, fishing, marine mammals, bald eagles, marine navigation, and forest management.

Begich, Boggs at Portage Glacier Visitor Center - The 200-seat theater features a 35mm movie about glaciers and their effects on landscapes and life in coastal Alaska and Portage Valley. Nature walks and ice worm hikes conducted by forest interpreters.

Tongass Natl. Forest (Juneau RD, S# 9, map D4)
Information Center
Centennial Hall Convention Center
101 Egan Dr.
Juneau, AK 99801   907-586-8751
Exhibits on historical use of forest resources. Audiovisual programs and cultural demonstrations have a "Sharing Nature's Bounty" theme.

Mendenhall Glacier Visitors Center
Juneau Ranger District (S# 9, map D4)
8465 Old Dairy Rd.
Juneau, AK 99801   907-586-8800
Circular Observatory with a year-around view of the glacier and its effect on the environment. Exhibits and audiovisual programs. Forest interpreters conduct guided walks featuring salmon spawning and glacial succession.

U.S. Army Corps of Engineers (COE)

Alaska District Point of Contact
Chena River Lakes (S# 1, map B3)
PO Box 55270
North Pole, AK 99705   907-488-2748

U.S. Fish & Wildlife Service

Two free brochures, *National Wildlife Refuges of Alaska*, and *Summary of Regulations on Alaska Refuges*, provide a good overview on the refuges in Alaska (85 percent of

ALASKA NOTES

Summary

There are 85 federal, 36 state, and 4 private recreation areas or local administrative offices covered in this state chapter. Of these, 99 appear in the Information Chart and 26 are covered in the notes. The special indexes feature 68 federally designated wilderness areas and wild rivers, and 9 agency published outdoor maps.

The Public Lands Information Centers, USFS Visitor Centers, USGS Earth Science Information Centers listed here are significant sources of visitor information.

Public Lands Information Centers

Alaska's parks, forests, wildlife refuges, and other public lands include more than 200 million acres. Joint federal/state agency information centers are located in Anchorage, Tok, and Fairbanks. A new Center is under construction in Ketchican. Center summer hours are 9 a.m. to 7 p.m. seven days a week, and 10 a.m. to 5 p.m. Tuesday through Saturday during the Winter.

Alaska Public Lands Info. Center
605 West Fourth Avenue
Anchorage AK 99501   907-271-2737

Alaska Public Lands Info. Center
Box 359
Tok, AK 99780   907-883-5667

Alaska Public Lands Info. Center
250 Cushman, Suite 1A
Fairbanks, AK 99701   907-451-7352

1 inch = approx. 178 mi. or 286 km

USFWS refuge land area in the United States). Access to all but the Kenai and Tetlin refuges is by boat or plane. Check with refuge personnel for current information about access, activities permitted, and visitor regulations.

The Alaska Maritime NWR (S# 2, map C2) information covers the NWRs Alaska Peninsula Unit, Bering Sea Unit, Chukchi Sea Unit, and Gulf of Alaska Unit. All are administered from the Homer office.

National Trail

The Iditarod National Historic Trail is a system of historic trails covering 2,450 miles (3,945 km). The best known segment is used for the annual 1,150-mile Iditarod Dogsled Race between Anchorage (map A3) and Nome (map B1). Most of the area along the route as shown on the Alaska map is only usable during the winter. For current information contact:
BLM Anchorage District Office (S# 2, map C2)
6881 Abbott Loop Road
Anchorage, AK 99507
or   907-267-1246
Idaditarod Trail Committee (map C2)
PO Box 870800
Wasilla, AK 99687   907-376-5155

Wilderness/Wild River Index

The Alaska map shows the location of most of the 43 wilderness areas and 25 wild rivers. Detailed agency published maps are the best source for on-the-ground wilderness and wild river access. Look up the local agency offices, referred to by S# and map coordinates in this index, in the information chart pages for access details and maps. Larger areas are shown on the map.

Wilderness Areas

The following wilderness areas are managed by the one or more of the Tongass National Forest Area or Ranger District offices located throughout southeast Alaska and listed in the Information Chart:
Admiralty Island Wilderness - 937,396 acres
Coronation Island Wilderness - 19,232 acres
Endicott River Wilderness - 98,729 acres
Maurelle River Wilderness - 4,937 acres
Misty Fiords National Monument Wilderness - 2,142,243 acres
Petersburg Creek-Duncan Salt .Chuck Wilderness - 46,777 acres
Russell Fiord Wilderness - 348,701 acres
South Baranof Wilderness - 319,568 acres
South Prince of Wales Wilderness - 90,996 acres
Stikine-Le Conte Wilderness - 448,841 acres
Tebenkof Bay Wilderness - 66,839 acres
Tracy Arm-Fiords Terror Wilderness - 653,179 acres
Warren Island Wilderness - 11,181 acres
West Chichagof-Yakobi Wilderness - 264,747 acres

The next eleven wilderness areas are managed by the Alaska Maritime National Wildlife Refuge (S# 2, map C2):
Aleutian Islands Wilderness - 1,300,000 acres
Bering Sea Wilderness - 81,340 acres
Bogoslof Wilderness - 175 acres
Chamisso Wilderness - 455 acres
Forrester Island Wilderness - 2,832 acres
Hazy Islands Wilderness - 32 acres

Saint Lazaria Wilderness - 65 acres
Semidi Wilderness - 250,000 acres
Simeonof Wilderness - 25,855 acres
Tuxedni Wilderness - 5,556 acres
Unimak Wilderness - 910,000 acres

The ten wilderness areas which follow are managed by other National Wildlife Refuges. Under each listing the name of a local office or information source is given and the map symbol number and coordinates appear in parenthesis. Use the symbol number to find the office address and telephone number in the Information Chart.
Andreafsky Wilderness - 1,300,000 acres and Nunivak Wilderness - 600,000 acres
Yukon Delta NWR (S# 17, map B3)
Arctic Wildlife Refuge Wilderness - 8,000,000 acres
Arctic NWR (S# 6, map A3)
Becharof Wilderness - 400,000 acres
Becharof NWR (S# 5, map C2)
Innoko Wilderness - 1,240,000 acres
Innoko NWR (S# 7, map B2)
Izembek Wilderness - 300,000 acres
Izembek NWR (S# 8, map C1)
Kenai Wilderness - 1,350,000 acres
Kenai NWR (S# 10, MAP C2)
Koyukuk Wilderness - 400,000 acres
Koyukuk/Nowitna NWR (S# 12, map B2)
Selawik Wilderness - 240,000 acres
Selawik NWR (S# 13, map A2)
Togiak Wilderness - 2,270,000 acres
Togiak NWR (S# 15, map C1)

The next eight wilderness areas are located within and are a part of selected National Park Service areas.
Denali Wilderness - 1,900,000 acres
Denali NP & Preserve (S# 6, B2)
Gates of the Arctic Wilderness - 7,052,000 acres
Gates of the Arctic NP & Preserve (S# 7, map A2)
Glacier Bay Wilderness - 2,770,000 acres
Glacier Bay NP & Preserve (S# 8, map C4)
Katmai Wilderness - 3,473,000 acres
Katmai NP & Preserve (S# 9, map C2)
Kobuk Valley Wilderness - 190,000 acres
Kobuk Valley National Park (S# 12, map A2)
Lake Clark Wilderness - 2,470,000 acres
Lake Clark NP & Preserve (S# 13, C2)
Noatak Wilderness - 5,800,000 acres
Noatak National Preserve (S# 14, map A2)
Wrangell-St. Ellis Wilderness - 8,700,000 acres
Wrangell-St. Ellis NP & Preserve (S# 16, map C3)

Wild Rivers
Alagnac Wild River
Katmai National Park and Preserve (S# 9)
Alatna Wild River
Gates of the Arctic NP & Preserve (S# 7)
Andreafsky Wild River
Yukon Delta NWR (S# 16)
Aniakchak Wild River
Aniakchak NM & Preserve (S# 3)
Beaver Creek Wild River
BLM Steese/White Mountain District (S# 11) & Yukon Flats NWR (S# 17)
Birch Creek Wild River

BLM Arctic District (S# 4)
Charlie Wild River
Yukon Charlie Rivers Natl. Preserve (S# 17)
Chilkadrotna Wild River
Lake Clark NP & Preserve (S# 13)
Delta Wild River
BLM Glennallen District (S# 5)
Forty Mile Wild River
BLM Arctic District (S# 4)
Gulkana Wild River
BLM Glennallen District (S# 5)
Ivishak Wild River
Arctic NWR (S# 6)
The John, Kobuk, Koyukuk North Fork, & Noatak Wild Rivers
Gates of the Arctic NP & Preserve (S# 7)
Mulchatna Wild River
Lake Clark NP & Preserve (S# 13)
Nowitna Wild River
Koyukuk/Nowitna NWR (S# 12)
Salmon Wild River (Alaska)
Kobuk Valley National Park (S# 12)
Selawik Wild River
Selawik NWR (S# 13)
Sheenjek Wild River
Arctic NWR (S# 6)
Tinayguk Wild River
Gates of the Arctic NP & Preserve (S# 7)
Tlikakila Wild River
Lake Clark NP & Preserve (S# 13)
Unalakleet Wild River
BLM Anchorage District (S# 2)
Wind Wild River
Arctic NWR (S# 6)

USGS Earth Science Information Centers
USGS Anchorage-ESIC
4230 University Dr., Rm. 101
Anchorage, AK 99508   907-786-7011

USGS Anchorage-ESIC
605 W. 4th Ave., Rm. G-84
Anchorage, AK 99501   907-271-2754

Outdoor Map Index
National Park Service (USGS Maps)
Denali Natl. Park. Scale: 1 inch = 4 miles, 1 cm = 2.5 km

U.S. Forest Service Maps
Chugach National Forest [1983]
Scale: 1 inch = 8.0 miles (1 cm = 5.1 km)
Size: 18x39 inches (46x99 cm)
Hoonah (Tongass Natl. Forest)
Scale: 1 inch = 0.7 mile (1 cm = 0.4 km)
Size: 18x36 inches (46x91 cm)
Misty Fiords (Tongass Natl. Forest)
Scale: 1 inch = 4.0 miles (1 cm = 2.5 km)
Size: 21x42 inches (53x106 cm)
Mitkof Island (Tongass NF)
Scale: 1 inch = 0.7 mile (1 cm = 0.4 km)
Size: 18x36 inches (46x91 cm)
Prince of Wales (Tongass NF)
Scale: 1 inch = 4.0 miles (1 cm = 2.5 km)
Size: 21x42 inches (53x106 cm)
Tongass National Forest [1990]

Scale: 1 inch = 14.0 miles (1 cm = 8.9 km)
Size: 18x36 inches (46x91 cm)

Bureau of Land Management Maps
The typical state BLM map grid shown in the other western state chapters in this Guide, is not available for Alaska. Contact the state office in Anchorage (see BLM S# 1) for map information. An Alaska National Interest Lands Conservation Act (ANILCA) map, a Land Status Map, and U.S. Survey and Master Title Plats are available.

State Agencies
Department of Natural Resources (DNR)
400 Willoughby
Juneau, AK 99801   907-465-2400
The Alaska Divisions of Parks and Outdoor Recreation, and Forestry, function under this department.

Alaska Division of Parks & Outdoor Recreation (S# 1, map C2)
Alaska has the largest park system land area in the United States with more than three million acres, or almost one-third of America's state park acreage.
Selected parks are covered in the Guide and range from scenic roadside campgrounds to large parks including State Marine Parks (SMP), State Recreation Areas (SRA), State Recreation Sites (SRS), and Wilderness Parks (WP).

Ask for the free Alaska State Parks brochure. It features a map and includes park location to nearest town, size of park, facilities, visitor safety, and other details.

An overnight fee is charged at developed campsites. There are rental cabins at Chena River State Recreation Area (SRA) and Nancy Lake SRA. Cabins at Oliver Inlet and Shuyak Island are only accessible by plane or boat. Reservations are not required at any park facilities except the rental cabins.

Division of Forestry
3601 C Street, Suite 1058
Anchorage, AK 99503   907-762-2117
There is no State Forest recreation program in Alaska.

Department of Fish & Game (DFG)
PO Box 3-2000
Juneau, AK 99802   907-465-4100
The Alaska Divisions of Wildlife Conservation and Sport Fish function under this department.

Alaska Division of Wildlife Conservation (ADWC) (S# 1, map D4)
Information chart and road map coverage is limited to the ADWC offices. The State of Alaska is divided into 26 large Game Management Units that contain a mixture of state, federal agency, and native corporation owned lands. Free brochures and maps describing game management units are available.

For hunting and Nongame Wildlife Program information contact the agency offices listed in the information chart. Alaska has a variety of hunting licenses. Permits to hunt many units are by drawing. Check with department offices for current hunting regulations and about the various types of permits.

At some wildlife viewing locations permits are required and may be issued by drawing. An example are the bear viewing permits for McNail River State Game Sanctuary. In 1992, more than 1,600 people from around the world applied and 125 permits were issued. Contact ADWC - Region 2 (see S# 3, map C2).

A free booklet Alaska Fish & Game Facts contains state wildlife statistics. Comprehensive game harvest statistics are not available in a single publication. Contact a regional agency biologist for harvest information.

You may subscribe to the bi-monthly 36 page full color Alaska Fish & Game magazine for $9 a year. $15 for two years. Mail to: AF&G, Box 3-2000, Juneau, AK 99802.

Alaska Division of Sport Fish
PO Box 3-2000
Juneau, AK 99802   907-465-4180
Contact this division for sport fishing information.

Alaska Dept. of Commerce & Economic Development
Alaska Division of Tourism
Box E
Juneau, AK 99811   907-465-2010
in Anchorage   907-344-0541
Current travel information and free travel guides and maps are available from this office.

Guide Licensing and Control Board
Box D-Lic
Juneau, AK 99811   907-465-2534
For information about qualifications and on licensed guides and outfitters contact the board.

Private Organization
Tribal Land Area in Alaska
Metlakatla Indian Community of the Annette Islands Reserve - Fishing, hunting, camping, boating, hiking.
Metlakatla Indian Community Council (S# 1, map D4)
PO Box 8
Metlakatla, AK 99926   907-886-4441

The Nature Conservancy
Alaska Field Office (map C2)
601 W. Fifth Ave., Suite 550
Anchorage, AK 99501   907-276-3133
There are no TNC preserves open to the public.

ANCA Location in Alaska
Campbell Creek E E Center (S# 2, map C2)
6881 Abbott Loop Rd.
Anchorage, AK, 99507

Alaska State Chamber of Commerce
217 Second St., #201   Phone 907-586-2323
Juneau, AK 99801   Fax 907-463-5515

INFORMATION CHART LEGEND - SYMBOLS & LETTER CODES

- ■ means **YES** & □ means **Yes with disability provisions**
- **sp** means **spring**, March through May
- **S** means **Summer**, June through August
- **F** means **Fall**, September through November
- **W** means **Winter**, December through February
- **T** means **Two (2)** or **Three (3)** Seasons
- **A** means **All Four (4)** Seasons
- **na** means **Not Applicable or Not Available**
- Note: empty or blank spaces in the chart mean **NO**

Note: Refer to yellow block on page 7 (top right) for location name and address abbreviations. If a symbol number has a star ★ that symbol is not shown on the map.

U.S. Forest Service Supervisor & Ranger Dist. Offices . . NFS
U.S. Army Corps of Engineers Rec. Areas & Offices . . COE
USFWS National Wildlife Refuges & Offices . . . . NWR
National Park Service Parks & other NPS Sites . . . . . NPS
Bureau of Land Management Rec. Areas & Offices . . . BLM
Bureau of Reclamation Rec. Areas & Reg. Offices . . . BOR
State Parks (also see State Agency notes) . . . . SPS
State Wildlife Areas (also see State Agency notes) . . . SWA
Private Preserves, Nature Centers & Tribal Lands
The Wild Rivers — and Wilderness Areas

FACILITIES, SERVICES, RECREATION OPPORTUNITIES & CONVENIENCES

S#	MAP	LOCATION NAME (state initials if more than one) with ADDRESS and/or LOCATION DATA	TELEPHONE	ACRES / ELEVATION
		U.S. Forest Svc., Alaska Region, FOB, 709 W. Ninth St., PO Box 21628, Juneau 99802	907-586-8806	na / na
1	D4	Chugach National Forest Sup. 201 E. 9th Ave, Suite 206, Anchorage 99501	907-271-2500	5,600,000 / 14,000
2	C2	Cordova Ranger D., 612 2nd Street, PO Box 280, Cordova 99574	907-424-7661	na / na
3	C3	Glacier Ranger D. (see notes on VC), Monarch Mine Rd, PO Box 129, Girdwood 99587 [S of Anchorage]	907-783-3242	na / na
4	C2	Seward Ranger D., 334 4th Ave., PO Box 390, Seward 99664	907-224-3374	na / na
5	C2	Tongass NF, Chatham Area, 204 Siginaka Way, Sitka 99835	907-747-6671	8,000,000 / 0-8,770
6	D4	Admiralty Island NM & Kootznoowoo Wilderness Area, 8461 Old Dairy Road, Juneau 99801	907-586-8790	964,282 / 0-4,023
7	D4	Hoonah Ranger D., PO Box 135, Hoonah 99829	907-945-3631	636,137 / 0-3,768
8	D4	Juneau Ranger D. (see notes on VC), 8465 Old Dairy Rd., Juneau 99801	907-586-8800	3,462,043 / 0-8,584
9	D4	Sitka Ranger D., 204 Siginaka Way, Sitka 99835	907-747-6671	na / na
10	D4	Yakutat Ranger D., PO Box 327, Yakutat 99689	907-784-3359	1,227,958 / 0-8,770
11	C3	Tongass NF, Ketchikan Area, Federal Building, Ketchikan 99901	907-225-3101	5,155,000 / 0-5,400
12	D4	Craig Ranger D., Tongass NF, PO Box 500, Craig 99921	907-826-3271	na / na
13	D4	Ketchikan Ranger D., Tongass NF, 3031 Tongass Ave., Ketchikan 99901	907-225-2148	na / na
14	D4	Misty Fiords Nat'l. Monument, Tongass NF, 3031 Tongass, Ketchikan 99901	907-225-2148	2,400,000 / 0-8,000
15	D4	Thorne Bay Ranger D., Tongass NF, PO Box 1, Thorne Bay 99919	907-828-3304	na / na
16	D4	Tongass NF, Stikine Area, PO Box 309, Petersburg 99833	907-772-3841	3,261,640 / 0-9,000
17	D4	Petersburg Ranger D., PO Box 1328, Petersburg 99833	907-772-3871	1,680,250 / 0-9,000
18	D4	Wrangell Ranger D., PO Box 51, Wrangell 99929	907-874-2323	1,581,390 / 0-6,500
19	B3	**COE, Alaska District**, point of contact for: Chena River Lakes, PO Box 55270, North Pole 99705	907-488-2748	na / na
1	C2	**USFWS Region 7**, 1011 E. Tudor Road, Anchorage 99503 [Region is the state of Alaska only]	907-786-3487	na / na
1	C2	Alaska Maritime NWR, 509 Sterling Hwy., Homer 99603 [see chapter notes about NWR units]	907-235-6961	3,500,000 / 0-6,000
2	D2	Aleutian Islands Unit, AMNWR, mail to: Naval AS, PSC 486, Box 5251, FPO AP 96506-5251, Adak	907-592-2406	2,700,000 / 0-7,500
6	C2	Alaska Peninsula NWR, PO Box 277, King Salmon 99613	907-246-3339	3,800,000 / 0-8,000
7	C2	Becharof NWR, PO Box 277, King Salmon 99613	907-246-3339	1,200,000 / 0-5,000
8	A3	Arctic NWR, FOB & Courthouse, Room 266, 101-12th Ave., Box 20, Fairbanks 99701 [NE of Fairbanks]	907-456-0250	19,200,000 / 0-9,050
9	B2	Innoko NWR, Box 69, McGrath 99627	907-524-3251	3,850,000 / 100-2,300
10	C1	Izembek NWR, Box 127, Cold Bay 99571 [adjacent community of Cold Bay near tip of Alaska Peninsula]	907-532-2445	315,000 / 0-6,000
11	B2	Kanuti NWR, 101 12th Ave., Box 11, Fairbanks 99701 [NW of Fairbanks, Field Station/VC at Bettles]	907-456-0329	1,430,000 / 500-3,000
12	C2	Kenai NWR, PO Box 2139, Soldotna 99669	907-262-7021	1,970,000 / 0-6,100
13	C2	Kodiak NWR, 1390 Buskin River Road, Kodiak 99615 [refuge is 25 mi from any road]	907-487-2600	1,600,000 / 0-4,500
14	B2	Koyukuk/Nowitna NWR, PO Box 287, Galena 99741 [Koyukuk 10 mi N / Galena; Nowitna, 50 mi E / Galena]	907-656-1231	7,300,000 / 200-3,520
15	A2	Selawik NWR, PO Box 270, Kotzebue 99752 [2nd St, Bldg. #160]	907-442-3799	2,700,000 / 0-1,869
16	B2	Tetlin NWR, PO Box 779, Tok 99780	907-883-5312	730,000 / 1,600-8,100
17	C1	Togiak NWR, PO Box 270, Dillingham 99576	907-842-1063	4,300,000 / 0-5,200
18	B1	Yukon Delta NWR, PO Box 346, Bethel 99559	907-543-3151	19,600,000 / 0-3,000
19	B3	Yukon Flats NWR, 101-12th Ave., Room 110, Box 14, Fairbanks 99701	907-456-0440	8,630,000 / 300-5,000
1	C2	**Nat'l. Park Svc., Alaska Region**, c/o AK Public Lands Info. Ctr., 605 W. 4th Ave. Anchorage 99501	907-271-2737	na / na
2	C2	Alagnak Wild River, c/o Katmai Nat'l. Park & Preserve, PO Box 7, King Salmon 99613	907-246-3305	24,038 / na
3	C1	Aniakchak Nat'l. Mon. & Preserve, PO Box 7, King Salmon 99613 [SW of King Salmon, map C2]	907-246-3305	591,000 / na
4	A1	Bering Land Bridge Nat'l. Preserve, PO Box 220, Nome 99762 [N of Nome, map B1]	907-443-2522	2,785,000 / 0-2,700
5	A2	Cape Krusenstern National Monument, PO Box 1029, Kotzebue 99752	907-442-3760	660,000 / na
6	B2	Denali National Park & Preserve, PO Box 9, Denali Park 99755	907-683-2686	6,000,000 / 500-20,320
7	A2	Gates of the Arctic NP & Preserve, PO Box 74680, Fairbanks 99707 [NE of Kotzebue, map A2]	907-456-0281	8,472,517 / 400-8,500
8	C4	Glacier Bay Nat'l. Park & Preserve, PO Box 140, Gustavus 99826	907-697-2230	3,225,000 / 0-15,320
9	C2	Katmai Nat'l. Park & Preserve, PO Box 7, King Salmon 99613	907-246-3305	3,716,000 / na
10	C2	Kenai Fjords National Park, PO Box 1727, Seward 99664	907-224-3175	670,000 / 0-6,000
11	C4	Klondike Gold Rush Nat'l. Hist. Park, PO Box 517, Skagway 99840 [at corner of 2nd & Broadway St.]	907-983-2921	13,191 / 0-3,740
12	A2	Kobuk Valley National Park, PO Box 1029, Kotzebue 99752	907-442-3760	1,750,000 / na
13	C2	Lake Clark NP & Preserve, 4230 University Dr., Suite 311, Anchorage 99508 [W of Anchorage]	907-271-3751	4,040,000 / 0-10,200

★ INFORMATION CHART ★

AGENCY/MAP LEGEND... INITIALS, MAP SYMBOLS, COLOR CODES

U.S. Forest Service Supervisor & Ranger Dist. Offices	NFS [61]
U.S. Army Corps of Engineers Rec. Areas & Offices	COE [31]
USFWS National Wildlife Refuges & Offices	NWR [40]
National Park Service Parks & other NPS Sites	NPS [7]
Bureau of Land Management Rec. Areas & Offices	BLM [26]
Bureau of Reclamation Rec. Areas & Reg. Offices	BOR [8]
State Parks (also see State Agency notes)	SPS [52]
State Wildlife Areas (also see State Agency notes)	SWA [19]
Private Preserves, Nature Centers & Tribal Lands	[15]

The Wild Rivers ~~~ and Wilderness Areas

Note: Refer to yellow block on page 7 (top right) for location name and address abbreviations.

INFORMATION CHART LEGEND - SYMBOLS & LETTER CODES

■ means YES & □ means Yes with disability provisions
sp means spring, March through May
S means Summer, June through August
F means Fall, September through November
W means Winter, December through February
T means Two (2) or Three (3) Seasons
A means All Four (4) Seasons
na means Not Applicable or Not Available

Note: empty or blank spaces in the chart mean NO and ★ that symbol is not shown on the map.

Column categories (FACILITIES, SERVICES, RECREATION OPPORTUNITIES & CONVENIENCES)

INFO OFFICE (IO) / VISITOR CENTER (VC); IO / VC: Open Saturday / Sunday; ENTRY FEE not camping or permit fee, etc.; CONCESSIONAIRE SERVICES or permits; FREE LITERATURE or brochures, maps, etc.; AGENCY GUIDED TOURS, scheduled / by res.; INTERPRETIVE or EDUCATIONAL DISPLAY; NATURE STUDY PROGRAMS; WILDFLOWER VIEWING AREA or DRIVE; ARCHAEOLOGICAL / GEOLOGICAL SITES; HISTORIC SITES; INTERPRETIVE TRAILS; WILDLIFE VIEWING TRAILS; ENDANGERED SPECIES ARE COMMON; WILDLIFE IS ABUNDANT OR COMMON; DEVELOPED PICNIC AREAS / PICNIC SITES; NO-CHARGE CAMPGROUNDS / CAMPSITES; WILDERNESS AREAS / CAMPSITES; WALKING / HIKING TRAILS; BICYCLING PERMITTED; HORSEBACK RIDING, w/ your own horse; OFF-ROAD Motorized Vehicle Area / use OK; FISHING OK, license / permit reqd.; BOATING IN SEASON, ramps, marinas, etc.; NON-MOTORIZED WATERCRAFT OK, check limits; MOTORIZED WATERCRAFT OK; HUNTING IN SEASON, license / permit reqd.; WINTER SPORTS OPPORTUNITIES; PARK & WALK-IN ONLY AREA; DAY USE ONLY, no overnight; DRINKING WATER; RESTROOMS

Location Data

S#	MAP	LOCATION NAME (state initials if more than one) with ADDRESS and/or LOCATION DATA	TELEPHONE	ACRES / ELEVATION
14	A2	Noatak National Preserve, PO Box 1029, Kotzebue 99752 [N of Kotzebue]	907-442-3760	6,000,000 / na
15	D4	Sitka National Historical Park, 106 Metlakatla, PO Box 738, Sitka 99835 [SE of Sitka]	907-747-6281	107 / 10
16	C3	Wrangell-St. Elias NP & Preserve, PO Box 29, Glennallen 99588 [SE of Glennallen]	907-822-5235	13,200,000 / 0-18,000
17	B3	Yukon-Charley Rivers N. Preserve, PO Box 167, Eagle 99738 [NW of Eagle]	907-547-2233	2,524,000 / 700-6,435
1	C2	**BLM Alaska State Office**, 222 W. 7th Avenue, #13, Anchorage 99513	907-271-5555	na / 100
★2	C2	Anchorage District Office, 6881 Abbott Loop Road, Anchorage 99507	907-267-1204	16,000,000 / 0-100
★3	C2	Campbell Tract, 6881 Abbott Loop Rd., Anchorage 99507	907-267-1204	100 / 100
4	B3	Arctic District Office, 1150 University Ave., Fairbanks 99709	907-474-2302	34,000,000 / 1,000-9,000
5	C3	Glennallen District Office, PO Box 147, Glennallen 99588	907-822-3217	5,000,000 / 1,000-5,000
6	C3	Denali-Clearwater SRA, near Paxton	907-822-3217	2,000,000 / 2,000-5,000
7	B3	Kobuk District Office, 1150 University Ave., Fairbanks 99709	907-474-2332	17,000,000 / 1,000-7,000
8	A2	Kotzebue Field Station, PO Box 1049, Kotzebue 99752	907-442-3430	2,000,000 / 0-6,000
9	B1	Nome Field Station, PO Box 952, Nome 99762	907-443-2177	1,000,000 / 0-6,000
10	B1	Kigluiak Mountains, near Nome	907-443-2177	500,000 / 2,000-6,000
11	B3	Steese/White Mtn. District Office, 1150 University Ave., Fairbanks 99709	907-356-5367	7,000,000 / 1,000-7,000
12	B3	Steese National Conservation Area, near Fairbanks	907-474-2352	1,000,000 / 1,000-6,000
13	B3	White Mountains NRA, near Fairbanks	907-474-2352	1,000,000 / 1,500-5,000
14	B3	Tok Field Station, PO Box 309, Tok 99780	907-883-5121	2,000,000 / 2,000-4,000
15	B3	Fortymile SRA, Tok [North of Tok, map C3]	907-883-5121	2,000,000 / 1,000-6,000
16	B3	Ft. Egbert/Eagle Historic District, Eagle	907-883-5121	10 / 1,000
1	C2	**DNR, Parks & Outdoor Rec. Div HQ.** SC Reg for Anchorage Pks, 3601 C St, PO Box 107001, Anchorage 99510	907-762-2617	na / na
2	C2	Kenai Peninsula Region Office, Mile 85 Sterling Hwy., PO Box 1247, Soldotna 99669	907-262-5581	na / na
3	C2	Caines Head SRA (access by boat), nearest town is, Seward	907-262-5581	5,961 / na
4	C2	Captain Cook SRA (7 areas), nearest town is, Kenai	907-262-5581	3,466 / na
5	C2	Kachemak Bay SP/WP, (access by plane & boat), nearest town is, Homer	907-262-5581	368,290 / 0-5,500
6	C2	Kenai River Spl.Mgt. Area (9 areas), nearest towns, Sterling, Soldotna &, Kenai	907-262-5581	1,866 / na
7	C2	Kodiak Region Office, Mile 3.5 Mill Bay Rd., SR Box 380047, Kodiak 99615	907-486-6339	12,000 / 0-600
8	C2	Buskin River SRS, 4.5 mi. W of Rezanof Dr., Kodiak	907-486-6339	196 / na
9	C2	Shuyak Island SP, (access by plane & boat), Kodiak	907-486-6339	11,000 / na
10	C2	Mat-Su/Valdez/Copper Basin Reg. Off. & Finger Lake SRS, HC 32 Box 6706, Wasilla 99687	907-745-3975	47 / 200
11	C2	Denali SP (6 areas), nearest town is, Trapper Creek	907-745-3975	324,240 / na
12	C3	Dry Creek SRS, nearest town is, Glennallen	907-745-3975	372 / na
13	C2	Montana Creek SRS, nearest town is, Talkeetna	907-745-3975	82 / na
14	C2	Nancy Lake SRA (4 areas), nearest town is, Willow	907-745-3975	22,685 / na
15	B3	Northern Region Office, 3700 Airport Way, Fairbanks 99709	907-451-2695	na / 30
16	B3	Chena River SRA (6 areas), nearest town is, Fairbanks	907-451-2695	254,080 / 620-4,420
17	B3	Eagle Trail SRS, nearest towns are North Pole and, Fairbanks	907-451-2695	640 / 1,700
18	B3	Harding Lake SRA, nearest town is, Tok	907-451-2695	169 / 720
19	D4	Southeast Region Office, 400 Willoughby Bldg., 3rd Floor, Juneau 99801	907-465-4563	na / na
20	C4	Chilkat SP, nearest town is, Haines	907-465-4563	6,045 / na
21	C4	Chilkoot Lake SRS, nearest town is, Haines	907-465-4563	80 / na
22	D4	Shelter Island SMP, (access Lynn Canal), Juneau	907-465-4563	3,560 / na
23	C2	SW Reg. Off. & Chugach SP (7 areas), 3601 C St., Suite 1280, PO Box 107001, Anchorage 99510	907-345-5014	500,000 / 0-8,500
24	C1	Wood-Tikchik SP & Reg Office (access by plane/boat), PO Box 3022, Dillingham (nearest town) 99576	907-842-2375	1,555,200 / 37-5,100
1	D4	**Div. of Wildlife Conservation,** 1255 West 8th St., PO Box 25526, Juneau 99802	907-465-4190	na / na
2	D4	ADWC - Region 1, 802 Third St., Douglas Island, Douglas 99824	907-465-4265	na / na
3	C2	ADWC - Region 2, 333 Raspberry Rd., Anchorage 99518	907-267-2179	na / na
4	B3	ADWC - Region 3, 1300 College Rd., Fairbanks 99701	907-456-5156	na / na
5	C2	ADWC - Region 4, Kodiak Island, Kodiak 99615	907-486-4969	na / na

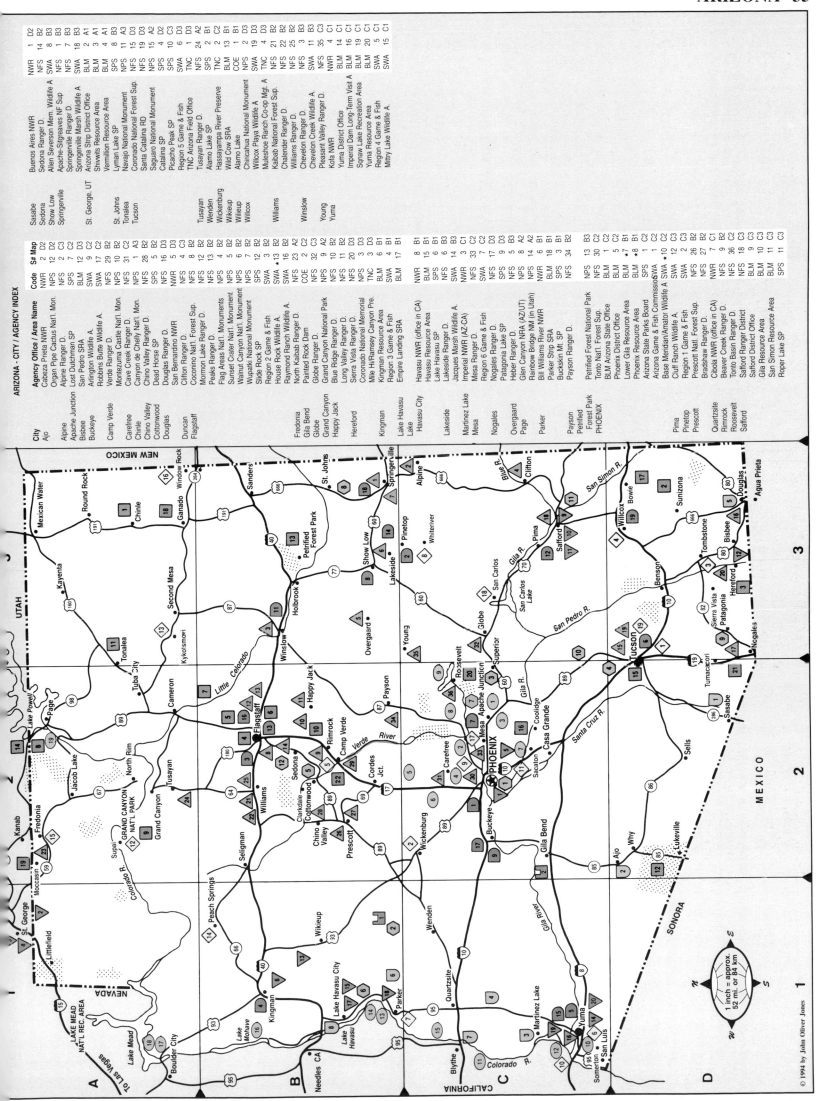

ARIZONA - CITY / AGENCY INDEX

City	Agency Office / Area Name	Code	S# Map
Ajo	Cabeza Prieta NWR	NWR	2 D2
	Organ Pipe Cactus Natl. Mon.	NPS	12 D2
Alpine	Alpine Ranger D.	NFS	5 C3
Apache Junction	Lost Dutchman SP	SPS	7 C2
Bisbee	San Pedro SRA	BLM	12 D3
Buckeye	Arington Wildlife A.	SWA	17 C2
Camp Verde	Robbins Butte Wildlife A.	SWA	17 C2
	Verde Ranger D.	NFS	29 B2
Carefree	Cave Creek Natl. Mon.	NPS	10 B2
Chinle	Canyon de Chelly Natl. Mon.	NPS	31 A3
Chino Valley	Chino Valley Ranger D.	NFS	1 B2
Cottonwood	Dead Horse SP	SPS	28 B2
Douglas	Douglas Ranger D.	NFS	16 D3
	San Bernardino NWR	NWR	5 D3
Duncan	Clifton Ranger D.	NFS	4 C3
Flagstaff	Coconino Natl. Forest Sup.	NFS	8 B2
	Mormon Lake Ranger D.	NFS	13 B2
	Peaks Ranger D.	NFS	12 B2
	Flag Areas Natl. Monuments	NPS	4 B2
	Sunset Crater Natl. Monument	NPS	6 B2
	Walnut Canyon Natl. Monument	NPS	7 B2
	Wupatki National Monument	NPS	12 B2
	Slide Rock SP	SPS	3 B2
	Region 2 Game & Fish	SWA	3 *13 B2
	House Rock Wildlife A.	SWA	16 A2
	Raymond Ranch Wildlife A.	NFS	23 A2
Fredonia	North Kaibab Ranger D.	COE	2 C2
Gila Bend	Painted Rock Dam	NFS	32 C3
Globe	Globe Ranger D.	NFS	9 A2
Grand Canyon	Grand Canyon National Park	NPS	10 B1
Happy Jack	Long Valley Ranger D.	NFS	11 B2
Hereford	Sierra Vista Ranger D.	NFS	20 D3
	Coronado National Memorial	NPS	3 D3
	Mile Hi/Ramsey Canyon Pre.	TNC	3 D3
Kingman	Kingman Resource Area	BLM	6 B1
	Region 3 Game & Fish	SWA	4 B1
Lake Havasu City	Empire Landing SRA	BLM	17 B1
	Havasu NWR (office in CA)	NWR	8 B1
Lake Havasu	Havasu Resource Area	BLM	15 B1
Lake	Lake Havasu SP	SPS	6 B3
Lakeside	Lakeside Ranger D.	NFS	14 C3
Martinez Lake	Jacques Marsh Wildlife A.	SWA	3 C1
	Imperial NWR (AZ-CA)	NWR	7 C2
Mesa	Mesa Ranger D.	NFS	33 D3
	Region 6 Game & Fish	SWA	7 C2
Nogales	Nogales Ranger D.	NFS	17 D3
	Patagonia Lake SP	SPS	5 D3
Overgaard	Heber Ranger D.	NFS	5 B3
Page	Glen Canyon NRA (AZ/UT)	NPS	8 A2
	Rainbow Bridge NM (in Utah)	NPS	14 A2
Parker	Bill Williams River NWR	NWR	6 B1
	Parker Strip SRA	BLM	18 B1
Payson	Buckskin Mt. SP	SPS	18 B1
	Payson Ranger D.	NFS	34 B2
Petrified Forest Park	Petrified Forest National Park	NPS	13 B3
PHOENIX	Tonto Natl. Forest Sup.	NFS	30 C2
	BLM Arizona State Office	BLM	1 C2
	Phoenix District Office	BLM	5 C2
	Lower Gila Resource Area	BLM	*7 B1
	Phoenix Resource Area	BLM	*8 B1
	Arizona State Parks Board	SWA	1
	Arizona Game & Fish Commission	SWA	1
	Base Meridian/Amator Wildlife A	SWA	*10 C2
Pima	Cluff Ranch Wildlife A.	SWA	12 C3
Pinetop	Region 1 Game & Fish	SWA	26 B2
Prescott	Prescott Natl. Forest Sup.	NFS	27 C1
	Bradshaw Ranger D.	NWR	9 B1
Quartzsite	Beaver Creek Ranger D.	NFS	5 B2
Rimrock	Cibola NWR (office in CA)	NWR	18 C2
Roosevelt	Tonto Basin Ranger D.	NFS	9 C2
Safford	Safford District Office	NFS	36 C2
	Gila Resource Area	BLM	10 C3
	San Simon Resource Area	BLM	10 C3
	Roper Lake SP	SPS	11 C3

	Code	S#	Map
Sasabe	Buenos Aires NWR	NWR	1 D2
Sedona	Sedona Ranger D.	NFS	14 B2
Show Low	Allen Severson Mem. Wildlife A.	SWA	8 B3
Springerville	Apache-Sitgreaves NF Sup.	NFS	7 B3
	Springerville Ranger D.	NFS	7 B3
	Springerville Marsh Wildlife A.	SWA	18 B3
St. George, UT	Arizona Strip District Office	BLM	2 A1
	Shivwits Resource Area	BLM	3 A1
	Vermillion Resource Area	BLM	4 A1
St. Johns	Lyman Lake SP	SPS	11 A3
Tonalea	Navajo National Monument	NPS	15 D3
Tucson	Coronado National Forest Sup.	NFS	15 A2
	Santa Catalina RD	NPS	15 A2
	Saguaro National Monument	NPS	15 A2
	Catalina SP	SPS	4 D2
	Picacho Peak SP	SPS	10 C3
	Region 5 Game & Fish	SWA	6 D3
	TNC Arizona Field Office	TNC	13 D3
Tusayan	Tusayan Ranger D.	SPS	2 B1
Wenden	Alamo Lake SP	NFS	13 B1
Wickenburg	Hassayampa River Preserve	COE	1 B1
Wikieup	Wild Cow SRA	BLM	3 D3
Willcox	Alamo Lake	SWA	19 D3
	Chincahua National Monument	TNC	4 D3
	Wilcox Playa Wildlife A.	NFS	21 B2
	Muleshoe Ranch Co-op Mgt. A.	NFS	25 B2
Williams	Chalender Ranger D.	SWA	11 B3
	Williams Ranger D.	NFS	35 C3
	Chevelon Ranger D.	NWR	14 C1
Winslow	Chevelon Creek Wildlife A.	BLM	16 C1
	Pleasant Valley Ranger D.	BLM	18 C1
Young	Kofa NWR	BLM	20 C1
Yuma	Yuma District Office	SWA	5 C1
	Imperial Dam Long-Term Visit A	SWA	15 C1
	Sqnaw Lake Recreation Area		
	Yuma Resource Area		
	Region 4 Game & Fish		
	Mltry Lake Wildlife A.		

© 1994 by John Oliver Jones

1 inch = approx. 52 mi. or 84 km

ARIZONA NOTES

Summary

There are 108 federal, 33 state, and 20 private recreation areas or local administrative offices covered in this state chapter. Of these, 104 appear in the Information Chart and 57 are covered in the notes. The special indexes feature 50 federally designated wilderness areas and wild rivers, and 59 agency published outdoor maps including the 42 maps on the BLM map grid.

Federal Agencies

U.S. Forest Service

Arizona is in the Southwestern Region (see New Mexico chapter - U.S. Forest Svc., Southwestern Region listing).

Sabino Canyon Visitor Center   602-749-8700
(see S# 19, Santa Catalina RD of the Coronado NF)
Exhibits here interpret the geology, history, and botany of the Santa Catalina Mountains.

Columbine Visitor Station   602-428-4150
(see S# 18, Safford RD of the Coronado NF)
At the top of the Pinaleno Mountains and 19 miles up Hwy. 366 from the SH 191 junction. Open 9am to 6 pm Memorial Day through Labor Day and on weekends in September from 9am to 5pm. Interpretive displays, walking and interpretive trails, and abundant wildlife.

National Park Service

Arizona National Park sites are administered as part of several National Park Service regions. Piping Spring Natl. Monument is administered by the Rocky Mountain Region in Denver, Colorado. Canyon de Chelly, Navajo, Sunset Crater, and Wupatki Natl. Monuments are administered from the Southwest Region in Santa Fe, New Mexico. The other NPS locations in Arizona are administered by the Western Region in San Francisco, California.

Additional NPS Locations in Arizona

Casa Grande National Monument (472 acres)
(S# 16, map C2)
PO Box 518
Coolidge, AZ 85228   602-723-3172

Fort Bowie National Historic Site (1,000 acres)
(S# 17, map D3)
PO Box 158
Bowie, AZ 85605   602-847-2500

Hohokam Pima National Monument
Not open to public. Contact Casa Grande Natl. Monument for current information.

Hubbell Trading Post National Historic Site (160 acres)
(S# 18, map A3)
PO Box 150
Ganado, AZ 86505   602-755-3475

Pipe Spring National Monument (40 acres)
(S# 19, map A2)
Moccasin, AZ 85730   602-643-7105

Tonto National Monument (1,120 acres)
(S# 20, map D2)
PO Box 707
Roosevelt, AZ 85545   602-467-2241

Tumacacori NH Park (17 acres) (S# 21, map D2)
PO Box 67
Tumacacori, AZ 85640   602-398-2341

Tuzigoot Natl. Monument (801 acres) (S# 22, map C2)
PO Box 68 (near Cottonwood)
Clarkdale, AZ 86324   602-634-5564

Wilderness/Wild River Index

Local offices are listed with their symbol number and map coordinates, followed by the names of wilderness areas under their jurisdiction. Use the symbol numbers to find the office address and telephone number in the Information Chart. Areas are listed under more than one office when jurisdiction overlaps. The wilderness areas shown on the Arizona map and are indicated here with an asterisk.

Wilderness Areas

Apache-Sitgreaves National Forests (S# 1, map B3)
Bear Wallow Wilderness - 11,080 acres
Escudilla Wilderness - 5,200 acres
Mt. Baldy Wilderness - 7,079 acres
Coconino National Forest (S# 8, map B2)
Fossil Springs Wilderness - 11,550 acres
Kachina Peaks Wilderness - 18,200 acres
Kendrick Mountain Wilderness - 6,510 acres
Munds Mountain Wilderness - 18,150 acres
Red Rock-Secret Mountain Wilderness* - 43,950 acres
Strawberry Crater Wilderness - 10,141 acres
Sycamore Canyon Wilderness - 55,937 acres
West Clear Creek Wilderness - 13,600 acres
Wet Beaver Wilderness - 6,700 acres
Coronado National Forest (S# 15, map D3)
Chiricahua Wilderness* - 87,700 acres
Galiuro Wilderness* - 76,317 acres
Miller Peak Wilderness - 20,190 acres
Mount Wrightson Wilderness - 25,260 acres
Pajarita Wilderness - 7,420 acres
Pusch Ridge Wilderness - 56,933 acres
Rincon Mountain Wilderness* - 38,590 acres
Santa Teresa Wilderness - 26,780 acres
Kaibab National Forest (S# 21, map B2)
Kanab Creek Wilderness* - 63,760 acres
Kendrick Mountain Wilderness - 6,510 acres
Saddle Mountain Wilderness* - 40,600 acres
Sycamore Canyon Wilderness - 55,937 acres
Prescott National Forest (S# 26, map B2)
Apache Creek Wilderness - 5,420 acres
Castle Creek Wilderness - 26,030 acres
Cedar Bench Wilderness - 14,950 acres
Granite Mountain Wilderness - 9,800 acres
Juniper Mesa Wilderness - 7,600 acres
Pine Mountain Wilderness - 20,061 acres
Sycamore Canyon Wilderness - 55,937 acres
Woodchute Wilderness - 5,600 acres
Tonto National Forest (S# 30, map C2)
Four Peaks Wilderness - 53,500 acres
Hellsgate Wilderness - 36,780 acres
Matatzal Wilderness* - 251,950 acres
Pine Mountain Wilderness - 20,061 acres
Salome Wilderness - 18,950 acres
Salt River Canyon Wilderness* - 32,800 acres
Sierra Ancha Wilderness - 20,850 acres
Superstition Wilderness - 159,757 acres

BLM Arizona Strip District (S# 2, map A1)
Note: Office is located in St. George, Utah
Aravaipa Canyon Wilderness - 6,670 acres
Beaver Dam Mountains Wilderness* - 17,000 acres
Cottonwood Point Wilderness - 6,500 acres
Grand Wash Cliffs Wilderness* - 36,300 acres
Kanab Creek Wilderness - 8,850 acres
Mount Logan Wilderness - 14,600 acres
Mount Trumbull Wilderness - 7,900 acres
Paiute Wilderness - 84,700 acres
Paria Canyon-Vermillion
Cliffs Wilderness* - 90,000 acres

National Park Service Wilderness Areas:
Chiricahua Natl. Monument (S# 2, map D3)
Chiricahua Wilderness* - 9,440 acres
Organ Pipe Cactus Natl. Monument (S# 12, map D2)
Organ Pipe Cactus Wilderness* - 312,600 acres
Petrified Forest National Park (S# 13, map B3)
Petrified Forest Wilderness* - 50,260 acres
Saguaro Natl. Monument (S# 15, map A2)
Saguaro Wilderness* - 71,400 acres

Wild River

Prescott National Forest (S# 26, map B2)
Verde Wild River (map B2)

Bureau of Reclamation

Nineteen recreation areas are listed here and symbolized on the Arizona state map.

S#	MAP	LOCATION NAME
Arizona:		
1	C2	Apache Lake
2	C2	Bartlett Reservoir
3	C2	Canyon Lake
4	C2	Horsemen's Park
5	C2	Horseshoe Reservoir
6	C2	Lake Pleasant
7	C2	Saguaro Lake
8	C2	Salt River Project Canals
9	C2	Theodore Roosevelt Lake
Arizona/California:		
		The Imperial Reservoir Area -
10	C1	Mittry Lake Wildlife Area
11	C1	Picacho State Recreation Area
12	C1	Senator Wash Res./Squaw Lake
		The Havasu Area -
13	B1	Lake Havasu Rec. Area
14	B1	Parker Dam
15	C1	Parker Strip
Arizona/Nevada:		
16	B1	Davis Dam
17	A1	Hoover Dam
18	A1	Lake Mead Natl. Rec. Area
Arizona/Utah:		
19	A2	Lake Powell & Glen Canyon Dam/NRA

National Park Service
Outdoor Map Index
Glen Canyon Natl. Recreation Area [1969]

U.S. Forest Service Maps

Apache-Sitgreaves National Forest
Scale: 1 inch = 2.0 miles (1 cm = 1.3 km)
Coconino National Forest
Scale: 1 inch = 2.0 miles (1 cm = 1.3 km)
Coronado National Forest, North
Scale: 1 inch = 2.0 miles (1 cm = 1.3 km)
Coronado National Forest, South
Scale: 1 inch = 2.0 miles (1 cm = 1.3 km)
Coronado NF, Douglas Ranger D.
Scale: 1 inch = 2.0 miles (1 cm = 1.3 km)
Kaibab National Forest, North
Scale: 1 inch = 2.0 miles (1 cm = 1.3 km)
Kaibab National Forest, South
Scale: 1 inch = 2.0 miles (1 cm = 1.3 km)
Mazatzal Wilderness
Scale: 1 inch = 1.0 mile (1 cm = 0.6 km)
Mt. Baldy Wilderness
Scale: 1 inch = 2.7 miles (1 cm = 1.7 km)

Scale: 1 inch = 4.0 miles (1 cm = 2.5 km)
Size: 32x36 inches (81x91 cm)
Grand Canyon National Park [1962]
Scale: 1 inch = 1.0 mile (1 cm = 0.6 km)
Size: 38x60 inches (96x152 cm)
Petrified Forest National Park [1981]
Scale: 1 inch = 0.8 miles (1 cm = 0.5 km)
Size: 24x40 inches (61x101 cm)

Prescott National Forest (black-and-white)
Scale: 1 inch = 2.0 miles (1 cm = 1.3 km)
Pusch Ridge Wilderness
Scale: 1 inch = 2.7 miles (1 cm = 1.7 km)
Superstition Wilderness
Scale: 1 inch = 1.0 mile (1 cm = 0.6 km)
Tonto National Forest
Scale: 1 inch = 2.0 miles (1 cm = 1.3 km)

Bureau of Land Management Maps

Two full-color State of Arizona maps are available at the state office in Phoenix (see BLM S# 1). The $7 map is 4x5 feet and covers a scale 1:1,000,000 (1 in. = 8 mi.). The same map in 1:500,000 scale (1 in. = 16 mi.) is $5 and map size is 24x28 inches. The Arizona BLM map grid below shows the 42 available intermediate maps.

State Agencies

Arizona State Parks Board (ASPB) (S# 1, map C2)
The Board manages Arizona Parks. *Arizona State Parks* (21 parks) and *Arizona Campground Directory* guides are available free. There is an entrance fee at all parks. Camping fees vary. Reservations are taken for Group-use areas only. Other guide books covering Arizona's trails, lakes, rivers, and streams, are sold by the ASPB. Ask for an order form.

BLM ARIZONA map grid (longitude 115°–109°, latitude 37°–31°) — 1:100,000 intermediate scale map sheets (name, year, code; T = topographic, P = planimetric):

- Overton 1978 P
- Lake Mead 1979 T
- Boulder City 1978 P
- Davis Dam 1979 P
- Needles 1978
- Parker 1978 T
- Blythe 1978 P
- Yuma 1979
- Littlefield 1978 P
- Mount Trumbull 1978 P
- Peach Springs 1979 P
- Valentine 1979 P
- Bagdad 1979 T
- Alamo Lake 1979 T
- Salome 1978 P
- Trigo Mountains 1988 P
- Tinajas Altas Mtns. 1984 T
- Fredonia 1978 P
- Grand Canyon 1978 T
- Valle 1983 T
- Williams 1990 T
- Prescott 1987 T
- Bradshaw Mountains 1984 T
- Phoenix North 1979 T
- Phoenix South 1984 T
- Little Horn Mountains 1982 T
- Dateland 1982 T
- Cabeza Prieta Mtns. 1982 T
- Lukeville 1983
- Glen Canyon Dam 1980 P
- Tuba City
- Cameron
- Flagstaff 1985 T
- Sedona 1982 T
- Payson 1983 T
- T. Roosevelt Lake 1982 T
- Mesa 1979
- Casa Grande 1979 T
- Gila Bend 1982 T
- Ajo 1982 T
- Sells 1979 T
- Atascosa Mountains 1979 T
- Kayenta
- Pinon
- Polacca
- Winslow 1984 T
- Holbrook 1982 P
- Show Low 1984 T
- Globe 1979
- Seneca
- Mammoth 1978 P
- Silver Bell Mountains 1977 T
- Tucson 1979 P
- Nogales 1979 P
- Rock Point
- Canyon De Chelly
- Ganado
- Sanders 1973 T
- Saint Johns 1983 P
- Springerville 1984 T
- Nutrioso 1984
- Clifton 1973 P
- Safford 1973 P
- Wilcox 1978 P
- Fort Huachuca 1979 P
- Chiricahua Peak 1979 P
- Douglas 1977

BLM ARIZONA
1:100,000 INTERMEDIATE SCALE MAPS
SURFACE & SURFACE / MINERAL SERIES
T (topographic) P (planimetric)
T topographic / P planimetric / Base Map Not Available

Arizona Game & Fish Dept. (GFD) (S# 1, map C2)

The *Arizona Hunting Regulations* describes each of the wildlife areas in the Regulations Management Unit Boundaries section. A free booklet titled *Desert Survival* is available. Game harvest and drawing statistics are available annually. The monthly agency magazine, *Wildlife Views*, may be purchased at any Game & Fish office and is available by subscription for $6.50 a year. The agency HQ and six regional offices are listed in the Information Chart. Twelve Wildlife Areas (map S# 8-19) are listed here with their map coordinates and nearby city. Some brochures are available featuring local maps and recreation details.

S#	MAP	Wildlife Area Name, Location
8	B3	Allen Steverson Memorial WA, Show Low
9	C2	Arlington Wildlife Area, Buckeye
★10	C2	Base Meridian/Amator WA, Phoenix
11	B3	Chevron Creek WA, Winslow
12	C3	Cluff Ranch WA, Pima
13	B2	House Rock WA, Flagstaff
14	B3	Jacques Marsh WA, Lakeside
15	C1	Mittry Lake WA, Yuma
16	B2	Raymond Ranch WA, Flagstaff
17	C2	Robbins Butte WA, Buckeye
18	B3	Springerville Marsh WA, Springerville
19	D3	Wilcox Playa WA, Wilcox

State Land Department (Forestry Division)
1616 W. Adams
Phoenix, AZ 85007   602-542-4621
There is no state forest recreation program in Arizona.

The Arizona Office of Tourism
1100 W. Washington
Phoenix, AZ 85007   602-542-8087
Current travel information and free travel guides and maps are available from this office. A *We've Been Thinking About You* guide describes attractions at the state's parks. An official Arizona Dept. of Transportation highway map is available. Map coordinates are provided for listed points of interest. National Forest, Indian Reservation, National Park, and National Recreation Areas are color-coded and scenic routes are identified. Red symbols and location names mark State Parks, Recreation Areas, and where camping is permitted.

Arizona Highways, a monthly Arizona travel magazine, is available for $16 a year from Arizona Highways, 2039 W. Lewis Ave., Phoenix, AZ 85009, phone 602-258-1000 or the in-state WATS phone 1-800-543-5432.

Private Organizations

Tribal Land Areas in Arizona
Yavapai-Apache Indian Community of the Camp Verde Indian Reservation - Camping, hiking, touring.
Yavapai-Apache Community Council (S# 5, map B2)
PO Box 1188
Camp Verde, AZ 86322   602-567-3649

Cocopah Tribe of the Cocopah Indian Reservation - Fishing, hunting, camping, boating, hiking, touring.
Cocopah Tribal Council (S# 6, map C1)
Box B-n G
Somerton, AZ 85350   602-627-2102

Colorado River Tribes of the Colorado River Indian Reservation - Fishing, hunting, camping, boating, touring.
Colorado River Tribal Council (AZ/CA) (S# 7, map B/C1)
Route 1, Box 23-B
Parker, AZ 85344   602-669-9211

White Mountain Apache Tribe of the Fort Apache Indian Reservation - Fishing, hunting, camping, boating, hiking, touring.
White Mountain Apache Tribal Council (S# 8, map C3)
PO Box 7C0
Whiteriver, AZ 85941   602-338-4346

Fort McDowell Mohave-Apache Indian Community of the Fort McDowell Indian Reservation - Fishing, camping, boating.
Mohave-Apache Community Council (S# 9, map C2)
PO Box 17779
Fountain Hills, AZ 85268   602-990-0995

Quechan Tribe of the Fort Yuma Indian Reservation - Fishing, hunting, camping, boating.
Quechan Tribal Council (AZ/CA) (S# 10, map C1)
PO Box 1352
Yuma, AZ 85364   619-572-213

Gila River Pima-Maricopa Community of the Gila River Indian Reservation - Camping, boating, touring.
Gila River Indian Community Council (S# 11, map C2)
PO Box 97
Sacaton, AZ 85247   602-562-3311

Havasupai Tribe of the Havasupai Indian Reservation - Camping, hiking, touring.
Havasupai Tribal Council (S# 12, map A2)
PO Box 10
Supai, AZ 85344   602-448-2961

Hopi Tribe of the Hopi Indian Reservation - Camping, hiking, touring.
Hopi Tribal Council (S# 13, map A3)
PO Box 123
Kykotsmovi, AZ 86039   602-734-2445

Hualapai Tribe of the Hualapai Indian Reservation - Fishing, hunting, camping, boating, hiking.
Hualapai Tribal Council (S# 14, map B1)
PO Box 168
Peach Springs, AZ 86434   602-769-2286

Kaibab Band of Paiute Indians of the Kaibab Indian Reservation - Hunting, camping, hiking.
Kaibab Paiute Tribal Council (S# 15, map A2)
Tribal Affairs Bldg.
Pipe Springs Route
Fredonia, AZ 86022   602-643-7245

Navajo Tribe of the Navajo Indian Reservation - Fishing, hunting, camping, boating, hiking, touring.
Navajo Tribal Council (AZ/NM/UT) (S# 16, map A3)
PO Box 308
Window Rock, AZ 86515   602-871-4941

Salt River Pima-Maricopa Indian Community of the Salt River Indian Reservation - Fishing, camping, boating.
Salt River Pima-Maricopa Indian Community Council (S# 17, map C2)
Route 1, Box 216
Scottsdale, AZ 85256   602-941-7277

San Carlos Apache Tribe of the San Carlos Indian Reservation - Fishing, hunting, camping, boating, hiking.
San Carlos Tribal Council (S# 18, map C3)
PO Box O
San Carlos, AZ 85550   602-475-2361

ANCA Location in Arizona
Arizona-Sonora Desert Museum (S# 19, map D3)
2021 N. Kinney Rd.
Tucson, AZ 85743   602-883-1380

Arizona State Chamber of Commerce
1221 E. Osborn Rd., #100
Phoenix, AZ 85014   Phone 602-248-9172
Fax 602-265-1262

★ INFORMATION CHART ★

INFORMATION CHART LEGEND - SYMBOLS & LETTER CODES
- ■ means **YES** & □ means **Yes with disability provisions**
- **sp** means spring March through May
- **S** means Summer, June through August
- **F** means Fall, September through November
- **W** means Winter, December through February
- **T** means Two (2) or Three (3) Seasons
- **A** means All Four (4) Seasons
- **na** means Not Applicable or Not Available
- Note: empty or blank spaces in the chart mean **NO**

AGENCY/MAP LEGEND . . . INITIALS, MAP SYMBOLS, COLOR CODES
- U.S. Forest Service Supervisor & Ranger Dist. Offices NFS (61)
- U.S. Army Corps of Engineers Rec. Areas & Offices . COE (31)
- USFWS National Wildlife Refuges & Offices . . . . . . NWR (40)
- National Park Service Parks & other NPS Sites . . . . NPS (7)
- Bureau of Land Management Rec. Areas & Offices . . BLM (26)
- Bureau of Reclamation Rec. Areas & Reg. Offices . . BOR (8)
- State Parks (also see State Agency notes) . . . . SPS (52)
- State Wildlife Areas (also see State Agency notes) . . SWA (19)
- Private Preserves, Nature Centers & Tribal Lands . . . (15)
- The Wild Rivers ▦ and Wilderness Areas ▦

Note: Refer to yellow block on page 7 (top right) for location name and address abbreviations. If a symbol number has a star ★ that symbol is not shown on the map.

Column headers (facilities, services, recreation opportunities & conveniences):
INFO OFFICE (IO) / VISITOR CENTER (VC); IO / VC OPEN SATURDAY / SUNDAY; ENTRY FEE / ENTRANCE FEE; CONCESSIONAIRE SERVICES AVAILABLE; INTERPRETIVE or EDUCATIONAL SERVICES; FREE LITERATURE or EDUCATIONAL DISPLAY; AGENCY GUIDED TOURS / STUDY PROGRAMS; NATURE EDUCATION; WILDFLOWER VIEWING IN SEASON; WILDLIFE VIEWING SITES; WILDLIFE IS ABUNDANT OR COMMON; ENDANGERED SPECIES ARE COMMON; DEVELOPED PICNIC AREAS; NO-CHARGE CAMPGROUNDS / PICNIC SITES; DEVELOPED CAMPGROUNDS / CAMPSITES; WALKING / HIKING TRAILS; WILDERNESS AREAS / WILD RIVERS; BICYCLING OPPORTUNITIES; HORSEBACK RIDING, at one's own risk; OFF-ROAD MOTORIZED RIDING; FISHING; HUNTING IN SEASON, by res.; BOATING FACILITIES, ramps, marinas, etc.; MOTORIZED WATERCRAFT OK, check limits; NON-MOTORIZED WATERCRAFT OK; SWIMMING AREA / USE ONLY / WALK-IN ONLY AREA; PARK & SPORTS OPPORTUNITIES; DAY USE ONLY AREA; DRINKING WATER; RESTROOMS

S#	MAP	LOCATION NAME (state initials if more than one) with ADDRESS and/or LOCATION DATA	TELEPHONE	ACRES / ELEVATION
1	B3	**Apache-Sitgreaves Nat'l. Forest Sup.**, PO Box 640, Springerville 85938 [on Mountain Ave.]	602-333-4301	2,000,000 / 3,500-11,500
2	C3	Alpine Ranger D., PO Box 469, Alpine 85920	602-339-4384	400,000 / 4,500-10,900
3	B3	Chevelon Ranger D., HC-62, Box 600, Winslow 86047	602-289-2471	200,000 / 6,000-8,000
4	C3	Clifton Ranger D., HC 1 733, Duncan 85534	602-687-1301	510,000 / 4,100-9,200
5	B3	Heber Ranger D., PO Box 368, Overgaard 85933	602-535-4481	383,000 / 6,300-7,750
6	B3	Lakeside Ranger D., 2022 *W* White Mountain Bl., RR #3, Box B-50, Lakeside 85929	602-368-5111	265,000 / 6,800
7	B3	Springerville Ranger D., PO Box 640, Springerville 85938 [in town at corner of S Mountain Ave. & Airport Rd.]	602-333-4372	400,000 / 5,500-11,600
8	B2	Coconino Nat'l. Forest Sup., 2323 E. Greenlaw Lane, Flagstaff 86004	602-556-7400	1,821,495 / 3,500-12,633
9	B2	Beaver Creek Ranger D., HC 64, Box 240, Rimrock 86335 [off I-17, 45 mi S of Flagstaff]	602-567-4501	300,000 / 2,800-6,000
10	B2	Blue Ridge Ranger D., Int. Hwy. 87 & Lake Mary Rd., HC 31, Box 300, Happy Jack 86024	602-477-2255	200,000 / 7,000-8,500
11	B2	Long Valley Ranger D., Lake Mary Rd., HC 31, PO Box 68, Happy Jack 86024	602-354-2216	350,000 / 5,600-8,400
12	B2	Mormon Lake Ranger D., 4825 S. Lake Mary Road, Flagstaff 86001	602-556-7474	na / na
13	B2	Peaks Ranger D., 5075 N. Highway 89, Flagstaff 86004	602-526-0866	525,000 / 4,800-12,643
14	B2	Sedona Ranger D., off Hwy. 89, PO Box 300, Sedona 86336	602-282-4119	2'6,000 / 4,000-6,000
15	D3	Coronado National Forest Sup., Federal Building, 300 West Congress, Tucson 85701	602-670-6483	2,475,000 / 2,300-11,000

AGENCY/MAP LEGEND . . . INITIALS, MAP SYMBOLS, COLOR CODES

- U.S. Forest Service Supervisor & Ranger Dist. Offices NFS
- U.S. Army Corps of Engineers Rec. Areas & Offices . COE
- USFWS National Wildlife Refuges & Offices . . . . NWR
- National Park Service Parks & other NPS Sites . . . . . NPS
- Bureau of Land Management Rec. Areas & Offices . . BLM
- Bureau of Reclamation Rec. Areas & Reg. Offices . . . BOR
- State Parks (also see State Agency notes) . . . . SPS
- State Wildlife Areas (also see State Agency notes) . . SWA
- Private Preserves, Nature Centers & Tribal Lands . .
- The Wild Rivers and Wilderness Areas

★ INFORMATION CHART ★

INFORMATION CHART LEGEND - SYMBOLS & LETTER CODES

- ■ means **YES** & □ means **Yes with disability provisions**
- **sp** means **sp**ring, March through May
- **S** means **S**ummer, June through August
- **F** means **F**all, September through November
- **W** means **W**inter, December through February
- **T** means **T**wo (2) or **T**hree (3) Seasons
- **A** means **A**ll Four (4) Seasons
- **na** means Not Applicable or Not Available
- Note: empty or blank spaces in the chart mean **NO**

Note: Refer to yellow block on page 7 (top right) for location name and address abbreviations. If a symbol number has a star ★ that symbol is not shown on the map.

FACILITIES, SERVICES, RECREATION OPPORTUNITIES & CONVENIENCES

S#	MAP	LOCATION NAME (state initials if more than one) with ADDRESS and/or LOCATION DATA	TELEPHONE	ACRES / ELEVATION	INFO OFFICE (IO) / VISITOR CENTER (VC)	IO / VC OPEN SATURDAY / SUNDAY	ENTRY FEE, not camping or permit fee	CONCESSIONAIRE SERVICES AVAILABLE	INTERPRETIVE or EDUCATIONAL DISPLAY	FREE LITERATURE, brochures, maps, etc.	AGENCY GUIDED TOURS, scheduled / by res.	NATURE EDUCATION / STUDY PROGRAMS	WILDFLOWER VIEWING AREA or DRIVE	ARCHAEOLOGICAL / GEOLOGICAL SITES	HISTORIC SITES	INTERPRETIVE TRAILS	WILDLIFE IS ABUNDANT OR COMMON	ENDANGERED SPECIES ARE COMMON	WILDLIFE VIEWING SITES, blinds, signs, etc.	DEVELOPED PICNIC AREAS / PICNIC SITES	DEVELOPED CAMPGROUNDS / CAMPSITES	NO-CHARGE CAMPGROUNDS / CAMPSITES	WILDERNESS AREAS / WILD RIVERS	WALKING / HIKING TRAILS	SWIMMING PERMITTED, at one's own risk	BICYCLING OPPORTUNITIES...areas, trails	HORSEBACK RIDING, w/ your own horse	OFF-ROAD Motorized Vehicle Area / Use OK	FISHING IN SEASON, license / permit reqd.	BOATING FACILITIES, ramps, marinas, etc.	MOTORIZED WATERCRAFT OK, check limits	NON-MOTORIZED WATERCRAFT OK	HUNTING IN SEASON, license / permit reqd.	WINTER SPORTS OPPORTUNITIES	PARK & WALK-IN ONLY AREA	DAY USE ONLY, no overnight	DRINKING WATER	RESTROOMS	S#
16	D3	Douglas Ranger D., Leslie Canyon Rd., RR #1, Box 228-R, Douglas 85607	602-364-3468	450,000 / 4,500-9,800	■					■					■					■	■		■	■	■		■		■			■	■						16
17	D3	Nogales Ranger D., 2251 N. Grand Ave., Nogales 85621 [I-16 S to Nogales exit, go 1 mi, office on left past Circle K]	□ 602-281-2296	369,562 / 3,400-9,453	■					■					■		T			□	□	T	■	■		■	■		□	□	■	■	■				■	□	17
18	C3	Safford Ranger District (& Columbine VC), PO Bldg., 3rd Fl., PO Box 709, Safford 85548 [SW corner Hwy 70 at 5th Ave.]	□ 602-428-4150	415,000 / 4,000-11,000	□	S			■	■		■	S	■	■	■	A			□	□	T	■	■	■	■	■	■	■	■	■	■	■	■			□	□	18
19	D3	Santa Catalina RD, 5700 N. Sabino Canyon Road, Tucson 85715 [Sabino Canyon VC, see notes]	602-749-8700	250,000 / 2,300-9,200	■					■				■	■				■	■	■		■	■	■	■	■	■	■				■						19
20	D3	Sierra Vista Ranger D., 5990 South Hwy. 92, Hereford 85615	602-378-0311	360,000 / 4,500-9,466	■					■				■	■				■	■	■		■		■		■	■	■	■	■	■	■						20
21	B2	Kaibab National Forest Sup., 800 South 6th Street, Williams 86046	602-635-2681	1,560,411 / 5,100-10,418	□			□	■	■		□		■	■	□				□	□		■	■		■	■	■	□	□	■	■	■	■			□	□	21
22	B2	Chalender Ranger D., 501 West Bill Williams Ave., Williams 86046	602-635-2676	270,552 / na	□					■				□	□	□	A			□	□		■	■		■	■	■	■	■	■	■	■	■			□	□	22
23	A2	North Kaibab Ranger D., PO Box 248, Fredonia 86022 [off Hwy. 89A]	602-643-7395	650,000 / na	□	T		□	■	■		□	A	■	□		A			□	□		■	■		■	■	■					■	■			□	□	23
24	A2	Tusayan Ranger D., PO Box 3088, Tusayan 86023 [off SR 64 from I-40]	602-638-2443	360,000 / na	□			□		■				■	■	□	A			□	□			■		■	■	■	■			■	■	■			□	□	24
25	B2	Williams Ranger D., Rt. #1, Box 142, Williams 86046 [off I-40 at B. Williams Ave.]	602-635-2633	279,859 / na	□					■		□		■	■					□	□		■	■		■	■	■	□	□	■	■	■	■			□	□	25
26	B2	Prescott Natl. Forest Sup., 344 South Cortez St., Prescott 86303	602-445-1762	1,238,000 / 3,000-8,000	■					■				■	■					■	■		■	■	■	■	■	■	■	■		■	■						26
27	B2	Bradshaw Ranger D., 2230 East Highway 69, Prescott 86301	602-445-7253	370,000 / 3,500-7,800	■										■					■	■		■	■		■	■		■	■		■	■						27
28	B2	Chino Valley Ranger D., 735 N Hwy. 89, PO Box 485, Chino Valley 86323	602-636-2302	500,000 / 3,000-7,300	■									■	■								■		■		■		■				■						28
29	B2	Verde Ranger D., PO Box 670, Camp Verde 86322	602-567-4121	320,000 / 2,800-7,800	■									■	■					■	■		■		■		■		■	■		■	■						29
30	C2	Tonto Nat'l. Forest Sup., 2324 E. McDowell Road, PO Box 5348, Phoenix 85010 [just W of 24th Street & McDowell]	602-225-5200	2,900,000 / 1,800-7,900	□			□	■	■		□	T	■		■				□	□	A	■	■	■	■	■	■	□	□	■	■	■			■	□	□	30
31	C2	Cave Creek Ranger D., PO Box 5068, Carefree 85377	602-488-3441	550,000 / 2,000-6,800	□					■			sp			■				□	□	A	■	■	■	■	■		■	□	■	■	■					□	31
32	C3	Globe Ranger D., Six Shooter Canyon Rd., Rt. #1, Box 33, Globe 85501	602-425-7180	450,000 / 2,200-7,800	□					■			sp	■	■					■	■		■	■	■	■	■		■			■	■				■	■	32
33	C2	Mesa Ranger D., 26 N. MacDonald, PO Box 5800, Mesa 85211 [one block north of Main St.]	602-835-1161	440,000 / 1,300-7,100	■			□	■	■			sp			■				■	■	W	■	■	■	■	■		■	■	■	■	■				■	■	33
34	B2	Payson Ranger D., 1009 East Highway 260, Payson 85541	602-474-2269	450,000 / 2,500-7,900	□					■			T	■						□	□	A	■	■	■	■	■	■	■				■			■	□	□	34
35	C3	Pleasant Valley Ranger D., PO Box 450, Young 85554 [0.25 mi S of SH 88 on FR 63]	602-462-3311	427,000 / 2,800-7,500	■					■			T		■					■	■	A	■	■	■	■	■	■	■				■					□	35
36	C2	Tonto Basin Ranger D., Hwy. 88, PO Box 649, Roosevelt 85545	602-467-2236	530,000 / 2,100-7,100	□			□		■		□	sp	■						□	□	A		■	■	■	■		■	□	■	■	■				□	□	36
		COE, Los Angeles District, PO Box 2711, Los Angeles, CA 90053	213-894-5635	na / na	■					■																										■	■	■	
1	B1	Alamo Lake, S of Wilieup [adjacent Alamo Lake State Park]	213-894-5635	na / na																■	■	A							■	■	■	■					■	■	1
2	C2	Painted Rock Dam, W of Gila Bend	213-894-5635	na / na																																			2
1	D2	**Buenos Aires NWR**, PO Box 109, Sasabe 85633	602-823-4251	114,500 / 3,500-4,600	■					■	■													■		■	■						■		■	■	■		1
2	D2	Cabeza Prieta NWR, 1611 N. Second Ave., Ajo 85321	602-387-6483	860,010 / 650-3,000	■					■					■					■			■										■				■		2
3	C1	Imperial NWR (AZ-CA), PO Box 72217, Martinez Lake 85365	602-783-3371	25,765 / 180	□	T			■	■	■			■	■		A		■	■			■	■	■	■	■		□	□	■	■	■			■	■	■	3
4	C1	Kofa NWR, 356 W. 1st. St., PO Box 6290, Yuma 85366 [refuge located 30 mi. N of Yuma on US 95]	602-783-7861	700,000 / 680-4,877	□				■	■						■			■				■	■			■						■						4
5	D3	San Bernardino NWR (2 sections), 1408 10th Street, Douglas 85607	602-364-2104	3,640 / 3,900-5,800	■					■				■	■																		■		■	■			5
6	B1	Bill Williams River NWR, 60911 Hwy. 95, Parker 85344 [between Havasu and Parker, office at mile post 161 on US 95]	602-667-4144	6,105 / 500-1,000	■					■							sp												■		■	■	■		■	■			6
7	C1	Cibola NWR (office in CA), PO Box AP, Blythe, CA 92226, near Quartzsite [SE of Blythe]	602-857-3253	16,667 / 240	■					■	■	■				□	W		■								■		■	■	■	■	■			■	■		7
8	B1	Havasu NWR (office in CA), 1406 Bailey Ave., Suite B, PO Box 3009, CA 92363, Lake Havasu City [NW of City]	619-326-3853	38,900 / 430-2,200	■			■		■													■		■				■	■	■	■	■			■	■		8
1	A3	**Canyon de Chelly National Monument**, PO Box 588, Chinle 86503	602-674-5500	83,840 / 5,500	□			■		■				■						■	■		■	■			■	■											1
2	D3	Chiricahua National Monument, Dos Cabezas Route, Box 6500, Willcox 85643 [SE of Willcox]	602-824-3560	11,985 / na	□	A	A		■	■		■		□	□	□	T			□	□			■			■											□	2
3	D3	Coronado N Mem., 4101 East Montezuma Canyon Rd., Hereford 85615 [5 mi S off Hwy. 92 & 16 mi S of Sierra Vista]	602-366-5515	4,976 / 4,700-7,676	□	A			■	■	□	□	T	■		□	A		□	□				■												■	□	□	3
4	B2	Flag Areas Nat'l. Monuments, 2717 N. Stevens Blvd., Suite #3, Flagstaff 86004	602-527-7152	41,000 / 7,000	■					■										■																■			4
5	B2	Sunset Crater Nat'l. Monument, Flagstaff [on Hwy. 89, 15 mi N of Flagstaff]	602-527-7042	3,100 / 6,900	■					■				■	■					■				■												■			5
6	B2	Walnut Canyon Nat'l. Monument, Walnut Canyon Rd., (off I-40, 8 mi. E of), Flagstaff 86004	602-526-3367	2,600 / 6,700	■					■				■	■					■				■												■			6
7	B2	Wupatki National Monument, Flagstaff [on Hwy. 89 40 mi N of Flagstaff]	602-527-7040	35,300 / 5,100	■					■				■	■					■				■												■			7
8	A2	Glen Canyon NRA (AZ/UT), PO Box 1507, Page 86040 [weekend ph. 645-2511]	602-645-2471	1,236,880 / 3,100-7,440	□	A		□	■	■	□	□	T	■	■	■	A			□	□			■	■	■	■		■	■	■	■	■				□	□	8
9	A2	Grand Canyon National Park, PO Box 129, Grand Canyon 86023	602-638-7888	1,218,000 / 7,000-8,000	□	A	A	□	■	■	□	□		■	■	□	A			□	□			■			■		■	■	■	■		■				□	9
10	B2	Montezuma Castle Nat'l. Monument, PO Box 219, Camp Verde 86322	602-567-3322	858 / 3,200	■	A	A		■	■				■		□				■																■			10
11	A3	Navajo National Monument, HC 71, Box 3, Tonalea 86044	602-672-2366	360 / na	■					■				■						■	■														■				11
12	D2	Organ Pipe Cactus Nat'l. Monument, Rt. #1, Box 100, Ajo 85321 [S of Why on SR 85]	602-387-6849	330,689 / 1,044-4,808	■					■				■	■				■	■	■		■	■			■												12
13	B3	Petrified Forest National Park, PO Box 2217, Petrified Forest Park 86028 [26 mi E of Holbrook on I-40]	602-524-6228	93,533 / 5,300-6,235	□	A	A	□	■	■				□	□	□	T			□			■	■			■									■	□	□	13
14	A2	Rainbow Bridge NM (in Utah), c/o Glen Canyon NRA, PO Box 1507, Page 86040 [boat / hike in access only; tours available]	602-645-2511	160 / 3,600-5,000					■	■		□		■		□								■							■	■			■	■		□	14
15	A2	Saguaro National Monument, 3693 South Old Spanish Trail, Tucson 85730	602-296-8576	83,574 / 2,720-8,666	□	A	A		■	■	□	□	A	■	■	□	A		■	□	■	A	■	■		■	■											□	15
1	C2	**BLM Arizona State Office**, 3707 N. 7th Street, PO Box 16563, Phoenix 85011	602-640-5504	na / na	■					■														■												■	■		1
2	A1	Arizona Strip District Office, 390 North, 3050 East, St. George, UT 84770	801-673-3545	2,850,000 / 1,800-8,000	■					■				■	■					■	■		■		■		■	■				■	■						2

#	Grid	Name / Address	Phone	Acres / Elev.
5	C2	Phoenix District Office, 2015 W. Deer Valley Road, Phoenix 85027	602-863-4464	9,000,000 / 1,130
6	B1	Kingman Resource Area, 2475 Beverly Ave., Kingman 86401	602-757-3161	2,500,000 / 3,330
*7	B1	Lower Gila Resource Area, 2015 W. Deer Valley Road, Phoenix 85027	602-863-4464	5,500,000 / 1,130
*8	B1	Phoenix Resource Area, 2015 W. Deer Valley Road, Phoenix 85027	602-863-4464	1,000,000 / 1,130
9	C3	Safford District Office, 425 E. 4th Street, Safford 85546	602-428-4040	1,500,000 / 2,930
10	C3	Gila Resource Area, 425 E. 4th Street, Safford 85546	602-428-4040	750,000 / 2,930
11	C3	San Simon Resource Area, 425 E. 4th Street, Safford 85546	602-428-4040	750,000 / 2,930
12	D3	San Pedro SRA, near Bisbee	602-855-8017	na / na
13	B1	Wild Cow SRA, near Wikieup		na / na
14	C1	Yuma District Office, 3150 Winsor Ave., Yuma 85365	602-726-6300	500,000 / 50-130
15	C1	Havasu Resource Area, 3189 Sweetwater Ave., PO Box 685, Lake Havasu City 86403	602-855-8017	500,000 / 400-5,100
16	C1	Imperial Dam Long-Term Visitor Area, near the Imperial Dam, 25 mi. N of Yuma	602-726-6300	2,805 / 100
17	B1	Empire Landing SRA, near Lake Havasu	602-855-8017	2,500,000 / 400
18	B1	Parker Strip SRA, near Parker	602-855-8017	25,385 / 400
19	C1	Squaw Lake Recreation Area, near Imperial Dam, 22 mi. N of Yuma	602-726-6300	10 / 100
20	C1	Yuma Resource Area, 3150 Winsor Ave., Yuma 85365	602-726-6300	3,500 / 180-200

Arizona State Parks Board. 800 W. Washington, Suite 415, Phoenix 85007

#	Grid	Name / Address	Phone	Acres / Elev.
1	C2		602-542-4174	na / na
2	B1	Alamo Lake SP, Wenden [38 mi. N of Wenden, map C1]	602-669-2088	5,642 / 1,250
3	B1	Buckskin Mt. SP, 11 mi. N of Parker	602-667-3231	1,676 / 420
4	D2	Catalina SP, 9 mi. N of Tucson	602-628-5798	5,511 / 2,650
5	B2	Dead Horse SP, Cottonwood	602-634-5283	320 / 3,300
6	B1	Lake Havasu SP, HQ at, Lake Havasu City	602-855-7851	11,839 / 450
7	C2	Lost Dutchman SP, 5 mi. NE of Apache Junction	602-982-4485	330 / 2,000
8	B3	Lyman Lake SP, 11 mi. S of St. Johns	602-337-4441	1,180 / 6,000
9	D3	Patagonia Lake SP, 16 mi. NE of Nogales	602-287-6965	640 / 4,000
10	D3	Picacho Peak SP, 40 mi. N of Tucson	602-466-3183	3,400 / 2,000
11	C3	Roper Lake SP, 6.5 mi. SE of Safford	602-428-6760	319 / 3,130
12	B2	Slide Rock SP, S of Flagstaff	602-282-3034	43 / 4,930

Arizona Game & Fish Commission. 2221 West Greenway Rd., Phoenix 85023

#	Grid	Name / Address	Phone	Acres / Elev.
1	C2		602-942-3000	na / na
2	C3	Region 1 Game & Fish, HC 62, Box 57201, Pinetop 85935	602-367-4281	na / na
3	B2	Region 2 Game & Fish, 3500 S. Lake Mary Rd., Flagstaff 86001	602-774-5045	na / na
4	B1	Region 3 Game & Fish, 5325 N. Stockton Hill Rd., Kingman 86401	602-692-7700	na / na
5	C1	Region 4 Game & Fish, 9140 E. County, 10 1/2 St., Yuma 85365	602-342-0091	na / na
6	D3	Region 5 Game & Fish, 555 N. Greasewood Rd., Tucson 85745	602-628-5376	na / na
7	C2	Region 6 Game & Fish, 7200 E. University Blvd., Mesa 85207	602-981-9400	na / na

TNC Arizona Field Office. 300 E. University Blvd., Suite 230, Tucson 85705

#	Grid	Name / Address	Phone	Acres / Elev.
1	D3		602-622-3861	na / na
2	C2	Hassayampa River Preserve, 49614 Hwy. 60, PO Box 1162, Wickenburg 85358 [mile 114 on Hwy 60, closed Mon. & Tues.]	602-684-2772	340 / 2,000
3	D3	Mile Hi/Ramsey Canyon Preserve, 27 Ramsey Canyon Rd., RR #1, Box 84, Hereford 85615 [limited visitor capacity]	602-378-2785	300 / 5,525-6,300
4	D3	Muleshoe Ranch Co-op Mgt. Area, RR #1, Box 1542, Willcox 85643 [Co-op Management Area - TNC, US-S, BLM]	602-384-2626	54,660 / 3,300-7,660

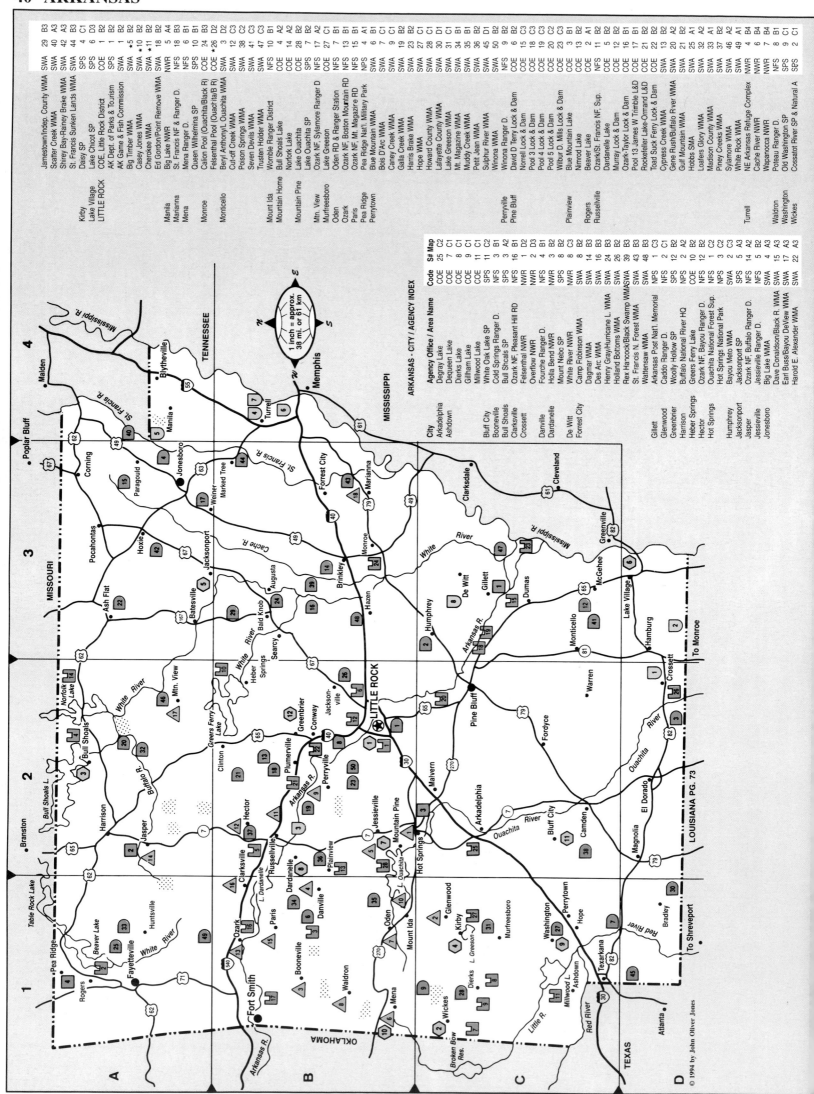

	Code	S#	Map
Jamestown/Indep. County WMA	SWA	29	B3
Scatter Creek WMA	SWA	40	A3
Shirey Bay-Rainey Brake WMA	SWA	42	B3
St. Francis Sunken Lands WMA	SWA	44	B3
Daisy SP	SPS	4	C1
Lake Chicot SP	SPS	6	D3
COE, Little Rock District	COE	1	B2
AK Dept. of Parks & Tourism	SPS	1	B2
AK Game & Fish Commission	SWA	1	B2
Big Timber WMA	SWA	*5	B2
Casey Jones WMA	SWA	*10	B2
Cherokee WMA	SWA	*11	B2
Ed Gordon/Point Remove WMA	SWA	18	B2
Big Lake NWR	NWR	5	A4
St. Francis NF & Ranger D.	NFS	18	B3
Mena Ranger D.	NFS	5	B1
Queen Wilhelmina SP	SPS	10	B1
Calion Pool (Ouachita/Black R)	COE	24	B3
Felsenthal Pool (Ouachita/B R)	COE	*26	D2
Beryl Anthony/L. Ouachita WMA	SWA	3	D2
Cut-off Creek WMA	SWA	12	C3
Poison Springs WMA	SWA	38	C1
Seven Devils WMA	SWA	41	C3
Trusten Holder WMA	SWA	47	C3
Womble Ranger District	NFS	10	B1
Bull Shoals Lake	COE	14	A2
Norfork Lake	COE	28	A2
Lake Ouachita	COE	19	B1
Lake Ouachita SP	SPS	7	B1
Ozark NF, Sylamore Ranger D	NFS	17	A2
Lake Greeson	COE	27	C1
Oden RD & Ranger Station	NFS	7	B1
Ozark NF, Boston Mountain RD	NFS	13	B1
Ozark NF, Mt. Magazine RD	NFS	15	A1
Pea Ridge Nat'l. Military Park	NPS	4	A1
Blue Mountain WMA	SWA	6	B1
Bois D'Arc WMA	SWA	8	C1
Caney Creek WMA	SWA	9	C1
Galla Creek WMA	SWA	19	B2
Harris Brake WMA	SWA	23	B2
Hope WMA	SWA	27	C1
Howard County WMA	SWA	30	D1
Lafayette County WMA	SWA	31	C1
Mt. Magazine WMA	SWA	34	B1
Muddy Creek WMA	SWA	35	B1
Petit Jean WMA	SWA	36	D1
Sulphur River WMA	SWA	45	D1
Winona WMA	SWA	50	B2
David D Terry Lock & Dam	COE	9	B2
Norrell Lock & Dam	COE	15	C3
Pool 3 Lock & Dam	COE	18	C3
Pool 4 Lock & Dam	COE	19	C3
Pool 5 Lock & Dam	COE	20	C2
Wilbur D. Mills Lock & Dam	COE	23	C3
Blue Mountain Lake	COE	13	B2
Nimrod Lake	COE	2	A1
Beaver Lake	COE	1	B2
Ozark/St. Francis NF, Sup.	NFS	11	B1
Dardanelle Lake	COE	5	B2
Murray Lock & Dam	COE	12	B2
Ozark-Taylor Lock & Dam	COE	16	B1
James W Trimble L&D	COE	17	B1
Rockefeller Lake-Ormand L&D	COE	21	B2
Toad Suck Ferry Lock & Dam	COE	22	B2
Cypress Creek WMA	SWA	13	A3
Gene Rush/Buffalo River WMA	SWA	20	A2
Gulf Mountain WMA	SWA	21	B2
Hobbs SMA	SWA	25	A1
Loafers Glory WMA	SWA	32	A2
Madison County WMA	SWA	33	A1
Piney Creeks WMA	SWA	37	B2
Sylamore WMA	SWA	46	A2
White Rock WMA	SWA	49	A1
NE Arkansas Refuge Complex	NWR	4	B4
Cache River NWR	NWR	6	B4
Wapanocca NWR	NWR	7	B4
Poteau Ranger D.	NFS	8	B1
Old Washington SP	SPS	9	C1
Cossatot River SP & Natural A	SPS	2	C1

	City	Code	S#	Map
Kirby				
Lake Village				
LITTLE ROCK				
Manila				
Marianna				
Mena				
Monroe				
Monticello				
Mount Ida				
Mountain Home				
Mount Pine				
Mtn. View				
Murfreesboro				
Oden				
Ozark				
Paris				
Pea Ridge				
Perrytown				
Perryville				
Pine Bluff				
Plainview				
Rogers				
Russellville				
Turrell				
Waldron				
Washington				
Wickes				

ARKANSAS - CITY / AGENCY INDEX

City	Agency Office / Area Name	Code	S#	Map
Arkadelphia	Degray Lake	COE	25	C2
Ashdown	Dequeen Lake	COE	7	C1
	Dierks Lake	COE	8	C1
	Gillham Lake	COE	9	C1
Bluff City	Millwood Lake	COE	11	C1
Booneville	White Oak Lake SP	SPS	11	C2
Bull Shoals	Cold Springs Ranger D.	NFS	3	B1
Clarksville	Bull Shoals SP	SPS	3	A2
Crossett	Ozark NF, Pleasant Hill RD	NFS	16	B1
	Felsenthal NWR	NWR	1	D2
Danville	Overflow NWR	NWR	4	B1
Dardanelle	Fourche Ranger D.	NFS	3	B2
De Witt	Holla Bend NWR	NWR	3	B2
Forest City	Mount Nebo SP	SPS	8	C3
	White River NWR	NWR	8	B2
	Camp Robinson WMA	SWA	14	B3
	Dagmar WMA	SWA	16	B3
	Des Arc WMA	SWA	24	B3
	Henry Gray/Hurricane L. WMA	SWA	39	B3
	Holland Bottoms WMA	SWA	48	B3
Gillett	Rex Hancock/Black Swamp WMA	SWA	43	B3
Glenwood	St. Francis N. Forest WMA	SWA	1	C3
Greenbrier	Wattensaw WMA	SWA	2	C1
Harrison	Arkansas Post Nat'l. Memorial	NPS	5	A2
Heber Springs	Caddo Ranger D.	NFS	12	B2
Hector	Woolly Hollow SP	SPS	2	C2
Hot Springs	Buffalo National River HQ	NPS	5	A3
	Greers Ferry Lake	COE	10	B2
Humphrey	Ozark NF, Bayou Ranger D.	NFS	12	B2
Jacksonport	Ouachita National Forest Sup.	NFS	1	C2
Jasper	Hot Springs National Park	NPS	2	C2
Jessieville	Bayou Meto WMA	SWA	5	A3
Jonesboro	Jacksonport SP	SPS	5	A3
	Ozark NF, Buffalo Ranger D.	NFS	14	A2
	Jessieville Ranger D.	NFS	4	A3
	Big Lake WMA	SWA	15	A3
	Dave Donaldson/Black R. WMA	SWA	17	A3
	Earl Buss/Bayou DeView WMA	SWA	22	C1
	Harold E. Alexander WMA	SWA		

© 1994 by John Oliver Jones

ARKANSAS NOTES

Summary

There are 60 federal, 53 state, and 2 private recreation areas or local administrative offices covered in this state chapter. Of these, 112 appear in the Information Chart and 3 are covered in the notes. The special indexes feature 12 federally designated wilderness areas and 7 agency published outdoor maps.

U.S. Forest Service

Arkansas is in the Southern Region (see Georgia chapter - U.S. Forest Svc., Southern Region listing).

The Blanchard Springs Caverns and Visitors Center (phone 501-269-3229) near Mountain View is located in the Sylamore Ranger District (S# 17, map A2) of the Ozark National Forest. Free brochures describe interpretive cave tours and camping facilities at the Caverns.

National Park Service

Additional NPS Location in Arkansas

Fort Smith Natl. Historic Site (75 acres) (S# 5, map B1)
PO Box 1406
Forth Smith, AR 72902   501-783-3961

Wilderness Index

These areas are indicated on the Arkansas map.

Ouachita National Forest (S# 1, map B2)
Black Fork Mountain Wilderness - 7,568 acres
Caney Creek Wilderness - 14,460 acres
Dry Creek Wilderness - 6,310 acres
Flatside Wilderness - 10,105 acres
Poteau Mountain Wilderness - 10,884 acres
Ozark-St. Francis NF Sup (S# 11, map B2)
East Fork Wilderness - 10,777 acres
Hurricane Creek Wilderness - 15,177 acres
Leatherwood Wilderness - 16,956 acres
Richard Creek Wilderness - 11,882 acres
Upper Buffalo Wilderness - 11,746 acres
Big Lake NWR (S# 5, map A4)
Big Lake Wilderness - 2,144 acres
Buffalo National River (NPS S# 2, map A2)
Buffalo Wilderness - 10,529 acres

Outdoor Map Index

U.S. Forest Service

Caney Creek Wilderness, Ouachita NF [1976]
Ouachita National Forest [1987]
Ouachita National Recreation Trail [1986]
Ozark National Forest [1988]
Ozark NF - Sylamore Ranger District [1984]
St. Francis National Forest [1982]
Upper Buffalo Wilderness-Ozark/St Francis NF [1981]

State Agencies

Arkansas Dept. of Parks & Tourism (S# 1, map B2)
The Arkansas State Parks guide describes facilities available at Arkansas's 45 parks. It includes a locator map, written directions to each park, plus services and user fee information. Other free travel guides and maps are available, including the Arkansas Tour Guide describing regional attractions and information on special interest activities, and an Arkansas Camper's Guide.

An official Arkansas state highway map is available from park headquarters. Symbols indicate scenic byways, highways, and campgrounds. Wildlife management areas and national forests boundaries are shown in color.

The headquarters office and Cossatot River State Park & Natural Area (S# 2) are covered in the Arkansas Information Chart. A selection of ten other state park locations are noted here with their symbol numbers and map coordinates.

S#	MAP	PARK NAME, CITY
3	A2	Bull Shoals State Park, Bull Shoals
4	C1	Daisey SP, Kirby
5	A3	Jacksonport SP, Jacksonport
6	D3	Lake Chicot SP, Lake Village
7	B2	Lake Ouachita SP, Mountain Pine
8	B2	Mount Nebo SP, Dardanelle
9	C1	Old Washington SP, Washington
10	B1	Queen Wilhemina SP, Mena
11	C2	White Oak Lake SP, Bluff City
12	B2	Woolly Hollow SP, Greenbrier

Arkansas Forestry Commission

PO Box 4523, Asher Station
Little Rock, AR 72214   501-664-2531
There is no state forest recreation program in Arkansas.

Arkansas Game & Fish Commission (S# 1, map B2)

The Hunt Arkansas fold-out brochure provides details on game species at most wildlife management areas and six National Wildlife Refuges. A free quarterly magazine, Arkansas Game & Fish Magazine, is available.

Private Organizations

Arkansas State Chamber of Commerce
412 South Cross St.
PO Box 3645   Phone 501-374-9225
Little Rock, AR 72203-3645   Fax 501-372-2722

The Nature Conservancy
Arkansas Field Office
300 Spring Bldg., Suite 717
Little Rock, AR 72201   501-372-2750

Contact the field office for current information about preserves in Arkansas and visitation.

★ INFORMATION CHART ★

INFORMATION CHART LEGEND - SYMBOLS & LETTER CODES

- ■ means YES & □ means Yes with disability provisions
- **sp** means spring, March through May
- **S** means Summer, June through August
- **F** means Fall, September through November
- **W** means Winter, December through February
- **T** means Two (2) or Three (3) Seasons
- **A** means All Four (4) Seasons
- **na** means Not Applicable or Not Available

Note: empty or blank spaces in the chart mean **NO**

AGENCY/MAP LEGEND . . . INITIALS, MAP SYMBOLS, COLOR CODES

U.S. Forest Service Supervisor & Ranger Dist. Offices NFS 61
U.S. Army Corps of Engineers Rec. Areas & Offices . COE 31
USFWS National Wildlife Refuges & Offices . . . . NWR 40
National Park Service Parks & other NPS Sites . . . . . NPS 7
Bureau of Land Management Rec. Areas & Offices . . BLM 26
Bureau of Reclamation Rec. Areas & Reg. Offices . . . BOR 8
State Parks (also see State Agency notes) . . . . SPS 52
State Wildlife Areas (also see State Agency notes) . . SWA 19
Private Preserves, Nature Centers & Tribal Lands . . 15
The Wild Rivers ～ and Wilderness Areas

Note: Refer to yellow block on page 7 (top right) for location name and address abbreviations.

			INFORMATION CHART LEGEND	
		■	means YES & □ means Yes with disability provisions	

FACILITIES, SERVICES, RECREATION OPPORTUNITIES & CONVENIENCES

S#	MAP	LOCATION NAME (state initials if more than one) with ADDRESS and/or LOCATION DATA	TELEPHONE	ACRES / ELEVATION	S#
1	C2	Ouachita National Forest Sup., PO Box 1270, Hot Springs 71902	501-321-5202	1,613,120 / 540-2,660	1
2	B5	Choctaw Ranger D., HC 64, Box 3467, Heavener, OK 74937 [1 mi S of Heavener on W side of Hwy. 259]	918-653-2991	97,400 / 540-2,666	2
2	C1	Caddo Ranger D., PO Box 369, Glenwood 71943	501-356-4186	144,490 / 600-2,300	2
3	B1	Cold Springs Ranger D., PO Box 417, Booneville 72927 [Hwy. 10 East]	501-675-3233	154,000 / 1,000	3
4	B1	Fourche Ranger D., Hwy. 10 East, PO Box 459, Danville 72833	501-495-2844	140,000 / 400-2,000	4
5	B2	Jessieville Ranger D., 8607 Hwy. 7 North, PO Box 189, Jessieville 71949	501-984-5313	120,000 / 600-2,000	5
6	B2	Mena Ranger D., Hwy. 71N, Rt. #3, Box 220, Mena 71953	501-394-2382	188,000 / 1,000-2,680	6
7	B2	Oden Ranger D. & Ranger Station, Rt. #9, Box 16, Oden 71961 [1 mi W of Oden on SR 88]	501-326-4322	183,000 / 600-2,200	7
8	B1	Poteau Ranger D., PO Box 100, Waldron 72958	501-637-4174	190,000 / 1,000-3,000	8
9	B2	Winona Ranger D., 1039 Hwy. 10 North, Perryville 72126	501-889-5176	108,000 / 400-1,900	9
10	B1	Womble Ranger District, PO Box 255, Mount Ida 71957 [1.5 mi E of Mount Ida on Hwy. 270]	501-867-2101	160,000 / 600-1,300	10
11	B1	Ozark-St. Francis N. Forests, Sup., 605 W. Main St., PO Box 1008, Russellville 72801	501-968-2354	1,144,056 / na	11
12	B2	Ozark NF, Bayou Ranger D., Hwy. 27, Rt. #1, Box 36, Hector 72843	501-284-3150	na / na	12
13	B1	Ozark NF, Boston Mountain RD, Hwy. 23 N, PO Box 76, Ozark 72949	501-667-2191	na / na	13
14	A2	Ozark NF, Buffalo Ranger D., Hwy. 7 N, PO Box 427, Jasper 72641	501-446-5122	na / na	14
15	B1	Ozark NF, Mt. Magazine Ranger D., Hwy. 22 E & Kalamazoo Rd., PO Box 511, Paris 72855	501-963-3076	na / na	15
16	B2	Ozark NF, Pleasant Hill Ranger D., Hwy. 21 N, PO Box 190, Clarksville 72830	501-754-2864	na / na	16
17	A2	Ozark NF, Sylamore Ranger D., Hwy. 14 N, Henderson Bldg., PO Box 1279, Mtn. View 72560	501-269-3228	na / na	17
18	B3	St. Francis NF & Ranger D., Hwy. 44 S, Rt. #4, Box 14-A, Marianna 72360	501-295-5278	20,977 / na	18
1	B2	COE, Little Rock District, PO Box 867, Little Rock 72203	501-324-5673	na / na	1
2	A1	Beaver Lake, PO Box 2044, Rogers 72757 [near Pea Ridge]	501-636-1210	na / na	2
3	B1	Blue Mountain Lake, HC 68, Box 604, Plainview 72857	501-272-4324	na / na	3
4	A2	Bull Shoals Lake, PO Box 369, Mountain Home 72653 [E of Bull Shoals]	501-425-2700	na / na	4
5	B1	Dardanelle Lake, Ark.Riv.Nav.Sys., PO Box 1087, Russellville 72801	501-968-5008	na / na	5
6	B2	David D. Terry Lock & Dam, Ark.Riv., Ark.Riv., PO Box 7835, Pine Bluff 71611 [NE of Little Rock]	501-534-0451	na / na	6

★ INFORMATION CHART ★

AGENCY/MAP LEGEND ... INITIALS, MAP SYMBOLS, COLOR CODES

U.S. Forest Service Supervisor & Ranger Dist. Offices NFS ... 61
U.S. Army Corps of Engineers Rec. Areas & Offices ... COE ... 31
USFWS National Wildlife Refuges & Offices ... NWR ... 40
National Park Service Parks & other NPS Sites ... NPS ... 7
Bureau of Land Management Rec. Areas & Offices ... BLM ... 26
Bureau of Reclamation Rec. Areas & Reg. Offices ... BOR ... 8
State Parks (also see State Agency notes) ... SPS ... 52
State Wildlife Areas (also see State Agency notes) ... SWA ... 19
Private Preserves, Nature Centers & Tribal Lands
The Wild Rivers ~~~ and Wilderness Areas ... 15

Note: Refer to yellow block on page 7 (top right) for location name and address abbreviations.

INFORMATION CHART LEGEND - SYMBOLS & LETTER CODES

■ means YES & □ means Yes with disability provisions
sp means spring, March through May
S means Summer, June through August
F means Fall, September through November
W means Winter, December through February
T means Two (2) or Three (3) Seasons
A means All Four (4) Seasons
na means Not Applicable or Not Available
Note: empty or blank spaces in the chart mean NO

If a symbol number has a star ★ that symbol is not shown on the map.

S#	MAP	LOCATION NAME (state initials if more than one) with ADDRESS and/or LOCATION DATA	TELEPHONE	ACRES / ELEVATION	S#
7	C1	Dequeen Lake, Rt. 1, Box 37 A, Ashdown 71822 [near Wickes]	501-898-3343	na / na	7
8	C1	Dierks Lake, Rt. 1, Box 37 A, Ashdown 71822 [SE of Wickes]	501-898-3343	na / na	8
9	C1	Gillham Lake, Rt. 1, Box 37 A, Ashdown 71822 [SE of Wickes]	501-898-3343	na / na	9
10	B1	Greers Ferry Lake, PO Box 1088, Heber Springs 72543	501-362-2416	na / na	10
11	C1	Millwood Lake, Rt. 1, Box 37 A, Ashdown 71822	501-898-3343	na / na	11
12	B2	Murray Lock & Dam, Ark.Riv.Nav.Sys., PO Box 1087, Russellville 72801 [near Little Rock]	501-968-5008	na / na	12
13	B2	Nimrod Lake, HC 68, Box 604, Plainview 72857	501-272-4324	na / na	13
14	A2	Norfork Lake, PO Box 369, Mountain Home 72653 [E of Bull Shoals]	501-425-2700	na / na	14
15	C3	Norrell Lock & Dam, Ark.Riv.Nav.Sys., PO Box 7835, Pine Bluff 71611 [near Dumas]	501-534-0451	na / na	15
16	B1	Ozark-Taylor Lock & Dam, Ark.Riv.Na, PO Box 1087, Russellville 72801 [at Ozark]	501-667-2129	na / na	16
17	B1	Pool 13 James W Trimble L&D, Ark.Ri, PO Box 1087, Russellville 72801 [at Fort Smith]	501-667-2129	na / na	17
18	C3	Pool 3 Lock & Dam, Ark.Riv.Nav.Sys., PO Box 7835, Pine Bluff 71611 [SE of Pine Bluff]	501-534-0451	na / na	18
19	C3	Pool 4 Lock & Dam, Ark.Riv.Nav.Sys., PO Box 7835, Pine Bluff 71611 [SE of Pine Bluff]	501-534-0451	na / na	19
20	C2	Pool 5 Lock & Dam, Ark.Riv.Nav.Sys., PO Box 7835, Pine Bluff 71611 [NW of Pine Bluff]	501-534-0451	na / na	20
21	B2	Rockefeller Lake-Ormand L&D Ark.Riv, PO Box 1087, Russellville 72801 [near Plumerville]	501-968-5008	na / na	21
22	B2	Toad Suck Ferry Lock & Dam, Ark.Riv, PO Box 1087, Russellville 72801 [near Conway]	501-968-5008	na / na	22
23	C3	Wilbur D. Mills Lock & Dam, Ark.Riv, PO Box 7835, Pine Bluff 71611 [E of Dumas]	501-534-0451	na / na	23
		COE, Vicksburg District, 3515 I-20 Frontage Rd., Vicksburg, MS 39181	601-631-5286	na / na	
24	B3	Calion Pool [Ouachita-Black Rivers], 3505 South Grand St., Monroe 71202	318-322-6391	na / na	24
25	C2	Degray Lake, 30 Ip Circle, Arkadelphia 71923	501-246-5501	na / na	25
26	D2	Felsenthal Pool [Ouachita-Black Rivers], 3505 South Grand St., Monroe 71202	318-322-6391	na / na	26
27	C1	Lake Greeson, Route 1, Murfreesboro 71958 [near Kirby]	501-285-2151	na / na	27
28	B2	Lake Ouachita, Post Office Box 4, Mountain Pine 71956	501-767-2101	na / na	28
1	D2	**Felsenthal NWR**, PO Box 1157, Crossett 71635	501-364-3167	65,000 / na	1
2	D3	Overflow NWR, PO Box 1157, Crossett 71635	501-364-3167	11,000 / na	2
3	B4	Holla Bend NWR, Rt. #1, Box 59, Dardanelle 72834 [office at refuge. 9 mi. SE of Dardanelle on Hwy 155]	501-229-4300	6,368 / 285-320	3
4	B4	Northeast Arkansas Refuge Complex, PO Box 279, Turrell 72384 [Hwy. 42 E, 0.25 mi S of Turrell]	501-343-2595	na / na	4
5	A4	Big Lake NWR (subject to flooding), PO Box 67, Manila 72442 [on Hwy. 18, 2 mi. E of Manila]	501-564-2429	11,038 / 240	5
6	B4	Cache River NWR, PO Box 279, Turrell 72384 [Dixie Farm Unit is 6 mi S of Gregory on E side of Hwy 33]	501-343-2595	22,000 / na	6
7	B4	Wapanocca NWR, PO Box 279, Turrell 72384 [Hwy. 42 E, 0.25 mi S of Turrell]	501-343-2595	5,484 / na	7
8	C3	White River NWR, 321 W. 7th Street, Box 308, De Witt 72042 [office in De Witt, refuge subject to annual flooding]	501-946-1468	154,000 / 130-190	8
1	C3	**Arkansas Post Nat'l. Memorial**, Rt. #1, Box 16, Gillett 72055 [5 mi S of Gillett on SR 165/1, 2 mi E on CR 169 to park]	501-548-2207	389 / 160-175	1
2	A2	Buffalo Nat'l. River HQ, PO Box 1173, Harrison 72602 [Tyler Bend VC off Hwy 65 between Gilbert/Marshall, ph. 439-2502]	501-741-5443	95,730 / 375-2,385	2
3	C1	Hot Springs National Park, PO Box 1860, Hot Springs 71902 [VC is in former Fordyce Bathhouse downtown on Hwy. 7]	501-623-1433	5,839 / 600-1,400	3
4	A1	Pea Ridge Nat'l. Military Park, Hwy. 62 E, Pea Ridge 72751	501-451-8122	4,300 / 1,407	4
1	B2	**Arkansas Dept. of Parks & Tourism**, No. 1 Capitol Mall, Little Rock 72201 [see Chapter Notes for park details]	501-682-1191	na / na	1
2	C1	Cossatot River St. Park & Natural A, c/o Park Superintendent, Rt. #1, Box 170-A, Wickes 71973	501-385-2201	4,414 / 1,020	2
1	B2	**Arkansas Game & Fish Commission**, 2 Natural Resources Dr., Little Rock 72205	501-223-6300	na / na	1
2	C3	Bayou Meto WMA, Rt. #1, Box 188A, Humphrey 72073 [15 mi. SW of Stuttgart]	501-633-6393	33,901 / na	2
3	D2	Beryl Anthony/Lower Ouachita WMA, 104 N. Hyatt, Monticello 71655 [15 mi. W of Crossett]	501-367-9530	7,500 / na	3
4	A3	Big Lake WMA, 1704 Rosemond, Jonesboro 72401 [5 mi. W of Manila]	501-972-5438	11,447 / na	4
*5	C1	Big Timber WMA, c/o Game & Fish Comm. HQ, Little Rock [in Hot Springs & Clark Cos.]	501-223-6359	22,000 / na	*5
6	B1	Blue Mountain WMA, PO Box 6637, Perrytown 71801 [17 mi. from Danville]	501-777-5580	9,860 / na	6
7	C1	Bois D'Arc WMA, PO Box 6637, Perrytown 71801 [16 mi. S of Hope]	501-777-5580	5,843 / na	7
8	B2	Camp Robinson WMA, 1718 Lindauer Rd., Forrest City 72335 [S of Conway]	501-633-6393	29,221 / na	8
9	C1	Caney Creek WMA, PO Box 6637, Perrytown 71801 [12 mi. SE of Mena]	501-777-5580	85,000 / na	9
*10	B2	Casey Jones WMA, c/o Game & Fish Comm. HQ, Little Rock	501-223-6359	143,000 / na	*10
*11	B2	Cherokee WMA, c/o Game & Fish Comm. HQ, Little Rock	501-223-6359	135,000 / na	*11
12	C3	Cut-off Creek WMA, 104 N. Hyatt, Monticello 71655 [25 mi. E of Monticello]	501-367-9530	8,732 / na	12
13	B2	Cypress Creek WMA, PO Box 1008, Russellville 72801 [8 mi. N of Plumerville]	501-968-2354	1,335 / na	13

Column headings for the symbol grid (FACILITIES, SERVICES, RECREATION OPPORTUNITIES & CONVENIENCES):
INFO OFFICE (IO) / VISITOR CENTER (VC); IO / VC OPEN SATURDAY / SUNDAY; ENTRY FEE, not camping / permit fee; INTERPRETIVE or EDUCATIONAL SERVICES; FREE LITERATURE or brochures, maps; AGENCY GUIDED TOURS, scheduled / by res.; INTERPRETIVE SERVICES / STUDY PROGRAMS; NATURE EDUCATION / CONCESSIONAIRE SERVICES; WILDFLOWER VIEWING AREA / DISPLAY; ARCHAEOLOGICAL / HISTORIC SITES; INTERPRETIVE TRAILS; WILDLIFE VIEWING SITES, blinds; ENDANGERED SPECIES; ABUNDANT OR COMMON SPECIES ARE COMMON; DEVELOPED PICNIC SITES; NO-CHARGE CAMPGROUNDS / PICNIC SITES; DEVELOPED CAMPGROUNDS / CAMPSITES; WILDERNESS AREAS / WILD RIVERS; WALKING PERMITTED / HIKING TRAILS; BICYCLING OPPORTUNITIES, at one's own risk; HORSEBACK RIDING, w/ your own horse; OFF-ROAD Motorized Vehicle Area / Use OK; SWIMMING PERMITTED, areas, trails; FISHING OPPORTUNITIES, at one's own risk; NON-MOTORIZED WATERCRAFT OK; MOTORIZED WATERCRAFT OK, check limits; HUNTING IN SEASON, license / permit req'd; WINTER SPORTS OPPORTUNITIES OK; BOATING: ramps, marinas, etc.; PARK USE ONLY, check limits; DAY USE ONLY, no overnight; DRINKING WATER; RESTROOMS

14	B3	Dagmar WMA, 1718 Lindauer Rd., Forrest City 72335 [6 mi. W of Brinkley]	501-633-6393	8,062 / na		■					■	■	■		■			14
15	A3	Dave Donaldson/Black River WMA, 1704 Rosemond, Jonesboro 72401 [10 mi. S of Corning]	501-972-5438	22,798 / na							■	■	■		■			15
16	B3	Des Arc WMA, 1718 Lindauer Rd., Forrest City 72335 [4 mi. N of Des Arc]	501-633-6393	750 / na							■	■	■		■	■		16
17	A3	Earl Buss/Bayou DeView WMA, 1704 Rosemond, Jonesboro 72401 [4 mi. from Weiner]	501-972-5438	4,419 / na							■	■	■		■			17
18	B2	Ed Gordon/Point Remove WMA, c/o Game & Fish Comm. HQ, Little Rock 77205 [N of Morrilton]	501-968-2354	8,450 / na							■	■	■		■			18
19	B2	Galla Creek WMA, PO Box 6637, Perrytown 71801 [4 mi. S of Pottsville]	501-968-2354	3,358 / na											■			19
20	A2	Gene Rush/Buffalo River WMA, PO Box 1008, Russellville 72801 [15 mi. NW of Marshall]	501-968-2354	21,781 / na						■	■			■	■			20
21	B2	Gulf Mountain WMA, PO Box 1008, Russellville 72801 [12 mi. SW of Clinton]	501-968-2354	11,102 / na						■	■			■	■			21
22	A3	Harold E. Alexander WMA, 1704 Rosemond, Jonesboro 72401 [6 mi. S of Hardy]	501-972-5438	12,741 / na							■			■	■			22
23	B2	Harris Brake WMA, PO Box 6637, Perrytown 71801 [1 mi. S of Perryville]	501-777-5580	2,866 / na							■	■	■		■			23
24	B3	Henry Gray/Hurricane Lake WMA, 1718 Lindauer, Forrest City 72335 [5 mi. E of Bald Knob]	501-633-6393	17,421 / na							■	■	■		■			24
25	A1	Hobbs SMA, PO Box 1008, Russellville 72801 [12 mi. SE of Rogers]	501-968-2354	12,000 / na			■			■	■		■		■			25
26	B2	Holland Bottoms WMA, 1718 Londauer Rd., Forrest City 72335 [adjacent to Jacksonville]	501-633-6393	5,625 / na							■	■	■		■			26
27	C1	Hope WMA, PO Box 6637, Perrytown 71801 [3 mi. N of Hope]	501-777-5580	2,116 / na											■	■	■	27
28	C1	Howard County WMA, PO Box 6637, Perrytown 71801 [10 mi. N of Dierks]	501-777-5580	27,000 / na											■			28
29	B3	Jamestown/Independence County WMA, 1704 Rosemond, Jonesboro 72401 [N of Bald Knob]	501-972-5438	1,051 / na											■			29
30	D1	Lafayette County WMA, PO Box 6637, Perrytown 71801 [2 mi. E of Bradley]	501-777-5580	32,000 / na				■			■	■	■		■			30
31	C1	Lake Greeson WMA, PO Box 6637, Perrytown 71801 [4 mi. N of Murfreesboro]	501-777-5580	38,000 / na				■	■	■	■	■	■	■	■			31
32	A2	Loafers Glory WMA, PO Box 1008, Russellville 72801 [10 mi. NE of Marshall]	501-968-2354	1,740 / na											■			32
33	A1	Madison County WMA, PO Box 1008, Russellville 72801 [12 mi. N of Huntsville]	501-968-2354	13,270 / na											■			33
34	B1	Mt. Magazine WMA, PO Box 6637, Perrytown 71801 [W of Dardanelle]	501-777-5580	98,985 / na			■	■	■	■	■				■			34
35	B1	Muddy Creek WMA, PO Box 6637, Perrytown 71801 [10 mi. N of Mt. Ida]	501-777-5580	146,206 / na				■	■	■					■			35
36	B2	Petit Jean WMA, PO Box 6637, Perrytown 71801 [10 mi. S. of Dardanelle]	501-777-5580	15,460 / na				■			■	■	■		■			36
37	B2	Piney Creeks WMA, PO Box 1008, Russellville 72801 [16 mi. N of Russellville]	501-968-2354	180,000 / na				■	■	■	■			■	■			37
38	C2	Poison Springs WMA, 104 N. Hyatt, Monticello 71655 [25 mi. W of Camden]	501-367-9530	19,510 / na							■	■	■		■			38
39	B3	Rex Hancock/Black Swamp WMA, 1718 Lindauer Rd., Forrest City 72335 [10 mi. S of Augusta]	501-633-6393	5,700 / na							■		■		■			39
40	A3	Scatter Creek WMA, 1704 Rosemond, Jonesboro 72401 [9 mi. NW of Paragould]	501-972-5438	1,200 / na											■			40
41	C3	Seven Devils WMA, 104 N. Hyatt, Monticello 71655 [12 mi. E of Monticello]	501-367-9530	494 / na							■	■	■		■			41
42	A3	Shirey Bay-Rainey Brake WMA, 1704 Rosemond, Jonesboro 72401 [SW of Hoxie]	501-972-5438	10,668 / na							■	■	■		■			42
43	B3	St. Francis Nat'l. Forest WMA, 1718 Lindauer Rd., Forrest City 72335 [20 mi. S of Forrest City]	501-633-6393	20,946 / na	■	■	■	■	■	■	■	■	■		■			43
44	B3	St. Francis Sunken Lands WMA, 1704 Rosemond, Jonesboro 72401 [near Marked Tree]	501-972-5438	15,659 / na							■	■	■		■			44
45	D1	Sulphur River WMA, PO Box 6637, Perrytown 71801 [16 mi. S of Texarkana]	501-777-5580	16,542 / na							■	■	■		■			45
46	A2	Sylamore WMA, PO Box 1008, Russellville 72801 [7 mi. N of Mtn. View]	501-968-2354	125,000 / na			■	■	■	■	■	■	■	■	■			46
47	C3	Trusten Holder WMA, 104 N. Hyatt, Monticello 71655 [35 mi. SE of DeWitt]	501-367-9530	13,379 / na							■	■	■		■			47
48	B3	Wattensaw WMA, 1718 Lindauer Rd., Forrest City 72335 [3 mi. N of Hazen]	501-633-6393	17,461 / na							■	■	■		■			48
49	A1	White Rock WMA, PO Box 1008, Russellville 72801 [13 mi. N of Ozark]	501-968-2354	280,000 / na				■	■	■	■	■	■	■	■			49
50	B2	Winona WMA, PO Box 6637, Perrytown 71801 [4 mi. S of Perryville]	501-777-5580	160,000 / na				■	■	■	■				■			50

CALIFORNIA - CITY / AGENCY INDEX

City	Agency Office / Area Name	Code	S#	Map
Adelanto	El Mirage SRA	BLM	12	G3
Adin	Big Valley Ranger D.	NFS	47	B3
Agoura Hills	Santa Monica Mountains NRA	NPS	15	G2
Alpine	Descanso Ranger District	NFS	9	H3
Alturas	Modoc National Forest Sup.	NFS	46	B3
	Modoc NWR	NWR	9	B3
	Alturas Resource Area	BLM	22	B3
Arcadia	Angeles Nat'l. Forest Sup.	NFS	2	G3
Arcata	Arcata Resource Area	BLM	29	A1
	Eureka Slough WA	SWA	10	A1
Baker	Dumont Dunes SRA	BLM	11	F4
	Soda Springs SRA	BLM	13	F4
Bakersfield	Greenhorn Ranger D.	NFS	66	F3
	Bakersfield Dist. Office	BLM	2	F3
	Caliente Resource Area	BLM	4	F2
Barstow	Barstow Desert Info. Center	BLM	8	G3
	Barstow Resource Area	BLM	9	G3
	Calico Early Man Site SRA	BLM	10	F3
	Stoddard/Johnson Valley ORV A	BLM	14	G3
Big Bar	Big Bar Ranger D.	NFS	71	B1
Big Bear City	Big Bear Valley Preserve	TNC	3	G3
Bishop	Inyo National Forest Sup.	NFS	18	E3
	White Mountain Ranger D.	NFS	22	E3
	Bishop Resource Area	BLM	3	E3
	Battle Creek WA	SWA	22	E3
Blairsden	Beckwourth RD/Mohawk RS	NFS	52	C3
Blythe	Cibola NWR (located in AZ)	NWR	1	H5
Brawley	Imperial Sand Dunes SRA	BLM	16	H4
Bridgeport	Bridgeport Ranger D.	NFS	99	D3
Bridgeville	Mad River Ranger D.	NFS	86	B1
CA Hot Springs	Hot Springs Ranger D.	NFS	67	F3
Calipatra	Imperial WA	SWA	27	H4
Calipatria	Salton Sea NWR	NWR	14	H4
	Coachella Valley NWR	NWR	15	G4
Camino	Eldorado NF Information Center	NFS	14	C2
Camptonville	Downieville Ranger D.	NFS	94	C2
Canby	Devil's Garden Ranger D.	NFS	48	B3
Carmel	Point Lobos State Reserve	SPS	9	E1
Cedarville	Warner Mountain Ranger D.	NFS	50	B3
	Suprise Resource Area	BLM	26	B3
	High Rock Canyon SRA	BLM	27	B3
Challenge	La Porte RD/Challenge RS	NFS	54	C2
Chester	Almanor Ranger D.	NFS	32	B2
Chico	Vina Plains Preserve	TNC	17	B2
Clearlake	Anderson Marsh State Hist. Park	SPS	2	C1
Clovis	Sierra National Forest Sup.	NFS	78	E2
Cobb	Boggs Lake Preserve	TNC	4	C1
Corcoran	Creighton Ranch Preserve	TNC	6	E2
Corning	Corning Ranger D.	NFS	42	B2
Corona	Trabuco Ranger District	NFS	11	G3
Covelo	Covelo Ranger D.	NFS	43	B1
Crescent City	Redwood National Park	NPS	14	A1
Death Valley	Death Valley NM (CA/NV)	NPS	3	F4
Delano	Kern NWR	NWR	3	F2
Doyle	Doyle WA	SWA	9	C3
Dunlap	Hume Lake Ranger D.	NFS	68	E3
El Centro	El Centro Resource Area	BLM	15	H4
Etna	Salmon River Ranger D.	NFS	27	A2
Eureka	Six Rivers Nat'l. Forest Sup.	NFS	83	B1
	Samoa Dunes Recreation Area	BLM	30	B1
	Patrick's Point State Park	SPS	8	A1
	Prairie Creek Redwoods State P	SPS	10	A1
Fairfield	Hill Slough WA	SWA	18	D2
Fall River Mill	Cinder Flats WA	SWA	8	B2
Fall River Mills	Hat Creek Ranger D.	NFS	34	B2
Fawnskin	Big Bear Ranger D.	NFS	60	G3
Flintridge	Arroyo Seco Ranger D.	NFS	3	G3
Folsom	Folsom Resource Area	BLM	5	C2
Foresthill	Foresthill Ranger D.	NFS	95	C2
Fort Jones	Scott River Ranger D.	NFS	28	A2
Frazier Park	Mt. Pinos Ranger D.	NFS	37	F2
Fresno	Region 4, Dept. Fish and Game	SWA	5	E2
Galt	Cosumnes River Preserve	TNC	5	D2
Gasquet	Smith River Nat'l. Rec. Area	NFS	84	A1
Georgetown	Georgetown Ranger D.	NFS	15	C2
Geyserville	L. Sonoma Warm Springs Dam	COE	19	C1
Glendora	Mt. Baldy Ranger D.	NFS	4	G3
Goleta	Los Padres National Forest Sup.	NFS	35	F2
Greenville	Greenville Ranger D.	NFS	53	B2
Groveland	Groveland Ranger D.	NFS	90	D2
Happy Camp	Happy Camp Ranger D.	NFS	25	A2
Hathaway Pines	Calaveras Ranger D.	NFS	89	D2
Hayfork	Hayfork Ranger D.	NFS	72	B1
Hollister	Hollister Resource Area	BLM	6	D2
Idyllwild	San Jacinto Ranger D.	NFS	63	G3
Imperial Beach	Southern CA Coastal Complex	NWR	23	H3
	Sweetwater Marsh NWR	NWR	24	H3
	Tijuana Slough NWR	NWR	★25	H3
Kernville	Cannell Meadow Ranger D.	NFS	65	F3
King City	Monterey Ranger D.	NFS	36	E2
Klamath River	Oak Knoll Ranger D.	NFS	26	A2
Lee Vining	Mono Lake RD/Mono Basin VC	NFS	20	D3
	Mono Lake Tufa State Res.	SPS	5	D3
Lemon Cove	Lake Kaweah	COE	17	E3
Lodi	White Slough WA	SWA	16	D2
Loleta	Humboldt Bay NWR	NWR	17	B1
Lone Pine	Mt. Whitney Ranger D.	NFS	21	E3
Long Beach	Region 5, Dept. Fish and Game	SWA	6	G3
Los Angeles	COE, Los Angeles District	COE	1	G3
	Brea Dam	COE	2	G3
	Carbon Canyon Dam	COE	3	G3
	Fullerton Dam	COE	4	G3
	Hansen Dam	COE	★5	G3
	Mojave River Dam	COE	6	G3
	Prado Dam	COE	7	G3
	Salinas Dam/Santa Margarita L.	COE	8	F2
	Santa Fe Dam Recreation Area	COE	9	G3
	Sepulveda Dam	COE	10	G2
	Whittier Narrows Dam/Legg L.	COE	★11	G3
Los Banos	San Luis NWR	NWR	20	D2
	Kesterson NWR	NWR	21	D2
	Merced NWR	NWR	22	D2
	Grizzly Island WA	SWA	23	D2
Lost Hills	Paine Wildflower Preserve	TNC	8	F2
Ludlow	Camp Cady WA	SWA	26	G4
	Marble Mountains WA	SWA	28	G4
Lytle Creek	Cajon Ranger D/Lytle Creek RS	NFS	61	G3
Macdoel	Butte Valley WA	SWA	7	A2
	Indian Tom WA	SWA	11	A2
Macdowel	Goosenest Ranger D.	NFS	24	A2
Mammoth Lakes	Mammoth RD & Visitor Center	NFS	19	D3
	Devils Postpile Nat'l. Monument	NPS	4	D3
Martinez	John Muir Nat'l. Historic Site	NPS	6	A5
McCloud	McCloud Ranger D.	NFS	73	B2
	McCloud River Preserve	TNC	13	B2
Mentone	San Gorgonio RD/Mill Creek RS	NFS	62	G3
Mi-Wok Village	Mi-Wok Ranger D.	NFS	91	D2
Milford	Milford RD/Laufman RS	NFS	55	C3
Mill Valley	Muir Woods National Monument	NPS	11	A4
Mineral	Lassen Volcanic National Park	NPS	9	B2
Morro Bay	Morro Bay State Park	SPS	6	F2
Moss Landing	Elkhorn Slough Preserve	TNC	11	D1
Mt. Shasta	Mt. Shasta Ranger D.	NFS	74	A2
Murrieta	Santa Rosa Plateau Preserve	TNC	16	G3
N. Palm Springs	Palm Springs-South Coast RA	BLM	18	G3
Needles	Havasu NWR (85% in AZ)	NWR	2	G5
	Needles Resource Area	BLM	17	G5
Nevada City	Tahoe National Forest Sup.	NFS	93	C2
	Nevada City Ranger D.	NFS	96	C2
Newark	Farallon NWR (No Public Use)	NWR	8	A4
	San Francisco Bay NWR	NWR	16	B5
	Salinas River NWR	NWR	18	D1
	San Pablo Bay NWR	NWR	19	A5
North Fork	Minarets Ranger D.	NFS	81	E3
Novato	Petaluma Marsh WA	SWA	20	A5
Oakdale	Stanislaus River Parks	COE	23	D2
Oakhurst	Mariposa Ranger D.	NFS	80	E3
Oasis	Santa Rosa WA	SWA	30	H4
Ojai	Ojai Ranger D.	NFS	38	G2
Onyx	Jawbone/Butterbredt ORV Area SRA	BLM	20	F3
Orland	Black Butte Lake	COE	13	B2
Orleans	Ukonom Ranger D.	NFS	29	A1
	Orleans Ranger D.	NFS	87	A1
Oroville	Oroville Ranger D.	NFS	56	C2
	Spenceville WA	SWA	15	C2
Paicines	Pinnacles Nat'l. Monument	NPS	12	E2
	Little Panoche WA	SWA	24	E2
Penngrove	Fairfield Osborn Preserve	TNC	12	C1
Piedra	Pine Flat Lake	COE	22	E3
Pioneer	Amador Ranger D.	NFS	13	D2
Pixley	Pixley Vernal Pools Preserve	TNC	9	E2
Placerville	Eldorado Nat'l. Forest Sup.	NFS	12	C2
	Placerville Ranger D.	NFS	17	C2
Platina	Yolla Bolla Ranger D.	NFS	77	B2

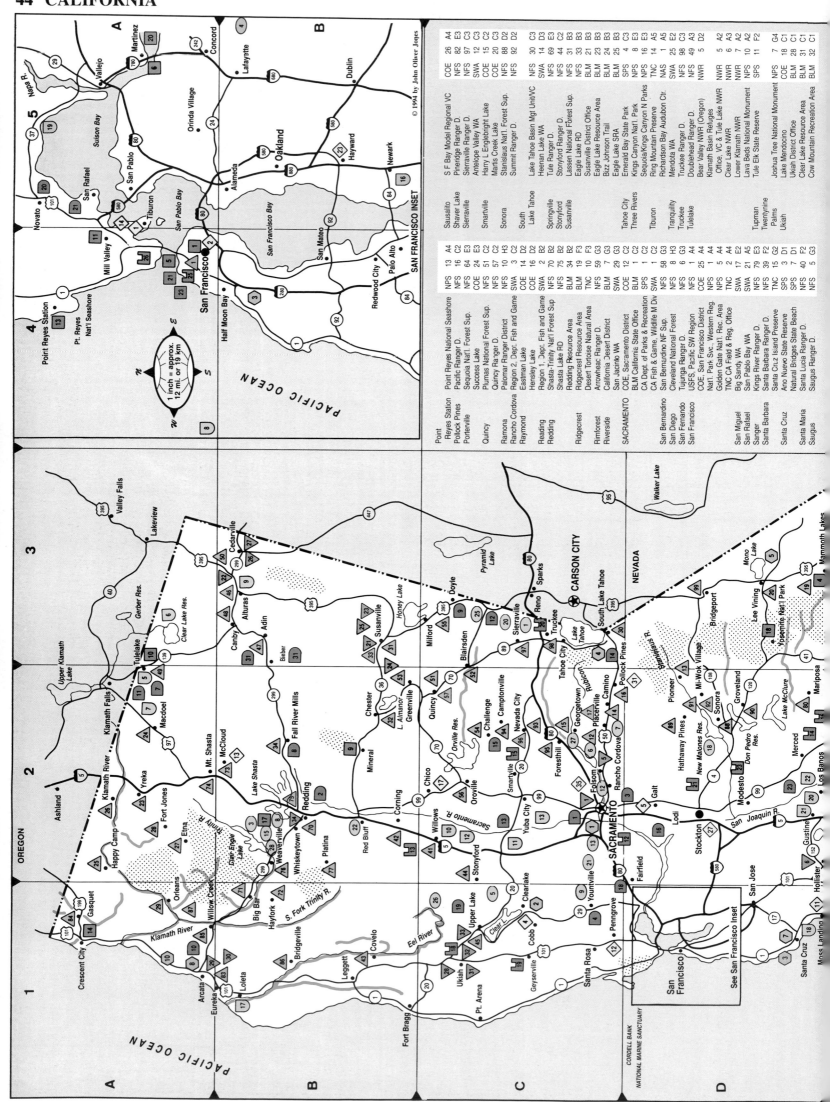

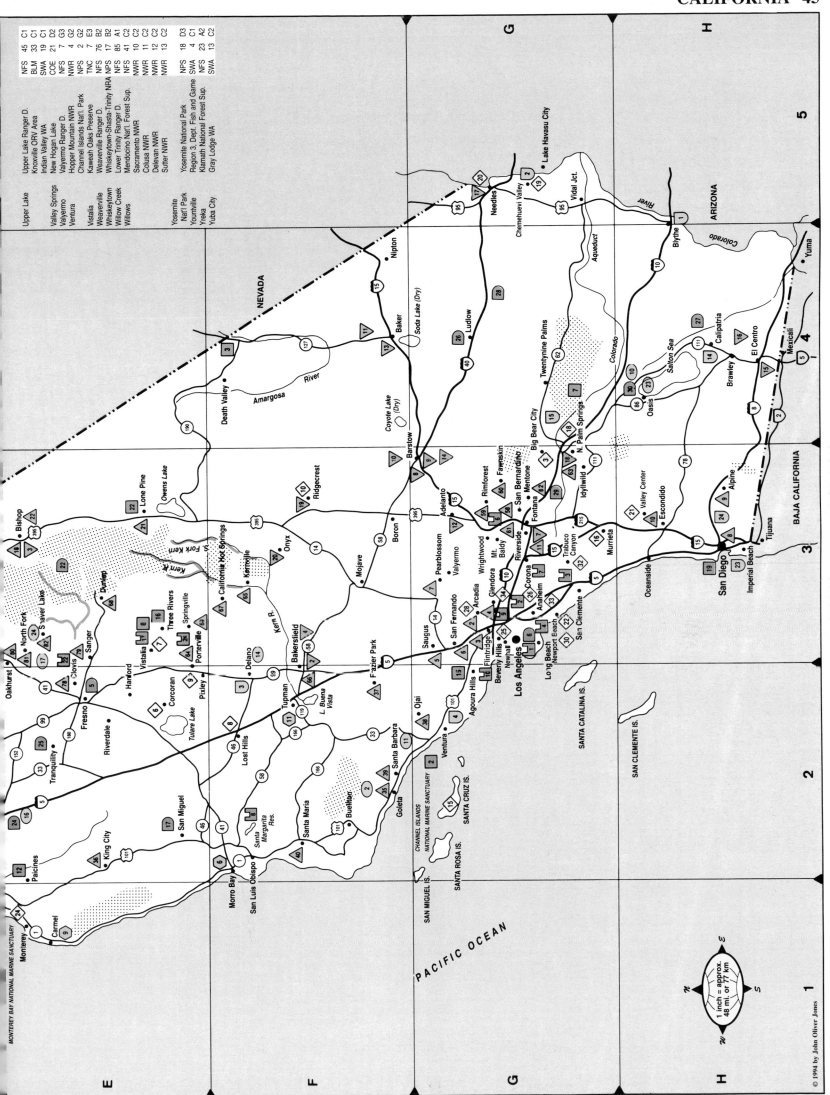

CALIFORNIA NOTES

Summary

There are 258 federal, 44 state, and 36 private recreation areas or local administrative offices covered in this state chapter. Of these, 236 appear in the Information Chart and 102 are covered in the notes. The special indexes feature 70 federally designated wilderness areas and wild rivers, and 147 agency published outdoor maps.

Federal Agencies

U.S. Forest Service

Angeles National Forest (see S# 2) has the following visitor center and information stations (not on map).

Chilao Visitor Center 818-796-5541
Star Route
La Canada, CA 91111
Located at the restored Chilao Ranger Station on Hwy. 2 and open on weekends year around. Four nature trails.

Big Pines Visitor Center & Info Station
PO Box 1011
Wrightwood, CA 92397 619-249-3504
The station is located in the historic Big Pines Clubhouse and is open 5 days a week year long (closed Tuesdays and Wednesdays). Hours are 8 a.m. to 4:30 p.m. There are exhibits, a self-guided interpretive trail and a hiking trail which connect to the Pacific Crest Trail. Location is two miles west of Wrightwood on Hwy. 2 at the gateway to the high country of the San Gabriel Mountains.

Inyo National Forest (see S# 18) has four visitor centers.

Inter-Agency Visitors Center
PO Box R
Lone Pine, CA 93545 619-876-4252
Multiple Agency funded and operated VC to provide orientation to the local areas of the east side of the Sierra Mountains. Natural and cultural history information.

Schulman Grove Visitor Center at 10,000 feet elevation in the White Mountains (see S# 22, White Mountain Ranger District) is the focal point for "the oldest living thing on earth" the bristlecone pine. Follow "discovery trail" and the methuselah walk through the "grove of the ancient." Daily talks by forest interpreters are given late May to September. Call 619-873-2500 for details.

Mammoth Visitor Center (see S# 19, Mammoth RD). Exhibits, inperpretive programs, and audio-visual programs cover the diverse values of the Inyo NF, and the various opportunities for year-round recreation in the district. There are several interpretive sites, self-guided nature trails, wayside exhibits and kiosks that highlight geological, cultural, and natural history of the area.

Mono Basin Visitors Center (see S# 20, Mono Lake Ranger District). Two art galleries, library, and herbarium house rotating exhibits, and research and specimens from the Mono Basin and vicinity.

Shasta Lake Visitors Center 916-275-1587
14250 Holiday Rd.
Redding, CA 96003
Located at the south end of the Shasta Unit of the Whiskeytown-Shasta-Trinity NRA (see Natl. Park Service S# 17) north of Redding at Mountain Gate off I-5 near the Shasta Lake Ranger District (see S# 75) to the Sahsta Trinity NF. Year-round recreation information. The Center also provides permits for wood cutting, campfires, and Christmas trees.

Lake Tahoe Visitors Center (Lake Tahoe Basin Management Unit, see S# 30) features a variety of indoor and outdoor exhibits and five nature trails. An important attraction is the Stream Profile Chamber which offers an opportunity to view spawning salmon and trout in season. Open May through October. VC phone is 916-573-2674.

Meyers Inter-Agency Information Center is located along the Tahoe Basin in Meyers, CA (Lake Tahoe Basin Management Unit, see S# 30). Self-service, 24 hour, year-round orientation and recreation information and exhibits.

Information Stations:
Mt. Baldy Village is open Friday through Sunday from 9 a.m. to 4 p.m. The phone number is 714-982-2829. and

U.S. Army Corps of Engineers (COE)

South Pacific Division
630 Sansome Street, Room 1216
San Francisco, CA 94111-2206 415-705-1444
In California the Los Angeles, Sacramento, and San Francisco District Offices manage COE projects in California and Arizona (see information charts).

USFWS National Wildlife Refuges

The Klamath Basin Refuges headquarters at the Tule Lake NWR administers three refuges in Oregon, Bear Valley, Klamath Forest, and Upper Klamath. The San Francisco Bay Refuge Complex includes an Environmental Education Center located at the southern tip of the bay, fifteen miles from the complex office. Most of the acreage of the Cibola and Havasu NWRs is located in Arizona. They are administered from refuge offices in California, and coverage is duplicated in the Arizona chapter.

The Chula Vista Nature Center (near San Diego) is situated within the Sweetwater Marsh NWR and is accessible from Chula Vista by shuttle bus only. The Center address is 1000 Gunpowder Point Dr., Chula Vista, CA 92010 (telephone 619-422-2481).

National Park Service

Additional NPS Locations in California
Cabrillo National Monument (137 acres)
PO Box 6670 (S# 19, map H3)
San Diego, CA 92106 619-372-0200

Eugene O'Neill National Historic Site (13 acres)
c/o John Muir NHS (S# 20, map A5)
4204 Alhambra Ave.
Martinez, CA 94553 501-838-0249

Fort Point National Historic Site (29 acres) 415-556-1693
PO Box 29333 (S# 21, map A4)
Presidio of San Francisco, CA 94129

Manzanar National Historic Site (S# 22, map E3) 619-786-2331
Lone Pine, CA
New NPS site approved March 2, 1992.

San Francisco Maritime NHP (50 acres) 415-556-1659
Fort Mason, Bldg. 201 (S# 23, map A4)
San Francisco, CA 94123

Bureau of Reclamation - USDI

Mid-Pacific Region 916-978-4919
FOB, 2800 Cottage Way
Sacramento, CA 95825
This office administers bureau recreation areas in west central and northern California, a portion of southern Oregon, and Nevada (except southern Nevada).

Bureau of Reclamation Recreation Areas

Twenty-eight recreation areas are listed here and symbolized on the California state map.

S#	MAP	LOCATION NAME
1	C3	Boca Res.
2	F2	Cachuma Lake
3	B2	Clair Engle Natl. Recreation Area
4	B5	Contra Loma Res.
5	C1	East Park Res.
6	C2	Folsom Lake
7	C2	Jenkinson Lake
8	B2	Keswick Res.
9	C1	Lake Berryessa
10	H4	Lake Cahuilla
11	F2	Lake Casitas
12	C2	Lake Natoma
13	C2	Lake Solano
14	F3	Lake Woollomes
15	B2	Lewiston Natl. Recreation Area
16	E2	Los Banos Res.
17	E3	Millerton Lake
18	D2	New Melones Lake
*19	C2	Nimbus Fish Hatchery
20	C3	Prosser Creek Res.
21	C2	Putah Creek Fishing Site
22	B2	Red Bluff Diversion Dam & Res.
23	H4	Salton Sea State Recreation Area
24	E3	Squaw Leap Management Area
25	C3	Stampede Res.
26	C1	Stony Gorge Res.
27	C2	Sugar Pine Res.
28	B2	Trinity River Fish Hatchery

USDC, Natl. Oceanic & Atmospheric Admin. (NOAA)

National Ocean Service
For National Marine Sanctuary (NMS) information contact the following offices:

Channel Islands NMS
113 Harbor Way
Santa Barbara, CA 93109 805-966-7107
or
Sea Center
211 Stearns Wharf
Santa Barbara, CA 93101 805-962-0885

Cordell Bank NMS is located about 50 miles northwest of San Francisco. Gulf of the Farallones NMS is located about 20 miles west to Point Reyes, CA. Mainland public facilities are planned for both sanctuaries.

Monterey Bay NMS
A recently designated sanctuary located adjacent Monterey, CA. No public facilities.

USGS Earth Science Information Centers

USGS Los Angeles-ESIC 213-894-2850
Federal Bldg., Rm. 7638
300 N. Los Angeles St.
Los Angeles, CA 90012

USGS Menlo Park-ESIC 415-329-4309
Bldg., 3, MS 532, Rm. 3128
345 Middlefield Rd.
Menlo Park, CA 94025

USGS San Francisco-ESIC 415-705-1010
504 Custom House
555 Battery St.
San Francisco, CA 94111

Wilderness/Wild River Index

In this index more than one agency office may manage a listing (wild river or wilderness), or a single office may be in charge of several listings. The index structure varies to reflect variations. Office names are followed by S# and map coordinate information in parenthesis.

Wilderness

Angeles National Forest (S# 2, map G3)
Cucamonga Wilderness - 12,981 acres, also San Bernardino NF (S# 58, map G3)
San Gabriel Wilderness - 36,118 acres
Sheep Mountain Wilderness - 43,600 acres, also San Bernardino NF (S# 58, map G3)
Cleveland National Forest (S# 8, map H3)
Agua Tibia Wilderness - 15,933 acres
Hauser Wilderness - 8,000 acres
Pine Creek Wilderness - 13,100 acres
San Mateo Canyon Wilderness - 39,540 acres
Eldorado National Forest Info Center (S# 14, map C2)
Desolation Wilderness - 63,475 acres
Mokelumne Wilderness - 104,461 acres, also Stanislaus NF (S# 88, map D2) and Toiyabe NF, Bridgeport RD (S# 99, map D3)
Inyo National Forest (S# 18, map E3)
Ansel Adams Wilderness - 228,669 acres, also Sierra NF (S# 78, map E2)
Golden Trout Wilderness - 303,287 acres, also Sequoia NF (S# 64, map E3)
Hoover Wilderness - 48,601 acres, also Toiyabe NF (CA/OR), Bridgeport RD (S# 99, map D3)
John Muir Wilderness - 580,675 acres, also Sierra NF (S# 78, map E2)
South Sierra Wilderness - 63,000 acres, also Sequoia NF (S# 64, map E3)
Klamath National Forest (S# 23, map A2)
Marble Mountain Wilderness - 241,744 acres
Russian Wilderness - 12,000 acres
Lassen National Forest (31, map B3)
Caribou Wilderness - 20,625 acres
Ishi Wilderness - 41,600 acres
Thousand Lakes Wilderness - 16,355 acres
Los Padres National Forest (S# 35, map F2)
Dick Smith Wilderness - 65,130 acres
Machesna Mountain Wilderness - 19,880 acres
San Rafael Wilderness - 150,610 acres
Santa Lucia Wilderness - 18,679 acres
Venatna Wilderness - 164,144 acres
Mendocino National Forest (S# 41, map C2)
Snow Mountain Wilderness - 37,000 acres
Yolla Bolly-Middle Eel Wilderness - 145,404 acres, also Shasta-Trinity NF (S# 70, map B2) and Six Rivers NF (S# 83, map B1)
Modoc National Forest (S# 46, map B3)
South Warner Wilderness - 70,385 acres
Plumas National Forest (S# 51, map C2)
Bucks Lake Wilderness - 21,000 acres
Rogue River National Forest (see Oregon chapter, S# 32, map D2)
Red Buttes Wilderness (CA/OR) - 16,150 acres
San Bernardino National Forest (S# 58, map G3)
San Gorgonio Wilderness - 56,722 acres
San Jacinto Wilderness - 32,040 acres
Santa Rosa Wilderness - 20,160 acres
Sequoia National Forest (S# 64, map E3)
Dome Land Wilderness - 94,686 acres
Jennie Lakes Wilderness - 10,500 acres
Monarch Wilderness - 45,000 acres, also Sierra NF (S# 78, map E2)
Shasta-Trinity National Forests (S# 70, map B2)
Castle Crags Wilderness - 7,300 acres
Chanchelulla Wilderness - 8,200 acres
Mount Shasta Wilderness - 37,000 acres
Trinity Alps Wilderness - 495,377 acres, also Klamath NF (S# 23, map A2) and Six Rivers NF (S# 83, map B1)
Sierra National Forest (S# 78, map E2)
Dinkey Lakes Wilderness - 30,000 acres
Kaiser Wilderness - 22,700 acres
Siskiyou NF (see Oregon Chapter, S# 37, map D1), also in California Klamath NF (S# 23, map A2) and Six Rivers NF (S# 83, B1), the Siskiyou Wilderness (CA/OR) - 153,000 acres
Six Rivers National Forest (S# 83, B1)
North Fork Wilderness - 8,100 acres
Stanislaus National Forest (S# 88, map D2)
Emigrant Wilderness - 112,119 acres
Tahoe National Forest (S# 93, map C2)
Granite Chief Wilderness - 25,000 acres
Toiyabe NF (CA/OR), Bridgeport RD (S# 99, map D3)
Carson-Iceberg Wilderness - 160,000 acres
Farallon NWR (see USFWS San Francisco Bay NWR S# 16, map B5)
Farallon Natl. Wilderness - 141 acres
Joshua Tree Natl. Monument (S# 7, map G4)
Joshua Tree Wilderness - 429,690 acres
Lassen Volcanic Natl. Park (S# 9, map B2)
Lassen Volcanic Wilderness - 78,982 acres
Lava Beds Natl. Monument (S# 10, map A3)
Lava Beds Wilderness - 28,460 acres
Pinnacles Natl. Monument (S# 12, map E2)
Pinnacles Wilderness - 12,952 acres

Toiyabe NF, Bridgeport Ranger District [1984]
Trinity Alps Wilderness
Ventana Wilderness
Yolla Bolly Middle Eel (Shasta/Mendocino)

Bureau of Land Management Maps

The state office (BLM S# 1) is in Sacramento. The 107 intermediate scale maps listed in the grid are available in both surface and mineral editions. The Long Beach map has not been published to date.

State Agencies

California Dept. of Parks & Recreation (S# 1, map C2)
A California State Parks Guide (251 state parks) is available. Entry fees are charged at most parks. Selected parks are covered in the Information Chart.

California Dept. of Fish and Game (S# 1, map C2)
Contact this Department regarding, Game, Marine Resources, and Inland Fisheries. A variety of free literature is available covering regulations and sites. A bi-monthly magazine, *Outdoor California*, is available by subscription for $6.50 per year. A list of the management areas open to hunting is available in the hunting regulations pamphlet. Fees are charged to hunt on some areas. Selected wildlife areas (WAs) are listed here and shown on the map, HQ and regional offices in the chart.

S#	MAP	WA NAME & LOCATION
7	A2	Butte Valley WA, Macdoel
8	B2	Cinder Flats WA, Fall River Mill
9	C3	Doyle WA, Doyle
10	A1	Eureka Slough WA, Arcata
11	A2	Indian Tom WA, Macdoel
12	C3	Antelope Valley WA, Sierraville
13	C2	Gray Lodge WA, Yuba City
14	D3	Heenan Lake WA, South Lake Tahoe
15	C2	Spenceville WA, Oroville
16	D2	White Slough WA, Lodi
17	E2	Big Sandy WA, San Miguel
18	D2	Hill Slough WA, Fairfield
19	C1	Indian Valley WA, Upper Lake
20	A5	Petaluma Marsh WA, Novato
21	A5	San Pablo Bay WA, San Rafael
22	E3	Battle Creek WA, Bishop
23	D2	Grizzly Island WA, Los Banos
24	E2	Little Panoche WA, Paicines
25	E2	Mendota WA, Tranquility
26	G4	Camp Cady WA, Ludlow
27	H4	Imperial WA, Calipatria
28	G4	Marble Mountains WA, Ludlow
29	G3	San Jacinto WA, Riverside
30	H4	Santa Rosa WA, Oasis
31	B3	Ash Creek WA, Bieber

Outdoor Map Index

National Park Service (USGS Maps)

Channel Islands National Park [1973]
Scale: 1 inch = 0.4 miles (1 cm = 0.3 km)
Death Valley National Monument [1977]
Scale: 1 inch = 4.0 miles (1 cm = 2.5 km)
Size: 24x37 inches (61x94 cm)
Lassen Volcanic National Park [1957]
Scale: 1 inch = 1.0 miles (1 cm = 0.6 km)
Point Reyes National Seashore [1973]
Scale: 1 inch = 0.8 miles (1 cm = 0.5 km)
Sequoia & Kings Canyon Natl. Parks [1958]
Scale: 1 inch = 2.0 miles (1 cm = 1.3 km)
Yosemite National Park [1958]
Scale: 1 inch = 2.0 miles (1 cm = 1.3 km)
Yosemite Valley [1970]
Scale: 1 inch = 0.4 miles (1 cm = 0.3 km)

U.S. Forest Service

For the Toiyabe National Forest District maps (Bridgeport RD listed here under California), see Nevada map index.

Angeles National Forest
Scale: 1 inch = 2.0 miles (1 cm = 1.3 km)
Ansel Adams Wilderness
Carson-Iceberg Wilderness, Stanislaus/Toiyabe NF
Cleveland National Forest
Scale: 1 inch = 2.0 miles (1 cm = 1.3 km)
Eldorado National Forest
Scale: 1 inch = 2.0 miles (1 cm = 1.3 km)
Emigrant Wilderness
Golden Trout & South Sierra Wilderness
Inyo National Forest
Scale: 1 inch = 2.0 miles (1 cm = 1.3 km)
John Muir & Sequoia-Kings Canyon NP
Klamath National Forest
Scale: 1 inch = 2.0 miles (1 cm = 1.3 km)
Lake Tahoe Basin Mgt. Unit
Lassen National Forest
Scale: 1 inch = 2.0 miles (1 cm = 1.3 km)
Los Padres National Forest
Scale: 1 inch = 2.0 miles (1 cm = 1.3 km)
Marble Mountain Wilderness
Mendocino National Forest
Scale: 1 inch = 2.0 miles (1 cm = 1.3 km)
Modoc National Forest
Scale: 1 inch = 2.0 miles (1 cm = 1.3 km)
Plumas National Forest
Scale: 1 inch = 2.0 miles (1 cm = 1.3 km)
San Bernardino National Forest
Scale: 1 inch = 2.0 miles (1 cm = 1.3 km)
Sequoia National Forest
Scale: 1 inch = 2.0 miles (1 cm = 1.3 km)
Shasta-Trinity National Forest
Scale: 1 inch = 2.0 miles (1 cm = 1.3 km)
Sierra National Forest
Scale: 1 inch = 2.0 miles (1 cm = 1.3 km)
Six Rivers National Forest
Scale: 1 inch = 2.0 miles (1 cm = 1.3 km)
South Warner Wilderness
Stanislaus National Forest
Scale: 1 inch = 2.0 miles (1 cm = 1.3 km)
Tahoe National Forest
Scale: 1 inch = 2.0 miles (1 cm = 1.3 km)

Dept. of Forestry & Fire Protection
Resources Bldg. - 1416 Ninth St.
PO Box 94246   916-445-3976
Sacramento, CA 94244
Contact this office for state forest recreation literature.

California Resources Agency
1416 Ninth Street, Room 1311
Sacramento, CA 95814   916-445-5656
Contact this agency for information on Wild Rivers as noted in the Wilderness/Wild River Index above.

Klamath River
California Resources Agency
(see State Agencies below)
Hoopa Valley Indian Reservation, PO Box 817, Hoopa, CA 95546
Klamath National Forest (S# 23, map A2)
Merced River
BLM Bakersfield District Office (S# 2, map F3)
Sierra National Forest (S# 78, map E2)
Yosemite National Park (S# 18, map D3)
Smith River
California Resources Agency
(see State Agencies below)
Six Rivers National Forest (S# 83, map B1)
Trinity River
BLM CA State Office (S# 1, map C2)
California Resources Agency
(see State Agency notes)

Point Reyes Natl. Seashore (S# 13, A4)
Phillip Burton Wilderness - 25,370 acres
Sequoia & Kings Canyon Natl. Park (S# 16, map E3) - 736,980 acres
Yosemite Natl. Park (S# 18, map D3) - 677,600 acres

BLM Ukiah District Office (S# 28, map C1)
Ishi Wilderness - 240 acres
Trinity Alps Wilderness - 4,623 acres
Yolla Bolly-Middle Eel Wilderness - 8,500 acres
BLM Bakersfield District Office (S# 2, map F3)
Machesna Mountain Wilderness - 120 acres
Santa Lucia Wilderness - 1,733 acres

Wild Rivers

American (Lower) Wild River
California Resources Agency
(see State Agencies below)
American River, North Fork
BLM CA State Office (S# 1, map C2)
Tahoe National Forest (S# 93, map C2)
Eel River
BLM CA State Office (S# 1, map C2)
California Resources Agency
(see State Agencies below)
Mendocino National Forest (S# 41, map C2)
Six Rivers National Forest (S# 83, map B1)

Feather River, North Fork
Plumas National Forest (S# 51, map C2)
Kern River
Sequoia National Forest (S# 64, map E3)
Sequoia (& Kings Canyon) National Park (S# 16, map E3)
Kings River
Sequoia National Forest (S# 64, map E3)
(Sequoia &) Kings Canyon National Park (S# 16, map E3)
Sierra National Forest (S# 78, map E2)

Hoopa Valley Indian Reservation, PO Box 817, Hoopa, CA 95546
Shasta-Trinity National Forest (S# 70, map B2)
Six Rivers National Forest (S# 83, map B1)
Tuolumne River
BLM CA State Office (S# 1, map C2)
Stanislaus National Forest (S# 88, map D2)
Yosemite National Park (S# 18, map D3)

BLM CALIFORNIA
1:100,000 INTERMEDIATE SCALE MAPS
SURFACE & SURFACE / MINERAL SERIES
P = (planimetric only) / Base Map Not Published

Map grid (quad name, year, series code), longitude markers: 125° 124° 123° 122° 121° 120° 119° 118° 117° 116° 115° 114°; latitude markers: 42° 41° 40° 39° 38° 37° 36° 35° 34° 33°

Crescent City 1985 T
Happy Camp 1985 T
Yreka 1979 T
Tule Lake 1975 P
Cedarville 1975 P
Orick 1982 T
Hoopa 1985 T
Mount Shasta 1979 T
McArthur 1978 T
Alturas 1978 T
Eureka 1979 T
Hayfork 1982 T
Redding 1979 T
Burney 1976 T
Eagle Lake 1978 T
Cape Mendocino 1979 T
Garberville 1979 T
Red Bluff 1979 T
Lake Almanor 1976 T
Susanville 1976 T
Covelo 1981 T
Chico 1980 T
Portola 1979 T
Ukiah 1981 T
Willows 1975 T
Yuba City 1979 T
Truckee 1979 T
Smith Valley 1978 P
Point Arena 1981 T
Lakeport 1975 T
Healdsburg 1972 T
Sacramento 1978 P
Placerville 1979 P
Bridgeport 1975 P
Excelsior Mountains 1973 P
Goldfield 1978 P
Last Chance Range 1978 P
Beatty 1978 P
Death Valley Junction 1978 P
Owlshead Mountains 1979 P
Mesquite Lake 1979 P
Davis Dam 1979 P
Napa 1985 T
Lodi 1978 T
San Andreas 1980 T
Yosemite Valley 1978 P
Benton Range 1976 P
Saline Valley 1976 P
Darwin Hills 1976 P
Ridgecrest 1978 P
Cuddeback Lake 1978 P
Soda Mountains 1978 P
Ivanpah 1979 P
Needles 1978 P
Parker 1979 P
Bodega Bay
San Francisco 1985 T
Stockton 1978 T
Oakdale 1977 P
Bishop 1978 P
Mount Whitney 1978 P
Three Rivers 1978 P
Isabella Lake 1978 P
Victorville 1978 P
Newberry Springs 1978 P
Amboy 1978 P
Sheep Hole Mountains 1978 P
Eagle Mountains 1978 P
Blythe 1978 P
Palo Alto 1985 T
San Jose 1978 T
Merced 1982 P
Fresno 1984 P
Vialia 1978 P
Delano 1978 P
Tehachapi 1978 P
Lancaster 1978 P
San Bernardino 1978 P
Big Bear Lake 1978 P
Palm Springs 1978 P
Salton Sea 1978 P
Trigo Mountains 1979 P
Monterey
Mendota 1982 P
Coolinga 1979 P
Paso Robles 1978 P
Taft 1978 P
Cuyama 1978 P
Los Angeles 1978 P
Santa Ana 1985 T
Barrego Valley 1982 P
Yuma 1979 P
Point Sur 1984 T
Shaver Lake 1980 P
Santa Maria
Santa Barbara
Long Beach
El Cajon 1979 P
El Centro 1978 T
Cambria 1984 T
San Luis Obispo 1984 T
Point Conception 1984
Laguna Harbor 1978
Santa Catalina Isl.
Oceanside 1984 T
San Diego 1983 T
Santa Rosa Island
San Nicolas Island

Office of Tourism
PO Box 9278
Van Nuys, CA 91409 1-800-862-2543
A state highway map is included in the tourism package. Scenic roads, state parks, recreation areas, and campsites are indicated by symbols.

Private Organizations

TNC California Field Office
785 Market St.
San Francisco, CA 94103 415-777-0487
A guidebook titled *California Wild Lands* is available for $9.95. It describes 23 nature conservancy areas in California, including a physical description and history of each area, biological and ecological information, significance of the area's preservation, local maps, directions to the preserve, seasonal information, description of facilities, and weather conditions.

Tribal Land Areas in California
Agua Caliente Band of Cahuilla Indians of the Agua Caliente Indian Reservation - Camping, hiking.
Agua Caliente Tribal Council (S# 18, map G4)
960 East Tahquitz Way, #106
Palm Springs, CA 92262 619-325-5673

Chemehuevi Tribe of the Chemehuevi Indian Reservation - Fishing, hunting, camping, boating, touring.
Chemehuevi Tribal Council (S# 19, map G5)
PO Box 1976
Chemehuevi Valley, CA 92363 619-858-4531

Fort Mojave Tribe of the Fort Mojave Indian Reservation - Fishing, camping, boating.
Fort Mojave Tribal Council (California/Arizona/Nevada)
500 Merriman Ave. (S# 20, map G5)
Needles, CA 92363 619-326-4591

La Jolla Band of Luiseno Mission Indians of the La Jolla Indian Reservation - Fishing, camping, touring.
La Jolla General Council (S# 21, map H3)
Star Route, Box 158
Valley Center, CA 92082 619-742-3771

ANCA Locations in California
Environmental Nature Center (S# 22, map G3)
1601 16th Street
Newport Beach, CA 92509 714-645-8489

Hayward Shoreline Interpretive Center (S# 23, map B5)
4901 Breakwater Ave.
Hayward, CA 94545 415-881-6751

Monterey Bay Aquarium (S# 24, map E1)
886 Cannery Row
Monterey, CA 93940 408-648-4800

Placerita Canyon Nature Center (S# 25, map G3)
19152 North Placerita Canyon Rd.
Newhal, CA 91312 805-259-7721

Oak Canyon Nature Center (S# 26, map G3)
6700 Walnut Canyon Rd.
Anaheim, CA 92807 714-998-8380

Oak Grove Nature Center (S# 27, map D2)
4520 West 8 Mile Rd.
Stockton, CA 95209 209-953-8814

John Panatier Nature Center (S# 28, map G3)
PO Box 60
Arcadia, CA 91006 818-355-9938

Lewis Robidoux Nature Center (S# 29, map G3)
5370 Riverview Drive
Riverside, CA 92509 714-683-4880

Shipley Nature Center (S# 30, map G3)
PO Box 190
Huntington Beach, CA 92648 714-960-8847

Sly Park Environmental Education Center
5600 Sly Park Rd. (S# 31, map D2)
Pollock Pines, CA 95726 916-644-2071

Starr Ranch Sanctuary (S# 32, map G3)
PO Box 967
Trabuco Canyon, CA 92678 714-858-0309

Turtle Rock Nature Center (S# 33, map G3)
PO Box 19575
Irvine, CA 92713-0575 714-854-8151

Whittier Narrows Nature Center (S# ★34, N of Glendora)
1000 North Durfee Ave.
South El Monte, CA 91733 818-444-1872

Effie Yeaw Nature Center (S# 35, map C2, N of Folsom)
PO Box 597
Carmichael, CA 95609-0579 916-489-4918

California State Chamber of Commerce
1215 K St., 12th Floor
PO Box 1736 Phone 916-444-6670
Sacramento, CA 95812-1736 Fax 916-444-6685

AGENCY/MAP LEGEND . . . INITIALS, MAP SYMBOLS, COLOR CODES

U.S. Forest Service Supervisor & Ranger Dist. Offices NFS 61
U.S. Army Corps of Engineers Rec. Areas & Offices . COE 31
USFWS National Wildlife Refuges & Offices . . . . NWR 40
National Park Service Parks & other NPS Sites . . . . . NPS 7
Bureau of Land Management Rec. Areas & Offices . . BLM 26
Bureau of Reclamation Rec. Areas & Reg. Offices . . . BOR 8
State Parks (also see State Agency notes) . . . . SPS 52
State Wildlife Areas (also see State Agency notes) . . SWA 19
Private Preserves, Nature Centers & Tribal Lands . . 15
The Wild Rivers and Wilderness Areas

***Note:** Refer to yellow block on page 7 (top right) for location name and address abbreviations. If a symbol number has a star ★ that symbol is not shown on the map.*

★ INFORMATION CHART ★

INFORMATION CHART LEGEND - SYMBOLS & LETTER CODES

- ■ means **YES** & □ means **Yes with disability provisions**
- **sp** means **sp**ring, March through May
- **S** means **S**ummer, June through August
- **F** means **F**all, September through November
- **W** means **W**inter, December through February
- **T** means **T**wo (2) or **T**hree (3) Seasons
- **A** means **A**ll Four (4) Seasons
- **na** means Not Applicable or Not Available

Note: empty or blank spaces in the chart mean **NO**

S#	MAP	LOCATION NAME (state initials if more than one) with ADDRESS and/or LOCATION DATA	TELEPHONE	ACRES / ELEVATION	INFO OFFICE (IO) / VISITOR CENTER (VC)	IO / VC OPEN SATURDAY / SUNDAY	ENTRY FEE, not camping or permit fee	CONCESSIONAIRE SERVICES AVAILABLE	INTERPRETIVE or EDUCATIONAL DISPLAY	FREE LITERATURE, brochures, maps, etc.	AGENCY GUIDED TOURS, scheduled / by res.	NATURE EDUCATION / STUDY PROGRAMS	WILDFLOWER VIEWING AREA or DRIVE	ARCHAEOLOGICAL / GEOLOGICAL SITES	HISTORIC SITES	INTERPRETIVE TRAILS	WILDLIFE IS ABUNDANT OR COMMON	ENDANGERED SPECIES ARE COMMON	WILDLIFE VIEWING SITES, blinds, signs, etc.	DEVELOPED PICNIC AREAS / PICNIC SITES	DEVELOPED CAMPGROUNDS / CAMPSITES	NO-CHARGE CAMPGROUNDS / CAMPSITES	WILDERNESS AREAS / WILD RIVERS	WALKING / HIKING TRAILS	SWIMMING PERMITTED, at one's own risk	BICYCLING OPPORTUNITIES...areas, trails	HORSEBACK RIDING, w/ your own horse	OFF-ROAD Motorized Vehicle Area / Use OK	FISHING IN SEASON, license / permit reqd.	BOATING FACILITIES, ramps, marinas, etc.	MOTORIZED WATERCRAFT OK, check limits	NON-MOTORIZED WATERCRAFT OK	HUNTING IN SEASON, license / permit reqd.	WINTER SPORTS OPPORTUNITIES	PARK & WALK-IN ONLY AREA	DAY USE ONLY, no overnight	DRINKING WATER	RESTROOMS	S#
1	A4	**U.S. Forest Svc., Pacific SW Region**, 630 Sansome Street, San Francisco 94111	415-705-2874	na / na	■					■														■												■	■		1
2	G3	Angeles Nat'l. Forest Sup., 701 N. Santa Anita Ave., Arcadia 91006 [see notes for Visitor Center information]	818-574-5200	693,000 / 800-10,064	■			■		■	■	■		■	■					■	■		■	■	■	■	■	■	■	■	■	■	■	■				■	2
3	G3	Arroyo Seco Ranger D., Oak Grove Park, Flintridge 91011	818-790-1151	na / na	■			■		■	■	■		■	■					■	■		■	■		■	■	■	■				■	■				■	3
4	G3	Mt. Baldy Ranger D., 110 N. Wabash Ave., Glendora 91740	818-335-1251	na / na	■					■	■	■		■	■					■	■		■	■		■	■	■	■				■					■	4
5	G3	Saugus Ranger D., 30800 Bouquet Canyon Rd., Saugus 91350	805-296-9710	na / na	■			■		■				■	■					■	■			■	■	■	■	■	■				■					■	5
		Toiyabe National Forest Sup. (CA/NV), 1200 Franklin Way, Sparks, NV 89431	702-331-6444	3,800,000 / 4,000-12,000	■					■				■	■					■	■		■	■	■	■	■	■	■	■	■	■	■	■				■	
6	G3	Tujunga Ranger D., 12371 N. Little Tujunga Canyon Rd., San Fernando 91342	818-899-1900	na / na	■					■				■	■					■	■			■		■	■						■					■	6
7	G3	Valyermo Ranger D., Valyermo Rd., PO Box 15, Valyermo 93563	805-944-2187	na / na	■			■		■	■	■		■	■					■	■		■	■	■	■			■				■					■	7
8	H3	Cleveland National Forest, 10845 Rancho Bernardo Rd., Suite 200, San Diego 92127	619-673-6180	420,000 / 2,000-6,200	□			□	■	■	■		sp	□		□	A			■	□		■	■	■	■	■	■	■				■				□	□	8
9	H3	Descanso Ranger District, 3348 Alpine Blvd., Alpine 92001 [off Hwy. 8, east from San Diego]	619-445-6235	na / na	□	A		□	■	■	■				□	■	A			■	□		■	■		■	■	■	■				■				□	□	9
10	H3	Palomar Ranger District, 1634 Black Canyon Rd, Ramona 92065	619-788-0250	na / na	■				■	■			sp			□				■	■		■	■	■	■	■		■				■				■	□	10
11	G3	Trabuco Ranger District, 1147 E. Sixth Street, Corona 91719	714-736-1811	na / na	■					■						■				■	■		■	■		■	■	■	■				■				■	■	11
12	C2	Eldorado Nat'l. Forest Sup., 100 Forni Rd., Placerville 95667	916-622-5061	583,000 / 3,000-8,500	■			■		■					■				■	■	■		■	■	■	■	■	■	■	■	■	■	■	■				■	12
13	D2	Amador Ranger D., 26820 Silver Dr. & Hwy. 88, Star Route 3, Pioneer 95666	209-295-4251	175,000 / 3,500-8,500	■			■		■				■						■	■		■		■		■	■	■	■	■	■	■	■			■	■	13
14	C2	Eldorado Nat. Forest Information Ce, 3070 Camino Heights Drive, Camino 95709	916-644-6048	586,000 / 1,500-10,000	■			■		■		■		■	■					■	■		■	■	■		■	■	■	■	■	■	■	■				■	14
15	C2	Georgetown Ranger D., 7600 Wentworth Springs Rd., Georgetown 95634	916-333-4312	100,000 / 3,000-6,700	■			■		■										■	■				■	■	■	■	■	■	■	■	■				■	■	15
16	C2	Pacific Ranger D., Pollock Pines 95726	916-644-2349	137,000 / 5,000-8,000	■			■		■				■	■				■	■	■		■		■		■	■	■	■	■	■	■	■			■	■	16
17	C2	Placerville Ranger D., 3491 Carson Court, Placerville 95667	916-644-2324	171,000 / 3,000-6,000	■			■		■	■	■		■	■					■	■		■		■	■	■	■	■	■	■	■	■	■			■	■	17
18	E3	Inyo National Forest Sup., 873 N. Main Street, Bishop 93514 [see notes for Visitor Centers information]	619-873-2400	2,000,000 / 4,000-14,495	□					■	■	■		■	■				■	■	■		■	■	■	■	■	■	■	■	■	■	■	■				■	18
19	D3	Mammoth RD & Visitor Center, PO Box 148, Mammoth Lakes 93546	619-924-5500	na / na	□	A		□	■	■	□	□	A	■	□	□	A		■	□	□		■	■	■	■	■	■	□	□	■	■	■	■		■	□	□	19
20	D3	Mono Lake RD & Mono Basin Visitor C, PO Box 429, Lee Vining 93541	619-647-3000	na / na	□				■	■	□	□		□	□	□			■	□	□	A	■	■	■	■	■	■	■	■	■	■	■	■		■	■	■	20
21	E3	Mt. Whitney Ranger D., PO Box 8, Lone Pine 93545	619-876-6200	na / na	■	S		□	■	■		■		■					■	■	■		■	■	■	■	■	■	■		■	■	■				■	■	21
22	E3	White Mountain Ranger D., 798 N. Main St., Bishop 93514	619-873-2500	na / na	■					■	■	■		■		□			■	■	■		■	■		■	■	■	■	■	■	■	■	■		■	■	■	22
23	A2	Klamath National Forest Sup., 1312 Fairlane Rd., Yreka 96097	916-842-6131	1,700,000 / 500-9,000	■					■	■	■		■	■					■	■		■	■	■	■	■	■	■	■	■	■	■	■				■	23
24	A2	Goosenest Ranger D., 37805 Highway 97, Macdowel 96058	916-398-4391	na / na	■					■				■	■					■	■		■	■	■	■	■	■	■	■	■	■	■	■				■	24
25	A2	Happy Camp Ranger D., Hwy 96, PO Box 377, Happy Camp 96039	916-493-2243	na / na	■					■				■	■					■	■		■	■	■	■	■	■	■	■	■	■	■	■				■	25
26	A2	Oak Knoll Ranger D., 22541 - Highway 96, Klamath River 96050	916-465-2241	375,000 / 1,500-7,500	□					■					■	■	A			□	□	A	■	■	■	■	■	■	■	■		■	■	■			□	□	26
27	A2	Salmon River Ranger D., Hwy. 3, PO Box 280, Etna 96027	916-467-5757	365,930 / 1,150-8,480	□				■	■										■	■		■	■	■	■	■		■			■	■	■			■	■	27
28	A2	Scott River Ranger D., 11263 N. Highway 3, Fort Jones 96032	916-468-5351	na / na	■					■				■	■					■	■		■	■	■	■	■	■	■	■	■	■	■	■				■	28
29	A1	Ukonom Ranger D., PO Drawer 410, Orleans 95556	916-627-3291	na / na	■					■				■	■					■	■		■	■	■	■	■	■	■	■	■	■	■	■				■	29

No.	Grid	Name / Address	Phone	Acres / Elevation
31	B3	Lassen National Forest Sup., 55 South Sacramento St., Susanville 96130 [85 mi NW of Reno, NV on Hwy 395]	916-257-2151	1,136,830 / na
32	B2	Almanor Ranger D., 900 E. Hwy. 36, PO Box 767, Chester 96020	916-258-2141	500,000 / 1,000-9,000
33	B3	Eagle Lake RD, c/o USDA Forest Serv., 55 South Sacramento St., Susanville 96130	916-257-2151	290,000 / 3,000-8,000
34	B2	Hat Creek Ranger D., PO Box 220, Fall River Mills 96028 [joint NPS/USFS VC at Manzanita Lake]	916-336-5521	440,000 / 3,500-8,700
35	F2	Los Padres National Forest Sup., 6144 Calle Real, Goleta 93117	805-683-6711	1,963,251 / 0-8,831
36	E2	Monterey Ranger D., 406 S. Mildred, King City 93930	408-385-5434	326,683 / 0-5,000
37	F2	Mt. Pinos Ranger D., Star Route, Box 400, Frazier Park 93225	805-245-3731	497,064 / 4,000-8,83'
38	G2	Ojai Ranger D., 1190 E. Ojai Ave., Ojai 93023	805-646-4348	311,294 / 240-7,570
39	F2	Santa Barbara Ranger D., Star Route, Los Prietos, Santa Barbara 93105	805-967-3481	286,000 / 500-6,800
40	F2	Santa Lucia Ranger D., 1616 N. Carlotti Dr., Santa Maria 93454	805-925-9538	538,139 / 600-6,828
41	C2	Mendocino Nat'l. Forest Sup., 420 E. Laurel St., Willows 95988	916-934-3316	900,000 / 500-7,000
42	B2	Corning Ranger D., 22000 Corning Rd., PO Box 1019, Corning 96021	916-824-5196	na / na
43	B1	Covelo Ranger D., Rt. #1, Box 62-C, Covelo 95428	707-983-6118	na / na
44	C2	Stonyford Ranger D., Stites Ladoga Rd., Stonyford 95979	916-963-3128	na / na
45	C1	Upper Lake Ranger D., Middlecreek Rd., PO Box 96, Upper Lake 95485	707-275-2361	na / na
46	B3	Modoc National Forest Sup., 441 N. Main Street, Alturas 96101	916-233-5811	2,000,000 / 4,000-9,800
47	B3	Big Valley Ranger D., PO Box 159, Adin 96006	916-299-3215	na / na
48	B3	Devil's Garden Ranger D., PO Box 5, Canby 96015	916-233-4611	na / na
49	A3	Doublehead Ranger D., PO Box 369, Tulelake 96134	916-667-2247	na / na
50	B3	Warner Mountain Ranger D., PO Box 220, Cedarville 96104	916-279-6116	na / na
51	C3	Plumas National Forest Sup., 159 Lawrence St., PO Box 11500, Quincy 95971	916-283-2050	1,400,000 / 1,000-8,300
52	C3	Beckworth RD/Mohawk RS, Mohawk Road, PO Box 7, Blairsden 96013	916-836-2575	185,000 / 3,800-8,300
53	B2	Greenville-Ranger D., 410 Main St., PO Box 329, Greenville 95947	916-284-7126	216,000 / 3,000-8,300
54	C2	La Porte RD/Challenge RS, 10087 LaPorte Rd., PO Drawer 369, Challenge 95925	916-675-2462	180,000 / 1,000-7,500
55	C3	Milford RD/Laufman RS, Milford 96121 [2 mi W of Hwy. 395 on Milford Grade]	916-253-2223	231,000 / 5,000-8,300
56	C2	Oroville Ranger D., 875 Mitchell Avenue, Oroville 95965	916-534-6500	156,000 / 1,000-7,000
57	C2	Quincy Ranger D., 39696 Hwy. 70, Quincy 95971	916-283-0555	234,000 / 2,200-7,200
58	G3	San Bernardino Nat'l. Forest Sup., 1824 Commercenter Circle, San Bernardino 92408	714-383-5588	819,000 / 1,000-11,500
59	G3	Arrowhead Ranger D., State Hwy. 18, Rimforest 92378	714-337-2444	80,000 / 5,000-7,000
60	G3	Big Bear Ranger D., PO Box 290, Fawnskin 92333	714-866-3437	146,300 / 4,400-9,952
61	G3	Cajon Ranger D. & Lytle Creek RS, 1209 Lytle Creek Rd., Lytle Creek 92358	909-887-2576	125,000 / 2,200-8,800
62	G3	San Gorgonio Ranger D., Mill Creek VC, 34701 Mill Creek Rd., Mentone 92359 [Hwy 38 E of Redlands at cor. of Bryant]	909-794-1123	190,000 / 3,000-11,000
63	G3	San Jacinto Ranger D., Idyllwild Ranger Station, PO Box 518, Idyllwild 92349	909-659-2117	250,000 / 2,000-9,000
64	E3	Sequoia Nat'l. Forest Sup., 900 W. Grand Ave., Porterville 93257	209-784-1500	1,139,542 / 1,000-12,432
65	F3	Cannell Meadow Ranger D., Whitney Rd., PO Box 6105, Kernville 93238	619-376-3781	na / na
66	F3	Greenhorn Ranger D., 15701 Hwy 178, PO Box 6129, Bakersfield 93386	805-861-4212	na / na
67	F3	Hot Springs Ranger D., 43474 Mountain Rd., Rt. #4, Box 548, CA Hot Springs 93207	805-548-6503	na / na
68	E3	Hume Lake Ranger D., 35860 E. Kings Canyon Rd., Dunlap 93621	209-338-2251	na / na
69	E3	Tule Ranger D., 32588 Hwy. 190, Springville 93257	209-539-2607	na / na
70	B2	Shasta-Trinity Nat'l. Forest Sup., 2400 Washington Ave., Redding 96001	916-246-5222	2,121,547 / 1,067-14,162
71	B1	Big Bar Ranger D., Star Route #1, Box 10, Big Bar 96010	916-623-6106	na / na
72	B1	Hayfork Ranger D., Star Route 159, Hayfork 96041	916-628-5227	na / na
73	B2	McCloud Ranger D., PO Box 1620, McCloud 96057	916-964-2184	na / na
74	A2	Mt. Shasta Ranger D., 204 West Alma, Mt. Shasta 96067	916-926-4511	na / na
75	B2	Shasta Lake RD (see notes on VC), 14225 Holiday Rd., Redding 96003	209-275-1587	na / na
76	B1	Weaverville Ranger D., PO Box 1190, Weaverville 96093	916-623-2131	na / na
77	B1	Yolla Bolla Ranger D., Platina 96076	916-352-4211	na / na
78	E3	Six Rivers National Forest Sup., 1330 Bayshore Way, Eureka 95501	707-442-1721	958,470 / 0-7,000
79	E3	Smith River National Recreation Are, PO Box 228, Gasquet 95543	707-457-3131	330,800 / na
80	B2	Mariposa Ranger D., 41969 Hwy. 41, Oakhurst 93644	209-683-4665	na / na
81	E3	Minarets Ranger D., North Fork 93643	209-877-2218	na / na
82	E3	Pineridge Ranger D., PO Box 300, Shaver Lake 93664	209-841-3311	na / na
83	B1	Sierra National Forest Sup., FOB, 1600 Tollhouse Rd., Clovis 93612	209-487-5155	1,300,000 / 800-10,000
84	A1	Kings River Ranger D., 34849 Maxon Rd., Sanger 93657 [summer contact Dinkey Ranger Station, ph. 841-3404]	209-855-8321	na / na
85	A1	Lower Trinity Ranger D., PO Box 68, Willow Creek 95573	916-629-2118	183,870 / 650-5,000
86	B1	Mad River Ranger D., Star Route, Box 300, Bridgeville 95526	707-574-6233	230,800 / na
87	A1	Orleans Ranger D., Drawer B, Orleans 95556	707-627-3291	212,120 / 400
88	D2	Stanislaus Nat'l. Forest Sup., 19777 Greenley Road, Sonora 95370 [office at top of hill on Greenley Rd.]	209-532-3671	850,000 / 1,500-11,000
89	D2	Calaveras Ranger D., Hwy. 4, PO Box 500, Hathaway Pines 95233	209-795-1381	200,000 / 2,000-10,000
90	D2	Groveland Ranger D., Hwy. 120-Star Route, PO Box 75 G, Groveland 95321 [8 mi E of Groveland or Hwy. 20]	209-962-7825	200,000 / 1,500-6,000
91	D2	Mi-Wok Ranger D., PO Box 100, Mi-Wok Village 95346 [15 mi E of Sonora on Hwy 108E, in Mi-Wok Village]	209-586-3234	200,000 / 1,500-6,000
92	D2	Summit Ranger D., Star Route, Box 1295, Sonora 95370 [Hwy 108E 30 mi E of Sonora at Dodge Ridge Pinecrest turn-off]	209-965-3434	250,000 / 5,000-12,000
93	C2	Tahoe National Forest Sup., Hwy. 49, 631 Coyote St., PO Box 6063, Nevada City 95959	916-265-4531	1,211,000 / 2,500-7,000
94	C2	Downieville Ranger D., 15924 Hwy. 49, Camptonville 95922	916-288-3231	na / na

★ INFORMATION CHART ★

INFORMATION CHART LEGEND - SYMBOLS & LETTER CODES
- ■ means YES & □ means Yes with disability provisions
- sp means spring, March through May
- S means Summer, June through August
- F means Fall, September through November
- W means Winter, December through February
- T means Two (2) or Three (3) Seasons
- A means All Four (4) Seasons
- na means Not Applicable or Not Available

Note: empty or blank spaces in the chart mean NO

If a symbol number has a star ★ that symbol is shown on the map.

AGENCY/MAP LEGEND ... INITIALS, MAP SYMBOLS, COLOR CODES
- U.S. Forest Service Supervisor & Ranger Dist. Offices NFS
- U.S. Army Corps of Engineers Rec. Areas & Offices . COE
- USFWS National Wildlife Refuges & Offices .... NWR
- National Park Service Parks & other NPS Sites ..... NPS
- Bureau of Land Management Rec. Areas & Offices .. BLM
- Bureau of Reclamation Rec. Areas & Reg. Offices .. BOR
- State Parks (also see State Agency notes) .... SPS
- State Wildlife Areas (also see State Agency notes) . SWA
- Private Preserves, Nature Centers & Tribal Lands...
- The Wild Rivers — and Wilderness Areas

Note: Refer to yellow block on page 7 (top right) for location name and address abbreviations.

Column group: **FACILITIES, SERVICES, RECREATION OPPORTUNITIES & CONVENIENCES**

S#	MAP	LOCATION NAME (state initials if more than one) with ADDRESS and/or LOCATION DATA	TELEPHONE	ACRES / ELEVATION
95	C2	Foresthill Ranger D., 22830 Auburn-Foresthill Rd., Foresthill 95631	916-367-2224	na / na
96	C2	Nevada City Ranger D., Hwy. 49, 631 Coyote St., PO Box 6063, Nevada City 95959	916-265-4538	na / na
97	C3	Sierraville Ranger D., Hwy. 89, PO Box 95, Sierraville 96126	916-994-3401	na / na
98	C3	Truckee Ranger D., PO Box 909, Truckee 95734	916-587-3558	na / na
		Toiyabe National Forest Sup. (CA/NV), 1200 Franklin Way, Sparks, NV 89431	702-331-6444	3,800,000 / 4,000-12,000
99	D3	Bridgeport Ranger D., Hwy. 395, PO Box 595, Bridgeport 93517	619-932-7070	970,000 / 5,000-12,000
1	G3	COE, Los Angeles District, PO Box 2711, Los Angeles 90053	213-894-5635	na / na
2	G3	Brea Dam, PO Box 2711, Los Angeles 90053	213-894-5635	na / na
3	G3	Carbon Canyon Dam, PO Box 2711, Los Angeles 90053	213-894-5635	na / na
4	G3	Fullerton Dam, PO Box 2711, Los Angeles 90053	213-894-5635	na / na
*5	G3	Hansen Dam, PO Box 2711, Los Angeles 90053	213-894-5635	na / na
6	G3	Mojave River Dam, PO Box 2711, Los Angeles 90053	213-894-5635	na / na
7	G3	Prado Dam, PO Box 2711, Los Angeles 90053	213-894-5635	na / na
8	F2	Salinas Dam & Santa Margarita Lake, PO Box 2711, Los Angeles 90053 [near San Luis Obispo]	213-894-5635	na / na
9	G3	Santa Fe Dam Recreation Area, PO Box 2711, Los Angeles 90053	213-894-5635	na / na
10	G2	Sepulveda Dam, PO Box 2711, Los Angeles 90053	213-894-5635	na / na
*11	G3	Whittier Narrows Dam & Legg Lake, PO Box 2711, Los Angeles 90053	213-894-5635	na / na
12	C2	COE, Sacramento District, 1325 "J" Street, Sacramento 95814	916-557-5281	na / na
13	B2	Black Butte Lake, Star Route 30, Orland 95963	916-865-4781	na / na
14	D2	Eastman Lake, PO Box 67, Raymond 93653	209-689-3255	na / na
15	C2	Harry L Englebright Lake, PO Box 6, Smartville 95977	916-639-2342	na / na
16	D2	Hensley Lake, PO Box 85, Raymond 93653	209-673-5151	na / na
17	E3	Lake Kaweah, Box 44270, Lemon Cove 93244	209-597-2301	na / na
18	C1	Lake Mendocino, 1160 Lake Mendocino Dr, Ukiah 95482	707-462-7581	na / na
19	C1	Lake Sonoma Warm Springs Dam, 3333 Skaggs Springs Rd, Geyserville 95441	707-433-9483	na / na
20	C3	Martis Creek Lake, PO Box 6, Smartville 95977 [near Truckee]	916-639-2342	na / na
21	D2	New Hogan Lake, 2713 Hogan Dam Road, Valley Springs 95252	209-772-1343	na / na
22	E3	Pine Flat Lake, PO Box 117, Piedra 93649	209-787-2589	na / na
23	D2	Stanislaus River Parks, PO Box 1229, Oakdale 95361	209-881-3517	na / na
24	E3	Success Lake, Box 1072, Porterville 93258	209-784-0215	na / na
25	A4	COE, San Francisco District, 211 Main St., San Francisco 94105	415-332-3871	na / na
26	A4	S F Bay Model Regional Visitor Cent, 2100 Bridgeway Blvd, Sausalito 94965	415-332-3871	na / na
1	H5	Cibola NWR (located in Cibola Arizo, PO Box AP, Blythe 92226	602-857-3253	16,667 / 240
2	G5	Havasu NWR (85% of NWR is in Arizon, 1406 Bailey Ave., Suite B, PO Box 3009, Needles 92363	619-326-3853	38,900 / 430-2,200
3	F2	Kern NWR, Jct. Garces Hwy. & Corcoran Rd., PO Box 670, Delano 93216 [19 mi. W of Delano]	805-725-2767	10,618 / 340-350
4	G2	Hopper Mountain NWR, 2493-A Patrola Rd., PO Box 5839, Ventura 93005 [adjacent to Los Padres Natl. Forest office]	805-644-5185	2,560 / 2,500
5	A2	Klamath Basin Refuges Office/VC & Tule Lake NWR, Rt. #1, Box 74, Tulelake 96134	916-667-2231	39,100 / 4,100
6	A3	Lower Klamath NWR, Rt. #1, Box 74, Tulelake 96134	916-667-2231	53,600 / 4,100-4,300
7	A2	Clear Lake NWR, Rt. #1, Box 74, Tulelake 96134	916-667-2231	211 / na
8	A4	Farallon NWR (No Public Use), PO Box 524, Newark 94560 [30 mi W off the coast of San Francisco]	510-792-0222	211 / na
9	B3	Modoc NWR, PO Box 1610, Alturas 96101 [3 mi. S on CR 115]	916-233-3572	6,280 / 4,400
10	C2	Sacramento NWR, Rt. #1, Box 311, Willows 95988 [exit I-5 at Norman Rd. go N 1.5 at entrance 7 mi S of Willows]	916-934-2801	10,783 / 95
11	C2	Colusa NWR, Rt. #1, Box 311, Willows 95988 [exit I-5 go E on Hwy. 20 7.5 mi to entrance]	916-934-2801	4,040 / 40-48
12	C2	Delevan NWR, Rt. #1, Box 311, Willows 95988 [exit I-5 at Maxwell Rd.go E 5 mi to viewing turnout, 9 mi N of Williams]	916-934-2801	5,634 / 55-60
13	C2	Sutter NWR, Rt. #1, Box 311, Willows 95988 [W from Yuba City, Hwy. 20 to G. Washington Bl., S on Schlag]	916-934-2801	2,591 / 30-35
14	H4	Salton Sea NWR, PO Box 120, Calipatria 92233	619-348-5278	2,500 / -230
15	G4	Coachella Valley NWR (closed to all entry), PO Box 120, Calipatria 92233	619-348-5278	2,589 / 200
16	B5	San Francisco Bay NWR, PO Box 524, Newark 94560	510-792-0222	18,219 / 0-300
17	B1	Humboldt Bay NWR, 1020 Ranch Rd., Loleta 95551 [at Hwy. 101 & Hookton Rd.]	707-733-5406	2,208 / na

20	D2	San Luis NWR, 340 "I" St., PO Box 2176, Los Banos 93635 [office is in town]	209-826-3508	7,340 / 70	□ ■ ■ A □ □ ■ □ ■ □	20
21	D2	Kesterson NWR, 340 I St., PO Box 2176, Los Banos 93635 [Hwy. 140, 6 mi. E fo Gustine]	209-826-3508	10,846 / 70	■ sp A ■ ■ ■	21
22	D2	Merced NWR, 340 I St., PO Box 2176, Los Banos 93635 [off Hwy. 59 on Sandy Mush Rd. near Merced]	209-826-3508	4,148 / 70	■ T □ ■ ■ ■ □	22
23	H3	Southern California Coastal Complex, PO Box 335, Imperial Beach 91933 [VC at 301 Caspian Way, Imperial Beach 91932]	619-575-1290	2,500 / na	□ A ■ ■ □ □ ■ □ A □ ■ ■ ■ □ ■ ■ □ □ □	23
24	H3	Sweetwater Marsh NWR, 1000 Gunpowder Pt Dr,in Chula Vista, PO Box 335, Imperial Beach 91933	619-422-2481	316 / na	■ ■ ■ ■ ■ ■	24
★25	H3	Tijuana Slough NWR, 301 Caspian Way, Imperial Beach 91932	619-575-1290	1,056 / na	■ ■ ■ ■ ■ ■ ■ ■	★25
1	A4	**Nat'l. Park Svc., Western Region**, Bldg. 201, Ft. Mason, Bay & Franklin Sts., San Francisco 94123	□ 415-556-0560	na / na	■ ■	1
2	G2	Channel Islands Nat'l. Park, 1901 Spinnaker Drive, Ventura 93001	805-644-8262	249,350 / na	■ ■ ■ ■ ■ ■ ■ ■ ■ ■ ■ ■	2
3	F4	Death Valley Nat'l. Mon. (CA/NV), Hwy. 190, Death Valley 92328	619-786-2331	2,067,600 / -300-11,000	□ A A □ ■ ■ sp □ □ □ sp □ □ S ■ ■ ■ □ □	3
4	D3	Devils Postpile Nat'l. Monument, PO Box 501, Mammoth Lakes 93546	619-934-2289	798 / 7,560	■ ■ ■ ■ ■ ■ ■ ■ ■ ■	4
5	A4	Golden Gate Nat'l. Recreation Area, Fort Mason, Bldg. 201, San Francisco 94123	415-556-0560	73,117 / 0-2,600	■ ■ ■ ■ ■ ■ ■ ■ ■ ■ ■ ■ ■ ■ ■	5
6	A5	John Muir Nat'l. Historic Site, 4202 Alhambra Avenue, Martinez 94553	415-228-8860	9 / na	■ ■ ■ ■ ■ ■	6
7	G4	Joshua Tree NM, 74485 Nat'l Monument Dr., Twentynine Palms 92277 [S side Hwy 62, E edge of town, off Utah Trail]	619-367-7511	559,950 / 1,200-5,185	□ A A ■ ■ ■ sp ■ ■ □ A □ □ A ■ ■ ■ ■ □	7
8	E3	Kings Canyon Nat'l. Park, c/o Sequoia & Kings Canyon NPs, Three Rivers 93271 [50 mi E of Fresno]	209-568-3341	458,800 / 4,100-13,500	■ ■ ■ ■ ■ ■ ■ ■ ■ ■	8
9	B2	Lassen Volcanic National Park, 38050 Hwy. 36 E., PO Box 100, Mineral 96063	916-595-4444	106,370 / 5,800-10,457	□ T T □ ■ ■ ■ S □ □ □ T ■ ■ □ T ■ ■ ■ ■ ■ ■ ■ ■ ■ □	9
10	A3	Lava Beds National Monument, PO Box 867, Tulelake 96134	916-667-2282	46,599 / 4,000-5,493	□ A ■ ■ □ □ ■ ■ A □ □ □ T ■ ■ ■ □ □	10
11	A4	Muir Woods NM, Mill Valley 94941 [17 mi N of San Francisco, 7 mi W off US 101 at CA 1/Stinson Bch., follow signs]	415-388-2595	559 / 1-1,200	□ □ ■ ■ □ ■ □ ■ ■ ■	11
12	E2	Pinnacles Nat'l. Monument, Paicines 95043	408-389-4485	16,265 / 1,000-3,000	■ ■ ■ ■ ■ ■ ■	12
13	A4	Point Reyes National Seashore, Point Reyes Station 94956 [take Bear Valley Rd. L off US 1 just N of Olema]	□ 415-663-1092	71,045 / 0-1,404	□ A □ ■ ■ □ □ sp □ □ □ A □ ■ A ■ ■ ■ ■ ■ ■ ■ ■ ■ □ □	13
14	A1	Redwood National Park, 1111 Second Street, Crescent City 95531	707-464-6101	110,178 / 0-3,097	■ ■ ■ ■ ■ ■ ■ ■ ■ ■ ■ ■ ■	14
15	G2	Santa Monica Mountains NRA, 30401 Agoura Rd., Suite 100, Agoura Hills 91301	818-597-9192	150,000 / na	■ ■ ■ ■ ■ ■ ■ ■ ■ ■ ■	15
16	E3	Sequoia & Kings Canyon Nat'l. Parks, Three Rivers 93271	209-565-3341	864,383 / 1,500-14,495	■ ■ ■ ■ ■ ■ ■ ■ ■ ■	16
17	B2	Whiskeytown-Shasta-Trinity NRA, PO Box 188, Whiskeytown 96095	916-241-6584	42,500 / 900-6,200	□ A ■ ■ ■ ■ ■ □ ■ T ■ ■ A ■ ■ ■ ■ ■ ■ ■ ■ ■ ■ ■ □	17
18	D3	Yosemite National Park, PO Box 577, Yosemite Nat'l Park 95389	□ 209-372-0200	748,542 / 2,000-13,000	□ A A □ ■ ■ □ □ T □ □ □ □ □ ■ ■ ■ ■ ■ ■ ■ ■ □ □	18
1	C2	**BLM California State Office**, 2800 Cottage Way, E-2807, Sacramento 95825	916-978-4754	17,100,000 / -282-14,500	■ ■ ■ ■ ■	1
2	F3	Bakersfield Dist. Office, FOB 800 Truxtun Ave., Room 311, Bakersfield 93301	805-861-4191	1,700,000 / 0-7,000	■ ■ ■	2
3	E3	Bishop Resource Area, 787 No. Main, Suite P, Bishop 93514	619-872-4881	750,000 / 3,000-7,000	■ ■ ■ ■ ■ ■ ■ ■ ■ ■ ■ ■ ■ ■	3
4	F2	Caliente Resource Area, 4301 Rosedale Highway, Bakersfield 93308	805-861-4236	500,000 / 0-6,000	■ ■ ■ ■ ■ ■ ■ ■ ■ ■	4
5	C2	Folsom Resource Area, 63 Natoma Street, Folsom 95630	916-985-4474	221,000 / 1,000-6,000	■ ■ ■ ■ ■ ■ ■ ■ ■ ■ ■ ■ ■	5
6	D2	Hollister Resource Area, PO Box 365, Hollister 95024	408-637-8183	310,000 / 200-2,000	■ ■ ■ ■ ■ ■ ■ ■ ■	6
7	G3	California Desert District, 6221 Box Springs Blvd., Riverside 92507	714-697-5217	12,500,000 / -200-11,000	■ ■ ■ ■ ■ ■ ■ ■ ■ ■ ■ ■	7
8	G3	Barstow Desert Information Center, 831 Barstow Road, Barstow 92311	619-256-8313	15 / 2,000	■ ■ ■ ■ ■	8
9	G3	Barstow Resource Area, 150 Coolwater Lane, Barstow 92311	619-256-3591	3,500,000 / 500-6,300	■ ■ ■ ■ ■ ■ ■ ■ ■ ■ ■ ■ ■	9
10	F3	Calico Early Man Site SRA, I-15 exit Mineola Rd., follow signs, 12 mi. N of Barstow	619-256-8313	400 / 2,200	■ ■ ■ ■ ■ ■ ■	10
11	F4	Dumont Dunes SRA, follow signs to dunes, off Hwy. 127, 34 mi. N of Baker	619-256-8313	30,000 / 2,100	■	11
12	G3	El Mirage SRA, follow signs off Hwy. 395, W of Adelanto	619-256-2729	3,000 / 2,500	■ ■ ■	12
13	F4	Soda Springs SRA, ZZYZX Rd. exit south off I-15, near Baker	619-256-8313	50 / 930	■ ■ ■ ■ ■ ■ ■	13
14	G3	Stoddard/Johnson Valley ORV Area, exit I-15 at Hodge or Sidewinder Rd, off Hwy. 247 at Camp Rock Rd., S of Barstow	619-256-8313	230,000 / 2,000-4,500	■ ■ ■	14
15	H4	El Centro Resource Area, 333 South Waterman Ave., El Centro 92243	619-352-5842	760,000 / -200-4,800	■ ■ ■ ■ ■ ■ ■ ■ ■ ■ ■ ■	15
16	H4	Imperial Sand Dunes SRA on SR 78, 25 mi. E of Brawley	619-352-5842	187,000 / 50	■ ■ ■ ■ ■ ■ ■ ■	16
17	G5	Needles Resource Area, 101 W. Spikes Road, PO Box 888, Needles 92363	619-326-3896	4,000,000 / 400-7,900	■ ■ ■ ■ ■ ■ ■ ■ ■ ■ ■ ■	17
18	G3	Palm Springs-South Coast Resource A, 63-500 Garnet Ave., N. Palm Springs 92258	619-251-0812	2,000,000 / -200-8,000	■ ■ ■ ■ ■ ■ ■ ■ ■ ■ ■ ■	18
19	F3	Ridgecrest Resource Area, 300 South Richmond Rd., Ridgecrest 93555	619-375-7125	2,500,000 / 1,100-11,000	■ ■ ■ ■ ■ ■ ■ ■ ■ ■ ■ ■	19
20	F3	Jawbone/Butterbredt ORV Area SRA, W of Hwy.14 & N of Jawbone Cyn Rd., or S of Hwy. 178 & E of Sequoia NF, Onyx	619-375-7125	250,000 / 2,000-5,000	■ ■ ■ ■ ■	20
21	B3	Susanville District Office, 705 Hall Street, Susanville 96130	916-257-5381	3,000,000 / 5,000	■ ■ ■ ■	21
22	B3	Alturas Resource Area, 608 West 12th St., Alturas 96101	916-233-4666	500,000 / 5,000	■ ■ ■ ■ ■ ■ ■ ■ ■ ■ ■ ■ ■	22
23	B3	Eagle Lake Resource Area, 2545 Riverside Drive, Susanville 96130	916-257-0456	1,100,000 / 5,000	■ ■ ■ ■ ■ ■ ■ ■ ■ ■ ■ ■ ■ ■ ■ ■ ■ ■ ■ ■	23
24	B3	Bizz Johnson Trail (25 mi. trail), off Hwy. 36 W of Susanville	916-257-0456	na / 4,200-5,600	■ ■ ■ ■ ■ ■ ■ ■ ■ ■ ■	24
25	B3	Eagle Lake SRA, W of Hwy. 139 & N of Susanville	916-257-0456	1,300,000 / 5,000	■ ■ ■ ■ ■ ■ ■ ■ ■ ■ ■ ■ ■ ■ ■ ■ ■	25
26	B3	Suprise Resource Area, 602 Cressler St., Cedarville 96104	916-279-6101	1,300,000 / 5,000	■ ■ ■ ■ ■ ■ ■ ■ ■ ■ ■ ■ ■ ■ ■	26
27	B3	High Rock Canyon SRA, located in Nevada, E of Cedarville	916-279-6101	80,000 / 5,000-6,000	■ ■ ■ ■ ■ ■ ■ ■	27
28	C1	Ukiah District Office, 555 Leslie Street, Ukiah 95482	707-462-3873	750,000 / 650-5,000	■ ■ ■ ■	28
29	A1	Arcata Resource Area, 1125 - 16th Street, Rm. 219, PO Box 1112, Arcata 95521	707-822-7648	250,000 / 800-5,000	■ ■ ■ ■ ■ ■ ■ ■ ■ ■ ■ ■ ■	29
30	B1	Samoa Dunes Recreation Area, near Eureka	704-822-7648	300 / 20	■ ■ ■ ■ ■ ■ ■	30
31	C1	Clear Lake Resource Area, 555 Leslie Street, Ukiah 95482	707-462-3873	180,000 / 650-3,300	■ ■ ■ ■ ■ ■ ■ ■ ■	31
32	C1	Cow Mountain Recreation Area, E of Hwy. 101 & N of Ukiah	707-462-3873	50,000 / 1,000-3,000	■ ■ ■ ■ ■ ■ ■	32
33	C1	Knoxville ORV Area, N of Hwy. 20 &, Upper Lake	707-462-3873	20,000 / 1,200	■ ■ ■ ■ ■	33
34	B2	Redding Resource Area, 355 Hemsted Drive, Redding 96002	916-246-5325	200,000 / 700-5,000	■ ■ ■ ■ ■ ■ ■ ■ ■ ■ ■ ■ ■ ■	34
1	C2	**Calif. Dept. of Parks & Recreation**, Office of Public Relations, PO Box 942896, Sacramento 94296	916-445-6477	na / na	■ ■ ■	1
2	C1	Anderson Marsh State Hist. Park, on Hwy. 53, between Lower Lake &, Clearlake	707-000-0000	17,545 / na	■ ■ ■ ■ ■ ■ ■ ■ ■ ■	2
3	D1	Ano Nuevo State Reserve, N of Santa Cruz	415-879-0595	1,192 / 0	■ ■ ■ ■ ■ ■ ■ ■	3
4	C3	Emerald Bay State Park, on Hwy. 89, 22 mi. S of Tahoe City	916-525-7277	593 / 6,800	■ ■ ■ ■ ■ ■ ■ ■ ■ ■ ■	4
5	D3	Mono Lake Tufa State Reserve, via Hwys. 395 & 120, 10 mi. SE of Lee Vining	619-647-6331	17,000 / 6,417	■ ■ ■ ■ ■ ■ ■ ■ ■ ■	5
6	F2	Morro Bay State Park, in, Morro Bay	805-772-2560	2,435 / 0	■ ■ ■ ■ ■ ■ ■ ■ ■ ■	6

52 CALIFORNIA / COLORADO

★ INFORMATION CHART ★

AGENCY/MAP LEGEND . . . INITIALS, MAP SYMBOLS, COLOR CODES
U.S. Forest Service Supervisor & Ranger Dist. Offices . NFS [61]
U.S. Army Corps of Engineers Rec. Areas & Offices . . COE [35]
USFWS National Wildlife Refuges & Offices . . . . . . NWR [40]
National Park Service Parks & other NPS Sites . . . . . NPS [7]
Bureau of Land Management Rec. Areas & Offices . . . BLM [26]
Bureau of Reclamation Rec. Areas & Reg. Offices . . . BOR [8]
State Parks (also see State Agency notes) . . . . SPS [52]
Private Preserves, Nature Centers & Tribal Lands . . .
State Wildlife Areas (also see State Agency notes) . . SWA [15]
The Wild Rivers —— and Wilderness Areas
Note: Refer to yellow block on page 7 (top right) for location name and address abbreviations.

INFORMATION CHART LEGEND - SYMBOLS & LETTER CODES
- ■ means YES & □ means YES with disability provisions
- **sp** means spring, March through May
- **S** means Summer, June through August
- **F** means Fall, September through November
- **W** means Winter, December through February
- **T** means Two (2) or Three (3) Seasons
- **A** means All Four (4) Seasons
- **na** means Not Applicable or Not Available
- Note: empty or blank spaces in the chart mean NO and/or that symbol is not shown on the map. If a symbol number has a star ★

Facility / convenience column headings (left to right):
INFO OFFICE (IO) / VISITOR CENTER (VC); IO / VC OPEN SATURDAY / SUNDAY; ENTRY FEE not camping or permit fee; FREE LITERATURE or EDUCATION, brochures, maps, etc.; AGENCY GUIDED TOURS, scheduled / by res; INTERPRETIVE SERVICES AVAILABLE; NATURE EDUCATION / STUDY PROGRAMS; WILDFLOWER VIEWING AREA or DRIVE; HISTORICAL / ARCHAEOLOGICAL SITES; INTERPRETIVE TRAILS; WILDLIFE IS ABUNDANT OR COMMON; ENDANGERED SPECIES ARE COMMON; DEVELOPED PICNIC AREAS / PICNIC SITES; NO-CHARGE CAMPGROUNDS / CAMPSITES; CHARGED CAMPGROUNDS / CAMPSITES; WALKING / HIKING TRAILS; WILDERNESS AREAS / WILD RIVERS; BICYCLING OPPORTUNITIES; HORSEBACK RIDING w/ your own horse; OFF-ROAD Motorized vehicle "...areas, trails; FISHING OPPORTUNITIES, at one's own risk; BOATING FACILITIES license / permit reqd; NON-MOTORIZED WATERCRAFT OK; MOTORIZED WATERCRAFT OK check limits; HUNTING IN SEASON, license / permit reqd; WINTER SPORTS OPPORTUNITIES; PARK & WALK-IN ONLY AREA; DAY USE ONLY / no overnight; DRINKING WATER; RESTROOMS

S#	MAP	LOCATION NAME (state initials if more than one) with ADDRESS and/or LOCATION DATA	TELEPHONE	ACRES / ELEVATION
7	D1	Natural Bridges State Beach, on West Cliff Drive in Santa Cruz	408-423-4609	65 / 0
8	A1	Patrick's Point State Park, on Hwy. 1, 25 mi. N of Eureka	707-667-3570	632 / 200
9	E1	Point Lobos State Reserve, on Hwy. 1, 3 mi. S of Carmel	408-624-4909	1,325 / 0
10	A1	Prairie Creek Redwoods State Park, on US 101, 50 mi. N of Eureka	707-488-2171	12,544 / 150
11	F2	Tule Elk State Reserve, 3 mi. W of I-5 off Stockdale Hwy., Tupman	209-822-2332	946 / 300
		Dept. of Fish & Game, Wildlife Mgt., 1416 Ninth Street, Sacramento 95814 [see notes for wildlife area details]		
1	C2	Region 1, Dept. Fish and Game, 601 Locust, Redding 96001	916-653-7664	na / na
2	B2	Region 2, Dept. Fish and Game, 1701 Nimbus Rd., Rancho Cordova 95670	916-225-2300	na / na
3	C2	Region 3, Dept. Fish and Game, 7329 Silverado Trail, Yountville 94599	916-355-0978	na / na
4	C1	Region 4, Dept. Fish and Game, 1234 E. Shaw Ave., Fresno 93710	707-944-5500	na / na
5	D2	Region 5, Dept. Fish and Game, 330 Golden Shore, Suite 50, Long Beach 90802	209-222-3761	na / na
6	G3	Richardson Bay Audubon Center, 376 Greenwood Beach Rd, Tiburon 94920	310-590-5132	na / na
1	A5	TNC California Field & Reg. Office, 785 Market Street, 3rd Floor, San Francisco 94103	415-388-2524	911 / 0
2	A4	Big Bear Valley Preserve, PO Box 2800, Big Bear City 92314	415-777-0487	
3	G3	Boggs Lake Preserve, contact Larry Serpa in Tiburon, N of Napa near Cobb	714-585-0717	250 / 6,700-8,500
4	C1	Cosumnes River Preserve, 6500 Desmond Road, Galt 95632	415-435-6465	153 / 2,787
5	D2		916-684-2816	3,000 / na
6	E2	Creighton Ranch Preserve, 3450 Ave 144, Corcoran 93212	209-992-2833	3,280 / na
7	E3	Kaweah Oaks Preserve, Road 182, Tulare County, Visalia	209-992-2833	324 / na
8	F2	Paine Wildflower Preserve, Corcoran Road, Kern County, near Lost Hills	209-992-2833	2,350 / na
9	E2	Pixley Vernal Pools Preserve, Road 168, Tulare County, Pixley	209-992-2833	40 / na
10	F3	Desert Tortoise Natural Area, c/o DTP Commission, PO Box 453, Ridgecrest 93556 [near California City]	619-377-4258	25,000 / 2,500
11	D1	Elkhorn Slough Preserve, Elkhorn Slough Foundation, PO Box 267, Moss Landing 95039	408-728-5939	650 / 0-150
12	C1	Fairfield Osborn Preserve, 6543 Lichau Road, Penngrove 94951	707-795-5069	210 / 1,300-2,200
13	B2	McCloud River Preserve, PO Box 409, McCloud 96057	916-926-4366	2,330 / 2,000
14	A5	Ring Mountain Preserve, North Coast Area Preserves Office, 3152 Paradise Dr., Rm. 101, Tiburon 94920	415-435-6465	377 / 610
15	G2	Santa Cruz Is. Preserve, c/o The Nature Conservancy, 213 Stearns Wharf, Santa Barbara 93101 [map F2]	805-962-9111	54,500 / 0-2,400
16	G3	Santa Rosa Plateau Preserve, 22115 Tenaja Road, Murrieta 92362	714-677-6951	3,100 / 1,700
17	B2	Vina Plains Preserve, contact Larry Serpa in Tiburon, N of Chico	415-435-6465	1,950 / na

COLORADO - CITY / AGENCY INDEX

City	Agency Office / Area Name	Code	S#	Map
Aguilar	Spanish Peaks SWA	SWA	46	C3
Alamosa	Alamosa NWR	NWR	1	C2
	Monte Vista NWR	NWR	2	C2
	San Luis Resource Area	BLM	5	C2
	Blanca SWA	BLM	20	C2
Alma	Alma SWA	SWA	30	B2
Almont	Almont Triangle SWA	SWA	50	B2
Artoles	Navajo SWA	SPS	64	D2
	Navajo SRA	SWA	43	D2
Aspen	Aspen Ranger D.	NFS	41	B2
Atwood	Atwood SWA	SWA	31	A3
Bayfield	Pine Ranger D.	NFS	3	D1
Bedrock	Dolores River SRMA	BLM	32	C1
Bond	Upper Colorado River SRMA	BLM	17	B2
Boulder	Boulder Ranger D.	NFS	14	A3
	TNC Colorado Field Office	TNC		A3
Brighton	Barr Lake SP	SPS		B2
Buena Vista	Clear Creek Reservoir SWA	SWA		B4
Burlington	South Republican SWA	SWA		A1
Campion	Lon Hagler SWA	SWA		A3

City	Agency Office / Area Name	Code	S#	Map
Canon City	San Carlos Ranger D.	NFS	22	C3
	Canon City District Office	BLM	2	C3
	Royal Gorge Resource A.	BLM	31	C3
Canyon City	Beaver Creek SWA	SWA	61	D2
Capulin	La Jara SWA	NFS	49	B2
Carbondale	Sopris Ranger D.	BLM	30	B2
	Thompson Creek SRMA	SWA	26	B1
Colbran	Plateau Creek SWA	NFS	11	B1
Collbran	Collbran Ranger D.	SPS	20	B3
Colorado Springs	Pikes Peak Ranger D.	SWA	5	B3
	SE Region, Div. of Wildlife	TNC	3	B3
Commerce City	Rocky Mtn. Arsenal Urban NWR	NWR	9	B3
Cortez	Hovenweep Nat'l. Monument	NPS	40	C1
	Anasazi SRMA	BLM	22	A2
Cowdrey	North Sand Hills SRMA	BLM	31	A2
Craig	Bears Ears Ranger D.	NFS	6	A1
	Craig District Office	BLM	8	A1
	Little Snake Resource A.	BLM	24	A1
	Upper Yampa River SRMA	SWA	20	A1
Creede	Creede Ranger D.	NFS	27	C2

City	Agency Office / Area Name	Code	S#	Map
Eagle	Eagle Ranger D.	NFS	46	B2
	Bull Gulch SRMA	BLM	26	B2
	Deep Creek SRMA	BLM	27	B2
	Eagle River SRMA	BLM	28	C2
Estes Park	Rocky Mountain Nat'l. Park	NPS	29	B2
	Hack Lake SWA	BLM	9	B1
Fairplay	South Park Ranger D.	NFS	58	B1
	High Creek Fen Preserve	SWA	10	A3
Flagler	Flagler Res SWA	TNC	34	B4
Florissant	Florissant Fossil Beds NM	SWA	6	B3
Fort Collins	Arapaho-Roosevelt NFs Sup.	NPS	5	A3
	Estes-Poudre Ranger D.	NWR	10	C2
	Redfeather Ranger D.	NPS	1	A3
	NE Region, Div. of Wildlife	BLM	3	B3
	Mountain Home Res. SWA	SPS	16	C2
Fort Garland	Colorado Springs SWA	SWA	5	C2
Fountain		NPS	7	A3
Fruita	Grand Valley SRMA	BLM	14	C2
Ft. Collins	Cherokee Park SWA (4 units)	BLM	36	C2
Gardner	Huerfano SWA	SWA	23	A1
Gateway	Gateway SRMA	SWA	48	B2
Glenwood Springs	Glenwood Springs RA	COE	3	C4
		SWA	35	C4
Golden	Golden Gate Canyon SP	SPS	6	B3
Granby	Sulphur Ranger D.	NFS	8	A2
	Deep Creek SRMA	BLM	27	B2
Grand Junction	Grand Junction Dist. Office	BLM	10	B1
	Grand Junction RA	BLM	12	B1
	Grand Mesa, Uncompahgre & Gunnison NFs Supervisor	NFS	35	B2
	Dominguez Canyon SRMA	NFS	32	B1
	Ruby Canyon/Black Ridge SRMA	BLV	4	B1
	Escalante SWA (9 units)	SWA		B1
Greeley	Pawnee National Grassland	NFS	10	A3
Gunnison	Cebolla Ranger D.	NFS	16	C2
	Curecanti National Rec. Area	NPS	5	C2
	Taylor River Ranger D.	NFS	7	A3
	Gunnison Basin RA	BLM	14	C2
	Cochetopa Canyon SRMA	BLM	36	C2
Hamilton	Cochetopa SWA	SWA	54	C2
Hartsel	Indian Run SWA	SWA	23	A1
Hasty	Tomahawk SWA	SWA	48	B2
Holly	John Martin Dam	COE	3	C4
	Holly SWA	SWA	35	C4
Hot Sulphur Springs	White River Nat'l. Forest Sup.	NFS	22	A2
	Hot Sulphur Springs SWA	SWA	8	A3
Hudson	Banner Lakes SWA	SWA	8	A3
Idaho Springs	Clear Creek Ranger D.	NFS	4	B3

City	Agency Office / Area Name	Code	S#	Map
Denver	USFWS Region 6 (Lakewood)	USFWS		
	Two Ponds Environmental Ctr.	NWR		
	NPS, Rocky Mtn. Region	NPS		
	NE Resource A. Office (Closed)	BLM		
	CO Div. Parks & Outdoor Rec.	SPS		
	Central Reg., Div. of Wildlife	SWA		
Dinosaur	Dinosaur Nat'l. Mon. (CO/UT)	NPS		
Dolores	Dolores Ranger District	BLM		
	Anasazi Heritage Center	SWA		
	Fish Creek SWA	NFS		
Durango	San Juan National Forest Sup.	NFS		
	Animas Ranger District	BLM		
	San Juan Resource A.	SWA		
	Perins Peak SWA	SWA		
Eads	Queens SWA (4 units)	SWA		

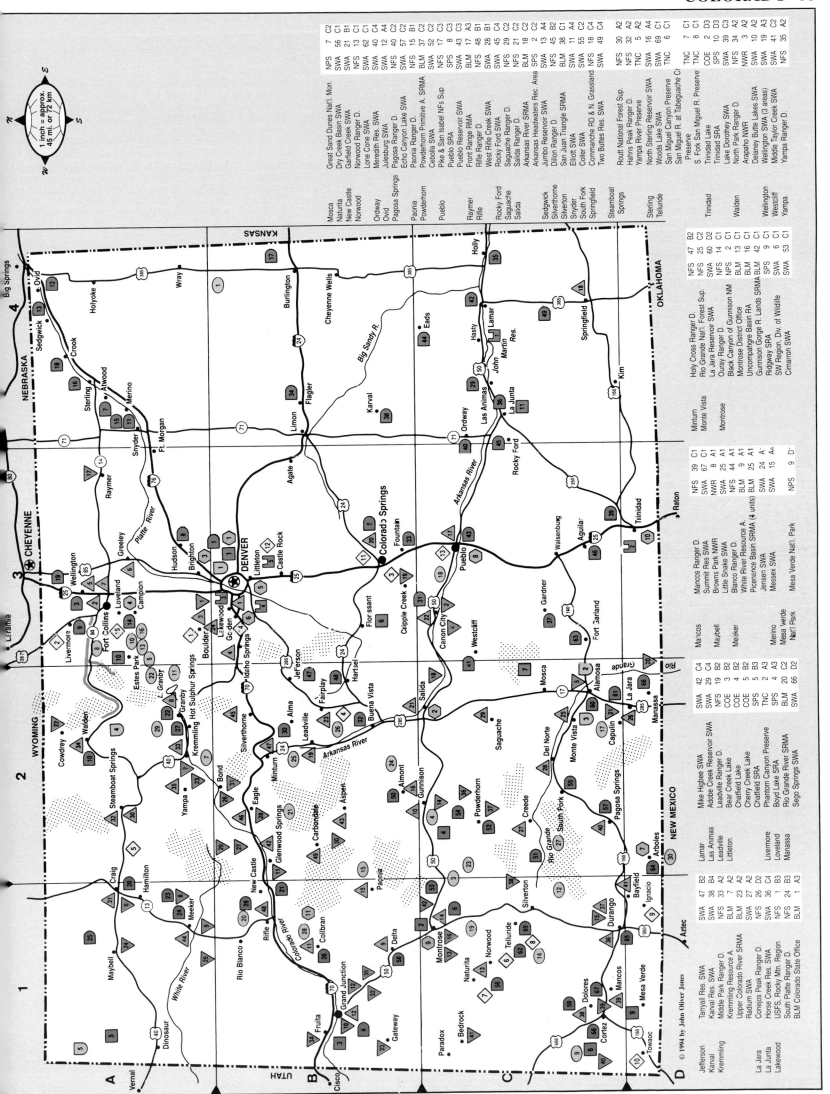

1 inch = approx.
45 mi. or 72 km

Great Sand Dunes Nat'l. Mon.	Mosca	NPS	7	C2
Dry Creek Basin SWA	Naturita	SWA	56	C1
Garfield Creek SWA	New Castle	SWA	21	B1
Norwood Ranger D.	Norwood	SWA	13	C1
Lone Cone SWA		SWA	62	C1
Meredith Res. SWA	Ordway	SWA	40	C4
Julesburg SWA	Ovid	SWA	12	A4
Pagosa Ranger D.	Pagosa Springs	NFS	40	C2
Echo Canyon Lake SWA		SWA	57	C2
Paonia Ranger D.	Paonia	NFS	15	B1
Powderhorn Primitive A. SRMA	Powderhorn	BLM	37	C2
Cebolla SWA		SWA	52	C2
Pike & San Isabel NFs Sup	Pueblo	NFS	17	C3
Pueblo SRA		SPS	8	C3
Pueblo SRMA		BLM	17	A3
Front Range RMA		BLM	48	B1
West Rifle Creek SWA	Raymer	SWA	28	A4
Rifle Ranger D.	Rifle	NFS	29	C2
Rocky Ford SWA	Rocky Ford	NFS	21	C4
Saguache Ranger D.	Saguache	NFS	18	C2
Salida Ranger D.	Salida	BLM	18	C2
Arkansas River SRMA		SPS	23	A4
Jumbo Reservoir SWA	Sedgwick	SWA	13	A4
Dillon Ranger D.	Silverthorne	NFS	45	B2
San Juan Triangle SRMA	Silverton	BLM	38	C1
Elliott SWA	Snyder	SWA	55	C2
Coller SWA	South Fork	SWA	18	C4
Commanche RD & N. Grassland	Springfield	NFS	49	C4
Two Buttes Res. SWA				
Routt National Forest Sup.	Steamboat Springs	NFS	30	A2
Hahns Peak Ranger D.		NFS	32	A2
Yampa River Preserve		TNC	5	A2
North Sterling Reservoir SWA	Sterling	SWA	16	A4
Woods Lake SWA		SWA	69	C1
San Miguel Canyon Preserve	Telluride	TNC	6	C1
San Miguel R. at Tabeguache Cr Preserve		TNC	7	C1
S. Fork San Miguel R. Preserve		TNC	8	C1
Trinidad Lake	Trinidad	NFS	25	D2
La Jara Reservoir SWA		SWA	60	D2
Ouray Ranger D.		NFS	14	C1
Black Canyon of Gunnison NM		NPS	2	B1
Montrose District Office	Walden	BLM	13	C1
Uncompahgre Basin RA		BLM	16	C1
Gunnison Gorge R. Lands SRMA		BLM	42	C1
Ridgway SRA		SPS	9	C1
SW Region, Div. of Wildlife		SWA	6	C1
Cimarron SWA		SWA	53	C1

Holy Cross Ranger D.	Minturn	NFS	39	C1
Rio Grande Nat'l. Forest Sup.	Monte Vista	SWA	67	C1
La Jara Reservoir SWA	Montrose	NWR	25	A1
Ouray Ranger D.		NFS	44	A1
Black Canyon of Gunnison NM		BLM	9	A1
Montrose District Office		BLM	25	A1
Uncompahgre Basin RA		SWA	24	A^
Gunnison Gorge R. Lands SRMA		SWA	15	A^
Mesa Verde Nat'l. Park	Nat'l Park	NPS	9	D^

Mancos Ranger D.	Mancos	SWA	47	B2
Summit Res SWA		SWA	38	B4
Browns Park NWR	Maybell	NFS	33	A2
Little Snake SWA		BLM	23	A2
Blanco Ranger D.	Meeker	BLM	27	A2
White River Resource A.		SWA	26	A2
Picenance Basin SRMA (4 units)		SWA	36	C4
Jensen SWA		SWA	1	B3
Messex SWA	Merino	NFS	1	B3
	Mesa Verde	BLM	1	A3

Mike Higbee SWA	Lamar	SWA	42	C4
Adobe Creek Reservoir D.	Las Animas	SWA	29	C4
Leadville Ranger D.	Leadville	NFS	19	B2
Bear Creek Lake	Littleton	COE	4	B2
Chatfield Lake		COE	5	B2
Cherry Creek Lake		COE	6	B2
Chatfield SRA		SPS	5	B3
Phantom Canyon Preserve	Livermore	TNC	2	A3
Boyd Lake SRA	Loveland	SPS	4	A3
Rio Grande River SRMA	Manassa	BLM	20	D2
Sego Springs SWA		SWA	66	D2

Tarryall Res. SWA	Jefferson	SWA	47	B2
Karval Res. SWA	Karval	SWA	38	B4
Middle Park Ranger D.	Kremmling	NFS	33	A2
Kremmling Resource A.		BLM	23	A2
Upper Colorado River SRMA		BLM	27	A2
Radium SWA		SWA	26	D2
Conejos Peak Ranger D.	La Jara	NFS	36	C4
Horse Creek Res. SWA	La Junta	SWA	36	C4
USFS, Rocky Mtn. Region	Lakewood	NFS	1	B3
South Platte Ranger D.		NFS	24	B3
BLM Colorado State Office		BLM	1	A3

Kansas

Nebraska

Wyoming

Oklahoma

New Mexico

Utah

Cheyenne

Laramie

Big Springs

Ovid
Sedgwick
Crook
Sterling
Atwood
Holyoke
Wray
Merino
Snyder
Ft. Morgan
Raymer
Wellington
Fort Collins
Livermore
Loveland
Campion
Greeley
Estes Park
Granby
L. Granby
Hot Sulphur Springs
Kremmling
Granby
Walden
Cowdrey
Steamboat Springs
Yampa
Hamilton
Craig
Maybell
Dinosaur
Vernal
Cisco
Fruita
Grand Junction
Gateway
Paradox
Bedrock
Rio Blanco
Meeker
Rifle
New Castle
Glenwood Springs
Carbondale
Aspen
Bond
Eagle
Minturn
Silverthorne
Leadville
Alma
Fairplay
Buena Vista
Jefferson
Hartsel
Idaho Springs
Golden
Boulder
Lakewood
Denver
Littleton
Brighton
Hudson
Castle Rock
Agate
Limon
Flagler
Burlington
Cheyenne Wells
Eads
Karval
Colorado Springs
Fountain
Florissant
Cripple Creek
Canon City
Westcliff
Gardner
Pueblo
Walsenburg
Aguilar
Trinidad
Raton
Hasty
Lamar
John Martin Res.
Las Animas
La Junta
Ordway
Rocky Ford
Holly
Springfield
Kim
Del Norte
Monte Vista
Alamosa
La Jara
Manassa
Arboles
Bayfield
Ignacio
Durango
Mancos
Mesa Verde
Cortez
Towaoc
Dolores
Norwood
Naturita
Telluride
Montrose
Delta
Collbran
Gunnison
Almont
Crested Butte
Powderhorn
Creede
South Fork
Pagosa Springs
Saguache
Salida
Mosca
Fort Garland
Steamboat Springs
Maybell
Platte River
Colorado River
White River
Arkansas River
Big Sandy R.
Rio Grande

COLORADO NOTES

Summary

There are 150 federal, 84 state, and 10 private recreation areas or local administrative offices covered in this state chapter. Of these, 106 appear in the Information Chart and 138 are covered in the notes. The special indexes feature 31 federally designated wilderness areas and wild rivers, and 74 agency published outdoor maps.

Federal Agencies

USFWS National Wildlife Refuges

The Arapaho NWR is also the administrative headquarters for the Bamforth, Hutton Lake, and Pathfinder NWRs in Wyoming.

National Park Service

Additional NPS Locations in Colorado

Bent's Old Fort NHS (800 acres) (S# 11, map C4)
35110 Hwy. 194 East
La Junta, CO 81050-9523   719-384-2596

Yucca House National Monument (10 acres)
Not open to the public at this time.
c/o Mesa Verde National Park
Mesa Verde National Park, CO 81321   303-529-4465

Bureau of Land Management

A 184 page book, *Recreation Futures for Colorado*, is available from the BLM Colorado State Office in Lakewood. It contains information about BLM Special Recreation Management Areas (SRMAs). The BLM state, district, and resource area offices appear in the Colorado information chart. The SRMAs are listed here with their S#, map coordinates and nearby city.

S#	MAP	LOCATION NAME, CITY
17	A3	Front Range SRMA, Raymer
18	C2	Arkansas River SRMA, Salida
19	B3	Gold Belt Complex SRMA, Cripple Creek
20	C2	Blanca SRMA, Alamosa
21	D2	Rio Grande River SRMA, Manassa
22	A3	North Sand Hills SRMA, Cowdrey
23	A2	Upper Colorado River SRMA, Kremmling
24	A1	Upper Yampa River SRMA, Craig
25	A1	Piceance Basin SRMA, Meeker
26	B2	Bull Gulch SRMA, Eagle
27	B2	Deep Creek SRMA, Eagle
28	B2	Eagle River SRMA, Eagle
29	B2	Hack Lake SRMA, Eagle
30	B2	Thompson Creek SRMA, Carbondale
31	A2	Upper Colorado River SRMA, Bond
32	B1	Dominguez Canyon SRMA, Grand Junction
33	B1	Gateway SRMA, Gateway
34	B1	Grand Valley SRMA, Fruita
35	B1	Ruby Canyon -Black Ridge SRMA, Grand Junction
36	C2	Cochetopa Canyon SRMA, Gunnison
37	C2	Powderhorn Primitive Area SRMA, Powderhorn
38	C1	San Juan Triangle SRMA, Silverton
39	C1	Anasazi Heritage Center, Dolores
40	C1	Anasazi SRMA, Cortez
41	C1	Dolores River SRMA, Bedrock
42	C1	Gunnison Gorge Rec. Lands SRMA, Montrose

Bureau of Reclamation - USDI

Denver Federal Center
PO Box 25007
Denver, CO 80225-0007   303-236-7000

The Bureau maintains a unique Hydraulics Laboratory at the Denver Federal Center. The public is welcome to tour the laboratory when group tours are given. Group tours occur on weekdays between 8:00 a.m. and 3:00 p.m.

Write to Public Affairs at the above address or call (303) 236-5995 for information. The laboratory is in Building 56, a part of the Federal Center Complex in the city of Lakewood at the intersection of 6th Avenue and Union.

Bureau of Reclamation Recreation Areas

Thirty recreation areas are listed here and symbolized on the Colorado state map.

S#	MAP	LOCATION NAME
1	B4	Bonny Res.
2	A3	Carter Lake
3	C1	Crawford Res.
4	C2	Curecanti Unit
5	A3	East Portal Res.
*6	A3	Flatiron Res.
7	A2	Green Mountain Res.
8	A3	Horsetooth Res.
9	C1	Jackson Gulch Res.
10	A3	Lake Estes
11	A2	Lake Granby
12	C1	Lemon Res.
13	A3	Marys Lake
14	C1	McPhee Res.
15	B2	Paonia Res.
16	A3	Pinewood Lake
17	C2	Platoro Res.
18	C3	Pueblo Res.
19	C1	Ridgeway Res.
20	B1	Rifle Gap Res.
21	B2	Ruedi Res.
22	A2	Shadow Mountain Lake
23	C2	Silver Jack Res.
24	B2	Taylor Park Res.
25	B2	Turquoise Lake
26	B2	Twin Lakes
27	C1	Vallecito Res.
28	B1	Vega Res.
29	A2	Willow Creek Res.
30	D2	Colorado/New Mexico Navajo Res.

Wilderness/Wild River Index

In this index more than one agency office may manage a wild river or wilderness, and a single office may be in charge of several. The index structure varies to reflect variations. Office names are followed by S# and map coordinate information in parentheses.

Wilderness Areas

Arapaho & Roosevelt National Forests Sup. (S# 2, map A3)
Cache La Poudre Wilderness - 9,238 acres
Comanche Peak Wilderness - 66,781 acres
Eagles Nest Wilderness - 133,325 acres, and by White River NF (S# 42, map B2), who also manage
Indian Peaks Wilderness - 70,374 acres
Mount Evans Wilderness - 74,401 acres, and by Pike & San Isabel NF Sup. (S# 17, map C3), who also manage Neota Wilderness - 9,924 acres, with Routt NF (S# 30, map A2), who also manage
Never Summer Wilderness - 13,702 acres
Rawah Wilderness - 73,020 acres
Grand Mesa, Uncompahgre & Gunnison NF Sup. (S# 9, map B1)
Big Blue Wilderness - 98,320 acres
Collegiate Peaks Wilderness - 166,654 acres, also managed by Pike & San Isabel NF Sup. (S# 17, map C3), and White River NF (S# 42, map B2) who also manage La Garita Wilderness - 103,986 acres, with Rio Grande NF (S# 25, map C2) who also manage
Lizard Head Wilderness - 41,189 acres, with San Juan NF (S# 36, map C1) who manage the Maroon Bells-Snowmass Wilderness - 180,498 acres, with White River NF (S# 42, map B2)
Mount Sneffels Wilderness - 16,505 acres, who also manage the Raggeds Wilderness - 59,519 acres, and West Elk Wilderness - 176,092 acres
Pike & San Isabel Natl. Forests Sup. (S# 17, map C3)
Holy Cross Wilderness - 122,037 acres, with White River NF (S# 42, map B2)
Lost Creek Wilderness - 105,090 acres
Mount Massive Wilderness - 27,980 acres
Rio Grande National Forest (S# 25, map C2) and San Juan National Forest (S# 36, map C1) manage
South San Juan Wilderness - 127,690 acres
Weminuche Wilderness - 459,604 acres
Routt National Forest (S# 30, map A2)
Flat Tops Wilderness - 235,035 acres, with White River NF (S# 42, map B2) who manage
Mount Zirkel Wilderness - 139,819 acres
Platte River Wilderness - 770 acres
Hunter-Fryingpan Wilderness - 74,250 acres

Leadville National Fish Hatchery. Contact USFWS Regional Office in Denver (S# 1, map B3). Hatchery is located west of Leadville, CO (map B2) and manages
Leadville Wilderness - 2,560 acres

Black Canyon of the Gunnison Natl. Monument (NPS S# 2, map C1)
Black Canyon of the Gunnison Wilderness - 11,180 acres
Great Sand Dunes Natl. Monument (S# 7, map B3) manages
Great Sand Dunes Wilderness - 33,450 acres
Mesa Verde National Park (S# 9, map D1)
Mesa Verde Wilderness - 8,100 acres

Wild River

Cache la Poudre Wild River
Arapaho & Roosevelt National Forests (S# 2, map A3)

Outdoor Map Index

National Park Service (USGS Maps)

Black Canyon of the Gunnison NM [1950]
Scale: 1 inch = 0.4 mile (1 cm = 0.3 km)
Size: 23x30 inches (58x76 cm)
Dinosaur Natl. Monument (CO & UT) [1971]
Scale: 1 inch = 1.0 mile (1 cm = 0.6 km)
Size: 30x51 inches (76x129 cm)
Great Sand Dunes Natl. Monument [1967]
Scale: 1 inch = 0.4 mile (1 cm = 0.3 km)
Size: 28x33 inches (71x63 cm)
Mesa Verde National Park [1967]
Scale: 1 inch = 0.4 mile (1 cm = 0.3 km)
Size: 46x54 inches (116x137 cm)
Rocky Mountain National Park [1967]
Scale: 1 inch = 1.0 mile (1 cm = 0.6 km)
Size: 28x39 inches (71x99 cm)

U.S. Forest Service Maps

The regional office in Colorado offers two wilderness maps, Colorado Wilderness [1980] and Wyoming Wilderness [1984]. There are some free travel maps available. Two travel maps are combined with Visitor Maps and are printed in color. They are The Uncompahgre and Grand Mesa NF maps. The Arapaho & Roosevelt National Forests map is available in paper or plasticized (water-proof).

Arapaho & Roosevelt National Forests
Scale: 1 inch = 0.5 mile (1 cm = 0.3 km)
Comanche National Grassland
Grand Mesa National Forest
Scale: 1 inch = 0.5 mile (1 cm = 0.3 km)
Gunnison Basin Area
Scale: 1 inch = 0.5 mile (1 cm = 0.3 km)
Pawnee National Grassland
Pike National Forest
Scale: 1 inch = 0.5 mile (1 cm = 0.3 km)
Rio Grande National Forest
Scale: 1 inch = 0.5 mile (1 cm = 0.3 km)
Routt National Forest
Scale: 1 inch = 0.5 mile (1 cm = 0.3 km)
San Isabel National Forest
Scale: 1 inch = 0.5 mile (1 cm = 0.3 km)
San Juan National Forest
Scale: 1 inch = 0.5 mile (1 cm = 0.3 km)
Uncompahgre National Forest
Scale: 1 inch = 0.5 mile (1 cm = 0.3 km)
White River National Forest
Scale: 1 inch = 0.5 mile (1 cm = 0.3 km)

Bureau of Land Management Maps

The BLM state office is in Lakewood (BLM S# 1). A Colorado Resource map in 1:500,000 scale (1 in. = 8 miles) is available and the map size is 52x44 inches. The intermediate scale maps shown on the map grid are 42x30 inches (107x76 cm).

USGS Earth Science Information Centers

USGS Denver-ESIC
169 Federal Bldg.
1961 Stout St.
Denver, CO 80294   303-844-4169

USGS Lakewood-ESIC
Box 25046, Federal Ctr. MS 504
Bldg. 25, Rm. 1813
Denver, CO 80225   303-236-5829

State Agencies

Colorado Department of Natural Resources
1313 Sherman St., Room 718
Denver, CO 80203   303-866-3311
This is the parent agency for the Parks and Outdoor Recreation, and Wildlife Divisions.

BLM COLORADO

1:100,000 INTERMEDIATE SCALE MAPS
SURFACE & SURFACE / MINERAL SERIES
P (planimetric)   S (surface/mineral only)

109°	108°	107°	106°	105°	104°	103°	(102°)
Canyon of Ladore 1988	Craig 1988	Walden 1985	Fort Collins 1988	Eaton 1986	Sterling 1978 P	Julesburg 1978 P	
Rangely 1987	Meeker 1988	Steamboat Springs 1988	Estes Park 1986	Greeley 1986 S	Fort Morgan 1978 S	Wray 1986 S	
Douglas Pass 1987	Glenwood Springs 1988	Vail 1985	Denver West 1986	Denver East 1986 S	Last Chance 1978 P	Bonny Reservoir 1978 P	
Grand Junction 1985	Carbondale 1988	Leadville 1985	Bailey 1986	Castle Rock 1986 S	Limon 1985 S	Burlington 1982 P	
Delta 1985	Paonia 1985	Gunnison 1986	Pikes Peak 1986	Colorado Springs 1985	Karval 1987	Cheyenne Wells 1987	
Nucla 1985	Montrose 1986	Soguache 1988	Canon City 1988	Pueblo 1985	Las Animas 1977	Lamar 1982	
Dove Creek 1986	Silverton 1986	Del Norte 1986	Blanca 1986	Walsenburg 1986	La Junta 1986	Two Buttes Reservoir 1977 P	
Cortez 1986	Durango 1986	Antonito 1987	Alamosa 1988	Trinidad 1988	Kim 1987 S	Springfield 1977 S,P	

Division of Parks and Outdoor Recreation

(S# 1, map B3)
A Colorado State Parks Guide (36 state parks) is available free. It describes each park, contains a state map showing their locations, and indicates facilities and activities using a bar chart. There is a $3 daily entry fee with additional fees for camping.

Chatfield State Recreation Area (S# 5, map B3) offers the recreationist a variety of outdoor opportunities, including balloon flights on Saturday mornings, weather permitting.

Division of Wildlife (S# 1, map B3)

A *Directory of Colorado Division of Wildlife Properties* provides information on 253 WMAs. Harvest, licensing statistics, and programs status are given in an annual report. A bi-monthly full color magazine, *Colorado Outdoors*, is available by subscription for $8.50 per year. Call 303-294-7469 for information about subscribing.

The headquarters and five regional offices are covered in the information chart. A selection of state wildlife areas (SWAs) are noted here and shown on the map.

S#	MAP	State Wildlife Area Name, Location
7	A4	Atwood SWA, Atwood
8	A3	Banner Lakes SWA, Hudson
9	A3	Cherokee Park SWA (4 units), Ft. Collins
10	A2	Delaney Butte Lakes SWA, Walden
11	A4	Elliott SWA, Snyder
12	A4	Julesburg SWA, Ovid
13	A4	Jumbo Reservoir SWA, Sedgwick
14	A3	Lon Hagler SWA, Campion
15	A4	Messex SWA, Merino
16	A4	North Sterling Reservoir SWA, Sterling
17	B4	South Republican SWA, Burlington
18	A4	Tamarack Ranch SWA, Crook
19	A3	Wellington SWA (3 areas), Wellington
20	A1	Elkhead Lake SWA, Craig
21	B1	Garfield Creek SWA, New Castle
22	A2	Hot Sulphur Springs SWA (6 units), Hot Sulphur Springs
23	A1	Indian Run SWA, Hamilton
24	A1	Jensen SWA, Meeker
25	A1	Little Snake SWA, Maybell
26	B1	Plateau Creek SWA, Collbran
27	A2	Radium SWA, Kremmling
28	B1	West Rifle Creek SWA, Rifle
29	C4	Adobe Creek Reservoir SWA, Las Animas
30	B2	Alma SWA, Alma
31	C3	Beaver Creek SWA, Canyon City
32	B2	Clear Creek Reservoir SWA, Buena Vista
33	B2	Colorado Springs SWA, Fountain
34	B4	Flagler Res. SWA, Flagler
35	C4	Holly SWA, Holly
36	C4	Horse Creek Res. SWA, La Junta
37	C3	Huerfano SWA, Gardner
38	B4	Karval Res. SWA, Karval
39	C3	Lake Dorothey SWA, Trinidad
40	C4	Meredith Res. SWA, Ordway
41	C2	Middle Taylor Creek SWA, Westcliff
42	C4	Mike Higbee SWA, Lamar
43	C3	Pueblo Reservoir SWA, Pueblo
44	C4	Queens SWA (4 units), Eads
45	C4	Rocky Ford SWA, Rocky Ford
46	C3	Spanish Peaks SWA, Aguilar
47	B2	Tarryall Res. SWA, Jefferson
48	B2	Tomahawk SWA, Hartsel
49	C4	Two Buttes Res. SWA, Springfield
50	B2	Almont Triangle SWA, Almont
51	C2	Brown Lakes SWA, Creede
52	C2	Cebolla SWA, Powderhorn
53	C1	Cimarron SWA, Montrose
54	C2	Cochetopa SWA, Gunnison
55	C2	Coller SWA, South Fork
56	C1	Dry Creek Basin SWA, Naturita
57	C2	Echo Canyon Lake SWA, Pagosa Springs
58	B1	Escalante SWA (9 units), Delta
59	C1	Fish Creek SWA, Dolores
60	C2	La Jara Reservoir SWA, Monte Vista
61	C2	La Jara SWA, Capulin
62	C1	Lone Cone SWA, Norwood
63	C2	Mountain Home Res. SWA, Fort Garland
64	D2	Navajo Res. SWA, Arboles
65	C1	Perins Peak SWA, Durango
66	D2	Sego Springs SWA, Manassa
67	C1	Summit Res. SWA, Mancos
68	C1	Totten Reservoir SWA, Cortez
69	C1	Woods Lake SWA, Telluride

Guide & Outfitter Licensing

Information may be obtained by contacting:
Outfitter Licensing Board
1525 Sherman St., Rm. 606
Denver, CO 80203   303-866-3898

ANCA Locations in Colorado

Bear Creek Nature Center (S# 11, map B3)
245 Bear Creek Rd.
Colorado Springs, CO 80906   719-520-6387

Theodore L. Carson Nature Center (S# 12, map B3)
6315 South University
Littleton, CO 80123   303-730-1022

The Greenway & Nature Center (S# 13, map C3)
5200 West 11th Street
Pueblo, CO 81003   719-545-9114

Jefferson County Nature Center (S# 14, map B3)
910 Colorow Rd.
Golden, CO 80401   303-526-0855

Northern Colorado Nature Center (S# 15, map A3)
2400 South Colorado Rd., #9
Fort Collins, CO 80525

State Forest Service

203 Forestry Bldg.
Colorado State University
Fort Collins, CO 80523   303-491-6303
There is no state forest recreation program in Colorado.

Colorado Tourism Board

PO Box 38700, Dept. MACEIO
Denver, CO 8C238   1-800-433-2656
Current tourist information and free travel guides and maps are available from this office. A Colorado Dept. of Highways map has symbols for scenic and historic byways, public campgrounds, and outdoor recreation areas. National forests and parks, state forests, and Indian reservations are marked in color.

Private Organizations

Tribal Land Areas in Colorado

Southern Ute Tribe of the Southern Ute Indian Reservation - Fishing, hunting, camping.
Southern Ute Tribal Council (S# 9, map D1)
PO Box 737
Ignacio, CO 81137   303-563-4525

Ute Mountain Ute Tribe of the Ute Mountain Indian Reservation - Fishing, camping, hiking.
Ute Mountain Ute Tribal Council (S# 10, map D1)
(Colorado/New Mexico/Utah)
General Delivery
Towaoc, CO 81344   303-565-3751

Colorado Assn. of Commerce & Industry

(State Chamber of Commerce)
1776 Lincoln St., #1200
Denver, CO 80203-1029
Phone 303-831-7411
Fax 303-860-1439

★ INFORMATION CHART ★

INFORMATION CHART LEGEND - SYMBOLS & LETTER CODES

■ means YES & □ means Yes with disability provisions
sp means spring, March through May
S means Summer, June through August
F means Fall, September through November
W means Winter, December through February
T means Two (2) or Three (3) Seasons
A means All Four (4) Seasons
na means Not Applicable or Not Available

Note: empty or blank spaces in the chart mean NO

Note: Refer to yellow block on page 7 (top right) for location name and address abbreviations. If a symbol number has a star ★ that symbol is not shown on the map.

AGENCY/MAP LEGEND ... INITIALS, MAP SYMBOLS, COLOR CODES

U.S. Forest Service Supervisor & Ranger Dist. Offices   NFS [61]
U.S. Army Corps of Engineers Rec. Areas & Offices . COE [31]
USFWS National Wildlife Refuges & Offices ......   NWR [40]
National Park Service Parks & other NPS Sites ..... NPS [7]
Bureau of Land Management Rec. Areas & Offices   BLM [26]
Bureau of Reclamation Rec. Areas & Reg. Offices .. BOR [8]
State Parks (also see State Agency notes) ...... SPS [52]
State Wildlife Areas (also see State Agency notes) .. SWA [19]
Private Preserves, Nature Centers & Tribal Lands [15]
The Wild Rivers — and Wilderness Areas

FACILITIES, SERVICES, RECREATION OPPORTUNITIES & CONVENIENCES

S#	MAP	LOCATION NAME (state initials if more than one) with ADDRESS and/or LOCATION DATA	TELEPHONE	ACRES / ELEVATION
1	B3	U.S. Forest Svc., Rocky Mtn. Region, 11177 W. 8th Ave., PO Box 25127, Lakewood 80225	303-236-9431	22,000,000 / na
2	A3	Arapaho & Roosevelt N. Forests Sup., 240 W. Prospect, Fort Collins 80526	303-498-1100	1,464,000 / 6,000-14,000
3	A3	Boulder Ranger D., 2995 Baseline Rd., Room 110, Boulder 80303	303-444-6600	160,000 / 6,000-13,000
4	A3	Clear Creek Ranger D., 101 Chicago Creek, Idaho Springs 80452	303-567-2901	173,000 / 7,000-14,000
5	B3	Estes-Poudre Ranger D., 148 Remington St., Fort Collins 80524	303-482-3822	256,000 / 6,000-13,000
6	A3	Pawnee National Grassland, 660 "O" Street, Greeley 80631	303-353-5004	193,000 / 5,000
7	A3	Redfeather Ranger D., 210 E. Olive St., Fort Collins 80524	303-498-1375	374,000 / 6,000-13,000
8	A3	Sulphur Ranger D., 62429 Hwy. 40, Granby 80446	303-887-3331	308,000 / 8,000-13,000
9	B1	Grand Mesa, Uncompahgre & Gunnison, Nat'l. Forests Supervisor, 2250 Hwy. 50, Delta 81416	303-874-7691	2,953,186 / 7,000-14,400
10	C2	Cebolla Ranger D., 216 N. Colorado, Gunnison 81230	303-641-0471	632,700 / 8,000-14,310
11	B1	Collbran Ranger D., PO Box 330, Collbran 81624	303-487-3534	294,000 / 8,000-11,200
12	B1	Grand Junction Ranger D., 764 Horizon Dr., Grand Junction 81506	303-242-8211	400,000 / 6,000-11,000
13	B1	Norwood Ranger D., 1760 E. Grand, PO Box 388, Norwood 81423	303-327-4261	397,676 / 7,000-14,000
14	C1	Ouray Ranger D., 2505 S. Townsend, Montrose 81401	303-249-3711	330,407 / 6,200-14,300
15	B1	Paonia Ranger D., N. Rio Grande Ave., Paonia	303-527-4131	480,000 / 7,500-12,500

★ INFORMATION CHART ★

AGENCY/MAP LEGEND . . . INITIALS, MAP SYMBOLS, COLOR CODES

U.S. Forest Service Supervisor & Ranger Dist. Offices NFS
U.S. Army Corps of Engineers Rec. Areas & Offices . COE
USFWS National Wildlife Refuges & Offices . . . . NWR
National Park Service Parks & other NPS Sites . . . . . NPS
Bureau of Land Management Rec. Areas & Offices . . . BLM
Bureau of Reclamation Rec. Areas & Reg. Offices . . . BOR
State Parks (also see State Agency notes) . . . . SPS
State Wildlife Areas (also see State Agency notes) . . . SWA
Private Preserves, Nature Centers & Tribal Lands . . . .
The Wild Rivers ∼ and Wilderness Areas

Refer to yellow block on page 7 (top right) for location name and address abbreviations.

INFORMATION CHART LEGEND - SYMBOLS & LETTER CODES

■ means YES & □ means Yes with disability provisions
sp means spring, March through May
S means Summer, June through August
F means Fall, September through November
W means Winter, December through February
T means Two (2) or Three (3) Seasons
A means All Four (4) Seasons
na means Not Applicable or Not Available
Note: empty or blank spaces in the chart mean NO
and . . . that symbol is not shown on the map.

S#	MAP	LOCATION NAME (state initials if more than one) with ADDRESS and/or LOCATION DATA	TELEPHONE	ACRES / ELEVATION	S#
16	C2	Taylor River Ranger D., 216 N. Colorado, Gunnison 81230	303-641-0471	694,260 / 8,000-14,300	16
17	C3	Pike & San Isabel Nat'l. Forest Sup., 1920 Valley Drive, Pueblo 81008	303-545-8737	2,756,437 / 3,500-14,433	17
18	C4	Commanche Ranger D & Nat'l. Grassla, 27162 Hwy. 287, Springfield 81073	719-523-6591	418,963 / 3,500-6,300	18
19	B2	Leadville Ranger D., 2015 North Poplar, Leadville 80461	719-486-0752	286,303 / 9,100-14,433	19
20	B3	Pikes Peak Ranger D., 601 S. Weber St., Colorado Springs 80903	719-636-1602	237,981 / 5,600-14,110	20
21	C2	Salida Ranger D., 325 W. Rainbow Blvd., Salida 81201	719-539-3591	445,102 / 7,200-14,420	21
22	C3	San Carlos Ranger D., 326 Dozier St., Canon City 81212	719-275-4119	386,060 / 6,500-14,345	22
23	B2	South Park Ranger D., NW of Jct. of Hwys. 9 & 285, Fairplay 80440	719-836-2031	473,168 / 10,000-14,286	23
24	B2	South Platte Ranger D., 11177 West 8th Ave., Lakewood 80225	303-236-7386	396,801 / 8,000-14,264	24
25	B3	Rio Grande Nat'l. Forest Sup., 1803 W. Highway 160, Monte Vista 81144	719-852-5941	1,850,000 / 7,800-14,000	25
26	D2	Conejos Peak Ranger D., Rt. #1, Box 520 G, La Jara 81140 [Hwy. 285 N of La Jara]	719-274-5193	710,937 / 8,200-14,000	26
27	C2	Creede Ranger D., Third & Creede Ave., PO Box 270, Creede 81130	719-658-2556	550,836 / 8,400-13,821	27
28	C2	Del Norte Ranger D., PO Box 40, Del Norte 81132	719-657-3321	303,741 / 7,800-13,289	28
29	C2	Saguache Ranger D., 46525 State Hwy. 114, PO Box 67, Saguache 81149	719-655-2553	na / na	29
30	A2	Routt National Forest Sup., 29587 W. US 40, Suite 20, Steamboat Springs 80487	303-879-1722	1,356,111 / 6,750-13,553	30
31	A2	Bears Ears Ranger D., 356 Ranney St., Craig 81652	303-824-9438	101,286 / na	31
32	A2	Hahns Peak Ranger D., 57 10th St., Box 1212, Steamboat Springs 80477	303-879-1870	331,136 / 6,750-12,100	32
33	A2	Middle Park Ranger D., 210 South 6th St., Box 1210, Kremmling 80459	303-724-9004	219,370 / na	33
34	A2	North Park Ranger D., 612 5th St., Box 158, Walden 80480	303-723-4707	218,611 / 8,000-12,000	34
35	A2	Yampa Ranger D., 300 Roselawn, Box 7, Yampa 80483	303-638-4516	139,901 / 8,000-12,500	35
36	C1	San Juan National Forest Sup., 701 Camino Del Rio, Durango 81301 [South entrance to town in Federal Bldg.]	303-247-4874	na / na	36
37	C1	Animas Ranger District, 701 Camino Del Rio, Room 301, Durango 81301	303-247-4874	357,264 / 6,300-14,000	37
38	C1	Dolores Ranger District, 100 N. 6th St., Box 210, Dolores 81323	303-882-7296	468,714 / 6,300-14,000	38
39	C1	Mancos Ranger D., 41595 E. Hwy. 160, PO Box 330, Mancos 81328	303-533-7716	152,263 / 6,300-14,000	39
40	C2	Pagosa Ranger D., 2nd & Pagosa St., Box 310, Pagosa Springs 81147	303-264-2268	541,229 / 6,300-14,000	40
41	D1	Pine Ranger D., 367 S. Pearl St., PO Box 439, Bayfield 81122	303-884-2512	337,643 / 6,300-14,000	41
42	B2	White River Nat'l. Forest Sup., Old Federal Bldg., Box 948, Glenwood Springs 81602	303-945-2521	1,011,000 / 7,000-14,065	42
43	B2	Aspen Ranger D., 806 W Hallam St., Aspen 81611	303-925-3445	256,255 / 7,480-14,065	43
44	A1	Blanco Ranger D., 317 E. Market, Meeker 81641	303-878-4039	346,000 / 9,100-12,000	44
45	B2	Dillon Ranger D., 135 Hwy., 9, Blue River Center, PO Box 620, Silverthorne 80498	303-468-5400	280,000 / 8,000-14,000	45
46	B2	Eagle Ranger D., 125 W. 5th St., PO Box 720, Eagle 81631	303-328-6388	320,000 / 8,000-13,000	46
47	B2	Holy Cross Ranger D., 401 Main St., PO Box 190, Minturn 81645	303-827-5715	341,000 / 7,000-14,000	47
48	B1	Rifle Ranger D., 0094 County Road 244, Rifle 81650	303-625-2371	350,000 / 7,000-11,375	48
49	B2	Sopris Ranger D., 620 Main St., PO Box 309, Carbondale 81623	303-963-2266	400,000 / 6,500-14,000	49

COE, Albuquerque District, PO Box 1580, Albuquerque, NM 87103 505-766-2724 na / na

S#	MAP				S#
1	C4	John Martin Dam, Star Route, Hasty 81044	719-336-3476	na / na	1
2	D3	Trinidad Lake, PO Box 771, Trinidad 81082	719-846-7990	na / na	2

COE, Omaha District, 215 N. 17th St., Omaha, NE 68102 402-221-4137 na / na

3	B2	Bear Creek Lake, 9307 Colorado Hwy. 121, Littleton 80123	303-979-4120	na / na	3
4	B2	Chatfield Lake, 9307 Colorado Hwy. 121, Littleton 80123	303-979-4120	na / na	4
5	B2	Cherry Creek Lakk, 9307 Colorado Hwy. 121, Littleton 80123	303-979-4120	na / na	5

USFWS Region 6 (Lakewood), 134 Union Blvd., Denver Fed. Ctr., Denver 80225 [CO, KS, MT, NE, ND, SD, UT, WY] 303-236-7904 na / 88,888

1	C2	Alamosa NWR, 9383 El Rancho Lane, Alamosa 81101 [from Alamosa go 3 mi E on Hwy 160, 2 mi S on El Rancho Lane]	719-589-4021	11,169 / 7,500	1
2	C2	Monte Vista NWR, c/o Alamosa NWR, 9383 El Rancho Lane, Alamosa 81101 [6 mi S of Monte Vista on Hwy 15]	719-589-4021	14,188 / 7,600	2
3	A2	Arapaho NWR, PO Box 457, Walden 80480 [9 mi. S of Walden on Hwy. 125]	303-723-8202	18,250 / 8,000-8,200	3
5	A1	Browns Park NWR, 1318 Highway 318, Maybell 81640	303-365-3613	13,450 / 5,500-6,300	5
*6	B3	Rocky Mtn. Arsenal Urban NWR (access restricted), Bldg. 111, Commerce City 80022 [suburb, NE of Denver]	303-289-0232	na / na	*6
*7	B3	Two Ponds Environmental Center (located in Arvada), Bldg. 25486, Denver Fed. Ctr., Denver 80225	303-236-7904	na / na	*7

Nat'l. Park Svc., Rocky Mountain Region, PO Box 25287, Denver 80225

| 1 | B3 | Black Canyon of the Gunnison NM, 2233 East Main, Montrose 81401 | 303-249-7036 | 20,766 / 8,200 | 1 |

Grid	#	Name / Address	Phone	na / elev.
B1	3	Colorado National Monument, Fruita 81521	303-858-3617	20,454 / 4,620-7,00_
C2	4	Curecanti National Recreation Area, 102 Elk Creek, Gunnison 81230	303-641-0406	42,114 / 7,600-9,000
A1	5	Dinosaur Nat'l. Monument (CO/UT), PO Box 210, Dinosaur 81610	303-374-2216	211,140 / 4,800-9,006
B3	6	Florissant Fossil Beds NM, PO Box 185, Florissant 80816 [on Teller County Rd, 2 mi S of Florissant & Hwy 24]	719-748-3253	5,998 / 8,000-8,800
C2	7	Great Sand Dunes Nat'l. Monument, 11500 Hwy. 150, Mosca 81146	719-378-2312	38,662 / 8,200
C1	8	Hovenweep Nat'l. Monument, McElmo Rt., Cortez 81321	303-529-4465	784 / 5,240-6,000
D1	9	Mesa Verde Nat'l. Park, Mesa Verde Nat'l Park 81330	303-529-4461	52,085 / 7,000-8,500
A3	10	Rocky Mountain Nat'l. Park Estes Park 80517 [2.5 mi W of Estes Park on US 36]	303-586-2371	265,729 / 7,800-14,255

BLM Colorado State Office, 2850 Youngfield Street, Lakewood 80215

Grid	#	Name / Address	Phone	na / elev.
△	1		303-239-3670	na / na
C3	2	Canon City District Office, 3170 E. Main Street, PO Box 2200, Canon City 81215	719-275-0631	na / ra
B3	*3	Northeast Resource Area Office [Closed, contact state office in Lakewood]		na / ra
C3	4	Royal Gorge Resource A. (see notes, S# 17-19), 3170 E. Main St., PO Box 2200, Canon City 81215	719-275-0631	700,000 / ra
C2	5	San Luis Resource Area (see notes, S# 20-21), 1921 State Street, Alamosa 81101	719-589-4975	520,000 / ra
A1	6	Craig District Office, 455 Emerson Street, Craig 81625	303-824-8261	3,200,000 / ra
A2	7	Kremmling Resource A. (see notes, S# 22-23), 1116 Park Ave., PO Box 68, Kremmling 80459	303-724-3437	1,000,000 / ra
A1	8	Little Snake Resource A. (see notes, S# 24), 1280 Industrial Ave., Craig 81625	303-824-4441	1,200,000 / ra
A1	9	White River Resource A. (see notes, S# 25), 73544 Highway 64, PO Box 928, Meeker 81641	303-878-3601	1,000,000 / na
B1	10	Grand Junction Dist. Office, 2815 "H" Rd., Grand Junction 81506	303-243-6552	1,860,000 / 4,700-9,000
B2	11	Glenwood Springs RA (see notes, S# 26-31), 50629 Hwys. 6 & 24, PO Box 1009, Glenwood Springs 81602	303-945-2341	680,000 / na
B1	12	Grand Junction RA (see notes, S# 32-35), 2850 "H" Rd., Grand Junction 81506	303-243-6561	1,200,000 / na
C1	13	Montrose District Office, 2465 S. Townsend Ave., Montrose 81401	303-249-7791	6,000,000 / 5,800-14,000
C2	14	Gunnison Basin RA (see notes, S# 36-38), 216 N. Colorado, Gunnison 81230	303-641-0471	2,000,000 / na
C1	15	San Juan Resource A. (see notes, S# 39-40), FOB, 701 Camino Del Rio, Room 102, Durango 81301	303-247-4082	2,000,000 / na
C1	16	Uncompahgre Basin RA (see notes, S# 41-42), 2505 S. Townsend Ave. (Recreation Hot Line 249-6306), Montrose 81401	303-249-7791	2,000,000 / na

Colorado Div. Parks & Outdoor Recre., 1313 Sherman St., Room 618, Denver 80203

Grid	#	Name / Address	Phone	na / elev.
△	1		303-866-3437	na / 5,280
C2	2	Arkansas Headwaters Recreation Area (150 mi. long area), PO Box 126, Salida 81201	719-539-7289	na / 4,900-9,500
A3	3	Barr Lake SP, 13401 Piccadilly Rd., Brighton 80601	303-659-6005	2,600 / 5,103
A3	4	Boyd Lake SRA, 3720 N. County Rd. 11-C, Loveland 80537	303-669-1739	1,950 / 5,003
B3	5	Chatfield SRA, 11500 N. Roxborough Park Rd., Littleton 80125	303-791-7275	5,300 / 5,503
B3	6	Golden Gate Canyon SP, Rt. #6, Box 280, Golden 80403	303-592-1502	10,500 / 8,500-1,203
D2	7	Navajo SRA, Box 1697, Arboles 81121	303-883-2208	5,050 / 6,103
C3	8	Pueblo SRA, 640 Pueblo Reservoir Rd., Pueblo 81005	719-561-9320	na / na
C1	9	Ridgway SRA, 1332 E. Oak Grove Rd., Montrose 81401	303-626-5822	na / na
D3	10	Trinidad SRA, Rt. #3, Box 360, Trinidad 81082	719-846-6951	na / na
B1	11	Vega SRA, PO Box 186, Collbran 81624	303-487-3407	na / na

Colorado Div. of Wildlife, 6060 Broadway, Denver 80216 [see notes]

Grid	#	Name / Address	Phone	na / elev.
B3	1	Central Region, Div. of Wildlife, 6060 Broadway, Denver 80216	303-297-1192	na / na
B3	*2	Northeast Region, Div. of Wildlife, 317 W. Prospect Ave., Fort Collins 80526	303-291-7227	na / na
B1	3	Northwest Region, Div. of Wildlife, 711 Independent Ave., Grand Junction 81505	303-484-2836	na / na
B3	4	Southeast Region, Div. of Wildlife, 2126 North Weber, Colorado Springs 80907	303-248-7175	na / na
B3	5	Southwest Region, Div. of Wildlife, 2300 S. Townsend Ave., Montrose 81401	719-473-2945	na / na
C1	6		303-249-3431	na / 5,240

TNC Colorado Field Office (FO), 1244 Pine Street, Boulder 80302

Grid	#	Name / Address	Phone	na / elev.
△	1			
A3	2	Phantom Canyon Pre., 633 S. College (tours by reservation), Fort Collins 80524 [30 mi N, W on Hwy. 287 near Livermore]	303-498-0180	1,600 / 6,700
B3	3	Aiken Canyon Preserve, c/o TNC CO Field Office, 15 mi S of Colorado Springs [on W side of SH 115]	303-444-2950	1,400 / 6,500-8,500
B2	4	High Creek Fen Preserve, c/o TNC CO Field Office, 8 mi S of Fairplay [0.2 mi S of mile post 175 on US Hwy 285]	303-444-2950	1,000 / 9,300-9,400
A2	5	Yampa River Preserve, PO Box 775528, Steamboat Springs 80477 [5 mi E of Hayden, park W & S of bridge over Yampa R]	303-875-1546	315 / 6,400-6,800
B1	6	San Miguel Canyon Pre (winter c/o FO), PO Box 3140, Telluride 81435 [5 mi W of Placerville on SH 145]	303-728-5291	279 / 6,900-7,300
C1	7	San Miguel R. at Tabeguache Cr. (winter c/o FO), address see S# 6, [10 mi S of Naturita on SH 145, mi posts 71 & 74]	303-728-5291	259 / 5,100-5,300
C1	8	S. Fork San Miguel R. Pre (winter c/o FO), add. see S# 6, [10 mi S of Telluride, 0.5 mi S of Telluride, Illium Valley Rd]	303-728-5291	67 / 8,550-8,750

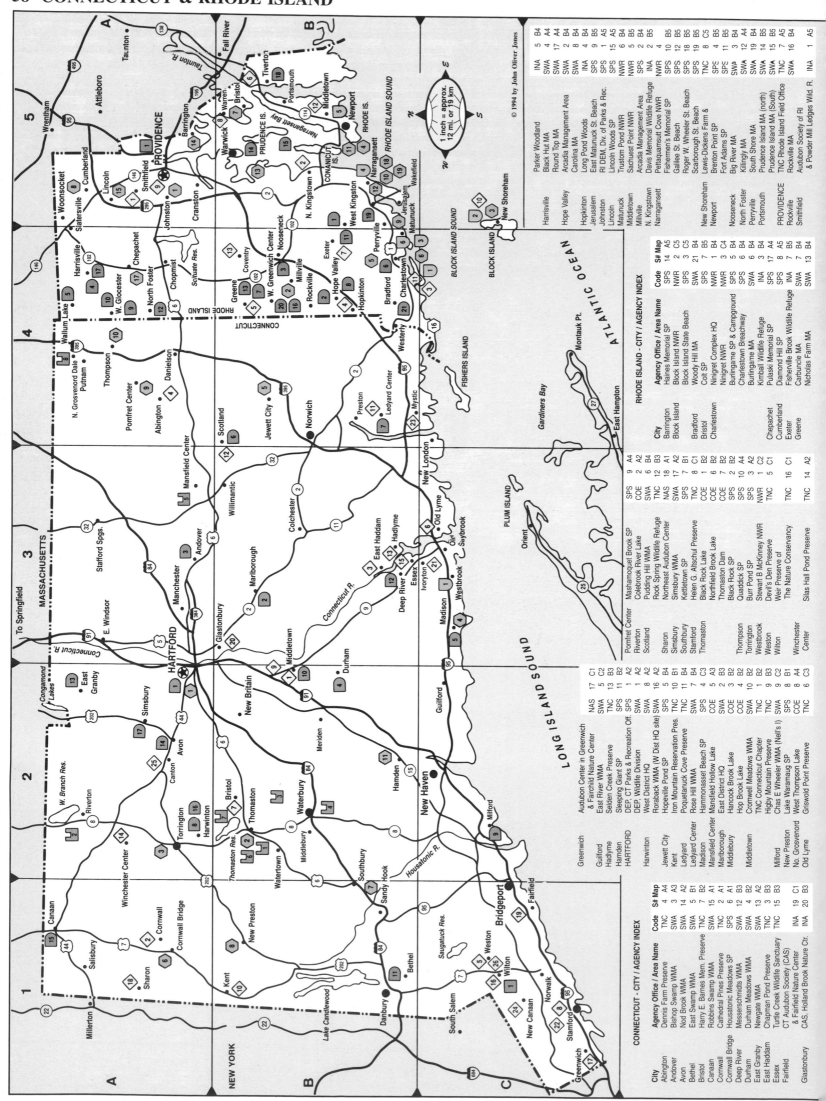

© 1994 by John Oliver Jones

1 inch = approx.
12 mi. or 19 km.

CONNECTICUT NOTES

Summary

There are 10 federal, 31 state, and 28 private recreation areas or local administrative offices included in the Connecticut coverage. Of these, 58 appear in the Information Chart and 11 are covered in the notes.

Federal Agencies

National Park Service Location in Connecticut

Weir Farm National Historic Site (62 acres)
735 Nod Hill Road (NPS S# 1, map C1)
Wilton, CT 06897   203-834-1896

State Agencies

Department of Environmental Protection

State Office Bldg.
165 Capitol Ave.
Hartford, CT 06106   203-566-5599

This is the parent agency for the Bureau of Fisheries and Wildlife, Wildlife Division, and the Bureau of Parks and Forests, Parks Division and State Forester. The Bureau

personnel can provide a variety of free literature about fishing, hunting, and other outdoor recreation activities and facilities in Connecticut.

Bureau of Parks and Forests (S# 1, map A2)

A guide to Connecticut Public Recreation Areas (77 state parks and 30 state forests) is available free. It describes each area, contains a map showing locations, and indicates facilities and activities.

Connecticut Wildlife Division (S# 1, map A2)

Maps and information on 92 wildlife areas are listed in the free *Hunting and Trapping Field Guide*. Permit and harvest data is available annually. A bi-monthly publication, *Scope*, is available from the division for a $4 donation.

Department of Economic Development

Tourism Division
210 Washington St.
Hartford, CT 06106   203-566-3948

Publications available include a *Vacation Guide*, *Discover Connecticut*, *Explore Connecticut and Group Tour Planning Guide*. An official transportation map is available from this office. Symbols show information centers, picnic areas, boat launch sites, hiking trails and regulated hunting areas. State park and forest boundaries are shown in color.

Private Organizations

TNC-Connecticut Chapter (see chart, S# 1, map B2)

55 High St.
Middletown, CT 06457   203-344-0716

A free brochure briefly describes 16 visitable preserves. A book with more details on these sites, and other TNC preserves in Connecticut, may be purchased from the Chapter for $9.67 plus $1 for shipping and handling.

ANCA Locations in Connecticut

Bushy Hill Nature Center (S# 21, map C3)
PO Box 577
Ivoryton, CT 06442   203-767-0843

Darien Nature Center (S# 22, map C1)
PO Box 1603
Darien, CT 06820-1603   203-655-7459

Denison Pequotsepos Nature Center (S# 23, map B4)
PO Box 122
Mystic, CT 06355-0122   203-536-1216

New Canaan Nature Center (S# 24, map C1)
144 Oenoke Rd.
New Canaan, CT 06840   203-966-9577

Roaring Brook Nature Center (S# 25, map A2)
70 Gracey Rd.
Canton, CT 06019   203-693-0263

Woodcock Nature Center (S# 26, map C1)
56 Deer Run Rd.
Wilton, CT 06897   203-762-7280

Connecticut Bus. & Ind. Assn. (State Ch. of Comm.)
370 Asylum St.   Phone 203-244-1900
Hartford, CT 06103   Fax 203-278-8562

RHODE ISLAND NOTES

Summary

There are 7 federal, 43 state, and 13 private recreation areas or local administrative offices included in the Rhode Island coverage. Of these, 56 appear in the Information Chart and 7 are covered in the notes.

Federal Agencies

National Park Service Location in Rhode Island

Roger Williams National Memorial (4.6 acres)
(S# 1, map A5)
282 North Main Street
Providence, RI 02903   401-528-5385

State Agencies

Department of Environmental Management

9 Hayes St.
Providence, RI 02903   401-277-2774

The divisions of this Department are listed below. Each is located at another address as noted here or in the Information Chart.

Division of Parks & Recreation (S# 1, map A5)

A *Rhode Island State Parks Guide* (18 state parks) is available free. The guide describes each area, contains a locator map, and includes information on facilities and activities.

Division of Forest Environment

1037 Hartford Pike
North Scituate, RI 02857   401-647-3367
A few areas listed in the Guide under wildlife or parks are located within division areas, notably the Arcadia and

George Washington Management Areas. For additional information and forest recreation literature contact this office.

Division of Fish & Wildlife (Field HQ is S# 1, map B5)

A monthly newsletter *Briefings* is available free. A *Hunting Guide to Rhode Island's Wildlife Management Areas* is a basic reference.

RI Tourism Division

7 Jackson Walkway
Providence, RI 02903   401-277-2601

Private Organizations

ANCA Locations in Rhode Island

Frosty Dew Naure Center (S# 11, map B4)
PO Box 160
Charlestown, RI 02813

Norman Bird Sanctuary (S# 12 map B5)
583 Third Beach Rd.
Middletown, RI 02840

Parker Woodland Wildlife Refuge (S# 13, map B4)
Maple Valley Rd.
Coventry, RI 02827

No State Chamber of Commerce in Rhode Island
There are local Chamber of Commerce offices throughout the state.

S#						
Tiverton	Sapowet MA	SWA	18	B5		
W. Glocester	Ruecker Wildlife Refuge	INA	6	B5		
	Durfee Hill MA	SWA	9	A4		
W. Greenwich	George Washington MA	SWA	10	A4		
W. Greenwich Center	Wickaboxet MA	SWA	20	B4		
Wallum Lake	Buck Hill MA	SWA	5	A4		
Warren	Touisset Marsh Wildlife Refuge	INA	8	B5		
Warwick	Goddard Memorial SP	SPS	13	B5		
West Kingston	DEM. Div. of Fish & Wildlife	SWA	1	B5		
	Great Swamp Management A. & Field Office	SWA	11	B5		
Westerly	Misquamicut St. Beach	SPS	16	C4		

★ INFORMATION CHART ★

INFORMATION CHART LEGEND - SYMBOLS & LETTER CODES

- ■ means YES & □ means Yes with disability provisions
- **sp** means spring, March through May
- **S** means Summer, June through August
- **F** means Fall, September through November
- **W** means Winter, December through February
- **T** means Two (2) or Three (3) Seasons
- **A** means All Four (4) Seasons
- **na** means Not Applicable or Not Available

Note: empty or blank spaces in the chart mean NO

AGENCY/MAP LEGEND . . . INITIALS, MAP SYMBOLS, COLOR CODES

U.S. Forest Service Supervisor & Ranger Dist. Offices	NFS	△61
U.S. Army Corps of Engineers Rec. Areas & Offices .	COE	H 31
USFWS National Wildlife Refuges & Offices	NWR	◆ 40
National Park Service Parks & other NPS Sites	NPS	▼ 7
Bureau of Land Management Rec. Areas & Reg. Offices	BLM	● 26
Bureau of Reclamation Rec. Areas & Reg. Offices . .	BOR	○ 8
State Parks (also see State Agency notes)	SPS	◉ 52
State Wildlife Areas (also see State Agency notes) .	SWA	⬡ 19
Private Preserves, Nature Centers & Tribal Lands . .		⬡15
The Wild Rivers ⌇ and Wilderness Areas		

Note: Refer to yellow block on page 7 (top right) for location name and address abbreviations. If a symbol number has a star ★ that symbol is not shown on the map.

S#	MAP	LOCATION NAME (state initials if more than one) with ADDRESS and/or LOCATION DATA	TELEPHONE / ACRES / ELEVATION
		CONNECTICUT CHART LISTINGS	
		COE, New England District, 424 Trapelo Road, Waltham, MA 02254	617-647-8107 na / na
1	B2	Black Rock Lake, 331 Hill Road, Thomaston 06787	203-283-5540 na / na
2	A2	Colebrook River Lake, PO Box 58, Riverton 06065	203-379-8234 na / na
3	B2	Hancock Brook Lake, Route 63, Middlebury 06762	203-729-8840 na / na
4	B2	Hop Brook Lake, Route 63, Middlebury 06762	203-729-8840 na / na
5	A3	Mansfield Hollow Lake, RFD #2, Mansfield Cent 06250	203-423-5603 na / na
6	B2	Northfield Brook Lake, 331 Hill Road, Thomaston 06787	203-283-5540 na / na
7	B2	Thomaston Dam, 331 Hill Road, Thomaston 06787	203-283-5540 na / na
8	A4	West Thompson Lake, RFD #1 300, No. Grosvenord 06255 [N of Putnam]	203-923-2982 na / na
1	C2	**Stewart B. McKinney NWR (6 units)**, 733 Old Clinton Rd., PO Box 1030, Westbrook 06498	203-399-2513 130 / 80
1	A2	**DEP, CT Parks & Recreation Office**, 165 Capitol Ave., Room 265, Hartford 06106	203-566-2304 na / na
2	A2	Black Rock SP (season ph.283-8088), Route 6, 2 mi. W of Thomaston 06787	203-566-2304 444 / na
3	A2	Burr Pond SP, Burr Mt. Road, 5 mi. N of Torrington 06790	203-482-1817 438 / na
4	C3	Hammonasset Beach SP, Box 271, Madison 06443 [1 mi. S. of I-95 exit 62]	203-245-2785 923 / na

The FACILITIES, SERVICES, RECREATION OPPORTUNITIES & CONVENIENCES columns include: INFO OFFICE (IO) / VISITOR CENTER (VC), IO / VC OPEN SATURDAY / SUNDAY / by res., ENTRY FEE / VC FEE not camping or permit fee, CONCESSIONAIRE SERVICES AVAILABLE, FREE LITERATURE or brochures, maps, etc., INTERPRETIVE SERVICES AVAILABLE, AGENCY GUIDED TOURS / STUDY PROGRAMS, NATURE EDUCATION, brochures, maps, scheduled / by res., WILDFLOWER VIEWING AREA / DISPLAY, ARCHAEOLOGICAL / GEOLOGICAL SITES, HISTORIC SITES, INTERPRETIVE TRAILS, WILDLIFE VIEWING / STUDY SITES, ENDANGERED SPECIES ARE COMMON / ABUNDANT OR DRIVE COMMON, DEVELOPED PICNIC AREAS, ON-CHARGE CAMPGROUNDS / PICNIC AREAS, CHARGE CAMPGROUNDS / CAMPSITES, WILDERNESS AREAS / WILD RIVERS, WALKING PERMITTED, w/ your own trails, HIKING TRAILS, BICYCLING PERMITTED, at one's own risk, HORSEBACK RIDING, w/ your own horse, OFF-ROAD Motorized Vehicle Area / Use OK, FISHING IN SEASON, license, check limits, SWIMMING WATER, BOATING FACILITIES, ramps / marinas, etc., MOTORIZED WATERCRAFT OK, NON-MOTORIZED WATERCRAFT OK, check limits, HUNTING IN SEASON, license / permit reqd., WINTER SPORTS OPPORTUNITIES, PARK & WALK-IN ONLY AREA, DAY USE ONLY, no overnight, DRINKING WATER, RESTROOMS

★ INFORMATION CHART ★

AGENCY/MAP LEGEND . . . INITIALS, MAP SYMBOLS, COLOR CODES

U.S. Forest Service Supervisor & Ranger Dist. Offices . . NFS △61
U.S. Army Corps of Engineers Rec. Areas & Offices . . COE △31
USFWS National Wildlife Refuges & Offices . . . . NWR △40
National Park Service Parks & other NPS Sites . . . . . . NPS △7
Bureau of Land Management Rec. Areas & Offices . . . BLM △26
Bureau of Reclamation Rec. Areas & Reg. Offices . . . BOR △8
State Parks (also see State Agency notes) . . . . SPS △52
State Wildlife Areas (also see State Agency notes) . . . SWA △19
Private Preserves, Nature Centers & Tribal Lands
The Wild Rivers ∼∼∼ and Wilderness Areas ░░░ △15

Note: Refer to yellow block on page 7 (top right) for location name and address abbreviations.

INFORMATION CHART LEGEND - SYMBOLS & LETTER CODES

■ means YES, & □ means **Yes** with disability provisions
sp means **spring**, March through May
S means **Summer**, June through August
F means **Fall**, September through November
W means **Winter**, December through February
T means Two (2) or Three (3) Seasons
A means All Four (4) Seasons
na means Not Applicable or Not Available
Note: empty or blank spaces in the chart mean **NO**
that symbol number has a star ★

If a symbol number has a star ★ that symbol is not shown on the map.

S#	MAP	LOCATION NAME (state initials if more than one) with ADDRESS and/or LOCATION DATA	TELEPHONE	ACRES / ELEVATION
5	B4	Hopeville Pond SP, Rt. #201, 3 mi. E of Jewett City 06351	203-566-2304	554 / na
6	A1	Housatonic Meadows SP, Rt. #7 (season ph. 672-6772), 1 mi. N of Cornwall Bridge 06754	203-566-2304	452 / na
7	B1	Kettletown SP (season ph. 264-5169), George's Hill Rd., Southbury 06488 [5 mi. S. of I-84 exit 15]	203-566-2304	507 / na
8	B1	Lake Waramaug SP, 30 Lake Waramaug Rd., 5 mi. N of New Preston 06777	203-566-2304	95 / na
9	A4	Mashamoquet Brook SP, RFD #1, Wold Den Dr., Pomfret Center 06259	203-566-2304	838 / na
10	A4	Quaddick SP, Quaddick Town Farm Rd., Thompson 06277	203-566-2304	116 / na
11	B2	Sleeping Giant SP, 200 Mount Carmel Ave., 2 mi. N of Hamden 06518	203-789-7498	1,439 / na
1	A2	**DEP, Wildlife Division**, 165 Capitol Ave. Room 254, Hartford 06106	203-566-4683	na / na
2	B3	East District HQ, Wildlife Div., 209 Hebron Road, Marlborough 06447	203-295-9523	na / na
3	A3	Bishop Swamp WMA, Jurovaty Rd., Andover	203-295-9523	531 / na
4	B2	Durham Meadows WMA, near Durham	203-295-9523	571 / na
5	B1	East River WMA, near Guilford	203-295-9523	147 / na
6	C2	East Swamp WMA, near Bethel	203-485-0226	82 / na
7	B4	Pudding Hill WMA, near Scotland	203-295-9523	135 / na
7	B4	Rose Hill WMA, near Preston & Ledyard Center	203-295-9523	474 / na
8	A2	West District HQ, Wildlife Div., 230 Plymouth Road, Harwinton 06791	203-485-0226	na / na
9	C2	Charles E. Wheeler WMA (Nell's Is.), near Stratford & Milford	203-485-0226	1,069 / na
10	B2	Cromwell Meadows WMA, near Cromwell & Middletown	203-485-0226	486 / na
12	B3	Messerschmidts WMA, near Deep River	203-485-0226	421 / na
13	A2	Newgate WMA, near East Granby	203-485-0226	429 / na
14	A2	Nod Brook WMA, near Simsbury & Avon	203-485-0226	137 / na
15	A1	Robbins Swamp WMA, near Canaan	203-485-0226	1,120 / na
16	A2	Roraback WMA (West Dist. HQ site), near Harwinton	203-485-0226	2,100 / na
17	A2	Simsbury WMA, near Simsbury	203-485-0226	91 / na
1	B2	**TNC Connecticut Chapter**, 55 High Street, Middletown 06457	203-344-0716	na / na
2	A1	Cathedral Pines Preserve (contact Chapter Office, storm damage, trail may be closed), near Cornwall	203-344-0716	42 / na
3	B3	Chapman Pond Preserve(canoe access , contact Chapter Office, near East Haddam	203-344-0716	429 / na
4	A4	Dennis Farm Preserve, contact Chapter Office, near Abington	203-344-0716	382 / na
5	C1	Devil's Den Preserve, PO Box 1162, Weston 06883	203-226-4991	1,650 / 300-500
6	C3	Griswold Point Preserve, contact Chapter Office, near Old Lyme	203-344-0716	22 / na
7	B2	Harry E. Barnes Memorial Preserve, contact Chapter Office, near Bristol	203-344-0716	154 / na
8	C1	Helen G. Altschul Preserve, contact Chapter Office, near Stamford	203-344-0716	164 / na
9	B2	Higby Mountain Preserve, contact Chapter Office, near Middletown	203-344-0716	159 / na
10	B1	Iron Mountain Reservation Preserve, contact Chapter Office, near Kent	203-344-0716	276 / na
11	B4	Poquetanuck Cove Preserve, contact Chapter Office, near Ledyard Center	203-344-0716	234 / na
12	B3	Rock Spring Wildlife Refuge, contact Chapter Office, near Scotland	203-344-0716	444 / na
13	C1	Selden Creek Preserve(canoe access , contact Chapter Office, near Hadlyme	203-344-0716	55 / na
14	A2	Silas Hall Pond Preserve, contact Chapter Office, near Winchester Center	203-344-0716	94 / na
15	B3	Turtle Creek Wildlife Sanctuary, contact Chapter Office, near Essex	203-344-0716	93 / na
16	C1	Weir Preserve of The Nature Conserv., PO Box 7033, Wilton 06897	206-344-0716	110 / 600
17	C1	**Audubon Center in Greenwich & Fairchild Wildflower Garden**, 613 Riversville Rd., Greenwich 06831	203-869-5272	485 / na
18	A1	Northeast Audubon Center, Rt. #4, Box 171, Sharon 06069	203-364-0520	684 / na
19	C1	**Connecticut Audubon Society, Fairfield Nature Center & Larsen Sanctuary**, 2325 Burr St., Fairfield 06430	203-259-6305	152 / na
20	B3	Holland Brook Nature Center, 1361 Main St., Glastonbury 06033 [between Rt 2 (exit 7) & S Glastonbury on Rt. 17]	203-633-8402	38 / na
		RHODE ISLAND CHART LISTINGS		
1	B4	Ninigret Complex HQ, Rt. 1A, Shoreline Plaza, PO Box 307, Charlestown 92813	401-364-9124	na / na
2	C5	Block Island NWR, Corn Neck Rd., New Shoreham, Block Island [take ferry from Galilee, or fly from Westerly]	401-364-9124	30 / 50
3	C4	Ninigret NWR, Rt. 1, PO Box 307, Charlestown 02813 [Information Office in town at Shoreline Plaza on Rt. 1A]	401-364-9124	410 / 30
4	B5	Pettaquamscutt Cove NWR, near Tower Hill Rd., Narragansett	401-847-5511	170 / 10

RI DEM, Div. of Parks & Recreation, 2321 Hartford Ave., Johnston 02919

#	Grid	Location	Phone	Acres
1	A5			na / na
2	B4	Arcadia Management Area. managed by Div. of Forest Env., N & S of Rt. 165, also W of Millville	401-539-2356	14,000 / 150-550
3	C5	Block Island State Beach (ph.# is for mid-June/Labor Day), Corn Neck Rd., Block Island	401-466-2611	20 / na
4	B5	Brenton Point SP, Ocean Drive, Newport	401-847-2400	50 / na
5	B4	Burlingame State Park & Campground, Rt. #1, Charlestown	401-322-7994	2,100 / na
6	B4	Charlestown Breachway, Charlestown Beach Rd., Charlestown	401-364-7000	62 / na
7	B5	Colt SP, Hope Street, Rt. #114, Bristol	401-253-7482	466 / na
8	A5	Diamond Hill SP, Diamond Hill Rd., Cumberland	401-333-2437	427 / na
9	B5	East Matunuck St. Beach, Succotash Rd., Jerusalem	401-789-8585	102 / na
10	B5	Fishermen's Memorial SP, 1011 Point Judith Rd., Narragansett	401-789-8374	90 / na
11	B5	Fort Adams SP, Harrison Ave., Newport	401-847-2400	105 / na
12	B4	Galilee St. Beach, Galilee Rd., Narragansett	401-277-2632	10 / na
13	B5	Goddard Memorial SP, Ives Rd., Warrick	401-884-2010	490 / na
14	A5	Haines Memorial SP, Washington Rd., Barrington	401-253-7482	100 / na
15	A5	Lincoln Woods SP, Great Rd., Rt. #123, Lincoln	401-723-7892	630 / na
16	C4	Misquamicut St. Beach, Atlantic Ave. (phone is for mid-June/Labor Day), Westerly	401-596-9097	151 / na
17	A4	Pulaski Memorial SP (part of Geo. Washington Mgt. Area), on Rt. #44 at 102, 6 mi. W of Chepachet	401-568-2013	3,500 / na
18	B5	Roger W. Wheeler St. Beach, Sand Hill Cove Rd. (phone is for mid-June/Labor Day), Narragansett	401-789-3563	27 / na
19	B5	Scarborough St. Beach, Ocean Rd., Narragansett	401-789-2324	33 / na

DEM, Div. of Fish & Wildlife, Div. Field HQ, PO Box 218, West Kingston 02892

#	Grid	Location	Phone	Acres
1	B5		401-789-0218	na / na
2	B4	Arcadia Management Area - 2 units (South Forestry HQ), near Hope Valley	401-539-2356	13,738 / na
3	B4	Big River MA, near Nooseneck	401-539-2356	8,000 / na
4	A4	Black Hut MA, near Harrisville	401-568-2013	1,553 / na
5	A4	Buck Hill MA, near Wallum Lake	401-568-2013	2,060 / na
6	B4	Burlingame MA, near Charlestown	401-789-0281	1,380 / na
7	B4	Carbuncle MA, near Greene	401-539-2356	147 / na
8	B4	Carolina MA, near Hope Valley	401-568-2013	1,881 / na
9	A4	Durfee Hill MA, near W. Glocester	401-568-2013	1,183 / na
10	A4	George Washington MA (northern Forestry HQ), near W. Glocester	401-568-2013	3,482 / na
11	B5	Great Swamp Management Area & Field, near West Kingston	401-789-2081	3,243 / na
12	A4	Killingly MA, near North Foster	401-568-2013	400 / na
13	B4	Nicholas Farm MA, near Greene	401-789-0281	1,086 / na
14	B5	Prudence Island MA - North (access by boat), near Portsmouth	401-789-0281	1,044 / na
15	B5	Prudence Island MA - South, near Portsmouth	401-789-0281	690 / na
16	B4	Rockville MA, near Rockville	401-789-0281	789 / na
17	A4	Round Top MA, near Harrisville	401-568-8200	143 / na
18	B4	Sapowet MA, near Tiverton	401-789-0281	200 / na
19	B4	South Shore MA, near Perryville	401-789-0281	175 / na
20	B4	Wickaboxet MA, near W. Greenwich Center	401-539-2356	692 / na
21	B4	Woody Hill MA, near Bradford	401-769-0281	736 / na

Audubon Society of RI & Powder Mill Ledges Wildlife Refuge. 12 Sanderson Rd., Rt. #5, Smithfield 02917

#	Grid	Location	Phone	Acres
1	A5		401-231-6444	100 / na
2	B5	Davis Memorial Wildlife Refuge, Davisville Rd. (VC in Smithfield), N. Kingstown	401-231-6444	50 / na
3	B4	Kimball Wildlife Refuge, Watchaug Pond, Charlestown	401-231-6444	50 / na
4	B4	Long Pond Woods, Hopkinton	401-231-6444	na / na
5	B4	Parker Woodland 1670 Maple Valley Rd., Greene	401-397-4474	600 / na
6	B5	Ruecker Wildlife Refuge, 137 Seapowet Ave., Tiverton	401-231-6444	50 / na
7	B4	Fisherville Brook Wildlife Refuge, Pardon Joslin Rd., Exeter 02822	401-231-6444	600 / na
8	B5	Touisset Marsh Wildlife Refuge, Touisset Rd., Warren 02885	401-331-6444	60 / na

TNC Rhode Island Field Office, 240 Hope Street, Providence 02906 401-331-7110 na / na

#	Grid	Location	Phone	Acres
10	C5	Lewis-Dickens Farm & Rodman's Hollow Preserve, on Block Island near New Shoreham	401-331-7110	400 / na

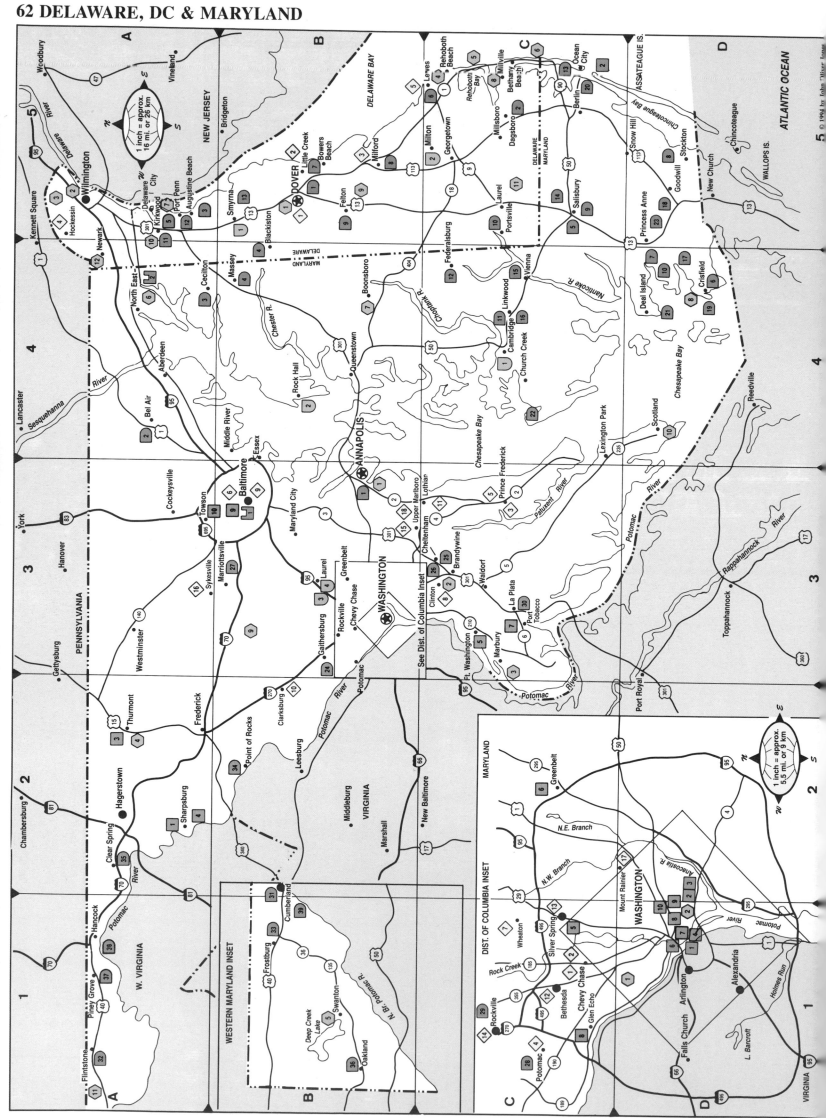

DELAWARE - CITY / AGENCY INDEX

City	Agency Office / Area Name	Code	S# Map
Augustine Beach	Augustine WA	SWA	3 A5
Bethany Beach	Fenwick Island SP	SPS	6 C5
Blackiston	Blackiston WA	SWA	4 B4
Dagsboro	Assawoman WA	SWA	2 C5
Delaware City	Fort Delaware SP	SPS	7 A5
DOVER	DNREC, Div. of Parks & Rec.	SPS	1 B5
	DNREC, Div. of Fish & Wildlife	SWA	1 B5
	Little Creek WA	SWA	7 B5
	TNC Delaware Field Office	TNC	
Felton	Killens Pond SP	SPS	9 B5
Kirkwood	N.G. Wilder WA	SWA	10 A4
Laurel	Lums Pond SP	SPS	11 C5
Lewes	Cape Henlopen SP	SPS	4 C5
Little Creek	Trap Pond SP	SWA	6 C5
Milford	Gordons Pond WA	SWA	16 C4
Millville	Port Mahon Wildlife Area	TNC	2 B5
Milton	Holts Landing SP	SPS	8 B5
Newark	Prime Hook NWR	NWR	8 C5
	Walter S. Carpenter SP	SPS	12 A4

Private Organizations

Delaware State Chamber of Commerce
1201 N. Orange St.
PO Box 671
Wilmington, DE 19899   302-654-0691

ANCA Locations in Delaware

Abbotts Nature Center (S# 3, map B5)
RD 4, Box 207
Milford, DE 19963   302-422-0847

Ashland Nature Center (S# 4, map A5)
PO Box 700
Hockessin, DE 19707   302-239-2334

Seaside Nature Center (S# 5, map B5)
42 Cape Henlopen Drive
Lewes, DE 19966   302-645-6852

DELAWARE NOTES

Summary

There are 2 federal, 27 state, and 6 private recreation areas or local administrative offices included in the Delaware coverage. Of these, 17 appear in the Information Chart and 18 are covered in the notes.

State Agencies

Department of Natural Resources and Environmental Control
89 Kings Highway
PO Box 1401
Dover, DE 19903   302-739-4506

Contact the Divisions listed here and in the Information Chart for information about recreation opportunities in Delaware.

Division of Parks & Recreation (S# 1, map B5)

A *Delaware State Parks Guide* (11 parks) is available free. Park user fees are charged from Memorial Day weekend through Labor Day.

Division of Fish & Wildlife (see chart S# 1, map B5)

Maps and brochures are available for each of the 12 State Wildlife Areas (WAs). The Guide map symbol number, map coordinates, WA name, and approximate location are listed below.

S# MAP	Name & Location
2 C5	Assawoman WA, Dagsboro
3 A5	Augustine WA, Augustine Beach
4 B4	Blackiston WA, Blackiston
5 A5	C & D Canal WA, Delaware City
6 C5	Gordons Pond WA, Lewes
7 B5	Little Creek WA, Dover
8 B5	Milford Neck WA, Milford
9 B5	N.G. Wilder WA, Felton
10 C5	Nanticoke WA, Portsville
11 A5	Reedy Island WA, Port Penn
12 A5	Silver Run WA, Port Penn
13 B5	Woodland Beach WA, Smyrna

Department of Agriculture
Attn: State Forester
2320 South DuPont Hwy.
Dover, DE 19901   302-736-4811

Contact the State Forester for recreation literature. The Blackbird, Ellendale, and Redden State Forests are open to public hunting.

Delaware Tourism Office
99 Kings Highway
PO Box 1401
Dover, DE 19903   1-800-441-8846

The official State Highway Map includes symbols for public boat access, charter boat fishing, campsites, picnic areas, fishing, water skiing, surfing, swimming, and recreational vehicle trails. State Parks and Wildlife Areas are shown in color.

DISTRICT OF COLUMBIA - CITY / AGENCY INDEX

City	Agency Office / Area Name	Code	S# Map
WASHINGTON	NPS, Nat'l. Cap. Reg.	NPS	1 D1
	Nat'l. Capital Parks, East	NPS	2 D2
	Fort Dupont Pk. & Activity C.	NPS	3 D2
	National Capital Parks, Central	NPS	4 D1
	Rock Creek Park & Nat'l. Capital Parks W	NPS	5 C1
	DC Parks & Recreation Adm. Office & PPE	SPS	1 D1
	Oxen Run Park	SPS	2 D1

DISTRICT OF COLUMBIA NOTES

Summary

There are 26 federal, 3 district, and 1 private recreation areas or local administrative offices included in the District of Columbia coverage. Of these, 7 appear in the Information Chart and 23 are covered in the notes.

Federal Agencies

Current outdoor recreation information and opportunities on agency lands and waters in the various states is best obtained from local agency offices with day-to-day local management responsibility in those states.

The main offices and headquarters administrative staff personnel of the federal agencies are located in Washington and the suburbs (nearby Maryland and Virginia). Those offices are listed here or in the respective Information Chart pages. Headquarter office personnel can provide information of a general nature.

MARYLAND - CITY / AGENCY INDEX

City	Agency Office / Area Name	Code	S# Map
ANNAPOLIS	DNR Dept. Forests, Parks & Nat. Heritage	SPS	1 E3
	MD DNR - Wildlife Division	SWA	1 E3
Baltimore	COE, Baltimore District	COE	1 E3
Bel Air	Wildlife Div., Central Region	SWA	2 A4
Berlin	Assateague Island National Seashore (MD/VA)		
Boonsboro	Greenbrier SP	NPS	2 C5
Brandywine	Calvert Cliffs SP	SPS	7 B4
	Bowen WMA	SWA	25 C3
Cambridge	Blackwater NWR	NWR	1 C4
	Fishing Bay WMA	SWA	11 C4
Cecilton	Earnville WMA	SWA	3 A4
Cheltenham	Cheltenham WMA	SWA	26 C3
Chesapeake City	Inlane Waterway to Delaware R.	COE	2 A4
Chevy Chase	TNC Maryland Field Office	TNC	1 C1
Church Creek	Woodend Wildlife San & Nat Ctr	INA	1 C1
Clear Spring	Taylor's Island WMA	SWA	22 C4
Crisfield	Indian Springs WMA	SWA	35 A2
	Janes Island SP	SPS	6 D4
	Cedar Island WMA	SWA	8 B1
	MD Marine Properties WMA	SWA	17 D4

Army Corps of Engineers (COE)
Pulaski Bldg.
20 Massachusetts Ave. NW
Washington, DC 20314-1000   202-272-0247

The nine COE Division Offices are listed in the state chapter notes. More than 460 District Offices and Lakeside Recreation Area Projects are covered in this Guide representing almost 4,400 recreation sites.

U.S. Fish & Wildlife Service (USFWS)
Division of Refuges
Interior Building
18th & C Streets, NW
Washington, DC 20240   703-358-2029

A foldout color map and recreation chart is available covering most refuge locations in the United States. The USFWS Regional Offices are included in the Information Charts.

National Park Service (NPS)
Interior Building
1849 C Street, NW
PO Box 37127
Washington, DC 20240   202-208-6843

A foldout U.S. National Park map and recreation chart is available from this office and regional and local NPS offices and visitor centers. Regional Offices are listed in the Information Charts.

A fold out National Trails System Map and Guide is available from NPS offices and visitor centers. The primary sources of information about specific National Scenic and Historic Trails include various associations and other non-profit organizations, the U.S. Forest Service, Bureau of Land Management, and selected offices of the National Park Service.

Selected larger park units with the most outdoor recreation potential are covered in the Information Charts in the state chapters. All other National Park Service locations are listed in the chapter notes under the heading **Additional NPS Locations**. Their approximate size in acres, address, and local telephone number are included as shown in this chapter (below).

In the District of Columbia metropolitan area the National Park Service's 300-plus park units in the metropolitan area are administered by three divisions. These are the National Capital Parks East, National Capital Parks Central (Constitution Gardens, The Mall, White House, etc.), and (Parks West) Rock Creek Park divisions. Division offices are listed in the Information Chart. Contact them for visitor information.

Additional NPS Locations in the District of Columbia

Those listed with a symbol number are shown on the District of Columbia map inset.

Constitution Gardens (52 acres)
c/o Nat'l. Capital Parks Central   202-426-6841

Ford's Theater (0.29 acre)
c/o Nat'l. Capital Parks Central   202-426-6924

Frederick Douglass NHS (8.5 acres)
1411 W Street, SW
Washington, DC 20020   202-426-5960

John F. Kennedy Center for the Performing Arts (17.5 acres) (S# 6, map D1)
National Park Service
2700 F Street, NW
Washington, DC 20566   202-416-7910

Lincoln Memorial (109.6 acres)
(S# 7, map D1) c/o Nat'l. Capital Parks Central   202-426-6841

Mary McLeod Bethune Council House NHS
Washington, DC
c/o Nat'l. Capital Region   202-619-7222

National Mall (146.4 acres)
c/o Nat'l. Capital Region   202-619-7222

Pennsylvania Ave. National Historic Site
c/o PA Ave. Development Corp., Suite 1220N
1331 Pennsylvania Ave., NW
Washington, DC 20004-1703   202-724-9091

Thomas Jefferson Memorial (18.4 acres) c/o Nat'l. Capital Parks Central   202-426-6841

Vietnam Veterans Memorial (2 acres) (S# 8, map D1) c/o Nat'l. Capital Parks Central   202-426-6841

Washington Monument (106 acres) (S# 9, map D1-2) c/o Nat'l. Capital Region   202-426-6841

White House (18 acres) (S# 10, map D1) c/o Nat'l. Capital Region   202-755-7798

USDA, U.S. Forest Service (USFS)
14th & Independence Ave., SW
PO Box 96090
Washington, DC 20090-6090   202-205-1760

A two page map of the United States (pages 18-19) shows USFS region boundaries, forest and grassland locations. This administrative offices is open from 8 a.m. to 4:30 p.m. Monday through Friday.

Bureau of Land Management (BLM)
Interior Building
18th & C Streets, NW
Washington, DC 20240   202-208-5717

All but a very few acres of BLM administered land is located in the west. A BLM map on page 22 shows the boundaries of BLM administrative Districts and Resource Areas in the west. BLM land holding boundaries are shaded. Eastern states offices are in the Mississippi, Ohio, Pennsylvania, Virginia, and Wisconsin chapters.

USDC, Natl. Oceanic & Atmospheric Admin. (NOAA)
National Ocean Service
Office of Ocean & Coastal Resource Management
Sanctuaries & Reserves Division
1825 Connecticut Ave.
Washington, DC 20235   202-606-4126
Francesca Cava, Chief

The California, Florida, Georgia, Louisiana, Massachusettes, and Texas chapter notes feature information about 11 NOAA Marine Sanctuaries.

Bureau of Reclamation (BOR)
C Street between 18th and 19th Streets, NW
Washington, DC 20240   202-343-4662

Bureau of Reclamation areas and offices are covered in the chapter notes. A fold out recreation map of the western United States showing BOR areas is available from this office, the Denver Colorado office, and the Regional Offices in California, Idaho, Montana, Nevada, and Utah chapter notes.

Unites States Geological Survey USGS

The local Earth Sciences Information Center is located in the Interior Bldg. on E Street NW, between between 18th and 19th Sts. The telephone number is 202-208-4047. This Center is open from 8 a.m. to 4 p.m. weekdays.

Information about ordering USGS maps is included under Agency Profiles in the front section of this Guide. To secure free USGS map indexes for any state you may call 1-800-USA-MAPS. Other USGS Information Centers are covered in the state chapter notes. The USGS headquarters is in Reston Virginia. See the Virginia chapter for details.

Bureau of Indian Affairs (BIA)
Office of Trust & Economic Development
Fish, Wildlife and Recreation Program
1849 "C" Street, NW
Washington, DC 20245   202-208-4088

This office is the central source for the most current information about contacting Tribal Councils and other tribal governing bodies throughout the United States in regard to outdoor recreation and gaming opportunities available to visitors.

District Agencies

District of Columbia Parks & Recreation
This agency manages more than 100 local neighborhood recreation sites comprising about 1,300 acres. Oxen Run Park and the DC Parks & Recreation office are listed in the Guide. Contact the DC Parks & Recreation office for neighborhood recreation site information.

A number of the District of Columbia sites are managed by the National Park Service. Contact the National Park district offices in this chapter for information.

Private Organizations
Many private conservation organizations have headquarters offices in Washington, DC, suburban Maryland, or Virginia. The National Wildlife Federation (NWF) publishes a Conservation Directory listing most of them. This directory may be ordered by calling the NWF at 1-800-432-6564.

District of Columbia Chamber of Commerce
1411 K St., NW
Washington, DC 20062   202-659-6000

MARYLAND NOTES
Summary
There are 16 federal, 52 state, and 19 private recreation areas or local administrative offices included in the Maryland coverage. Of these, 56 appear in the Information Chart and 31 are covered in the notes.

Federal Agencies

U.S. Fish & Wildlife Service
A new National Wildlife Visitor Center (see chart S# 4) is scheduled to open in late 1994. It will feature a major exhibit area including a variety of interactive exhibits dealing with global environmental issues, endangered species, habitats, and more. There will also be trails and outdoor study areas.

National Park Service
Additional NPS Locations in Maryland
Clara Barton National Historic Site (8.6 acres)
5801 Oxford Road (S# 8, map C1)
Glen Echo, MD 20812   301-492-6245

Fort McHenry NM and Historic Shrine (S# 9, map B3)
End of East Fort Ave.
Baltimore, MD 212230-5393   410-962-4290

Hampton National Historic Site (S# 10, map A3)
535 Hampton Lane
Towson, MD 21204   410-962-0688

Monocacy National Battlefield
Not open to the public at this time.
c/o Antietam National Battlefield (see chart)   301-662-3515

State Agencies
Department of Natural Rresources
*Resource Conservation Service
Tawes State Office Bldg.
Annapolis, MD 21410   410-841-5700
The Forest, Park, and Wildlife Services functions under this Department.

Forests and Parks
A Maryland State Parks Guide (36 state parks) is available free. The guide describes each area, contains a locator map, and includes information on facilities and activities. A selection of 10 state parks are shown on the Guide map. Their symbol number, map coordinates, name, and general location are listed here.

S#	MAP	Name & Location
2	C3	Calvert Hills SP, Brandywine
3	C3	Chapel Point SP, Marbury
4	A2	Cunningham Falls SP, Thurmont
5	B1	Deep Creek Lake SP, Swanton
6	A4	Elk Neck SP, North east
7	B4	Greenbrier SP, Boonsboro
8	D4	Janes Island SP, Crisfield
9	B3	Patuxent River SP, Gaithersburg
10	D4	Point Lookout SP, Scotland
11	A1	Rocky Gap SP, Flintstone

Wildlife Division (S# 1, map B3)
The basic reference for areas open to the public is Guide to Hunting and Trapping in Maryland. Annual harvest information is published on deer and turkey harvests. A quarterly publication, Tracks 'n Trails, is available by subscription for $3 per year.

Maryland Tourist Development
45 Calvert St.
Annapolis, MD 21401   in state call 410-925-3806   1-800-543-1036

Locust Grove Nature Center (S# 12, map C1)
7777 Democracy Blvd.
Bethesda, MD 20817   301-365-2530

Maydale Nature Center (S# 13, map C1)
1726 Briggs Chaney Rd.
Silver Spring, MD 20904   301-384-9447

Meadowside Nature Center (S# 14, map C1)
5100 Meadowside Lane
Rockville, MD 20855   301-924-4141

Merkle Wildlife Sanctuary (S# 15, map B3)
11704 Fenno Rd.
Upper Marlboro, MD 20772   301-747-8336

Piney Run Nature Center (S# 16, map A3)
30 Martz Rd.
Sykesville, MD 21784   301-795-3274

30th Street Nature Center (S# 17, map D2)
4210 30th Street
Mount Rainier, MD 20712   301-927-2163

Watkins Nature Center (S# 18, map B2)
301 Watkins Park Drive
Upper Marlboro, MD 20772   301-249-6202

Maryland Chamber of Commerce
275 West St., #400
Annapolis, MD 21401   Phone 410-269-0642   Fax 410-269-5427

Private Organizations

ANCA Locations in Maryland
Adventure Nature Study Area (S# 4, map C1)
10801 Glen Rd.
Potomac, MD 20854   301-279-0277

Battle Creek Nature Center (S# 5, map C3)
c/o County Courthouse
Prince Frederick, MD 20678   301-535-5327

Bragg Nature Center (S# 6, map B3)
6601 Baltimore National Pike
Baltimore, MD 21228

Brookside Nature Center (S# 7, map C1)
1400 Glenallen Ave.
Wheaton, MD 20902   301-888-1410

Clearwater Nature Center (S# 8, map C3)
11000 Thrift Rd.
Clinton, MD 20735   301-297-4575

Clyburn Arboretum (S# 9, map B3)
4915 Greenspring Ave.
Baltimore, MD 20209   301-396-0180

Hawk's Reach Nature Center (S# 10, map B2)
23701 Frederick Rd.
Clarksburg, MD 20871   301-972-9458

Jug Bay Wetlands Sanctuary (S# 11, map C3)
1361 Wrighton Rd.
Lothian, MD 20711   301-741-9330

★ INFORMATION CHART ★

AGENCY/MAP LEGEND . . . INITIALS, MAP SYMBOLS, COLOR CODES
U.S. Forest Service Supervisor & Ranger Dist. Offices   NFS   61
U.S. Army Corps of Engineers Rec. Areas & Offices   COE   31
USFWS National Wildlife Refuges & Offices   NWR   40
National Park Service Parks & other NPS Sites   NPS   7
Bureau of Land Management Rec. Areas & Offices   BLM   26
Bureau of Reclamation Rec. Areas & Reg. Offices   BOR   8
State Parks (also see State Agency notes)   SPS   52
State Wildlife Areas (also see State Agency notes)   SWA   19
Private Preserves, Nature Centers & Tribal Lands   15
The Wild Rivers   and Wilderness Areas

Note: Refer to yellow block on page 7 (top right) for location name and address abbreviations. If a symbol number has a star ★ that symbol is not shown on the

INFORMATION CHART LEGEND - SYMBOLS & LETTER CODES
■ means YES & □ means Yes with disability provisions
sp means spring, March through May
S means Summer, June through August
F means Fall, September through November
W means Winter, December through February
T means Two (2) or Three (3) Seasons
A means All Four (4) Seasons
na means Not Applicable or Not Available
Note: empty or blank spaces in the chart mean NO   ★ that symbol is not shown on the

FACILITIES, SERVICES, RECREATION OPPORTUNITIES & CONVENIENCES

Column categories (rotated headers):
INFO OFFICE (IO) / VISITOR CENTER (VC); IO / VC OPEN SATURDAY / SUNDAY; ENTRY FEE, not camping or permit fee; CONCESSIONAIRE; INTERPRETIVE OR EDUCATIONAL DISPLAY; FREE LITERATURE or brochures, maps, etc.; AGENCY GUIDED TOURS, scheduled / by res.; NATURE LITERATURE EDUCATION / STUDY PROGRAMS; WILDFLOWER VIEWING AREA or PROGRAMS; ARCHAEOLOGICAL / HISTORIC SITES; HISTORIC SITES / GEOLOGICAL SITES; WILDLIFE VIEWING AREA / GEOLOGICAL SITES; ENDANGERED SPECIES ARE COMMON; WILDLIFE IS ABUNDANT OR COMMON; DEVELOPED VIEWING SITES, blinds, signs, etc.; WILDERNESS AREAS / PICNIC SITES; NO-CHARGE CAMPGROUNDS / PICNIC SITES; DEVELOPED CAMPGROUNDS / CAMPSITES; WALKING / HIKING TRAILS; WILDERNESS AREAS / TRAILS; BICYCLING PERMITTED; HORSEBACK RIDING w/ your own horse; OFF-ROAD Motorized Vehicle Area / Use OK; SWIMMING OPPORTUNITIES / WILD RIVERS; BOATING OPPORTUNITIES, at one's own risk; FISHING IN SEASON, license / permit req'd; MOTORIZED WATERCRAFT OK, check limits; HUNTING IN SEASON, license / permit req'd; WINTER SPORTS OPPORTUNITIES; PARK & WALK-IN ONLY AREA; DAY USE ONLY, no overnight; DRINKING WATER; RESTROOMS

DELAWARE CHART LISTINGS

S#	MAP	LOCATION NAME (state initials if more than one) with ADDRESS and/or LOCATION DATA	TELEPHONE	ACRES / ELEVATION
1	B5	Bombay Hook NWR, RD #1, Box 147, Smyrna 1977 [office at refuge, 8 mi SE of Smyrna via RD 12, Rt. 9 & RD 85]	302-653-6872	15,000 / 10
2	C5	Prime Hook NWR, Rt. 3, Box 195, Milton 19968 [take SR 16 1 mi E of SR 1, turn L to Rd 236 - sign]	302-684-8419	8,818 / 0-30
1	B5	DNREC, Div. of Parks & Recreation, 89 Kings Highway, PO Box 1401, Dover 19903	302-739-4702	na / na
2	A5	Bellevue SP, NE of Wilmington	302-577-3390	459 / na
3	A5	Brandywine Creek SP, N of Wilmington	302-577-3534	840 / na
4	C5	Cape Henlopen SP, East of Lewes	302-645-8983	3,177 / na
5	C5	Delaware Seashore SP, between Bethany Beach & Rehoboth Beach	302-227-2800	2,287 / na
6	C5	Fenwick Island SP, S of Bethany Beach	302-539-9060	307 / na
7	A5	Fort Delaware SP (access by boat from Delaware City to Pea Patch Island), near Delaware City	302-834-7941	479 / na
8	C5	Holts Landing SP, N of Millville	302-539-9060	301 / na
9	B5	Killens Pond SP, S of Felton	302-284-4526	943 / na
10	A4	Lums Pond SP, near Kirkwood	302-368-6989	1,757 / na
11	C5	Trap Pond SP, near Laurel	302-875-5153	966 / na
12	A4	Walter S. Carpenter SP, N of Newark	302-731-1310	1,321 / na
1	B5	DNREC, Div. of Fish & Wildlife, Richard & Robbins Bldg., 89 Kings Hwy., PO Box 1401, Dover 19903 [see notes]	302-739-5295	na / na
1	B5	TNC Delaware Field Office, 319 S. State Street, Dover 19903	302-674-3550	na / na

Ref	Name / Address	Phone	Acres
1 D1	**Nat'l. Park Svc. Nat'l. Cap. Reg.**, 1100 Ohio Drive, S.W., Washington 20242	202-619-7222	na / na
2 D2	Nat'l. Capital Parks, East, 1900 Anacostia Drive, SE, Washington 20020	202-690-5185	na / na
3 D2	Ft. Dupont Park & Activity Center, 1900 Anacostia Dr. SE, Washington 20020 [at Minnesota Ave. & Randal Circle SE]	202-426-7723	376 / 253
4 D1	National Capital Parks, Central, 900 Ohio Drive, SW, Washington 20242	202-485-9880	na / na
5 C1	Rock Creek Park & Nat'l. Capital Pa., 5000 Glover Rd., NW, Washington 20015	202-426-6829	1,754 / 0-43?
1 D1	**DC Parks & Recreation Adm. Office**, 3149 16th St., NW, Washington 20010	202-673-7665	na / na
2 D1	Oxen Run Park, 4th & Mississippi Ave., SE, Washington [SE Washington]	202-562-2255	na / na

MARYLAND CHART LISTINGS

Ref	Name / Address	Phone	Acres
1 B3	**COE, Baltimore District**, PO Box 1715, Baltimore 21203	410-962-3693	na / na
2 A4	Inline Waterway to Delaware River, Chesapeake & Delaware Canal, Chesapeake City 21915 [adjacent town of North East]	301-885-5622	20,090 / 0
1 C4	**Blackwater NWR**, 2145 Key Wallace Drive, Cambridge 21613	410-228-2692	2,286 / 0-30
2 B4	Eastern Neck NWR, 1730 Eastereck Rd., Rock Hall 21661	410-639-7056	12,750 / na
3 C1	Patuxent Wildlife Research Ctr., N Tract VC Station, 230 Bald Eagle Dr., Laurel 20724 [off Rt. 198, 1.4 mi E of Pkwy.]	410-674-3304	12,750 / na
4 B3	Patuxent WRC N Wildlife VC (open fall 1994), 11400 American Holly Dr., Laurel 20708 [off Powder Mill Rd., E of Pkwy.]	301-497-0539	4,341 / na
1 A2	**Antietam National Battlefield**, Box 158, Sharpsburg 21782	301-432-5124	3,244 / 365
2 C5	Assateague Is. National Seashore (M, 7206 National Seashore Lane, Berlin 21811 [take MD SR 611, 6 mi S of US 50]	410-641-1441	39,630 / 0-20
3 A2	Catoctin Mountain Park, 6602 Foxville Road, Thurmont 21788	301-663-9388	5,770 / 900-1,800
4 C1	Chesapeake and Ohio Canal NHP, PO Box 4, Sharpsburg 21782	301-739-4200	20,781 / 50-610
5 C1	Ft. Washington/Piscataway Pks., c/o Nat'l. Cap. Pks. E, Washington, DC 20020, [Ft. Washington, off Indian Head Hwy.]	301-763-4600	4,341 / na
6 B3	Greenbelt Park, 6565 Greenbelt Road, Greenbelt 20770 [at exit 23 of Rt. 95 in Prince Georges Co.]	301-344-3948	1,176 / na
7 C3	Thomas Stone NHS, 6655 Rose Hill Rd., Port Tobacco 20677 [on Rose Hill Rd. bet. MD Rts. 6 & 225, 4 mi W of US 301]	301-934-6027	320 / na
1 B3	**DNR Dept. Forests, Parks & Natural Heritage**, Tawes State Office Bldg., Annapolis 21401 [see notes]	410-974-3771	na / na
2 A4	**DNR Wildlife Division**, 580 Taylor Ave., Annapolis 21401 [Tawes State Office Bldg.]	410-836-4550	na / na
3 A4	Central Region, 2 Bond St., Bel Air 21014	301-929-3650	190 / na
4 B4	Earlville WMA, Cecil County near, Cecilton	301-928-3650	3,800 / na
5 C5	Millington WMA, Kent County near, Massey	410-543-6595	na / na
6 C4	Eastern Region, 201 Baptist St., Suite 22, Salisbury 21801	410-651-2320	2,880 / na
7 D4	Cedar Island WMA, Somerset County near, Crisfield	410-651-2320	11,900 / na
8 D5	Deal Island WMA, Somerset County near, Princess Anne	410-651-2320	1,750 / na
9 C5	E.A. Vaughn WMA, Worcester County near, Stockton	410-651-2320	2,090 / na
10 D4	Ellis Bay WMA, Wicomico County near, Salisbury	410-749-2461	3,880 / na
11 D4	Fairmount WMA, Somerset County near, Princess Anne	410-376-3236	17,200 / na
12 C4	Fishing Bay WMA, Dorchester County near, Cambridge	410-376-3226	3,000 / na
13 C5	Idylwild WMA, Caroline County near, Federalsburg	410-651-2320	100 / na
14 C5	Isle of Wight WMA, Worcester County near, Ocean City	410-543-6595	115 / na
15 C4	Johnson WMA, Wicomico County near, Salisbury	410-376-3236	485 / na
16 C4	LeCompte WMA, Dorchester County near, Vienna	410-376-3236	313 / na
17 D4	Linkwood WMA, Dorchester County near, Linkwood	410-651-2320	1,030 / na
18 D5	Maryland Marine Properties WMA, Somerset County near, Crisfield	410-632-0572	505 / na
19 D4	Pocomoke River WMA, Worcester County near, Snow Hill	410-651-2320	922 / na
20 D4	Pocomoke Sound WMA (boat access onl, Somerset County near, Ocean City	410-543-6595	24 / na
21 D4	Sinepuxent Bay WMA (boat access onl, Worcester County near, Ocean City [closed in summer]	410-651-2320	2,969 / na
22 C4	South Marsh Island WMA (boat access, Somerset County near, Deal Island	410-376-3236	1,020 / na
23 D5	Taylor's Island (boat access only), Dorchester County near, Church Creek	410-651-2320	389 / na
24 C4	Wellington WMA, Somerset County near, Princess Anne	301-258-0817	na / na
25 C3	Southern Region, 11960 Clopper Rd., Gaithersburg 20878	301-258-0817	313 / na
26 C3	Bowen WMA (boat access only), Prince George's Co. near, Brandywine	301-372-8128	276 / na
27 C1	Cheltenham WMA, Prince George's Co. near, Cheltenham	410-258-0817	na / na
28 C1	Hugg-Thomas WMA, Howard County near, Marriottsville	301-258-0817	329 / na
29 C1	Islands of the Potomac WMA (boat ac, Montgomery County near, Potomac	301-258-0817	1,947 / na
30 C3	McKee-Beshers WMA, Montgomery County near, Rockville	301-258-0817	754 / na
31 B2	Myrtle Grove WMA, Charles County near, La Plata	301-777-2136	1,066 / na
32 A1	Western Region, Pershing St., Room 110, Cumberland 21502	301-478-2525	8,376 / na
33 B1	Billmeyer WMA, Allegany County near, Flintstone	301-777-2136	194 / na
34 B2	Dan's Mountain WMA, Allegany County near, Frostburg	301-777-2136	6,363 / na
35 A2	Heater's Island WMA (boat access on, Frederick County near, Point of Rocks	301-842-2702	1,763 / na
36 B1	Indian Springs WMA, Washington County near, Clear Spring	301-777-2136	2,151 / na
37 B1	Mt. Nebo WMA, Garrett County near, Oakland	301-777-2136	2,151 / na
38 A1	Sideling Hill WMA, Allegany County near, Piney Grove	301-777-2136	3,950 / na
39 B2	Sideling Hill WMA, Washington County near, Hancock	301-777-2136	
	Warrior Mountain WMA, Allegany County near, Cumberland		
1 C1	**Audubon NS of Cent Atl Sts & Woodend Wildlife San & NC**, 8940 Jones Mill Rd., Chevy Chase 20815 [call for directions]	301-652-9188	40 / 50
2 C1	TNC Maryland Field Office, Chevy Chase Metro Bldg., 2 Wisconsin Cir., Suite 410, Chevy Chase 20815	301-656-8673	na / na
3 C3	Battle Cr. Cypress Swamp Sanctuary, c/o Courthouse, 2880 Gray's Rd., Prince Frederick 20678	410-535-5327	100 / na

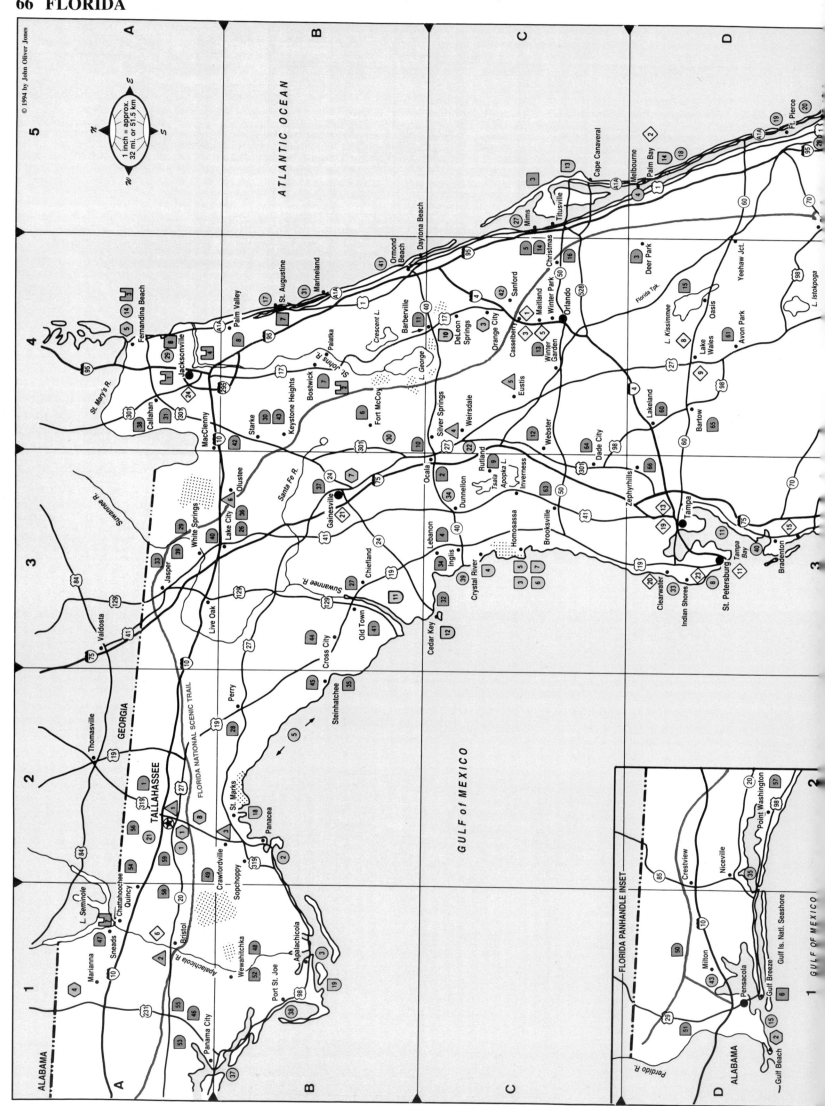

© 1994 by John Oliver Jones

1 inch = approx.
32 mi. or 51.5 km

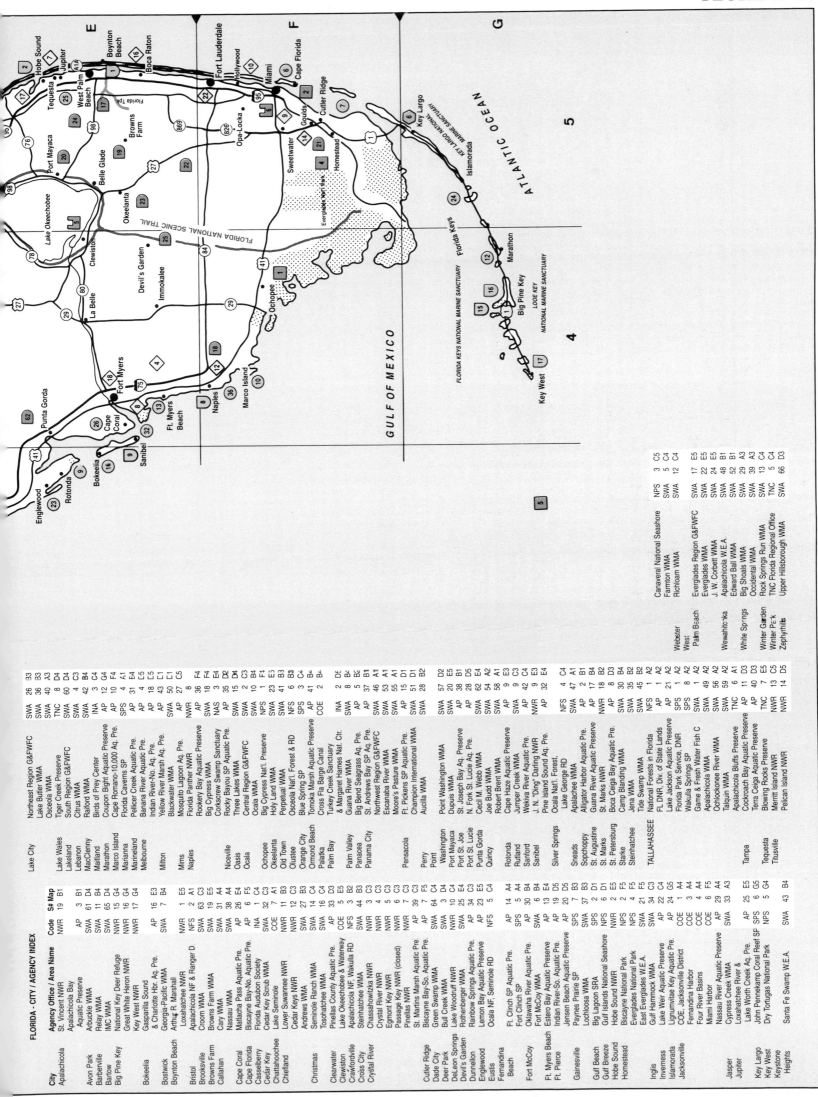

FLORIDA - CITY / AGENCY INDEX

City	Agency Office / Area Name	Code	S#	Map
Apalachicola	St. Vincent NWR	NWR	19	B1
	Apalachicola Bay Aquatic Preserve	AP	3	B1
Avon Park	Arbuckle WMA	AP	61	D4
Barberville	Relay WMA	SWA	11	B4
Bartow	IMC WMA	SWA	65	G4
Big Pine Key	National Key Deer Refuge	NWR	15	G4
	Great White Heron NWR	NWR	16	G4
	Key West NWR	NWR	17	G4
Bokeelia	Gasparilla Sound & Charlotte Hbr. Aq. Pre.	AP	16	E3
Bostwick	Georgia-Pacific WMA	SWA	7	B4
Boynton Beach	Arthur R. Marshall Loxahatchee NWR	NWR	1	E5
Bristol	Apalachicola NF & Ranger D.	NFS		A1
Brooksville	Croom WMA	SWA	63	C3
Browns Farm	Browns Farm WMA	SWA	19	E5
Callahan	Cary WMA	SWA	31	A4
	Nassau WMA	SWA	38	A4
Cape Coral	Matlacha Pass Aquatic Pre.	AP	26	E4
Cape Florida	Biscayne Bay-No. Aquatic Pre.	AP	6	F5
Casselberry	Florida Audubon Society	INA	1	C4
Cedar Key	Cedar Key Scrub WMA	SWA	32	C3
Chattahoochee	Lake Seminole	COE	7	A1
Chiefland	Lower Suwannee NWR	NWR	12	C3
	Cedar Keys NWR	NWR		C3
Christmas	Andrews WMA	SWA	27	B3
	Seminole Ranch WMA	SWA	14	C4
	Tosohatchee WMA	SWA	16	C4
Clearwater	Pinellas County Aquatic Pre.	AP	33	D3
	St. Martins Marsh Aquatic Pre.	AP	39	F5
Clewiston	Biscayne Bay-So. Aquatic Pre.	AP	7	F5
Crawfordville	Green Swamp WMA	SWA	64	C4
Cross City	Bull Creek WMA	SWA	10	C4
Crystal River	Lake Woodruff NWR	NWR	3	B4
	Rothenberger WMA	SWA	44	B3
	Rainbow Springs Aquatic Pre.	AP	34	C3
	Lemon Bay Aquatic Preserve	AP	23	E3
	Ocala NF, Seminole RD	NFS	5	C4
Cutler Ridge	Ft. Clinch SP Aquatic Pre.	AP	14	A4
Dade City	Ft. Clinch SP	SPS	30	B4
Deer Park	Oklawaha River WMA	SWA	6	B4
DeLeon Springs	Fort McCoy WMA	AP	13	E4
Devil's Garden	Estero Bay Aquatic Preserve	AP	20	D5
Dunnellon	Jensen Beach Aquatic Preserve	SPS	37	B3
Englewood	Paynes Prairie SP	SWA	2	D1
Eustis	Lochloosa WMA	SPS	6	D1
Fernandina Beach	Big Lagoon SRA	NWR	2	E5
Fort McCoy	Gulf Islands National Seashore	NPS	2	F5
Ft. Myers Beach	Biscayne National Park	SWA	21	F5
Ft. Pierce	Everglades National Park	SWA	34	C3
Gainesville	East Everglades W.E.A.	AP	22	C4
Gulf Beach	Gulf Hammock WMA	AP	29	A4
Gulf Breeze	Lake Weir Aquatic Preserve	SWA	33	A3
Homestead	Lignumvitae Key Aquatic Pre.			
	COE, Jacksonville District			
Inglis	Fernandina Harbor			
Inverness	Four River Basins			
Islamorada	Miami Harbor			
Jacksonville	Nassau River Aquatic Preserve			
Jasper	Loxahatchee River & Cypress Creek WMA	AP	25	E5
Jupiter	Lake Worth Creek Aq. Pre.	SPS	6	G5
Key Largo	John Pennekamp Coral Reef SP	NPS	5	G4
Key West	Dry Tortugas National Park			
Keystone Heights	Santa Fe Swamp W.E.A.	SWA	43	B4

City	Agency Office / Area Name	Code	S#	Map
Lake City	Northeast Region G&FWFC	SWA	26	B3
	Lake Butler WMA	SWA	36	B3
	Osceola WMA	SWA	40	A3
Lake Wales	Tiger Creek Preserve	TNC	60	D4
Lakeland	South Region G&FWFC	SWA	4	C3
Lebanon	Citrus WMA	SWA	42	B4
MacClenny	Raiford WMA	INA	2	D...
Maitland	Birds of Prey Center	AP	12	G4
Marathon	Coupon Bight Aquatic Preserve	AP	5	A1
Marco Island	Cape Romano-10,000 Aq. Pre.	SPS	4	A1
Marianna	Florida Caverns SP	AP	4	E5
Marineland	Pellicer Creek Aquatic Pre.	AP	18	E5
Melbourne	Banana River Aquatic Pre.	AP	43	C1
	Indian River-No. Aq. Pre.	SWA	50	C1
Milton	Yellow River Marsh Aq. Pre.	AP	27	C5
	Blackwater WMA	NWR	8	F4
Mims	Mosquito Lagoon Aq. Pre.	AP	36	F4
Naples	Florida Panther NWR	SWA	18	F4
	Rookery Bay Aquatic Preserve	NAS	3	E4
	Big Cypress WMA	AP	35	D2
	Corkscrew Swamp Sanctuary	SWA	15	D4
Niceville	Rocky Bayou SP Aquatic Pre.	SWA	2	C3
Oasis	Three Lakes WMA	SWA	10	B4
Ocala	Central Region G&FWFC	NPS	1	F1
Ochopee	Big Cypress Nat'l. Preserve	SWA	41	B3
Okeelanta	Holy Land WMA	SWA	6	B3
Olustee	Perpetual WMA	SPS	5	C4
Orange City	Osceola Nat'l. Forest & RD	AP	41	B4
Ormond Beach	Blue Spring SP	COE	2	B4
Palatka	Tomoka Marsh Aquatic Preserve	INA	2	DE
Palm Bay	Cross Fla Barge Canal	SWA	5	B...
Palm Valley	Turkey Creek Sanctuary & Margaret Hames Nat. Ctr.	AP	37	B1
Panacea	Guana River WMA	AP	46	A1
Panama City	Big Bend Seagrass Aq. Pre.	SWA	54	A2
	St. Andrews Bay SP Aq. Pre.	SWA	55	A1
Pensacola	Northwest Region G&FWFC	AP	15	D1
	Escanaba River WMA	SWA	28	B2
	Moore's Pasture WMA			
	Ft. Pickens SP Aquatic Pre.			
	Champion International WMA			
	Aucilla WMA			
Perry	Point Washington WMA	SWA	57	D2
Point	Dupuis WMA	SWA	20	E5
Point Washington	St. Joseph Bay Aq. Preserve	AP	38	B1
Port Mayaca	N. Fork St. Lucie WMA	AP	28	D5
Port St. Joe	Cecil M. Webb WMA	AP	62	E4
Port St. Lucie	Joe Budd WMA	SWA	53	A2
Punta Gorda	Robert Brent WMA	SWA	58	A1
Quincy	Cape Haze Aquatic Preserve	NFS	2	C4
Rotonda	Jumper Creek WMA	SWA	47	A1
Rutland	Wekiva River Aquatic Pre.	AP	2	B1
Sanford	J. N. "Ding" Darling NWR	AP	17	B4
Sanibel	Pine Island Sound Aq. Pre.	NWR	18	B2
Silver Springs	Ocala Nat'l. Forest	AP	8	D3
	Lake George RD	SWA	30	B4
Sneads	Apalachee WMA	SWA	45	B2
Sopchoppy	Alligator Harbor Aquatic Pre.	AP	9	C3
St. Augustine	Guana River Aquatic Preserve	AP	42	C4
St. Marks	St. Marks NWR	AP	9	E3
St. Petersburg	Boca Ceiga Bay Aquatic Pre.	AP	32	E4
Starke	Camp Blanding WMA			
Steinhatchee	Jena WMA			
	Tide Swamp WMA			
TALLAHASSEE	National Forests in Florida	NFS	1	A2
	FL DNR, Div. of State Lands	AP	21	A2
	Lake Jackson Aquatic Preserve	SPS	8	A2
	Florida Park Service, DNR	SWA	1	A2
	Wakulla Springs SP	SWA	49	A2
	Game & Fresh Water Fish C	SWA	56	A2
	Apalachicola WMA	SWA	59	A2
	Ochlockonee River WMA	TNC	6	A1
	Talquin WMA			
Tampa	Cockroach Bay Aquatic Preserve	AP	40	D3
	Terra Ceiga Bay Aquatic Preserve			
Tequesta	Blowing Rocks Preserve	TNC	7	E5
Titusville	Merritt Island NWR	NWR	13	C5
	Pelican Island NWR	NWR	14	D5

City	Agency Office / Area Name	Code	S#	Map
	Canaveral National Seashore	NPS	3	C5
	Farmton WMA	SWA	5	C4
	Richloam WMA	SWA	12	C4
Webster	Everglades Region G&FWFC	SWA	17	E5
	Everglades WMA	SWA	22	E5
	J. W. Corbett W.E.A.	SWA	24	E5
Wewahitchka	Apalachicola WMA	SWA	48	B1
	Edward Ball WMA	SWA	52	B1
White Springs	Big Shoals WMA	SWA	29	A3
Winter Garden	Occidental WMA	SWA	39	A3
Winter Park	Rock Springs Run WMA	SWA	13	C4
Zephyrhills	TNC Florida Regional Office	TNC	5	C4
	Upper Hillsborough WMA	SWA	66	D3

FLORIDA NOTES

Summary

There are 46 federal, 121 state, and 24 private recreation areas or local administrative offices covered in this state chapter. Of these, 162 appear in the Information Chart and 29 are covered in the notes. The special indexes feature 18 federally designated wilderness areas and wild rivers, and 3 agency published outdoor maps.

Florida Tourist Note: Emergency road phones are answered when picked up!

Federal Agencies

USFWS National Wildlife Refuges

Merritt Island NWR abuts the Canaveral National Seashore and NASA's Kennedy Space Center. Portions of the refuge may be closed during NASA Space Shuttle or satellite launch activity.

National Park Service

Additional NPS Locations in Florida

Castillo de San Marcos National Monument (20.5 acres) (S# 7, map A1)
1 Castillo Drive
St. Augustine, FL 32084 904-829-6506

Fort Caroline National Memorial (138 acres) (S# 8, map A1)
12713 Fort Caroline Road
Jacksonville, FL 32225 904-641-7155

Fort Matanzas National Monument (227 acres) (S# *9)
c/o Castillo de San Marcos National Monument
1 Castillo Drive
St. Augustine, FL 32084 904-829-6506

Timucuan Ecological and
Historic Preserve (46,000 acres) (S# *10)
c/o Fort Caroline National Memorial
12713 Fort Caroline Road
Jacksonville, FL 32225 904-641-7155

USDC, Natl. Oceanic & Atmospheric Admin. (NOAA)

National Ocean Service
For National Marine Sanctuary (NMS) information contact the Florida Department of Natural Resources (see State Agencies below).

Looe Key, Key Largo, and Florida Keys National Marine Sanctuaries are located in the area of the Florida Keys south of Miami. Looe Key and Key Largo onsite management is through a cooperative arrangement with the Florida Department of Natural Resources. Various recreational and commercial activities like diving, fishing, and underwater photography are permitted in sanctuary waters.

National Trail

The Florida National Scenic Trail covers 1,300 miles (2,090 km) from the lower portion of Big Cypress Preserve in south Florida, north and northwest to the west end of the panhandle of Florida. The trail location is shown on the USFS map on page 19. More than 1,000 miles of trail have been completed and there are a number of side loop trails to nearby points of interest.

For information contact the National Forests in Florida Supervisor (see S# 1, map A2), phone 904-681-7293.
Another information source is:
Florida Trail Association
PO Box 13708 in FL only 800-342-1882
Gainesville, FL 32604 or 904-378-8823

Wilderness/Wild River Index

Wilderness Areas

Apalachicola NF & RD (S# 2, map A1)
  Bradwell Bay Wilderness - 24,602 acres
  Mud Swamp/New River Wilderness - 7,800 acres
Ocala NF, Lake George RD (S# 4, map C4)
  Alexander Springs Wilderness - 7,700 acres
  Billies Bay Wilderness - 3,120 acres
  Juniper Prairie Wilderness - 13,260 acres
  Little Lake George Wilderness - 2,500 acres
Osceola NF & RD (S# 6, map B3)
  Big Gum Swamp Wilderness - 13,600 acres

Cedar Keys NWR (S# 11, map C3)
  Cedar Keys Wilderness - 397 acres
Chassahowitzka NWR (S# 3, map C3)
  Chassahowitzka Wilderness - 23,580 acres
Great White Heron NWR (S# 16, map G4)
  Florida Keys Wilderness - 1,900 acres
Key West NWR (S# 17, map G4)
  Florida Keys Wilderness - 2,019 acres
National Key Deer Refuge (S# 14, map G4)
  Florida Keys Wilderness - 2,278 acres
J.N. "Ding" Darling NWR
  Island Bay Wilderness - 20 acres
J.N. "Ding" Darling Wilderness - 2,619 acres
Lake Woodruff NWR (S# 9, map C4)
  Lake Woodruff Wilderness - 1,066 acres
Passenger Key NWR (S# 6, map C3)
  Passenger Key Wilderness - 2,500 acres
Pelican Island NWR (S# 13, map D5)
  Pelican Island Wilderness - 6 acres
Saint Marks NWR (S# 18, map B2)
  Saint Marks Wilderness - 17,350 acres

Everglades National Park (S# 4, map F5)
  Everglades Wilderness - 1,296,500 acres

Wild River

Loxahatchee Wild River
Florida Dept. of Natural Resources (see note below and DNR S# 25, map E5)

Outdoor Map Index

U.S. Forest Service Maps

Apalachicola National Forest [1985]
Ocala National Forest [1988]
Osceola National Forest [1980]

State Agencies

Florida Department of Natural Resources (DNR)
Marjory Stoneman Douglas Bldg.
3900 Commonwealth Blvd.
Tallahassee, FL 32399 904-488-1554
Information about the Loxahatchee Wild River (S# 25, map E5) is available from this office.

DNR, Division of State Lands (DSL)

Bureau of Submerged Lands (S# 1, map A2)
Florida's Aquatic Preserves are featured in the Information Chart and on the Florida map using a special symbol shape (round) and color (medium blue). Aquatic Preserves are mostly submerged lands. A number of the preserves lie adjacent to state parks and/or upland recreation sites which may offer various services and recreation facilities.

DNR, Division of Recreation & Parks

Florida Park Service (S# 1, map A2)
Selected State Parks are listed in the Information Chart. Free park and recreation site literature is available including a Florida State Parks Guide (105 state parks). It describes each park, and indicates the facilities and park activities available. Ask about Recreational Trails System brochures covering canoeing, hiking, bicycling, horseback riding, and jogging.

DNR, Division of Marine Resources 904-488-6058

Contact this division at DNR in Tallahassee for Marine Resources information.

Game & Fresh Water Fish Commission (G&FWFC)

(HQ - S# 1, map A2) Chart details on G&FWFC office locations indicate office facilities and services. Hunt maps and regulations for any of the departments wildlife management areas may be obtained from the regional offices. Permits are required for some hunts during the first nine days of the season. A $25 stamp is required when hunting in areas designated Type I.

A variety of publications is available from the G&FWFC. Florida Wildlife, a bi-monthly 36 page magazine, is available by subscription for $7 per year.

Department of Agriculture

Division of Forestry
3125 Conner Blvd.
Tallahassee, FL 32399 904-488-4274
Contact the Division for State Forest recreation literature.

Department of Commerce

Division of Tourism
Collins Building
Tallahassee, FL 32304 904-487-1462
The official Florida Transportation Department highway map is available here and at other state agency offices. Symbols and their map coordinates indicate state parks and recreation areas with and without campsites.

Private Organization

Tribal Land Areas in Florida
Miccosukee Tribe of the Miccosukee Indian Reservation - Fishing, hunting, boating, touring.
Miccosukee Business Committee (S# 9, map F5)
PO Box 440021
Tamiami Station
Miami, FL 33144 305-223-8380

Seminole Tribe of Florida - Fishing, camping.
Seminole Tribal Council (S# 10, map F5)
6073 Stirling Rd.
Hollywood, FL 33024 305-583-7112

ANCA Locations in Florida

Boyd Hill Nature Park (S# 11, map D3)
1101 Country Club Way South
St. Petersburg, FL 33705 813-893-7326

Briggs Nature Center (S# 12, map F4)
41 Shell Island Road
Naples, FL 33942 813-775-8569

Busch Gardens (S# 13, map D3)
PO Box 9158
Tampa, FL 33674-9158 813-988-5171

Castellow Hammock Nature Center (S# 14, map F5)
22301 SW 162 Ave.
Goulds, FL 33170 305-245-4321

Crowley Museum & Nature Center (S# 15, map D3)
16405Myakka Road
Sarasota, FL 34240 813-322-1000

Gumbo Limbo Nature Center (S# 16, map E5)
1801 North Ocean Blvd.
Boca Raton, FL 33432 407-337-1473

Hobe Sound Nature Center (S# 17, map E5)
PO Box 214
Hobe Sound, FL 33475 407-546-2067

Lee County Nature Center (S# 18, map E4)
3450 Ortiz Ave.
Fort Myers, FL 33906 813-275-3435

Lowry Park Zoological Garden (S# 19, map D3)
7530 North Blvd.
Tampa, FL 33604 813-935-8552

Moccasin Lake Nature Center (S# 20, map D3)
2750 Park Trail Lane
Clearwater, FL 34619-5601 813-462-6024

Morningside Nature Center (S# 21, map B3)
3540 East University Ave.
Gainesville, FL 32605 904-374-2170

Secret Woods Nature Center (S# 22, map F5)
2701 West State Road 84
Fort Lauderdale, FL 33025 305-792-8528

Suncoast Seabird Sanctuary (S# 23, map D3)
18328 Gulf Blvd.
Indian Shores, FL 34635 813-391-6211

Tree Hill Nature Center (S# 24, map A4)
7152 Lone Star Road
Jacksonville, FL 3221* 904-724-4646

Florida State Chamber of Commerce
136 So. Bronough St.
PO Box 11309 Phone 904-425-1200
Tallahassee, FL 32302-3309 Fax 904-425-1260

★ INFORMATION CHART ★

AGENCY/MAP LEGEND... INITIALS, MAP SYMBOLS, COLOR CODES

- U.S. Forest Service Supervisor & Ranger Dist. Offices ... NFS
- U.S. Army Corps of Engineers Rec. Areas & Offices ... COE
- USFWS National Wildlife Refuges & Offices ... NWR
- National Park Service Parks & other NPS Sites ... NPS
- Bureau of Land Management Rec. Areas & Offices ... BLM
- FL Aquatic Preserves (also see State Agency notes) ... AP
- State Parks (also see State Agency notes) ... SPS
- State Wildlife Areas (also see State Agency notes) ... SWA
- Private Preserves, Nature Centers & Tribal Lands
- The Wild Rivers ⟿ and Wilderness Areas ▓▒

INFORMATION CHART LEGEND - SYMBOLS & LETTER CODES

- ■ means YES & □ means Yes with disability provisions
- sp means spring, March through May
- S means Summer, June through August
- F means Fall September through November
- W means Winter, December through February
- T means Two (2) or Three (3) Seasons
- A means All Four (4) Seasons
- na means Not Applicable or Not Available
- Note: empty or blank spaces in the chart mean NO

Note: Refer to yellow block on page 7 (top right) for location name and address abbreviations. If a symbol number has a star ★ that symbol is not shown on the map.

LOCATION DATA

MAP	S#	LOCATION NAME (state initials if more than one) with ADDRESS and/or LOCATION DATA	TELEPHONE	ACRES / ELEVATION
A2	1	National Forests in Florida, 325 John Knox rd., Suite F-100, Tallahassee 32303	904-942-9300	1,134,089 / 10C
A1	2	Apalachicola NF & Ranger D., SH 20, PO Box 579, Bristol 32321 [S side of Hwy 20, adjacent to high school]	904-643-2283	287,635 / 10C
B2	3	Apalachicola NF, Wakulla Ranger D., Rt. #6, Box 7860, Crawfordville 32327 [E off Hwy. 319 at CR 267 & 2.25 mi S]	904-926-3561	276,333 / 10C
C4	4	Ocala NF, Lake George RD, 17147 East Hwy. 40, Silver Springs 34488 [N off Hwy. 40, 8 mi E of Ocklocknee R. bridge]	904-625-2520	203,493 / 100
C4	5	Ocala Nat'l. Forest, Seminole RD, 40929 State Road 19, Eustis 32784 [E off Hwy. 19, .075 mi N of Umatilla]	904-669-3153	179,673 / 100
B3	6	Osceola Nat'l. Forest & Ranger D., US 90, PO Box 70, Olustee 32072 [S off Hwy. 90, 1 mi W of Olustea]	904-752-2577	186,955 / 100
B4	2	COE, Jacksonville District, 400 W. Bay St., PO Box 4970, Jacksonville 32232	904-791-2215	na / na
B4	3	Cross Fla Barge Canal, PO Box 1317, Palatka 32178	904-328-2737	na / na
A4	4	Fernandina Harbor, PO Box 4970, Jacksonville 32232	904-232-2215	na / na
A4	4	Four River Basins, PO Box 4970, Jacksonville 32232	904-232-2215	na / na
E5	5	L. Okeechobee/WW, 525 Ridgelawn Rd., Clewiston 33440 [St. Lucie, Port Mayaca, Moore Haven, Ortona/WP Franklin ...ocks]	813-983-3335	na / na
F5	6	Miami Harbor, PO Box 4970, Jacksonville 32232	904-232-2215	na / na
	7	COE, Mobile District, 109 Saint Joseph St., PO Box 2288, Mobile, AL 36628	205-694-3720	na / na
A1	1	Lake Seminole, PO Box 96, Chattahoochee 32324	912-662-2001	145,000 / 12-17
E5	1	Arthur R. Marshall Loxahatchee NWR., Rt. #1, Box 278, Boynton Beach 33437	407-732-3684	145,000 / 12-17
E5	2	Hobe Sound NWR, PO Box 645, Hobe Sound 33475	407-546-6141	1,000 / 0-35
C3	3	Chassahowitzka NWR, 1502 SE Kings Bay Dr., Crystal River 34429	904-563-2088	30,500 / 0-10
C3	4	Crystal River NWR, 1502 SE Kings Bay Dr., Crystal River 34429	904-563-2088	40 / 0-5
C3	5	Egmont Key NWR, 1502 SE Kings Bay Dr., Crystal River 34429	904-563-2088	350 / 0-10
C3	6	Passage Key NWR (closed to public), 1502 SE Kings Bay Dr., Crystal River 34429	904-563-2088	30 / 0-10
C3	7	Pinellas NWR, 1502 SE Kings Bay Dr., Crystal River 34429	904-563-2088	500 / 0-10
C3	8	Florida Panther NWR (contact mgr.), 3860 Tollgate Blvd., Suite 30, Naples 33942 [not open to public]	813-353-8442	26,900 / na
E3	9	J. N. "Ding" Darling NWR, One Wildlife Drive, Sanibel 33957	813-472-1100	5,030 / 4
C4	10	Lake Woodruff NWR, 4490 Grand Ave., PO Box 488, DeLeon Springs 32130	904-985-4673	19,545 / na
B3	11	Lower Suwannee NWR, Rt. 1, Box 1193C, Chiefland 32626	904-493-0238	50,000 / 10
C3	12	Cedar Keys NWR, Rt. 1, Box 1193C, Chiefland 32626	904-493-0238	800 / 50
C5	13	Merritt Island NWR, PO Box 6504, Titusville 32782 [4 mi E of Titusville on SR 402]	407-861-0667	140,000 / 0-15
D5	14	Pelican Island NWR (not open to pub), PO Box 6504, Titusville 32782	407-861-0667	4,760 / 0-3
G4	15	National Key Deer Refuge, PC Box 430510, Big Pine Key 33043 [W end of Watson Blvd.]	305-872-2239	8,000 / 1-8
G4	16	Great White Heron NWR (boat access), PO Box 430510, Big Pine Key 33043	305-872-2239	7,400 / na
G4	17	Key West NWR (boat access only), PO Box 430510, Big Pine Key 33043	305-872-2239	2,019 / na
G2	18	St. Marks NWR, PO Box 68, St. Marks 32355 [25 mi S of Tallahassee along coast, S of US 98]	904-925-6121	65,000 / 0-45
B2	19	St. Vincent NWR, 479 Market St., PO Box 447, Apalachicola 32329 [N on market St. to boat basin]	904-653-8808	12,358 / na
F4	1	Big Cypress National Preserve, Star Route, Box 110, Ochopee 33943	813-695-2000	716,000 / 3
F5	2	Biscayne National Park, PO Box 1369, Homestead 33090	305-247-7275	173,000 / 4
C5	3	Canaveral National Seashore, 308 Julia St., Titusville 32796	407-267-1110	57,627 / na
F5	4	Everglades National Park, PO Box 279, Homestead 33030	305-242-7700	1,506,539 / na
G4	5	Dry Tortugas National Park, PO Box 6208, Key West 33041 [formerly Ft. Jefferson National Historic Site]	305-242-7700	64,700 / 0-4
D1	6	Gulf Islands National Seashore, 1801 Gulf Breeze Parkway, Gulf Breeze 32561 [VC 2 mi E of Gulf Breeze on US Hwy. 93]	904-934-2600	135,000 / 0-50
A2	1	DNR, Div. of State Lands, Bur. of Submerged Lands, MS 125, 3900 Commonwealth Ave., Tallahassee 32393	904-487-4436	na / na
B1	2	Alligator Harbor Aquatic Preserve, c/o FSU Marine Laboratory, Rt. #1, Box 456, Sopchoppy 32361	904-697-2218	14,402 / na
B1	3	Apalachicola Bay Aquatic Preserve, near Apalachicola	904-697-2218	80,000 / na
D5	4	Banana River Aquatic Preserve, Brevard County, near Melbourne	407-984-4807	29,700 / na
B2	5	Big Bend Seagrass Aquatic Preserve, along the Gulf Coast, from Yankeetown NW to, Panacea	904-697-2218	945,412 / na
D1	6	Biscayne Bay-No. Aquatic Preserve, from Cape Florida, to Monroe-Dade County Line, Cape Florida	305-451-4777	227,000 / na
F5	7	Biscayne Bay-So. Aquatic Preserve, part of Biscayne Bay No., near Cutler Ridge	305-451-4777	na / na
D3	8	Boca Ceiga Bay Aquatic Preserve, in Pinellas County near St. Petersburg	813-622-7364	22,000 / na
E3	9	Cape Haze Aquatic Preserve, in Charlotte County near Rotonda	813-283-2424	11,289 / na
F4	10	Cape Romano-10,000 Aquatic Preserve, in Collier County near Marco Island	813-283-2424	27,642 / na
D3	11	Cockroach Bay Aquatic Preserve, Hillsborough County, 8402 Laurel Fair Circle, Suite 212, Tampa 33610	813-622-7364	8,583 / na

★ INFORMATION CHART ★

AGENCY/MAP LEGEND . . . INITIALS, MAP SYMBOLS, COLOR CODES

U.S. Forest Service Supervisor & Ranger Dist. Offices NFS △61△
U.S. Army Corps of Engineers Rec. Areas & Offices . COE △31△
USFWS National Wildlife Refuges & Offices . . . . NWR △40△
National Park Service Parks & other NPS Sites . . . . . . NPS △7△
Bureau of Land Management Rec. Areas & Offices . . BLM △26△
FL Aquatic Preserves (also see State Agency notes) . . AP △35△
State Parks (also see State Agency notes) . . . . SPS △52△
State Wildlife Areas (also see State Agency notes) . . SWA △19△
Private Preserves, Nature Centers & Tribal Lands . . ▨△15△
The Wild Rivers ～～ and Wilderness Areas

Note: Refer to yellow block on page 7 (top right) for location name and address abbreviations.

INFORMATION CHART LEGEND - SYMBOLS & LETTER CODES

■ means **YES** & ☐ means **Yes with disability provisions**

- **sp** means **spring**, March through May
- **S** means **Summer**, June through August
- **F** means **Fall**, September through November
- **W** means **Winter**, December through February
- **T** means **Two (2)** or **Three (3)** Seasons
- **A** means **All Four (4)** Seasons
- **na** means **Not Applicable or Not Available**

Note: empty or blank spaces in the chart mean **NO**
★ that symbol is not shown on the map.

S#	MAP	LOCATION NAME (state initials if more than one) with ADDRESS and/or LOCATION DATA	TELEPHONE	ACRES / ELEVATION	S#
12	G4	Coupon Bight Aquatic Preserve, in Monroe County near Marathon	305-451-4777	9,000 / na	12
13	E4	Estero Bay Aquatic Preserve, in Lee County near Ft. Myers Beach	813-283-2424	11,300 / na	13
14	A4	Ft. Clinch SP Aquatic Preserve, in Nassau County near Fernandina Beach	904-348-2710	9,000 / na	14
15	D1	Ft. Pickens SP Aquatic Preserve, Escambia & Santa Rosa Counties, 41 N Jefferson St., Suite 402, Pensacola 32591	904-444-8608	34,000 / na	15
16	E3	Gasparilla Sound-Charlotte Hbr. AP, Lee & Charlotte Counties, 13960 Stringfellow Blvd., Bokeelia 33922	813-283-2424	80,000 / na	16
17	B4	Guana River Aquatic Preserve, in St. Johns County near St. Augustine	904-348-2710	11,500 / na	17
18	D5	Indian River-No. Aquatic Preserve (from Malabar to Vero Beach), 12 E. Melbourne Ave., Suite A, Melbourne 32901	407-984-4807	27,800 / na	18
19	D5	Indian River-So. Aquatic Preserve (Vero Beach to Ft.Pierce Inlet), 4842 South US 1, Ft. Pierce 34982	407-468-4097	12,000 / na	19
20	D5	Jensen Beach Aquatic Preserve, Martin, Palm Beach & St. Lucie Cos., 4842 South US 1, Ft. Pierce 34982	407-468-4097	26,000 / na	20
21	A2	Lake Jackson Aquatic Preserve, Leon County, 3900 Commonwealth Blvd., Tallahassee 32301	904-487-4436	4,710 / na	21
22	C4	Lake Weir Aquatic Preserve, Marion Co. near Weirsdale, c/o 107 N Park Ave., Suite 6, Inverness 32650	904-637-4210	6,380 / na	22
23	E5	Lemon Bay Aquatic Preserve, Lemon & Sarasota Cos., near Englewood	813-283-2424	10,000 / na	23
24	G5	Lignumvitae Key Aquatic Preserve, Lignumvitae Key in Monroe County, near Islamorada	305-451-4777	8,320 / na	24
25	E5	Loxahatchee River-L. Worth Creek AP, Martin & Palm Beach Cos., near Jupiter	407-468-4097	9,000 / na	25
26	E4	Matlacha Pass Aquatic Preserve, Lee County, Cape Coral	813-283-2424	14,000 / na	26
27	C5	Mosquito Lagoon Aquatic Preserve, Brevard & Volusia Cos., near Mims	407-984-4807	36,000 / na	27
28	D5	N. Fork St. Lucie Aquatic Preserve, Martin & St. Lucie Cos., near Port St. Lucie	407-468-4097	6,100 / na	28
29	A4	Nassau River Aquatic Preserve, Highland Bldg., Suite 201, 4151 Woodcock Dr., Jacksonville 32207	904-348-2710	85,000 / na	29
30	B4	Oklawaha River Aquatic Preserve, Marion County near Fort McCoy	904-637-4210	na / na	30
31	B4	Pellicer Creek Aquatic Preserve, Flagler & St. John Cos., near Marineland	904-348-2710	505 / na	31
32	E4	Pine Island Sound Aquatic Preserve, Lee County, near Sanibel	813-283-2424	62,000 / na	32
33	D3	Pinellas County Aquatic Preserve, Pinellas County, near Clearwater	813-622-7364	336,265 / na	33
34	C3	Rainbow Springs Aquatic Preserve, Marion County, PO Box 1316, Dunnellon 32630	904-489-5297	4,000 / na	34
35	D2	Rocky Bayou SP Aquatic Preserve, Okaloosa County, Niceville	904-444-8608	480 / na	35
36	F4	Rookery Bayou Aquatic Preserve, Collier County, Naples	813-283-2424	32,035 / na	36
37	B1	St. Andrews Bay SP Aquatic Preserve, Bay County, Panama City	904-444-8608	25,000 / na	37
38	B1	St. Joseph Bay Aquatic Preserve, Gulf County, Port St. Joe	904-697-2218	74,000 / na	38
39	C3	St. Martins Marsh Aquatic Preserve, Marsh & Citrus Cos., 10550 W. Fort Is. Trail, Crystal River 32629	904-563-1136	23,123 / na	39
40	D3	Terra Ceiga Aquatic Preserve (near Bradenton), 8402 Laurel Fair Circle, Suite 212, Tampa 33610	813-622-7364	25,786 / na	40
41	B4	Tomoka Marsh Aquatic Preserve, Volusia County, Ormond Beach	407-330-6727	7,000 / na	41
42	C4	Wekiva River Aquatic Preserve, Lake, Orange & Seminole Cos., 8300 West SR 46, Sanford 32771	407-330-6727	19,000 / na	42
43	D1	Yellow River Marsh Aquatic Preserve, Santa Rosa County, near Milton	904-444-8608	16,435 / na	43
1	A2	**DNR, Florida Park Service.** Mail Station 525, 3900 Commonwealth Blvd., Tallahassee 32399	904-488-8241	na / na	1
2	D1	Big Lagoon SRA, near Gulf Beach	904-488-8241	na / na	2
3	C4	Blue Spring SP, near Orange City	904-488-8241	na / na	3
4	A1	Florida Caverns SP, near Marianna	904-488-8241	na / na	4
5	A4	Fort Clinch SP, near Fernandina Beach	904-488-8241	na / na	5
6	G5	John Pennekamp Coral Reef SP, near Key Largo	904-488-8241	na / na	6
7	B3	Paynes Prairie SP, near Gainesville	904-488-8241	na / na	7
8	A2	Wakulla Springs SP, near Tallahassee	904-222-7279	na / na	8
1	A2	**Florida Game & Fresh Water Fish Commission,** 620 S. Meridian St., Tallahassee 32399 [Farris Bryant Bldg.]	904-488-4676	na / na	1
2	C3	Central Region G&FWFC, 1239 SW 10th St., Ocala 32674	904-732-1225	na / na	2
3	D4	Bull Creek WMA, near Deer Park	904-732-1225	22,206 / na	3
4	C3	Citrus WMA, near Lebanon	904-732-1225	41,000 / na	4
5	C4	Farmton WMA, W of Titusville	904-732-1225	52,170 / na	5
6	B4	Fort McCoy WMA, near Fort McCoy	904-732-1225	12,482 / na	6
7	B4	Georgia-Pacific WMA, near Bostwick	904-732-1225	11,000 / na	7
8	B4	Guana River WMA, near Palm Valley	904-732-1225	8,700 / na	8
9	C3	Jumper Creek WMA, near Rutland	904-732-1225	10,068 / na	9
10	B4	Ocala WMA, near Ocala	904-732-1225	382,000 / na	10

#	Grid	Site	Phone	Acres
12	C4	Richloam WMA, near Webster	904-732-1225	na / na
13	C4	Rock Springs Run WMA, near Winter Garden	904-732-1225	9,000 / na
14	C4	Seminole Ranch WMA, NE of Christmas	904-732-1225	6,000 / na
15	D4	Three Lakes WMA, N of Oasis	904-732-1225	43,000 / na
16	C4	Tosohatchee WMA, near Christmas	904-732-1225	28,000 / na
17	E5	Everglades Region G&FWFC, 551 N. Military Trail, West Palm Beach 33406	407-640-6100	na / na
18	F4	Big Cypress WMA, in Collier & Monroe Cos., E of Naples	407-640-6100	564,320 / 0
19	E5	Browns Farm WMA, off Canal, near Browns Farm	407-640-6100	4,460 / 0
20	E5	Dupuis WMA, S of SR 76, near Port Mayaca	407-640-6100	21,935 / 0
21	F5	East Everglades W.E.A., in Dade County, near Homestead	407-640-6100	62,560 / 0
22	E5	Everglades WMA, W Dade, Broward & Palm Bch. Cos., W of US 27 and SW of West Palm Beach	407-640-6100	671,831 / 0
23	E5	Holy Land WMA, off US 27, south of Okeelanta	407-640-6100	35,350 / 0
24	E5	J. W. Corbett WMA, off SR 710 (the Beeline), near West Palm Beach	407-640-6100	57,892 / 0
25	E4	Rothenberger WMA, near Miami Canal, SE of Devil's Garden	407-640-6100	27,810 / 0
26	B3	Northeast Region G&FWFC, Rt. #7, Box 440, Lake City 32055	904-758-0525	na / ra
27	B3	Andrews WMA, Levy County, on US 19, 5 mi. N of Chiefland	904-758-0525	3,800 / ra
28	B2	Aucilla WMA, Taylor Co., on Hwy. 98, 17 mi. W of Perry	904-758-0525	74,000 / ra
29	A3	Big Shoals WMA, Hamilton Co., on CR 135, 2 mi. NE of White Springs	904-758-0525	3,500 / ra
30	B4	Camp Blanding WMA, Clay Co., on SR 16, 8 mi. E of Starke	904-758-0525	62,340 / ra
31	A4	Cary WMA, Nassau Co., on US 301, S of Callahan	904-758-0525	3,400 / na
32	C3	Cedar Key Scrub WMA, Levy Co., 4 mi. from, Cedar Key	904-758-0525	4,000 / na
33	A3	Cypress Creek WMA, Hamilton Co., on SR 6, 18 mi. E of Jasper	904-758-0525	19,934 / na
34	C3	Gulf Hammock WMA, Levy Co., on SR 40A, 3 mi. W of Inglis	904-758-0525	26,950 / na
35	B2	Jena WMA, Dixie Co., on CR 358, 1 mi. S of Steinhatchee	904-758-0525	27,714 / na
36	B3	Lake Butler WMA, Baker, Columbia & Union Cos., on US 90, 3 mi. E of Lake City	904-758-0525	106,479 / na
37	B3	Lochloosa WMA, Alachua Co., on SR 20, 11 mi. E of Gainesville	904-758-0525	31,751 / na
38	A4	Nassau WMA, Nassau Co., on Hwy., A1A, 4 mi. NW of Callahan	904-758-0525	40,168 / na
39	A3	Occidental WMA, Hamilton Co., on US 441, 7 mi. N of White Springs	904-758-0525	1,400 / na
40	A3	Osceola WMA, Columbia Co., on US 90, 3 mi. E of Lake City	904-758-0525	177,762 / na
41	B3	Perpetual WMA, Dixie Co., on CR 349, 10 mi. SW of Old Town	904-758-0525	41,380 / na
42	B4	Raiford WMA, Union Co., on SR 125, 10 mi. S of MacClenny	904-758-0525	9,000 / na
43	B4	Santa Fe Swamp W.E.A., Clay Co., 5 mi. NE of Keystone Heights	904-758-0525	5,500 / na
44	B3	Steinhatchee WMA, Dixie Co., 1 mi. N of Cross City	904-758-0525	32,700 / na
45	B2	Tide Swamp WMA, Taylor Co., on CR 361, 2 mi. N of Steinhatchee	904-758-0525	18,879 / na
46	A1	Northwest Region G&FWFC, 6938 Hwy. 2321, Panama City 32409	904-265-3676	na / ne
47	A1	Apalachee WMA, SW of Tallahassee in Jackson Co., near Sneads	904-265-3676	7,952 / na
48	B1	Apalachicola W.E.A., lower Apalachicola River S of Wewahitchka	904-265-3676	46,992 / na
49	A2	Apalachicola WMA, in a 4 county area SW of Tallahassee	904-265-3676	558,380 / na
50	D1	Blackwater WMA, in Santa Rosa & Okaloosa Cos. N of Milton	904-265-3676	186,395 / na
51	D1	Champion International WMA, in Escanaba County N of Pensacola	904-265-3676	21,078 / na
52	B1	Edward Ball WMA, in Gulf County S of Wewahitchka	904-265-3676	66,270 / na
53	A1	Escanaba River WMA, near Panama City	904-265-3676	56,188 / na
54	A2	Joe Budd WMA, in Gadsden County near Quincy	904-265-3676	7,383 / na
55	A1	Moore's Pasture WMA, in Bay County near Panama City	904-265-3676	42,810 / na
56	A2	Ochlockonee River WMA, in Leon County near Tallahassee	904-265-3676	2,790 / na
57	D2	Point Washington WMA, Bay & Walton Cos. near Point Washington	904-265-3676	88,280 / na
58	A1	Robert Brent WMA, in Liberty & Gadsden Cos. S of Quincy	904-265-3676	79,979 / na
59	A2	Talquin WMA, in Leon County W of Tallahassee	904-265-3676	2,993 / na
60	D4	South Region G&FWFC, 3900 Drane Field Rd., Lakeland 33803	813-644-9269	na / na
61	D4	Arbuckle WMA, E of Old Avon Rd., on L. Arbuckle Rd. near Avon Park	813-644-9269	13,500 / 60
62	E4	Cecil M. Webb WMA, I-75, exit 27 near Punta Gorda	813-644-9269	65,340 / 40
63	C3	Croom WMA, on Croom Rd. 5 mi. E of Brooksville	813-644-9269	20,560 / 50
64	C4	Green Swamp WMA, 6.3 mi. N of US 98 on SR 471 near Dade City	813-644-9269	48,050 / 30
65	D4	IMC WMA, S of SR 640 on SR 555 near Bartow	813-644-9269	720 / 40
66	D3	Upper Hillsborough WMA, 1.5 mi. W of US 98 on Hwy. 54 near Zephyrhills	813-644-9269	5,180 / 30

Florida Audubon Society (Administrative Office), 460 Hwy. 436, Suite 200, Casselberry 32707

#	Grid	Site	Phone	Acres
1	C4		407-260-8300	na / na
2	D5	Turkey Cr. Sanct./Margaret Hem., PO Box 060175, Palm Bay 329061 [E on Malabar Bl. and over Turkey Creek Bridge]	407-952-3443	30 / na
3	C4	Birds of Prey Ctr, 1101 Audubon Way, Maitland 32751 [off I-4 Lee Rd., L on Wymore, R on Kennedy, L on East Ave.]	407-644-0190	3 / na
4	E4	**NAS Corkscrew Swamp Sanct.**, Sanctuary Road, Rt #6, Box 1875-A, Naples 33964 [I-75 exit 17/CR 864 25 mi NE of Naples]	813-657-3771	11,000 / 20
5	C4	**TNC Florida Regional Office**, 2699 Lee Road, Suite 500, Winter Park 32789	904-628-5887	na / na
6	A1	Apalachicola Bluffs Preserve, c/o NW FL Land Steward, 625 North Adams St., Tallahassee 32301 [N of Bristol]	904-222-0199	6,267 / na
7	E5	Blowing Rocks Preserve, 575 S Beach Rd., CR 707, Juniper I., PO Box 3795, Tequesta 33469	407-575-2297	73 / 0-25
8	D4	Tiger Creek Preserve, c/o Central FL Land Steward, 225 E. Stuart Ave., PO Box 1319, Lake Wales 33859	813-678-1551	4,400 / 100

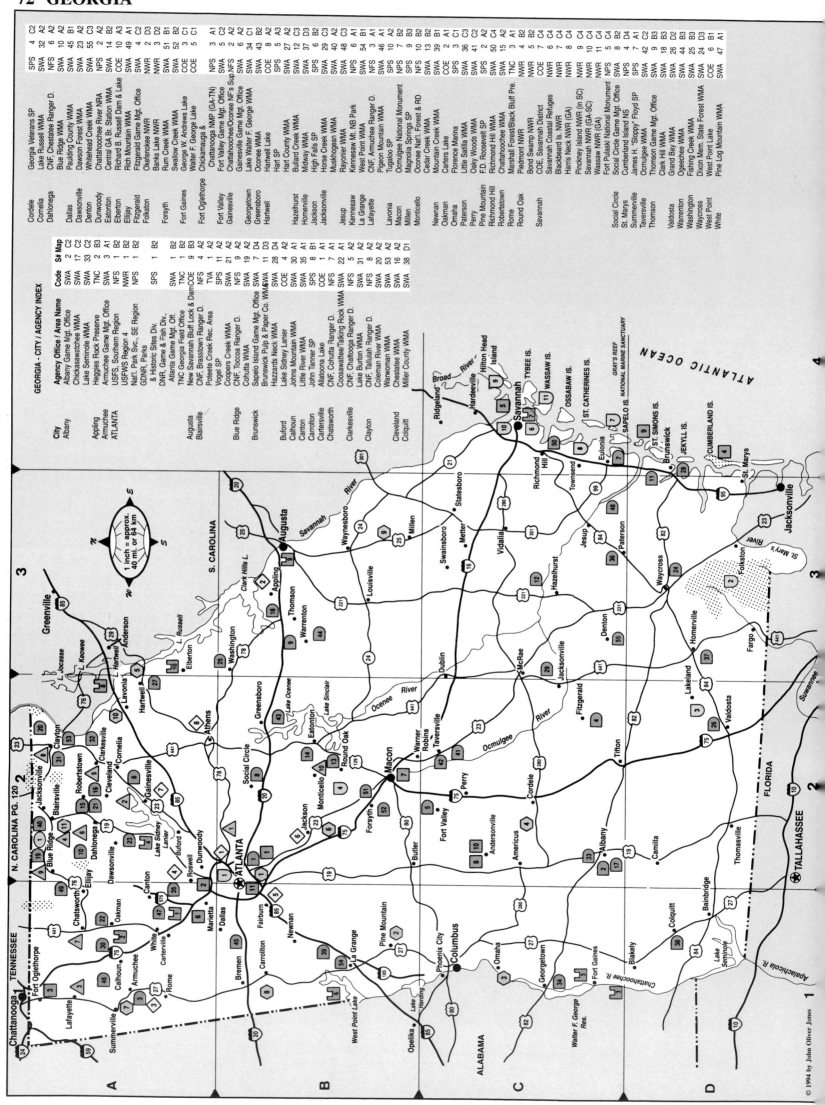

GEORGIA NOTES

Summary

There are 46 federal, 67 state, and 9 private recreation areas or local administrative offices covered in this state chapter. Of these, 52 appear in the Information Chart and 70 are covered in the notes. The special indexes feature 13 federally designated wilderness areas and wild rivers, and 5 agency published outdoor maps.

Federal Agencies

U.S. Forest Service

The Brasstown Bald Visitor Center features a unique building atop the highest peak in the state serves as a 360 degree scenic overlook. Exhibits here interpret the cultural and natural history of the southern Appalachian Mountains, and the role the USFS plays in resource management and conservation. Contact the Chattahoochee National Forest (CNF) Brasstown Ranger District Office (see S# 4, map A2) near Bairsville for access details.

U.S. Army Corps of Engineers (COE)

South Atlantic Division
77 Forsyth Street, SW, Room 313
Atlanta, GA 30335-6801   404-331-6746

The Jacksonville, Florida, Mobile, Alabama, Savannah, Georgia, and Wilmington, North Carolina District Offices manage COE projects in the South Atlantic area (see information charts).

USFWS National Wildlife Refuges

The Savannah Coastal Refuges Complex manages seven refuges. Two of them, Tybee NWR and Wolf Island NWR, are closed to the public at this time. The Pinckney Island NWR is located in South Carolina but it is listed in this chapter. These refuges extend along a 100-mile stretch of Georgia-South Carolina coastline.

National Park Service

Additional NPS Locations in Georgia

Andersonville National Historic Site (495 acres)
(S# 8, map C2)
Route 1, Box 85
Andersonville, GA 31711   912-924-0343

Fort Frederica National Monument (216 acres)
(S# 9, map D4)
Route 9, Box 286-C
St. Simmons Island, GA 31522   912-638-3639

Jimmy Carter National Historic Site
(70 acres) (S# 10, map C2)
c/o Andersonville National Historic Site
Route 1, Box 85
Andersonville, GA 31711   912-824-3413

Martin Luther King, Jr. National Historic Site (23 acres)
(S# 11, map B2)
522 Auburn Ave., NE
Atlanta, GA 30312   404-331-3920

USDC, Natl. Oceanic & Atmospheric Admin. (NOAA)

National Ocean Service
For Natl. Marine Sanctuary (NMS) information contact:

Gray's Reef National Marine Sanctuary
PO Box 13687
Savannah, GA 31416
Gray's Reef lies about 18 miles east of Sapelo Island (see Georgia map C4).

Wilderness/Wild River Index

Wilderness Areas

Chattahoochee (& Oconee) NF Sup. (S# 2, map A2)
Big Frog Wilderness - 83 acres
Brasstown Wilderness - 11,405 acres
Cohutta Wilderness - 35,247 acres
Ellicott Rock Wilderness - 2,181 acres
Raven Cliffs Wilderness - 8, 562 acres
Rich Mountain Wilderness - 9,649 acres
Southern Nantahala Wilderness - 12,439 acres
Tray Mountain Wilderness - 9,702 acres

Blackbeard Island NWR (S# 7, map C4)
Blackbeard Island Wilderness - 3,000 acres
Okeefenokee NWR (S# 2, map D3)
Okeefenokee Wilderness - 353,981 acres
Savannah Coastal Refuges (S# 10, map C4)
Wolf Island Wilderness - 5,126 acres

Cumberland Island Natl. Seashore (S# 4, map D4)
Cumberland Island Wilderness - 8,840 acres

Wild Rivers

Chattooga Wild River - also in NC and SC
Chattahoochee National Forest (S#2, map A2)

Outdoor Map Index

U.S. Forest Service Maps

States within the USFS Southern Region are Alabama, Arkansas, Florida, Georgia, Kentucky, Louisiana, Mississippi, N. and S. Carolina, Tennessee, Texas, and Virginia. USFS maps are listed under those states as appropriate.

Appalachian Trail, GA Section, Chattahoochee NF [1981]
Chattahoochee National Forest [1988]
Scale: 1 inch = 2.0 miles (1 cm = 1.3 km)
Chattooga National Wild & Scenic River [1981]
Cohutta Wilderness-Chattahoochee/Cherokee [1981]
Oconee National Forest [1981]

State Agencies

Department of Natural Resources

205 Butler St., SE
Suite 1252, East Towers
Atlanta, GA 30334   404-656-6374
Coastal Resources, Parks, and Game and Fish Divisions operate under this agency in Georgia.

Parks, Recreation & Historical Sites Division

A free tourist kit, *Georgia On My Mind*, includes a color guide to Georgia's state parks (51 state parks) and historic sites, with information on facilities and activities available, and user fees. A state road map is included.

A selected number of Georgia Parks are listed below and are indicated on the Guide map.

S#	MAP	Name & Location
1	B2	Parks, Rec. & Hist. Div., Atlanta
2	B1	F.D. Roosevelt SP, Pine Mountain
3	C1	Florence Marina, Omaha
4	C2	Georgia Veterans SP, Cordele
5	A3	Hart SP, Hartwell
6	B2	High Falls SP, Jackson
7	A1	James H. "Sloppy" Floyd SP, Summerville
8	B1	John Tanner SP, Carrolton
9	B3	Magnolia Springs SP, Millen
10	A2	Tugaloo SP, Lavonia
11	A2	Vogel SP, Blairsville

Game and Fish Division (GFD)

(S# 1, map B2)
A hunting map, WMA access information, and regulations are part of the hunting regulations. Permits are required for some quota hunts. A quarterly outdoor report with limited circulation is published.

The information Chart lists the division HQ and eight Georgia Game Management Offices. The below listed WMAs are featured on the Georgia map.

S#	MAP	Name & Location
10	A2	Blue Ridge WMA, Dahlonega
11	D3	Brunswick Pulp & P. Co. WMA, Brunswick
12	C3	Bullard Creek WMA, Hazelhurst
13	B2	Cedar Creek WMA, Monticello
14	B2	Central GA Branch Station WMA, Eatonton
15	A2	Chattahoochee WMA, Robertstown
16	A2	Chestatee WMA, Cleveland
17	C2	Chickasawatchee WMA, Albany
18	B3	Clark Hill WMA, Thomson
19	A2	Cohutta WMA, Blue Ridge
20	A2	Coleman River WMA, Clayton
21	A2	Coopers Creek WMA, Blairsville
22	A1	Coosawattee/Talking Rock WMA, Chatsworth
23	A2	Dawson Forest WMA, Dawsonville
24	C3	Dixon Mem. State Forest WMA, Waycross
25	A2	Fishing Creek WMA, Washington
26	D2	Grand Bay WMA, Valdosta
27	A2	Hart County WMA, Hartwell
28	D4	Hazzards Neck WMA, Brunswick
29	C3	Horse Creek WMA, Jacksonville
30	A1	Johns Mountain WMA, Calhoun
31	A2	Lake Burton WMA, Clarksville
32	A2	Lake Russell WMA, Cornelia
32	C1	Lake Seminole WMA, Albany
33	C2	Lake Walter F. George WMA, Georgetown
35	A1	Little River WMA, Canton
36	C3	Little Satilla WMA, Paterson
37	D3	Midway WMA, Homerville
38	D*	Miller County WMA, Colquitt
39	B*	Mountain Creek WMA, Newnan
40	A2	Muskhogean WMA, Jacksonville
41	C2	Oaky Woods WMA, Perry
42	C2	Ocmulgee WMA, Taversville
43	B2	Oconee WMA, Greensboro
44	B3	Ogeechee WMA, Warrenton
45	B1	Paulding County WMA, Dallas
46	A1	Pigeon Mountain WMA, Lafayette
47	A1	Pine Log Mountain WMA, White
48	C3	Rayonier WMA, Jesup
49	A1	Rich Mountain WMA, Ellijay

S#	MAP	Name & Location
50	C4	Richmond Hill WMA, Richmond Hill
51	B2	Rum Creek WMA, Forsyth
52	B2	Swallow Creek WMA, Forsyth
53	A2	Warwoman WMA, Clayton
54	B1	West Point WMA, La Grange
55	C3	Whitehead Creek WMA, Denton

Georgia Forestry Commission

There is no state forest recreation program in Georgia.

Tourist Division

PO Box 1776
Atlanta, GA 30301   404-656-3590
out of state   1-800-847-4842
The official Dept. of Transportation road map has symbols for state park or natural areas, camp sites, and historic sites. Park, forest, or preserve land boundaries are shown in color.

Private Organizations

ANCA Locations in Georgia

Chattahoochee Nature Center (S# 4, map A2)
9135 Willeo Road
Roswell, GA 30075   404-992-2055

Cochran Mill Nature Center (S# 5, map B1)
PO Box 911
Fairburn, GA 30213   404-964-1421

Dauset Trails Nature Center (S# 6, map B2)
Route 5, Box 38
Jackson, GA 30233   404-775-6798

Elachee Nature Science Center (S# 7, map A2)
2125 Elachee Drive
Gainesville, GA 30504   404-775-6798

Sandy Creek Nature Center (S# 8, map A2)
Old Commerce Road
Athens, GA 30607   404-354-2930

Business Council of Georgia

(State Chamber of Commerce)
233 Peachtree St., #200   Phone 404-223-2264
Atlanta, GA 30303-1504   Fax 404-223-2290

★ INFORMATION CHART ★

AGENCY/MAP LEGEND . . . INITIALS, MAP SYMBOLS, COLOR CODES

U.S. Forest Service Supervisor & Ranger Dist. Offices . NFS [61]
U.S. Army Corps of Engineers Rec. Areas & Offices . . COE [31]
USFWS National Wildlife Refuges & Offices . . . . NWR [40]
National Park Service Parks & other NPS Sites . . . . . NPS [7]
Bureau of Land Management Rec. Areas & Offices . . . BLM [26]
Tennessee Valley Authority Offices & Sites . . . . TVA [8]
State Parks (also see State Agency notes) . . . . SPS [52]
State Wildlife Areas (also see State Agency notes) . . SWA [19]
Private Preserves, Nature Centers & Tribal Lands . . . [15]
The Wild Rivers ——— and Wilderness Areas ▒▒▒

Note: Refer to yellow block on page 7 (top right)

INFORMATION CHART LEGEND - SYMBOLS & LETTER CODES

■ means YES & □ means Yes with disability provisions
sp means spring, March through May
S means Summer, June through August
F means Fall, September through November
W means Winter, December through February
T means Two (2) or Three (3) Seasons
A means All Four (4) Seasons
na means Not Applicable or Not Available

Note: empty or blank spaces in the chart mean NO and ★ that symbol is not shown on the map.

If a symbol number has a ★ (top right) for location name and address abbreviations.

S#	MAP	LOCATION NAME (state initials if more than one) with ADDRESS and/or LOCATION DATA	TELEPHONE	ACRES / ELEVATION
1	B2	**U.S. Forest Svc., Southern Region,** 1720 Peachtree Road NW, Atlanta 30367	404-347-4191	na / na
2	A2	Chattahoochee & Oconee NFs Sup., 508 Oak Street, NW, Gainesville 30501 [ask about Visitor Centers]	404-536-0541	750,000 / 1,200-5,000
3	A1	CNF, Armuchee RD, 806 E. Villanow St., PO Box 465, Lafayette 30728 [0.25 mi E of US 27 bypass, right side street]	706-638-1085	64,508 / 600-1,800
4	A2	CNF, Brasstown Ranger D., Hwy. 19/129 South, Blairsville 30512	706-745-6928	108,000 / 1,750-4,780
5	A2	CNF, Chattooga RD, Hwy. 197 N. Burton Rd., PO Box 196, Clarkesville 30523 [0.5 mi from Clarkesville on SR 197 N]	706-754-6221	105,000 / 800-3,200
6	A2	CNF, Chestatee Ranger D., 1015 Tipton Dr., PO Box 2080, Dahlonega 30533	404-864-6173	na / na
7	A1	CNF, Cohutta Ranger D., 401 Old Ellijay Road, Chatsworth 30705	404-695-6736	108,000 / 850-4,150
8	A2	CNF, Tallulah Ranger D., Hwy 441, PO Box 438, Clayton 30525	706-782-3320	164,000 / 1,200-4,696
9	A2	CNF, Toccoa Ranger D., E. Main St., Owenby Bldg., Suite 5, Blue Ridge 30513	706-632-3031	115,000 / 1,700-4,100
10	B2	Oconee Nat'l. Forest & Ranger D., 349 Forsythe St., Monticello 31064	404-468-2244	110,000 / 600-600
11	B2	Ozark-St. Francis N. Forests, Sup., 605 W. Main St., PO Box 1008, Russellville, AR 72801	501-968-2354	1,144,056 / na
1	A1	**COE, Mobile District,** 109 St. Joseph St., PO Box 2288, Mobile, AL 36628	205-694-3720	na / na
2	A1	Allatoona Lake, PO Box 487, Cartersville 30120	404-382-4700	na / na
3	C1	Carters Lake, PO Box 96, Oakman 30732	706-334-2248	na / na
		George W. Andrews Lake, Rt. 1, Box 176, Fort Gaines 31751	912-768-2516	na / na
4	A2	Lake Sidney Lanier, PO Box 567, Buford 30518	404-945-9531	na / na
5	C1	Walter F. George Lake, Rt. 1, Box 176, Fort Gaines 31751	912-768-2516	na / na
6	B1	West Point Lake, 500 Resource Management Drive, West Point 31833	706-645-2937	na / na
7	C4	COE, Savannah District, PO Box 889, Savannah 31402	912-944-5997	na / na
8	A2	Hartwell Lake, PO Box 278, Hartwell 30643	706-376-4788	na / na
9	B3	New Savannah Bluff Lock & Dam, Rt. 3, Box 49, Augusta 30906	706-793-9403	na / na
10	A3	Richard B. Russell Dam & Lake, Rt. 4, Box 224b, Elberton 30635	404-283-8731	na / na
1	B2	**USFWS Region 4,** R.B. Russell FOB, 75 Spring St. SW, Atlanta 30303 [AL, AR, FL, GA, KY, LA, MS, NC, SC, TN, PR]	404-331-3588	na / na
2	D3	Okefenokee NWR, Rt. #2, Box 338, Folkston 31537 [11 mi SW of Folkston off Hwys. 121/23]	912-496-3331	396,000 / 114-128
3	D2	Banks Lake NWR, (adm. by Okefenoke N, Rt. #2, Box 338, Folkston 31537 [W of Lakeland off Hwy. 122]	912-496-3331	3,500 / 0-200
4	B2	Piedmont NWR, Round Oak/Juliette Rd., Rt. 1, Box 670, Round Oak 31038	912-986-5441	35,000 / 640
5	D2	Bond Swamp NWR (not open to public), Rt. 1, Box 670, Round Oak 31038	912-986-5441	4,500 / 270
6	C4	Savannah Coastal Refuges, 1000 Business Center Dr., Suite 10, Savannah 31405 [Chatham Pkwy. S, 1.5 mi off I-16]	912-652-4415	53,340 / na
7	C4	Blackbeard Is. NWR (GA, see Coastal Refuges above, Savannah [18 mi. from Harris Neck]	912-652-4415	5,618 / na
8	C4	Harris Neck NWR (GA), see Coastal Refuges above, Savannah [off I-95, Hwy. 17 E then 131, Townsend]	912-652-4415	2,765 / na
9	C4	Pinckney Island NWR (in So. Carolin, see Coastal Refuges above, Savannah [on US 278, 0.5 mi. W of Hilton Hd. Is.]	912-652-4415	4,053 / na
10	C4	Savannah NWR (GA-SC), see Coastal Refuges above, Savannah [off I-95 at exit 5 take Hwy. 17 South to NWR]	912-652-4415	25,608 / na
11	C4	Wassaw NWR (GA, access by boat), see Coastal Refuges above, Savannah [near Savannah]	912-652-4415	10,070 / na
1	B2	**Nat'l. Park Svc.,** SE Region, Richard B. Russell FOB, Room 1004, 75 Spring St. SW, Atlanta 30303	404-331-5187	na / na
2	A2	Chattahoochee River NRA, 1978 Island Ford Pkwy, Dunwoody 30350 [from I-285 take SR 400 N, exit #6 & follow signs]	404-399-8070	4,100 / 800-1,000
3	A1	Chickamauga & Chattanooga NMP (GA/TN), PO Box 2128, Fort Oglethorpe 30742 [VC on US 27 in Ft. Oglethorpe]	706-866-9241	8,100 / 600-2,200
4	D4	Cumberland Island Nat'l. Seashore, PO Box 806, St. Marys 31558	912-882-4335	36,415 / 15
5	C4	Fort Pulaski National Monument, PO Box 30757, Savannah 31410 [15 mi E of Savannah, off Hwy. 80 East]	912-786-5787	5,623 / na
6	A1	Kennesaw Mt. National Battlefield P., 900 Kennesaw Mtn. Dr., Kennesaw 30144	404-427-4686	2,884 / 1,100-1,808
7	B2	Ocmulgee National Monument, 1207 Emery Highway, Macon 31201	912-752-8257	683 / na
1	A2	**TVA - Central District,** 1101 Congress Parkway, Athens, TN 37303	615-632-2088	na / na
1	A2	Poteete Creek Rec. Area, NW of Blairsville (GA Hwy. 325)	615-745-1783	na / na
1	B2	**DNR, Parks & Historic Sites Div.** (see notes), 205 Butler St., Atlanta 30334 [from out of state call 800-542-7275]	800-342-7275	na / na
1	B2	**DNR, Game & Fish Div.** Atlanta Game, 205 Butler St., SE, Atlanta 30334 [office in Floyd Towers East, Suite 1362]	404-656-3522	na / na
2	C2	Albany Game Management Office, 2024 Newton Rd., Albany 31708	912-430-4254	na / na
3	A1	Armuchee Game Management Office, 2592 Floyd Springs Rd., NE, Armuchee 30105	404-295-6041	na / na
4	C2	Fitzgerald Game Management Office, Rt. #1, Box 1820, Fitzgerald 31750	404-423-2988	na / na
5	C2	Fort Valley Game Management Office, Rt. #3, Box 75, Fort Valley 31030	912-825-6354	na / na
6	A2	Gainesville Game Management Office, 2150 Dawsonville Hwy., Gainesville 30501	404-535-5700	na / na
7	D4	Sapelo Island Game Mgt. Office, 1 Conservation Way, Brunswick 31523	912-262-3173	na / na

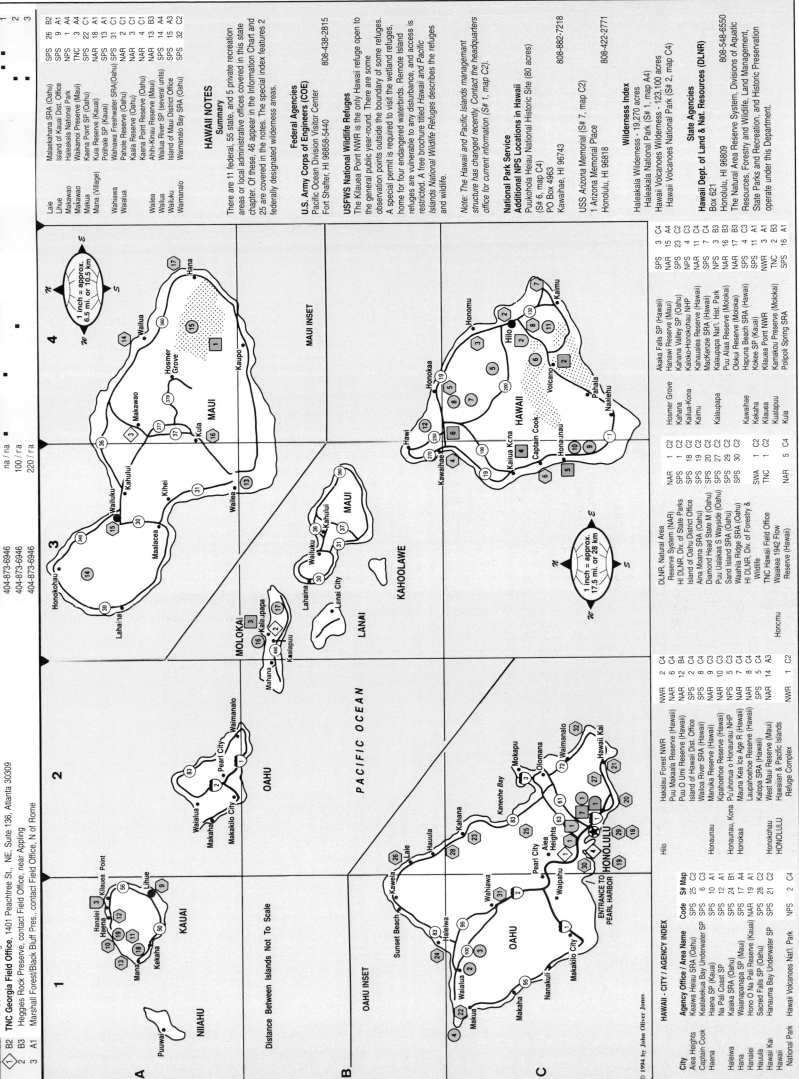

Thomson Game Management Office, Thomson 404-595-4211
TNC Georgia Field Office, 1401 Peachtree St., NE, Suite 136, Atlanta 30309 404-873-6946
Heggies Rock Preserve, contact Field Office, near Appling 404-873-6946
Marshall Forest/Black Bluff Pres., contact Field Office, N of Rome 404-873-6946

City	Agency Office / Area Name	Code	S#	Map
Laie	Maleekahana SRA (Oahu)	SPS	26	B2
Lihue	Island of Kauai Dist. Office	SPS	9	A1
Makawao	Haleakala National Park	NPS	1	A4
Makawao	Waikamo Preserve (Maui)	TNC	3	A4
Makua	Kaena Point SP (Oahu)	SPS	22	C1
Mana (Village)	Kuia Reserve (Kauai)	NAR	18	A1
	Polihale SP (Kauai)	SPS	13	A1
Wahiawa	Wahiawa Freshwater SRA(Oahu)	SPS	31	C1
Waialua	Pahole Preserve (Oahu)	NAR	2	C1
	Kaala Reserve (Oahu)	NAR	4	C1
Wailea	Kaena Point Reserve (Oahu)	NAR	13	B3
Wailua	Ahihi-Kinau Reserve (Maui)	SPS	15	A4
Wailuku	Wailua River SP (several units)	SPS	15	A3
Waimanalo	Island of Maui District Office	SPS	32	C2
	Waimanalo Bay SRA (Oahu)			

HAWAII NOTES

Summary

There are 11 federal, 55 state, and 5 private recreation areas or local administrative offices covered in this state chapter. Of these, 46 appear in the Information Chart and 25 are covered in the notes. The special index features 2 federally designated wilderness areas.

Federal Agencies

U.S. Army Corps of Engineers (COE)
Pacific Ocean Division Visitor Center
Fort Shafter, HI 96858-5440   808-438-2815

USFWS National Wildlife Refuges

The Kilauea Point NWR is the only Hawaii refuge open to the general public year-round. There are some observation points outside the boundary of some refuges. A special permit is required to visit the wetland refuges, home for four endangered waterbirds. Remote Island refuges are vulnerable to any disturbance, and access is restricted. A free brochure titled *Hawaii and Pacific Islands National Wildlife Refuges* describes the refuges and wildlife.

Note: The Hawaii and Pacific Islands managemant structure has changed recently. Contact the headquarters office for current information (S# 1, map C2).

National Park Service
Additional NPS Locations in Hawaii
Puukohola Heiau National Historic Site (80 acres)
(S# 6, map C4)
PO Box 4963
Kawaihae, HI 96743   808-882-7218

USS Arizona Memorial (S# 7, map C2)
1 Arizona Memorial Place
Honolulu, HI 96818   808-422-2771

Wilderness Index

Haleakala Wilderness - 19,270 acres
Haleakala National Park (S# 1, map A4)
Hawaii Volcanoes Wilderness - 123,100 acres
Hawaii Volcanoes National Park (S# 2, map C4)

State Agencies

Hawaii Dept. of Land & Nat. Resources (DLNR)
Box 621
Honolulu, HI 96809   808-548-6550
The Natural Area Reserve System, Divisions of Aquatic Resources, Forestry and Wildlife, Land Management, State Parks and Recreation, and Historic Preservation operate under this Department.

Distance Between Islands Not To Scale

1 inch = approx. 6.5 mi. or 10.5 km

1 inch = approx. 17.5 mi. or 28 km

© 1994 by John Oliver Jones

HAWAII - CITY / AGENCY INDEX

City	Agency Office / Area Name	Code	S#	Map
Aiea Heights	Keaiwa Heiau SRA (Oahu)	SPS	25	C2
Captain Cook	Kealakekua Bay Underwater SP	SPS	10	C3
Haena	Haena SP (Kauai)	SPS	12	A1
	Na Pali Coast SP	SPS	24	B1
Haleiwa	Kaiaka SRA (Oahu)	SPS	17	A4
Hana	Waianapanapa SP (Maui)	SPS	19	A4
Hanalei	Hono O Na Pali Reserve (Kauai)	NAR	19	A1
Haula	Sacred Falls SP (Oahu)	SPS	28	C2
Hawaii	Hanauma Bay Underwater SP	SPS	21	C2
National Park	Hawaii Volcanoes Natl. Park	NPS	2	C4

City	Agency Office / Area Name	Code	S#	Map
Hilo	Hakalau Forest NWR	NWR	2	C4
	Puu O Umi Reserve (Hawaii)	NAR	6	C4
	Puu Makaala Reserve (Hawaii)	NAR	12	B4
	Island of Hawaii Dist. Office	SPS	2	C4
Honaunau	Wailoa River SRA (Hawaii)	SPS	8	C4
	Manuka SP (Hawaii)	NAR	9	C3
	Kipahoehoe Reserve (Hawaii)	NAR	10	C3
Honaunau, Kona	Pu'uhonua o Honaunau NHP	NPS	5	C3
Honokaa	Mauna Kea Ice Age R (Hawaii)	NAR	7	C4
	Laupahoehoe Reserve (Hawaii)	NAR	8	C4
Honokohau	Kalopa SRA (Hawaii)	SPS	5	C4
HONOLULU	West Maui Reserve (Maui)	NAR	14	A3
	Hawaiian & Pacific Islands Refuge Complex	NWR	1	C2

	Agency Office / Area Name	Code	S#	Map
	DLNR, Natural Area Reserve System (NAR)	NAR	1	C2
	HI DLNR, Div. of State Parks	SPS	1	C2
	Island of Oahu District Office	SPS	18	C2
	Aina Moana SRA (Oahu)	SPS	20	C2
	Diamond Head State M (Oahu)	NAR	9	C3
	Puu Ualakaa S Wayside (Oahu)	SPS	27	C2
	Sand Island SRA (Oahu)	SPS	29	C2
	Waahila Ridge SRA (Oahu)	SPS	30	C2
	HI DLNR, Div. of Forestry & Wildlife	SWA	11	A1
	TNC Hawaii Field Office	TNC	1	C2
	Waiakea 1942 Flow Reserve (Hawaii)	NAR	5	C4

City	Agency Office / Area Name	Code	S#	Map
Hilo	Akaka Falls SP (Hawaii)	SPS	3	C4
	Hanawa Reserve (Maui)	NAR	15	A4
Hosmer Grove	Kahana Valley SP (Oahu)	SPS	23	C2
Kahana	Kaloko-Honokohau NHP	NPS	4	C4
Kailua-Kona	Kahaualea Reserve (Hawaii)	NAR	11	C4
Kaimu	MacKenzie SRA (Hawaii)	SPS	7	C4
Kalaupapa	Puu Alaia Natl. Hist. Park	NPS	3	B3
	Puu Alii Reserve (Molokai)	NAR	16	B3
	Olokui Reserve (Molokai)	NAR	17	B3
Kawaihae	Hapuna Beach SRA (Hawaii)	SPS	4	C3
Kekaha	Kokee SP (Kauai)	SPS	11	A1
Kilauea	Kilauea Point NWR	NWR	3	A1
Kualapuu	Kamakou Preserve (Molokai)	TNC	2	B3
Kula	Polipoli Spring SRA (Hawaii)	SPS	16	A1

Natural Area Reserves System (S# 1, map C2))

1151 Punchbowl St.
Honolulu, HI 96813
808-548-7417

The Guide features Hawaii's Natural Area Reserve System consisting of 18 reserves totaling more than 108 thousand acres. They are identified on the Guide map using a round medium blue symbol. Symbol numbers, map coordinates, names and locations are given here in the notes. Most reserves are remote and inaccessible. Others require 4-wheel-drive for access. Call the Natural Area Reserves office for current access information.

S#	MAP	Reserve & Location
2	C1	Pahole Reserve (Oahu), Waialua
3	C1	Kaala Reserve (Oahu), Waialua
4	C1	Kaena Point Reserve (Oahu), Waialua
5	C4	Waiakea 1942 Flow Res. (Hawaii), Honomu
6	C4	Puu Makaala Reserve (Hawaii), Hilo
7	C4	Mauna Kea Ice Age Res. (Hawaii), Honokaa
8	C4	Laupahoehoe Reserve (Hawaii), Honokaa

S#	MAP	Reserve & Location
9	C3	Manuka Reserve (Hawaii), Honaunau
10	C3	Kipahoehoe Reserve (Hawaii), Honaunau
11	C4	Kahaualea Reserve (Hawaii), Kaimu
12	B4	Puu O Umi Reserve (Hawaii), Hilo
13	B3	Ahihi-Kinau Reserve (Maui), Wailea
14	A3	West Maui Reserve (Maui), Honokohau
15	A4	Hanawi Reserve (Maui), Hosmer Grove
16	B3	Puu Aliaa Reserve (Molokai), Kalaupapa
17	B3	Olokui Reserve (Molokai), Kalaupapa
18	A1	Kuia Reserve (Kauai), Mana
19	A1	Hono O Na Pali Reserve (Kauai), Hanalei

DLNR, Division of State Parks (S# 1, map C2)

A comprehensive brochure providing information on 66 state parks on five islands is available. Included are directions to each of the parks, facilities and activities, and safety tips. Selected parks are listed in the Guide.

DLNR, Division of Forestry & Wildlife (DFW)

In addition to wildlife management, the DFW is responsible for forest and forest resources management. The agency recreation program includes building and maintaining hiking trails, access roads, shelters, vista points, hunting grounds, and other recreational facilities. Hunting opportunities on the islands are limited due to extensive private land ownership.

Recreational maps for five islands are available. These provide detailed information on hiking, hunting, and park accommodations. A fold-out Natural Area Reserve System brochure is also available. The DFW publishes a quarterly newsletter, *Hawaii's Forests and Wildlife*.

DLNR, Division of Aquatic Resources

1151 Punchbowl St.
Honolulu, HI 96813   808-548-4000
0Contact this division for fish and fishing information.

Hawaii Visitors Bureau

PO Box 8527
Honolulu, HI 96815   808-923-1811
The bureau literature contains information on government, history, culture, transportation, communications, and island geography.

Private Organizations

ANCA Location in Hawaii
Hawaii Nature Center (S# 4, map C2)
2131 Makiki Heights Drive
Honolulu, HI 96822   808-973-0100

Hawaii Chamber of Commerce
735 Bishop St.
Honolulu, HI 96813   808-522-8800

★ INFORMATION CHART ★

INFORMATION CHART LEGEND - SYMBOLS & LETTER CODES

■ means **YES** & □ means **Yes with disability provisions**
sp means **spring**, March through May
S means **Summer**, June through August
F means **Fall**, September through November
W means **Winter**, December through February
T means **Two (2) or Three (3) Seasons**
A means **All Four (4) Seasons**
na means **Not Applicable or Not Available**
Note: empty or blank spaces in the chart mean **NO**
★ *that symbol is not shown on the map.*
Note: *If a symbol number has a star ★*

AGENCY/MAP LEGEND . . . INITIALS, MAP SYMBOLS, COLOR CODES

U.S. Forest Service Supervisor & Ranger Dist. Offices NFS [6]
U.S. Army Corps of Engineers Rec. Areas & Offices COE [H]
USFWS National Wildlife Refuges & Offices NWR [40]
National Park Service Parks & other NPS Sites NPS [7]
Bureau of Land Management Rec. Areas & Offices BLM [26]
Hawaii Natural Area Reserves [23]
State Parks (also see State Agency notes) SPS [52]
State Wildlife Areas (also see State Agency notes) SWA [19]
Private Preserves, Nature Centers & Tribal Lands
The Wild Rivers ~~~ and Wilderness Areas ::::: [15]
Note: Refer to yellow block on page 7 (top right) for location name and address abbreviations.

FACILITIES, SERVICES, RECREATION OPPORTUNITIES & CONVENIENCES

S#	MAP	LOCATION NAME (state initials if more than one) with ADDRESS and/or LOCATION DATA	TELEPHONE	ACRES / ELEVATION
1	C2	Hawaiian & Pacific Is. Ref. Complex, 300 Ala Moana Blvd., PO Box 50167, Honolulu 96850	808-541-1201	na / na
2	C4	Hakalau Forest NWR, FOB, 154 Waianuenue Ave., Room 219, Hilo 96720 [on Keanakolu Rd., 16 mi N of Hwy 200]	808-969-9909	16,518 / 3,000-6,000
3	A1	Kilauea Point NWR, Kilauea Rd., PO Box 87, Kilauea, Kauai 96754 [2 mi. off Hwy. 56]	808-828-1413	169 / na
1	A4	Haleakala National Park, PO Box 369, Makawao 96768 [summit of East Maui on SR 378; recorded info ph. 572-7749]	808-572-9306	28,655 / 0-10,000
2	C4	Hawaii Volcanoes Nat'l. Park, mail to; Hawaii National Park 96718 [located at Volcano HI]	808-967-7311	229,177 / 0-13,670
3	B3	Kalaupapa Nat'l. Historical Park, Kalaupapa 96742	808-567-6102	10,902 / 0-4,000
4	C4	Kaloko-Honokohau NHP, 73-4786 Kanalani St., Kailua-Kona 96740 [new office]	808-329-6881	1,160 / 0-30
5	C3	Pu'uhonua o Honaunau NHP & Puukohol, Heiau NHS, PO Box 129, Honaunau, Kona 96726	808-328-2326	182 / 0-835
1	C2	DLNR, Natural Area Reserve System, 1151 Punchbowl St., Honolulu 96813 [see notes]	808-548-7417	na / na
1	C2	DLNR, Div. of State Parks, 1151 Punchbowl, PO Box 621, Honolulu 96809	808-548-7455	na / na
2	C4	Island of Hawaii District Office, 75 Aupuni Street, PO Box 936, Hilo 96721	808-933-4200	na / na
3	C4	Akaka Falls State Park (Hawaii), 3.6 mi. SW of Honomu	808-933-4200	65 / na
4	B4	Hapuna Beach State Rec. Area (Hawaii, on Queen Kaahumanu Hwy., 2.3 mi. S of Kawaihae	808-933-4200	61 / na
5	C4	Kalopa SRA (Hawaii), at the end of Kalopa Road, 5 mi. SE of Honokaa	808-933-4200	100 / na
6	C3	Kealakekua Bay Underwater SP, Hawaii [access by sea from Capt. Cook or Keei Junct., near Captain Cook]	808-933-4200	315 / na
7	C4	MacKenzie SRA (Hawaii), 9 mi. NE of Kaimu	808-933-4200	13 / na
8	C4	Wailoa River SRA (Hawaii), at end of Piilani St. in downtown, Hilo	808-933-4200	150 / na
9	A1	Island of Kauai District Office, 3060 Eiwa Street, PO Box 1671, Lihue 96766	808-241-3444	na / na
10	A1	Haena SP (Kauai), at end of Kuhio Hwy. in, Haena	808-241-3444	62 / na
11	A1	Kokee SP (Kauai), 15 mi. N of Kekaha	808-241-3444	4,345 / 4,000
12	A1	Na Pali Coast SP (several units) Hawaii (ask for directions), near Haena	808-241-3444	6,175 / na
13	A1	Polihale SP (Kauai), at end of a dirt road, 5 mi. from, Mana (Village)	808-241-3444	137 / na
14	A4	Wailua River SP (several units) Maui, [off Hwy. 56, along banks of Wailua River] near Wailua	808-241-3444	1,126 / na
15	A3	Island of Maui District Office, 54 S. High St., Wailuku 96793	808-243-5354	na / na
16	A1	Polipoli Spring SRA, 9.7 mi. upland from, Kula	808-243-5354	10 / 6,200
17	A4	Waianapanapa SP (Maui) [3 hr. drive, 53 mi. E. of Kahului Airport) near Hana	808-243-5354	120 / na
18	C2	Island of Oahu District Office, 1151 Punchbowl Street, PO Box 621, Honolulu 96809	808-548-7455	na / na
19	C2	Aina Moana SRA (Oahu), Hwy, 92, 1501 Ala Moana Blvd., Honolulu	808-548-7455	43 / na
20	C2	Diamond Head State Monument (Oahu), off Diamon Head Rd, Honolulu	808-548-7455	475 / na

Hawaii Recreation Areas (continued)

S#	MAP	LOCATION NAME	acres / use	phone
22	C1	Kaena Point SP (Oahu), at the end of Hwy. 930, Mokua	853 / ra	808-548-7455
23	C1	Kahana Valley SP (Oahu), Kahana	5,220 / ra	808-548-7455
24	B1	Kaiaka SRA (Oahu), Haleiwa	53 / ra	808-548-7455
25	C2	Keaiwa Heiau SRA (Oahu), Aiea Heights	384 / ra	808-548-7455
26	B2	Malaekahana SRA (Oahu), about 2 mi. N of Laie	110 / ra	808-548-7455
27	C2	Puu Ualakaa State Wayside (Oahu), 3 mi. up Round Top Dr. from, Makiki St. in, Honolulu	50 / ra	808-548-7455
28	C2	Sacred Falls SP (Oahu), 1 mi. S of Hauula	1,374 / ra	808-548-7455
29	C2	Sand Island SRA (Oahu), Sand Island, Honolulu	140 / ra	808-548-7455
30	C2	Waahila Ridge SRA (Oahu), St. Louis Heights, Honolulu	50 / ra	808-548-7455
31	C1	Wahiawa Freshwater SRA (Oahu), off Hwy. 80 near Wahiawa	66 / ra	808-548-7455
32	C2	Waimanalo Bay SRA (Oahu), near Waimanalo	75 / na	808-548-7455
1	C2	DLNR, Div. of Forestry & Wildlife, 1151 Punchbowl St., Honolulu 96813 [Kalanimoku Bldg., Room 325]	na / na	808-548-8850
2	C2	TNC Hawaii Field Office, 1116 Smith Street, Suite 201, Honolulu 96817	na / na	808-537-4508
2	B3	Kamakou Preserve, c/o Field Office, or, PO Box 220, Kualapuu, Molokai 96757	2,774 / 2,000-4,000	808-567-6680
3	A4	Waikamoi Preserve, c/o Field Office, or Makawao, PO Box 1716, Makawao, Maui 96768	5,230 / 3,800-7,500	808-572-7849

Payette National Forest [1984]
Salmon National Forest [1979]
Sawtooth NF & Scenic R Map Guide [1987]
Selway-Bitterroot Wilderness [1985]
Targhee NF-Island Park, Ashton, Teton Basin, and Palisades RDs [1984]
Targhee NF, Dubois RD [1985]

Bureau of Land Management Maps

The BLM grid shows intermediate scale maps. Two Idaho color maps are available. A 1:500,000 scale map (1 inch = 8 miles, size 3x5 feet), and a 1:1,000,000 scale map (1 inch = 16 miles, size 2x3 feet).

BLM IDAHO
1:100,000 INTERMEDIATE SCALE MAPS
SURFACE & SURFACE / MINERAL SERIES
T (topographic)
/ Base Map Not Available

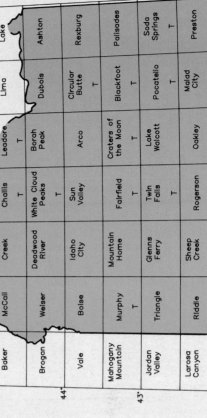

Nez Perce National Forest [1986]
Scale: 1 inch = 0.5 mile (1 cm = 0.3 km)

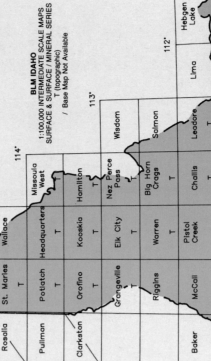

Wild Rivers

Clearwater River, Middle Fork
 Clearwater National Forest (S# 18, map B1)
 Nez Perce National Forest (S# 33, map C1)
 Bitterroot National Forest (see Montana S# 8, map B1)
Rapid River
 Hells Canyon Natl. Recreation Area (S# 63, map C1)
Saint Joe River
 Idaho Panhandle National Forest (S# 25, map B1)
Salmon River, Middle Fork
 Challis National Forest (S# 13, map D2)
Salmon River
 Salmon National Forest (S# 46, map C2)
Snake River
 Hells Canyon Natl. Recreation Area (S# 63, map C1)

Outdoor Map Index

National Park Service (USGS Maps)
Craters of the Moon Natl. Monument [1983]
 Scale: 1 inch = 0.5 mile (1 cm = 0.3 km)
 Size: 24x33 inches (61x83 cm)
Yellowstone Natl. Park (ID-MT-WY) [1961]
 Scale: 1 inch = 2.0 miles (1 cm = 1.3 km)
 Size: 38x41 inches (96x104 cm)

U.S. Forest Service Maps
Bitterroot NF (ID - MT) [1981]
 Scale: 1 inch = 0.5 mile (1 cm = 0.3 km)
Boise National Forest [1987]
Caribou NF, Montpelier/Soda Springs RD [1988]
Caribou NF, Pocatello & Malad RDs [1988]
Challis National Forest [1986]
Clearwater National Forest [1990]
 Scale: 1 inch = 0.5 mile (1 cm = 0.3 km)
Frank Church-R of NR, North Wilderness [1984]
 Scale: 1 inch = 0.5 mile (1 cm = 0.3 km)
Frank Church-R of NR, South Wilderness [1984]
 Scale: 1 inch = 0.5 mile (1 cm = 0.3 km)
ID Panhandle NFs - Coeur d'Alene [1989]
 Scale: 1 inch = 0.5 mile (1 cm = 0.3 km)
ID Panhandle NFs - Kaniksu [1988]
 Scale: 1 inch = 0.5 mile (1 cm = 0.3 km)
ID Panhandle NFs - St. Joe [1988]
 Scale: 1 inch = 0.5 mile (1 cm = 0.3 km)
Mid-For: Salmon-Wild & Scenic River [1985]

Bureau of Reclamation Recreation Areas

These areas are symbolized on the Idaho state map.

S#	MAP	LOCATION NAME
1	E2	American Falls Res.
2	E2	Anderson Ranch Res.
3	D1	Arrowrocks Res.
4	D1	Black Canyon Res.
5	D3	Carter Slough
6	D1	Cascade Res.
7	D1	Deadwood Res.
8	D3	Island Park Res.
9	D1	Lake Lowell
10	C1	Lake Waha
11	E3	Lake Walcott
12	E2	Little Wood Rever Res.
13	D1	Mann Creek Res.
14	E3	Minidoka Dam
15	E3	Montour Wildlife Rec. Mgt. Area
16	B1	Reservoir A
17	D3	Ririe Dam and Res.
18	C1	Soldiers Meadow Res.
19	E4	Idaho/Wyoming
		Palisades Res.

Wilderness/Wild River Index

Wilderness Areas
Frank Church-River of No Return Wilderness - 2,361,767 acres
 Boise National Forest (S# 1, map D1)
 Challis National Forest (S# 13, map D2)
 Nez Perce National Forest (S# 33, map C1)
 Payette National Forest (S# 40, map C1)
 Salmon National Forest (S# 46, map C2)
 Bitterroot National Forest (see Montana S# 8, map B1)
Gospel Hump Wilderness - 205,766 acres
 Nez Perce National Forest (S# 33, map C1)
Hells canyon Wilderness - 83,800 acres
 Nez Perce National Forest (S# 33, map C1)
 Payette National Forest (S# 40, map C1)
Sawtooth Wilderness 217,088 acres
 Boise National Forest (S# 1, map D1)
 Challis National Forest (S# 13, map D2)
 Sawtooth National Forest (S# 51, map E2)
Selway-Bitterroot Wilderness - 1,089,017
 Clearwater National Forest (S# 18, map B1)
 Nez Perce National Forest (S# 33, map C1)
 Bitterroot National Forest (see Montana S# 8, map B1)

IDAHO NOTES

Summary

There are 167 federal, 41 state, and 10 private recreation areas or local administrative offices covered in this state chapter. Of these, 190 appear in the Information Chart and 28 are covered in the notes. The special indexes feature 12 federally designated wilderness areas and wild rivers, and 91 agency published outdoor maps.

Federal Agencies

U.S. Forest Service

Three national forests in northern Idaho are in the Northern Region (see Montana chapter - U.S. Forest Svc., Northern Region listing, S# 1). There are seven forests in southern Idaho in the Intermountain Region (see USFS, Intermountain Region listing in Utah chapter).

Lolo Pass VC (S# 23, Powell RD of the Clearwater NF) Off Hwy. 12 at top of pass. Post office address is Lolo, MT. Historic trail interpretation includes the Nez Perce National and Lewis and Clark Trails and their role in history, and Lochsa River orientation and interpretation.

Lochsa Visitors Center (see S# 19, Locha RD/Kooskia RS of the Clearwater NF) at Kooskia, ID. Guided tours and demonstrations of a historic ranger station. Interpretation of devastating Idaho Fires of 1919.

Redfish Lake & Sawtooth Visitor Centers in the Sawtooth National Recreation Area (see S# 55), VC phone 208-726-8291. The VCs feature exhibits, photos, maps, book sales, an audio-visual program which interprets local human and natural history, and recreation information.

National Park Service

Additional NPS Location in Idaho
City of Rocks National Reserve (14,407 acres)
(S# 4, map E2)
963 Blue Lakes Blvd., Suite 1
Twin Falls, ID 83301 208-733-8398

Bureau of Reclamation - USDI

Pacific Northwest Region
FBO, U.S. Court House
Box 043 - 550 W. Fort St.
Boise, ID 83724 208-334-1938
This region administers recreation areas in Washington, Oregon, Idaho, western Montana, and western Wyoming.

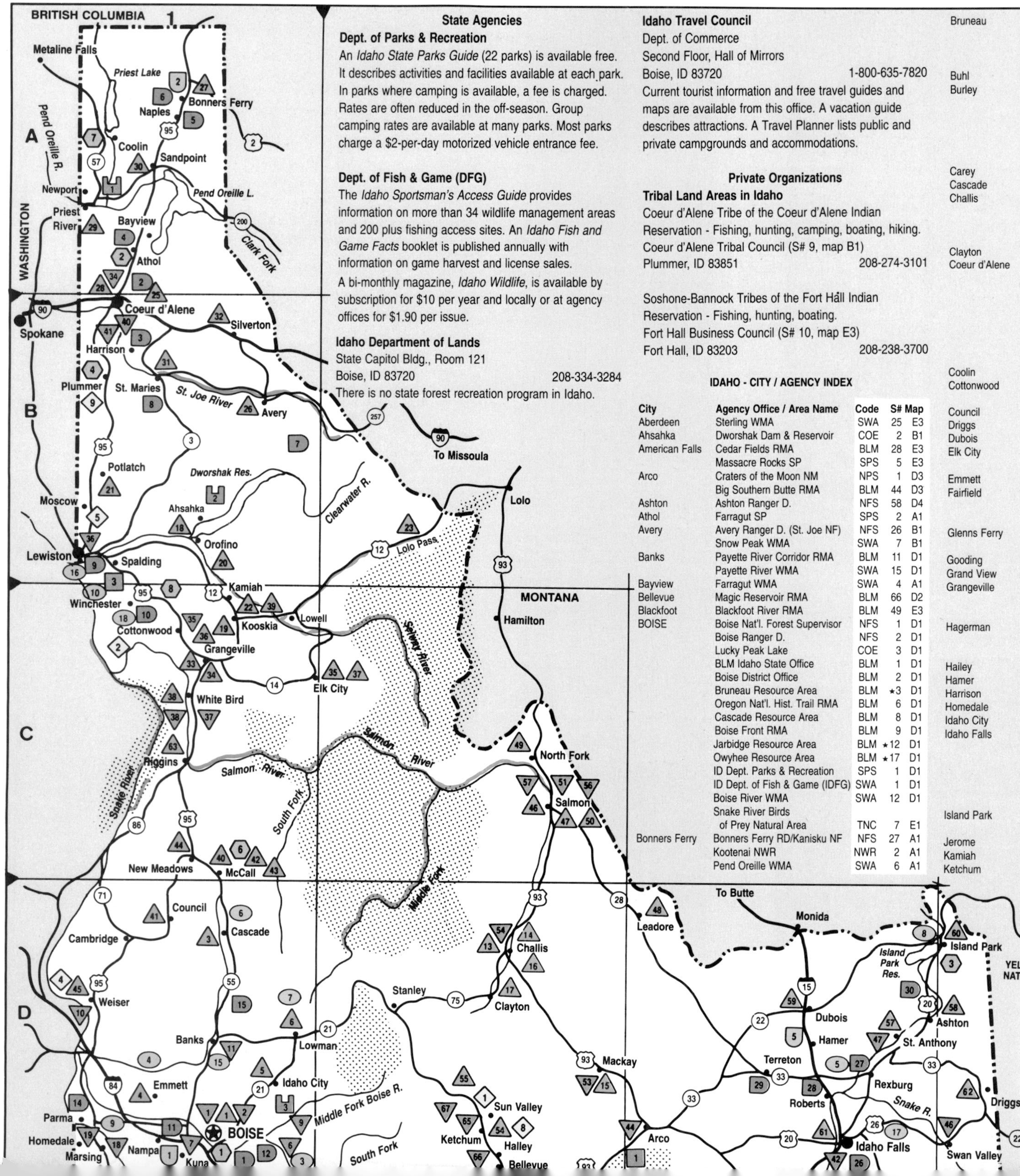

State Agencies

Dept. of Parks & Recreation
An *Idaho State Parks Guide* (22 parks) is available free. It describes activities and facilities available at each park. In parks where camping is available, a fee is charged. Rates are often reduced in the off-season. Group camping rates are available at many parks. Most parks charge a $2-per-day motorized vehicle entrance fee.

Dept. of Fish & Game (DFG)
The *Idaho Sportsman's Access Guide* provides information on more than 34 wildlife management areas and 200 plus fishing access sites. An *Idaho Fish and Game Facts* booklet is published annually with information on game harvest and license sales.
A bi-monthly magazine, *Idaho Wildlife*, is available by subscription for $10 per year and locally or at agency offices for $1.90 per issue.

Idaho Department of Lands
State Capitol Bldg., Room 121
Boise, ID 83720 208-334-3284
There is no state forest recreation program in Idaho.

Idaho Travel Council
Dept. of Commerce
Second Floor, Hall of Mirrors
Boise, ID 83720 1-800-635-7820
Current tourist information and free travel guides and maps are available from this office. A vacation guide describes attractions. A Travel Planner lists public and private campgrounds and accommodations.

Private Organizations

Tribal Land Areas in Idaho
Coeur d'Alene Tribe of the Coeur d'Alene Indian Reservation - Fishing, hunting, camping, boating, hiking.
Coeur d'Alene Tribal Council (S# 9, map B1)
Plummer, ID 83851 208-274-3101

Soshone-Bannock Tribes of the Fort Hall Indian Reservation - Fishing, hunting, boating.
Fort Hall Business Council (S# 10, map E3)
Fort Hall, ID 83203 208-238-3700

IDAHO - CITY / AGENCY INDEX

City	Agency Office / Area Name	Code	S#	Map
Aberdeen	Sterling WMA	SWA	25	E3
Ahsahka	Dworshak Dam & Reservoir	COE	2	B1
American Falls	Cedar Fields RMA	BLM	28	E3
	Massacre Rocks SP	SPS	5	E3
Arco	Craters of the Moon NM	NPS	1	D3
	Big Southern Butte RMA	BLM	44	D3
Ashton	Ashton Ranger D.	NFS	58	D4
Athol	Farragut SP	SPS	2	A1
Avery	Avery Ranger D. (St. Joe NF)	NFS	26	B1
	Snow Peak WMA	SWA	7	B1
Banks	Payette River Corridor RMA	BLM	11	D1
	Payette River WMA	SWA	15	D1
Bayview	Farragut WMA	SWA	4	A1
Bellevue	Magic Reservoir RMA	BLM	66	D2
Blackfoot	Blackfoot River RMA	BLM	49	E3
BOISE	Boise Nat'l. Forest Supervisor	NFS	1	D1
	Boise Ranger D.	NFS	2	D1
	Lucky Peak Lake	COE	3	D1
	BLM Idaho State Office	BLM	1	D1
	Boise District Office	BLM	2	D1
	Bruneau Resource Area	BLM	★3	D1
	Oregon Nat'l. Hist. Trail RMA	BLM	6	D1
	Cascade Resource Area	BLM	8	D1
	Boise Front RMA	BLM	9	D1
	Jarbidge Resource Area	BLM	★12	D1
	Owyhee Resource Area	BLM	★17	D1
	ID Dept. Parks & Recreation	SPS	1	D1
	ID Dept. of Fish & Game (IDFG)	SWA	1	D1
	Boise River WMA	SWA	12	D1
	Snake River Birds of Prey Natural Area	TNC	7	E1
Bonners Ferry	Bonners Ferry RD/Kanisku NF	NFS	27	A1
	Kootenai NWR	NWR	2	A1
	Pend Oreille WMA	SWA	6	A1
Bruneau	Jacks Creek RMA	BLM	5	E1
	Bruneau/Jarbidge Rivers RMA	BLM	14	E1
	Jarbidge Forks RMA	BLM	15	E1
	C.J. Strike WMA	SWA	13	E1
Buhl	Jarbidge Ranger D.	NFS	24	E2
Burley	Burley Ranger D.	NFS	52	E2
	Burley District Office	BLM	24	E2
	Snake River Resource Area	BLM	27	E2
	Jim Sage Mountain RMA	BLM	29	E2
	Milner RMA	BLM	30	E3
	Raft River Crossing RMA	BLM	31	E3
Carey	Carey Lake WMA	SWA	19	E2
Cascade	Cascade Ranger D.	NFS	3	D1
Challis	Challis National Forest Sup.	NFS	13	D2
	Challis Ranger D.	NFS	14	D2
	Middle Fork Ranger D.	NFS	16	D2
	Upper Salmon River RMA	BLM	54	D2
Clayton	Yankee Fork Ranger D.	NFS	17	D2
Coeur d'Alene	Idaho Panhandle Nat'l. Forests	NFS	25	B1
	Fernan Ranger District of Coeur D'Alene NF	NFS	28	B1
	Coeur d'Alene District Office	BLM	34	A1
	Emerald Empire Resource Area	BLM	39	B1
	Beauty Bay RMA	BLM	40	B1
	Lower Coeur d'Alene River RMA	BLM	41	B1
	Region 1 - IDFG	SWA	2	A1
Coolin	Priest Lake SP (3 units)	SPS	7	A1
Cottonwood	Cottonwood Resource Area	BLM	35	C1
	Garden Creek Preserve	TNC	2	C1
Council	Council Ranger D.	NFS	41	D1
Driggs	Teton Basin Ranger D.	NFS	62	D4
Dubois	Dubois Ranger D.	NFS	59	D3
Elk City	Elk City Ranger D.	NFS	35	C2
	Red River Ranger D./Ranger S	NFS	37	C2
Emmett	Emmett Ranger D.	NFS	4	D1
Fairfield	Fairfield Ranger D.	NFS	53	E2
	Camas Prairie Centennial Marsh WMA	SWA	18	E2
Glenns Ferry	Bennett Mountain Winter Recreation Area RMA	BLM	13	E2
Gooding	Gooding City of Rocks RMA	BLM	60	E2
Grand View	C.J. Strike Reservoir RMA	BLM	4	E1
Grangeville	Nez Perce National Forest Sup.	NFS	33	C1
	Clearwater Ranger D.	NFS	34	C1
	Moose Creek Ranger D.	NFS	36	C1
Hagerman	Owlsley Bridge ORV RMA	BLM	16	E2
	Bilingsley Creek WMA	SWA	17	E2
	Hagerman WMA	SWA	20	E2
Hailey	Stapp-Soldier Creek Preserve	TNC	8	D2
Hamer	Camas NWR	NWR	5	D3
Harrison	Coeur d'Alene River WMA	SWA	3	B1
Homedale	Jump Creek RMA	BLM	19	D1
Idaho City	Idaho City Ranger D.	NFS	5	D1
Idaho Falls	Palisades Ranger D.	NFS	61	D3
	Idaho Falls District Office	BLM	42	D3
	Big Butte Resource Area	BLM	43	D3
	Medicine Lodge Resource Area	BLM	45	D3
	Region 6 - IDFG	SWA	26	D3
	Tex Creek WMA	SWA	31	E3
Island Park	Island Park Ranger D.	NFS	60	D4
	Harriman SP	SPS	3	D4
Jerome	Region 4 - IDFG	SWA	16	E2
Kamiah	Pierce Ranger D.	NFS	22	C1
Ketchum	Ketchum Ranger D.	NFS	54	D2
	Sawtooth National Recreation Area & Redfish Lake VC	NFS	55	D2
	Bald Mountain RMA	BLM	65	D2
	North Ketchum RMA	BLM	67	D2
Kooskia	Lochsa RD & VC, Kooskia RS	NFS	19	C1
	Selway Ranger D. & Fenn RS	NFS	39	C1
Kuna	Snake River Birds of Prey RMA	BLM	7	D1
Leadore	Leadore Ranger D.	NFS	48	D3
Lewiston	Clearwater River RMA	BLM	36	B1
	Region 2 - IDFG	SWA	9	B1
Lolo, MT	Powell RD/RS & Lolo Pass VC	NFS	23	B2
Lowman	Lowman Ranger D.	NFS	6	D1
Mackay	Lost River Ranger D.	NFS	15	D2
	Mackay Reservoir RMA	BLM	53	D2
Malad City	Malad RD/Curlew N. Grassland	NFS	9	E3
	Deep Creek Resource Area	BLM	25	E3
Marsing	Blackstock RMA	BLM	18	D1
	North Fork Owyhee Backcountry RMA	BLM	20	E1
	Owyhee R. Canyonlands RMA	BLM	22	D1
McCall	Payette National Forest Sup.	NFS	40	C1
	Krassel Ranger D.	NFS	42	C1
	McCall Ranger D.	NFS	43	C1
	Pondersa SP	SPS	6	C1
Montpelier	Montpelier Ranger D.	NFS	10	E4
	Bear Lake NWR	NWR	4	E4
	Montpelier WMA	SWA	23	E4
Moscow	Idler's Rest Preserve	TNC	5	B1
Mountain Home	Mountain Home Ranger D.	NFS	7	E1
Murphy	Owyhee Front RMA	BLM	21	E1
Nampa	Deer Flat NWR	NWR	1	D1
	Region 3 - IDFG	SWA	11	D1
Naples	McArthur Lake WMA	SWA	5	A1
New Meadows	New Meadows Ranger D.	NFS	44	C1
Newport	Albeni Falls Dam & Lake Pend Oreille	COE	1	A1
North Fork	North Fork Ranger D.	NFS	49	C2
Orofino	Clearwater Nat'l. Forest Sup.	NFS	18	B1
	North Fork Ranger D.	NFS	20	B1
Parma	Fort Boise WMA	SWA	14	D1
Picabo	Silver Creek Preserve	TNC	6	E2
Plummer	Heyburn SP	SPS	4	B1
Pocatello	Caribou National Forest Sup.	NFS	8	E3
	Pocatello Ranger D.	NFS	11	E3
	Southeast ID Refuge Complex	NWR	3	E3
	Hawkins Reservoir RMA	BLM	26	E3
	Pocatello Resource Area	BLM	48	E3
	Pocatello ORV RMA	BLM	50	E3
	Region 5 - IDFG	SWA	22	E3
	Portneuf WMA	SWA	24	E3
Potlatch	Palouse Ranger District	NFS	21	B1
Priest River	Priest Lake RD (Kanisku NF)	NFS	29	A1
Rexburg	Cartier Slough WMA	SWA	27	D3
Riggins	Hells Canyon Nat'l. Rec. Area	NFS	63	C1
Roberts	Market Lake WMA	SWA	28	D3
Rogerson	Salmon Falls Cr. Canyon RMA	BLM	32	E2
	Salmon Falls Creek Res. RMA	BLM	33	E2
Rupert	Minidoka NWR	NWR	7	E2
Salmon	Salmon National Forest Sup.	NFS	46	C2
	Cobalt Ranger D.	NFS	47	C2
	Salmon Ranger D.	NFS	50	C2
	Salmon District Office	BLM	51	C2
	Challis Resource Area	BLM	52	C2
	Lemhi Resource Area	BLM	55	C2
	Continental Divide National Scenic Trail RMA	BLM	56	C2
	Lewis & Clark National Historic Trail RMA	BLM	57	C2
Sandpoint	Sandpoint RD (Kanisku NF)	NFS	30	A1
Shoshone	Shoshone District Office	BLM	58	E2
	Bennett Hills Resource Area	BLM	59	E2
	T-Maze Caves RMA	BLM	62	E2
	Thorn Creek RMA	BLM	63	E2
	Monument Resource Area	BLM	64	E2
Silver City	Silver City RMA	BLM	23	E1
Silverton	Wallace RD (Coeur D'Alene NF)	NFS	32	B1
Soda Springs	Soda Springs Ranger D.	NFS	12	E3
Spalding	Nez Perce Nat'l. Hist. Park	NPS	3	B1
St. Anthony	Targhee National Forest Sup.	NFS	57	D3
	St. Anthony Sand Dunes RMA	BLM	47	D3
	Sand Creek WMA	SWA	30	D3
St. Maries	St. Maries RD (St. Joe NF)	NFS	31	B1
	St. Maries WMA	SWA	8	B1
Sun Valley	TNC Idaho Field Office	TNC	1	D2
Swan Valley	South Fork Snake River RMA	BLM	46	D4
Terreton	Mud Lake WMA	SWA	29	D3
Twin Falls	Sawtooth National Forest Sup.	NFS	51	E2
	Twin Falls Ranger D.	NFS	56	E2
	Hagerman Fossil Beds NM	NPS	2	E2
	Snake River Rim RMA	BLM	61	E2

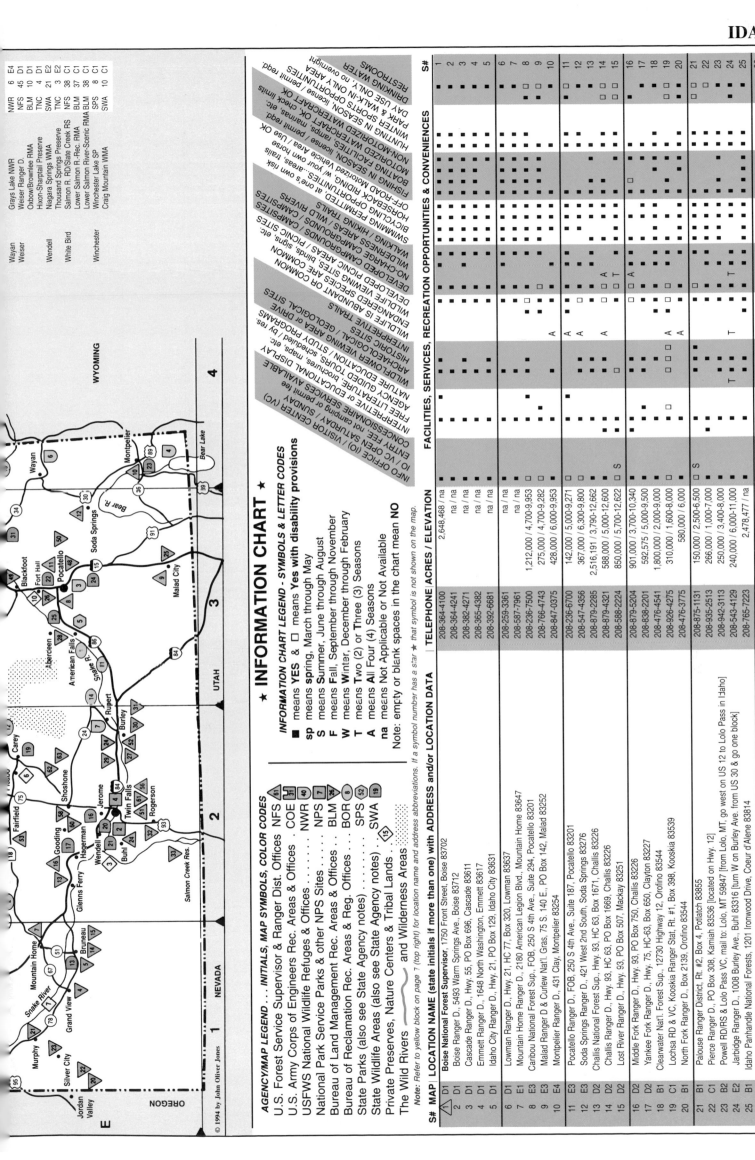

★ INFORMATION CHART ★

INFORMATION CHART LEGEND - SYMBOLS & LETTER CODES

- ■ means YES & □ means Yes with disability provisions
- sp means spring, March through May
- S means Summer, June through August
- F means Fall, September through November
- W means Winter, December through February
- T means Two (2) or Three (3) Seasons
- A means All Four (4) Seasons
- na means Not Applicable or Not Available

Note: empty or blank spaces in the chart mean NO

Note: Refer to yellow block on page 7 (top right) for location name and address abbreviations. If a symbol number has a star ★ that symbol is not shown on the map.

AGENCY/MAP LEGEND . . . INITIALS, MAP SYMBOLS, COLOR CODES

- U.S. Forest Service Supervisor & Ranger Dist. Offices . . NFS
- U.S. Army Corps of Engineers Rec. Areas & Offices . . COE
- USFWS National Wildlife Refuges & Offices . . . . . . NWR
- National Park Service Parks & other NPS Sites . . . . . NPS
- Bureau of Land Management Rec. Areas & Offices . . . BLM
- Bureau of Reclamation Rec. Areas & Reg. Offices . . . BOR
- State Parks (also see State Agency notes) . . . . SPS
- State Wildlife Areas (also see State Agency notes) . . . SWA
- Private Preserves, Nature Centers & Tribal Lands
- The Wild Rivers — and Wilderness Areas

© 1994 by John Oliver Jones

S#	MAP	LOCATION NAME (state initials if more than one) with ADDRESS and/or LOCATION DATA	TELEPHONE/ ACRES / ELEVATION
1	D1	Boise National Forest Supervisor, 1750 Front Street, Boise 83702	208-364-4100 / 2,648,468 / na
2	D1	Boise Ranger D., 5493 Warm Springs Ave., Boise 83712	208-364-4241 / na / na
3	D1	Cascade Ranger D., Hwy. 55, PO Box 696, Cascade 83611	208-382-4271 / na / na
4	D1	Emmett Ranger D., 1648 North Washington, Emmett 83617	208-365-4382 / na / na
5	D1	Idaho City Ranger D., Hwy. 21, PO Box 129, Idaho City 83631	208-392-6681 / na / na
6	D1	Lowman Ranger D., Hwy. 21, HC 77, Box 320, Lowman 83637	208-259-3361 / na / na
7	E1	Mountain Home Ranger D., 2180 American Legion Blvd., Mountain Home 83647	208-587-7961 / na / na
8	E3	Caribou National Forest Sup., FOB, 250 S 4th Ave., Suite 294, Pocatello 83201	208-236-7500 / 1,212,000 / 4,700-9,953
9	E4	Malad Ranger D & Curlew Nat'l. Gras., 75 S. 140 E., PO Box 142, Malad 83252	208-766-4743 / 275,000 / 4,700-9,282
10	E4	Montpelier Ranger D., 431 Clay, Montpelier 83254	208-847-0375 / 428,000 / 6,000-9,953
11	E3	Pocatello Ranger D., FOB, 250 S 4th Ave., Suite 187, Pocatello 83201	208-236-6700 / 142,000 / 5,000-9,271
12	E3	Soda Springs Ranger D., 421 West 2nd South, Soda Springs 83276	208-547-4356 / 367,000 / 6,300-9,800
13	D2	Challis National Forest Sup., Hwy. 93, HC 63, Box 1671, Challis 83226	208-879-2285 / 2,516,191 / 3,790-12,662
14	D2	Challis Ranger D., Hwy. 93, HC 63, PO Box 1669, Challis 83226	208-879-4321 / 588,000 / 5,000-12,600
15	D2	Lost River Ranger D., Hwy. 93, PO Box 507, Mackay 83251	208-588-2224 / 850,000 / 5,700-12,622
16	D2	Middle Fork Ranger D., Hwy. 93, PO Box 750, Challis 83226	208-879-5204 / 901,000 / 3,700-10,340
17	D2	Yankee Fork Ranger D., Hwy. 75, HC-63, Box 650, Clayton 83227	208-838-2201 / 592,575 / 5,000-9,500
18	B1	Clearwater Nat'l. Forest Sup., 12730 Highway 12, Orofino 83544	208-476-4541 / 1,800,000 / 1,600-9,000
19	C1	Lochsa RD & VC, Kooskia Ranger Stat., Rt. #1, Box 398, Kooskia 83539	208-926-4275 / 310,000 / 1,600-8,000
20	B1	North Fork Ranger D., Box 2139, Orofino 83544	208-476-3775 / 580,000 / 6,000
21	B1	Palouse Ranger District, Rt. #2, Box 4, Potlatch 83855	208-875-1131 / 150,000 / 2,500-6,500
22	C1	Pierce Ranger D., PO Box 308, Kamiah 83536 [located on Hwy. 12]	208-935-2513 / 266,000 / 1,000-7,000
23	B2	Powell RD/RS & Lolo Pass VC, mail to: Lolo, MT 59847 [from Lolo, MT, go west on US 12 to Lolo Pass in Idaho]	208-942-3113 / 250,000 / 3,400-8,000
24	E2	Jarbidge Ranger D., 1008 Burley Ave., Buhl 83316 [turn W on Burley Ave. from US 30 & go one block]	208-543-4129 / 240,000 / 6,000-11,000
25	B1	Idaho Panhandle National Forests, 1201 Ironwood Drive, Coeur d'Alene 83814	208-765-7223 / 2,478,477 / na
26	B1	Avery Ranger D. (St. Joe NF), St. Joe River Road, HC Box 1, Avery 83802	208-245-4517 / 510,618 / na
27	B1	Bonners Ferry RD (Kaniksu NF), Rt. #4, Box 4860, Bonners Ferry 83805 [office in town]	208-267-5561 / 414,511 / na
28	B1	Fernan Ranger D. (Coeur D'Alene NF), 2502 East Sherman Ave., Coeur d'Alene 83814	208-765-7381 / 354,107 / na
29	A1	Priest Lake Ranger D. (Kaniksu NF), Rt. #5, Box 207, Priest River 83856 [on W side of lake]	208-443-2512 / 322,527 / na
30	A1	Sandpoint Ranger D. (Kaniksu NF), 1500 Hwy. 2, Sandpoint 83864	208-263-5111 / 304,726 / na

Wayan
Weiser

Wendell

White Bird

Winchester

Grays Lake NWR	NWR	6	E4
Weiser Ranger D.	NFS	45	D1
Oxbow/Brownlee RMA	BLM	10	D1
Hixon-Sharptail Preserve	TNC	4	D1
Niagara Springs WMA	SWA	21	E2
Thousand Springs Preserve	TNC	3	E2
Salmon R. RD/Slate Creek RS	NFS	38	C1
Lower Salmon R.-Rec. RMA	BLM	37	C1
Lower Salmon River-Scenic RMA	BLM	38	C1
Winchester Lake SP	SPS	8	C1
Craig Mountain WMA	SWA	10	C1

★ INFORMATION CHART ★

AGENCY/MAP LEGEND . . . INITIALS, MAP SYMBOLS, COLOR CODES

U.S. Forest Service Supervisor & Ranger Dist. Offices NFS △
U.S. Army Corps of Engineers Rec. Areas & Offices . COE ◻
USFWS National Wildlife Refuges & Offices . . . . NWR ⬡
National Park Service Parks & other NPS Sites . . . . . NPS ◯
Bureau of Land Management Rec. Areas & Offices . BLM ◻
Bureau of Reclamation Rec. Areas & Reg. Offices . . . BOR ◯
State Parks (also see State Agency notes) . . . . SPS ◯
State Wildlife Areas (also see State Agency notes) . . SWA ◻
Private Preserves, Nature Centers & Tribal Lands . . . ◻
The Wild Rivers ~~~ and Wilderness Areas ▓▓▓
Note: Refer to yellow block on page 7 (top right) for location name and address abbreviations. If a symbol number has a star ★ that symbol is not shown on the map.

INFORMATION CHART LEGEND - SYMBOLS & LETTER CODES

■ means YES & ◻ means Yes with disability provisions
sp means spring, March through May
S means Summer, June through August
F means Fall, September through November
W means Winter, December through February
T means Two (2) or Three (3) Seasons
A means All Four (4) Seasons
na means Not Applicable or Not Available
Note: empty or blank spaces in the chart mean **NO**

Column headers (FACILITIES, SERVICES, RECREATION OPPORTUNITIES & CONVENIENCES):
BOATING IN SEASON, license / permit req'd. · MOTORIZED WATERCRAFT OK, permit req'd. · NON-MOTORIZED WATERCRAFT OK · HUNTING IN SEASON, license / permit req'd. · WINTER SPORTS OPPORTUNITIES OK · PARK & WALK-IN ONLY AREA · DAY USE ONLY AREA · DRINKING WATER ONLY · RESTROOMS · FISHING OPPORTUNITIES OK / Use Ok · OFF-ROAD Motorized Vehicle Area / Use Ok · HORSEBACK RIDING...at one's own risk · BICYCLING PERMITTED...areas, trails · SWIMMING PERMITTED / by res. · WALKING / HIKING TRAILS · WILDERNESS AREAS / WILD RIVERS · NO-CHARGE CAMPGROUNDS / CAMPSITES · DEVELOPED PICNIC AREAS / PICNIC SITES · WILDLIFE VIEWING SITES, birds, etc. · ENDANGERED SPECIES ARE COMMON · WILDLIFE IS ABUNDANT OR COMMON · INTERPRETIVE TRAILS · HISTORIC SITES · ARCHAEOLOGICAL SITES / GEOLOGICAL SITES · WILDFLOWER VIEWING AREA or DRIVE · NATURE EDUCATION / STUDY PROGRAMS · NATURE GUIDED TOURS / STUDY PROGRAMS · FREE LITERATURE or permit · INTERPRETIVE or SUNDAY · CONCESSIONAIRE SERVICES AVAILABLE · AGENCY GUIDED SERVICES AVAILABLE · ENTRY FEE not camping or permit fee · IO / VC OPEN SATURDAY / SUNDAY · INFO OFFICE (IO) / VISITOR CENTER (VC)

S#	MAP	LOCATION NAME (state initials if more than one) with ADDRESS and/or LOCATION DATA	TELEPHONE	ACRES / ELEVATION
31	B1	St. Maries Ranger D. (St. Joe NF), PO Box 407, St. Maries 83861 [office in town]	208-245-2531	204,906 / na
32	B1	Wallace RD (Coeur D'Alene NF), PO Box 14, Silverton 83867	208-752-1221	367,082 / na
33	C1	Nez Perce National Forest Sup., Rt. #2, Box 475, Grangeville 83530 [on SH 13, east end of town]	208-983-1950	2,200,000 / 2,000-8,500
34	C1	Clearwater Ranger D., Rt. #2, Box 475, Grangeville 83530 [on SH 13, east end of town]	208-983-1963	na / 4,000-7,000
35	C2	Elk City Ranger D., USDA Forest Service Dr., PO Box 416, Elk City 83525	208-842-2245	na / 4,000-8,000
36	C1	Moose Creek Ranger D., PO Box 464, Grangeville 83530 [above Post Office]	208-983-2712	na / 4,000-8,500
37	C2	Red River Ranger D. & Ranger S., Red River Rt., Box 23, Elk City 83525 [on Road 222, 13 mi S of town]	208-842-2255	na / 4,000-9,000
38	C1	Salmon River RD & Slate Creek Range, HC 01, Box 70, White Bird 83554 [on Hwy. 93, 13 mi S of town]	208-839-2211	na / 2,000-8,500
39	C1	Selway Ranger D. & Fenn Ranger Stat, HCR 1, Box 91, Kooskia 83539 [on Road 223, 4 mi E of Lowell]	208-926-4258	na / 3,000-8,000
40	C1	Payette National Forest Sup., 106 West Park St., PO Box 1026, McCall 83638	208-634-0700	2,300,000 / 3,000-9,600
41	D1	Council Ranger D., PO Box 567, Council 83612	208-253-4215	410,000 / 3,000-8,000
42	D1	Krassel Ranger D., PO Box 1026, McCall 83638	208-634-0600	1,200,000 / 3,500-9,500
43	C1	McCall Ranger D., 202 W. Lake St., PO Box 1026, McCall 83638	208-634-0400	600,000 / 5,000-9,300
44	D1	New Meadows Ranger D., 700 Virginia, Box J, New Meadows 83654	208-347-2141	270,000 / 3,600-8,800
45	D1	Weiser Ranger D., 275 East Seventh, Weiser 83672	208-549-2420	136,770 / 3,000-7,800
46	D2	Salmon NF Sup., Forest Svc. Bldg., Hwy 93 S, PO Box 729, Salmon 83467 [1 mi S of Hwy 28 on 93, bldg, blue roof]	208-756-2215	1,800,000 / 5,000-10,000
47	D3	Cobalt Ranger D., 311 McPherson St. (winter), PO Box 729, Salmon 83467	208-756-2240	627,555 / 7,000
48	D3	Leadore Ranger D., Hwy. 28, Box 180, Leadore 83464	208-768-2371	319,913 / 7,000
49	D3	North Fork Ranger D., Hwy. 93, PO Box 780, North Fork 83466	208-865-2383	598,904 / 7,000
50	C2	Salmon Ranger D., 604 Sharkey St., PO Box 729, Salmon 83467	208-756-3724	256,510 / 7,000
51	E2	Sawtooth National Forest Sup., 2647 Kimberly Rd. East, Twin Falls 83301	208-737-3200	2,200,000 / 4,000-12,000
52	E2	Burley Ranger D., 2621 South Overland Ave., Burley 83318	208-678-0430	327,800 / 4,000-9,000
53	E2	Fairfield Ranger D., PO Box 189, Fairfield 83327	208-764-2202	415,700 / 4,400-9,700
54	D2	Ketchum Ranger D., Sun Valley Road, PO Box 2356, Ketchum 83340	208-622-5371	328,400 / 5,500-12,000
55	D2	Sawtooth Nat'l Rec. Area & Redfish, Hwy. 75, Star Route, Ketchum 83340	208-726-7672	756,000 / 6,000-12,000
56	E2	Twin Falls Ranger D., 2647 Kimberly Road East, Twin Falls 83301	208-737-3200	309,000 / 4,000-8,000
57	D3	Targhee National Forest Sup., 420 North Bridge St., PO Box 208, St. Anthony 83445	208-624-3151	1,800,000 / 5,200-11,100
58	B4	Wallowa-Whitman Nat'l. Forest Sup., 1550 Dewey Ave., PO Box 907, Baker City, OR 97814	503-523-6391	2,396,049 / 900-9,393
58	D4	Ashton Ranger D., 30 South Yellowstone Hwy., PO Box 228, Ashton 83420	208-652-7442	348,630 / 5,300-9,720
59	D3	Dubois Ranger D., PO Box 46, Dubois 83423	208-374-5422	450,905 / 6,200-12,200
60	D4	Island Park Ranger D., PO Box 20, Island Park 83429	208-558-7301	858,327 / 6,100-9,800
61	D3	Palisades Ranger D., 3659 E. Ririe Hwy., Idaho Falls 83401	208-523-1412	458,797 / 5,120-10,025
62	D3	Teton Basin Ranger D., PO Box 127, Driggs 83422	208-354-2431	263,727 / 6,400-11,100
63	C1	Hells Canyon National Recreation Ar, Box 832, Riggins 83549 [S end of Riggins, W side of Hwy 95]	208-628-3916	652,488 / 1,000-9,393
		COE, Seattle District, PO Box 3755, Seattle, WA 98124	206-764-3442	
1	A1	Albeni Falls Dam & Lake Pend Oreill, PO Box 310, Newport 99156	208-437-3133	na / na
1		COE, Walla Walla District, City County Airport, Walla Walla, WA 99362	509-522-6714	na / na
2	B1	Dworshak Dam & Reservoir, PO Box 48, Ahsahka 83520	208-476-3294	na / na
3	D1	Lucky Peak Lake, HC 33, Box 1020, Boise 83706	208-343-0671	na / na
1	D1	**Deer Flat NWR**, 13751 Upper Embankment Road, Nampa 83686	208-467-9278	11,430 / 2,550
2	A1	Kootenai NWR, HRC 60, Box 283, Bonners Ferry 83805 [5 mi W of Bonners Ferry off Hwy 95, follow signs to office]	208-267-3888	3,000 / 1,800
3	E3	Southeast Idaho Refuge Complex, 1246 Yellowstone Ave., A-4, Pocatello 83201	208-237-6615	na / na
4	E4	Bear Lake NWR, 370 Webster, PO Box 9, Montpelier 83254	208-847-1757	18,000 / 5,920
5	D3	Camas NWR, 2150 E. 2350 N., Hamer 83425 [3 mi N on Frontage Rd, 2 mi W]	208-662-5423	10,500 / 4,900
6	E4	Grays Lake NWR, 74 Grays Lake Road, Wayan 83285 [access is difficult in winter]	208-574-2755	19,000 / 6,400-6,600
7	E2	Minidoka NWR, Rt. #4, Box 290, Rupert 83350 [12 mi NE of town, use SH 24; best viewed by boat sp/S, bad roads]	208-436-3589	20,720 / 4,100-4,300
1	D3	**Craters of the Moon National Monument**, US Hwy. 93, PO Box 29, Arco 83213	208-527-3257	53,545 / 5,900
2	E2	Hagerman Fossil Beds Nat'l. Mon., 963 Blue Lakes Blvd., Twin Falls 83301	208-733-8398	4,307 / 3,000
2	B1	Nez Perce National Historical Park, PO Box 93, Spalding 83551 [11 mi E of Lewiston on Hwy. 95]	208-843-2261	2,109 / 800-1,500
17	D1	BLM Idaho State Office, 3380 Americana Terrace, Boise 83706	208-384-3000	11,868,000 / na

No.	Grid	Name / Address	Acres / Elev.	Phone
*3	D1	Bruneau Resource Area, 3948 Development Ave., Boise 83705	2,037,000 / na	208-384-3300
4	E1	C.J. Strike Reservoir RMA, near Grand View	7,000 / 2,500	208-384-3300
5	E1	Jacks Creek RMA, near Bruneau	29,000 / 3,000	208-384-3300
6	D1	Oregon National Historic Trail RMA, near Boise	28,000 / 3,500	208-384-3300
7	D1	Snake River Birds of Prey RMA, near Kuna	27,000 / 2,500	208-384-3300
8	D1	Cascade Resource Area, 3948 Development Ave., Boise 83705	488,000 / na	208-384-3300
9	D1	Boise Front RMA, near Boise	12,000 / 3,500	208-384-3300
10	D1	Oxbow/Brownlee RMA, near Weiser	40,000 / 2,100	208-384-3300
11	D1	Payette River Corridor RMA, near Banks	19,000 / 2,800	208-384-3300
*12	D1	Jarbidge Resource Area, 3948 Development Ave., Boise 83705	1,695,000 / na	208-384-3300
13	E2	Bennett Mtn. Winter Rec. Area RMA, near Glenns Ferry	56,700 / 3,500	208-384-3300
14	E1	Bruneau/Jarbidge Rivers RMA, near Bruneau	55,000 / 4,500	208-384-3300
15	E1	Jarbridge Forks RMA, near Bruneau	4,300 / 5,000	208-384-3300
16	E2	Owsley Bridge ORV RMA, near Hagerman	2,700 / 3,000	208-384-3300
*17	D1	Owyhee Resource Area, 3948 Development Ave., Boise 83705	1,518,000 / na	208-384-3300
18	D1	Blackstock RMA, near Marsing	6,900 / 2,500	208-384-3300
19	D1	Jump Creek RMA, near Homedale	8,300 / 2,700	208-384-3300
20	E1	North Fork Owyhee Backcountry RMA, near Jordan Valley, OR, S of Marsing	55,000 / 5,000	208-384-3300
21	E1	Owyhee Front RMA, near Murphy	185,000 / 3,000	208-384-3300
22	D1	Owyhee River Canyonlands RMA, near Jordan Valley, OR, off US Hwy. 95, 50 mi. S of Marsing	37,000 / 5,000	208-384-3300
23	E1	Silver City RMA, near Silver City	1,200 / 6,200	208-284-3300
24	E1	Burley District Office, Rt. #3, Box 1, Burley 83318	1,341,000 / na	208-678-5514
25	E3	Deep Creek Resource Area, Rt. #3, Box 181, Malad City 83252	341,000 / na	208-766-4766
26	E3	Hawkins Reservoir RMA, near Pocatello	2,000 / 5,500	208-766-4766
27	E2	Snake River Resource Area, Rt. #3, Box 1, Burley 83318	1,000,000 / na	208-678-5514
28	E3	Cedar Fields RMA, near American Falls	2,300 / 4,500	208-678-5514
29	E2	Jim Sage Mountain RMA, near Burley	11,200 / 6,000	208-678-5514
30	E3	Milner RMA, near Burley	2,100 / 4,400	208-678-5514
31	E3	Raft River Crossing RMA, near Burley	600 / 4,500	208-678-5514
32	E2	Salmon Falls Creek Canyon RMA, near Rogerson	7,300 / 4,000	208-678-5514
33	E2	Salmon Falls Creek Reservoir RMA, near Rogerson	49,400 / 5,000	208-678-5514
34	A1	Coeur d'Alene District Office, 1808 N. Third Street, Coeur d'Alene 83814	249,000 / na	208-769-5000
35	C1	Cottonwood Resource Area, Rt. #3, Box 181, Cottonwood 83522	132,000 / na	208-962-3246
36	B1	Clearwater River RMA, near Lewiston	3,000 / 1,000	208-962-3246
37	C1	Lower Salmon River-Recreational RMA, near White Bird	16,000 / 1,600	208-962-3246
38	C1	Lower Salmon River-Scenic RMA, near White Bird	13,000 / 1,400	208-962-3246
39	B1	Emerald Empire Resource Area, 1808 N. Third Street, Coeur d'Alene 83814	117,000 / na	208-769-5000
40	B1	Beauty Bay RMA, near Coeur d'Alene	300 / 2,200	208-769-5000
41	B1	Lower Coeur d'Alene River RMA, near Coeur d'Alene	900 / 2,500	208-769-5000
42	D3	Idaho Falls District Office, 940 Lincoln Road, Idaho Falls 83401	2,021,000 / na	208-524-7500
43	D3	Big Butte Resource Area, 940 Lincoln Road, Idaho Falls 83401	1,102,000 / na	208-524-7500
44	D3	Big Southern Butte RMA, near Arco	5,800 / 7,600	208-524-7500
45	D3	Medicine Lodge Resource Area, 940 Lincoln Road, Idaho Falls 83401	653,000 / na	208-524-7500
46	D4	South Fork Snake River RMA, near Swan Valley	15,400 / 5,500	208-524-7500
47	D3	St. Anthony Sand Dunes RMA, near St. Anthony	36,900 / 5,500	208-524-7500
48	E3	Pocatello Resource Area, FOB, U.S. Courthouse, 250 S. 4th Ave., Suite 172, Pocatello 83201	265,000 / na	208-236-6860
49	E3	Blackfoot River RMA, near Blackfoot	16,000 / 6,500	208-236-6860
50	E3	Pocatello ORV RMA, near Pocatello	32,900 / 5,500	208-236-6860
51	C2	Salmon District Office, PO Box 430, Salmon 83467	1,296,000 / na	208-756-5400
52	C2	Challis Resource Area, PO Box 430, Salmon 83467	799,000 / na	208-756-5400
53	D2	Mackay Reservoir RMA, near Mackay	1,000 / 6,100	208-756-5400
54	D2	Upper Salmon River RMA, near Challis	7,500 / 4,500	208-756-5400
55	C2	Lemhi Resource Area, PO Box 430, Salmon 83467	497,000 / na	208-756-5400
56	C2	Continental Divide N. Scenic Trail , near Salmon	1,000 / 7,500	208-756-5400
57	C2	Lewis & Clark N. Historic Trail RMA, near Salmon	400 / 7,000	208-756-5400
58	E2	Shoshone District Office, 400 West "F" Street, PO Box 2B, Shoshone 83352	1,915,000 / na	208-886-2206
59	E2	Bennett Hills Resource Area, 400 West "F" Street, PO Box 2B, Shoshone 83352	772,000 / na	208-886-2206
60	E2	Gooding City of Rocks RMA, near Gooding	10,000 / 5,000	208-886-2206
61	E2	Snake River Rim RMA, near Twin Falls	5,000 / 3,500	208-886-2206
62	E2	T-Maze Caves RMA, near Shoshone	9,800 / 4,500	208-886-2206
63	E2	Thorn Creek RMA, near Shoshone	2,000 / 5,500	208-886-2206
64	E2	Monument Resource Area, 400 West "F" Street, PO Box 2B, Shoshone 83352	1,143,000 / na	208-886-2206
65	D2	Bald Mountain RMA, near Ketchum	1,300 / 7,500	208-886-2206
66	D2	Magic Reservoir RMA, near Bellevue	15,400 / 4,800	208-886-2206

AGENCY/MAP LEGEND ... INITIALS, MAP SYMBOLS, COLOR CODES

- U.S. Forest Service Supervisor & Ranger Dist. Offices . NFS [61]
- U.S. Army Corps of Engineers Rec. Areas & Offices . COE [31]
- USFWS National Wildlife Refuges & Offices ... NWR [40]
- National Park Service Parks & other NPS Sites ... NPS [7]
- Bureau of Land Management Rec. Areas & Offices .. BLM [36]
- Bureau of Reclamation Rec. Areas & Reg. Offices .. BOR [8]
- State Parks (also see State Agency notes) ...... SPS [52]
- State Wildlife Areas (also see State Agency notes) .. SWA [19]
- Private Preserves, Nature Centers & Tribal Lands ...
- The Wild Rivers ~~~ and Wilderness Areas

Note: Refer to yellow block on page 7 (top right) for location name and address abbreviations.

★ INFORMATION CHART ★

INFORMATION CHART LEGEND - SYMBOLS & LETTER CODES

- ■ means YES & □ means Yes with disability provisions
- **sp** means spring, March through May
- **S** means Summer, June through August
- **F** means Fall, September through November
- **W** means Winter, December through February
- **T** means Two (2) or Three (3) Seasons
- **A** means All Four (4) Seasons
- **na** means Not Applicable or Not Available

Note: empty or blank spaces in the chart mean NO ... ★ that symbol is not shown on the map. If a symbol number has a star.

Column group headings: **FACILITIES, SERVICES, RECREATION OPPORTUNITIES & CONVENIENCES**

Column headers (vertical): DRINKING WATER; RESTROOMS; DAY USE ONLY / no overnight; PARK & WALK-IN ONLY AREA; WINTER SPORTS OPPORTUNITIES; HUNTING IN SEASON, license / permit req'd.; NON-MOTORIZED WATERCRAFT OK; MOTORIZED WATERCRAFT OK, check limits; BOATING FACILITIES, ramps, marinas, etc. / permit req'd.; FISHING OPPORTUNITIES, license / permit req'd.; OFF-ROAD RIDING, at one's own risk; HORSEBACK RIDING, ...areas, trails; BICYCLING OPPORTUNITIES; WALKING / HIKING TRAILS; WILDERNESS AREAS / WILD RIVERS; WILDLIFE PERMITTED / CAMPSITES; NO-CHARGE CAMPGROUNDS / CAMPSITES; DEVELOPED PICNIC AREAS / PICNIC SITES; WILDLIFE VIEWING SITES, birds, etc.; ENDANGERED SPECIES ARE COMMON; WILDLIFE IS ABUNDANT OR COMMON; WILDLIFE INTERPRETIVE TRAILS; ARCHAEOLOGICAL / GEOLOGICAL SITES; HISTORIC SITES; WILDFLOWER VIEWING AREA or DRIVE; NATURE EDUCATION / STUDY PROGRAMS; INTERPRETIVE VISUAL / EDUCATION; AGENCY GUIDED TOURS, scheduled / by res.; FREE LITERATURE, brochures, maps, etc.; INTERPRETIVE or EDUCATIONAL SERVICES; CONCESSIONAIRE SERVICES AVAILABLE; INFO OFFICE / VISITOR CENTER (VC); IO / VC OPEN SATURDAY / SUNDAY; ENTRY FEE / VC

S#	MAP	LOCATION NAME (state initials if more than one) with ADDRESS and/or LOCATION DATA	TELEPHONE	ACRES / ELEVATION
67	D2	North Ketchum RMA, near Ketchum	208-886-2206	300 / 5,500
(1)	D1	**Idaho Dept. Parks & Recreation**, 7800 Fairview Ave., State House (for mail & zip), Boise 83720	208-327-7444	na / na
1	A1	Farragut SP, E. 13400 Ranger Rd., Athol 83801	208-683-2425	4,733 / 2,050-2,500
2	D4	Harriman SP, HC 66, Box 33, Island Park 83429	208-558-7368	4,700 / 4,330-6,100
3	B1	Heyburn SP, Rt. #1, Box 139, Plummer 83851	208-686-1308	7,825 / 2,200
4	E3	Massacre Rocks SP, 3592 N. Park Lane, American Falls 83211	208-548-2672	565 / 4,400
5	C1	Pondersa SP, PO Box A, McCall 83638	208-634-2164	1,280 / 5,050-5,200
6	A1	Priest Lake SP (3 units), Indian Creek Bay, # 423, Coolin 83821	208-443-2200	463 / 2,440
7	C1	Winchester Lake SP, PO Box 186, Winchester 83555	208-924-7563	418 / 3,900
(1)	D1	**Idaho Dept. of Fish & Game** (IDFG), 600 South Walnut St., PO Box 25, Boise 83707	208-334-3700	10 / 2,700
2	A1	Region 1 - IDFG, 2320 Government Way, Coeur d'Alene 83814	208-765-3111	1 / 2,200
3	A1	Coeur d'Alene River WMA, 3 mi. E of Harrison	208-765-3111	5,046 / 2,200
4	A1	Farragut WMA, 4 mi. W of Bayview	208-765-3111	1,445 / 2,100
5	A1	McArthur Lake WMA, 4 mi. S of Naples	208-765-3111	1,201 / 2,050
6	A1	Pend Oreille WMA, near Bonners Ferry	208-765-3111	4,318 / 2,090
7	B1	Snow Peak WMA, Shoshone Co. near Avery	208-765-3111	na / na
8	B1	St. Maries WMA, 7 mi. S of St. Maries	208-765-3111	10,627 / 2,220
9	C1	Region 2 - IDFG, 1540 Warner Ave., Lewiston 83501	208-743-6502	2 / 740
10	C1	Craig Mountain WMA, Nez Perce Co., near Winchester	208-743-6502	24,202 / 800-5,200
11	D1	Region 3 - IDFG, 109 West 44th St., Boise 83714 [office moving to Nampa]	208-327-7025	2 / 2,700
12	D1	Boise River WMA, 1 mi. NE of Boise	208-327-7025	20,000 / 2,800-6,000
13	E1	C.J. Strike WMA, 4 mi. W of Bruneau	208-327-7025	8,300 / 2,500
14	D1	Fort Boise WMA, 5 mi. NW of Parma	208-327-7025	1,400 / 2,240
15	E2	Payette River WMA, in Gem, Payette & Canyon Cos., near Banks	208-327-7025	2,041 / 2,230-2,260
16	E2	Region 4 - IDFG, 868 East Main St., Jerome 83338	208-324-4350	2 / 3,600
17	E2	Billingsley Creek WMA, 2 mi. NE of Hagerman	208-324-4350	275 / 2,960
18	E2	Camas Prairie Centennial Marsh WMA, in Camas County, near Fairfield	208-324-4350	2,328 / 5,000
19	E2	Carey Lake WMA, 1 mi. E of Carey	208-324-4350	430 / 4,600
20	E2	Hagerman WMA, 3 mi. SE of Hagerman	208-324-4350	877 / 2,900
21	E2	Niagara Springs WMA, 7 mi. S of Wendell	208-324-4350	957 / 2,950-3,360
22	E3	Region 5 - IDFG, 1345 Barton Rd., Pocatello 83204	208-232-4703	4 / 4,470
23	E4	Montpelier WMA, 1 mi. E of Montpelier	208-232-4703	1,588 / 5,920-7,600
24	E3	Portneuf WMA, 12 mi. S of Pocatello	208-232-4703	3,104 / 4,700-7,500
25	E2	Sterling WMA, 2 mi. E of Aberdeen	208-232-4703	3,304 / 4,400
26	D3	Region 6 - IDFG, 1515 Lincoln Rd., Idaho Falls 83401	208-522-7783	3 / 4,710
27	D3	Cartier Slough WMA, 10 mi. W of Rexburg	208-232-4703	1,000 / 4,970
28	D3	Market Lake WMA, 1 mi. N of Roberts	208-522-7783	5,000 / 4,780
29	D3	Mud Lake WMA, 2 mi. N of Terreton	208-522-7783	8,000 / 4,780
30	D3	Sand Creek WMA, 15 mi. N of St. Anthony	208-522-7783	15,000 / 6,200
31	E3	Tex Creek WMA, 20 mi. SE of Idaho Falls	208-522-7783	18,000 / 5,120-7,290
◇1	D2	**TNC Idaho Field Office**, PO Box 165, Sun Valley 83353	208-726-3007	14 / 5,400
1	C1	Garden Creek Preserve, contact Field Office, W of Cottonwood	208-726-3007	11,685 / 800-5,000
2	D1	Thousand Springs Preserve, 120 Thousand Springs Grade, Wendell 83355	208-536-6797	4,200 / 2,900
3	B1	Hixon-Sharptail Preserve, contact Field Office, near Weiser	208-726-3007	4,200 / 3,300
4	B1	Idler's Rest Preserve, c/o U. of ID, Col. of Forestry, Dept. of Wildland Rec. Mgt., Moscow 83843	208-885-7911	40 / 4,000
5	E2	Silver Creek Preserve, PO Box 624, Picabo 83353	208-788-2203	3,200 / 4,800
6	E1	Snake Rvr. Birds of Prey Nat'l Area, contact Field Office, or a BLM office in Boise, S of Boise	208-726-3007	380 / 2,000
7	D2	Stapp-Soldier Creek Preserve, contact Field Office, E of Halley, Hailey	208-726-3007	120 / 4,600

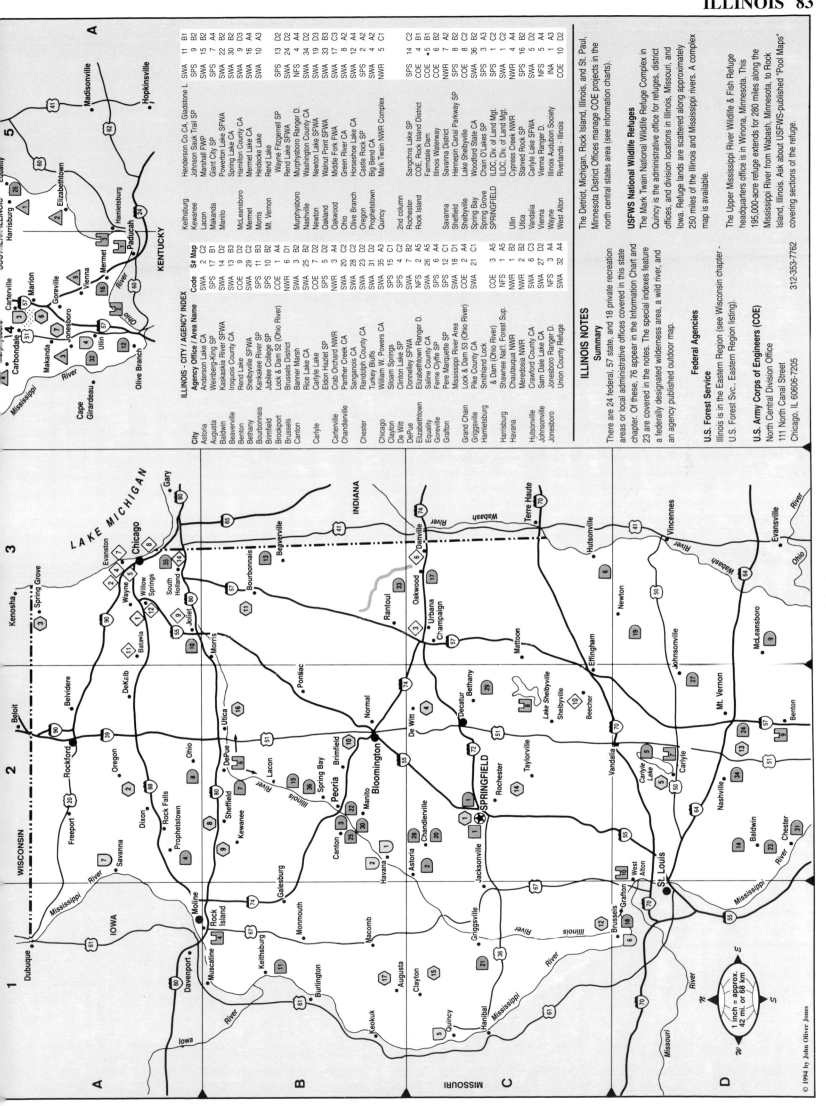

ILLINOIS - CITY / AGENCY INDEX

City	Agency Office / Area Name	Code	S#	Map
Astoria	Anderson Lake CA	SWA	3	C2
Augusta	Weinberg-King SP	SPS	17	B1
Baldwin	Kaskaskia River SFWA	SWA	14	D2
Beaverville	Iroquois County CA	SWA	13	B3
Benton	Rend Lake	COE	9	D3
Bethany	Shelbyville SFWA	SWA	29	C2
Bourbonnais	Kankakee River SP	SPS	11	B3
Brimfield	Jubilee College SP	SPS	10	B2
Brookport	Lock & Dam 52 (Ohio River)	COE	1	A4
Brussels	Brussels District	NWR	6	D1
Canton	Banner Marsh	SWA	25	B2
	Rice Lake CA	SWA	25	B2
Carlyle	Carlyle Lake	COE	5	D2
	Eldon Hazlet SP	SPS	7	D2
Carterville	Crab Orchard NWR	NWR	3	A4
Chandlerville	Panther Creek CA	SWA	20	C2
	Sanganois CA	SWA	28	C2
Chester	Randolph County CA	SWA	23	D2
	Turkey Bluffs	SWA	31	D2
Chicago	William W. Powers CA	SWA	35	A3
Clayton	Siloam Springs	SPS	15	C1
De Witt	Clinton Lake CA	SWA	4	C2
DePue	Donnelley SFWA	SWA	7	B2
Elizabethtown	Elizabethtown Ranger D.	NFS	2	A5
Equality	Saline County CA	SWA	26	A4
Goreville	Ferne Clyffe SP	SPS	6	A4
Grafton	Pere Marquette SP	SPS	12	C1
	Mississippi River Area	SWA	18	D1
Grand Chain	Lock & Dam 53 (Ohio River)	COE	2	A4
Griggsville	Pike County CA	SWA	21	C1
Hamletsburg	Smithland Lock & Dam (Ohio River)	COE	3	A5
Harrisburg	Shawnee Nat'l. Forest Sup.	NFS	1	B1
Havana	Chautauqua NWR	NWR	1	B2
	Meredosia NWR	NWR	2	B2
Hutsonville	Crawford County CA	SWA	27	D2
Johnsonville	Sam Dale Lake CA	SWA		
Jonesboro	Jonesboro Ranger D.	NFS	3	A4
	Union County Refuge	SWA	32	A4

City / Agency Office / Area Name	Code	S#	Map
Keithsburg — Henderson Co CA, Gladstone L.	SWA	11	B1
Kewanee — Johnson Sauk Trail SP	SPS	9	B2
Lacon — Marshall FWP	SWA	15	B2
Makanda — Giant City SP	SPS	7	A4
Manito — Powerton Lake CA	SWA	30	B2
— Spring Lake CA	SWA	9	D3
McLeansboro — Hamilton County CA	SWA	22	D3
Mermet — Mermet Lake CA	SWA	16	A4
Morris — Heidecke Lake	SWA	10	A3
Mt. Vernon — Rend Lake			
Murphysboro — Wayne Fitzgerrell SP	SPS	13	D2
— Rend Lake SFWA	SWA	24	D2
— Murphysboro Ranger D.	NFS	4	A4
Nashville — Washington County CA	SWA	34	D2
Newton — Newton Lake SFWA	SWA	19	D3
Oakland — Walnut Point SFWA	SWA	33	B3
Oakwood — Middle Fork FWA	SWA	17	C3
Ohio — Green River CA	SWA	8	A2
Olive Branch — Horseshoe Lake CA	SWA	12	A4
Oregon — Castle Rock SP	SPS	2	A2
Prophetstown — Big Bend CA	SWA	4	A2
Quincy — Mark Twain NWR Complex	NWR	5	C1

2nd column

City / Agency Office / Area Name	Code	S#	Map
Rochester — Sangchris Lake SP	SPS	14	C2
Rock Island — COE, Rock Island District	COE	4	B1
— Farmdale Dam	COE	*5	B1
— Illinois Waterway	COE	7	A2
Savanna — Savanna District	NWR	7	A2
Sheffield — Hennepin Canal Parkway SP	SPS	8	B2
Shelbyville — Lake Shelbyville	COE	8	C2
Spring Grove — Chain O'Lakes SP	SPS	36	B2
SPRINGFIELD — ILDC, Div. of Land Mgt.	SPS	1	C2
— ILDC, Div. of Land Mgt.	SPS	1	C2
Ullin — Cypress Creek NWR	NWR	4	B2
Utica — Starved Rock SP	SPS	1	B2
Vandalia — Carlyle Lake SFWA	SWA	16	B2
Vienna — Vienna Ranger D.	NFS	4	D2
Wayne — Illinois Audubon Society	NFS	1	A3
West Alton — Riverlands - Illinois	INA	1	A3
—	COE	10	D2

ILLINOIS NOTES

Summary

There are 24 federal, 57 state, and 18 private recreation areas or local administrative offices covered in this state chapter. Of these, 76 appear in the Information Chart and 23 are covered in the notes. The special indexes feature a federally designated wilderness area, a wild river, and an agency published outdoor map.

The Detroit, Michigan, Rock Island, Illinois, and St. Paul, Minnesota District Offices manage COE projects in the north central states area (see information charts).

USFWS National Wildlife Refuges

The Mark Twain National Wildlife Refuge Complex in Quincy is the administrative office for refuges, district offices, and division locations in Illinois, Missouri, and Iowa. Refuge lands are scattered along approximately 250 miles of the Illinois and Mississippi rivers. A complex map is available.

The Upper Mississippi River Wildlife & Fish Refuge headquarters office in Winona, Minnesota. This 195,000-acre refuge extends for 280 miles along the Mississippi River from Wabash, Minnesota, to Rock Island, Illinois. Ask about USFWS-published "Pool Maps" covering sections of the refuge.

Federal Agencies

U.S. Forest Service

Illinois is in the Eastern Region (see Wisconsin chapter - U.S. Forest Svc., Eastern Region listing).

U.S. Army Corps of Engineers (COE)

North Central Division Office
111 North Canal Street
Chicago, IL 60606-7205
312-353-7762

National Park Service
NPS Location in Illinois
Lincoln Home National Historic Site (12 acres)
(S# 1, map C2)
413 South Eighth Street
Springfield, IL 62701 · 217-492-4241

The Fisheries, Forest, and Wildlife Division function under this department.

Division of Land Management (Parks)
An *Illinois State Recreational Areas Guide* is available free. It describes the facilities and activities available in 67 State Parks, Historic Sites, State Forests, Conservation Areas and Fish and Wildlife Areas. A small state map is provided showing the general location of the areas. There is no entry fee but there are camping fees.

Wilderness Area
Crab Orchard Wilderness - 4,050 acres
Crab Orchard NWR (S# 2, map A4)

Division of Forest Resources
Northwest Office Plaza, Suite 2
Springfield, IL 62706 · 217-782-2361
Contact the Division office for state forest recreation literature.

Wild River
Middle Fork of the Vermilion River
Illinois Dept. of Conservation (see office listing below)

Division of Wildlife Resources (DWR)
Two basic references are *Guide to Public Hunting Areas in Illinois* and *Illinois Fishing Guide*. Various types of areas provide hunting opportunities. They include Conservation Areas (CA), State Fish & Wildlife Areas (SF&WA), and Fish and Wildlife Areas (FWA).

Outdoor Map Index
U.S. Forest Service Map
Shawnee National Forest [1988]
Scale: 1 inch = 4.0 miles (1 cm = 2.5 km)
Size: 33x50 inches (83x127 cm)

State Agencies
Illinois Dept. of Conservation
Lincoln Tower Plaza
524 S. Second St.
Springfield, IL 62701-1787 · 217-782-6302

Nature Preserves Commission
Lincoln Tower Plaza
524 S. Second St.
Springfield, IL 62701-1787
Manage Nature Preserves in Illinois. Contact this office for literature and access information.

Dept. of Commerce and Community Affairs
Office of Tourism · 312-793-2094
Chicago, IL · or 1-800-223-0121

Private Organizations
ANCA Locations in Illinois
Alexander Stillman Nature Center (S# 2, map A3)
33 West Penny Road
South Barrington, IL 60010 · 312-381-6201

Anita Purves Nature Center (S# 3, map C3)
1505 North Broadway
Urbana, IL 61801 · 217-384-4062

Crabtree Nature Center (S# 4, map A3)
Route 3, Stover Road
Barrington, IL 60010 · 708-381-6592

Fullerburg Woods Nature Center (S# 5, map A3)
3609 Spring Road
Oak Brook, IL 60521 · 708-790-4900

Kennekuk Nature Center (S# 6, map C3)
RR #1, Box 215
Danville, IL 61832 · 217-442-1691

Ladd Arboretum/Ecology Center (S# 7, map A3)
2024 McCormick Blvd.
Evanston, IL 60201 · 708-864-5181

North Park Village Nature Center (S# 8, map A3)
5801 North Pulaski Road
Chicago, IL 60646 · 312-583-8970

Pilcher Park Nature Center (S# 9, map A3)
3000 West Jefferson St.
Joliet, IL 60435 · 815-741-7277

Plum Creek Nature Center (S# 10, map C2)
RR #2, Box 241
Beecher, IL 60401 · 312-946-2216

Red Oak Nature Center (S# 11, map A3)
2342 South River
Batavia, IL 60510 · 312-897-1808

Red Schoolhouse Nature Center (S# 12, map A3)
9800 South 104th Ave.
Willow Springs, IL 60480 · 708-839-6897

River Trail Nature Center (S# *13, map A3)
3120 North Milwaukee Ave.
Northbrook, IL 60062 · 312-824-8630

Sand Ridge Nature Center (S# 14, map A3)
15890 Paxton
South Holland, IL 60473 · 708-868-0606

Spring Brook Nature Center (S# *15, map A3)
130 Forest Ave.
Itasca, IL 60143 · 312-733-5572

Spring Valley Nature Sanctuary (S# *16, map A3)
1111 East Schaumburg Road
Schaumburg, IL 60194 · 708-980-2100

Willowbrook Wildlife Haven (S# *17, map A3)
Park Blvd.
Glen Ellyn, IL 60137 · 708-790-4913

Illinois State Chamber of Commerce
20 N. Wacker Dr., #1960
Chicago, IL 60606-3083 · Phone 312-372-7373
Fax 312-372-7382

★ INFORMATION CHART ★

AGENCY/MAP LEGEND . . . INITIALS, MAP SYMBOLS, COLOR CODES

U.S. Forest Service Supervisor & Ranger Dist. Offices	NFS **61**
U.S. Army Corps of Engineers Rec. Areas & Offices . .	COE **31**
USFWS National Wildlife Refuges & Offices	NWR **40**
National Park Service Parks & other NPS Sites	NPS **7**
Bureau of Land Management Rec. Areas & Offices	BLM **26**
Bureau of Reclamation Rec. Areas & Reg. Offices	BOR **8**
State Parks (also see State Agency notes)	SPS **52**
State Wildlife Areas (also see State Agency notes) . . .	SWA **19**
Private Preserves, Nature Centers & Tribal Lands . . .	**15**

The Wild Rivers ⌇⌇⌇ and Wilderness Areas ▨▨▨

Note: Refer to yellow block on page 7 (top right) for location name and address abbreviations.

INFORMATION CHART LEGEND - SYMBOLS & LETTER CODES

- ■ means YES & □ means Yes with disability provisions
- sp means spring, March through May
- S means Summer, June through August
- F means Fall, September through November
- W means Winter, December through February
- T means Two (2) or Three (3) Seasons
- A means All Four (4) Seasons
- na means Not Applicable or Not Available

Note: empty or blank spaces in the chart mean NO

Note: a symbol number has a star ★ that symbol is not shown on the map.

S#	MAP	LOCATION NAME (state initials if more than one) with ADDRESS and/or LOCATION DATA	TELEPHONE ACRES / ELEVATION
△	A5	**Shawnee Nat'l. Forest Sup.**, 901 S. Commercial St., Harrisburg 62946	618-253-7114 · 270,000 / 350-1,000
2	A5	Elizabethtown Ranger D., Rt. #2, Box 4, Elizabethtown 62931	618-287-2201 · 61,000 / 350-800
3	A4	Jonesboro Ranger D., 521 N. Main Street, Jonesboro 62952	618-833-8576 · 50,000 / 350-1,000
4	A4	Murphysboro Ranger D., Box 787, Murphysboro 62966	618-687-1731 · 56,000 / 350-700
5	A4	Vienna Ranger D., Rt. #1, Box 288B, Vienna 62995	618-658-2111 · 96,000 / 350-1,000
▭		**COE, Louisville District**, PO Box 59, Louisville, KY 40201	502-582-6692 · na / na
1	A4	Lock & Dam 52 (Ohio River), PO Box 277, Brookport 62910	618-564-3151 · na / na
2	A4	Lock & Dam 53 (Ohio River), RR #1, Grand Chain 62941	618-742-6213 · na / na
3	A5	Smithland Lock & Dam (Ohio River), PO Box 401, Hamletsburg 62944	618-564-2315 · na / na
4	B1	COE, Rock Island District, Clock Tower Bldg., PO Box 2004, Rock Island 61204	309-788-6361 · na / na
★5	B1	Farmdale Dam, Clock Tower Building, Rock Island 61204	309-788-6361 · na / na
6	B2	COE, St. Louis District, 1222 Spruce St., St. Louis, MO 63103	314-331-8622 · na / na
7	D2	Carlyle Lake, 801 Lake Road, Carlyle 62231	618-594-2484 · na / na
8	C2	Lake Shelbyville, RR 4, Box 128B, Shelbyville 00006	217-774-3951 · na / na
9	D2	Rend Lake, RR #3, Benton 62812	618-724-2493 · na / na
10	D2	Riverlands - Illinois, PO Box 337, West Alton 63386	314-899-0405 · na / na
①	B2	**Chautauqua NWR**, RR #2, Box 61-B, Havana 62644 [take Manito Blacktop and go 6 mi N of Havana to refuge]	309-535-2290 · 4,500 / 430-470
2	B2	Meredosia NWR, RR #2, Box 61-B, Havana 62644 [just N & NE of Meredosia]	309-535-2290 · na / 424-460

Illinois Waterway, Clock Tower Building, Rock Island 61204 [along Illinois river bet. Griggsville and Chicago]

(Information chart data columns: FACILITIES, SERVICES, RECREATION OPPORTUNITIES & CONVENIENCES — column headers include: INFO OFFICE (IO) / VISITOR CENTER (VC); IO / VC OPEN SATURDAY / SUNDAY; ENTRY FEE, not camping fee / ENTRY FEE (EF); CONCESSIONAIRE SERVICES; INTERPRETIVE GUIDED TOURS; FREE LITERATURE: brochures, maps, etc.; AGENCY LITERATURE AVAILABLE; NATURE EDUCATION / STUDY PROGRAMS; WILDFLOWER VIEWING AREA or DRIVE; ARCHAEOLOGICAL / GEOLOGICAL SITES; HISTORIC SITES; INTERPRETIVE TRAILS; WILDLIFE VIEWING AREA / STUDY; ENDANGERED SPECIES ARE COMMON; WILDLIFE IS ABUNDANT OR COMMON; DEVELOPED PICNIC AREAS / PICNIC SITES; NO-CHARGE CAMPGROUNDS / CAMPSITES; WILDERNESS AREAS / WILD RIVERS; WALKING / HIKING TRAILS; BICYCLING OPPORTUNITIES; OFF-ROAD MOTORING; HORSEBACK RIDING / TRAILS; SWIMMING PERMITTED, at one's own risk; FISHING IN SEASON / by res.; BOATING IN SEASON, w/ your own horse; NON-MOTORIZED WATERCRAFT OK; MOTORIZED WATERCRAFT OK, check limits; WINTER SPORTS OPPORTUNITIES; PARK & USE ONLY, WALK-IN ONLY AREA; DRINKING WATER; RESTROOMS)

		Name / Address	Phone	Acres
5	C1	Mark Twain NWR Complex, 1704 N. 24th St., Quincy 62301	217-224-8580	na / na
6	D1	Brussels Dist HQ, HCR Box 107, Brussels 62013 [take Brussels Ferry (Hwy 100) in Calhoun Co, go 4 mi W/N of Grafton]	618-883-2524	8,000 / 422
7		Upper Miss. River NW & Fish Refuge, 51 East 4th St., Room 101, Winona, MN 55987	507-452-4232	200,000 / na
7	A2	Savanna District, Post Office Bldg., Savanna 61074	815-273-2732	46,000 / 600

ILDC, Div. of Land Management (Parks), 600 N. Grand Ave. West, Springfield 62706 — 217-782-6752 — na / na

		Name / Address	Phone	Acres
1	C2	Castle Rock SP, 1365 W. Castle Rd., Oregon 61061	815-732-7329	1,995 / na
2	A2	Chain O'Lakes SP, 39947 N. State Park Rd., Spring Grove 60081	708-587-5512	6,063 / na
3	A3	Clinton Lake SP, RR #1, Box 4, De Witt 61735	217-935-8722	9,907 / na
4	C2	Eldon Hazlet SP, 1351 Ridge St., Carlyle 62231	618-594-3015	3,000 / na
5	D2	Ferne Clyffe SP, Box 120, Goreville 62939	618-995-2411	1,125 / na
6	A4	Giant City SP, PO Box 70, Makanda 62958	618-457-4836	3,694 / na
7	A4	Hennepin Canal Parkway SP, RR #2, Box 201, Sheffield 61361	815-454-2328	5,777 / na
8	B2	Johnson Sauk Trail SP, RR #3, Kewanee 61443	309-853-5589	1,361 / na
9	B2	Jubilee College SP, 13921 W. Route 150, Brimfield 61517	309-446-3758	3,800 / na
10	B2	Kankakee River SP, PO Box 37, Bourbonnais 60914	815-933-1383	3,783 / na
11	B3	Pere Marquette SP, Box 158, Grafton 62037	618-786-3323	7,500 / na
12	C1	Rend Lake Wayne Fitzgerrell SP, RR #1, Box 73, Whittington 62897, SW of Mt. Vernon	618-629-2320	3,302 / na
13	D2	Sangchris Lake SP, RR #1, Box 58, Rochester 62563	217-498-9208	3,576 / na
14	C1	Siloam Springs, RR #1, Box 204, Clayton 62324	217-894-6205	3,323 / na
15	C1	Starved Rock SP, Box 116, Utica 61373	815-667-4726	2,630 / na
16	B2	Weinberg-King SP, PO Box 203, Augusta 62311	217-392-2345	772 / na
17	B1			

ILDC, Div. of Land Management (Conservation and other Areas), 600 N. Grand Ave. West, Springfield 62706 — 217-782-6752 — na / na

		Name / Address	Phone	Acres
1	C2	Anderson Lake CA (near Browning), RR #1, Astoria 61501	309-759-4484	2,135 / na
2	C2	Banner Marsh (near Banner), c/o Rice Lake CA, RR #3, Box 91, Canton 61520	309-647-9184	1,879 / na
3	B2	Big Bend CA, c/o Prophetstown St. Park, PO Box 181, Prophetstown 61277	815-537-2926	1,188 / na
4	A2	Carlyle Lake SFWA, RR #2, Vandalia 62471	618-425-3533	5,680 / na
5	B2	Crawford County CA, RR #1, Hutsonville 62433	618-563-4405	1,130 / na
6	C3	Donnelley SFWA (near Hennepin), Box 52, DePue 61322	815-447-2353	643 / na
7	B2	Green River CA, RR #1, Box 92, Harmon 61042, near Ohio	815-379-2324	2,330 / na
8	A2	Hamilton County CA, RR #4, McLeansboro 62859	618-773-4340	1,683 / na
9	D3	Heidecke Lake, 5010 N. Jugtown, Morris 60450	815-942-6352	2,468 / na
10	A3	Henderson Co. CA (Gladstone Lake), RR #1, Keithsburg 61442	309-374-2496	87 / na
11	B1	Horseshoe Lake CA, Box 85, Miller City 62962, near Olive Branch	618-776-5689	9,550 / na
12	B2	Iroquois County CA, near Beaverville 60912	815-435-2218	1,920 / na
13	B3	Kaskaskia River SFWA, RR #1, Box 49, Baldwin 62217	618-785-2555	10,096 / na
14	D2	Marshall FWP, RR #1, Box 236, Lacon 61540	309-246-8351	5,658 / na
15	B2	Mermet Lake CA, RR #1, Box 126, Belknap 62908, near Mermet	618-524-5577	2,580 / na
16	A4	Middle Fork FWA, c/o Kickapoo St. Park, RR #1, Box 374, Oakwood 61858	217-442-4915	2,843 / na
17	C3	Mississippi River Area, RR #1, Box 182, Grafton 62037	618-376-3303	33,794 / na
18	D1	Newton Lake SFWA, RR #4, Box 329, Newton 62448	518-783-3478	780 / na
19	D3	Panther Creek CA, RR #2, Box 80, Chandlerville 62627	309-546-2628	759 / na
20	C2	Pike County CA, RR #1, Box 54, Griggsville 62340	217-833-2811	862 / na
21	C2	Powerton Lake SFWA (near Pekin), c/o Spring Lake CA, RR #1, Box 248, Manito 61546	309-968-7135	1,426 / na
22	D2	Randolph County CA, RR #1, Box 345, Chester 62233	618-826-2706	1,031 / na
23	D2	Rend Lake SFWA, mail to: RR 1, Box 73, Whittington 62897, SW of Mt. Vernon	618-629-2320	6,895 / na
24	D3	Rice Lake CA, RR #3, Box 91, Canton 61520	309-647-9184	5,660 / na
25	B2	Saline County CA, RR #1, Box 30, Equality 62934	618-276-4405	1,248 / na
26	A5	Sam Dale CA, RR #1, Johnsonville 62850	618-835-2292	1,301 / na
27	B2	Sanganois CA, RR #2, Box 80, Chandlerville 62627	309-546-2628	9,460 / na
28	C2	Shelbyville SFWA, RR #1, Box 42A, Bethany 61914	217-665-3112	7,016 / na
29	C2	Spring Lake CA, RR #1, Box 248, Manito 61546	309-968-7135	2,301 / na
30	B2	Turkey Bluffs, RR #1, Box 345, Chester 62233	618-826-2706	2,264 / na
31	B2	Union County Refuge, RR #2, Box 628, Jonesboro 62952	618-833-8711	6,202 / na
32	A4	Walnut Point SFWA, RR #2, Box 250, Oakland 61943	217-346-3336	577 / na
33	B3	Washington County CA, RR #3, Nashville 62263	618-327-3137	1,417 / na
34	D2	William W. Powers CA, 12800 S. Avenue O, Chicago 60633	312-646-3270	614 / na
35	A3	Woodford State CA, RR #1, Low Point 61545, near Spring Bay	309-822-8861	2,900 / na

		Name / Address	Phone	Acres
1	A3	Illinois Audubon Society & Barbara Dunham-Dole Wildlife Sanctuary, PO Box 608, Wayne 60184 [call for directions]	708-584-6290	30 / 700

S#	MAP	PARK NAME & LOCATION
2	A2	Bass Lake SB, Knox
3	D2	Brown County SP, Nashville
4	A3	Chain O'Lakes SP, Albion
5	D3	Clifty Falls SP, Madison
6	E1	Harmonie SP, New Harmony
7	A2	Indiana Dunes SP, Chesterton
8	E2	Lincoln SP, Lincoln City
9	C2	McCormick's Creek SP, Spencer
10	C3	Mounds SP, Anderson
11	B3	Ouabache SP, Bluffton
12	A3	Pokagon SP, Angola
13	A2	Potato Creek SP, North Liberty
14	C2	Shades SP, Waveland
15	D1	Shakamak SP, Jasonville
16	D2	Spring Mill SP, Mitchell
17	C3	Summit Lake SP, New Castle
18	A2	Tippecanoe River SP, Winamac
19	C1	Turkey Run SP, Marshall
20	D3	Versailles SP, Versailles
21	C3	Whitewater Memorial SP, Liberty

INDIANA NOTES

Summary

There are 18 federal, 41 state, and 29 private recreation areas or local administrative offices covered in this state chapter. Of these, 58 appear in the Information Chart and 30 are covered in the notes. The special indexes feature a federally designated wilderness area and 2 agency published outdoor maps.

Federal Agencies

U.S. Forest Service

Indiana is in the Eastern Region (see Wisconsin chapter - U.S. Forest Svc., Eastern Region listing).

Note: A local U.S. Forest Service recreation specialist advises use of an off-road vehicle in Indiana is illegal. Those who are apprehended doing so are subject to arrest.

National Park Service

Additional NPS Locations in Indiana

George Rogers Clark National Historic Park (26 acres) (S# 2, map D1)
401 South Second Street
Vincennes, IN 47591   812-882-1776

Lincoln Boyhood National Memorial (200 acres) (S# 3, map E2)
Lincoln City, IN 47552   812-937-4541

Wilderness Index

Charles C. Deam Wilderness - 12,935
Wayne-Hoosier National Forest Sup. (S# 1, map D2)

Outdoor Map Index

National Park Service (USGS Map)

Indiana Dunes National Lakeshore [1980]
Scale: 1 inch = 0.8 mile (1 cm = 0.5 km)

U.S. Forest Service Map

Hoosier National Forest [1989]
Scale: 1 inch = 2.0 miles (1 cm = 1.3 km)
Size: 29x57 inches (73x144 cm)

State Agencies

Department of Natural Resources (DNR)

402 W. Washington St., #C256
Indianapolis, IN 46204-2212   317-232-4200
State Parks, Forestry, Fish and Wildlife, Nature Preserves, Outdoor Recreation, and other divisions operate under the DNR. A magazine, *Outdoor Indiana*, is published 11 times a year. It is available by subscription for $10 or at DNR offices for $1.58 per issue.

Division of State Parks

A DNR Recreation Guide is available free. It provides information on State Parks, State Forests, Reservoirs, Nature Explores, Museums and Historic Sites, and Fish and Wildlife Properties. Selected State Parks are shown on the Guide map and listed here with the map symbol number and coordinates, park name, and location.

Division of Forestry

613 State Office Bldg.
Indianapolis, IN 46204
Contact the Division office for state forest recreation literature.

Division of Fish & Wildlife (DFW)

A free catalog of publications lists DFW pamphlets categorized in Management Series, Life Series, Information Leaflets, and General Publications. Various publications pertaining to fishing and hunting rules and regulations are also listed.

Division of Tourism

Indianapolis, IN   317-232-8860
                           or 1-800-289-6646

Private Organizations

TNC-Indiana Field Office

A guide book is available from the office for $15.75. It describes 123 preserve projects in Indiana.

ANCA Locations in Indiana

Clifty Falls Nature Center (S# 25, map D3)
1501 Green Road
Madison, IN 47250

Eagle Creek Nature Center (S# 26, map C2)
6515 Delong Road
Indianapolis, IN 46278   317-291-5618

Rum Village Nature Center (S# 27, map A2)
2716 Sampson St.
South Bend, IN 46614   219-284-9455

Wesselman Park Nature Center (S# 28, map E1)
551 North Boeke Road
Evansville, IN 47711   812-479-0771

Indiana Chamber of Commerce

One N. Capitol Ave., #200
Indianapolis, IN 46204-2248   Phone 317-264-3110
                                 Fax 317-264-6855

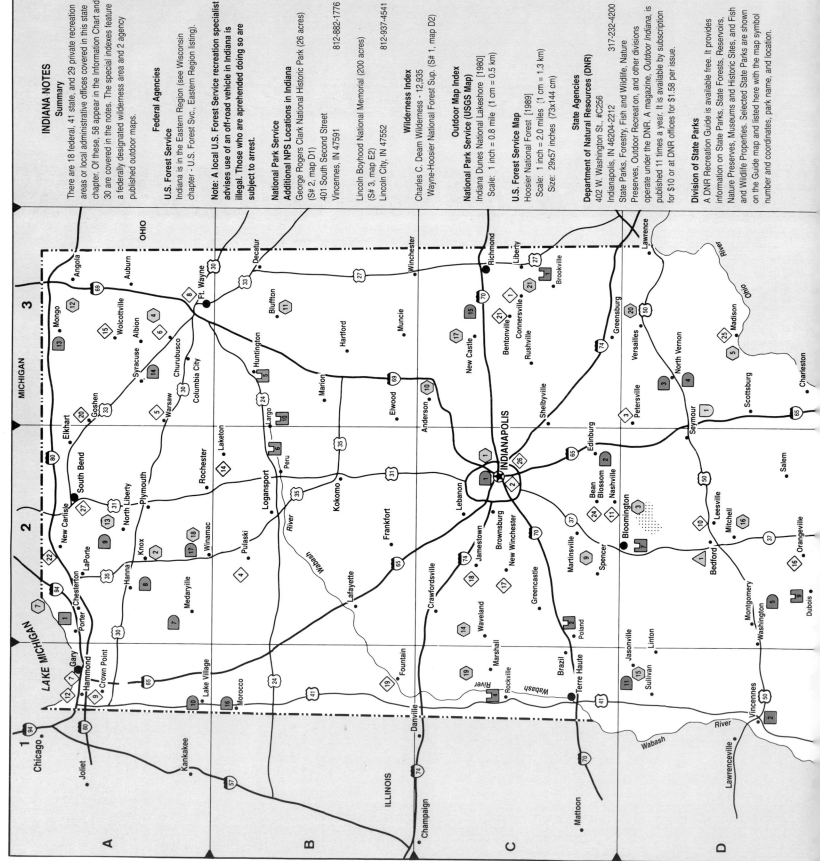

INDIANA - CITY / AGENCY INDEX

City	Agency Office / Area Name	Code	S#	Map
Albion	Chain O'Lakes SP	SPS	4	A3
Anderson	Mounds SP	SPS	10	C3
Angola	Pokagon SP	SPS	12	A3
Bean Blossom	Whip-poor-will Woods Pre	TNC	24	D2
Bedford	Wayne-Hoosier NF Supervisor	NFS	1	D2
Bentonville	Shrader-Weaver Woods Pre	TNC	21	C3
Bloomington	Monroe Lake	COE	7	D2
Bluffton	Ouabache SP	SPS	11	B3
Brookville	Brookville Lake	COE	1	C3
Brownstown	Brownstown Ranger D.	NFS	2	E2
Cannelton	Cannelton Lock & Dam	COE	3	E2
Chesterton	Indiana Dunes SP	SPS	7	A2
Churubusco	Crooked Lake Preserve	TNC	6	A3
Connersville	Mary Gray Bird Sanctuary & Indiana Audubon Sanct.			
Corydon	Indian Creek Woods Preserve	INA	1	C3
Crown Point	Gibson Woods Preserve	TNC	13	E2
Dubois	Patoka Lake	COE	9	D2
Edinburg	Atterbury FWA	SWA	2	C2
Fountain	Portland Arch Preserve	TNC	19	B1
Ft. Wayne	Fox Island Preserve	TNC	8	A2
Gary	Deep River Preserve	TNC	7	A1
Goshen	Shoup-Parsons Swamp Woods P	TNC	20	A3
Hammond	Hoosier Prairie Preserve	TNC	12	A1
Hanna	Kankakee FWA	SWA	4	A2
Huntington	Huntington Lake	COE	5	B3
INDIANAPOLIS	IDNR, Div. of State Parks	SPS	1	C2
INDIANAPOLIS	IDNR, Div. of Fish & Wildlife	TNC	13	C2
Jamestown	Pine Hills Preserve	TNC	18	C2
Jasonville	Shakamak SP	SPS	15	D1
Knox	Bass Lake SB	SPS	2	A2
Lagro	Salamonie Lake	COE	10	B3
Lake Village	LaSalle FWA	SWA	14	A1
Laketon	Laketon Bog Preserve	TNC	10	B2
LaPorte	Kingsbury FWA	SWA	21	A2
Leesville	Hemlock Bluff Preserve	TNC	10	D2
Liberty	Whitewater Memorial SP	SPS	21	C3
Lincoln City	Lincoln SP	SPS	5	D2
Madison	Clifty Falls SP	SPS	5	D3
Marshall	Turkey Run SP	SPS	19	C1
Medaryville	Jasper-Pulaski FWA	SWA	7	A2
Mitchell	Spring Mill SP	SPS	16	D2
Mongo	Pigeon River FWA	SWA	13	A3
Montgomery	Glendale FWA	SWA	5	D2
Morocco	Willow Slough FWA	SWA	16	B1
Mount Vernon	Hovey Lake FWA	SWA	6	E1
Mt. Vernon	Uniontown Lock & Dam	COE	11	E1
Nashville	Brown County SP	SPS	3	D2
New Carlisle	Hitz-Rhodehamel Woods Pre	TNC	11	A2
New Castle	Spicer Lake Preserve	SPS	1	C2
New Harmony	Harmonie SP	SPS	6	E1
New Winchester	Oscar & Ruth Hall Woods Pre	TNC	17	C2
Newburgh	Newburgh Lock & Dam	COE	8	E1
North Liberty	Potato Creek SP	SPS	13	A2
North Vernon	Brush Creek FWA	SWA	3	D3
Orangeville	Crosley FWA	SWA	4	D3
Peru	Orangeville Rise Preserve	TNC	16	D2
Petersville	Mississinewa Lake	COE	6	B2
Poland	Anderson Falls Preserve	TNC	3	D3
Porter	Cagles Mill Lake	COE	2	C2
Porter	Indiana Dunes National Lakeshore	NPS	1	A2
Pulaski	Berns-Meyer Woods Preserve	TNC	1	B2
Rockville	Cecil M. Harden Lake	COE	4	C1
Seymour	Muscatatuck NWR	NWR	1	D3
Spencer	McCormick's Creek SP	SPS	9	C2
Sullivan	Minnehaha FWA	SWA	11	D1
Syracuse	Tri-County FWA	SWA	14	A3
Tell City	Tell City Ranger D.	NFS	3	E2
Versailles	Versailles SP	SPS	20	D3
Warsaw	Chapman Lake Wetlands Pre	TNC	5	B3
Waveland	Shades SP	SPS	14	C2
Winamac	Tippecanoe River SP	SPS	18	A2
Winamac	Winamac FWA	SWA	17	A2
Winslow	Patoka FWA	SWA	12	E1
Wolcottville	Olin Lake Preserve	TNC	15	A3

AGENCY/MAP LEGEND... INITIALS, MAP SYMBOLS, COLOR CODES

U.S. Forest Service Supervisor & Ranger Dist. Offices NFS
U.S. Army Corps of Engineers Rec. Areas & Offices . COE
USFWS National Wildlife Refuges & Offices .... NWR
National Park Service Parks & other NPS Sites ...... NPS
Bureau of Land Management Rec. Areas & Offices .. BLM
Bureau of Reclamation Rec. Areas & Reg. Offices ... BOR
State Parks (also see State Agency notes) .... SPS
State Wildlife Areas (also see State Agency notes) .. SWA
Private Preserves, Nature Centers & Tribal Lands ...
The Wild Rivers ⌇ and Wilderness Areas

Note: Refer to yellow block on page 7 (top right) for location name and address abbreviations.

★ INFORMATION CHART ★

INFORMATION CHART LEGEND - SYMBOLS & LETTER CODES

■ means YES & □ means Yes with disability provisions
sp means spring, March through May
S means Summer, June through August
F means Fall, September through November
W means Winter, December through February
T means Two (2) or Three (3) Seasons
A means All Four (4) Seasons
na means Not Applicable or Not Available

Note: empty or blank spaces in the chart mean NO ★ that symbol is not shown on the map.

© 1994 by John Oliver Jones

1 inch = approx. 29 mi. = 47 km

S#	MAP	LOCATION NAME (state initials if more than one) with ADDRESS and/or LOCATION DATA	TELEPHONE	ACRES / ELEVATION
	D2	Wayne-Hoosier National Forests Supervisor, 811 Constitution Ave., Bedford 47421	812-275-5987	413,798 / na
	E2	Brownstown Ranger D., 608 W. Commerce St., Brownstown 47220	812-358-2675	116,893 / na
	E2	Tell City Ranger D., 15th & Washington Sts., Tell City 47586	812-547-7051	97,008 / na
1	C3	COE, Louisville District, PO Box 59, Louisville, KY 40201	502-582-6292	na / na
1	C3	Brookville Lake, PO Box 230, Brookville 47012	317-647-6701	na / na
2	C2	Cagles Mill Lake, RFD 2, Poland 47868	317-795-4439	na / na
3	E2	Cannelton Lock & Dam (Ohio River), Rt.1, Box 213, Cannelton 47520	812-547-2962	na / na
4	C1	Cecil M. Harden Lake, RR 1, Box 296, Rockville 47872	317-344-1570	na / na
5	B3	Huntington Lake, 735 N. Warren Rd., Huntington 46750	219-356-8648	na / na
6	B2	Mississinewa Lake, RR 1, Box 202-A, Peru 46970	317-473-5946	na / na
7	D2	Monroe Lake, 1620 E. Monroe Dam Ct., Bloomington 47401	812-824-9136	na / na
8	E1	Newburgh Lock & Dam (Ohio River), 6877 State Road 66, Newburgh 47630	812-853-8470	na / na
9	C2	Patoka Lake, 4512 N. Cuzco Road, Dubois 47527	812-678-3761	na / na
10	B3	Salamonie Lake, RR 1, Lagro 46941	219-782-2358	na / na
11	E1	Uniontown Lock & Dam (Ohio River), 16501 Raven Road, Mt. Vernon 47620	812-838-5836	na / na
1	D3	Muscatatuck NWR, Rt. #7, Box 189A, Seymour 47274 [3 mi E of I-65/US 50 jct. on US 50]	812-522-4352	8,000 / 540-620
1	A2	Indiana Dunes National Lakeshore, 1100 N. Mineral Springs Rd., Porter 46304	219-926-7561	13,945 / 580-700
1	C2	IDNR, Div. of State Parks, 616 State Office Bldg., Indianapolis 46204	317-232-4124	na / na
1	C2	IDNR, Div. of Fish & Wildlife, 402 W. Washington, Room 273, Indianapolis 46204	317-232-4080	na / na
2	C2	Atterbury FWA, in Johnson County, Edinburg 46124	812-526-2051	5,512 / na
3	D3	Brush Creek FWA, c/o Crosley FWA, RR #2, Box 87, North Vernon 47265	812-346-5596	1,860 / na
4	D3	Crosley FWA, RR #2, Box 87, North Vernon 47265	812-346-5596	4,084 / na
5	D2	Glendale FWA, RR #2, Box 300, Montgomery 47558	812-644-7711	8,021 / na
6	E1	Hovey Lake FWA, RR #5, Mount Vernon 47620	812-838-2927	4,298 / na
7	A2	Jasper-Pulaski FWA, RR #1, Box 216, Medaryville 47957	219-843-4841	8,022 / na

FACILITIES, SERVICES, RECREATION OPPORTUNITIES & CONVENIENCES

(Diagonal column headers, reading across the chart:)
INFO CENTER (IC) / VISITOR CENTER (VC)
IO / VC OPEN SATURDAY / SUNDAY
ENTRY FEE, not camping or permit fee
CONCESSIONAIRE SERVICES OK
FREE LITERATURE, brochures, maps, etc.
AGENCY GUIDED TOURS / STUDY PROGRAMS
NATURE LITERATURE / trochures, scheduled / by res.
WILDFLOWER EDUCATION / STUDY PROGRAMS
ARCHAEOLOGICAL / GEOLOGICAL SITES
INTERPRETIVE TRAILS
HISTORIC SITES
WILDLIFE VIEWING SITES, birds, etc.
ENDANGERED SPECIES ARE COMMON
WILDLIFE IS ABUNDANT OR COMMON
DEVELOPED PICNIC AREAS, signs, etc.
NO-CHARGE CAMPGROUNDS / PICNIC AREAS
DEVELOPED CAMPGROUNDS / CAMPSITES
WILDERNESS AREAS / WILD RIVERS
WALKING / HIKING TRAILS
BICYCLING OPPORTUNITIES
HORSEBACK RIDING, w/ your own horse
OFF-ROAD VEHICLE Area / Use OK
FISHING, license, permit reqd.
SWIMMING PERMITTED, at one's own risk
NON-MOTORIZED WATERCRAFT OK
BOATING FACILITIES, ramps, marinas, etc.
MOTORIZED WATERCRAFT OK, check limits
HUNTING IN SEASON, license / permit reqd.
WINTER SPORTS OPPORTUNITIES
PARK w / WALK-IN ONLY AREA
DAY USE ONLY, no overnight
DRINKING WATER
RESTROOMS

★ INFORMATION CHART ★

AGENCY/MAP LEGEND ... INITIALS, MAP SYMBOLS, COLOR CODES

U.S. Forest Service Supervisor & Ranger Dist. Offices . NFS
U.S. Army Corps of Engineers Rec. Areas & Offices . COE
USFWS National Wildlife Refuges & Offices .... NWR
National Park Service Parks & other NPS Sites ..... NPS
Bureau of Land Management Rec. Areas & Offices .. BLM
Bureau of Reclamation Rec. Areas & Reg. Offices .. BOR
State Parks (also see State Agency notes) .... SPS
State Wildlife Areas (also see State Agency notes) . SWA
Private Preserves, Nature Centers & Tribal Lands.
The Wild Rivers ⎯ and Wilderness Areas

Note: Refer to yellow block on page 7 for location name and address abbreviations.

INFORMATION CHART LEGEND - SYMBOLS & LETTER CODES

■ means **YES** & □ means **Yes with disability provisions**
sp means spring, March through May
S means Summer, June through August
F means Fall, September through November
W means Winter, December through February
T means Two (2) or Three (3) Seasons
A means All Four (4) Seasons
na means Not Applicable or Not Available

Note: empty or blank spaces in the chart mean **NO** ⎯ that symbol is not shown on the map.

If a symbol number has a star ★ that symbol is not shown on the map.

FACILITIES, SERVICES, RECREATION OPPORTUNITIES & CONVENIENCES

S#	MAP	LOCATION NAME (state initials if more than one) with ADDRESS and/or LOCATION DATA	TELEPHONE	ACRES / ELEVATION
8	A2	Kankakee FWA, 16591 S. 250 West, Hanna 46340	219-896-3522	3,328 / na
9	A2	Kingsbury FWA, 5344 S. Hupp Rd., LaPorte 46350	219-393-3612	6,059 / na
10	A1	LaSalle FWA, RR #1, Box 80, Lake Village 46349	219-992-3019	3,643 / na
11	D1	Minnehaha FWA, RR #5, Box 21C, Sullivan 47882	812-268-6640	12,500 / na
12	E1	Patoka FWA, RR #1, Winslow 47598	812-789-2724	7,300 / na
13	A3	Pigeon River FWA, Box 71, Mongo 46771	219-367-2164	11,500 / na
14	A3	Tri-County FWA, RR #2, Box 522, Syracuse 46567	219-834-4461	3,486 / na
15	C3	Wilbur Wright FWA, RR #4, Box 5A, New Castle 47362	317-529-9581	854 / na
16	B1	Willow Slough FWA, RR #1, Box 86, Morocco 47963	219-285-2704	9,938 / na
17	B1	Winamac FWA, RR #4, Box 115, Winamac 46996	219-285-2704	9,938 / na
1	C3	**Mary Gray Bird Sanctuary & Indiana Audubon Society**, RR #6, Box 162, Connersville 47331	317-825-9788	700 / 975
2	C2	**TNC Indiana Field Office**. 1330 W. 38th Street, Indianapolis 46208	317-923-7547	na / na
3	D3	Anderson Falls Preserve (contact Field Office), near Petersville	317-923-7547	44 / 700-750
4	B2	Berns-Meyer Woods Preserve (contact Field Office), near Pulaski	317-923-7547	20 / 690
5	A3	Chapman Lake Wetlands Preserve (contact Field Office), near Warsaw	317-923-7547	232 / 830-840
6	A3	Crooked Lake Preserve (contact Field Office), near Churubusco	317-923-7547	100 / 930-950
7	A1	Deep River Preserve, contact Lake County Parks & Rec. in Crown Point [near Gary]	317-923-7547	39 / 650
8	A3	Fox Island Preserve, contact Allen County, Parks & Rec. near Ft. Wayne	317-923-7547	814 / 750-775
9	A1	Gibson Woods Preserve, contact Lake County Parks & Rec. in Crown Point [near S. Gary]	317-923-7547	129 / 595-600
10	D2	Hemlock Bluff Preserve (contact Field Office), near Leesville	317-923-7547	45 / 700-800
11	C2	Hitz-Rhodehamel Woods Preserve (contact Field Office), near Nashville	317-923-7547	271 / 750-1,000
12	A1	Hoosier Prairie Preserve (contact Field Office), near Hammond	317-923-7547	439 / 620-625
13	E2	Indian Creek Woods Preserve, contact Harrison Co. Parks & Rec. in Corydon, preserve is near Corydon	317-923-7547	116 / 550-877
14	B2	Laketon Bog Preserve (contact Field Office), near Laketon	317-923-7547	32 / 760
15	A3	Olin Lake Preserve (contact Field Office), near Wolcottville	317-923-7547	304 / 900-930
16	D2	Orangeville Rise Preserve (contact Field Office), near Orangeville	317-923-7547	3 / 532
17	C2	Oscar & Ruth Hall Woods Preserve (contact Field Office), near New Winchester	317-923-7547	128 / 750-850
18	C2	Pine Hills Preserve (contact Field Office), near Jamestown [VC at Shades State Park]	317-923-7547	470 / 650-750
19	B1	Portland Arch Preserve (contact Field Office), near Fountain	317-923-7547	454 / 550-600
20	A3	Shoup-Parsons Swamp Woods Preserve (contact Field Office), near Goshen	317-923-7547	17 / 800
21	C3	Shrader-Weaver Woods Preserve (contact Field Office), near Bentonville	317-923-7547	108 / 1,020-1,050
22	A2	Spicer Lake Preserve (contact Field Office), near New Carlisle	317-923-7547	167 / 750
23	E1	Twin Swamps Preserve (contact Field Office), near Mt. Vernon	317-923-7547	600 / 360
24	C2	Whip-poor-will Woods Preserve (contact Field Office), near Bean Blossom	317-923-7547	719 / 900-950

Column headers (symbol columns, vertical):

INFO OFFICE (IO) / VISITOR CENTER (VC); IO / VC OPEN SATURDAY / SUNDAY; ENTRY FEE, not camping or permit fee; CONCESSIONAIRE SERVICES AVAILABLE; INTERPRETIVE or EDUCATIONAL DISPLAY; FREE LITERATURE AVAILABLE; NATURE LITERATURE, brochures, maps, etc.; AGENCY GUIDED TOURS, scheduled / by res.; WILDFLOWER VIEWING AREA; NATURE EDUCATION / STUDY PROGRAMS; ARCHAEOLOGICAL / GEOLOGICAL SITES; HISTORIC SITES; INTERPRETIVE TRAILS; WILDLIFE VIEWING TRAILS; WILDLIFE IS ABUNDANT OR COMMON; ENDANGERED SPECIES ARE COMMON; WILDLIFE VIEWING SITES, blinds, signs, etc.; DEVELOPED PICNIC AREAS / PICNIC SITES; NO-CHARGE CAMPGROUNDS / CAMPSITES; CAMPGROUNDS / CAMPSITES; WILDERNESS AREAS / WILD RIVERS; SWIMMING PERMITTED; WALKING / HIKING TRAILS; BICYCLING OPPORTUNITIES at one's own risk; HORSEBACK RIDING... areas, trails; OFF-ROAD Motorized RIDING, w/ your own horse or vehicle Area / Use OK; FISHING OPPORTUNITIES at one's own risk; BOATING FACILITIES: ramps, marinas, etc.; MOTORIZED WATERCRAFT OK, check limits; NON-MOTORIZED WATERCRAFT OK; HUNTING IN SEASON, license / permit reqd.; WINTER SPORTS OPPORTUNITIES; PARK & WALK-IN ONLY AREA; DAY USE ONLY, no overnight; DRINKING WATER; RESTROOMS

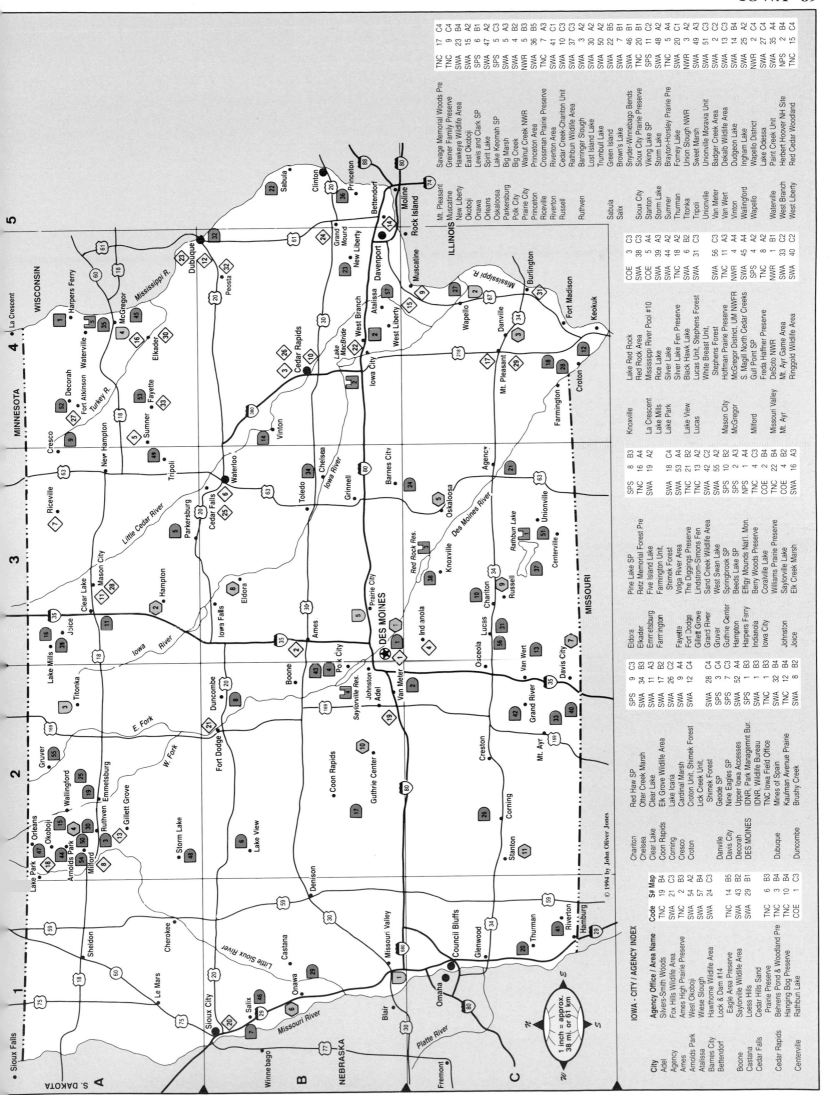

© 1994 by John Oliver Jones

1 inch = approx.
38 mi. or 61 km

IOWA NOTES

Summary
There are 13 federal, 71 state, and 34 private recreation areas or local administrative offices covered in this state chapter. Of these, 83 appear in the Information Chart and 37 are covered in the notes.

Federal Agencies

USFWS National Wildlife Refuges
The Upper Mississippi River Wildlife & Fish Refuge headquarters office is in Winona, Minnesota. This 195,000-acre refuge extends for 260 miles along the Mississippi River from Wabasha, Minnesota, to Rock Island, Illinois. Ask about the special USFWS-published "Pool Maps" covering sections of the refuge and recreation information in Iowa.

State Agencies

Iowa Department of Natural Resources (IDNR)
E. Ninth and Grand Ave.
Wallace State Office Bldg.
Des Moines, IA 50319-0034   515-281-5145
The Fish and Wildlife, Parks, Recreation and Preserves, and Forests and Forestry divisions oprate under the DNR.

IDNR, Park Management Bureau
An Iowa State Parks Guide (82 state parks) is available free. There are no park entry fees.

IDNR, State Forester
Wallace State Office Bldg.
Des Moines, IA 50319   515-281-8656
Contact the State Forester for forest recreation literature.

IDNR, Wildlife Bureau
The Iowa Public Hunting Areas brochure covers more than 300 public hunting areas. These are wildlife areas, marshes, lakes, waterfowl production, and general access areas. Most with more than 1,000 acres are featured in the chart. A monthly magazine, Iowa Conservation, is available for $2 per copy.

Iowa Travel Development Division
250 Jewett Bldg.
Des Moines, IA 50309   515-281-3100
The official Iowa Transportation Map is available from this office. There are symbols for parks, wildlife areas, and preserves. State forests are shown in green.

Private Organizations

TNC-Iowa Field Office
A leaflet is available from the field office about the preserve locations listed below. Contact the office for current visitor information.

S#	MAP	PRESERVE & LOCATION
2	B3	Ames High Prairie Preserve, near Ames
3	B4	Behrens Pond & Woodland Preserve, near Cedar Rapids
4	C3	Berry Woods Preserve, near Indianola
5	A4	Brayton-Horsley Prairie Pre., near Sumner
6	B3	Cedar Hills Sand Prairie Preserve, near Cedar Falls
7	A3	Crossman Prairie Preserve, near Riceville
8	A2	Freda Haffner Preserve, near Milford
9	C4	Greiner Family Preserve, near Muscatine
10	B4	Hanging Bog Preserve, near Cedar Rapids
11	A3	Hoffman Prairie Preserve, near Mason City
12	A2	Kaufman Avenue Prairie, in Dubuque
13	A2	Lindstrom-Simons Fen, near Gillett Grove
14	B5	Lock & Dam #14 Eagle Area Preserve, near Bettendorf
15	C4	Red Cedar Woodland, S of West Liberty
16	A4	Retz Memorial Forest Preserve, near Elkader
17	C4	Savage Mem. Woods Pre., near Mt. Pleasant
18	A2	Silver Lake Fen Preserve, near Lake Park
19	B2	Silvers-Smith Woods, near Adel
20	B1	Sioux City Prairie Preserve, near Sioux City
21	B2	The Diggings Preserve, near Sioux City
22	B4	Williams Prairie Preserve, near Iowa City

ANCA Locations in Iowa

E.B. Lyons Nature Center (S# 23, map A4)
8999 Bellevue Heights
Dubuque, IA 52001   319-556-0620

Eden Valley Nature Center (S# 24, map B4)
PO Box 161
Grand Mound, IA 52751-0161   319-847-7202

Hartman Reserve Nature Center (S# 25, map B3)
657 Reserve Drive
Cedar Falls, IA 50613   319-45-1516

Indian Creek Nature Center (S# 26, map B4)
6665 Otis Ridge
Cedar Rapids, IA 52403   319-362-0664

Lake Meyer Nature Center (S# 27, map A4)
Route 2
Fort Atkinson, IA 52144   319-534-7145

Lime Creek Nature Center (S# 28, map A3)
3501 Lime Creek Road
Mason City, IA 50401   515-423-5309

Oakland Mills Nature Center (S# 29, map C4)
RR #4, Box 96
Mount Pleasant, IA 52641   319-986-5067

Osborne Nature Center (S# 30, map A4)
RR #2, Box 65-A
Elkader, IA 52043   319-245-1516

Starr's Cave Nature Center (S# 31, map C4)
3299 Irish Ridge Road
Burlington, IA 52601   319-753-5808

Swiss Valley Nature Center (S# 32, map B4)
13768 Swiss Valley Road
Peosta, IA 52068   319-556-6745

Wildwood Nature Center (S# 33, map A4)
RR #1
Fayette, IA 52142   319-422-5146

Iowa Dept. of Economic Dev. (Chamber of Commerce)
200 E. Grand
Des Moines, IA 50309
Phone 515-242-4700
Fax 515-242-4749

★ INFORMATION CHART ★

AGENCY/MAP LEGEND . . . INITIALS, MAP SYMBOLS, COLOR CODES

U.S. Forest Service Supervisor & Ranger Dist. Offices . NFS [61]
U.S. Army Corps of Engineers Rec. Areas & Offices . COE [31]
USFWS National Wildlife Refuges & Offices . . . . . . NWR [40]
National Park Service Parks & other NPS Sites . . . . . NPS [7]
Bureau of Land Management Rec. Areas & Offices . BLM [39]
Bureau of Reclamation Rec. Areas & Reg. Offices . BOR [8]
State Parks (also see State Agency notes) . . . . SPS [52]
State Wildlife Areas (also see State Agency notes) . . SWA [19]
Private Preserves, Nature Centers & Tribal Lands [15]
The Wild Rivers and Wilderness Areas

Note: Refer to yellow block on page 7 (top right) for location name and address abbreviations. If a symbol number has a star ★ that symbol is not shown on the map.

INFORMATION CHART LEGEND - SYMBOLS & LETTER CODES

■ means YES & □ means Yes with disability provisions
sp means spring, March through May
S means Summer, June through August
F means Fall, September through November
W means Winter, December through February
T means Two (2) or Three (3) Seasons
A means All Four (4) Seasons
na means Not Applicable or Not Available
Note: empty or blank spaces in the chart mean NO

Facility/service column headers (FACILITIES, SERVICES, RECREATION OPPORTUNITIES & CONVENIENCES): INFO OFFICE (IO) / VISITOR CENTER (VC); IO / VC OPEN SATURDAY / SUNDAY; ENTRY FEE / no camping or permit fee; INTERPRETIVE or EDUCATIONAL SERVICES AVAILABLE; CONCESSIONAIRE SERVICES AVAILABLE; FREE LITERATURE / brochures, maps, etc.; AGENCY (VC); NATURE EDUCATION / STUDY PROGRAMS; WILDFLOWER VIEWING AREA or DRIVE; NATURE EDUCATION / guided tours, scheduled / by res.; INTERPRETIVE TRAILS; HISTORIC SITES; ARCHAEOLOGICAL / GEOLOGICAL SITES; WILDLIFE VIEWING AREA or DRIVE; ENDANGERED SPECIES; WILDLIFE IS ABUNDANT OR COMMON; WILDLIFE VIEWING SITES, blinds, signs, etc.; NO-CHARGE CAMPGROUNDS; DEVELOPED CAMPGROUNDS / PICNIC AREAS; WILDERNESS AREAS / HIKING TRAILS; WALKING / HIKING TRAILS; DEVELOPED PICNIC AREAS; SWIMMING AREA / WILD RIVERS; CAMPSITES; CAMPSITES; BICYCLING OPPORTUNITIES; HORSEBACK RIDING; OFF-ROAD MOTORIZED RIDING; MOTORIZED RIDING 'w/ your own horse …areas, trails; WALKING PERMITTED at one's own risk; HUNTING IN SEASON, license / permit req'd; FISHING FACILITIES, license / permit req'd; BOATING FACILITIES / ramps, marinas etc.; NON-MOTORIZED WATERCRAFT OK; MOTORIZED WATERCRAFT OK, check limits; WINTER SPORTS OPPORTUNITIES; PARK & WALK-IN ONLY AREA; DAY USE ONLY, no overnight; DRINKING WATER; RESTROOMS.

S#	MAP	LOCATION NAME (state initials if more than one) with ADDRESS and/or LOCATION DATA	TELEPHONE	ACRES / ELEVATION
		COE, Kansas City District, 601 E. 12th St., 716 Federal Bldg., Kansas City, MO 64106	816-426-6816	na / na
1	C3	Rathbun Lake, Corps Of Engineers, RR 3, Centerville 52544	515-647-2464	na / na
2	B4	Coralville Lake, 2353 Prairie Du Chien, Iowa City 52240	319-338-3543	na / na
3	C3	COE, Rock Island District, Clock Tower Bldg., PO Box 2004, Rock Island, IL 61204	309-788-6361	na / na
3	B2	Lake Red Rock, RR 3, Box 149A, Knoxville 50138	515-828-7522	na / na
4	B2	Saylorville Lake, 5600 NW 78th Ave., Johnston 50131	515-276-4656	na / na
5	A4	COE, St. Paul District, 180 E. Kellog Blvd. East, Rm. 1421, St. Paul, MN 55101	612-220-0325	na / na
	B1	Mississippi River Pool No. 10, 300 S. 1st St., La Crescent 55947	507-895-6341	na / na
1	B1	DeSoto NWR, RR #1, Box 114, Missouri Valley 51555 [on Hwy. 30 5m E Blair NE/6m W I-29 ex 75]	712-642-4121	7,820 / 990-1,010
2	C4	Mark Twain NWR Complex, 1704 N. 24th St., Quincy, IL 62301	217-224-8580	na / na
	C4	Wapello District (3 Divisions), 10728 County Road X61, Wapello 52653 [two Divisions closed during Fall]	319-523-6982	5,200 / na
3	A2	Union Slough NWR, 1710 360th St., Titonka 50480	515-928-2523	2,845 / na
4	A4	Upper Miss. River NW, PO Box 460, McGregor 52157	507-452-4232	200,000 / na
	A4	McGregor Dist., Upper Miss River NW, PO Box 460, McGregor 52157	319-873-3423	80,000 / 600
5	B3	Walnut Creek NWR, PO Box 399, Prairie City 50228 [office 2.5 mi S of city on W 109th St. South]	515-994-2415	
1	A4	Effigy Mounds National Monument, RR #1, Box 25A, Harpers Ferry 52146 [3 mi N of Marquette on SR 76]	319-873-3491	1,481 / 350
2	B4	Herbert Hoover NH Site, Parkside Dr. & Main St., PO Box 607, West Branch 52358 [0.5 mi. N of I-80 at exit #254]	319-643-2541	187 / 750
1	B3	IDNR, Park Managemnt Bureau, Wallace State Office Bldg., E. 9th & Grand, Des Moines 50319		na / na
3	A3	Beeds Lake SP, off Hwy. 3, 3 mi. NW of Hampton 50441	515-281-6157	319 / na
	A3	Geode SP, RR #2, off county road, 4 mi. SW of Danville 52623	515-456-2047	na / na
	C4		515-392-4601	1,641 / na

#	Code	Site / Location	Acres	Phone
6	B1	Lewis and Clark SP, off Hwy. 324, 3 mi. NW of Onawa 51040	176 / na	712-423-2829
7	C3	Nine Eagles SP, RR #1, off county road, 6 mi. SE of Davis City 50065	1,119 / na	515-442-2855
8	B3	Pine Lake SP, RR #3, Box 45, Eldora 50627	572 / na	515-858-5832
9	C3	Red Haw SP, RR #1, Box 212, on Hwy. 34, 1 mi. E of Chariton 50049	420 / na	515-774-5632
10	B2	Springbrook SP, RR #1, Box 142, Hwy. 25 & 384, 8 mi. NE of Guthrie Center 50115	786 / na	515-747-3591
11	C2	Viking Lake SP, RR #1, Box 91, off county road, 4 mi. SE of Stanton 51573	1,000 / na	712-829-2235
1	B3	**IDNR, Wildlife Bureau**, Wallace State Office Bldg., E 9th & Grand Ave., Des Moines 50319	na	515-281-5145
2	C2	Badger Creek Area, 4 mi. SE of Van Meter	1,150 / na	515-281-5145
3	A2	Barringer Slough, 2 mi. W & 1 mi. N of Ruthven	1,071 / na	515-281-5145
4	B2	Big Creek, 1 mi. N of Polk City	3,100 / na	515-281-5145
5	A3	Big Marsh, 5 mi. N of Parkersburg	2,826 / na	515-281-5145
6	B2	Black Hawk Lake (VC phone 657-2639), c/o IDNR Dist. Off., Lake View 50535	1,228 / 1,000	712-657-8712
7	B1	Brown's Lake, 1.5 mi. W of Salix	1,156 / na	515-281-5145
8	B2	Brushy Creek, 6 mi. S of Duncombe	4,187 / na	515-281-5145
9	A4	Cardinal Marsh, 2 mi. SE of Cresco	1,165 / na	515-281-5145
10	C3	Cedar Creek-Chariton Unit, Stephens Forest, near Russell	3,076 / 1,000	515-281-5145
11	A3	Clear Lake, edge of Clear Lake	3,643 / na	515-281-5145
12	C4	Croton Unit, Shimek Forest, 2 mi. SE of Croton	1,594 / 712	515-281-5145
13	C3	DeKalb Wildlife Area, 4 mi. SW of Van Wert	1,060 / na	515-281-5145
14	B4	Dudgeon Lake, 1 mi. N of Vinton	1,364 / na	515-281-5145
15	A2	East Okoboji, E edge of Okoboji	1,873 / na	712-336-1840
16	A3	Elk Creek Marsh, 3 mi. N of Joice	2,000 / na	515-281-5145
17	B2	Elk Grove Wildlife Area, 11 mi. SW of Coon Rapids	1,600 / na	515-281-5145
18	C4	Farmington Unit, Shimek Forest, NE & E of Farmington	1,217 / 712	515-281-5145
19	A2	Five Island Lake, 1 mi. N of Emmetsburg	1,104 / na	515-281-5145
20	C1	Forney Lake, 2.5 mi. NW of Thurman	1,127 / na	515-281-5145
21	C3	Fox Hills Wildlife Area, 2 mi. S of Agency	1,297 / 1,000	515-281-5145
22	B5	Green Island, 6 mi. N of Sabula	3,294 / na	515-281-5145
23	B4	Hawkeye Wildlife Area, 2 mi. W & 1.5 mi. N of New Liberty	13,500 / 700	515-281-5145
24	C3	Hawthorne Wildlife Area, 1 mi. S of Barnes City	1,682 / 1,000	515-281-5145
25	A2	Ingham Lake, 5 mi. E of Wallingford	1,002 / na	515-281-5145
26	C4	Lake Icaria, 4 mi. N of Corning	2,000 / na	515-281-5145
27	C4	Lake Odessa, 4.5 mi. E of Wapello	3,828 / 536	319-523-3102
28	C4	Lick Creek Unit, Shimek Forest, 1 mi. N of Croton	2,355 / 712	515-281-5145
29	B1	Loess Hills, 3.5 mi. W of Castana	2,724 / na	515-281-5145
30	A2	Lost Island Lake, 1 mi. W & 3 mi. N of Ruthven	1,260 / na	515-281-5145
31	C3	Lucas Unit, Stephens Forest, 1 mi. SW of Lucas	991 / 1,000	515-281-5145
32	B4	Mines of Spain, 1 mi. S of Dubuque	1,260 / na	515-281-5145
33	C2	Mt. Ayr Game Area, 4 mi. W & 1 mi. S of Mt. Ayr	1,158 / na	515-281-5145
34	B3	Otter Creek Marsh, 1 mi. NW of Chelsea	3,399 / 1,000	515-281-5145
35	A4	Paint Creek Unit, Yellow River Forest, 3 mi. SE of Waterville	3,357 / na	515-281-5145
36	B5	Princeton Area, 1 mi. N of Princeton	1,178 / na	515-281-5145
37	C3	Rathbun Wildlife Area, 10 mi. SE of Russell	15,629 / 900	515-281-5145
38	C3	Red Rock Area, 7 mi. N of Knoxville	25,542 / na	515-281-5145
39	A3	Rice Lake, 2 mi. SE of Lake Mills	1,831 / na	515-281-5145
40	C2	Ringgold Wildlife Area, 6 mi. E & 8 mi. S of Mt. Ayr	1,040 / na	515-281-5145
41	C1	Riverton Area, 1 mi. W of Riverton	2,493 / na	515-281-5145
42	B2	Sand Creek Wildlife Area, 4 mi. NW of Grand River	1,835 / na	515-281-5145
43	B2	Saylorville Wildlife Area, near Madrid & Boone	10,904 / na	515-281-5145
44	A4	Silver Lake, S edge of Lake Park	1,141 / na	515-281-5145
45	A4	S. Magill North Cedar Creeks, 5 mi. S of McGregor	1,635 / na	515-281-5145
46	B1	Snyder-Winnebago Bends, 2 mi. SE of Salix	2,865 / na	712-336-1840
47	A2	Spirit Lake, N edge of Orleans	5,684 / na	515-281-5145
48	A2	Storm Lake, S of Storm Lake	3,367 / na	515-281-5145
49	A3	Sweet Marsh, 1 mi. E of Tripoli	2,242 / na	515-281-5145
50	A2	Trumbull Lake, 1 mi. W & 5 mi. N of Ruthven	1,224 / na	515-281-5145
51	A4	Unionville Moravia Unit, Stephens Forest, areas around Unionville	1,879 / 1,000	515-281-5145
52	A4	Upper Iowa Accesses, down stream from Decorah	3,068 / na	515-281-5145
53	A4	Volga River Area, 5 mi. NE of Fayette	5,324 / na	515-281-5145
54	A2	West Okoboji, W edge of Arnolds Park	3,949 / na	712-336-1840
55	A2	West Swan Lake, 2 mi. S & 1 mi. E of Gruver	1,195 / na	515-281-5145
56	C3	White Breast Unit, Stephens Forest, 3 mi. S & 2 mi. W of Lucas	3,256 / 1,000	515-281-5145
57	B4	Wiese Slough, 2 mi. E of Atalissa	1,700 / na	515-281-5145
◇	B3	**TNC Iowa Field Office**, 431 E. Locust, Suite 200, Des Moines 50309 [see notes for 21 Preserves]	na / na	515-244-5044

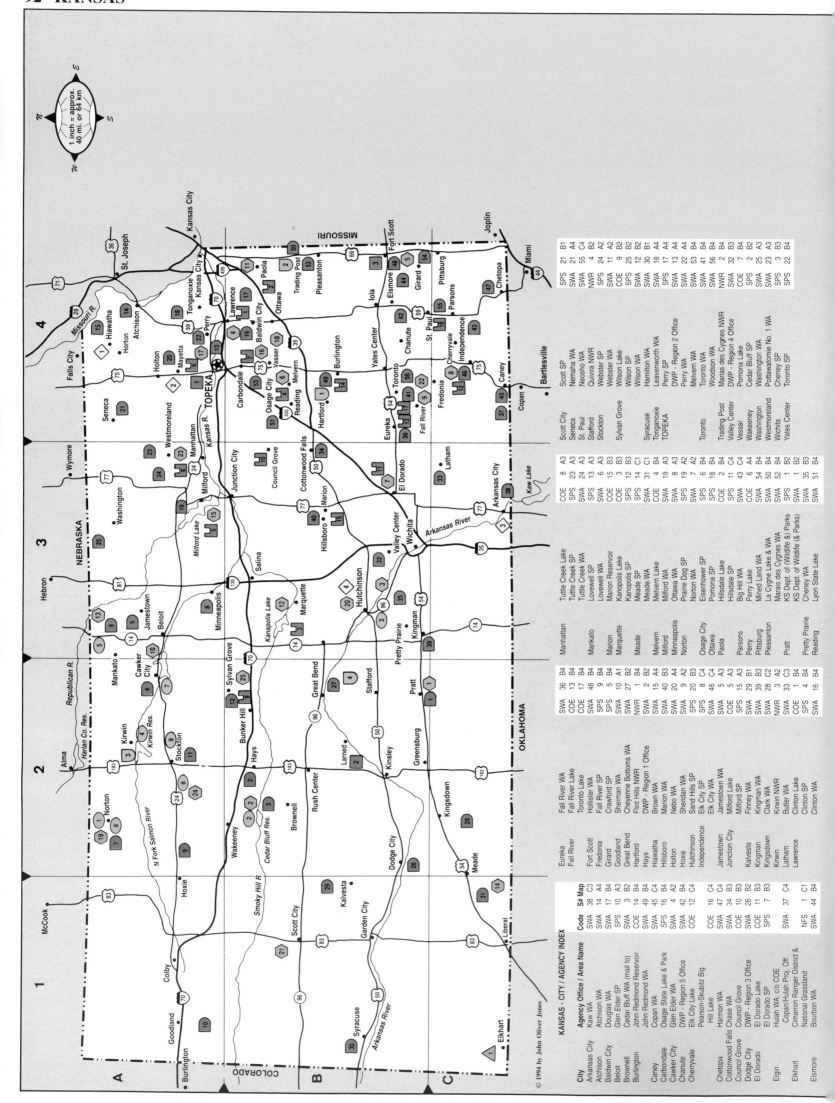

KANSAS NOTES

Summary

There are 25 federal, 83 state, and 5 private recreation areas or local administrative offices covered in this state chapter. Of these, 103 appear in the Information Chart and 10 are covered in the notes. The Outdoor Map Index features the Cimarron National Grassland map.

Federal Agencies

U.S. Forest Service

Kansas is in the Rocky Mountain Region (see Colorado chapter - U.S. Forest Svc., Rocky Mountain Region listing).

National Park Service

NPS Locations in Kansas

Brown vs. Board of Education NHS (S# 1, map A4)
Topeka, KS
402-221-3431
A new NPS site approved October 26, 1992.

Fort Larned National Historic Site (718 acres)
(S# 2, map B2)
Route 3
Larned, KS 67550
316-285-6911

Fort Scott National Historic Site (17 acres)
(S# 3, map B4)
Old Fort Blvd.
Fort Scott, KS 66701
316-223-0310

Bureau of Reclamation Recreation Areas

Nine recreation areas are listed here and symbolized on the Kansas state map.

S#	MAP	LOCATION NAME
1	A2	Almena Diversion Dam
2	B2	Cedar Bluffs Res.
3	B3	Cheney Res.
4	A2	Kirwin Res.
5	A3	Lovewell Res.
6	A2	Keith Sebelius Lake
7	A2	Waconda Lake
8	A2	Webster Res.
9	A2	Woodston Diversion Dam

Outdoor Map Index

U.S. Forest Service Map
Cimarron National Grassland
Scale: 1 inch = 0.5 mile (1 cm = 0.3 km)

State Agencies

The departments listed here operate as a part of the Kansas Parks and Public Lands Division. Local park and wildlife areas are often adjacent or close to one another and may be managed from one local office. Some park/WMA offices are indicated in the Information Chart listings. In the Information Chart pages, WMAs and parks are listed separately under their common headquarters.

Dept. of Wildlife & Parks (DWP)

A bi-monthly magazine, Kansas Wildlife and Parks, is available on newsstands, and by subscription for $8 per year. A Visitors Guide has extensive coverage of Kansas State Parks. A Hunting Guide to Kansas lists 71 state and federally administered areas open to the public. Kansas Outdoors, a fold-out brochure, lists 103 areas, including lakes and reservoirs.

Department of Forestry

2610 Claflin Road
Manhattan, KS 66502
913-537-7050
There is no state forest recreation program in Kansas.

Department of Commerce

Travel & Tourism Development
400 W. 8th, 5th Floor
Topeka, KS 66603
913-296-2009
A Visitors Guide with information on attractions, specific activities, special events and trip planning is available free. There is also a free Fun Map & Events Calendar. The official Kansas Transportation Map is available from this office. The map has symbols for state parks and fishing lakes.

Private Organizations

Tribal Land Areas in Kansas

Kickapoo Tribe of the Kickapoo Indian Reservation - Camping.

Kickapoo of Kansas Tribal Council (S# 1, map A4)
Route 1, Box 157A
Horton, KS 66349
913-486-2131

Prairie Band of Potawatomi Indians of Kansas - Fishing, hunting, camping.
Prairie Band Potawatomi Tribal Council (S# 2, map A4)
Route 2, Box 50A
Mayetta, KS 66509
913-966-2255

ANCA Locations in Kansas

Chaplin Nature Center (S# 3, map C3)
Route 1, Box 216
Arkansas City, KS 67005
316-442-7227

Dillon Nature Center (S# 4, map B3)
3002 east 30th Street
Hutchinson, KS 67502
316-663-7411

Kansas Chamber of Commerce
500 Bank IV Tower
Topeka, KS 66603
Phone 913-357-6321
Fax 913-357-4732

AGENCY/MAP LEGEND . . . INITIALS, MAP SYMBOLS, COLOR CODES

Agency	Initials	Symbol
U.S. Forest Service Supervisor & Ranger Dist. Offices	NFS	61
U.S. Army Corps of Engineers Rec. Areas & Offices	COE	31
USFWS National Wildlife Refuges & Offices	NWR	40
National Park Service Parks & other NPS Sites	NPS	7
Bureau of Land Management Rec. Areas & Offices	BLM	26
Bureau of Reclamation Rec. Areas & Reg. Offices	BOR	8
State Parks (also see State Agency notes)	SPS	52
State Wildlife Areas (also see State Agency notes)	SWA	19
Private Preserves, Nature Centers & Tribal Lands		15
The Wild Rivers ~~~~ and Wilderness Areas		

Note: Refer to page 7 (top right) for location name and address abbreviations. If a symbol number has a star ★ that symbol is not shown on the map.

★ INFORMATION CHART ★

INFORMATION CHART LEGEND - SYMBOLS & LETTER CODES

■ means YES & □ means Yes with disability provisions
sp means spring, March through May
S means Summer, June through August
F means Fall, September through November
W means Winter, December through February
T means Two (2) or Three (3) Seasons
A means All Four (4) Seasons
na means Not Applicable or Not Available
Note: empty or blank spaces in the chart mean NO

FACILITIES, SERVICES, RECREATION OPPORTUNITIES & CONVENIENCES

S#	MAP	LOCATION NAME (state initials if more than one) with ADDRESS and/or LOCATION DATA	TELEPHONE	ACRES / ELEVATION
⚠ C1		Pike & San Isabel National Forest Supervisor, 1920 Valley Drive, Pueblo, CO 81008	303-545-8737	2,756,437 / 3,500-14,433
		Cimarron Ranger District & National Grassland, 242 Hwy. 56 East, Elkhart 67950	316-697-4621	108,337 / 3,200-3,600
(H)		COE, Kansas City District, 601 E. 12th St., 716 Federal Bldg., Kansas City, MO 64106	816-426-6816	na / na
1	B4	Clinton Lake, Rt. 1, Box 120G, Lawrence 66044	913-843-7665	na / na
2	B4	Hillsdale Lake, Box 205, Paola 66071	913-783-4366	na / na
3	B3	Kanopolis Lake, Rt. 1, Marquette 67464	913-546-2294	na / na
4	B4	Melvern Lake, RR #1, Box 370, Melvern 66510	913-549-3318	na / na
5	A3	Milford Lake, Rt. 3 Box 303, Junction City 66441	913-238-5714	na / na
6	A4	Perry Lake, RR 1, Box 115, Perry 66073	913-597-5144	na / na
7	B3	Pomona Lake, RFD 1, Vassar 66543	913-453-2201	na / na
8	A3	Tuttle Creek Lake, 5020 Tuttle Creek Blvd., Manhattan 66502	913-539-8511	na / na
9	B2	Wilson Lake, RR 1, Box 241, Sylvan Grove 67481	913-658-2551	na / na
10		COE, Tulsa District, PO Box 61, Tulsa, OK 74121	918-581-7349	na / na
11	B3	Council Grove, Rt. 2, Box 110, Council Grove 66846	316-767-5195	na / na
12	B3	El Dorado Lake, RR 3, El Dorado 67042	316-321-9974	na / na
13	C4	Elk City Lake, PO Box 426, Cherryvale 67335	316-336-2741	na / na
14	B4	Fall River Lake, PO Box 37, Fall River 67047	316-658-4445	na / na
15	B3	John Redmond Reservoir, RR 1, Box 91, Burlington 66839	316-364-8613	na / na
16	B3	Marion Reservoir, RR #1, Box 102, Marion 66861	316-382-2101	na / na
16	C4	Pearson-Skubitz Big Hill Lake, PO Box 426, Cherryvale 67335	316-336-2741	na / na

★ INFORMATION CHART ★

INFORMATION CHART LEGEND - SYMBOLS & LETTER CODES

- ■ means YES & □ means Yes with disability provisions
- **sp** means spring, March through May
- **S** means Summer, June through August
- **F** means Fall, September through November
- **W** means Winter, December through February
- **T** means Two (2) or Three (3) Seasons
- **A** means All Four (4) Seasons
- **na** means Not Applicable or Not Available

Note: empty or blank spaces in the chart mean **NO**. ... that symbol is not shown on the map.

AGENCY/MAP LEGEND ... INITIALS, MAP SYMBOLS, COLOR CODES

- U.S. Forest Service Supervisor & Ranger Dist. Offices . . NFS
- U.S. Army Corps of Engineers Rec. Areas & Offices . . COE
- USFWS National Wildlife Refuges & Offices . . . . NWR
- National Park Service Parks & other NPS Sites . . . . . . NPS
- Bureau of Land Management Rec. Areas & Offices . . . . BLM
- Bureau of Reclamation Rec. Areas & Reg. Offices . . . . BOR
- State Parks (also see State Agency notes) . . . . SPS
- State Wildlife Areas (also see State Agency notes) . . . . SWA
- Private Preserves, Nature Centers & Tribal Lands . . .
- The Wild Rivers — and Wilderness Areas

Note: Refer to yellow block on page 7 (top right) for location name and address abbreviations. If a symbol number has a star ★

S#	MAP	LOCATION NAME / LOCATION DATA	TELEPHONE	ACRES / ELEVATION
17	B4	Toronto Lake, PO Box 37, Fall River 67047	316-658-4445	na / na
1	B4	Flint Hills NWR, PO Box 128, Hartford 66854 [8 mi. S of I-35 on KS Hwy. 130]	316-392-5553	18,463 / 1,036-1,068
2	B4	Marias des Cygnes NWR (new, not open), PO Box 128, Hartford 66854 [located in Trading Post, KS]	316-392-5553	5,300 / na
3	A2	Kirwin NWR, Rt. #1, Box 103, Kirwin 67644	913-543-6673	10,780 / 1,700
4	B2	Quivira NWR, Rt. #3, Box 48A, Stafford 67578	316-486-2393	21,820 / na
		Kansas Dept. of Wildlife & Parks, Parks & Public Lands Div., RR #2, Box 54A, Pratt 67124 [1 mi SE of Pratt]		
1	B2		316-672-5911	na / na
2	B2	Cedar Bluff SP, Rt. #2, Box 76-A, Ellis 67637 [23 mi. SE of Wakeeney]	913-726-3212	1,715 / 2,150-2,230
3	B3	Cheney SP, 20 mi. NW of Wichita	316-755-2711	2,495 / na
4	B4	Clinton SP, 4 mi. W of Lawrence	913-842-8562	1,425 / na
5	B4	Crawford SP, 9 mi. N of Girard	316-362-3671	439 / na
6	B4	Eisenhower SP, Melvern Res., Rt. #2, Box 306, Osage City 66523 [8 mi. SW of Lyndon]	913-528-4102	1,785 / 1,036
7	B3	El Dorado SP, 5 mi. E of El Dorado	316-321-7180	3,800 / na
8	C4	Elk City SP, c/o KDWP, PO Box 945, 5 mi. NW of Independence 67301	316-331-6820	857 / 810
9	B4	Fall River SP, 17 mi. NW of Fredonia	316-658-4818	917 / 950
10	A3	Glen Elder SP, 10 mi. W of Beloit	913-545-3345	1,350 / 1,456
11	B4	Hillsdale SP, Rt. #3, Box 205A, Paola 66071	913-783-4507	12,893 / 917
12	B3	Kanopolis SP, RR #1, Box 260, Marquette 67464 [11 mi. NW of Marquette]	913-546-2565	1,585 / na
13	A3	Lovewell SP, 15 mi. NE of Mankato	913-753-4305	1,126 / na
14	C1	Meade SP, Box K, 13 mi. SW of Meade 67864	316-296-2281	443 / na
15	A3	Milford SP, 3 mi. NW of Junction City	913-238-3014	1,084 / 1,144
16	B4	Osage State Lake & Park, S of Carbondale	913-828-4933	506 / 1,000
17	A4	Perry SP, 16 mi. NE of Topeka	913-246-3449	1,679 / na
18	A4	Pomona SP, 16 mi. W of Ottawa	913-828-4933	490 / 1,000
19	A2	Prairie Dog SP, Box 431, Norton 67654 [4 mi. W & 1 mi. S of Norton]	913-877-2953	1,028 / 2,285
20	B3	Sand Hills SP, 3 mi. NE of Hutchinson	316-755-2711	1,223 / na
21	B1	Scott SP, RR #1, Scott City 67871 [12 mi. N of Scott City]	316-872-2061	1,120 / na
22	A4	Toronto SP, 17 mi. SW of Yates Center	316-637-2213	1,050 / na
23	A3	Tuttle Creek SP, 5 mi. N of Manhattan	913-539-7941	1,156 / na
24	A2	Webster SP, Rt. #2, Box 153, 8 mi. W of Stockton 67669	913-425-6775	880 / 1,866-1,880
25	B2	Wilson SP, 8 mi. N of Wilson, Rt. #1, Box 181, Sylvan Grove 67481	913-658-2465	788 / na
		Kansas Dept. of Wildlife & Parks, Wildlife Div., RR #2, Box 54A, Pratt 67124 [1 mi SE of Pratt]		
1	B2		316-672-5911	na / na
2	B2	DWP - Region 1 Office, on Hwy. 183 bypass, PO Box 338, Hays 67601	913-628-8614	na / na
3	B2	Cedar Bluff WA, mail to) Rt. #2, Box 76-A, Ellis, KS 67637 [on K-147 N of Brownell]	913-628-8614	11,834 / 2,070-2,260
4	B2	Glen Elder WA, areas around Cawker City	913-545-3345	12,500 / 1,456
5	A3	Jamestown WA, 3.5 mi. N & 2 mi. W of Jamestown	913-753-4305	2,728 / 1,500
6	A3	Lovewell WA, 12 mi. NE of Mankato	913-753-4305	5,215 / 1,600
7	A3	Norton WA, 6 mi. W & 2 mi. S of Norton	913-877-2953	6,913 / 2,285
8	A3	Ottawa WA, 5 mi. N & 1 mi. E of Bennington, RR #2, Minneapolis 67467	913-546-2343	611 / na
9	A2	Sheridan WA, (mail to) Rt. #2, Box 76-A, Ellis, KS 67637 [11 mi. E of Hoxie]	913-726-3212	335 / na
10	A1	Sherman WA, (mail to) Rt. #2, Box 76-A, Ellis, KS 67637 [10 mi. S & 2 mi. W of Goodland]	913-726-3212	1,547 / na
11	A2	Webster WA, 8 mi. W of Stockton	913-439-8310	7,539 / 1,866-1,880
12	A2	Wilson WA, 7 mi. NW of Bunker Hill, Rt. #1, Box 181, Sylvan Grove 67481	913-658-2465	8,039 / na
13	A4	DWP - Region 2 Office, 3300 SW 29th, Topeka 66614	913-273-6740	179 / na
14	A4	Atchison WA, 5 mi. N & 2 mi. W of Atchison	913-273-6740	129 / na
15	A4	Brown WA, 8 mi. E of Hiawatha	913-367-7811	129 / na
16	B4	Clinton WA, SW of Lawrence	913-887-6882	9,923 / na
17	B4	Douglas WA, 1 mi. N & 1 mi. E of Baldwin City	913-842-8562	500 / na
18	A4	Leavenworth WA, 3 mi. W & 1 mi. N of Tonganoxie	913-842-8652	332 / na
19	A3	Milford WA (areas NW of the dam), Milford	913-461-5402	17,963 / na

#	Map	Name	Acreage (public/managed)	Phone
22	A4	Perry WA, 20 mi. NE of Topeka	10,984 / na	913-945-6615
23	A3	Pottawatomie No. 1 WA, 5 mi. N of Westmoreland	190 / na	913-539-7941
24	A3	Tuttle Creek WA, 20 mi. N of Manhattan	10,469 / na	913-539-7941
25	A3	Washington WA, 7 mi. N & 3 mi. W of Washington	457 / na	316-238-3014
26	B2	DWP - Region 3 Office, 808 Hwy. 56, Dodge City 67801	na / 2,594	316-227-8609
27	B2	Cheyenne Bottoms WA, Rt. #3, Box 301, Great Bend 67530 [5 mi. S & 5 mi. E of Great Bend]	19,857 / 1,800	316-793-7730
28	C2	Clark WA, 9 mi. S & 1 mi. W of Kingsdown	1,040 / na	316-227-8609
29	B1	Finney WA, 8 mi. N & 3 mi. W of Kalvesta	863 / na	316-227-8609
30	B1	Hamilton WA, 3 mi. W & 2 mi. N of Syracuse	432 / na	316-227-8609
31	C1	Meade WA, 8 mi. S & 5 mi. W of Meade	400 / na	316-227-8609
32	B2	DWP - Region 4 Office, 8420 N. Broadway, PO Box 317, Valley Center 67417	10 / na	316-755-2711
33	C3	Butler WA, 3 mi. W & 1 mi. N of Latham	351 / na	316-755-2711
34	B3	Chase WA, 1.5 mi. W of Cottonwood Falls	452 / na	316-755-2711
35	B3	Cheney WA, 7 mi. E of Pretty Prairie	5,249 / na	316-755-2711
36	B4	Fall River WA, 7 mi. SE of Eureka	9,352 / 958	316-583-6783
37	C4	Hulah WA, c/o COE Copan/Hulah Proj., Rt. #1, Box 260, Copan, OK 74022 [located E & W of Elgin]	844 / 700	918-532-4334
38	C3	Kaw WA, SE of Arkansas City	4,341 / na	316-755-2711
39	B3	Kingman WA, 7 mi. W of Kingman	4,043 / na	316-755-2711
40	B3	Marion WA, 5 mi. NE of Hillsboro	3,522 / na	316-755-2711
41	B4	Toronto WA, 1 mi. W or 1 mi. S of Toronto	4,366 / na	316-637-2213
42	B4	DWP - Region 5 Office, 1500 W 7th, PO Box 777, Chanute 66720	na / na	316-431-0380
43	C4	Big Hill WA, 8 mi. W & 4 mi. S of Parsons	1,320 / na	316-331-6820
44	B4	Bourbon WA, 4.5 mi. E of Elsmore	350 / na	316-362-3671
45	C4	Copan WA, 0.5 mi. W of Caney	2,360 / na	316-331-6820
46	C4	Elk City WA, 3 mi. W of Independence	10,966 / 810	316-331-6820
47	C4	Harmon WA, 2 mi. N of Chetopa	102 / 900	316-231-3173
48	B4	Hollister WA, 6 mi. W & 2 mi. S of Fort Scott	2,432 / na	316-362-3671
49	B4	John Redmond WA, NW of Burlington	1,597 / 1,039	913-528-4102
50	B4	La Cygne Lake & WA, Rt. #2, Box 132, near Pleasanton 66075 [5 mi. E of La Cygne]	4,600 / 800	913-352-8941
51	B4	Lyon State Lake, 5 mi. W & 1 mi. N of Reading	562 / 1,000	913-528-4102
52	B4	Marais des Cygnes WA, Rt. #2, Box 132, Pleasanton 66075 [5 mi. N of Pleasanton]	7,235 / 800	913-352-8941
53	B4	Melvern WA, 40 mi. S of Topeka	10,016 / na	316-699-9372
54	B4	Mined Land WA, Crawford & Cherokee Counties, near Pittsburg	14,250 / 910	316-231-3173
55	C4	Neosho WA, 5 mi. E of St. Paul	3,243 / na	316-362-3671
56	B4	Woodson WA, 5 mi. E of Toronto	2,800 / na	316-637-2213

KENTUCKY NOTES

Summary

There are 37 federal, 66 state, and 10 private recreation areas or local administrative offices covered in this state chapter. Of these, 76 appear in the Information Chart and 37 are covered in the notes. The special indexes feature 2 federally designated wilderness areas and 4 agency published outdoor maps.

Federal Agencies

U.S. Forest Service

Kentucky is in the Southern Region (see Georgia chapter - U.S. Forest Svc., Southern Region listing).

Tennessee Valley Authority (TVA)

Probably the best known TVA recreation area is the Land Between the Lakes or LBL, 170,000 acres located between Kentucky Lake and Lake Barkley in western Kentucky and Tennessee. Daily programs, camping, a nature center, and one of the largest buffalo herds east of the Mississippi River are a few of the attractions. For information and maps, including the annually published LBL "Calendar of Events," contact:

TVA/Land-Between-The-Lakes
100 Van Morgan Drive
Golden Pond, KY 42211-9000   502-924-1243

There are 15 recreation maps of TVA reservoirs (some are in the process of revision) listed in the *TVA Maps Price Catalog*. The first page of that catalog features a map showing the office location in Chattanooga, Tennessee. The catalog and maps are available from:

TVA Maps & Surveys Department
100 Haney Building
311 Broad St.
Chattanooga, TN 37402   615-751-MAPS

Wilderness Index

There are two wilderness areas in the Daniel Boone National Forest (S# 1, map B4) as follows:

Beaver Creek Wilderness - 4,756
Clifty Wilderness - 13,300

Outdoor Map Index

National Park Service (USGS Map)

Mammoth Cave National Park [1972]

Scale: 1 inch = 0.4 mile (1 cm = 0.3 km)
Size: 46x53 inches (116x134 cm)

U.S. Forest Service Maps

Daniel Boone NF, North Half [1984]
Daniel Boone NF, Redbird District [1982]
Daniel Boone NF, South Half [1984]

State Agencies

Kentucky State Nature Preserves Commission

This chapter includes Kentucky's Nature Preserves. A round medium blue symbol and Information Chart color code are used to identify them. Free preserve brochures feature a local area map. Some preserves are located within state parks. Those parks are not included in the selected state parks listed in the Guide.

KY Dept. of Parks

The State Parks (15 resort parks, 29 others), special events, and rate guides are available free. A park guide describes parks, contains a locator map, and includes information on facilities and activities. There are fees for camping and other activities but no entry fees.

KY Dept. of Fish & Wildlife Resources (DFWR)

#1 Game Farm Road
Frankfort, KY 40601   502-564-4336

A bi-monthly magazine, *Kentucky Afield - The Magazine,* is available by subscription for $5 per year. A free booklet titled *A Guide To Public Wildlife Areas In Kentucky* describes 59 areas open to the public.

Selected areas, their Guide map symbol numbers and coordinates, name and approximate location are listed below. They are open at least part of the year to hikers, picnickers, birdwatchers, and others looking for quiet places to enjoy nature.

S#	MAP	WMA Name & Location
2	B1	Ballard County WMA, Paducah
3	C1	Barkley Lake WMA, S of Princeton
4	C3	Barren Lake WMA, Lucas
5	C4	Beaver Creek WMA, Greenwood
6	B4	Beech Creek WMA, Manchester
7	B5	Buckhorn Lake WMA, Hazard
8	B4	Central Kentucky WMA, Richmond
9	A4	Clay WMA, Carlisle
10	C5	Cranks Creek WMA, Harlan
11	A4	Curtis Gates Lloyd WMA, Crittenden
12	B5	Dale Hollow WMA, Dale Hollow Lake
13	A5	Grayson Lake WMA, Olive Hill
14	B3	Green River WMA, Jamestown
15	B2	Higginson-Henry WMA, Morganfield
16	A4	John A. Kleber WMA, Frankfort
17	B2	Jones-Keeney WMA, Dawson Springs
18	C1	Kentucky Lake WMA, Murray
19	B2	L. B. Davison WMA, Owensboro
20	B4	Lake Cumberland WMA, Somerset
21	B1	Land Between the Lakes WMA, Gilbertsville
22	A4	Mullins WMA, Crittenden
23	B3	Nolin Lake WMA, Hodgenville
24	B1	Peal WMA, S of Barlow
25	B5	Pine Mountain WMA, Whitesburg
26	B3	Rough River WMA, W of Elizabethtown
27	B2	Sloughs WMA (3 tracts), Henderson
28	A3	Twin Eagle WMA, Perry Park
29	B2	White City WMA, Madisonville
30	C1	Winford WMA, Mayfield
31	B2	Yellowbank WMA, Owensboro

Kentucky Division of Forestry

Frankfort, KY 40601   502-564-4496

There is no state forest recreation program in Kentucky.

KY Dept. of Travel Development

Capital Plaza Office Tower   1-800-225-9747
Frankfort, KY 40601   502-564-4930

The official Kentucky Dept. of Highways road map has symbols for state resort parks, state and national parks, and roadside parks with full facilities. National forest areas are shown in green.

Private Organizations

ANCA Locations in Kentucky

Fort Campbell Nature Center (S# 7, map C2)
Outdoor Recreation Branch
Fort Campbell, KY 42223-5000   502-798-2741

Nature & Conservation Center (S# 8, map A3)
PO Box 7414
Louisville, KY 40207-7414   502-429-9666

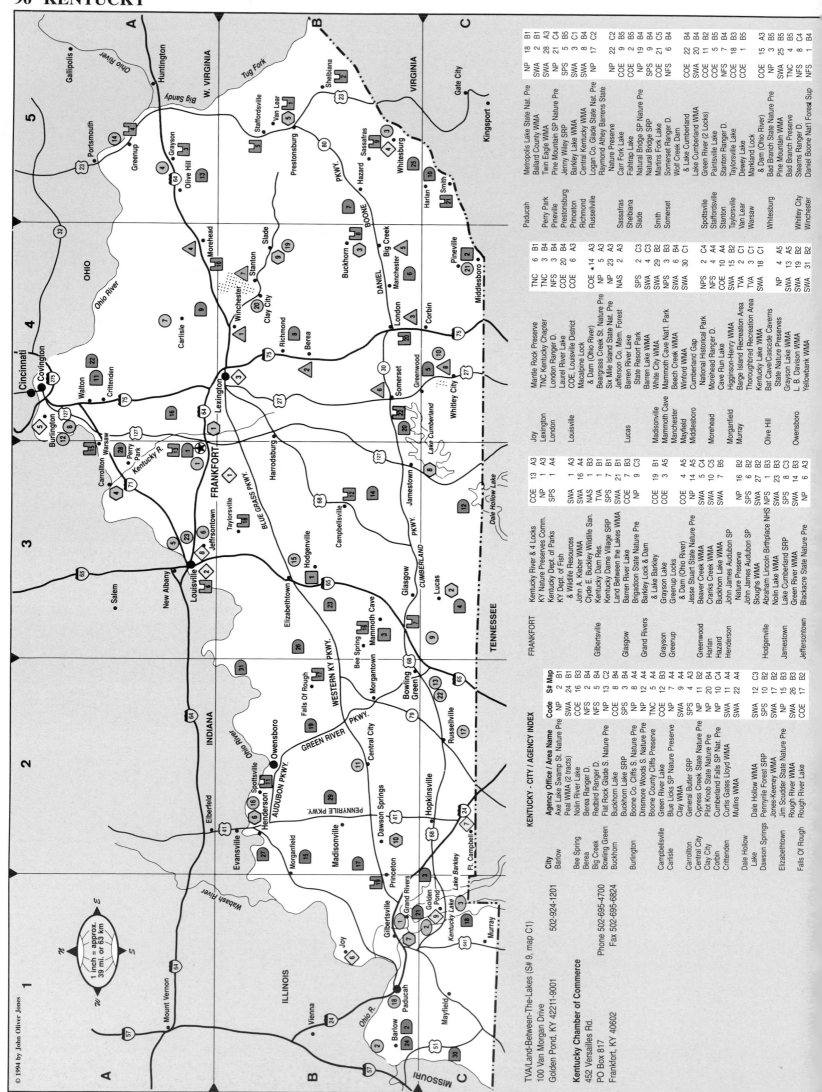

★ INFORMATION CHART ★

AGENCY/MAP LEGEND . . . INITIALS, MAP SYMBOLS, COLOR CODES

U.S. Forest Service Supervisor & Ranger Dist. Offices . NFS
U.S. Army Corps of Engineers Rec. Areas & Offices . . COE
Tennessee Valley Authority Offices & Sites . . . . TVA
National Park Service Parks & other NPS Sites . . . . . . NPS
Bureau of Land Management Rec. Areas & Offices . . . BLM
KY Nature Preserves (also see State Agency notes) . . . NP
State Parks (also see State Agency notes) . . . . SPS
State Wildlife Areas (also see State Agency notes) . . . SWA
Private Preserves, Nature Centers & Tribal Lands . . . .
The Wild Rivers ⌒ and Wilderness Areas

INFORMATION CHART LEGEND - SYMBOLS & LETTER CODES

■ means YES & □ means Yes with disability provisions
sp means spring, March through May
S means Summer, June through August
F means Fall, September through November
W means Winter, December through February
T means Two (2) or Three (3) Seasons
A means All Four (4) Seasons
na means Not Applicable or Not Available

Note: empty or blank spaces in the chart mean **NO**

INFO OFFICE (IO) / VISITOR CENTER (VC)
IO / VC OPEN SATURDAY / SUNDAY
ENTRY FEE / PERMIT FEE
CONCESSIONAIRE SERVICES AVAILABLE
FREE LITERATURE / BROCHURES, maps, etc.
AGENCY LITERATURE or permit fee
NATURE EDUCATION
WILDFLOWER VIEWING / STUDY PROGRAMS
WILDLIFE VIEWING / GUIDED TOURS, scheduled / by res.
ARCHAEOLOGICAL / GEOLOGICAL SITES
HISTORIC SITES
INTERPRETIVE TRAILS
WILDLIFE IS ABUNDANT OR COMMON
ENDANGERED SPECIES ARE COMMON
WILDLIFE VIEWING SITES, blinds, etc.
DEVELOPED PICNIC AREAS / signs, etc.
NO-CHARGE CAMPGROUNDS / CAMPSITES
FEE-CHARGE CAMPGROUNDS / CAMPSITES
WILDERNESS AREAS / HIKING TRAILS
WALKING / HIKING PERMITTED
BICYCLING PERMITTED w/ your own bike
OFF-ROAD Motorized Vehicle Area / your own risk
HORSEBACK RIDING, w/ your own horse
FISHING IN SEASON / license / permit reqd.
BOATING FACILITIES / ramps, marinas, etc.
MOTORIZED WATERCRAFT OK / check limits
NO-MOTORIZED WATERCRAFT OK
WINTER SPORTS OPPORTUNITIES
HUNTING IN SEASON, license / permit reqd.
PARK & WALK-IN ONLY AREA
DAY USE ONLY, no overnight
DRINKING WATER
RESTROOMS

Note: *Refer to yellow block on page 7 (top right) for location name and address abbreviations. If a symbol number has a star ★ that symbol is not shown on the map.*

S#	MAP	LOCATION NAME (state initials if more than one) with ADDRESS and/or LOCATION DATA	TELEPHONE	ACRES / ELEVATION
		Daniel Boone National Forest Sup., 100 Vaught Road, Winchester 40391	606-745-3100	672,361 / 1,200-2,700
1	B4	Berea Ranger D., 1835 Big Hill Road, Berea 40403	606-986-8434	83,661 / na
2	B4	London Ranger D., US 25 South, PO Box 907, London 40743	606-864-4164	94,549 / na
3	B4	Morehead Ranger D., 2375 Ky. 801 South, Morehead 40351	606-784-6428	117,073 / na
4	A4	Redbird Ranger D., HC 68, Box 65, Big Creek 40914	606-598-2192	143,363 / na
5	B4			
6	B4	Somerset Ranger D., 156 Realty Lane, Somerset 42501	606-679-2018	72,712 / na
7	B4	Stanton Ranger D., 705 W College Ave., Stanton 40380	606-663-2852	59,360 / na
8	C4	Stearns Ranger D., Hwy. 27 N., PO Box 429, Whitley City 42653	606-376-5323	111,597 / na
1	B5	**COE, Huntington District**, 502 8th St., Huntington, WV 25701	304-529-5607	na / na
		Dewey Lake, HC 70, Box 540, Van Lear 41265	606-789-4521	na / na
2	B5	Fishtrap Lake, Rt. #1, Box 501, Shelbiana 41562	606-437-7496	na / na
3	A5	Grayson Lake, Rt. 2, Box 258, Grayson 41143	606-474-5815	na / na
4	A5	Greenup Locks & Dam (Ohio River), 5121 New Dam Road, Greenup 41144	606-473-7441	na / na
5	B5	Paintsville Lake, PO Box 520, Staffordsville 41256	606-297-6312	na / na
6	A3	COE, Louisville District, PO Box 59, Louisville 40201	502-582-6292	na / na
7	B3	Barren River Lake, 11088 Finney Rd., Glasgow 42141	502-646-2055	na / na
8	B3	Buckhorn Lake, Buckhorn Lake, Buckhorn 41721	606-398-7251	na / na
9	B5	Carr Fork Lake, HCR 32, Box 520, Sassafras 41759	606-642-3308	na / na
10	A4	Cave Run Lake, 150 KY Hwy. 826, Morehead 40351	606-784-9709	na / na
11	B2	Green River (2 Locks), Green River Lock 1, Spottsville 42458	502-826-7360	na / na
12	B3	Green River Lake, 544 Lake Road, Campbellsville 42718	502-465-4463	na / na
★13	A3	Kentucky River & 4 Locks, 1021 Kentucky Ave., Frankfort 40601	502-223-8338	na / na
★14	A3	Macalpine Lock & Dam (Ohio River), 805 N 27th Street, Louisville 40212	502-774-3514	na / na
15	A3	Markland Lock & Dam (Ohio River), RFD 1, Warsaw 41095	606-567-7661	na / na
16	B3	Nolin River Lake, 2150 Nolin Dam Road, Bee Spring 42207	502-286-4511	na / na
17	B2	Rough River Lake, RR 1, Falls Of Rough 40119	502-257-2061	na / na
18	B3	Taylorsville Lake, 2825 Overlook Rd., Taylorsville 40071	502-477-8882	na / na
19	B1	Barkley Lock & Dam & Lake Barkley, Box 218, Grand Rivers 42045	502-362-4236	na / na
20	B1	Laurel River Lake, 1433 Laurel Lake Road, London 40741	606-864-6412	na / na
21	C5	Martins Fork Lake, HC 74, Box 763, Smith 40831	606-573-7655	na / na
22	B4	Wolf Creek Dam & Lake Cumberland, 1000 Boat Dock Road, Somerset 42501	606-679-6337	na / na
32		**TVA - Western District**, 202 West Blythe St., PO Box 280, Paris, TN 38242	901-642-2041	na / na
1	B1	Kentucky Dam Res., S of Gilbertsville [TN Hwy. 100]	901-642-2041	na / na
2	C1	Barge Island Recreation Area, N of Murray [KY Hwy. 962]	901-642-2041	na / na
3	C1	Thoroughbred Recreation Area, NE of Murray [KY Hwy. 280]	901-642-2041	na / na
1	B3	**Abraham Lincoln Birthplace NHS**, 2995 Lincoln Farm Rd., Hodgenville 42748	502-358-3137	116 / 750
2	C4	Cumberland Gap National Historical Site, PO Box 1848, Middlesboro 40965	606-248-2817	20,305 / 1,134-3,513
3	B3	Mammoth Cave Nat'l. Park, Mammoth Cave 42259	502-758-2251	52,420 / 421-902
1	B3	**KY Nature Preserves Commission**, 407 Broadway, Frankfort 40601	502-564-2886	na / na
2	B1	Axe Lake Swamp St. Nature Preserve, near Barlow	502-564-2886	150 / na
3	B5	Bad Branch State Nature Preserve, near Whitesburg	502-564-2886	440 / na
4	A5	Bat Cave/Cascade Caverns State NPs (within Carter Caves St. Resort Park), near Olive Hill	502-564-2886	150 / na
5	A3	Beargrass Creek St. Nature Preserve, in, Louisville	502-564-2886	40 / na
6	A3	Blackacre State Nature Preserve, near Jeffersontown	502-473-3295	170 / na
7	A3	Blue Licks SP Nature Preserve (within Blue Licks Battlefield SP), near Carlisle	502-564-2886	20 / na
8	A4	Boone Co. Cliffs S. Nature Preserve, near Burlington	502-564-2886	80 / na
9	C3	Brigadoon State Nature Preserve, near Glasgow	502-564-2886	90 / na
10	C4	Cumberland Falls SP Nat. Preserve (in Cumberland Falls State Park), W of Corbin	502-564-2886	1,290 / na
11	B2	Cypress Creek State Nature Preserve, near Central City	502-564-2886	100 / na
12	A4	Dinsmore Woods S. Nature Preserve, W of Burlington	502-564-2886	110 / na

FACILITIES, SERVICES, RECREATION OPPORTUNITIES & CONVENIENCES

★ INFORMATION CHART ★

AGENCY/MAP LEGEND ... INITIALS, MAP SYMBOLS, COLOR CODES

U.S. Forest Service Supervisor & Ranger Dist. Offices . NFS
U.S. Army Corps of Engineers Rec. Areas & Offices . COE
Tennessee Valley Authority Offices & Sites . . . . TVA
National Park Service Parks & other NPS Sites . . . . . NPS
Bureau of Land Management Rec. Areas & Offices . . . BLM
KY Nature Preserves (also see State Agency notes) . . . NP
State Parks (also see State Agency notes) . . . . SPS
Private Preserves, Nature Centers & Tribal Lands . . . SWA
The Wild Rivers —— and Wilderness Areas

Note: Refer to yellow block on page 7 (top right) for location name and address abbreviations.

INFORMATION CHART LEGEND - SYMBOLS & LETTER CODES

■ means YES & □ means Yes with disability provisions
sp means spring, March through May
S means Summer, June through August
F means Fall, September through November
W means Winter, December through February
T means Two (2) or Three (3) Seasons
A means All Four (4) Seasons
na means Not Applicable or Not Available

Note: empty or blank spaces in the chart mean NO
* that symbol is not shown on the map.

S#	MAP	LOCATION NAME (state initials if more than one) with ADDRESS and/or LOCATION DATA	TELEPHONE	ACRES / ELEVATION	S#
13	C2	Flat Rock Glade S. Nature Preserve, near Bowling Green	502-564-2886	60 / na	13
14	A5	Jesse Stuart State Nature Preserve, near Greenup	502-564-2886	730 / na	14
15	B3	Jim Scudder State Nature Preserve, near Elizabethtown	502-564-2886	60 / na	15
16	B2	John James Audubon SP Nat. Preserve (in Audubon State Park), N of Henderson	502-564-2886	330 / na	16
17	C2	Logan Co. Glade State Nat. Preserve, Russellville	502-564-2886	40 / na	17
18	B1	Metropolis Lake State Nat. Preserve, near Paducah	502-564-2886	120 / na	18
19	B4	Natural Bridge SP Nature Preserve, near Slade	502-564-2886	990 / na	19
20	B4	Pilot Knob State Nature Preserve, near Clay City	502-564-2886	310 / na	20
21	C4	Pine Mountain SP Nature Preserve (in Pine Mtn. State Resort Park), W of Pineville	502-564-2886	870 / na	21
22	C2	Raymond Athey Barrens SN Preserve, near Russellville	502-564-2886	60 / na	22
23	A3	Six Mile Island State Nat. Preserve (in the Ohio River), near Louisville	502-564-2886	80 / na	23
①	A4	KY Dept. of Parks, Capital Plaza Tower, 10th Floor, 500 Mero St., Frankfort 40601	800-255-7275	na / na	1
2	C3	Barren River Lake St. Resort Park, 1149 State Park Rd., Lucas 42156 (near Glasgow)	800-325-0057	2,187 / na	2
3	B4	Buckhorn Lake SRP (near Hazard), HC 36, Box 1000, Buckhorn 41721	800-325-0058	856 / na	3
4	A3	General Butler SRP, Box 325, Carrollton 41008	800-325-0078	809 / na	4
5	B5	Jenny Wiley SRP, HC 66, Box 200, Prestonsburg 41653	800-325-0142	1,651 / na	5
6	B1	John James Audubon SP, PO Box 576, Henderson 42420	502-564-2172	692 / na	6
7	B1	Kentucky Dame Village SRP (near Paducah, ph. 502-564-2172), PO Box 69, Gilbertsville 42044	800-325-0146	1,351 / na	7
8	C3	Lake Cumberland SRP, PO Box 380, Jamestown 42629	800-325-1709	3,117 / na	8
9	B4	Natural Bridge SRP, General Delivery, Slade 40376	800-325-1710	1,647 / na	9
⑩	B2	Pennyrile Forest SRP, 20781 Pennyrile Lodge Rd., Dawson Springs 42408	800-325-1711	863 / na	10
①	A3	Clyde E. Buckley Wildlife Res., #1 Game Farm Rd., Frankfort 40601 [Arnold L. Mitchell Bldg.]	502-564-4336	50 / na	1
1	B3	Clyde E. Buckley Wildlife Sanctuary, 1305 Germany Rd., Frankfort 40601	606-873-5711	275 / 550-850	1
2	A3	Jefferson Co. Mem. Forest, c/o Forest Ranger, 11311 Mitchell Hill Rd., Louisville 40118	502-363-4363	4,000 / na	2
3	B4	TNC Kentucky Chapter, 642 West Main St., Lexington 40508	606-259-9655	na / na	3
4	B5	Bad Branch Preserve (contact Chapter Office), near Whitesburg	606-259-9655	3,000 / 1,800-3,000	4
5	A4	Boone County Cliffs Preserve (contact Chapter Office), near Burlington	606-259-9655	74 / 800	5
6	B1	Mantle Rock Preserve (contact Chapter Office), near Joy	606-259-9655	191 / 500	6

LOUISIANA - CITY / AGENCY INDEX

City	Agency Office / Area Name	Code	S#	Map
Alexandria	Evangeline Ranger D.	NFS	4	B2
	Alexander Forest WMA	SWA	13	B2
Bastrop	Chemin-A-Haul SP	SPS	3	A2
	Georgia-Pacific WMA	SWA	8	A2
BATON ROUGE	LA State Parks	SPS	1	C3
	LA Dept. Wildlife & Fisheries	SWA	1	C3
	District 7 - LADWF	SWA	35	C3
	TNC Louisiana Field Office	TNC	1	C1
Bell City	Cameron Prairie NWR	NWR	1	C1
Bellevue	Bodcau WMA	SWA	37	A1
Bogalusa	Ben's Creek WMA	SWA	39	D4
Bohemia	Bohemia WMA	SWA	5	A1
Bossier City	Loggy Bayou WMA	SWA	20	B2
Columbia	Boeuf WMA	SWA	11	A1
Doyline	Lake Bistineau SP	SPS	17	A3
Epps	Poverty Point SCA	SPS	41	A2
Eros	Schoolhouse Springs Nature Pre	TNC	3	A2
Farmerville	D'Arbonne NWR	NWR	4	A2
	Upper Ouachita NWR	NWR	4	A2
	Louisiana WMD	SWA	18	B2
Ferriday	District 4 - LADWF	SWA	5	D2
Franklin	Cypremort Point SCA	SPS	19	D2
Gilbert	Big Lake WMA	SWA	2	B1

City	Area Name	Code	S#	Map
Glenmora	Lake Cocodrie Preserve	TNC	3	B3
Grand Isle	Grand Isle SP	SPS	10	D4
Hackberry	Sabine NWR	NWR	8	C1
Hammond	Sandy Hollow WMA	SWA	46	C3
Hickory	Charter Oak Nature Preserve	TNC	2	C4
Homer	Caney Ranger D.	NFS	2	A1
Houma	Lake Claiborne SP	SPS	12	A2
	Point-Au-Chien WMA	SWA	44	D3
Jackson	Tunica Hills Preserve	TNC	5	C3
	Peason Ridge WMA	SWA	16	B1
Kisatchie	Sherburne WMA	SWA	32	C2
Krotz Springs	Salvador WMA	SWA	45	D3
Lafitte	Lacassine NWR	NWR	3	C1
Lake Arthur	Sam Houston Jones SP	SPS	18	C1
Lake Charles	District 5 - LADWF	SWA	25	C1
Leesville	Vernon Ranger D.	NFS	6	B1
	Boise-Vernon WMA	SWA	14	B1
	Fort Polk WMA	SWA	15	B1
LePlace	Wisner WMA	SWA	47	D3
	Manchac WMA	SWA	41	C3
Mandeville	Fairview Riverside SP	SPS	6	C3
	Fontainebleau SP	SPS	7	C3
Marion	Union WMA	SWA	11	A2
Marksville	Lake Ophelia NWR	NWR	6	B2
Marthaville	Los Adais SCA	SPS	14	B1
	District 1 - LADWF	SWA	2	B1

City	Area Name	Code	S#	Map
Monroe	District 6 - LADWF	COE	1	A1
	Kisatchie Nat'l. Forest Sup.	COE	2	A1
	Catahoula Ranger D.			
	Joyce WMA	COE	3	A2
	Catahoula NWR			
	Jackson-Bienville WMA	COE	4	B2
	Red River WMA			
	Three Rivers WMA	COE	6	A1
	Grassy Lake WMA			
	Soda Lake WMA	COE	7	B1
	Sicily Island Hills WMA			
	Southeast Louisiana Refuges	COE	8	B1
	Atchafalaya NWR	COE	9	A1
	Bogue Chitto NWR	SWA	7	A2
	Shell Keys NWR	SWA	10	A2
Moreauville	Russell Sage WMA	SWA	31	B2
	Pomme De Terre WMA	SWA	33	B2
	Spring Bayou WMA	SWA	29	D3
Morgan City	Attakapas WMA	SWA	36	D3
Natchitoches	Atchafalaya Delta WMA	SWA	29	D3
	Kisatchie Ranger D.	NFS	5	B1
New Orleans	Jean Lafitte NHP & Preserve	NPS	9	D4
	Ft. St. Jean Baptiste SCA	SPS	8	C4
	Ft. Pike State Comm. Area	SPS	13	C4
Oakdale	Biloxi WMA	SWA	26	C4
	West Bay WMA	SWA	27	C4

	Area Name	Code	S#	Map
Opelousas	COE, Bayou Bodcau Reservoir	COE	1	A1
	COE, Caddo Lake	COE	2	A1
Pineville	COE, Columbia Pool			
	Ouachita/Black River	COE	3	A2
Pollock	COE, Jonesville Pool			
	Ouachita/Black River	COE	4	B2
Ponchatoula	COE, Pool 1			
Rhinehart	(Red River Waterway)	COE	6	A1
Ruston	COE, Pool 2			
	(Red River Waterway)	COE	7	B1
Shaw	COE, Red R. Waterway,			
	5 Locks/Dams, Pool	COE	8	B1
Shreveport	COE Wallace Lake	COE	9	A1
Sicily Island	District 2 - LADWF	SWA	7	A2
Slidell	Ouachita WMA	SWA	10	A2
	Pomme De Terre WMA	SWA	31	B2
St. Martinville	Spring Bayou WMA	SWA	33	B2
Sun	Attakapas WMA	SWA	24	B2
	Grassy Lake WMA	SWA	30	B2
Tallulah	Soda Lake WMA	SWA	6	A1
Tioga	Sicily Island Hills WMA	SWA	23	B2
Toomey	Southeast Louisiana Refuges	NWR	9	C4
Venice	Atchafalaya NWR	NWR	10	C2
	Bayou Sauvage NWR	NWR	*11	C4
	Bogue Chitto NWR	NWR	12	C4
	Shell Keys NWR	NWR	*15	C4
	White Kitchens Nature Pre	TNC	6	C4
	Lake Fausse Point SP	SPS	13	C2
	Pearl River (3 Locks & Dams)	COE	5	C4
	Tensas River NWR	NWR	16	A3
	District 3 - LADWF	SWA	42	B2
	Sabine Island WMA	SWA	12	B2
	Breton NWR	NWR	13	D4
	Delta NWR	NWR	14	D4
	Pass-A-Loutre WMA	SWA	42	D4

	Area Name	Code	S#	Map
Ville Platte	Chicot SP	SPS	4	C2
Walters	Saline WMA	SWA	22	B2
Washington	Thistlethwaite WMA	SWA	34	C2
Westwego	Bayou Segnette State Park	SPS	2	B2
Winnfield	Winn Ranger D.	NFS	7	B2
Zachary	Port Hudson SCA	SPS	16	C3
Zwolle	North Toledo Bend SP	SPS	15	B1
	Sabine WMA	SWA	17	B1

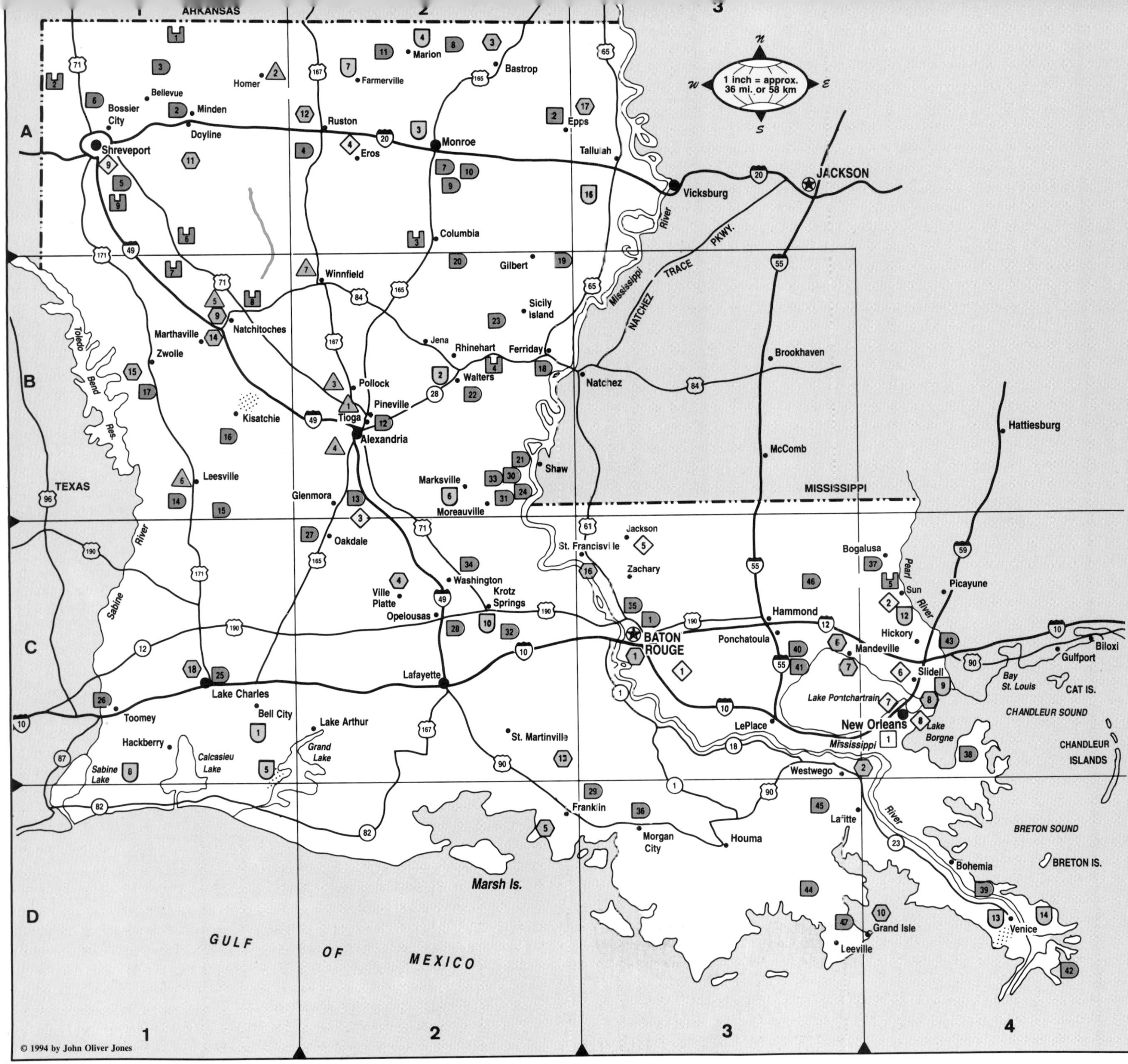

LOUISIANA NOTES

Summary

There are 35 federal, 67 state, and 10 private recreation areas or local administrative offices covered in this state chapter. Of these, 99 appear in the Information Chart and 13 are covered in the notes. The special indexes feature 3 federally designated wilderness areas and a wild river, and 2 agency published outdoor maps.

Federal Agencies

U.S. Forest Service

Louisiana is in the Southern Region (see Georgia chapter - U.S. Forest Svc., Southern Region listing).

National Park Service

Additional NPS Location in Louisiana

Poverty Point National Monument (911 acres)
c/o Poverty Point State Commerative Area
(S# 2, map A2)
PO Box 248
Epps, LA 71237   318-926-5492

USDC, Natl. Oceanic & Atmospheric Admin. (NOAA)

National Ocean Service

For information about the Flower Garden National Marine Sanctuary (LA & TX) which lies 120 miles south southwest of Galveston Texas, contact the following office.

NOAA, Sanctuaries and Reserves Division
1825 Connecticut Ave., NW, Suite 714
Washington, DC 20235   202-673-5122

Wilderness/Wild River Index

Wilderness Areas

Kisatchie Hills Wilderness - 8,700 acres
Kisatchie National Forest (S# 1, map B2)
Breton Wilderness - 5,000
Breton NWR (S# 2, map D4)
Lacassine Wilderness - 3,346
Lacassine NWR (S# 8, map C1)

Wild River

Saline Bayou Wild River
Kisatchie National Forest (S# 1, map B2)

Outdoor Map Index

U.S. Forest Service Maps

Kisatchie National Forest [1983]
Kisatchie NF, Caney Ranger D. [1983]

State Agencies

Dept. of Culture, Recreation & Tourism

Office of State Parks

A Guide to Louisiana State Parks and State Commemorative Areas is available free. The guide describes each area, contains a locator map, and includes information on facilities and activities. There is a $2 entry fee and fees for camping, cabins, and other activities. Special programs and benefits may be offered during the winter season.

Office of Tourism

PO Box 44291
Baton Rouge, LA 80804
                                  1-800-535-8388
in state call   504-925-3806

© 1994 by John Oliver Jones

Office of Tourism
The official Louisiana Dept. of Transportation & Development road map contains symbols for state parks with and without campsites, boat launching ramps, and recreational areas. The boundaries of wildlife areas, waterfowl or game refuges, and national forests are marked in distinct colors.

Dept. Wildlife & Fisheries (DWF)
Purchase of an annual $10 "Wild Louisiana Stamp" at any agency office is required for persons age 16 through 59 before they can visit any lands managed by the Department, unless they have a current hunting or fishing license. Money goes to a new Natural Heritage account

in the states conservation fund which is dedicated to non-game activities and improvements.

A bi-monthly magazine, *Conservationist*, is available on newsstands, and by subscription for $6 per year. A basic reference for hunters is *A Guide to Hunting in Louisiana*, which includes information on wildlife species.

Department of Agriculture
Office of Forestry
PO Box 1628
Baton Rouge, LA 70821   504-925-4500
Contact the Office of Forestry for recreation literature.

Private Organizations

The Nature Conservancy
Contact the Louisiana Field Office tour coordinator for visitor information and about visiting TNC preserves. Selected TNC preserves, their Guide map symbol numbers and coordinates, preserve name and general location are listed below. The Field Office listing answers in the Information Chart reflect the preserves as a group.

S#	MAP	PRESERVE NAME & LOCATION
2	C4	Charter Oak Nature Preserve, Hickory
3	B3	Lake Cocodrie Preserve, Glenmora
4	A2	Schoolhouse Springs Nature Preserve, Eros
5	C3	Tunica Hills Preserve, Jackson
6	C4	White Kitchens Nature Preserve, Slidell

ANCA Locations in Louisiana
Audubon Zoological Garden (S# 7, map C4)
PO Box 4327
New Orleans, LA 70178   504-861-2537

Louisiana Nature & Science Center (S# 8, map C4)
PO Box 870610
New Orleans, LA 70187-0610   504-246-5672

Walter Jacobs Nature Park (S# 9, map A1)
8012 Blanchard Furrh Road
Shreveport, LA 71107   318-929-2806

Louisiana Assn. of Bus. & Industry
3113 Valley Creek Dr.
PO Box 80258
Baton Rouge, LA 70898-0258
Phone 504-928-5388   Fax 504-929-6054

★ INFORMATION CHART ★

INFORMATION CHART LEGEND - SYMBOLS & LETTER CODES

- ■ means **YES** & □ means **Yes** with disability provisions
- **sp** means **spring**, March through May
- **S** means **Summer**, June through August
- **F** means **Fall**, September through November
- **W** means **Winter**, December through February
- **T** means **Two (2)** or **Three (3)** Seasons
- **A** means **All Four (4)** Seasons
- **na** means **Not Applicable** or **Not Available**

Note: empty or blank spaces in the chart mean **NO**

Note: Refer to yellow block on page 7 (top right) for location name and address abbreviations. If a symbol number has a ★ that symbol is not shown on the map.

AGENCY/MAP LEGEND . . . INITIALS, MAP SYMBOLS, COLOR CODES

U.S. Forest Service Supervisor & Ranger Dist. Offices NFS △61
U.S. Army Corps of Engineers Rec. Areas & Offices . COE ⬡31
USFWS National Wildlife Refuges & Offices . . . . . NWR ▱40
National Park Service Parks & other NPS Sites . . . . NPS ▭7
Bureau of Land Management Rec. Areas & Offices . . BLM ⬭26
Bureau of Reclamation Rec. Areas & Reg. Offices . . . BOR ◯8
State Parks (also see State Agency notes) . . . . SPS ◯52
State Wildlife Areas (also see State Agency notes) . . . SWA ◯19
Private Preserves, Nature Centers & Tribal Lands . . . . ◇15
The Wild Rivers ⌒⌒⌒ and Wilderness Areas ▨

Note: Refer to page 7 (top right) for location name and address abbreviations.

S#	MAP	LOCATION NAME (state initials if more than one) with ADDRESS and/or LOCATION DATA	TELEPHONE	ACRES / ELEVATION
1	⚠ B2	**Kisatchie Nat'l. Forest Sup.**, 2500 Shreveport Hwy., PO Box 5500, Pineville 71360	318-473-7160	600,000 / 200
2	A1	Caney Ranger D., 324 Beardsley, PO Box 479, Homer 71040	318-927-2061	32,000 / 200
3	B2	Catahoula Ranger D., Hwy. 165 & Ivy Street, PO Box 307, Pollock 71467	318-765-3554	120,000 / 200
4	B2	Evangeline Ranger D., 3727 Government St., Suite 111, Alexandria 71302	318-445-9396	97,000 / 200
5	B1	Kisatchie Ranger D., 229 Scarborough, PO Box 2128, Natchitoches 71457	318-352-2568	100,000 / 200
6	B1	Vernon Ranger D., 3362 Lake Charles Hwy., Leesville 71446	318-239-6576	85,000 / 200
7	B2	Winn Ranger D., Rt. #3, Box 36, Winnfield 71483	318-628-4664	165,000 / 200
1	A1	**COE, Vicksburg District**, 3515 I-20 Frontage Rd., Vicksburg, MS 39181	601-631-5286	na / na
1	A1	COE, Bayou Bodcau Reservoir, 3505 South Grand St., Monroe 71202	318-322-6391	na / na
2	A1	COE, Caddo Lake, 3505 South Grand St., Monroe 71202	318-322-6391	na / na
3	A2	COE, Columbia Pool, Ouachita/Black , 3505 South Grand St., Monroe 71202	318-322-6391	na / na
4	B2	COE, Jonesville Pool, Ouachita/Blac, 3505 South Grand St., Monroe 71202	318-322-6391	na / na
5	C4	COE, Pearl River (3 Locks & Dams), PO Box 790, Sun 70463	504-886-3141	na / na
6	A1	COE, Pool 1 (Red River Waterway), 3505 South Grand St., Monroe 71202	318-322-6391	na / na
7	B1	COE, Pool 2 (Red River Waterway), 3505 South Grand St., Monroe 71202	318-322-6391	na / na
8	B1	COE, Red R. Waterway, 5 Locks/Dams, 3505 South Grand St., Monroe 71202	318-322-6391	na / na
9	A1	COE, Wallace Lake, 3505 South Grand St., Monroe 71202	318-322-6391	na / na
1	C1	**Cameron Prairie NWR**, Rt. #1, Box 643, Bell City 70630 [Hwy. 27, N of Gibbstown Bridge, new facilities in 1994]	318-598-2216	9,621 / 2
2	B2	Catahoula NWR, PO Drawer Z, Rhinehart 71363 [on US 84, 12 mi SE of Jena]	318-992-5261	5,300 / 50
3	A2	D'Arbonne NWR, Rt. 2, Box 401B, Farmerville 71241 [Office at NWR, L side of Hwy. 143, 5 mi N of W. Monroe]	318-726-4222	17,000 / 100
4	A2	Upper Ouachita NWR, Rt. 2, Box 401B, Farmerville [office at D'Arbonne NWR]	318-726-4222	21,000 / 100
5	C1	Lacassine NWR, HCR 63, Box 186, Lake Arthur, 7 mi W on Hwy 14, then 5 mi S on Hwy 3056) [from Lake Arthur, 7 mi W on Hwy 14, then 5 mi S on Hwy 3056]	318-774-5923	32,625 / 0-10
6	B2	Lake Ophelia NWR, PO Box 256, Marksville 71351	318-253-4238	20,000 / na
7	A2	Louisiana WMD (new WMD, contact mgr.), Rt. #2, Box 401A, Farmerville 71241	318-726-4400	na / na
8	C1	Sabine NWR, Hwy. 27 S, 3000 Main St., Hackberry 70645	318-762-3816	125,000 / 1-8
9	C4	Southeast Louisiana Refuges, 1010 Gause Blvd., Bldg. 936, Slidell 70458	504-646-7555	na / na
10	C2	Atchafalaya NWR, 1010 Gause Blvd., Bldg. # 936, Slidell 70458 [near Krotz Springs]	504-646-7555	15,220 / 20
*11	C4	Bayou Sauvage NWR, 1010 Gause Blvd., Bldg. 936, Slidell 70458	504-646-7555	na / na
12	C4	Bogue Chitto NWR, 1010 Gause Blvd., Bldg.# 936, Slidell 70458	504-646-7555	36,155 / na
13	D4	Breton NWR, PO Box 924, Venice 70091	504-534-2235	5,000 / 10
14	D4	Delta NWR, PO Box 924, Venice 70091	504-534-2235	48,800 / 10
*15	C4	Shell Keys NWR, 1010 Gause Blvd., Bldg. 936, Slidell 70458	504-646-7555	na / na
16	A3	Tensas River NWR, Rt. #2, Box 295, Tallulah 71282 [exit I-20 at Tallulah or Waverly & follow signs]	318-574-2664	63,000 / na
1	D3	**Jean Lafitte NHP & Preserve**, 423 Canal St., Room 210, New Orleans 70130	504-589-3882	20,000 / 10

#	Grid	Name / Location	Phone	Acres / na
3	A2	Chemin-A-Haut SP, near Bastrop	504-342-8111	503 / na
4	C2	Chicot SP, near Ville Platte	504-363-2403	6,000 / na
5	D2	Cypremort Point SP, near Franklin	318-867-4510	na / na
6	C3	Fairview Riverside SP, near Mandeville	504-342-8111	100 / na
7	C3	Fontainebleau SP, near Mandeville	504-624-4443	2,809 / na
8	C4	Ft. Pike State Commemorative Area, near New Orleans	504-662-5703	95 / na
9	B1	Ft. St. Jean Baptiste SCA, near Natchitoches	504-357-3101	5 / na
10	D4	Grand Isle SP, near Grand Isle	504-787-2559	160 / na
11	A1	Lake Bistineau SP, near Doyline	504-745-3503	750 / na
12	A2	Lake Claiborne SP, near Homer	318-927-2976	620 / na
13	C2	Lake Fausse Point SP, near St. Martinville	318-229-4764	6,000 / na
14	D2	Los Adais SCA, near Marthaville	318-472-9449	14 / na
15	B1	North Toledo Bend SP, near Zwolle	318-645-4715	990 / na
16	C3	Port Hudson SCA, near Zachary	504-654-3775	643 / na
17	A3	Poverty Point SCA, near Epps	504-342-8111	400 / na
18	C1	Sam Houston Jones SP, near Lake Charles	504-855-2665	1,087 / na
1	C3	LA Dept. Wildlife & Fisheries Info., 2001 Quail Drive, PO Box 9800, Baton Rouge 70895	504-765-2800	3,000,000 / 200-500
2	A1	District 1 - LADWF, PO Box 915, Minden 71055	318-371-3050	32,471 / 300
3	A1	Bodcau WMA, near Bellevue	318-371-3050	na / na
4	A2	Jackson-Bienville WMA, US Hwy. 167, 12 mi. S of Ruston	318-371-3050	32,000 / 300
5	A1	Loggy Bayou WMA, off US Hwy. 71, 20 mi. S of Bossier City	318-371-3050	4,400 / 100-125
6	A1	Soda Lake WMA, 15 mi. N of Shreveport	318-371-3050	1,200 / 160-170
7	A2	District 2 - LADWF, PO Box 4004, Monroe 71211	318-343-4044	na / na
8	A2	Georgia-Pacific WMA, 5 mi. NW of Bastrop	318-343-4044	28,000 / 100
9	A2	Ouachita WMA, 12 mi. S of Monroe	318-343-4044	8,745 / 60
10	A2	Russell Sage WMA, 10 mi. E of Monroe	318-343-4044	17,220 / 60
11	A2	Union WMA, 3 mi. W of Marion	318-343-4044	12,397 / 200
12	B2	District 3 - LADWF, PO Box 278, Tioga 71477	318-487-5885	417,702 / 20-400
13	B2	Alexander Forest WMA, in Rapides Parish S of Alexandria	318-487-5885	7,800 / 150
14	B1	Boise-Vernon WMA, 15 mi. SW of Leesville	318-487-5885	56,000 / 250
15	B1	Fort Polk WMA, in Vernon Parish SE of Leesville	318-487-5885	109,855 / 350
16	B1	Peason Ridge WMA, S of Kisatchie	318-487-5885	33,000 / 350
17	B1	Sabine WMA, near Zwolle	318-487-5885	12,500 / 350
18	B2	District 4 - LADWF, PO Box 426, Ferriday 71334	318-757-4571	2,961,520 / 20-260
19	B2	Big Lake WMA, 12 mi. E of Gilbert	318-757-4571	19,210 / 55-65
20	B2	Boeuf WMA, 10 mi. SE of Columbia	318-757-4571	38,440 / 40-60
21	B2	Red River WMA, near Shaw	318-757-4571	28,320 / 35-55
22	B2	Saline WMA, near Walters	318-757-4571	60,275 / 35-50
23	B2	Sicily Island Hills WMA, 6 mi. W of Sicily Island	318-757-4571	6,500 / 35-230
24	B2	Three Rivers WMA, 10 mi. S of Shaw	318-757-4571	24,970 / 35-55
25	C1	District 5 - LADWF, 1213 N. Lakeshore Dr., Lake Charles 70601	318-491-2575	na / na
26	C1	Sabine Island WMA, NW of Toomey	318-491-2575	8,100 / na
27	C2	West Bay WMA, 3 mi. W of Oakdale	318-491-2575	55,185 / na
28	C2	District 6 - LADWF, PO Box 585, Opelousas 70571	318-948-0255	6,500 / na
29	D3	Attakapas WMA (access by boat), 20 mi. NW of Morgan City	318-828-4391	25,500 / na
30	D3	Grassy Lake WMA, W of Shaw	318-487-5055	13,608 / na
31	B2	Pomme De Terre WMA, 6 mi. E of Moreauville	318-487-5055	6,194 / na
32	C2	Sherburne WMA, SE of Krotz Springs	318-948-0255	37,000 / na
33	B2	Spring Bayou WMA, N of Mcreauville	318-487-5055	11,758 / na
34	C2	Thistlethwaite WMA, NE of Washington	318-948-0255	11,100 / na
35	C3	District 7 - LADWF, PO Box 9800, Baton Rouge 70898	504-765-2360	na / na
36	D3	Atchafalaya Delta WMA (access by boat), in St. Mary parish near Morgan City	318-369-3807	137,000 / -6-12
37	D3	Ben's Creek WMA, off LA Hwy. 10, 1 mi. W of Bogalusa	504-765-2360	na / 130-335
38	C4	Biloxi WMA, 30 mi. SE of New Orleans	504-765-2360	39,583 / na
39	D4	Bohemia WMA, Bohemia	504-765-2360	33,000 / 0-5
40	C3	Joyce WMA, SE of Ponchatoula	504-765-2360	13,569 / 0-5
41	C3	Manchac WMA (access by boat), 17 mi. NNE of LePlace	504-765-2360	8,325 / 0-5
42	D4	Pass-A-Loutre WMA (access by boat), 13 mi. down river from Venice	504-568-5886	66,000 / na
43	C4	Pearl River WMA, Honey Is. Swamp exit off I-59, 1 mi. E-NE of Slidell	504-765-2360	na / 0-20
44	D3	Point-Au-Chien WMA, 15 mi. SE of Houma	504-568-5886	30,000 / na
45	D3	Salvador WMA (access by boat), NW shore of L. Salvador near Lafitte	504-568-5886	31,000 / na
46	C3	Sandy Hollow WMA, off LA Hwy. 10, 20 mi. NE of Hammond	504-765-2360	3,457 / 180-270
47	D3	Wisner WMA (access by boat), near Leeville	504-765-2360	21,621 / 0-5
1	C3	TNC Louisiana Field Office, PO Box 4125, Baton Rouge 70821 [details cover preserves in notes]	504-338-1040	na / na

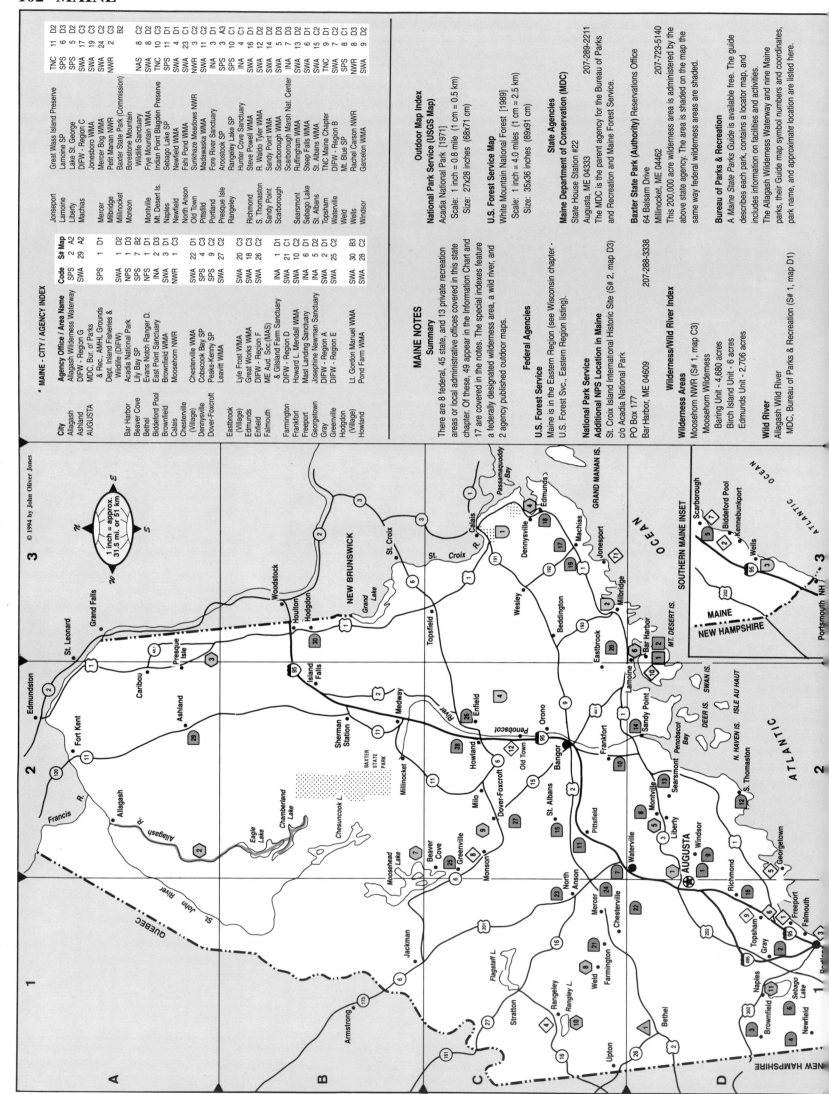

• MAINE - CITY / AGENCY INDEX •

City	Agency Office / Area Name	Code	S#	Map
Allagash	Allagash Wilderness Waterway	SPS	2	A2
Ashland	DIFW - Region G	SWA	29	A2
AUGUSTA	MDC, Bur. of Parks & Rec, AMHL Grounds	SPS	1	D1
	Dept. Inland Fisheries & Wildlife (DIFW)			
Bar Harbor	Acadia National Park	SWA	1	D2
Beaver Cove	Lily Bay SP	SPS	7	D3
Bethel	Evans Notch Ranger D.	NFS	1	B2
Biddeford Pool	East Point Sanctuary	INA	2	D3
Brownfield	Brownfield WMA	SWA	3	D1
Calais	Moosehorn NWR	NWR	1	C3
Chesterville (Village)	Chesterville WMA	SWA	22	D1
Dennysville	Cobscook Bay SP	SPS	4	C3
Dover-Foxcroft	Peaks-Kenny SP	SPS	9	C2
	Leavitt WMA	SWA	27	C2
Eastbrook (Village)	Lyle Frost WMA	INA	1	D1
Edmunds	Great Works WMA	SWA	21	C1
Enfield	DIFW - Region F	SWA	10	C2
Falmouth	ME Aud. Soc.(MAS) & Gisland Farm Sanctuary	INA	5	D2
Farmington	DIFW - Region D	INA	4	C1
Frankfort	Howard L. Mendall WMA	SWA	25	C2
Freeport	Mast Landing Sanctuary			
Georgetown	Josephine Newman Sanctuary			
Gray	DIFW - Region A			
Greenville	DIFW - Region B			
Hodgdon (Village)	Lt. Gordon Manuel WMA	SWA	30	B3
Howland	Pond Farm WMA	SWA	28	C2

City	Agency Office / Area Name	Code	S#	Map
Jonesport	Great Wass Island Preserve	TNC	11	D2
Lamoine	Lamoine SP	SPS	6	D3
Liberty	Lake St. George	SPS	5	D2
Machias	DIFW - Region C	SWA	17	C3
	Jonesboro WMA	SWA	19	C3
Mercer	Mercer Bog WMA	SWA	24	C2
	Petit Manan NWR	NWR	2	C3
Milbridge				
Millinocket	Baxter State Park (Commission)	NAS	8	C2
Monson	Borestone Mountain Wildlife Sanctuary	SWA	8	C2
Montville	Frye Mountain WMA	TNC	10	C3
Mt. Desert Is.	Indian Point Blagden Preserve	SPS	11	D1
Naples	Sebago Lake SP	SWA	4	C1
Newfield	Newfield WMA	NWR	23	C1
North Anson	Fahi Pond WMA	SWA	11	C2
Old Town	Sunkhaze Meadows NWR	INA	3	D1
Pittsfield	Madawaska WMA	SWA	16	C1
Portland	Fore River Sanctuary	SPS	4	C1
Presque Isle	Arostook SP	SPS	10	C1
Rangeley	Rangeley Lake SP	SWA	12	D2
Richmond	Hunter Cove Sanctuary	SWA	14	C2
S. Thomaston	Steve Powell WMA	INA	7	D3
Sandy Point	R. Waldo Tyler WMA	SWA	13	D2
Scarborough	Sandy Point WMA	SWA	6	D1
	Scarborough WMA	SWA	15	C2
Searsmont	Scarborough Marsh Nat. Center	TNC	9	D1
Sebago Lake	Ruffingham WMA	SPS	8	C1
St. Albans	St. Albans WMA	NWR	8	D3
Topsham	TNC Maine Chapter	SWA	9	D2
Waterville	Steep Falls WMA			
Weld	Mt. Blue SP			
Wells	Rachel Carson NWR			
Windsor	Garcelon WMA			

MAINE NOTES

Summary

There are 8 federal, 45 state, and 13 private recreation areas or local administrative offices covered in this state chapter. Of these, 49 appear in the Information Chart and 17 are covered in the notes. The special indexes feature a federally designated wilderness area, a wild river, and 2 agency published outdoor maps.

Federal Agencies

U.S. Forest Service

Maine is in the Eastern Region (see Wisconsin chapter - U.S. Forest Svc., Eastern Region listing).

National Park Service

Additional NPS Location in Maine
St. Croix Island International Historic Site (S# 2, map D3)
c/o Acadia National Park
PO Box 177
Bar Harbor, ME 04609   207-288-3338

Wilderness/Wild River Index

Wilderness Areas

Moosehorn NWR (S# 1, map C3)
Moosehorn Wilderness
Baring Unit - 4,680 acres
Birch Island Unit - 6 acres
Edmunds Unit - 2,706 acres

Wild River

Allagash Wild River
MDC, Bureau of Parks & Recreation (S# 1, map D1)

Outdoor Map Index

National Park Service (USGS Map)

Acadia National Park [1971]
Scale: 1 inch = 0.8 mile (1 cm = 0.5 km)
Size: 27x28 inches (68x71 cm)

U.S. Forest Service Map

White Mountain National Forest [1989]
Scale: 1 inch = 4.0 miles (1 cm = 2.5 km)
Size: 35x36 inches (89x91 cm)

State Agencies

Maine Department of Conservation (MDC)

State House Station #22
Augusta, ME 04333   207-289-2211
The MDC is the parent agency for the Bureau of Parks and Recreation and Maine Forest Service.

Baxter State Park (Authority) Reservations Office

64 Balsam Drive
Millinocket, ME 04462   207-723-5140
This 200,000 acre wilderness area is administered by the above state agency. The area is shaded on the map the same way federal wilderness areas are shaded.

Bureau of Parks & Recreation

A Maine State Parks Guide is available free. The guide describes each park, contains a locator map, and includes information on facilities and activities. The Allagash Wilderness Waterway and nine Maine parks; their Guide map symbol numbers and coordinates, park name, and approximate location are listed here.

© 1994 by John Oliver Jones

1 inch = approx. 31.5 mi. or 51 km

Park Name & Location

S#	MAP	Park Name & Location
2	A2	Allagash Wilderness Waterway, Allagash
3	A3	Aroostook SP, Presque Isle
4	C3	Cobscook Bay SP, Dennysville
5	D2	Lake St. George, Liberty
6	D3	Lamoine SP, Lamoine
7	B2	Lily Bay SP, Beaver Cove
8	C1	Mt. Blue SP, Weld
9	C2	Peaks-Kenny SP, Dover-Foxcroft
10	C1	Rangeley Lake SP, Rangeley
11	D1	Sebago Lake SP, Naples

Bureau of Forestry
State House Station #22
Augusta, ME 04333   207-289-2791
Contact the Bureau for state forest recreation literature.

Dept. of Inland Fisheries & Wildlife (DIFW)
(S# 1, map D2)
Brochures and maps are available for selected game and wildlife management areas. You may subscribe to *Maine Fish & Wildlife*, a quarterly magazine, for $14 a year.

Dept. of Marine Resources
State House, Station #21
Augusta, ME 04333
Contact the Department for marine resources information, rules and regulations.

Maine Publicity Bureau
State Development Office
State House Station #59   207-289-2423
Augusta, ME 04333
A free official Maine road map is available.

Private Organizations

TNC-Maine Chapter
The book, *Maine Forever*, is available from the Maine Chapter Office for $15.45 postpaid. It describes more than 40 preserves.   207-289-6550

Tribal Land Area in Maine
Penobscot Tribe of Maine - Fishing, hunting, camping, boating.
Penobscot Tribal Council (S# 12, map C2)
Six River Road
Indian Island Reservation
Old Town, ME 04468   207-827-7775

Maine Chamber of Commerce
126 Sewall St.
Augusta, ME 04330
Phone 207-623-4563
Fax 207-622-7723

AGENCY/MAP LEGEND ... INITIALS, MAP SYMBOLS, COLOR CODES

U.S. Forest Service Supervisor & Ranger Dist. Offices	NFS	61
U.S. Army Corps of Engineers Rec. Areas & Offices	COE	31
USFWS National Wildlife Refuges & Offices	NWR	40
National Park Service Parks & other NPS Sites	NPS	7
Bureau of Land Management Rec. Areas & Offices	BLM	76
Bureau of Reclamation Rec. Areas & Reg. Offices	BOR	8
State Parks (also see State Agency notes)	SPS	52
State Wildlife Areas (also see State Agency notes)	SWA	19
Private Preserves, Nature Centers & Tribal Lands		15
The Wild Rivers ~~~ and Wilderness Areas		

★ INFORMATION CHART ★

INFORMATION CHART LEGEND - SYMBOLS & LETTER CODES

■ means **YES** & □ means **Yes with disability provisions**
sp means spring, March through May
S means Summer, June through August
F means Fall, September through November
W means Winter, December through February
T means Two (2) or Three (3) Seasons
A means All Four (4) Seasons
na means Not Applicable or Not Available
Note: empty or blank spaces in the chart mean **NO**

FACILITIES, SERVICES, RECREATION OPPORTUNITIES & CONVENIENCES

S#	MAP	LOCATION NAME (state initials if more than one) with ADDRESS and/or LOCATION DATA	TELEPHONE	ACRES / ELEVATION
D1 (NFS)	D1	**White Mountain Nat'l. Forest Sup.**, 719 Main St., PO Box 638, Laconia, NH 03247	603-528-8721	769,000 / 800-6,288
	D1	Evans Notch Ranger D., Bridge St., Bethel 04217	207-824-2134	102,500 / na
1 (NWR)	C3	**Moosehorn NWR**, PO Box 1077, Calais 04619 [1 mi N of Calais off US 1]	207-454-7161	22,745 / 0-480
2	C3	Petit Manan NWR, Rt. 1, PO Box 279, Milbridge 04658	207-546-2124	3,335 / 0-135
3	D3	Rachel Carson NWR, RR 2, Box 751, Wells 04090 [Route 9 East]	207-646-9226	4,000 / 0-40
4	C2	Sunkhaze Meadows NWR, 1033 South Main St., Old Town 04468 [on US 2]	207-827-6138	9,337 / 120-240
1 (NPS)	D3	**Acadia National Park**, PO Box 177, Bar Harbor 04609	207-288-3338	38,000 / 0-1,500
1 (SPS)	D2	**MDC, Bur. of Parks & Rec.** (AMHL grounds), Hospital St, Harlow Bldg., Station 22, Augusta 04333	207-289-3821	na / na
2	D2	**Dept. Inland Fisheries & Wildlife** (DIFW), 284 State Street, State House Station 41, Augusta 04333	207-657-3258	na / na
2	D1	DIFW - Region A, 328 Shaker Rd., RR #1, Gray 04039	207-657-3258	na / na
3	D1	Brownfield WMA, 1.5 mi. NE of Brownfield	207-657-3258	5,514 / na
4	D1	Newfield WMA, 2 mi. W of Newfield	207-657-3258	4,374 / na
5	D3	Scarborough WMA, near Scarborough	207-657-3258	3,013 / na
6	D1	Steep Falls WMA, 2 mi. SW of Sebago Lake	207-657-3258	2,537 / na
7	C2	DIFW - Region B, office on Lyons Rd. in Sidney, mail to: RFD 1, Box G378, Waterville 04901	207-289-2536	na / na
8	D2	Frye Mountain WMA, Rt. 220, Montville	207-289-2536	5,176 / na
9	D2	Garcelon WMA (2 parcels), near Augusta &, Windsor	207-289-2536	2,997 / na
10	C2	Howard L. Mendall WMA, US Rt. 1A, S of Frankfort	207-289-2536	242 / na
11	B2	Madawaska WMA, on Madawaska Rd., 4 mi. N of Pittsfield	207-289-2536	295 / na
12	D2	R. Waldo Tyler WMA, on Buttermilk Lane, S. Thomaston	207-289-2536	533 / na
13	D2	Ruffingham WMA, Route 3, N of Searsmont	207-289-2536	610 / na
14	D2	Sandy Point WMA, N of Sandy Point	207-289-2536	540 / na
15	C2	St. Albans WMA, on Square Rd., near St. Albans	207-289-2536	540 / na
16	D1	Steve Powell WMA (islands & tidal flats in Kennebec River), near Richmond 04357	207-289-1150	1,753 / na
17	C3	DIFW - Region C, 68 Water St., Machias 04654	207-255-4715	na / na

Note: Refer to page 7 (top right) for location name and address abbreviations. If a symbol number has a star ★ that symbol is not shown on the map.

Maine (continued)

#	Map	Site / Address	Acres	Phone
18	C3	Great Works WMA, Route 86, Edmunds	641 / na	207-255-4715
19	C3	Jonesboro WMA, US Rt. 1A, 5 mi. W of Machias	716 / na	207-255-4715
20	C1	Lyle Frost WMA, SE of Eastbrook (Village)	1,818 / na	207-255-4715
21	C1	DIFW - Region D, Route 4, RFD #3, Box 3770, Farmington 04938	na / na	207-778-3324
22	D1	Chesterville WMA, S of Chesterville (Village)	468 / na	207-778-3324
23	C1	Fahi Pond WMA, Fahi Pond Rd., 4 mi. N of North Anson	281 / na	207-778-3324
24	C1	Mercer Bog WMA, US Rt. 2, 8 mi. E of Norridgewock, Mercer	317 / na	207-778-3324
25	C2	DIFW - Region E, Box 551, Greenville 04441	na / na	207-695-3756
26	D1	DIFW - Region F, Enfield Fish Hatchery, Box 66, Enfield 04433	na / na	207-732-4131
27	C2	Leavitt WMA, Rt. 15, 7.5 mi. S of Dover-Foxcroft	6,008 / na	207-732-4131
28	C2	Pond Farm WMA, Seboeis Rd., Howland	1,232 / na	207-732-4131
29	A2	DIFW - Region G, PO Box 416, Ashland 04732	na / na	207-435-3231
30	B3	Lt. Gordon Manuel WMA, S of Hodgdon (Village)	4,257 / na	207-435-3231
1	D1	Maine Audubon Society (MAS) & Gilsland Farm Sanctuary, 118 US Hwy. 1, Falmouth 04105 [at 118 on Old US Rt. 1]	60 / na	207-781-2330
2	D3	East Point Sanctuary, c/o MAS, Biddeford Pool [near Biddeford Pool]	30 / na	207-781-2220
3	D1	Fore River Sanctuary, c/o MAS, at end of Rowe Ave., Portland	76 / na	207-781-2330
4	C1	Hunter Cove Sanctuary, c/o MAS, on Rangeley Lake, Rangeley [near Rangeley]	100 / na	207-781-2330
5	D1	Josephine Newman Sanctuary, c/o MAS, Georgetown	119 / na	207-781-2330
6	D1	Mast Landing Sanctuary, c/o MAS, Upper Mast Landing Rd., Freeport	140 / na	207-781-2330
7	D3	Scarborough Marsh Nature Center, c/o MAS, Rt. 9, Scarborough [open mid-June to Labor Day]	3,100 / na	207-883-5100
8	C2	Borestone Mountain Wildlife Sanctuary (NAS), Elliotsville Rd., PO Box 112, Monson 04464 [winter ph. 997-3558]	1,600 / 700-2,000	207-997-3607
9	D1	TNC Maine Chapter, 122 Main Street, Topsham 04086	na / na	207-729-5181
10	D2	Indian Point Blagden Preserve, contact Field Office, on, Mt. Desert Is.	110 / na	207-288-4838
11	C3	Great Wass Island Preserve, contact Field Office, near Jonesport	1,543 / na	207-729-5181

MASSACHUSETTS - CITY / AGENCY INDEX

City	Agency Office / Area Name	Code	S#	Map
Acton	DFW NE District Office	SWA	33	A3
Ashby	Ashby WMA	SWA	34	A2
	Tully Lake	COE	12	A1
Athol	Millers River WMA	SWA	12	A1
	Lake Dennison RA	SPS	5	A2
Baldwinville	Barre Falls WMA	SWA	3	B2
Barre	Prince River WMA	SWA	17	B2
	Raccoon Hill WMA	SWA	4	B2
	Cook's Canyon Wildlife San	INA	17	B2
Becket	Becket WMA	SWA	54	D1
Belchertown	DFW CT Valley Dist. Office	SWA	23	B1
	Swift River WMA	SWA	6	B3
Bolton	Bolton Flats WMA	NPS	1	E2
Boston	NPS, N. Atlantic Reg.	SPS	1	E1
	Boston Nat'l Historical Park	TNC	24	E1
	DEM, Div. Forests & Parks	SWA	38	B3
	TNC MA Field Office	SPS	7	C5
Boxborough	Delaney WMA	SWA	18	B2
Brewster	Nickerson SP	SWA	5	C4
Brookfield	Quaboag River WMA	COE	43	C4
Buzzards Bay	Cape Cod Canal	SPS	6	A1
	DFW SE District Office	SWA	4	B2
Charlemont	Mohawk Trail State Forest	NWR	3	C5
Charlton	Bennett WMA	SWA	66	D2
Chatham	Monomoy NWR	SWA	62	D2
Cheshire	Stafford Hill WMA	SPS	25	A1
Chester	Kelly WMA	SWA	3	B3
Chicopee Falls	Chicopee Memorial SP	SWA	41	B3
Colrain	Catamount WMA	SWA	2	C4
Concord	Minute Man Nat'l Hist Park	INA	12	D4
	Pantry Brook WMA	INA	2	D4
Conway	Poland Brook WMA	SPS	11	D2
Duxbury	North Hill Marsh Wild San			
E. Falmouth	Ashumet Holly & Wild San			
East Otis	Tolland State Forest			
Easthampton	Arcadia Nature Center & Wildlife Sanctuary	INA	16	B1
Easton	Hockomock Swamp WMA	SWA	47	C3
Fall River	Fall River WMA	SWA	46	C3
Falmouth	Crane WMA	COE	7	B2
Fiskdale	Conant Brook Dam	COE	8	B2
Fitchburg	East Birmfield Lake	INA	18	A2
Gardner	Flat Rock Wildlife San	SWA	9	A2
Groveland	High Ridge WMA	SWA	37	A4
Hadley	Crane Pond WMA	NWR	1	B1
Hampden	Laughing Brook Education Center & Wildlife Sanctuary	INA	19	C1

City	Agency Office / Area Name	Code	S#	Map
Harvard	Oxbow NWR	NWR	5	A3
Hinsdale	Hinsdale Flats WMA	SWA	58	D1
Hubbardston	Barre Falls Dam	COE	2	B2
	Hubbardston WMA	SWA	10	B1
Huntington	Knightville Dam	COE	10	B1
	Littleville Lake	COE	63	B2
	Knightville WMA	SWA	61	D1
Lenox	Housatonic Valley WMA	INA	21	D1
Leominster	Pleasant Valley Wildlife San			
Lincoln	Lincoln Woods Wildlife Sanctuary & RPO	INA	15	A2
	MA Audubon Society	INA	1	B3
	Drumlin Farm Education Center & Wildlife Sanctuary			
Ludlow	Ludlow WMA	INA	6	B2
Marshfield	Black Pond N Pre. (Norwell)	SWA	26	B1
	South Shore Reg. Center	TNC	25	B4
Mashpee	Daniel Webster Wildlife San	INA	11	C4
Medfield	Quashnel Woods WMA	SWA	50	C5
Middleboro	Charles River WMA	SWA	36	B1
Middlefield	Rocky Gutter WMA	SWA	51	C4
Milton	Fox Den WMA	SWA	57	D2
	Blue Hills Reservation			
	Trailside Museum			
Montague	Spaulding Brook WMA	INA	3	F1
Nantucket Island	Nantucket NWR	NWR	30	A1
New Braintree	Winimussett Meadows WMA	SWA	22	B2
Newbury	Martin H. Burns WMA	SWA	40	A4
Newburyport	Parker River NWR	NWR	34	A4
Norfolk	Stony Brook Nature Center & Wildlife Sanctuary			
North Adams	Savoy Mountain SF	INA	13	B3
North Andover	Harold Parker WMA	SPS	10	C1
Northbridge	E. Kent Swift & W Hill WMA	SWA	39	A3
Northfield	Bennett Meadows WMA	SWA	24	A1
Northampton	Pauchaug Brook WMA	SWA	27	A1
	Satan's Kingdom	SWA	29	A1
Oakham	Conte Natl. Wildlife & Fish Refuge	NWR	7	A4
Oxford	Oakham WMA	SPS	10	C1
Paxton	Buffumville Lake	SWA	39	A3
Peru	Hodges Village Dam	SWA	24	A1
	Moose Hill WMA	SWA	27	A1
Phillipston	Peru WMA	SWA	29	A1
Pittsfield	Phillipston WMA			

City	Agency Office / Area Name	Code	S#	Map
Plymouth	Myles Standish WMA	SWA	49	C4
Princeton	Wachusett Meadow Wild San	INA	23	B2
Rowley	Bill Forward WMA	SWA	35	A4
Royalston	Birch Hill Dam	COE	3	A2
	Birch Hill WMA	SWA	5	A2
Rutland	Lawrence Brook WMA	SWA	11	A2
S. Wellfleet	Savage Hill WMA	SWA	21	B2
	Wellfleet Bay Wildlife Sanct	INA	14	C5
Salisbury	Salisbury Beach SR	SPS	9	A4
Savoy	Savoy WMA	SWA	65	C2
Sharon	Moose Hill Wildlife Sanct	INA	20	B3
	Broadmoor Wildlife Sanct	INA	5	C5
South Natick	Cape Cod Natl Seashore	NPS	2	B2
South Wellfleet	Westville Lake	COE	14	B2
Southbridge	Four Chimneys WMA	SWA	2	B3
Southborough	Great Meadows NWR	NWR	45	C3
Spencer	Erwin S. Wilder WMA	SWA	42	A2
Sudbury	Ipswich River Wildlife Sanct	INA	4	A2
Taunton	Hop Brook WMA	SWA	60	D1
Topsfield	Charles River Natural Valley Storage Project	COE	6	C3
Townsend	West Hill Dam	COE	13	D4
Tyngham	Felix Neck Wildlife Sanctuary	INA	8	D4
Uxbridge	West Meadows WMA	SWA	52	C4
	COE New England District	COE	1	E1
Vineyard Haven	Cochituate SP	SPS	3	B3
W. Bridgewater	Marconi WMA	SWA	48	C5
Waltham	Wendell Wilderness	INA	32	A1
Wayland	Endicott Reg. Center of MA Audubon Society (inactive)			
Wellfleet	DFW Central District Office	INA	7	A4
Wenham	MA Div. Fisheries & Wildlife	SWA	3	B2
West Boylston	Richardson WMA	SWA	20	B2
West Brookfield	Horseneck Beach SR	SWA	1	B3
Westport Point	Chalet WMA	SWA	4	A2
Windsor	Eugene D. Moran WMA	SWA	55	C1
Worcester	Quinsigamond SP	SPS	56	C1
Worthington	Broad Meadow Brook Sanct	INA	4	B2
	Hiram G. Fox (Canada Hill) WMA	SWA	59	D2

Boston Inset

© 1994 by John Oliver Jones

1 inch = approx. 4 mi. or 6.5 km

Map labels: Peabody, Lynn, Saugus, Wakefield, Stoneham, Woburn, Revere, Chelsea, Everett, Winthrop, Logan Int'l Airport, Boston, Somerville, Cambridge, Medford, Arlington, Lexington, Belmont, Watertown, Newton Corner, Brookline, Quincy, Milton, Needham, Dedham, Weymouth

Water features: Nahant Bay, Broad Sound, Mass. Bay, Boston Harbor, Quincy Bay, Hingham Bay, Neponset River, Mystic River, Charles River, Mystic Lakes

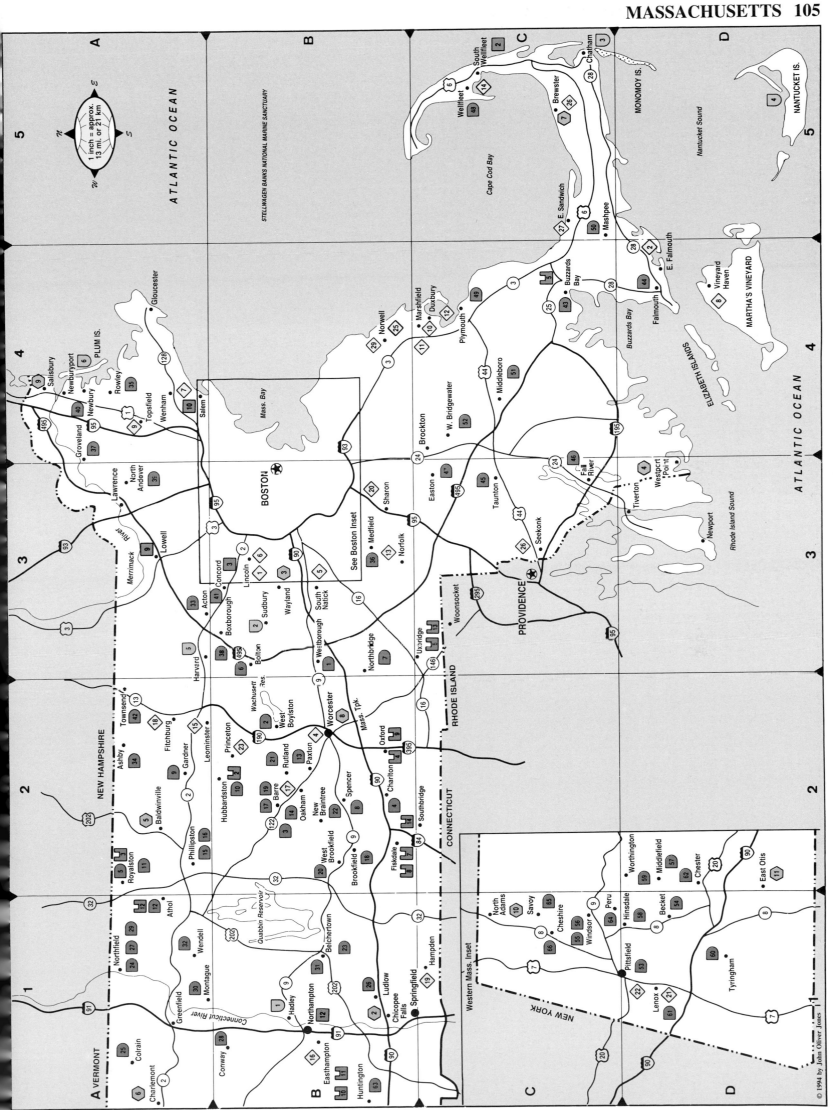

ATLANTIC OCEAN

STELLWAGEN BANKS NATIONAL MARINE SANCTUARY

1 inch = approx.
13 mi. or 21 km

N
W — E
S

Cape Cod Bay

MONOMOY IS.

Nantucket Sound

NANTUCKET IS.

South Wellfleet
Wellfleet
Chatham
Brewster
E. Sandwich
Mashpee
E. Falmouth
Falmouth
Buzzards Bay

MARTHA'S VINEYARD
Vineyard Haven

ELIZABETH ISLANDS

ATLANTIC OCEAN

Rhode Island Sound

Newport
Tiverton
Westport Point
Fall River
Seekonk
PROVIDENCE
Woonsocket
RHODE ISLAND

Gloucester
Salisbury
Newburyport
PLUM IS.
Newbury
Rowley
Topsfield
Wenham
Salem
Groveland
Lawrence
North Andover
Lowell
Merrimack River
NEW HAMPSHIRE

BOSTON
Mass. Bay
See Boston Inset

Concord
Lincoln
Acton
Boxborough
Sudbury
Wayland
South Natick
Harvard
Bolton
Westborough
Northbridge
Uxbridge

Norwell
Marshfield
Duxbury
Plymouth
Brockton
W. Bridgewater
Easton
Taunton
Middleboro
Sharon
Medfield
Norfolk

Worcester
West Boylston
Princeton
Leominster
Gardner
Fitchburg
Ashby
Townsend
Baldwinville
Phillipston
Royalston
Athol
Northfield
Wendell
Montague
Greenfield
Conway
Charlemont
Colrain
VERMONT
Connecticut River

Wachusett Res.
Rutland
Paxton
Spencer
Oakham
New Braintree
Barre
Hubbardston
West Brookfield
Brookfield
Fiskdale
Southbridge
Charlton
Oxford
Mass. Tpk.
CONNECTICUT

Belchertown
Quabbin Reservoir
Ludlow
Chicopee Falls
Springfield
Hampden
Northampton
Hadley
Easthampton
Huntington

Western Mass. Inset
North Adams
Savoy
Cheshire
Windsor
Pittsfield
Lenox
Tyringham
Peru
Hinsdale
Becket
Worthington
Middlefield
Chester
East Otis
NEW YORK

© 1994 by John Oliver Jones

MASSACHUSETTS NOTES

Summary

There are 36 federal, 79 state, and 29 private recreation areas or local administrative offices covered in this state chapter. Of these, 126 appear in the Information Chart and 18 are covered in the notes. A special index feature one federally designated wilderness area.

Federal Agencies

U.S. Army Corps of Engineers (COE)
New England Division Office
424 Trapelo Rd.
Waltham, MA 02254   617-647-8305
This division office manages COE projects in New England.

National Park Service

North Atlantic Regional Office
15 State Street
Boston, MA 02109   617-223-5200
A Visitor Center is located on the first floor at 15 State Street and is handicapped-accessible. The VC is open on weekends. Brochures for local NPS sites and a selection of popular parks in other parts of the U.S. are available.

Additional NPS Locations in Massachusetts

Adams National Historic Site (10 acres)
PO Box 531 (S# 4, map F2)
Quincy, MA 02269-0531   617-773-3177

Boston African American National Historic Site
46 Joy Street (S# 5, map E1)
Boston, MA 02114   617-720-0753

Frederick Law Olmsted National Historic Site (1.75 acres)
99 Warren Street (S# 6, map F1)
Brookline, MA 02146   617-566-1689

John Fitzgerald Kennedy National Historic Site
83 Beals Street (S# 7, map F1)
Brookline, MA 02146   617-566-7937

Longfellow National Historic Site (2 acres)
105 Brattle Street (S# 8, map E1)
Cambridge, MA 02138   617-876-4491

Lowell National Historic Park (137 acres)
246 Market Street (S# 9, map A3)
Lowell, MA 01853   508-459-1000

Salem Maritime National Historic Site (9 acres)
Custom House (S# 10, map A4)
174 Derby Street
Salem, MA 01970

Saugus Iron Works National Historic Site (9 acres)
244 Central Street (S# 11, map E2)
Saugus, MA 01906   617-233-0050

Springfield Armory National Historic Site (55 acres)
1 Armory Square (S# 12, map B1)
Springfield, MA 01105   413-734-8551

USDC, Natl. Oceanic & Atmospheric Admin. (NOAA)
National Ocean Service
For information about Stellwagen Banks National Marine Sanctuary (a new sanctuary) contact:
NOAA, Sanctuaries and Reserves Division
1825 Connecticut Ave. NW
Washington, DC 20235   202-673-5122

Wilderness Index

Monomoy Wilderness - 2,420 acres
Monomoy NWR (S# 3, map C5)

State Agencies

A number of Massachusetts bureaus, departments, and divisions operate under the:

Executive Office of Environmental Affairs
Leverett Saltonstall Bldg.
100 Cambridge St.
Boston, MA 02202   617-727-9800

Dept. of Environmental Management (DEM)
Division of Forests & Parks (S# 1, map E1)
100 Cambridge St.
Boston, MA 02202   617-727-3201
Selected State Forests and Parks are covered in the Information Chart. A Massachusetts State Parks Guide (146 locations) is available free. It describes each area, contains a locator map, and includes information on facilities and activities. There are day-use and camping fees. Inquire about special programs and benefits offered during the winter season.

Dept. of Fisheries, Wildlife and Environmental Law
Division of Fisheries and Wildlife (DFW) Field HQ
(S# 1, map B3 - Westboro)
Chart details on DFW office locations cover the office facilities and services. The DFW publishes guides and information brochures on a variety of subjects.

Maps and information on individual wildlife management areas are available. See Information Chart for area names. Harvest and license statistics are published every two to three years. A quarterly magazine, *Massachusetts Wildlife*, is available by subscription for $5 per year.

The Division of Marine Sports Fisheries may be reached through a DFW office at 100 Cambridge St., Boston, MA 02202 (Executive Office above), phone 617-727-3194

Office of Travel and Tourism
100 Cambridge St., 13th floor
Boston, MA 02202   617-727-3201
A Traveller's Guide to Massachusetts is available free from this office. The official Massachusetts road map is also available.

Private Organizations

Massachusetts Audubon Society (MAS)
The Society publishes comprehensive literature about MAS sanctuaries. The MAS Endicott Regional Center features a specially designed butterfly garden with many flowers. Artists frequently use the site in their work.

ANCA Locations in Massachusetts

Cape Cod Museum of Natural History (S# 26, map C5)
896 Main Street (Route 6A)
Brewster, MA 02631   508-896-3867

Green Briar Nature Center (S# 27, map C5)
6 Discovery Hill Road
East Sandwich, MA 02537   508-888-6870

New England Aquarium (S# 28, map E1)
Central Wharf
Boston, MA 02110   617-973-5200

South Shore Natural Science Center (S# 29, map B4)
PO Box 429
Norwell, MA 02061-0429   617-659-2559

No State Chamber of Commerce in Massachusetts

There are local Chamber of Commerce offices throughout the state.

★ INFORMATION CHART ★

INFORMATION CHART LEGEND - SYMBOLS & LETTER CODES

■ means YES & □ means Yes with disability provisions
sp means spring, March through May
S means Summer, June through August
F means Fall, September through November
W means Winter, December through February
T means Two (2) or Three (3) Seasons
A means All Four (4) Seasons
na means Not Applicable or Not Available
Note: empty or blank spaces in the chart mean NO

AGENCY/MAP LEGEND ... INITIALS, MAP SYMBOLS, COLOR CODES

U.S. Forest Service Supervisor & Ranger Dist. Offices NFS ... 61
U.S. Army Corps of Engineers Rec. Areas & Offices . COE ... 31
USFWS National Wildlife Refuges & Offices .... NWR ... 40
National Park Service Parks & other NPS Sites ..... NPS ... 7
Bureau of Land Management Rec. Areas & Offices . BLM ... 26
Bureau of Reclamation Rec. Areas & Reg. Offices . BOR ... 8
State Parks (also see State Agency notes) .... SPS ... 52
State Wildlife Areas (also see State Agency notes) . SWA ... 19
Private Preserves, Nature Centers & Tribal Lands ... 15
The Wild Rivers —— and Wilderness Areas

Note: Refer to yellow block on page 7 (top right) for location name and address abbreviations. If a symbol number has a star ★ that symbol is not shown on the map.

S#	MAP	LOCATION NAME (state initials if more than one) with ADDRESS and/or LOCATION DATA	TELEPHONE	ACRES / ELEVATION
1	E1	COE, New England District, 424 Trapelo Road, Waltham 02254	617-647-8107	na / na
2	B2	Barre Falls Dam, RFD #1, Hubbardston 01452	508-928-4712	na / na
3	A2	Birch Hill Dam, Route 68, Royalston 01331	508-249-4467	na / na
4	B2	Buffumville Lake, PO Box 155, Oxford 01540	508-248-5697	na / na
5	C4	Cape Cod Canal, Box J, Buzzards Bay 02532	508-759-4431	na / na
6	C3	Charles River Natural Valley Storag, RR #2, Box 45 E-1, Uxbridge 01569	508-278-2511	na / na
7	B2	Conant Brook Dam, E. Brimfield Lake, Fiskdale 01518	508-347-3705	na / na
8	B2	East Brimfield Lake, East Brimfield Lake, Fiskdale 01518	508-347-3705	na / na
9	B1	Hodges Village Dam, PO Box 155, Oxford 01540	508-248-5697	na / na
10	B1	Knightville Dam, RFD #1, Box 285, Huntington 01050	413-667-3430	na / na
11	B1	Littleville Lake, Littleville Road, Huntington 01050	413-667-3430	na / na
12	A1	Tully Lake, Tully Lake, RR #2, Athol 01331	508-249-9150	na / na
13	C3	West Hill Dam, RR #2, Box 45 E-1, Uxbridge 01569	508-278-2511	na / na
14	B2	Westville Lake, Westville Lake, Southbridge 01550	508-764-6424	na / na
1	B1	USFWS Region 5, 300 Westgate Center Drive, Hadley 01035 [CT, DE, MA, MD, ME, NH, NJ, NY, PA, RI, VA, VT, WV]	413-253-8200	na / na

Map	No.	Name / Location	Phone	Acres / Fee
C5	3	Monomoy NWR, Wiki Way, Morris Island, Chatham 02633	508-945-0594	2,750 / 0
D5	4	Nantucket NWR, Nantucket Island	508-443-4661	43 / 0
A3	5	Oxbow NWR, Still River Depot Rd., Harvard 01451	508-443-4661	711 / 300
A4	6	Parker River NWR, Northern Blvd., Plum Island, Newburyport 01950 [office at N end of Plum Is.]	508-465-5753	4,662 / 20
B1	7	Conte Natl. Wildlife & Fish Refuge (new, due to open in 1995), Vets. Med. Center, Northhampton 01060	413-582-3174	na / na
E2	1	**Boston National Historical Park**, Charlestown Navy Yard & 15 State St, Boston 02109	617-242-5642	41 / 0-55
C5	2	Cape Cod National Seashore, South Wellfleet 02663	508-349-3785	43,525 / na
B3	3	Minute Man National Historical Park, PO Box 160, Concord 01742	508-369-6993	748 / na
E1	1	**DEM, Div. Forests & Parks**, 100 Cambridge St., 19th Floor, Boston 02202	617-727-3180	na / na
B2	2	Chicopee Memorial SP, 570 Burnett Rd., Chicopee Falls 01020	413-594-9416	574 / na
B3	3	Cochituate SP, Rt. #30, 93 Commonwealth Road, Wayland 01778	508-653-9641	1,126 / na
D3	4	Horseneck Beach SR, PO Box 328, Westport Point 02791	508-636-8816	537 / na
A2	5	Lake Dennison RA, 34 New Winchendon Road, Baldwinville 01436	508-939-8962	9,400 / na
A1	6	Mohawk Trail State Forest, Rt. #2, PO Box 7, Charlemont 01339	413-339-5504	6,457 / na
C5	7	Nickerson SP, Rt. #6A, Brewster 02631	508-896-3491	1,955 / na
B2	8	Quinsigamond SP, 10 North Lake Ave., Worcester 01605	508-755-6880	51 / na
A4	9	Salisbury Beach SR, PO Box 5303, Salisbury 01952	508-462-4481	520 / 0-20
C1	10	Savoy Mountain SF, RFD #2, North Adams 01247	413-663-8469	11,112 / 1,990
D2	11	Tolland State Forest, PO Box 342, East Otis 01029	413-269-6002	8,000 / na
B3	1	**MA Div. of Fisheries & Wildlife** (Field HQ location), Westborough 01581 [on North Dr. off Rt. 135]	508-366-4470	na / na
B2	2	DFW Central District Office, Temple St., West Boylston 01583	508-835-3607	na / na
B2	3	Barre Falls WMA, near Barre	508-835-3607	2,000 / na
B2	4	Bennett WMA, near Charlton	508-835-3607	200 / na
A2	5	Birch Hill WMA, near Royalston	508-835-3607	7,000 / na
B3	6	Bolton Flats WMA, near Bolton	508-835-3607	1,000 / na
B3	7	E. Kent Swift & West Hill WMA, near Northbridge	508-835-3607	600 / na
B2	8	Four Chimneys WMA, near Spencer	508-835-3607	200 / na
B2	9	High Ridge WMA, near Gardner	508-835-3607	1,600 / na
B2	10	Hubbardston WMA, near Hubbardston	508-835-3607	1,000 / na
A2	11	Lawrence Brook WMA, near Royalston	508-835-3607	300 / na
A1	12	Millers River WMA, near Athol	508-835-3607	1,000 / na
B2	13	Moose Hill WMA, near Paxton	508-835-3607	500 / na
B2	14	Oakham WMA, near Oakham	508-835-3607	200 / na
B2	15	Phillipston WMA, near Phillipston	508-835-3607	1,500 / na
A2	16	Popple Camp WMA, near Phillipston	508-835-3607	500 / na
A2	17	Prince River WMA, near Barre	508-835-3607	378 / na
B2	18	Quaboag River WMA, near Brookfield	508-835-3607	1,100 / na
B2	19	Raccoon Hill WMA, near Barre	508-835-3607	400 / na
B2	20	Richardson WMA, near West Brookfield	508-835-3607	300 / na
B2	21	Savage Hill WMA, near Rutland	508-835-3607	300 / na
B2	22	Winimusett Meadows WMA, near New Braintree	508-835-3607	600 / na
B1	23	DFW Connecticut Valley Dist. Office, East Street, Belchertown 01007	413-323-7632	na / na
A2	24	Bennett Meadows WMA, near Northfield	413-323-7632	300 / na
A1	25	Catamount WMA, near Colrain	413-323-7632	300 / na
B1	26	Ludlow WMA, near Ludlow	413-323-7632	100 / na
A1	27	Pauchaug Brook WMA, near Northfield	413-323-7632	300 / na
B1	28	Poland Brook WMA, near Conway	413-323-7632	600 / na
A1	29	Satan's Kingdom, near Northfield	413-323-7632	500 / na
A1	30	Spaulding Brook WMA, near Montague	413-323-7632	400 / na
B1	31	Swift River WMA, East St., Belchertown	413-323-7632	1,400 / na
A1	32	Wendell Wilderness, near Wendell	413-323-7632	400 / na
B1	33	DFW Northeast District Office, Harris Street, Box 86, Acton 01720	508-263-4347	na / na
A3	34	Ashby WMA, near Ashby	508-263-4347	300 / na
A4	35	Bill Forward WMA, near Rowley	508-465-8012	1,000 / na
B3	36	Charles River WMA, near Medfield	508-263-4347	2,500 / na
A4	37	Crane Pond WMA, near Groveland	508-263-4347	2,500 / na
B3	38	Delaney WMA, near Boxborough	508-263-4347	500 / na
A3	39	Harold Parker WMA, near North Andover	508-263-4347	1,000 / na
A4	40	Martin H. Burns WMA, Orchard St., near Newbury	508-465-8012	1,500 / na
B3	41	Pantry Brook WMA, near Concord	508-263-4347	300 / na
A2	42	Squannacook WMA, near Townsend	508-263-4347	800 / na
C4	43	DFW Southeast District Office, RFD No. 3, Buzzards Bay 02532	508-759-3406	na / na
D4	44	Crane WMA, Rt. 151, Falmouth	508-759-3406	1,800 / na
C3	45	Erwin S. Wilder WMA, near Taunton	508-759-3406	500 / na

★ INFORMATION CHART ★

INFORMATION CHART LEGEND - SYMBOLS & LETTER CODES

- ■ means YES & □ means Yes with disability provisions
- **sp** means spring, March through May
- **S** means Summer, June through August
- **F** means Fall, September through November
- **W** means Winter, December through February
- **T** means Two (2) or Three (3) Seasons
- **A** means All Four (4) Seasons
- **na** means Not Applicable or Not Available

Note: empty or blank spaces in the chart mean **NO**

Note: that symbol is not shown on the map. If a symbol number has a star ★

AGENCY/MAP LEGEND... INITIALS, MAP SYMBOLS, COLOR CODES

- U.S. Forest Service Supervisor & Ranger Dist. Offices ... NFS
- U.S. Army Corps of Engineers Rec. Areas & Offices . COE
- USFWS National Wildlife Refuges & Offices .... NWR
- National Park Service Parks & other NPS Sites ...... NPS
- Bureau of Land Management Rec. Areas & Offices .. BLM
- Bureau of Reclamation Rec. Areas & Reg. Offices .. BOR
- State Parks (also see State Agency notes) .... SPS
- State Wildlife Areas (also see State Agency notes) .. SWA
- Private Preserves, Nature Centers & Tribal Lands ..
- The Wild Rivers —— and Wilderness Areas

Note: Refer to yellow block on page 7 (top right) for location name and address abbreviations.

S#	MAP	LOCATION NAME (state initials if more than one) with ADDRESS and/or LOCATION DATA	TELEPHONE	ACRES / ELEVATION
46	C3	Fall River WMA, Fall River-Freetown State Forest, Fall River	508-759-3406	800 / na
47	C3	Hockomock Swamp WMA, near Easton	508-759-3406	4,500 / na
48	C5	Marconi WMA, Capr Cod Natl. Seashore Park, Wellfleet	508-759-3406	2,000 / na
49	C4	Myles Standish WMA, Myles Standish State Forest, Plymouth	508-759-3406	2,000 / na
50	C5	Quashnet Woods WMA, near Mashpee	508-759-3406	400 / na
51	C4	Rocky Gutter WMA, Rocky Gutter St., Middleboro	508-759-3406	1,800 / na
52	C4	West Meadows WMA, near W. Bridgewater	508-759-3406	300 / na
53	D1	DFW Western District Office, Hubbard Avenue, Pittsfield 01201	413-447-9789	na / na
54	D1	Becket WMA, near Becket	413-447-9789	500 / na
55	C1	Chalet WMA, near Windsor	413-447-9789	1,400 / na
56	C1	Eugene D. Moran WMA, near Windsor	413-447-9789	900 / na
57	D2	Fox Den WMA, near Middlefield	413-447-9789	800 / na
58	D1	Hinsdale Flats WMA, near Hinsdale	413-447-9789	900 / na
59	D1	Hiram G. Fox (Canada Hill) WMA, near Worthington	413-447-9789	2,000 / na
60	D1	Hop Brook WMA, near Tyringham	413-447-9789	300 / na
61	D1	Housatonic Valley WMA, near Lenox	413-447-9789	500 / na
62	D2	Kelly WMA, near Chester	413-447-9789	300 / na
63	B2	Knightville WMA, near Huntington	413-447-9789	500 / na
64	C1	Peru WMA, near Peru	413-447-9789	1,500 / na
65	C2	Savoy WMA, near Savoy	413-447-9789	400 / na
66	C1	Stafford Hill WMA, near Cheshire	413-447-9789	500 / na
1	B3	**Massachusetts Audubon Society**, 208 South Great Road, Lincoln 01773 [Rt. 128 to Rt. 117 W, Rt. 126 E to Rt. 117]	617-259-9500	3 / na
2	D4	Ashumet Holly & Wildlife San., 286 Ashumet Rd., E. Falmouth 02536 [at Rts. 28 & 151 take 151 E 4 mi.]	508-563-6390	50 / na
3	F1	Blue Hills Res Trailside M & Chickatawbut E Ctr, 1904 Canton Ave., Milton 02186 [Rt. 128 exit 2B (Rt. 138), 0.5 mi on Rt.]	617-333-0690	6,500 / na
4	B2	Broad Meadow Brook Sanctuary, 414 Massasoit Rd., Worcester 01604 [call for directions]	508-753-6087	272 / 450
5	B3	Broadmoor Wildlife Sanctuary, 280 Eliot St., South Natick 01760 [Mass. Pike exit 16 (Rt. 16W)]	508-655-2296	600 / 180
6	B3	Drumlin Farm Education Center & Wil. Sanctuary, S. Great Rd., Lincoln 01773 [Rt. 117W from Rt. 128, or E fron Rt. 126]	617-259-9807	180 / na
7	A4	Endicott Reg. Center MA Audubon Soc. (inactive location), 346 Grapevine Rd., Wenham 01984	508-927-1122	35 / 50-60
8	D4	Felix Neck Wildlife Sanctuary, Edgartown Rd., PO Box 494, Vineyard Haven 02568	508-627-4850	350 / na
9	A4	Ipswich River Wildlife Sanctuary, 87 Perkins Row, Topsfield 01983 [I-95 to Rt. 1N to Rt. 97 S, 2nd left]	508-887-9264	2,500 / 150
10	C4	South Shore Regional Center, 2000 Main St., Marshfield 02050 [Rt. 3 exit 12 (Rt. 139E) or exit 13 (Rt 123E); to Rt. 3A]	617-837-9400	175 / 0-80
11	C4	Daniel Webster Wildlife Sanctuary, Marshfield 02050 [Rt. 139, Webster St., Winslow Cemetery Rd.]	617-837-9400	475 / 6-20
12	C4	North Hill Marsh Wildlife Sanctuary, Mayflower St., Duxbury	617-837-9400	140 / 40-100
13	B3	Stony Brook Nature Center & Wildlif, 108 North St., Norfolk 02056 [at Rts. 1A & 115, follow 115N 1.5 mi, 3rd left]	508-528-3140	241 / na
14	C5	Wellfleet Bay Wildlife Sanctuary, PO Box 236, S. Wellfleet 02663 [Rt. 6, west side, N of Eastham/Wellfleet Line]	508-349-2615	600 / 0-35
15	A2	Lincoln Woods Wildlife Sanctuary &, 226 Union St., Leominster 01453	508-355-4638	68 / na
16	B1	Arcadia N Ctr & WS, 127 Coombs Rd, Easthampton 01027 [I-95 ex 18, R to S 5, R on East St 1 m, R on Ford Hill Rd 1 m]	413-584-3009	550 / 120-140
17	B2	Cook's Canyon Wildlife Sanctuary, South St., Barre 01005	508-355-4638	45 / na
18	A2	Flat Rock Wildlife San, Fitchburg [at Rts. 2A, 13, & 31, follow 2A W to West St, take 2nd R onto Ashburnham - 1 mi]	508-355-4638	340 / 500
19	C1	Laughing Brook E Ctr & WS, 789 Main St., Hampden 01036 [from I-91 exit 2N / 4S take Rt 83 8.1 mi to Allen, L on Main]	413-566-8034	269 / na
20	B3	Moose Hill WS, 293 Moose Hill St., Sharon 02067 [I-95 S exit 10, L off ramp, R onto Rt. 27N 0.5 mi, L onto Moose Hill]	617-784-5691	1,435 / 534
21	D1	Pleasant Valley WS, 472 W Mountain Rd, Lenox 01240 [I-90 exit 2 (Rt7/20) 6.6 mi, L onto W Dugway Rd, follow signs]	413-637-0320	1,120 / 1,200-1,800
22	D1	Canoe Meadows Wildlife Sanctuary, Holmes Road, Pittsfield [I-90 exit 2 (Rts. 7/20), Holmes Rd.]	413-637-0320	262 / 900-1,000
23	B2	Wachusett Meadow Wildlife Sanctuary, 113 Goodnow Rd., Princeton 01541 [take Rt. 62 W 0.7 mi, turn R, entrance 1 mi.]	508-464-2712	1,031 / 975-1,312
24	E1	**TNC Massachusetts Field Office**, 201 Devonshire St., 5th Floor, Boston 02110	617-423-2545	na / na
25	B4	Black Pond Nat. Preserve (Norwell), managed by MA Audubon Soc., 2000 Main Street, Marshfield 02050	617-837-9400	94 / 50

MICHIGAN NOTES

Summary

There are 34 federal, 88 state, and 36 private recreation areas or local administrative offices covered in this state chapter. Of these, 113 appear in the Information Chart and 45 are covered in the notes. The special indexes feature 6 federally designated wilderness areas and wild rivers, and 6 agency published outdoor maps.

Federal Agencies

U.S. Forest Service

Michigan is in the Eastern Region (see Wisconsin chapter - U.S. Forest Svc., Eastern Region listing).

The Lumberman's Monument and Visitor Center includes outdoor logging related exhibits and feature a history of logging in the Lake states. Educational programs are available. Contact the Tawas Ranger District (S# 13, map C3) of the Huron-Manistee National Forest for details.

The Sylvania Visitor Center at the Watersmeet Ranger District (S# 21, map B1) of the Ottawa National Forest has a series of exhibits and audio-visual programs covering the discovery and development of forest lands and varied land uses. Information about recreation opportunities are also available.

USFWS National Wildlife Refuges

Shiawassee NWR also administers two refuges that are closed to the public. These are the 300-acre Wyandotte and 360-acre Michigan Islands NWRs. The latter is made up of Pismire, Shoe, Scarecrow, Thunder Bay, and Gull Islands.

National Park Service

Isle Royale National Park in Lake Superior is accessible by ferry (a six-hour ferry ride) from Houghton or Copper Harbor in northern Michigan. The mainland office is in Houghton. You may also reach the park in season from Grand Portage, Minnesota, a three-hour ferry ride.

Additional NPS Location in Michigan

Keweenaw National Historical Park   402-221-3431
New NPS site approved October 27, 1992.

Wilderness/Wild River Index

Wilderness Areas

Seney NWR (S# 1, map B2)
Seney Wilderness - 25,150 acres
Huron Islands - 147 acres
Shiawassee NWR (S# 4, map D3)
Michigan Islands - 12 acres (closed to public)
Isle Royale National Park (S# 1, map A1)
Isle Royale Wilderness - 131,880

Wild Rivers

Huron-Manistee National Forest Sup. (S# 7, map C2)
Au Sable Wild River and
Pere Marquette Wild River

Outdoor Map Index

National Park Service (USGS Maps)

Isle Royale National Park [1987]
Scale: 1 inch = 1.0 miles (1 cm = 0.6 km)
Pictured Rocks National Lakeshore

U.S. Forest Service Maps

Hiawatha National Forest [1981]
Scale: 1 inch = 4.0 miles (1 cm = 2.5 km)
Size: 28x34 inches (71x86 cm)
Huron National Forest [1982]
Scale: 1 inch = 4.0 miles (1 cm = 2.5 km)
Size: 26x42 inches (66x106 cm)
Manistee National Forest [1979]
Scale: 1 inch = 4.0 miles (1 cm = 2.5 km)
Size: 36x49 inches (91x124 cm)
Ottawa National Forest [1988]
Scale: 1 inch = 4.0 miles (1 cm = 2.5 km)
Size: 40x52 inches (101x132 cm)

State Agencies

Michigan Dept. of Natural Resources (DNR)

Parks Division (S# 1, map E3)

A Michigan State Parks Guide (94 parks) is available free. The guide describes each area, contains a locator map, and includes information on facilities and activities. There is a motor vehicle permit fee, plus fees for camping, cabins, and other activities. Selected parks, their Guide map symbol numbers and coordinates, park name, and approximate location are listed here.

S#	MAP	PARK NAME & LOCATION
2	E4	Bald Mountain SP, Lake Orion
3	B3	Cheboygan SP, Cheboygan
4	B2	Fayette SP, Garden
5	A1	Fort Wilkins SP, Copper Harbor
6	C3	Hartwick Pines SP, Grayling
7	E3	Holly SP, Holly
8	B2	Indian Lake (2 units), Manistique
9	C2	Ludington SP, Ludington
10	E3	Ortonville SP, Ortonville
11	D2	P.J. Hoffmaster SP, Muskegon
12	E3	Pinckney SP, Pinckney
13	A1	Porcupine Mtns. SP (2 units), Ontonagon
14	D4	Port Crescent SP, Port Austin
15	E3	Proud Lake SP, Milford
16	D2	Silver Lake SP, Mears
17	E3	Sterling SP, Monroe
18	B3	Tahquamenon Falls SP, Paradise
19	A1	Van Riper SP, Champion
20	E2	Warren Dunes SP, Sawyer
21	E3	Waterloo SP, Chelsea
22	B3	Wilderness SP, Mackinaw City

Michigan Dept. of Natural Resources (DNR)

Forest Management Division

Stevens T. Mason Bldg.
Box 30028
Lansing, MI 48909   517-373-1275
Contact the State Forester for recreation literature.

Michigan Dept. of Natural Resources (DNR)

Wildlife Division (S# 1, map E3)

The Division has district offices in 13 cities as follows: in the upper peninsula in Region 1 - Baraga, Crystal Falls, Escanaba, and Newberry; in the lower peninsula in Region 2 - Cadillac, Gaylord, Mio, and Claire; and in Region 3 - Grand Rapids, Plainwell, Imlay City, Jackson, and Pontiac Lake. These offices are not indicated on the state map or listed in the Information Chart pages.

Two free nongame brochures, Saving Your Natural Heritage of Wildlife & Plants and Bird Watching at Its Best, are available. A brochure titled Michigan's Public Lands covers 64 State Game Areas (SGA) and State Wildlife Areas (SWA), state recreation areas, and National Forest and Park lands. Annual game harvest and license information is available.

Consider subscribing Michigan Natural Resources Magazine. It is published by the agency nine times a year and the single issue price is $2.50.

Michigan Travel Bureau

PO Box 30226
Lansing, MI 48909   1-800-543-2937
A state map and a traveler's guide to Michigan are available free from this office.

Private Organizations

TNC-Michigan Field Office

The office has a preserve directory available for $6.

ANCA Locations in Michigan

Blandford Nature Center (S# 18, map D2)
1715 Hillburn NW
Grand Rapids, MI 49504   616-453-6192

Chippewa Nature Center (S# 19, map D3)
400 South Badour Road
Midland, MI 48640   517-631-0830

Degraaf Nature Center (S# 20, map E2)
600 Graafschap Road
Holland, MI 49423   616-396-2739

Fernwood Nature Center (S# 21, map E2)
13988 Rangeline Road
Niles, MI 49120   616-695-6491

Howard Christensen Nature Center (S# 22, map D2)
16160 Red Pine Drive
Kent City, MI 49330   616-887-1852

Independence Oaks Nature Center (S# 23, map E4)
9401 Shashabaw St.
Clarkston, MI 48016   313-739-6731

Jennison Nature Center (S# 24, map D3)
3582 State Park Drive
Bay City, MI 48706   517-667-0717

Kalamazoo Nature Center (S# 25, map E2)
7000 North Westnedge
Kalamazoo, MI 49007-9711   616-381-1574

Kensington Metropark Nature Center (S# 26, map E3)
2240 West Bruno Road
Milford, WI 48165   313-685-1561

Oakwoods Metropark Nature Center (S# 27, map E3)
PO Box 332
Flat Rock, MI 48173-0332   313-697-9181

Price Nature Center (S# 28, map D3)
111 South Michigan
Saginaw, MI 48602   517-790-5280

Sterling Heights Nature Center (S# 29, map E4)
40555 Utica
Sterling Heights, MI 48078   313-739-6731

Stony Creek Nature Center (S# 30, map E4)
4100 Inwood Road
Romeo, MI 48065   313-781-4621

Michigan Chamber of Commerce

600 S. Walnut St.   Phone 517-371-2100
Lansing, MI 48933   Fax 517-371-7224

Tribal Land Areas in Michigan

Bay Mills Community of the Sault Ste. Marie Band of the Chippewa Indians, Bay Mills Indian Reservation - Camping, boating.
Bay Mills Executive Council (S# 31, map B3)
Route 1
Brimley, MI 49715   906-248-3241

Grand Traverse Band of the Ottawa and Chippewa Indians of Michigan - Camping.
Grand Traverse Tribal Council (S# 32, map C2)
Route 1, Box 135
Suttons Bay, MI 49682   616-271-3538

Keweenaw Bay Indian Community of the L'Anse and Ontonagon Bands of Chippewa Indians - Fishing, hunting, camping, boating.
Keweenaw Bay Tribal Council (S# 33, map A1)
Center Building
Route 1, Box 45
Baraga, MI 49908   906-353-6623

Saginaw Chippewa Tribe of the Isabella Indian Reservation - Fishing, hunting, camping, boating, hiking.
Saginaw Chippewa Tribal Council (S# 34, map D3)
7070 East Broadway Rd.
Mt. Pleasant, MI 48858   517-772-5700

Sault Ste. Marie Tribe of Chippewa Indians of Michigan - Hiking.
Sault Ste. Marie Chippewa Tribal Council (S# 35, map B3)
206 Greenough St.
Sault Ste. Marie, MI 49783   906-635-6050

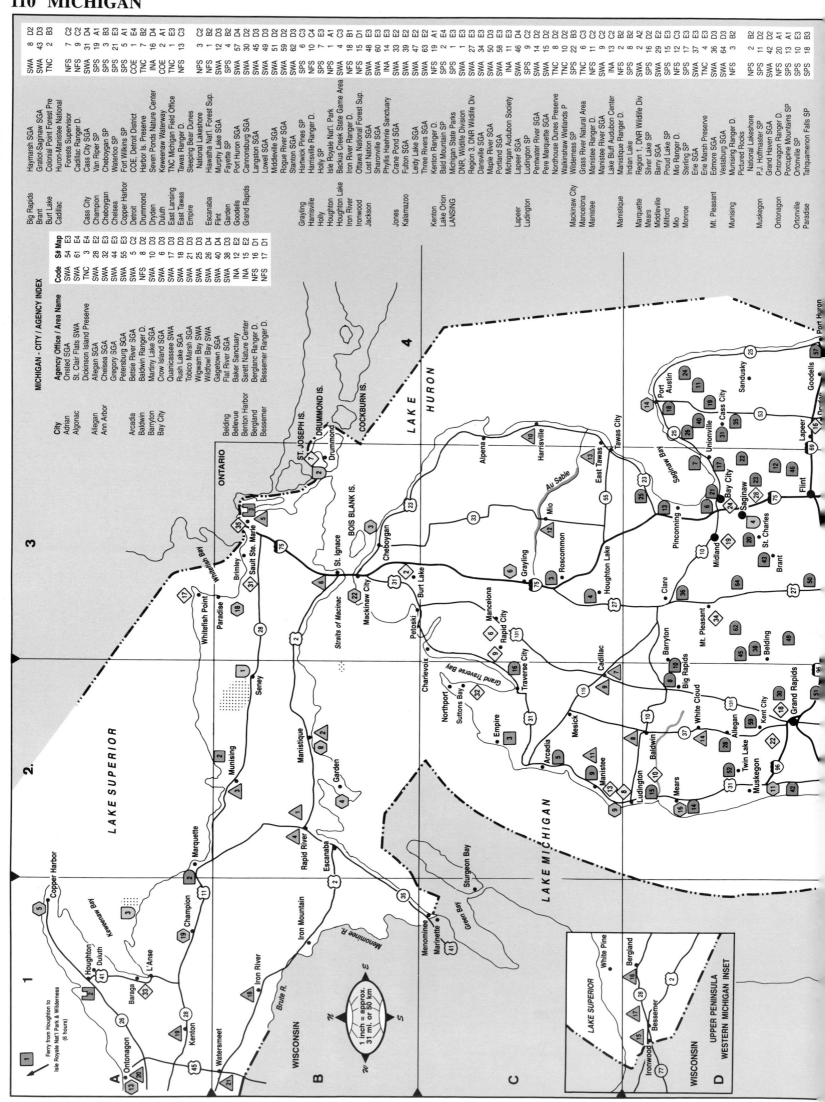

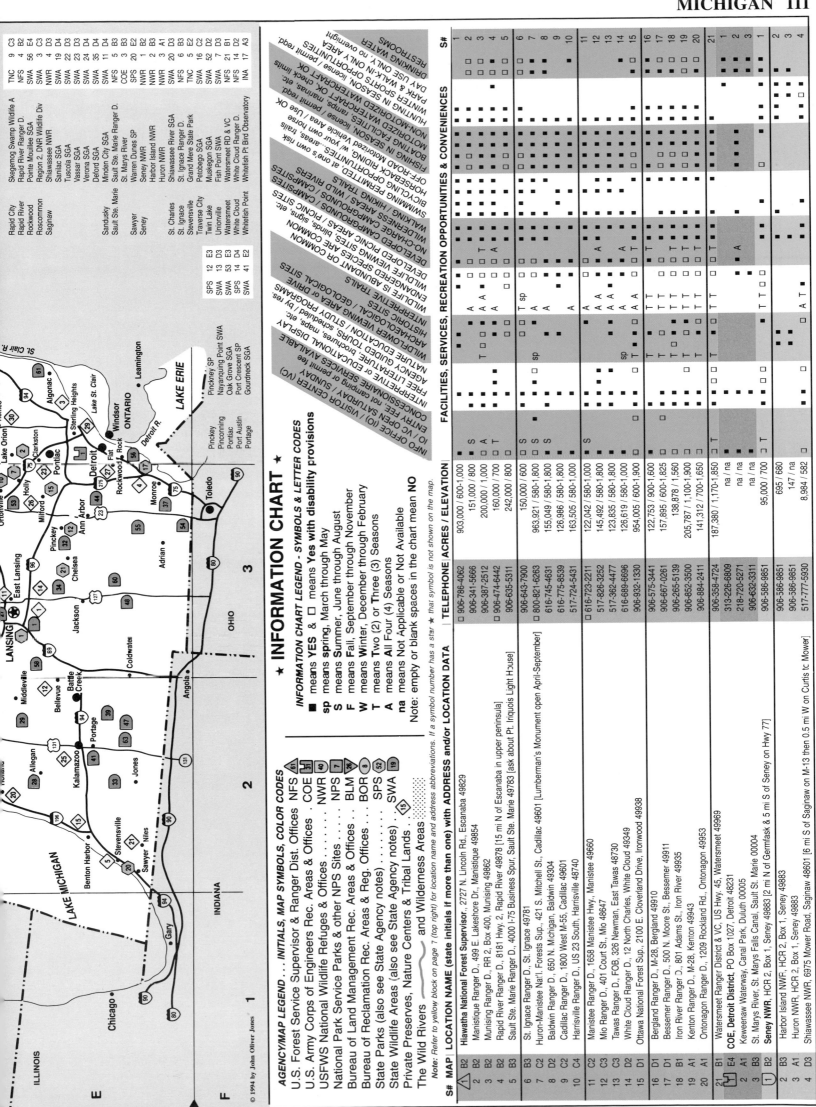

★ INFORMATION CHART ★

AGENCY/MAP LEGEND . . . INITIALS, MAP SYMBOLS, COLOR CODES

U.S. Forest Service Supervisor & Ranger Dist. Offices . . . NFS
U.S. Army Corps of Engineers Rec. Areas & Offices . . . COE
USFWS National Wildlife Refuges & Offices . . . . NWR
National Park Service Parks & other NPS Sites . . . . NPS
Bureau of Land Management Rec. Areas & Offices . . . BLM
Bureau of Reclamation Rec. Areas & Reg. Offices . . . BOR
State Parks (also see State Agency notes) . . . . SPS
State Wildlife Areas (also see State Agency notes) . . . SWA
Private Preserves, Nature Centers & Tribal Lands . . .
The Wild Rivers ⌒⌒⌒ and Wilderness Areas ⠿⠿

Note: Refer to yellow block on page 7 (top right) for location name and address abbreviations. If a symbol number has a star ★ that item is not shown on the map.

INFORMATION CHART LEGEND - SYMBOLS & LETTER CODES

■ means YES & ☐ means Yes with disability provisions
sp means spring, March through May
S means Summer, June through August
F means Fall, September through November
W means Winter, December through February
T means Two (2) or Three (3) Seasons
A means All Four (4) Seasons
na means Not Applicable or Not Available

Note: empty or blank spaces in the chart mean NO

VC / VISITOR CENTER (VC)
IO / IO: OPEN SATURDAY / SUNDAY
VC / VC OPEN SATURDAY / SUNDAY
ENTRY FEE / ENTRY FEE
INTERPRETIVE SERVICES AVAILABLE
AGENCY LITERATURE AVAILABLE
FREE LITERATURE, brochures, maps, etc.
NATURE EDUCATION / STUDY PROGRAMS
WILDFLOWER VIEWING AREA or DRIVE
ARCHAEOLOGICAL / GEOLOGICAL SITES
HISTORIC SITES
INTERPRETIVE TRAILS
WILDLIFE VIEWING AREA or DRIVE
ENDANGERED SPECIES ARE COMMON
WILDLIFE VIEWING SITES, blinds, signs, etc.
DEVELOPED PICNIC AREAS / PICNIC SITES
NO-CHARGE CAMPGROUNDS / CAMPSITES
DEVELOPED CAMPGROUNDS / CAMPSITES
WILDERNESS AREAS / HIKING TRAILS
WALKING TRAILS
BICYCLING PERMITTED
SWIMMING PERMITTED . . . areas, trails
HORSEBACK RIDING, w/ your own horse
MOTORIZED VEHICLE Area / Use OK
FISHING IN SEASON, license / permit req'd.
HUNTING IN SEASON, license / permit req'd.
MOTORIZED WATERCRAFT OK
NON-MOTORIZED WATERCRAFT OK
WINTER SPORTS OPPORTUNITIES
PARK & WALK-IN ONLY AREA
DAY USE ONLY, no overnight
RESTROOMS

© 1994 by John Oliver Jones

S#	MAP	LOCATION NAME (state initials if more than one) with ADDRESS and/or LOCATION DATA	TELEPHONE	ACRES / ELEVATION
1	B2	**Hiawatha National Forest Supervisor**., 2727 N. Lincoln Rd., Escanaba 49829	906-786-4062	903,000 / 600-1,000
2	B2	Manistique Ranger D., 499 E. Lakeshore Dr.., Manistique 49854	906-341-5666	151,000 / 800
3	B2	Munising Ranger D., RR 2, Box 400, Munising 49862	906-387-2512	200,000 / 1,000
4	B2	Rapid River Ranger D., 8181 Hwy. 2, Rapid River 49878 [15 mi N of Escanaba in upper peninsula]	906-474-6442	160,000 / 700
5	B3	Sault Ste. Marie Ranger D., 4000 I-75 Business Spur, Sault Ste. Marie 49783 [ask about Pt. Iriquois Light House]	906-635-5311	242,000 / 800
6	B3	St. Ignace Ranger D., St. Ignace 49781	906-643-7900	150,000 / 600
7	C2	Huron-Manistee Nat'l. Forests Sup., 421 S. Mitchell St., Cadillac 49601 [Lumberman's Monument open April-September]	800-821-6263	963,921 / 580-1,800
8	C2	Baldwin Ranger D., 650 N. Michigan, Baldwin 49304	616-745-4631	155,049 / 580-1,800
9	C2	Cadillac Ranger D., 1800 West M-55, Cadillac 49601	616-775-8539	126,986 / 580-1,800
10	C4	Harrisville Ranger D., US 23 South, Harrisville 48740	517-724-5431	163,505 / 580-1,000
11	C2	Manistee Ranger D., 1658 Manistee Hwy., Manistee 49660	616-723-2211	122,042 / 580-1,000
12	C3	Mio Ranger D., 401 Court St., Mio 48647	517-826-3252	145,492 / 580-1,800
13	C3	Tawas Ranger D., FOB, 326 Newman, East Tawas 48730	517-362-4477	123,835 / 580-1,800
14	C3	White Cloud Ranger D., 12 North Charles, White Cloud 49349	616-689-6696	126,619 / 580-1,000
15	D1	Ottawa National Forest Sup., 2100 E. Cloverland Drive, Ironwood 49938	906-932-1330	954,005 / 600-1,900
16	D1	Bergland Ranger D., M-28, Bergland 49910	906-575-3441	122,753 / 900-1,600
17	D1	Bessemer Ranger D., 500 N. Moore St., Bessemer 49911	906-667-0261	157,895 / 600-1,825
18	D1	Iron River Ranger D., 801 Adams St., Iron River 49935	906-265-5139	138,878 / 1,560
19	A1	Kenton Ranger D., M-28, Kenton 49943	906-852-3500	205,787 / 1,100-1,900
20	A1	Ontonagon Ranger D., 1209 Rockland Rd., Ontonagon 49953	906-884-2411	141,312 / 700-1,650
21	B1	Watersmeet Ranger District & VC, US Hwy. 45, Watersmeet 49969	906-358-4724	187,380 / 1,170-1,850
1	E4	**COE, Detroit District**, PO Box 1027, Detroit 48231	313-226-6809	na / na
2	A1	Keweenaw Waterway, Canal Park, Duluth 00005	218-720-5271	na / na
3	B3	St. Marys River, St. Marys Falls Canal, Sault St. Marie 00004	906-632-3311	na / na
1	B2	**Seney NWR**, HCR 2, Box 1, Seney 49883 [2 mi N of Germfask & 5 mi S of Seney on Hwy 77]	906-586-9851	95,000 / 700
2	B3	Harbor Island NWF, HCR 2, Box 1, Seney 49883	906-586-9851	695 / 680
3	A1	Huron NWR, HCR 2, Box 1, Seney 49883	906-586-9851	147 / na
4	D3	Shiawassee NWR, 6975 Mower Road, Saginaw 48601 [6 mi S of Saginaw on M-13 then 0.5 mi W on Curtis to Mower]	517-777-5930	8,984 / 582

Skegemog Swamp Wildlife A	Rapid City	TNC 9 C3
Rapid River Ranger D.	Rapid River	NFS 4 B2
Pointe Mouillee SGA	Rockwood	SWA 56 E4
Region 2, DNR Wildlife Div	Roscommon	SWA 3 C3
Shiawassee NWR	Saginaw	NWR 4 D3
Sanilac SGA		SWA 19 D4
Tuscola SGA		SWA 22 D3
Vassar SGA		SWA 24 D3
Verona SGA		SWA 35 D4
Deford SGA		SWA 11 D4
Minden City SGA	Sandusky	SWA 5 D4
Sault Ste. Marie Ranger D.	Sault Ste. Marie	NFS 5 B3
St. Marys River		COE 3 B3
Warren Dunes SP	Sawyer	SPS 20 E2
Seney NWR	Seney	NWR 1 B2
Harbor Island NWR		NWR 2 B3
Huron NWR		NWR 3 A1
Shiawassee River SGA	St. Charles	SWA 20 D3
St. Ignace Ranger D.	St. Ignace	NFS 6 B3
Grand Mere State Park	Stevensville	TNC 1 E2
Petobego SGA	Traverse City	SWA 16 C2
Muskegon SGA	Twin Lake	SWA 52 D2
Fish Point SWA	Unionville	SWA 7 D3
Watersmeet RD & VC	Watersmeet	NFS 21 B1
White Cloud Ranger D.	White Cloud	NFS 14 D2
Whitefish Pt Bird Observatory	Whitefish Point	INA 17 A3

		SPS 12 E3
		SWA 13 D3
Nayanquing Point SWA		SWA 53 E3
Oak Grove SGA		SPS 14 D4
Port Crescent SP		SWA 41 E2
Gourdneck SGA		
Pinckney SP	Pinckney	
Pinconning		
Port Austin		
Portage		

LAKE ERIE

ONTARIO

OHIO

INDIANA

ILLINOIS

LAKE MICHIGAN

St. Clair R.

★ INFORMATION CHART ★

INFORMATION CHART LEGEND - SYMBOLS & LETTER CODES

- ■ means YES & □ means Yes with disability provisions
- sp means spring, March through May
- S means Summer, June through August
- F means Fall, September through November
- W means Winter, December through February
- T means Two (2) or Three (3) Seasons
- A means All Four (4) Seasons
- na means Not Applicable or Not Available

Note: empty or blank spaces in the chart mean NO

★ that symbol is not shown on the map.

Note: *Refer to yellow block on page 7 (top right) for location name and address abbreviations. If a symbol number has a star*

AGENCY/MAP LEGEND ... INITIALS, MAP SYMBOLS, COLOR CODES

- U.S. Forest Service Supervisor & Ranger Dist. Offices .. NFS
- U.S. Army Corps of Engineers Rec. Areas & Offices . COE
- USFWS National Wildlife Refuges & Offices .... NWR
- National Park Service Parks & other NPS Sites .... NPS
- Bureau of Land Management Rec. Areas & Offices .. BLM
- Bureau of Reclamation Rec. Areas & Reg. Offices ... BOR
- State Parks (also see State Agency notes) .... SPS
- State Wildlife Areas (also see State Agency notes) ... SWA
- Private Preserves, Nature Centers & Tribal Lands ..
- The Wild Rivers — and Wilderness Areas

S#	MAP	LOCATION NAME (state initials if more than one) with ADDRESS and/or LOCATION DATA	TELEPHONE	ACRES / ELEVATION
1	A1	Isle Royale National Park, 87 North Ripley Street, Houghton 49931 [ferry access, closed November 1 to April 15]	906-482-0984	571,790 / 600-1,400
2	B2	Pictured Rocks National Lakeshore, PO Box 40, Munising 49862 [S shore L. Superior between Munising & Gr. Marais]	906-387-3700	71,397 / 600-800
3	C2	Sleeping Bear Dunes National Lakesh, 9922 Front St. (Hwy. M-72), PO Box 277, Empire 49630	616-326-5134	71,132 / 700
	E3	Michigan State Parks, Knapps Ctr, 300 S. Washington Sq., Suite 340, PO Box 30028, Lansing 48909	517-373-1270	na / na
1	E3	DNR, Wildlife Division, PO Box 30028, Lansing 48909	517-373-1263	na / na
2	A2	Region 1, MI DNR Wildlife Div., 1990 US 41 South, Marquette 49855	906-228-6561	na / na
3	C3	Region 2, MI DNR Wildlife Div., 8717 N Roscommon Rd., PO Box 128, Roscommon 48653	517-275-5151	na / na
4	C3	Backus Creek State Game Area (SGA), near Houghton Lake	517-275-5151	na / na
5	C2	Betsie River SGA, near Arcadia	517-275-5151	na / na
6	D3	Crow Island SGA (near Bay City), 503 N. Euclid Ave., Suite 9B, Bay City 48706	517-684-9141	2,064 / na
7	D3	Fish Point SWA, RFD, Unionville 48767	517-674-2511	2,217 / na
8	D3	Haymarsh SGA, near Big Rapids	517-275-5151	na / na
9	C2	Manistee River SGA, Oceana County, near Manistee	517-275-5151	na / na
10	D2	Martiny Lake SGA, near Barryton	517-275-5151	na / na
11	D4	Minden City SGA, 10 mi. NE of Sandusky	517-684-9141	6,265 / na
12	D3	Murphy Lake SGA, 20 mi. N of Flint	517-684-9141	na / na
13	D3	Nayanquing Point State Wildlife Are, 1570 Tower Beach Rd., Pinconning 48650	517-697-5101	1,420 / na
14	D2	Pentwater River SGA, S of Ludington	517-275-5151	na / na
15	C2	Pere Marquette SGA, S of Ludington	517-275-5151	178 / na
16	C2	Petobego SGA, E of Traverse City	517-275-5151	na / na
17	D3	Quanicassee SWA (includes 731 leased acres), 11 mi. E of Bay City	517-684-9141	949 / na
18	D3	Rush Lake SGA, 36 mi. NE of Bay City	517-684-9141	1,057 / na
19	D4	Sanilac SGA, 45 mi. E of Bay City & Saginaw	517-684-9141	1,120 / na
20	D3	Shiawassee River SGA, c/o St. Charles Field Office, 225 E. Spruce St., St. Charles 48655	517-865-6211	8,419 / na
21	D3	Tobico Marsh SGA, 5 mi. NW of Bay City	517-684-9141	1,791 / na
22	D3	Tuscola SGA, 25 mi. E of Saginaw	517-684-9141	8,383 / na
23*	D3	Vassar SGA, 20 mi. E of Saginaw	517-684-9141	30,959 / na
24	D4	Verona SGA, 40 mi. NE of Saginaw	517-684-9141	7,464 / na
25	D3	Wigwam Bay SWA, 25 mi. N of Bay City	517-684-9141	334 / na
26	D4	Wildfowl Bay SWA, 40 mi. NE of Bay City	517-684-9141	1,790 / na
27	E3	Region 3, MI DNR Wildlife Div., Gen. Off. Bldg, 3rd Fl. SSC, Box 30028, Lansing 48909	517-322-1300	na / na
28	E3	Allegan SGA (near Kalamazoo), 4590 118th Ave., R #3, Allegan 49010	616-673-2430	45,000 / na
29	E2	Barry SGA (near Grand Rapids), 1805 S. Yankee Springs Rd., Middleville 49333	616-795-3280	14,841 / na
30	D4	Cannonsburg SGA, 5 mi. NW of Grand Rapids	616-456-5071	1,331 / na
31	D4	Cass City SGA, 4017 E. Caro Rd., Cass City 48726	517-872-5300	963 / na
32	E3	Chelsea SGA, c/o Dist. Office in Jackson, near Ann Arbor	517-784-3188	640 / na
33	E3	Crane Pond SGA (near Kalamazoo), 60887 M-40, Jones 49061	616-244-5928	3,625 / na
34	E3	Dansville SGA, 14 mi. SE of Lansing	517-373-9358	4,200 / na
35	D3	Deford SGA, 30 mi. E of Bay City & Saginaw	517-684-9141	18,730 / na
36	E3	Edmore SGA, 12 mi. NE of Mt. Pleasant	616-456-5071	2,400 / na
37	E3	Erie SGA, 13 mi. SW of Monroe	313-379-9692	na / na
38	D3	Flat River SGA, Rt.2, 6640 Long Lake, Belding 48809	616-794-2658	11,000 / na
39	E2	Fulton SGA, 20 mi. SE of Kalamazoo	616-685-6851	552 / na
40	D4	Gagetown SGA, NE of Bay City	517-684-9141	na / na
41	E2	Gourdneck SGA, within 10 mi. of Kalamazoo & Portage	616-685-6851	2,025 / na
42	D2	Grand Haven SGA, 13 mi. S of Muskegon	616-456-5071	1,078 / na
43	E3	Gratiot-Saginaw SGA (near Ithaca), 13350 S. Meridian Rd. (other ph. 373-9358), Brant 48614	517-643-7000	15,323 / na
44	E3	Gregory SGA, 18 mi. SE of Ann Arbor	517-373-9358	3,474 / na
45	D3	Langston SGA, 30 mi. NE of Grand Rapids	616-456-5071	2,793 / na

The column header groups read: FACILITIES, SERVICES, RECREATION OPPORTUNITIES & CONVENIENCES

S#	MAP	WMA NAME & LOCATION	Phone	Acres / na
48	E3	Lost Nation SGA, 30 mi. S of Jackson	517-784-3188	2,374 / na
49	D3	Lowell SGA, 20 mi. E of Grand Rapids	616-456-5071	1,800 / na
50	D3	Maple River SGA, 30 mi. N of Lansing	517-373-9358	6,415 / na
51	D2	Middleville SGA, 15 mi. SE of Grand Rapids	616-685-6851	3,375 / na
52	D2	Muskegon SGA, 7600 E. Messinger Rd., Twin Lake 49457	616-788-5055	8,422 / na
53	E3	Oak Grove SGA, 26 mi. NW of Pontiac	517-373-9358	1,744 / na
54	E3	Onsted SGA, 15 mi. SE of Adrian	517-784-3188	512 / na
55	D3	Petersburg SGA, 25 mi. S of Ann Arbor	313-379-9692	442 / na
56	E4	Pointe Mouillee SGA (near Detroit), 37205 Mouilee Rd. R #2, Rockwood 48173	313-379-9692	3,769 / na
57	D4	Port Huron SGA (near Port Huron), 6181 Lapeer Rd., Goodells 48027	313-987-5398	6,180 / na
58	E3	Portland SGA, 20 mi. W of Lansing	616-456-5071	1,759 / na
59	D2	Rogue River SGA, 17 mi. NW of Grand Rapids	616-456-5071	5,587 / na
60	E3	Sharonville SGA, 15 mi. SE of Jackson	517-784-3188	2,248 / na
61	E4	St. Clair Flats SWA, 1803 Kirspin Rd., Harsen's Island, 48028 [near Algonac]	313-748-9504	6,624 / na
62	D3	Stanton SGA, 40 mi. NE of Grand Rapids	616-456-5071	4,303 / na
63	E2	Three Rivers SGA, 25 mi. S of Kalamazoo	616-685-6851	2,060 / na
64	D3	Vestaburg SGA, 20 mi. SE of Mt. Pleasant	616-456-5071	1,786 / na
1	E3	TNC Michigan Field Office, 2840 East Grand River, Suite 5, East Lansing 48823	517-332-1741	na / na
2	B3	Colonial Point Forest Preserve (contact Field Office), adjacent Burt Lake	517-332-1741	285 / na
3	E4	Dickinson Island Preserve (contact Field Office), near Algonac [on Dickinson Island]	517-332-1741	1,500 / na
4	E3	Erie Marsh Preserve (closed Oct-Nov, contact Field Office), near Monroe	517-332-1741	2,168 / na
5	E2	Grand Mere State Park (contact Field Office), near Stevensville	517-332-1741	1,184 / na
6	C3	Grass River Natural Area (contact FO, tour ph. 616-553-8709), W of Mancelona	517-332-1741	1,050 / na
7	B2	Harbor Is. Preserve (part of Seney NWR, contact FO), in Potaganissing Bay near Drummond	517-332-1741	695 / na
8	D2	Nordhouse Dunes Preserve (contact FO or Manistee Nat'l. Forest), near Ludington	517-332-1741	598 / na
9	C3	Skegemog Swamp Wildlife Area (contact Field Office), W of Rapid City	517-332-1741	2,700 / na
10	D2	Walkinshaw Wetlands Preserve (contact Field Office), S of Ludington	517-332-1741	1,031 / na
11	E3	Michigan Audubon Society, 6011 W. St. Joseph Hwy., Suite 403, PO Box 80527, Lansing 48908	517-886-9144	na / na
12	E2	Baker Sanctuary, 5 mi. S of Bellevue	517-886-9144	900 / na
13	C2	Lake Bluff Audubon Center, 2 mi. N of Manistee	616-723-2625	70 / na
14	E3	Phyllis Haehnle Sanctuary, 10 mi. NE of Jackson	517-886-9144	900 / na
15	E2	Sarett Nature Center, 2300 Benton Center Rd., Benton Harbor 49022	616-927-4832	400 / na
16	D4	Seven Ponds Nature Center, 3854 Crawford Rd., Dryden 48428	313-796-3419	250 / na
17	A3	Whitefish Point Bird Observatory, 10 mi. N of Paradise at Whitefish Point	906-492-3596	40 / na

★ INFORMATION CHART ★

INFORMATION CHART LEGEND - SYMBOLS & LETTER CODES

- ■ means **YES** & □ means **Yes with disability provisions**
- **sp** means **spring**, March through May
- **S** means **Summer**, June through August
- **F** means **Fall**, September through November
- **W** means **Winter**, December through February
- **T** means **Two (2)** or **Three (3) Seasons**
- **A** means **All Four (4) Seasons**
- **na** means **Not Applicable or Not Available**

Note: empty or blank spaces in the chart mean **NO**

★ that symbol is not shown on the map.

AGENCY/MAP LEGEND . . . INITIALS, MAP SYMBOLS, COLOR CODES

- U.S. Forest Service Supervisor & Ranger Dist. Offices .. NFS
- U.S. Army Corps of Engineers Rec. Areas & Offices .. COE
- USFWS National Wildlife Refuges & Offices .... NWR
- National Park Service Parks & other NPS Sites .... NPS
- Bureau of Land Management Rec. Areas & Offices .... BLM
- Bureau of Reclamation Rec. Areas & Reg. Offices .... BOR
- State Parks (also see State Agency notes) .... SPS
- State Wildlife Areas (also see State Agency notes) ... SWA
- Private Preserves, Nature Centers & Tribal Lands ....
- The Wild Rivers ——— and Wilderness Areas

Note: Refer to yellow block on page 7 (top right) for location name and address abbreviations. If a symbol number has a star ★ that symbol is not shown on the map.

FACILITIES, SERVICES, RECREATION OPPORTUNITIES & CONVENIENCES

S#	MAP	LOCATION NAME (state initials if more than one) with ADDRESS and/or LOCATION DATA	TELEPHONE	ACRES / ELEVATION	S#
	B2	**Chippewa National Forest Supervisor**, Rt. #3, Box 244, Cass Lake 56633	218-335-2226	na / na	1
	B2	Blackduck Ranger D., Pennington Route, Box 95, Blackduck 56630	218-835-4291	na / na	2
	B2	Cass Lake Ranger D., Rt. #3, Box 219, Cass Lake 56633	218-335-2283	na / na	3
	B2	Deer River Ranger D., Box 308, Deer River 56636	218-246-8233	na / na	4
	B2	Marcell Ranger D., Box 155, Marcell 56657	218-832-3161	na / na	5
	B3	Walker Ranger D., HCR 73, Box 15, Walker 56484	218-547-1044	na / na	6
	B3	Superior National Forest Sup., FOB, 5th Ave. W. & 1st St., PO Box 338, Duluth 55801	218-720-5324	3,000,000 / na	7
	A4	Gunflint Ranger D., PO Box 308, Grand Marais 55604	218-378-1750	na / na	8
	A3	Kawishiwi Ranger D., 118 S. 4th Ave. E., Ely 55731	218-365-7600	na / na	9
	A3	LaCroix Ranger D., Box 1085, Cook 55723 [90 mi N of Duluth on Hwy. 53]	218-666-5251	na / na	10
	B3	Laurentian Ranger D., 318 Forestry Rd., Aurora 55705	218-229-3371	na / na	11
	B3	Tofte Ranger D., Tofte 55615	218-663-7981	na / na	12
1	B3	**COE, Detroit District**, PO Box 1027, Detroit, MI 48231	313-226-6809	na / na	1
	B3	Duluth-Superior Harbor & Marine Mus, Canal Park, Duluth 55802	218-720-5277	na / na	1
2	C3	COE, St. Paul District, 180 E. Kellog Blvd., Rm. 1421, St. Paul 55101	612-220-0325	na / na	2
3	C1	Lac Qui Parle Lake, County Rd. 13, Watson	612-269-6303	na / na	3
4	C1	Lake Traverse, RR #2, Box 59, Wheaton 56296	612-563-4586	na / na	4
5	B2	Mississippi River Headwaters Lakes, Project, PO Box 130, Remer 56672	218-566-2306	na / na	5
6	C2	Mississippi River Pool U & L, St. A, Saint Anthony Falls, 300 S. 1st St., La Crescent 55947	507-895-6341	na / na	6
7	D3	Mississippi River Pool No. 1, 300 S. 1st St., La Crescent 55947	507-895-6341	na / na	7
8	D3	Mississippi River Pool No. 2, 300 S. 1st St., La Crescent 55947	507-895-6341	na / na	8
9	D3	Mississippi River Pool No. 3, 300 S. 1st St., La Crescent 55947	507-895-6341	na / na	9
10	D3	Mississippi River Pool No. 5, 300 S. 1st St., La Crescent 55947	507-895-6341	na / na	10
11	D3	Mississippi River Pool No. 5a, 300 S. 1st St., La Crescent 55947	507-895-6341	na / na	11
12	D3	Mississippi River Pool No. 7, 300 S. 1st St., Lacrescent 55947	507-895-6341	na / na	12
13	C1	Orwell Lake, RR #2, Box 59, Wheaton 56296	612-563-4586	na / na	13
1	C2	**USFWS Region 3**, Bishop Henry Whipple FOB, Ft. Snelling (Minneapolis) 55111 [IL, IN, IA, MI, MN, MO, OH, WI]	612-725-3519	na / na	1
2	A1	Agassiz NWR, Middle River 56737 [HQ is 11 mi N on MN Hwy. 32 & 11 mi E on CR 7 from Thief River Falls]	218-449-4115	61,450 / 1,137-1,156	2
3	C1	Big Stone NWR, 25 NW 2nd St., Ortonville 56278	612-839-3700	11,200 / 950	3
4	D2	Minnesota Valley NWR, 3815 E. 80th Street, Bloomington 55425 [exit I-494 at 34th Ave, follow signs]	612-335-2323	8,000 / 700	4
5	C1	Minnesota Waterfowl & Wetlands Mgt. Complex, Trunk Hwy. 210 E., Rt. #1, Box 76, Fergus Falls 56537	218-739-2291	na / na	5
6	B1	Detroit Lakes WMD, Rt. #3, Box 47D, Detroit Lakes 56501	218-847-4431	37,000 / 1,300	6
7	C1	Fergus Falls WMD, Rt. #1, Box 76, Fergus Falls 56537	218-739-2291	38,500 / 1,350	7
8	B1	Hamden Slough NWR, Rt. #1, Box 32, Audubon 56511	218-439-6319	2,700 / na	8
9	C2	Litchfield WMD (120 units), 971 E. Frontage Rd., Litchfield 55355 [office at Shopping Center, E on Hwy 12]	612-693-2849	30,000 / na	9
10	C1	Morris WMD (239 WPAs), Rt. #1, Box 877, Morris 56267	612-589-1001	na / na	10
11	B1	Rydell NWR (new refuge), Rt. #3, Box 47D, Detroit Lakes, MN 56537, Eskine	218-847-4431	na / na	11
12	D2	Windom WMD, Hwy. 71 South, Rt. #1, Box 273A, Windom 56101	507-831-2220	6,000 / 1,400	12
13	B2	Rice Lake NWR, Hwy. 65, Rt. #2, Box 67, McGregor 55760 [IO is 2 mi. W of East Lake Village]	218-768-2402	18,104 / na	13
14	C2	Sherburne NWR, 17076 293rd Ave., Zimmerman 55398	612-389-3323	30,000 / 1,000	14
15	B1	Tamarac NWR, HC 10, Box 145, Rochert 56578 [18 mi. NE of Detroit Lakes at jct. of CRs 26 & 29]	218-847-2641	42,724 / 1,442-1,710	15
16	D3	Upper Miss. River NW & Fish Refuge & Ref. Complex Office, 51 East 4th St., Room 101, Winona 55987	507-452-4232	200,000 / na	16
17	D3	Winona District, 51 East 4th St., Room 203, Winona 55987	507-452-4232	34,000 / na	17
1	A4	**Grand Portage National Monument**, PO Box 668, Grand Marais 55604	218-387-2788	710 / 601-1,305	1
2	D1	Pipestone National Monument, PO Box 727, Pipestone 56164	507-825-5464	283 / na	2
3	A3	Voyageurs Nat'l. Park, HRC 9, Box 600, International Falls 56649	218-283-9821	218,050 / 1,100	3
1	C3	**DNR, Div. of Parks & Recreation**, 500 Lafayette Rd., St. Paul 55155 [in MN toll free 800-652-9747]	612-296-4776	na / na	1
2	A3	Bear Head Lake SP, Star Rt. #2, Box 5700, near Ely 55731	218-365-7229	4,384 / na	2
3	D3	Beaver Creek Valley SP, Rt. #2, Box 57, near Caledonia 55921	507-724-2107	1,200 / na	3

S#	MAP	Name & Location	Phone	Acres
		Fraliard SP, 1500 Summit Ave, New Ulm 56073	507-354-8219	800 / na
5	C1	Glacial Lakes SP, Rt. #2, Box 126, near Starbuck 56381	612-239-2860	1,900 / na
6	C1			
7	B3	Jay Cooke SP, 500 East Hwy. 210, near Carlton 55718	218-384-4610	8,800 / na
8	D1	Lake Shetek SP, Rt. #1, Box 164, near Currie 56123	507-763-3256	1,200 / na
9	D2	Nerstrand Big Woods SP, 9700 170th St. East, Nerstrand 55053	507-334-8848	1,300 / na
10	C2	Sibley SP, 800 Sibley Park Rd. NE, New London 56273	612-354-2055	3,000 / na
11	C3	William O'Brien, 16821 O'Brien Trail N, Marine-on-St.Croix 55047	612-433-2421	1,330 / na
		DNR, Div. of Fish & Wildlife, 500 Lafayette St., DNR Bldg., Box 7, St. Paul 55155	612-296-6157	na / na
1	C3	Northwoods Audubon Center, Rt. #1, Box 288, Sandstone 55072	612-245-2648	535 / 1,100
2	C2	TNC, Minnesota Chapter Office, 1313 5th St., Rm. 320, Minneapolis 55414	612-379-2134	na / na
3	B1	Agassiz Dunes Preserve, contact Field Office, 2 mi. SW of Fertile	612-379-2134	435 / na
4	D2	Black Dog Fen Preserve, contact Ch. Office, off Cliff Rd., NE of I-35W & Hwy. 13, near Burnsville	612-379-2134	100 / na
5	D1	Blue Devil Valley Preserve, contact Chapter Office, near Granite Falls	612-379-2134	27 / na
6	B1	Bluestem Prairie Preserve, Western Preserves Office, RR #2, Box 240 (4 mi. SE of), Glyndon 56540	218-498-2679	2,458 / na

MISSISSIPPI NOTES

Summary

There are 45 federal, 45 state, and 2 private recreation areas or local administrative offices covered in this state chapter. Of these, 52 appear in the Information Chart and 40 are covered in the notes. The special indexes feature 4 federally designated wilderness areas and wild rivers, and 4 agency published outdoor maps.

Federal Agencies

U.S. Forest Service
Mississippi is in the Southern Region (see Georgia chapter - U.S. Forest Svc., Southern Region listing).

U.S. Army Corps of Engineers (COE)
Lower Mississippi Valley Division Office
PO Box 80
Vicksburg, MS 39181-0080   601-634-5885
The St. Louis, Missouri, and Vicksburg, Mississippi District Offices manage COE projects in the lower Mississippi valley area (see information charts).

Special COE Note:
Waterways Experiment Station
3909 Halls Ferry Road
Vicksburg, MS 39180-6199   601-634-3494

The COE maintains a unique (the only one of its kind in the world) 685-acre Waterways Experimental Station (WES) at Vicksburg. A free WES Complex Brochure describes six COE laboratories: Information Technology, Structures, Hydraulics, Environmental, Geotechnical, and the Coastal Engineering Research Center (CERC). It also depicts the two self-guided tours available to visitors and the tour stops, and includes a map of the complex.

Guided tours of the WES Complex are conducted at 10:00 a.m. and 2:00 p.m. Monday through Friday. Free self-guided unescorted tours of stops 1-3 are permitted daily and on weekends. Stops 4-6 are open from 7:45 a.m. to 4:15 p.m. weekdays only. Stop 1 is the Visitor's Facility with displays, picnic area, rest rooms, water fountain, and a drink machine.

For tour information or to request a WES brochure, contact: WES Public Affairs Office, PO Box 631, Vicksburg, MS 39181-0631 or call (601) 634-2502 during business hours. The main entrance to the WES complex is located two miles south of Interstate 20 on Halls Ferry Road in Vicksburg, Mississippi.

National Park Service
The 445 mile long Natchez Trace Parkway (S# 2) extends northeast from Natchez, Mississippi, through the northwest corner of Alabama and into central Tennessee where it ends just southwest of Nashville. The parkway is the route of the Natchez Trace National Scenic Trail (see USFS map page 18-19).

Additional NPS Locations in Mississippi
Brices Cross Roads National Battlefield Site (1 acre) c/o Natchez Trace Parkway (see chart)

Natchez National Historical Park (79 acres) (S# 4, map C1)
PO Box 1086
Natchez, MS 39121   601-446-5790

Tupelo National Battlefield (1 acre) c/o Natchez Trace Parkway (see chart)

Wilderness/Wild River Index

Wilderness Areas
Black Creek Wilderness - 4,560 acres and Leaf Wilderness - 940 acres DeSoto Natl. Forest, Black Creek RD (S# 5, map D2)
Gulf Islands Wilderness - 3,200 Gulf Islands National Seashore (S# 1, map D3)

Wild River
Black Creek DeSoto Natl. Forest, Black Creek RD (S# 5, map D2)

Outdoor Map Index

U.S. Forest Service Maps
Bienville National Forest [1983]
Delta & Homochitto National Forests
DeSoto National Forest [1985]
Holly Springs & Tombigbee NF [1985]

USGS Earth Science Information Centers
Stennis Space Center-ESIC
Bldg. 3101
Stennis Space Center, MS 39529   601-688-3544

State Agencies

Dept. of Wildlife, Fisheries and Parks (DWFP)
A Mississippi State Parks Guide (27 parks) is available free. The guide describes each area, contains a locator map, and includes information on facilities and activities at each park. Fees are charged for admission, lodging, and most activities.

A basic reference is the Hunt in Mississippi brochure, which includes WMAs and NWRs. Individual WMA brochures are available that feature local area maps and management details, including the local manager's address and telephone number.

Mississippi WMAs, their Guide map symbol numbers and coordinates, WMA name, and approximate location are listed here.

S#	MAP	NAME & LOCATION
2	B1	Anderson Tully WMA, near Mayersville
3	C2	Bienville WMA, near Morton
4	C3	Bucatunna Creek WMA, 12 mi. S of Meridian
5	A2	Calhoun County WMA, near Calhoun City
6	C2	Caney Creek WMA, near Forest
7	A3	Chickasaw WMA, near Houston
8	C2	Chickasawhay WMA, near Laurel
9	B2	Choctaw WMA, near Ackerman
10	C2	Copiah County WMA, near Hazlehurst
11	A3	Divide Section WMA, near Belmont
12	C1	Homochitto WMA, near Meadville
13	B1	Indian Bayou WA, near Rolling Fork
14	A3	John Bell Williams WMA, near Fulton
15	D3	Leaf River WMA, near McLain
16	B1	Leroy Percy WMA, near Hollandale
17	D2	Little Biloxi WMA, near McHenry
18	B2	Malmaison WMA, near Grenada
19	D2	Marion County WMA, near Columbia
20	A2	O'Keefe WA, near Lambert
21	C3	Okatibbee WA, near Collinsville
22	D2	Old River WMA, near Poplarville
23	D3	Pascagoula River WMA, near Vancleave
24	C2	Pearl River WMA, near Canton
25	D2	Red Creek WMA, near Wiggins
26	C1	Sandy Creek WMA, near Natchez
27	B1	Shipland WMA, near Mayersville
28	B1	Stoneville WMA, near Leland
29	B1	Sunflower WMA, near Holly Bluff
30	C2	Tallahala WMA, near Montrose
31	A2	Upper Sardis WMA, near Oxford
32	D2	Wolf River WMA, near Poplarville

Mississippi Forestry Commission
Suite 300, 301 Bldg.
Jackson, MS 39201   601-359-1386
There is no state forest recreation program in Mississippi.

Tourism Division
PO Box 22825
Jackson, MS 39205   601-359-3414
from out of state   1-800-647-2290

A traveler's Guide to Mississippi is available free from this office.

Private Organizations

Tribal Land Areas in Mississippi
Mississippi Band of Choctaw Indians, Choctaw Indian Reservation - Fishing, hunting, camping, boating.
Choctaw Tribal Council (S# 1, map B2/B3)
Route 7, Box 21
Philadelphia, MS 39350   601-656-5251

Mississippi Economic Council
(State Chamber of Commerce)
PO Box 23276   Phone 601-969-0022
Jackson, MS 39225-3276   Fax 601-353-0247

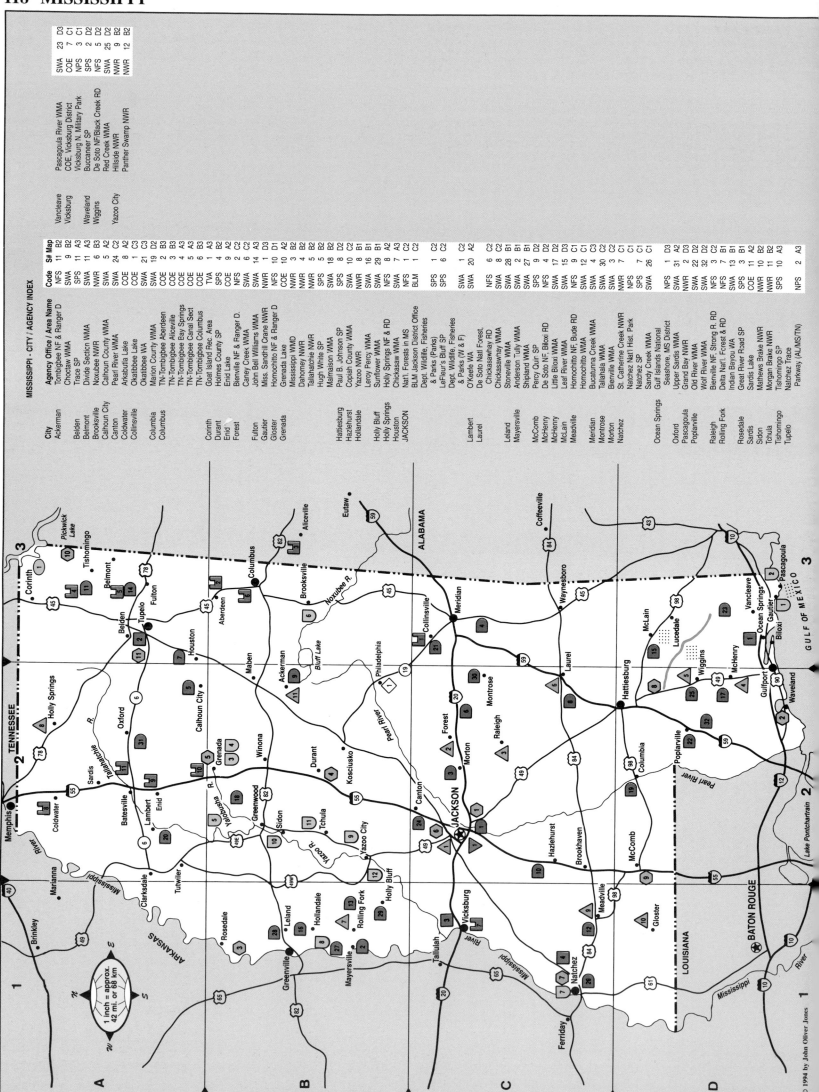

★ INFORMATION CHART ★

AGENCY/MAP LEGEND ... INITIALS, MAP SYMBOLS, COLOR CODES

U.S. Forest Service Supervisor & Ranger Dist. Offices .. NFS
U.S. Army Corps of Engineers Rec. Areas & Offices .. COE
USFWS National Wildlife Refuges & Offices .... NWR
National Park Service Parks & other NPS Sites ...... NPS
Bureau of Land Management Rec. Areas & Offices .. BLM
Tennessee Valley Authority Offices & Sites .... TVA
State Parks (also see State Agency notes) .... SPS
State Wildlife Areas (also see State Agency notes) .. SWA
Private Preserves, Nature Centers & Tribal Lands .
The Wild Rivers —— and Wilderness Areas

INFORMATION CHART LEGEND - SYMBOLS & LETTER CODES

■ means YES & □ means Yes with disability provisions
sp means spring, March through May
S means Summer, June through August
F means Fall, September through November
W means Winter, December through February
T means Two (2) or Three (3) Seasons
A means All Four (4) Seasons
na means Not Applicable or Not Available
Note: empty or blank spaces in the chart mean NO
That symbol is not shown on the map.
Refer to yellow block on page 7 (top right) for location name and address abbreviations. If a symbol number has a star ★

S#	MAP	LOCATION NAME (state initials if more than one) with ADDRESS and/or LOCATION DATA	TELEPHONE	ACRES / ELEVATION
1	C2	National Forests in Mississippi (Supervisor), FOB, 100 W. Capitol St., Suite 1141, Jackson 39269	601-965-4391	1,100,000 / na
2	C2	Bienville Nat'l. Forest & Ranger D., Rt. #2, Box 268A, Forest 39074	601-469-3811	85,700 / na
3	C2	Bienville NF, Strong River RD, 214 Mimosa Drive, PO Box 217, Raleigh 39153	601-782-4271	92,400 / na
4	D2	De Soto Nat'l. Forest, Biloxi RD, Rt. #1, Box 62, McHenry 39561	601-928-5291	117,500 / na
5	D2	De Soto NF, Black Creek Ranger D., 1436 W. Border & Frontage Rd., PO Box 248, Wiggins 39577	601-928-4422	232,900 / na
6	C2	De Soto NF, Chickasawhay Ranger D., 488 S. Magnolia St., PO Box 426, Laurel 39440	601-428-0594	150,300 / na
7	B1	Delta Nat'l. Forest D., Sharkey-Ag. Bldg., 402 Hwy. 61 North, Rolling Fork 39159	601-873-6256	59,500 / na
8	A2	Holly Springs NF & Ranger D., Hwy. 78 East, PO Box 400, Holly Springs 38635	601-252-2633	126,300 / na
9	C1	Homochitto NF, Bude Ranger D., Rt. #1, Meadville 39653	601-384-5876	91,600 / na
10	D1	Homochitto Nat'l. Forest & Ranger D., Hwy. 24E & Magnolia Street, PO Box 398, Gloster 39638	601-225-4281	97,200 / na
11	B2	Tombigbee Nat'l. Forest & Ranger D., Rt. #1, Box 98A, Ackerman 39735	601-285-3264	86,600 / na
1	C3	COE, Mobile District, 109 St. Joseph St., PO Box 2288, Mobile, AL 36628	205-694-3720	na / na
2	B3	Okatibbee Lake, PO Box 98, Collinsville 39325	601-626-8431	na / na
3	B3	Tennessee-Tombigbee Aberdeen, 3606 West Plymouth Rd., Columbus 39701	601-327-2142	na / na
4	A3	Tennessee-Tombigbee Aliceville, 3606 West Plymouth Rd., Columbus 39701	601-327-2142	na / na
5	A3	Tennessee-Tombigbee Bay Springs, 3606 West Plymouth Rd., Columbus 39701	601-327-2142	na / na
6	B3	Tennessee-Tombigbee Canal Section, 3606 West Plymouth Rd., Columbus 39701	601-327-2142	na / na
7	B3	Tennessee-Tombigbee Columbus, 3606 West Plymouth Rd., Columbus 39701	601-631-5286	na / na
8	C1	COE, Vicksburg District, 3515 I-20 Frontage Rd., Vicksburg 39181	601-562-6261	na / na
9	A2	Arkabutla Lake, Route 1, Box 572, Coldwater 38618	601-563-4571	na / na
10	A2	Enid Lake, PO Box 10, Enid 38927	601-226-5911	na / na
11	A2	Grenada Lake, Box 903, Grenada 38901	601-563-4531	na / na
	A2	Sardis Lake, PO Drawer 186, Sardis 38666		
1	D3	Mississippi Sandhill Crane NWR, 7200 Crane Lane, Gautier 39553	601-497-6322	20,000 / 0-25
2	D3	Grand Bay NWR, [new NWR being developed], Pascagoula [15 mi SE of MS Sandhill Crane NWR]	601-497-6322	12,000 / 0-15
3	B2	Mississippi WMD, Hwy. 8 West, PO Box 1070, Grenada 38901	601-226-8286	40,000 / 300
4	B2	Dahomey NWR, PO Box 1070, Grenada 38901	601-226-8286	na / na
5	B2	Tallahatchie NWR, PO Box 1070, Grenada 38901	601-226-8286	80 / na
6	B3	Noxubee NWR, Rt. #1, Box 142, Brooksville 39739	601-323-5548	46,590 / 220
7	C1	St. Catherine Creek NWR, PO Box 18639, Natchez 39122	601-442-6696	na / na
8	B1	Yazoo NWR, Rt. #1, Box 286, Hollandale 38748	601-839-2638	12,941 / 90-105
9	B1	Hillside NWR, NE of Yazoo City	601-839-2638	15,406 / 95-110
10	B1	Mathews Brake NWR, near Sidon	601-839-2638	2,418 / 110-120
11	B1	Morgan Brake NWR, Tchula [3 mi N of Tchula]	601-839-2638	7,301 / 95-110
12	C1	Panther Swamp NWR, Route 5, Box 25, Yazoo City 39194 [SE of Yazoo City]	601-746-5060	28,581 / 85-100
1	D3	Gulf Islands National Seashore, MS, 3500 Park Rd., Ocean Springs 39564	601-875-9057	400 / na
2	A3	Natchez Trace Parkway (ALMS/TN), RR #1, NT-143, Tupelo 38801 [extends through NW AL toward Nashville in TN]	601-680-4025	52,738 / 700-1,100
3	C1	Vicksburg Nat'l. Military Park, 3201 Clay Street, Vicksburg 39180	601-636-0583	1,620 / na
4	C1	Natchez National Historical Park, 504 S. Canal St., PO Box 1208, Natchez 39121	601-442-7047	80 / na
1		BLM Eastern States Office, 7450 Boston Blvd., Springfield, VA 22153	703-440-1200	na / na
1	C2	BLM Jackson District Office, 411 Briarwood Dr., Suite 404, Jackson 39206	601-977-5400	na / na
1	A3	TVA - Southern District, 170 Office Svc. Whse. Annex, Muscle Shoals, AL 35660 [S of Florence on US 43 E of TN R.]	205-386-2221	na / na
1		Goat Island Recreation Area, E of Corinth [TN Hwy. 128]	205-386-2223	na / na
1	C2	Dept. Wildlife, Fisheries & Parks (Parks), 2906 N. State St., Southport Mall, PO Box 451, Jackson 39205	601-364-2120	na / na
2	D2	Buccaneer SP, 1150 S. Beach Blvd., Waveland 39576	601-467-3822	400 / na
3	B1	Great River Road SP, Hwy. 35 N of Greenville, PO Box 292, Rosedale 38769	601-759-6762	730 / na
4	B2	Holmes County SP, 4 mi. S of Durant, Rt. #1, Box 153, Durant 39063	601-653-3351	450 / na
5	B2	Hugh White SP, 5 mi. E of Grenada, PO Box 725, Grenada 38901	601-226-4934	1,260 / na
6	C1	LeFleur's Bluff SP, I-55 exit 98B, 2140 Riverside Dr., Jackson 39216	601-987-3923	300 / na
7	C1	Natchez SP, 10 mi. N of Natchez, 230 B Wickcliff Rd., Natchez 39120	601-442-2658	3,410 / na

Column group at right: FACILITIES, SERVICES, RECREATION OPPORTUNITIES & CONVENIENCES

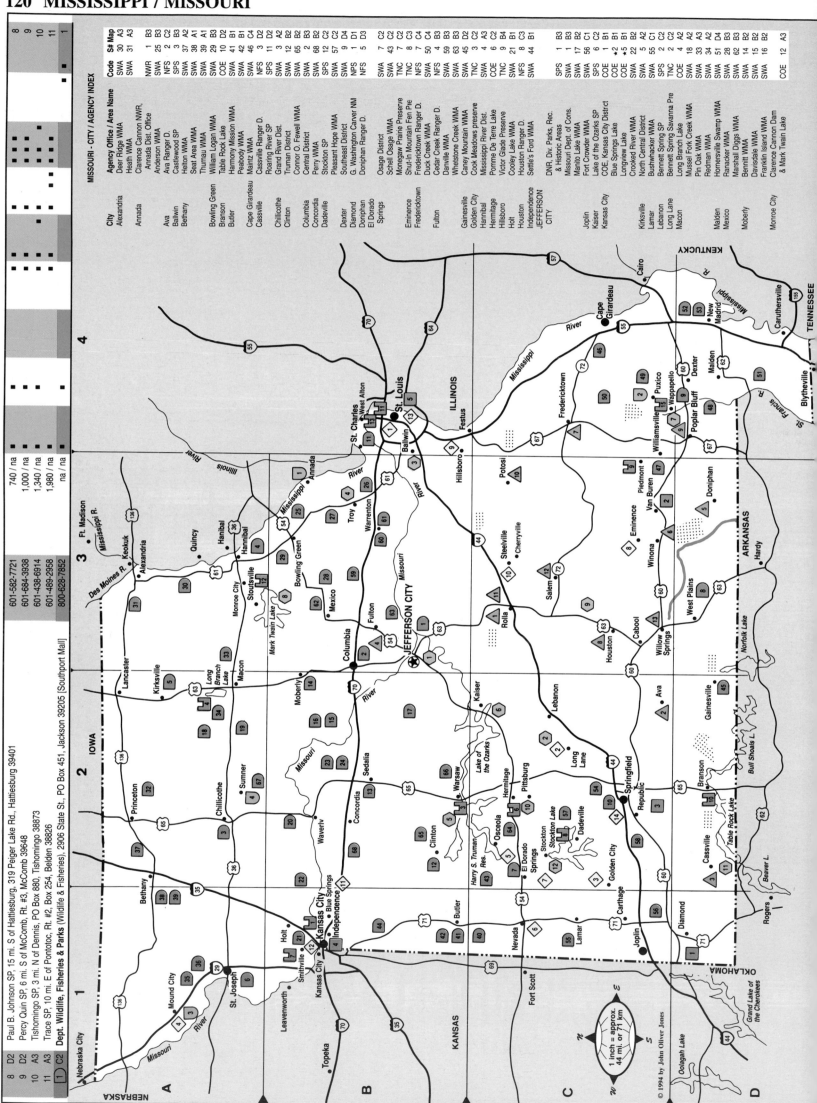

Continued Mississippi State Parks listing:

#	Map	Name / Location	Acres / na	Phone
8	D2	Paul B. Johnson SP, 15 mi. S of Hattiesburg, 319 Peiger Lake Rd., Hattiesburg 39401	740 / na	601-582-7721
9	D2	Percy Quin SP, 6 mi. S of McComb, Rt. #3, McComb 39648	1,000 / na	601-684-3938
10	A3	Tishomingo SP, 3 mi. N of Dennis, PO Box 880, Tishomingo 38873	1,340 / na	601-436-6914
11	A3	Trace SP, 10 mi. E of Pontotoc, Rt. #2, Box 254, Belden 38826	1,980 / na	601-489-2958
	C2	Dept. Wildlife, Fisheries & Parks (Wildlife & Fisheries), 2906 State St., PO Box 451, Jackson 39205 [Southport Mall]	na / na	800-628-7852

MISSOURI - CITY / AGENCY INDEX

City	Agency Office / Area Name	Code	S#	Map
Alexandria	Deer Ridge WMA	SWA	30	A3
	Heath WMA	SWA	31	A3
Annada	Clarence Cannon NWR, Annada Dist. Office	NWR	1	B3
		SWA	25	B3
Anderson	Anderson WMA	NFS	2	C2
Ava	Ava Ranger D.	SPS	3	B3
Ballwin	Castlewood SP	SWA	37	A2
Bethany	Helton WMA	SWA	38	A1
	Seat Area WMA	SWA	39	A1
	Thurnau WMA	SWA	29	A1
Bowling Green	William Logan WMA	COE	10	D2
Branson	Table Rock Lake	SWA	41	B1
Butler	Harmony Mission WMA	SWA	42	C1
	Peabody WMA	SWA	46	C4
Cape Girardeau	Maintz WMA	SWA	11	D2
Cassville	Cassville Ranger D.	SPS	3	A2
	Roaring River SP	SWA	12	B2
Chillicothe	Grand River Dist.	SWA	65	B3
Clinton	Truman District	SWA	2	B2
Columbia	Connor O. Fewell WMA	SWA	68	C2
Concordia	Central District	SPS	57	C2
Dadeville	Perry WMA	SWA	9	D4
Dexter	Stockton SP	NPS	1	D1
Diamond	Pleasant Hope WMA	NFS	5	D3
Doniphan	G. Washington Carver NM			
	Southeast District			
El Dorado Springs	Doniphan Ranger D.			
Eminence	Osage WMA	SWA	7	C2
Fredericktown	Schell Osage WMA	TNC	43	C2
Fulton	Monegaw Prairie Preserve	TNC	8	C3
Gainesville	Shut-In Mountain Fen Pre	NFS	7	C4
Golden City	Fredericktown Ranger D.	SWA	50	C4
Hannibal	Duck Creek WMA	NFS	4	B3
Hermitage	Cedar Creek Ranger D.	SWA	59	B3
Hillsboro	Danville WMA	SWA	63	B3
Holt	Whetstone Creek WMA	SWA	45	D2
Houston	Caney Mountain WMA	TNC	3	C2
Independence	Cook Meadows preserve	COE	6	C2
	Mississippi River Dist.	TNC	6	B4
	Pomme De Terre Lake	SWA	21	B1
	Victor Glade Preserve	NFS	8	C3
	Cooley Lake WMA	SWA	44	B1
	Houston Ranger D.			
	Settle's Ford Lake			
JEFFERSON CITY	DNR, Div. Parks, Rec. & Historic Areas	SPS	1	B3
	Missouri Dept. of Cons.	SWA	1	B2
Joplin	Manito Lake WMA	SWA	17	C1
Kaiser	Fort Crowder WMA	SPS	56	C1
Kansas City	Lake of the Ozarks SP	SPS	6	C2
	COE, Kansas City District	COE	1	B1
	Blue Springs Lake	COE	*2	B2
	Longview Lake	COE	*5	B1
Kirksville	Crooked River WMA	SWA	22	B2
Lamar	North Central District	SWA	55	C1
Lebanon	Bushwhacker WMA	TNC	2	C2
Long Lane	Bennett Spring SP	COE	4	A2
Macon	Bennett Spring Savanna Pre	SWA	18	A2
	Long Branch Lake	SWA	34	A2
Malden	Mussel Fork Creek WMA	SWA	51	D4
Mexico	Pin Oak WMA	SWA	62	B2
Moberly	Redman WMA	SWA	14	B2
	Homersville Swamp WMA	SWA	16	B2
Monroe City	Ranacker WMA	COE	12	A3
	Marshall Diggs WMA			
	Benitt WMA			
	Davisdale WMA			
	Franklin Island WMA			
	Clarence Cannon Dam & Mark Twain Lake			

© 1994 by John Oliver Jones

1 inch = approx. 44 mi. or 71 km

MISSOURI NOTES

Summary

There are 39 federal, 83 state, and 15 private recreation areas or local administrative offices covered in this state chapter. Of these, 61 appear in the Information Chart and 76 are covered in the notes. The special indexes feature 9 federally designated wilderness areas and wild rivers, and one agency published outdoor map.

Federal Agencies

U.S. Forest Service

Missouri is in the Eastern Region (see Wisconsin chapter - U.S. Forest Svc., Eastern Region listing).

National Park Service

Additional NPS Locations in Missouri

Harry S. Truman National Historic Site (1.41 acres)
(S# 4, map B1)
223 North Main Street
Independence, MO 64050   816-254-9929

Jefferson National Expansion Memorial (190 acres)
(S# 5, map B4)
11 North 4th Street
St. Louis, MO 63102   314-425-4465

USGS Earth Science Information Center

USGS Rolla-ESIC
1400 Independence Road
Rolla, MO 65401   314-341-0851

State Agencies

Dept. of Conservation (DC)

PO Box 180
Jefferson City, MO 65102-0180   314-751-4115
The Missouri Fisheries, Wildlife, and Forestry Divisions operate under the DC.

Division of Parks, Recreation and Historic Preservation (DPRHP)

A Missouri State Parks Guide (45 parks) is incorporated in this state chapter. It describes each area, and includes information on facilities and activities. There are also brochures on individual parks. There is a camping fee and off-season fees are lower.

State Forester

Missouri Dept. of Conservation
2901 West Truman Blvd.
PO Box 180
Jefferson City, MO 65102   314-751-411E
Contact the State Forester for recreation literature.

Wildlife Division

The Information Chart lists wildlife agency district offices. There are 164 offices. These lands are owned or leased and comprise more than 400,000 acres open to hunting in season, and other forms of outdoor recreation as appropriate. Check with the nearest district office or agency headquarters for specific information. The 55 larger WMAs, their map symbol numbers and coordinates, are listed below.

S#	MAP	WMA NAME & LOCATION
14	B2	Bennett WMA, Moberly
15	B2	Davisdale WMA, Moberly
16	B2	Franklin Island WMA, Moberly
17	B2	Manito Lake WMA, Jefferson City
18	A2	Mussel Fork Creek WMA, Macon
19	A2	Prairie Home WMA, Sumner
20	B2	Bunch Hollow WMA, Waverly
21	B1	Cooley Lake WMA, Holt
22	B2	Crooked River WMA, Kansas City
23	B2	Grand Pass WMA, Sedalia
24	B2	Little Compton WMA, Sedalia
25	B3	Anderson WMA, Annada
26	B3	B.K. Leach WMA (2 tracts), Troy
27	B3	Dupont WMA, Troy
28	B3	Ranacker WMA, Mexico
29	B3	William Logan WMA, Bowling Green
30	A3	Deer Ridge WMA, Alexandria
31	A3	Heath WMA, Alexandria
32	A2	Locust Creek, Princeton
33	A3	Pin Oak WMA, Macon
34	A2	Redman WMA, Macon
35	A1	Bob Brown WMA, Mound City
36	A1	Brickyard Hill WMA, St. Joseph
37	A2	Helton WMA, Bethany
38	A1	Seat Area WMA, Bethany
39	A1	Thurnau WMA, Bethany
40	C1	Four Rivers WMA, Nevada
41	B1	Harmony Mission WMA, Butler
42	B1	Peabody WMA, Butler
43	C2	Schell Osage WMA, ElDorado Springs
44	B1	Settle's Ford WMA, Independence
45	D2	Caney Mountain WMA, Gainesville
46	C4	Maintz WMA, Cape Girardeau
47	C3	Peck Ranch WMA, Van Buren
48	D4	Coon Island WMA, Poplar Bluff
49	C4	Crowley's Ridge WMA, Puxico
50	C4	Duck Creek WMA, Fredericktown

S#	MAP	WMA NAME & LOCATION
51	D4	Hornersville Swamp WMA, Malden
52	D4	Seven Island WMA, New Madrid
53	D4	Ten Mile Pond WMA, New Madrid
54	C2	Bois D'Arc WMA, Springfield
55	C1	Bushwhacker WMA, Lamar
56	C1	Fort Crowder WMA, Joplin
57	C2	Pleasant Hope WMA, Dadeville
58	C1	Talbot WMA, Republic
59	B3	Danville WMA, Fulton
60	B3	Little Lost Creek WMA, Warrenton
61	B3	Loutre Lake WMA, Warrenton
62	B3	Marshall Diggs WMA, Mexico
63	B3	Whetstone Creek WMA, Fulton
64	C2	Birdsong WMA, Osceola
65	B2	Connor O. Fewell WMA, Clinton
66	B2	Big Buffalo Creek WMA, Warsaw
67	A2	Lamine River WMA, Sumner
68	B2	Perry WMA, Concordia

The DC has a free catalog of available publications. Fishing and hunting regulations are not listed in the catalog. A monthly magazine, *Missouri Conservationist*, is available by subscription for $5 per year out of state, free in state.

Division of Tourism

Truman State Office Bldg.
PO Box 1055
Jefferson City, MO 65102   314-751-4133

The official Missouri Highway and Transportation Commission road map is available. Another road map, "Discover Outdoor Missouri," has an index to hundreds of public areas, with each site located by coordinates. Letter codes are used to indicate activities and available facilities.

Private Organizations

TNC-Missouri Chapter Office

A new 212-page book, *Discover Natural Missouri* ($12.95 plus $150 postage), is available at the TNC office or from local book stores in Missouri. It describes 34 TNC preserves in depth. Selected preserves are listed here and shown on the Guide map.

S#	MAP	PRESERVE NAME & LOCATION
2	C2	Bennett Spring Savanna Pre., Long Lane
3	C2	Cook Meadows Preserve, Golden City
4	A1	J.C. McCormack Loess Mounds, Mound City
5	C2	Lichen Glade Preserve, Osceola
6	C1	Marmaton River Bottoms Wet Prairie, Nevada
7	C2	Monegaw Prairie Pres, El Dorado Springs
8	C3	Shut-In Mountain Fen Preserve, Eminence
9	B4	Victor Glade Preserve, Hillsboro
10	C3	Zahorsky Woods Preserve, Steelville

ANCA Locations in Missouri

Burr Oak Woods Nature Center (S# 11, map B1)
1401 Park Road
Blue Springs, MO 64015   816-228-3766

Lakeside Nature Center (S# 12, map B1)
5600 East Gregory (Swope Park)
Kansas City, MO 64132   816-444-4656

St. Louis Zoological Park (S# 13, map B4)
Forest Park
St. Louis, MO 63110   314-781-0900

Springfield Nature Center (S# 14, map C2)
4600 South Chrisman
Springfield, MO 65804   417-882-4237

Missouri Chamber of Commerce
428 E. Capitol Ave.
PO Box 149
Jefferson City, MO 65102   Phone 314-634-3511
Fax 314-634-8855

Wilderness/Wild River Index

Wilderness Areas

Mark Twain National Forest (S# 1, map C3)
Bell Mountain Wilderness - 8,817 acres
Devils Backbone Wilderness - 6,595 acres
Hercules-Glades Wilderness - 12,314
Irish Wilderness - 16,500 acres
Paddy Creek Wilderness - 6,728 acres
Piney Creek Wilderness - 8,087 acres
Rockpile Mountain Wilderness - 4,089 acres

Mingo NWR (S# 2, map C4)
Mingo Wilderness - 7,730 acres

Wild River

Eleven Point Wild River
Mark Twain National Forest (S# 1, map C3)

Outdoor Map Index

U.S. Forest Service Maps

Mark Twain National Forest [1989]
Scale: 1 inch = 4.0 miles (1 cm = 2.5 km)
Size: 22x26 inches (56x66 cm)

Missouri City/Agency Index - continued

City	Agency Office / Area Name	Code	S#	Map
Mound City	Squaw Creek NWR	NWR	3	A1
	Bob Brown WMA	SWA	35	A1
	Jameson C. McCormack Loess Mounds	TNC	4	A1
Nevada	Four Rivers WMA	SWA	40	C1
	Marmaton River Bottoms Wet Prairie	TNC	6	C1
New Madrid	Seven Island WMA	SWA	52	D4
	Ten Mile Pond WMA	SWA	53	D4
Osceola	Birdsong WMA	SWA	64	C2
	Lichen Glade Preserve	TNC	5	C2
Piedmont	Clearwater Lake	COE	9	C3
Pittsburg	Pomme de Terre SP	SPS	9	C2
Poplar Bluff	Poplar Bluff Ranger D.	NFS	9	D4
	Coon Island WMA	SWA	48	D4
Potosi	Potosi Ranger D.	NFS	10	C3
Princeton	Locust Creek	SWA	32	A2
Puxico	Mingo NWR	NWR	2	C4
	Crowley's Ridge WMA	SWA	49	C4
Republic	Wilson's Creek Nat'l. Battlefield	NPS	3	C2
	Talbot WMA	SWA	58	C1
Rolla	Mark Twain Nat'l. Forest	NFS	1	C3
	Rolla Ranger D.	NFS	11	C3
Salem	Salem Ranger D.	NFS	12	C3
	Montauk SP	SPS	9	C3
Sedalia	West Central District	SWA	13	B2
	Grand Pass WMA	SWA	23	B2
	Little Compton WMA	SWA	24	B2
Smithville	Smithville Lake	COE	7	B1
Springfield	Southwest District	SWA	10	C2
	Bois D'Arc WMA	SWA	54	C2
St. Charles	St. Louis District	SWA	11	B4
St. Joseph	Northwest District	SWA	6	A1
	Brickyard Hill WMA	SWA	36	A1
St. Louis	COE, St. Louis District	COE	1	B4
	TNC Missouri Chapter Off	TNC	1	B4
Steelville	Zahorsky Woods Preserve	TNC	10	C3
Stockton	Stockton SP	COE	8	B2
Stoutsville	Mark Twain SP	SPS	8	B3
Sumner	Swan Lake NWR	NWR	8	A2
	Prairie Home WMA	SWA	19	A2
	Lamine River WMA	SWA	67	B2
Troy	Cuivre River SP	SPS	4	B3
	B.K. Leach WMA	SWA	26	B3
	Dupont WMA	SWA	27	B2
Van Buren	Ozark N. Scenic Riverways	NPS	5	C3
	Peck Ranch WMA	SWA	47	C3
Wappapello	Wappapello Lake	COE	15	C4
Warrenton	Little Lost Creek WMA	SWA	60	B3
	Loutre Lake WMA	SWA	61	B4
Warsaw	Harry S Truman Dam & Res	COE	3	B2
	Harry S Truman SP	SPS	5	B2
	Big Buffalo Creek WMA	SWA	66	B2
Waverly	Bunch Hollow WMA	SWA	20	B2
West Alton	Riverlands - Upper	COE	13	B4
	Riverlands - Lower	COE	14	B4
West Plains	Ozark District	SWA	7	D3
Williamsville	Lake Wappapello SP	SPS	8	D4
Willow Springs	Willow Springs Ranger D.	NFS	13	C3
Winona	Eleven Point Ranger D.	NFS	6	C3

★ INFORMATION CHART ★

INFORMATION CHART LEGEND - SYMBOLS & LETTER CODES

■ means **YES** & □ means **Yes** with disability provisions

- **sp** means **spring**, March through May
- **S** means **Summer**, June through August
- **F** means **Fall**, September through November
- **W** means **Winter**, December through February
- **T** means **Two** (2) or **Three** (3) Seasons
- **A** means **All Four** (4) Seasons
- **na** means **Not Applicable** or **Not Available**

Note: empty or blank spaces in the chart mean **NO**

Note: Refer to yellow block on page 7 (top right) for location name and address abbreviations. If a symbol number has a star ★ that symbol is not shown on the map.

AGENCY/MAP LEGEND . . . INITIALS, MAP SYMBOLS, COLOR CODES

- U.S. Forest Service Supervisor & Ranger Dist. Offices . . . NFS
- U.S. Army Corps of Engineers Rec. Areas & Offices . . . COE
- USFWS National Wildlife Refuges & Offices . . . NWR
- National Park Service Parks & other NPS Sites . . . NPS
- Bureau of Land Management Rec. Areas & Offices . . . BLM
- Bureau of Reclamation Rec. Areas & Reg. Offices . . . BOR
- State Parks (also see State Agency notes) . . . SPS
- State Wildlife Areas (also see State Agency notes) . . . SWA
- Private Preserves, Nature Centers & Tribal Lands
- The Wild Rivers . . . and Wilderness Areas

S#	MAP	LOCATION NAME (state initials if more than one) with ADDRESS and/or LOCATION DATA	TELEPHONE	ACRES / ELEVATION
		Mark Twain National Forest (Supervisor), 401 Fair Grounds Rd., Rolla 65401	314-364-4621	1,500,000 / 600-1,200
1	C3	Ava Ranger D., Business Rt. 5 South, Ava 65608	417-683-4428	141,000 / 600-1,200
2	C2	Cassville Ranger D., Hwy. 248 East, Cassville 65625	417-847-2144	75,000 / 600-1,200
3	D2	Cedar Creek Ranger D., Rt. F & Airport Rd., Fulton 65251	314-642-6726	90,000 / 600-1,200
4	B3	Doniphan Ranger D., 1104 Walnut, Doniphan 63935	314-996-2153	150,000 / 600-1,200
5	D3	Eleven Point Ranger D., Hwy. 19 North, Rt. #1, Box 182, Winona 65588	314-325-4233	172,000 / 600-1,200
6	C3	Fredericktown Ranger D., Hwys. 72 & 00, Fredericktown 63645	314-783-7225	80,000 / 600-1,200
7	C4	Houston Ranger D., 104 Hwy. 63 South, Houston 65483	417-967-4194	84,000 / 600-1,200
8	D3	Poplar Bluff Ranger D., 1420 Maud, Poplar Bluff 63901	314-785-1475	150,000 / 600-1,200
9	D4	Potosi Ranger D., Hwy. 8 West, Potosi 63664	314-438-5427	200,000 / 600-1,200
10	C3	Rolla Ranger D., Bridge School Rd. & Kings Highway, Rolla 65401	314-364-4501	110,000 / 600-1,200
11	C3	Salem Ranger D., 1221 S. Main, Salem 65560	314-729-6656	189,000 / 600-1,200
12	C3	Willow Springs Ranger D., Old Springfield Rd., Willow Springs 63793	417-469-3155	100,000 / 600-1,200
13		**COE, Kansas City District**, 601 E. 12th St., 716 Federal Bldg., Kansas City 64134		
★2	B1	Blue Springs Lake, 10698 E. 109th St, Kansas City 64134	816-426-6816	na / na
3	B2	Harry S. Truman Dam & Reservoir, Route 2, Box 29A, Warsaw 65355	816-438-7317	na / na
4	A2	Long Branch Lake, Rt. #4, Box 6, Macon 63552	816-385-2108	na / na
★5	B1	Longview Lake, 10698 E. 109th St., Kansas City 64134	816-761-6194	na / na
6	B1	Pomme De Terre Lake, Route 2, Box 2160, Hermitage 65668	417-745-6411	na / na
7	B1	Smithville Lake, 16311 DD Hwy., Smithville 64089	816-532-0174	na / na
8	C2	Stockton Lake, PO Box 610, Stockton 65785	417-276-3113	na / na
		COE, Little Rock District, PO Box 867, Little Rock, AR 72203	501-324-5673	na / na
9	C3	Clearwater Lake, RR 3, Box 3559 D, Piedmont 63957	417-223-7777	na / na
10	D2	Table Rock Lake, PO Box 1109, Branson 65616	417-334-4101	na / na
11	B4	COE, St. Louis District, 1222 Spruce St., St. Louis 63103	314-331-8622	na / na
12	A3	Clarence Cannon Dam & Mark Twain La., RR 2, Box 20A, Monroe City 63456	314-735-4097	na / na
13	B4	Riverlands - Upper, PO Box 337, West Alton 63386	314-899-0405	na / na
★14	B4	Riverlands - Lower, PO Box 337, West Alton 63386	314-899-0405	na / na
15	C4	Wappapello Lake, HC2 2, Box 2349, Wappapello 63966	314-222-8562	na / na
		Mark Twain NWR Complex, 1704 N. 24th St., Quincy, IL 62301	217-224-8580	na / na
1	B3	Clarence Cannon NWR, Annada Dist. O, PO Box 88, Annada 63330 [from Annada, 1 mi E off Hwy. 79, follow signs]	314-847-2333	3,750 / 410-450
2	C4	Mingo NWR, RR #1, Box 103, Puxico 63960	314-222-3589	22,000 / 300-400
3	A1	Squaw Creek NWR, PO Box 101, Mound City 64470 [from Mound City I-29 S 4.5 mi, exit 79, Hwy 159 W to NWR & HQ]	816-442-3187	7,180 / 850
4	A2	Swan Lake NWR, Rt. #1, Box 29A, Sumner 64681 [2 mi S of Sumner]	816-856-3323	10,600 / na
1	D1	**George Washington Carver National Monument**, PO Box 38, Diamond 64840	417-325-4151	210 / 1,080
2	B3	Ozark Nat'l. Scenic Riverways, PO Box 490, Van Buren 63965 [Hwy. 60 in Van Buren]	314-323-4236	80,788 / na
3	D2	Wilson's Creek Nat'l. Battlefield, Rt. #1, Box 75, Republic 65738	417-732-2662	1,750 / 1,150
		DNR, Div. Parks, Recreation & Historic Preservation, 205 Jefferson, PO Box 176, Jefferson City 65102	800-334-6946	na / na
1	B3	Bennett Spring SP, on Hwy. 64, 12 mi. W of Lebanon 65536	417-532-4338	3,064 / na
2	B3	Castlewood SP, St. Louis County, Kiefer Creek Rd., Ballwin 63011	314-527-6481	1,790 / na
3	B3	Cuivre River SP, on Hwy. 47, 3 mi. E of Troy 63379	314-528-7247	6,250 / na
4	B3	Harry S. Truman SP, off Hwy. 7, on Hwy. UU, W of Warsaw 65355	816-438-7711	1,440 / na
5	C2	Lake of the Ozarks SP, Camden & Miller Cos., E off Hwy. 42, Kaiser 65047	314-348-2694	17,152 / na
6	D4	Lake Wappapello SP, Hwy. 67 12 mi. N of Poplar Bluff, or on Hwy. 172, 9 mi. E of Williamsville 63967	314-297-3232	1,854 / na
7	B3	Mark Twain SP, Monroe County, Stoutsville 65283	314-565-3440	2,733 / na
8	C3	Montauk SP, 21 mi. SW of Salem 65560	314-545-2201	1,193 / na
9	C3	Pomme de Terre SP, Pittsburg 65724	417-852-4291	734 / na
10	D2	Roaring River SP, 8 mi. S of Cassville 65625	417-847-2539	3,513 / na
11	C2	Stockton SP, S of Stockton on Hwy. 215, near Dadeville 65635	417-276-4259	2,176 / na
1	R3	Missouri Dept. of Conservation, 2901 W. Truman Blvd., PO Box 180, Jefferson City 65102	314-751-4115	na / na

S#	MAP	District	Phone		Map #
3	A2	Grand River District (S# 20-24), Rt. #1, Box 122 B, Chillicothe 64601 [Hwy. 36, 11 mi E of Chillicothe]	816-646-6122	na / na	3
4	A3	Mississippi River Dist. (S# 25-29), Box 428, Hannibal 63401 [W of Hannibal]	314-248-2530	na / na	4
5	A2	North Central District (S# 30-34), 2500 Halliburton, Kirksville 63501	816-785-2420	na / na	5
6	A1	Northwest District (S# 35-39), 3408 Ashland, St. Joseph 64506	816-387-2360	na / na	6
7	C2	Osage District (S# 40-44), 722 E. Hwy. 54, PO Box 106, El Dorado Springs 64744	417-876-5226	na / na	7
8	D3	Ozark District (S# 45-47), PO Box 138, West Plains 65775	417-256-7161	na / na	8
9	D4	Southeast District (S# 48-53), 1207 North One Mile Rd., Dexter 63841	314-624-7483	na / na	9
10	C2	Southwest District (S# 54-58), 2630 N. Mayfair, Springfield 65803	417-895-6880	na / na	10
11	B4	St. Louis District (S# 59-63), August Busch Memorial Wildlife Area, 2360 Hwy. D, St. Charles 63303	314-441-4554	na / na	11
12	B2	Truman District (S# 64-65), PO Box 250, Clinton 64735	816-885-6981	na / na	12
13	B2	West Central District (S# 66-68), 1014 Thompson Blvd., Sedalia 65301	816-826-2192	na / na	13
◇	B4	TNC Missouri Chapter Office, 2800 S. Brentwood Blvd., St. Louis 63144 [Chart info for preserves listed in notes]	314-968-1105		1

MONTANA NOTES

Summary

There are 120 federal, 66 state and 16 private recreation areas or local administrative offices covered in this state chapter. Of these, 178 appear in the Information Chart and 24 are covered in the notes. The special indexes feature 18 federally designated wilderness areas and wild rivers, and 132 agency published outdoor maps.

U.S. Forest Service

The Aerial Fire Depot Smokejumpers Visitors Center and facilities are located a few miles north of Missoula off U.S. Hwy. 93 (also U.S. 10 & SR 200) and adjacent to Johnson Bell Field (the Missoula Airport). The Center is open to visitors from Memorial to Labor Day and from 8 a.m. to 4 p.m. Exhibits, videos, bookstore, and forest interpreter guided tours of the facilities are available. The phone number is (406) 329-4934.

Lolo Pass Visitors Center (see Idaho map and chart S# 23), Powell RD of the Clearwater National Forest) ◇

Hungry Horse Visitors Center (S# 23 Hungry Horse RD of the Flathead NF), Hungry Horse Road, Hungry Horse, MT
406-387-5243

VC is jointly operated with the Bureau of Reclamation. Views of dam and reservoir. Conducted tours of the Hungry Horse dam are available. Exhibits tell the story of water and the Hungry Horse watershed, from falling rain or snow to water flow to the Pacific Ocean via the Columbia River.

Madison River Earthquake Area Visitors Center (also see Hebgen Lake Ranger District, S# 31, map C2)
Hebgen Lake Road
W. Yellowstone, MT
406-646-7369

Orientation to recreation opportunities in the Yellowstone area. Interpretation of geological features with an emphasis on earthquakes and story of the Madison River Earthquake.

Nine Mile Remount Depot Visitors Center (S# 50, Ninemile Ranger D of the Lolo NF), A historic Forest Service Ranger Station and open May-October. Contemporary and historic use of pack stock is interpreted. Demonstrations of pack animal use and minimum impact camping, especially wilderness camping, are available.

USFWS National Wildlife Refuges

The Medicine Lake NWR office manages about 40 waterfowl production areas in northeastern Montana. A few Montana refuges have no facilities or are closed to the public. These are Lamesteer, Halfbreed Lake, Lake Thibadeau, and Creedman Coulee. The following Charles M. Russell NWR Wildlife Stations do not appear in the Guide map or in the Information Chart.

Federal Agencies

Fort Peck Wildlife Station
PO BOX 110
Fort Peck, MT 59223
406-526-3464

Jordan Wildlife Station
PO Box 63
Jordan, MT 59337
406-557-6145

Sand Creek Wildlife Station
PO Box 89
Roy, MT 59471
406-464-5181

Bureau of Land Management

The state office is responsible for BLM lands in Montana, and North and South Dakota. BLM offices and recreation lands in the Dakotas are covered in those state chapters.

Bureau of Reclamation - USDI

Great Plains Region
FOB, 316 N. 26th St.
PO Box 36900
Billings, MT 59101
406-657-6218

This office administers bureau recreation areas in central and eastern Montana, central and eastern Texas, part of Idaho, Wyoming, Colorado, and all of the Dakotas, Nebraska, Kansas, and Oklahoma.

Bureau of Reclamation Recreation Areas

Eighteen recreation areas are listed here and symbolized on the Montana state map.

S#	MAP	LOCATION NAME
1	C4	Anita Res.
2	C2	Barretts Diversion Dam
3	B2	Canyon Ferry Lake
4	C2	Clark Canyon Res.
5	B2	Freezout Lake
6	A3	Fresno Res.
7	B2	Gibson Res.
8	B2	Helena Valley Res.
9	A1	Hungry Horse Res.
10	C4	Huntley Diversion Dam
11	B5	Intake Diversion Dam
12	A2	Lake Elwell
13	A2	Lake Sherburne
14	B4	Nelson Res.
15	B2	Pishkin Res.
16	A4	Sleeping Buffalo Wildlife Management Area
17	B2	Willow Creek Res.
		Montana/Wyoming
18	C4	Bighorn Lake

Wilderness/Wild River Index

Wilderness Areas

Absaroka-Beartooth Wilderness - 920,310 acres
Custer national Forest (S# 13, MAP c4)
Gallatin National Forest (S# 27, map C3)
Anaconda-Pintler Wilderness - 157,874 acres
Beaverhead National Forest (S# 2, map C2)
Bitterroot National Forest (S# 8, map B31
Deerlodge National Forest (S# 16, map C2)
Bob Marshall Wilderness - 1,009, 356 acres
Flathead National Forest (S# 21, map A1)
Lewis & Clark National Forest (S# 43, map B2)
Cabinet Mountains Wilderness - 94,272 acres
Kootenai National Forest (S# 37, map A1)
Gates of the Mountains Wilderness - 28,562 acres
Helena National Forest (S# 33, map B2)
Great Bear Wilderness - 286,700 acres
Flathead National Forest (S# 21, map A1)
Lee Metcalf Wilderness - 248,994 acres
Beaverhead National Forest (S# 2, map C2)
Gallatin National Forest (S# 27, map C3)
Mission Mountains Wilderness - 73,877 acres
Flathead National Forest (S# 21, map A1)
Rattlesnake Wilderness - 34,844 acres
Lolo National Forest (S# 48, map B1)
Scapegoat Wilderness - 239,296 acres
Helena National Forest (S# 33, map B2)
Lewis & Clark National Forest (S# 43, map B2)
Selway-Bitterroot Wilderness - 251,343 acres
Bitterroot National Forest (S# 8, map B31
Welcome Creek Wilderness - 28,135 acres
Lolo National Forest (S# 48, map B1)
Medicine Lake Wilderness - 11,366 acres
Medicine Lake NWR (S# 11, map A5)
Red Rock Lakes Wilderness - 32,350 acres
Red Rock Lakes NWR (S# 18, map C2)
UL Bend Wilderness - 20,819 acres
UL Bend NWR (S# 8, map B4)

Lee Metcalf-Bear Trap Canyon Wilderness - 6,000 acres
BLM Butte District Office (S# 2, map C2)

Wild Rivers

Flathead Wild River
Flathead National Forest (S# 21, map A1) and
Glacier National Park (S# 4, map A1)
Upper Missouri National Wild & Scenic River
BLM Lewistown District Office (S# 16, map B3)

Outdoor Map Index

National Park Service (USGS Maps)

Custer Battlefield Natl Monument [1991]
Scale: 1 inch = 0.4 mile (1 cm = 0.3 km)
Size: 19x22 inches (48x56 cm)
Glacier National Park [1968]
Scale: 1 inch = 1.6 miles (1 cm = 1.0 km)
Size: 38x42 inches (96x106 cm)
Yellowstone Natl. Park (ID-MT-WY) [1961]
Scale: 1 inch = 2.0 miles (1 cm = 1.3 km)
Size: 38x41 inches (96x104 cm)

U.S. Forest Service Maps

The regional office is in Missoula. Inquire about Travel Plan maps. They are available for some forests as separate maps. Some are combined with the Visitor map. An order form is available for black-and-white forest contour maps in a 7.5-minute series. This map series is based on USGS quad maps and is indexed on Northern Region forest Visitor Maps.

Absaroka - Beartooth Wilderness [1986]
Scale: 1 inch = 0.5 mile (1 cm = 0.3 km)
Anaconda Pintler Wilderness [1983]
Scale: 1 inch = 0.5 mile (1 cm = 0.3 km)
Beaverhead National Forest, Travel Plan [1990]
Scale: 1 inch = 2.7 miles (1 cm = 1.7 km)
Bitterroot NF (ID - MT) [1981]
Scale: 1 inch = 0.5 mile (1 cm = 0.3 km)
Bob Marshall Wilderness Complex [1990]
Scale: 1 inch = 0.5 mile (1 cm = 0.3 km)
Custer NF, Ashland Division [1983]
Scale: 1 inch = 0.5 mile (1 cm = 0.3 km)
Custer NF, Beartooth [1986]
Scale: 1 inch = 0.5 mile (1 cm = 0.3 km)
Deerlodge National Forest [1990]
Scale: 1 inch = 0.5 mile (1 cm = 0.3 km)
Flathead National Forest [1991]
Scale: 1 inch = 0.5 mile (1 cm = 0.3 km)
Gallatin National Forest [1991]
Scale: 1 inch = 0.5 mile (1 cm = 0.3 km)
Gates of Mountains Wilderness [1983]
Scale: 1 inch = 0.5 mile (1 cm = 0.3 km)
Helena National Forest [1991]
Scale: 1 inch = 0.5 mile (1 cm = 0.3 km)
Kootenai-Kaniksu East NF [1985]
Scale: 1 inch = 0.5 mile (1 cm = 0.3 km)
Lewis & Clark NF, Jefferson Div. [1988]
Scale: 1 inch = 0.5 mile (1 cm = 0.3 km)
Lewis & Clark NF, Rocky Mtn. Div. [1988]
Scale: 1 inch = 0.5 mile (1 cm = 0.3 km)
Lolo National Forest [1991]
Scale: 1 inch = 0.5 mile (1 cm = 0.3 km)
Lolo-Seeley National Forest [1991]
Scale: 1 inch = 0.5 mile (1 cm = 0.3 km)
Mission Mountains Wilderness [1979]
Scale: 1 inch = 0.5 mile (1 cm = 0.3 km)
Selway-Bitterroot Wilderness [1980]
Scale: 1 inch = 0.5 mile (1 cm = 0.3 km)

Bureau of Land Management Maps

The Montana intermediate scale map grid is featured on page 125. A BLM map grid for North and South Dakota appears in the North Dakota chapter notes. BLM land in all three states is under the jurisdiction of the BLM State Office in Billings (Montana BLM S# 1). Other types of maps are available. Selected maps, including grid listed maps, are available at local BLM offices. A new map series, Recreation Access Guide (RAG) maps, are available for the Zortman, Fort Peck, Winnett, and Sand Springs areas. They are also available in surface and mineral map editions.

Another map series index grid for Montana (not included in the Guide or a part of this index) is available free from the Billings office. The 29 maps featured on it are in 1:169,000 scale. These are "Public Lands in Montana Maps" (Recreation). Each covers twice the area of a 1:100,000 series map and sells for $4 - a bargain.

Caution: There are two free map order forms available from the Billings office for ordering BLM maps. They are for the Public Lands in Montana maps and the intermediate scale maps shown on the grid on page 125. Both have map grid numbers you can use when ordering.

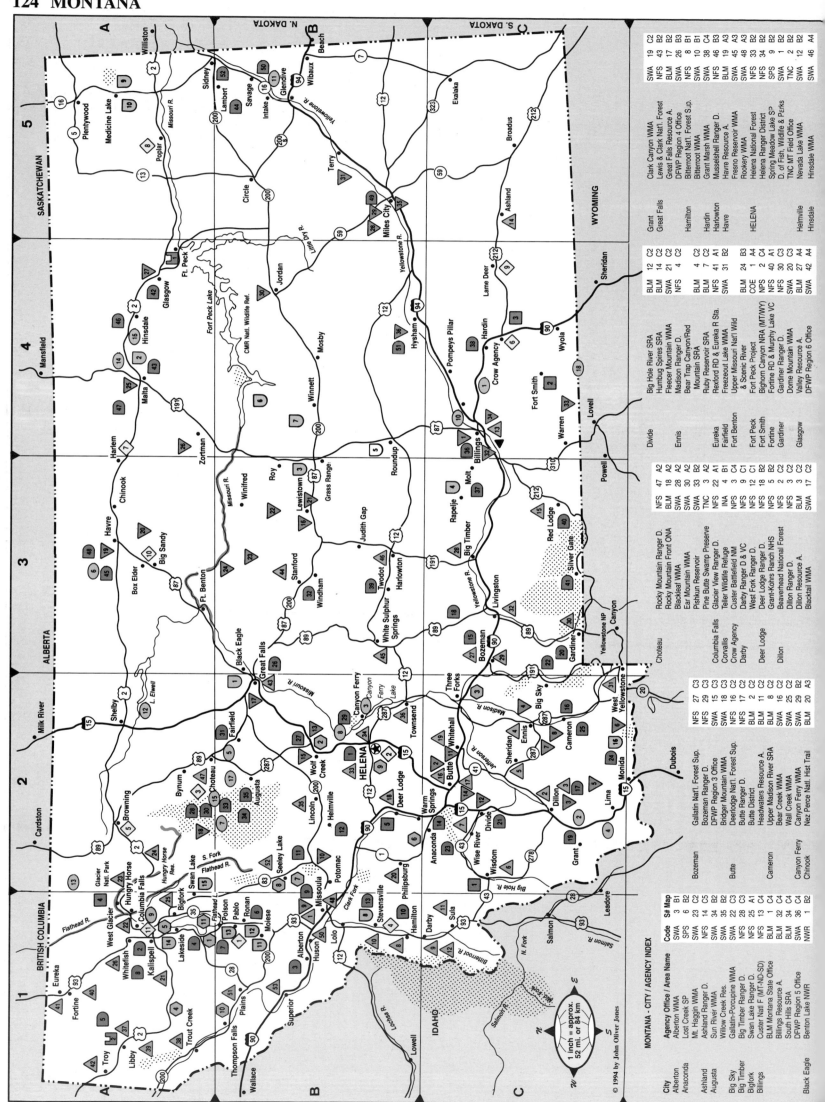

© 1994 by John Oliver Jones

Agency Office / Area Name Index (continued)

City	Agency Office / Area Name	Code	S#	Map
Hungry Horse	Hungry Horse RD	NFS	23	A2
	Spotted Bear Ranger D.	NFS	24	A2
Huson	Nine Mile RD &	NFS	50	B1
	Remount Depot VC	BLM	36	B4
Hysham	Howrey Island SRA	SWA	51	B4
Jorda	Isaac Homestead WMA	BLM	30	B4
	Jordan Field Station	NFS	21	A1
Kalispell	Flathead Nat'l. Forest Sup.	NWR	14	A1
	Northwest Montana WMD	NWR	15	A2
	Swan River NWR	SPS	5	A1
	Logan SP	SPS	5	A1
	Lone Pine SP	SWA	2	A1
	DFWP Region 1 Office	SWA	4	A1
Lakeside	Flathead Lake WMA	SWA	44	E5
Lambert	Fox Lake WMA	NFS	3	E3
Lewistown	Charles M. Russell NWR	BLM	16	B3
	Lewistown District	BLM	21	B3
	Judith Resource A.	BLM	22	B3
	Judith Mountains SRA	NFS	37	A1
Libby	Kootenai WMA	COE	2	A1
	Kootenai Nat'l. Forest	SWA	5	A1
	Fisher River & Libby RD's.			
	Libby Dam & Lake Koocanusa			
Lima	Red Rock Lakes NWR	NWR	16	C2
	Big Sheep Creek SRA	BLM	14	C2
Lincoln	Lincoln Ranger D.	NFS	35	B2
Livingston	Livingston Ranger D.	NFS	32	C3
Malta	Bowdoin NWR	NWR	25	A4
	Phillips Resource A.	BLM	43	A4
	Bowdoin WMA	SWA	47	A4
	Milk River WMA	SWA	47	A4
Medicine Lake	Medicine Lake NWR	NWR	9	A5
	Medicine Lake WPA's	NWR	10	A5
Miles City	Miles City Dist.	BLM	28	B5
	Big Dry Resource A.	BLM	29	B5
	Powder River Resource A.	BLM	35	B5
	DFWP Region 7 Office	SWA	49	B5
Missoula	U.S. Forest Svc., No. Reg	NFS	1	B1
	Lolo Nat'l. Forest Sup.	NFS	48	B1
	Missoula Ranger D. & Rattlesnake NRA	NFS	*49	B1
	Garnet Resource A.	BLM	9	B1
	DFWP Region 2 Office	SWA	9	B1
	National Bison Range NWR	NWR	11	B1
	Ninepipe NWR, c/o NBR	NWR	12	B1
Molese	Pablo NWR, c/o NBR	NWR	13	B1
Molt	Big Lake WMA	SWA	37	C3
Monida	Centennial Mountains SRA	BLM	34	C2
Pablo	Red Rock Lake WMA	SWA	24	C2
	Confederated Salish & Kootenai Tribes	TLA	1	B1
Philipsburg	Philipsburg Ranger D.	NFS	20	B2
Plains	Plains/Thompson Falls RD	NFS	51	B1
Polson	Big Arm SP	SPS	11	A1
	Wild Horse Island SP	SPS	1	A1
	Pablo WMA	SWA	7	B2
Potomac	Garnet Ghost Town SRA	BLM	10	B2
Rapelje	Hailstone NWR	NWR	4	C3
Red Lodge	Beartooth Ranger D.	NFS	15	C3
	Point of the Rocks WMA	SWA	40	C3
Ronan	Ninepipe WMA	SWA	6	B1
Roundup	Lake Mason NWR	NWR	5	B4
Savage	Elk Island WMA	SWA	50	B5
Seeley Lake	Seeley Lake Ranger D.	NFS	52	B2
	Placid Lake SP	SPS	9	B2
	Salmon Lake SP	SPS	8	B2
	Blackfoot-Clearwater WMA	SWA	11	B2
Sheridan	Sheridan Ranger D.	NFS	11	C2
Sidney	Seven Sisters WMA	SWA	52	B5
Silver Gate	Silver Gate WMA	SWA	41	C3
Stanford	Judith Ranger D.	NFS	44	B3
	Square Butte SRA	BLM	23	B3
Stevensville	Stevensville Ranger D.	NFS	10	B1
	Lee Metcalf NWR	NWR	8	B1
	Three Mile WMA	SWA	13	B1
Sula	Sula Ranger D.	NFS	11	C1
Superior	Superior Ranger D.	NFS	53	B1
Terry	Terry Badlands SRA	BLM	31	B5
Thompson Falls	Thompson Falls SP	SPS	10	B1
Three Forks	Lewis & Clark Caverns SP	SPS	3	C2
Townsend	Townsend Ranger D.	NFS	36	B2
Trout Creek	Cabinet Ranger D. & RS	NFS	38	A1
Troy	Three Rivers RD & Troy RS	NFS	42	A1
	Haymaker WMA	SWA	39	B3
Twodot	Warm Springs WMA	SWA	14	C2
Warren	Pryor Mountain Wild Horse Range	BLM	33	C4
West Glacier	Glacier National Park	NPS	4	A1
West	Hebgen Lake RD	NFS	31	C2
White Sulphur Springs	Kings Hill Ranger D.	NFS	45	B3
Whitefish	Tally Lake Ranger D.	NFS	26	A1
Whitehall	Ray Kuhns WMA	NFS	8	A1
Windham	Judith River WMA	NFS	19	C2
Winnett	UL Bend NWR	SWA	32	B3
	War Horse NWR	NWR	6	B4
Wisdom	Wisdom Ranger D.	NWR	7	B3
	Big Hole Nat'l. Battlefield	NFS	6	C2
Wise River	Wise River Ranger D.	NFS	5	C2
Wolf Creek	Holter Lake SRA	NFS	7	C2
	Sleeping Giant/Holter L SRA	BLM	13	B2
	Holter Lake SP	SPS	15	B2
	Beartooth WMA	SPS	2	B2
		SWA	27	B2
Zortman	Little Rocky Mountains SRA	BLM	26	A4

BLM Montana 1:100,000 Map Grid

Map-sheet names by longitude (north to south):

- **117°:** Bonner's Ferry, Sandpoint, Coeur D'Alene
- **116°:** Yak River, Libby, Thompson Falls, Wallace, Headquarters
- **115°:** Whitefish Range, Kalispell, Polson, Plaine, Missoula West, Hamilton, Nez Perce
- **114°:** Saint Mary, Hungry Horse Reservoir, Swan Peak, Seely Lake, Missoula East, Philipsburg, Wisdom, Salmon, Leadore, Borah Peak
- **113°:** Cut Bank, Valier, Choteau, Dearborn River, Elliston, Butte North, Butte South, Dillon, Lima, Dubois
- **112°:** Sweetgrass Hills, Conrad, Great Falls South, Canyon Ferry Dam, Townsend, Bozeman, Ennis, Hebgen Lake, Ashton
- **111°:** Great Falls North, Fort Benton, Belt, White Sulphur Springs, Ringling, Livingston, Gardiner, Yellowstone Park
- **110°:** Chester, Lonesome Lake, Winifred, Lewistown, Big Snowy Mountains, Harlowton, Big Timber, Red Lodge, Cody
- **109°:** Havre, Rocky Boy, Zortman, Winnett, Musselshell, Roundup, Billings, Bridger, Powell
- **108°:** Harlem, Dodson, Hardin, Lodge Grass, Sheridan (RAG)
- **107°:** Whitewater, Malta, Fort Peck Lake West, Sand Springs, Forsyth, Lame Deer, Burgess Junction, Recluse, Hysham
- **106°:** Opheim, Glasgow, Fort Peck Lake East, Jordan, Angela, Birney, Broadus, Devils Tower
- **105°:** Scobey, Wolf Point, Richey, Circle, Terry, Miles City, Powderville, Broadus
- **104°:** Plentywood, Culbertson, Sidney, Glendive, Wibaux, Baker, Ekalaka, Alzada

BLM MONTANA
1:100,000 INTERMEDIATE SCALE MAPS
SURFACE & SURFACE / MINERAL SERIES
RAG (Recreation Access Guide)
P (planimetric) / Base Map Not Available

---

the maps. If you use those forms and numbers, be sure to include the map name as grid numbers on the two forms (grids) overlap one another. For example, the #5 map in 1:100,000 scale is called Libby (in northwest Montana). In the 1:169,000 scale, the #5 map name is Havre (in north-central Montana).

Of special interest are the two Upper Missouri National Wild & Scenic River maps. Each features two river areas (maps) and are printed on both sides (a total of four map areas). Maps (areas) 1 & 2 cover the Missouri River from Fort Benton east for about 80 miles. Maps (areas) 3 & 4 continue east along the river for another 70 miles to McNulty Bottoms. These two maps, and the RAG maps, are printed on water-resistant paper.

Montana Department of Fish, Wildlife, & Parks (DFWP)

A free *Catalog of Publications* lists available literature on a variety of subjects, from birds to wildlife management areas. Comprehensive game harvest and drawing statistics are available for a small fee. The bi-monthly 36 page full color magazine, *Montana Outdoors*, is available at agency offices and on many newsstands at $2 a copy. A subscription is $7 a year.

A Montana State Parks Guide (37 state parks) is available free. It describes each park, contains a small state map showing their locations, and indicates facilities and activities with a picture legend. There are daily entry fees at most parks in season, and campground use fees.

Private Organizations

Tribal Land Areas in Montana

Free visitor publications available from The Confederated Salish & Kootenai Tribes office are the *Flathead Reservation Touring Guide* and *Hunting, Fishing, and Recreation Regulations*. A trail map is available.

Blackfeet Tribe of the Blackfeet Indian Reservation - Fishing, hunting, camping, biking, boating, hiking, touring.
Blackfeet Tribal Business Council (S# 5, map A2)
PO Box 850
Browning, MT 59417   406-338-7179

Crow Tribe of the Crow Indian Reservation - Fishing, hunting, camping, boating, touring.
Crow Tribal Council (S# 6, map C4)
Box 159
Crow Agency, MT 59022   406-638-2316

Fort Belknap Indian Community of the Fort Belknap Indian Reservation - Fishing, hunting, camping.
Fort Belknap Community Council (S# 7, map A4)
Box 249
Harlem, MT 59526   406-353-2205

Assiniboine and Sioux Tribes of the Fort Peck Indian Reservation - Fishing, hunting, camping, boating.
Fort Peck Executive Board (S# 8, map A5)
PO Box 1027
Poplar, MT 59255   406-768-5311

Northern Cheyenne Tribe of the Northern Cheyenne Indian Reservation - Camping.
Northern Cheyenne Tribal Council (S# 9, map C4)
PO Box 128
Lame Deer, MT 59043   406-477-6284

Chippewa-Cree Indians of the Rocky Boy's Indian Reservation - Fishing, camping.
Chippewa-Cree Business Committee (S# 10, map A3)
Box 544
Box Elder, MT 59521   406-395-4282

ANCA Location in Montana
Big Creek Outdoor Education Center (S# 11, map A1)
6500 North Fork Rd.
Columbia Falls, MT 59912   406-755-6078

Montana Chamber of Commerce
2030 11th Ave.
PO Box 1730
Helena, MT 59601   Phone 406-442-2405
                          Fax 406-442-2409

Division of Forestry
Department of State Lands
2705 Spurgin Rd.
Missoula, MT 59801   406-542-4300
There is no State forest recreation program in Montana.

Montana Dept. of Commerce
Tourism Office
1424 Ninth Ave.
Helena, MT 59620   406-444-2654
from out-of-state   1-800-541-1447
Current information and free travel guides and maps are available from this office. The *Vacation Guide* describes attractions and all State Parks. A *Travel Planner* lists accommodations, public and private campgrounds, and licensed outfitters and guides. Ask for the Montana Travel Planning Packet.

The Official Montana Transportation Department highway map is available here and from other state agencies at no charge. Scenic routes are identified. Red symbols and location names mark State Parks, Recreation Areas, campsites, and points of interest.

Guide & Outfitter Information
111 N. Jackson St.
Helena, MT 59620   406-444-3737
The Montana Department of Commerce (Board of Outfitters) licenses qualified Guides and Outfitters.
Passing an 8 hour test and carrying liability insurance are two of the licensing requirements. A descriptive list of all Montana licensed guides and outfitters is available.

★ INFORMATION CHART ★

AGENCY/MAP LEGEND ... INITIALS, MAP SYMBOLS, COLOR CODES

U.S. Forest Service Supervisor & Ranger Dist. Offices NFS [61]
U.S. Army Corps of Engineers Rec. Areas & Offices . COE [H]
USFWS National Wildlife Refuges & Offices .... NWR [40]
National Park Service Parks & other NPS Sites ...... NPS [7]
Bureau of Land Management Rec. Areas & Offices .. BLM [26]
Bureau of Reclamation Rec. Areas & Reg. Offices ... BOR [8]
State Parks (also see State Agency notes) .... SPS [52]
State Wildlife Areas (also see State Agency notes) .. SWA [19]
Private Preserves, Nature Centers & Tribal Lands ...
The Wild Rivers ____ and Wilderness Areas .....

Note: Refer to yellow block on page 7 (top right) for location name and address abbreviations. If a symbol number has a star ★ that symbol is not shown on the map.

INFORMATION CHART LEGEND - SYMBOLS & LETTER CODES

■ means YES & □ means Yes with disability provisions
sp means spring, March through May
S means Summer, June through August
F means Fall, September through November
W means Winter, December through February
T means Two (2) or Three (3) Seasons
A means All Four (4) Seasons
na means Not Applicable or Not Available

Note: empty or blank spaces in the chart mean NO

FACILITIES, SERVICES, RECREATION OPPORTUNITIES & CONVENIENCES

S#	MAP	LOCATION NAME (state initials if more than one) with ADDRESS and/or LOCATION DATA	TELEPHONE	ACRES / ELEVATION
1	B1	U.S. Forest Service, Northern Region, FOB, Pattee at Pine, PO Box 7669, Missoula 59807	406-329-3511	25,000,000 / na
2	C2	Beaverhead National Forest, 420 Barrett St., Dillon 59725	406-683-3900	2,147,000 / 5,000-11,000
3	C2	Dillon Ranger D., 420 Barrett St., Dillon 59725	401-683-3900	na / na
4	C2	Madison Ranger D., 5 Forest Service Road, Ennis 59729	406-682-4253	na / na
5	C2	Sheridan Ranger D., Box 428, Sheridan 59749	406-842-5432	na / na
6	C2	Wisdom Ranger D., Box 238, Wisdom 59761	406-689-3243	na / na
7	C2	Wise River Ranger D., Box 100, Wise River 59762	406-832-3178	na / na
8	B1	Bitterroot Nat'l. Forest Sup., 1801 N. First St., Hamilton 59840 [W side of US 93 across from Pain Clinic]	406-363-3131	1,650,310 / 3,500-9,800
9	C1	Darby Ranger D & VC, 712 Hwy. 93 North, Darby 59829 [E side of Hwy. 93 across from school]	406-821-3913	358,140 / na
10	B1	Stevensville Ranger D., 88 Main Street, Stevensville 59870 [junction Main St. & E Side Hwy.]	406-777-5461	250,250 / na
11	C1	Sula Ranger D., 7338 Hwy. 93 South, Sula 59871 [E side of US 93 & S of Sula store]	406-821-3201	259,800 / na
12	C1	West Fork Ranger D., 6735 West Fork Rd., Darby 59829 [W off US 93 on Hwy 473 on N side of road]	406-821-3269	782,120 / na
13	C4	Custer National Forest (MT-ND-SD), 2602 First Ave. N., PO Box 2556, Billings 59103	406-657-6361	2,446,130 / 1,000-12,800
14	C3	Ashland Ranger D., Hwy. 212, Box 168, Ashland 59003	406-784-2344	436,000 / 3,500-4,340
15	C3	Beartooth Ranger D., Hwy. 212, Rt. #2, Box 3420, Red Lodge 59068	406-446-2103	588,000 / 5,000-12,799
16	C2	Deerlodge Nat'l. Forest Sup., FOB, Main & Copper, PO Box 400, Butte 59703	406-496-3400	1,195,000 / 4,000-10,950
17	C2	Butte Ranger D., 1820 Meadowlark, Butte 59701	406-494-2147	169,000 / 5,200-10,070
18	B2	Deer Lodge Ranger D., 91 Frontage Road, Deer Lodge 59722	406-846-1770	205,000 / 5,300-10,160
19	B2	Jefferson Ranger D., 405 E. Legion, PO Box Of Whitehall 59759	406-287-3223	422,000 / 4,800-10,600
20	B2	Philipsburg Ranger D., PO Box H, Philipsburg 59858	406-859-3211	399,000 / 5,300-10,460
21	A1	Flathead Nat'l. Forest Sup., 1935 Third Ave. East, Kalispell 59901	406-755-5401	3,630,210 / 3,000-10,750
22	A1	Glacier View Ranger D., 744 Railroad St. E.N., PO Box W, Columbia Falls 59912	406-892-4372	344,680 / 5,500
23	A2	Hungry Horse RD, Hwy. 2 East, PO Box 190340, Hungry Horse 59919 [VC at Dam, open June 5th to Labor Day]	406-387-5243	448,465 / 3,560
24	A1	Spotted Bear Ranger D., PO Box 310, Hungry Horse 59919 [S and above Hungry Horse Reservoir]	406-752-7345	1,029,350 / 4,000
25	A1	Swan Lake Ranger D., 8350 Hwy. 35, PO Box 370, Bigfork 59911	406-837-5081	511,940 / 3,000-9,000
26	A1	Tally Lake Ranger D., 1335 Hwy. 93 W., Whitefish 59937	406-862-2508	295,775 / 5,500
27	C3	Gallatin Nat'l. Forest Sup., FOB, 10 W. Babcock, PO Box 130, Bozeman 59771	406-587-6701	1,735,412 / 3,500-12,800
28	C3	Big Timber Ranger D., PO Box A, Big Timber 59011	406-932-5155	347,103 / na
29	B2	Bozeman Ranger D., 601 Nikles, Bozeman 59715	406-587-6920	330,854 / na
30	C3	Gardiner Ranger D., Hwy. 89, PO Box 5, Gardiner 59030	406-848-7375	400,000 / na
31	B2	Hebgen Lake RD, Hwy. 191, PO Box 520, West Yellowstone 59758	406-646-7369	350,000 / na
32	C3	Livingston Ranger D., Hwy. 89, Rt. #2, Box 62, Livingston 59047	406-222-1892	307,455 / na
33	B2	Helena National Forest Supervisor, 2880 Skyway Dr., Helena 59601	406-449-5201	975,100 / 3,586-9,472
34	B2	Helena Ranger District, 2001 Poplar St., Helena 59601	406-449-5490	444,975 / na
35	B2	Lincoln Ranger D., Box 219, Lincoln 59639	406-362-4265	330,110 / na
36	B2	Townsend Ranger D., 415 S. Front, Box 29, Townsend 59644	406-266-3425	200,015 / na
37	A1	Kootenai Nat'l. Forest Supervisor's, 506 US Hwy. 2 West, Libby 59923	406-293-6211	2,245,000 / 1,900-8,700
38	A1	Cabinet Ranger D. & Ranger S., 2693 Hwy. 200, HCR 2, Box 210, Trout Creek 59874	406-827-3534	418,000 / 2,000-8,000
39	A1	Fisher River & Libby Ranger D's., at Canoe Gulch Ranger S., 2557 Hwy. 37, Libby 59923	406-293-7773	319,000 / 2,000-8,000
40	A1	Fortine Ranger D. & Murphy Lake, Ranger Station, PO Box 116, Fortine 59918	406-882-4451	258,000 / 2,000-8,000
41	A1	Rexford Ranger D. & Eureka Ranger S., PO Box 666, Eureka 59917	406-296-2536	311,000 / 2,400-5,000
42	A1	Three Rivers Ranger D. & Troy Range, 1437 N. Hwy. 2, Troy 59935	406-295-4693	611,000 / 1,800-8,000
43	B2	Lewis & Clark Nat'l. Forest Sup., 1101 15th St. No., Box 869, Great Falls 59403	406-791-7700	1,843,469 / 3,800-9,400
44	B3	Judith Ranger D., 109 Central Ave., Box 484, Stanford 59479	406-566-2292	362,667 / 4,600-9,200
45	B3	Kings Hill Ranger D., 204 W. Folsom, Box A, White Sulphur Springs 59645	406-547-3361	436,886 / 3,800-9,200
46	B3	Musselshell Ranger D., 809 2 NW, Box Of Harlowton 59036	406-632-4391	267,476 / 4,700-8,700
47	A2	Rocky Mountain Ranger D., 1102 Main Ave. NW, Box 340, Choteau 59422	406-466-5341	776,440 / 4,400-9,400
48	B1	Lolo Nat'l. Forest Sup., Building 24, Fort Missoula, Missoula 59801	406-329-3750	2,100,000 / 3,000-9,000
*49	B1	Missoula Ranger D. & Rattlesnake NR, Bldg. 24-A, Fort Missoula, Missoula 59801	406-329-3814	na / na
50	B1	Nine Mile RD & Remount Depot VC, 20325 Remount Road, Huson 59846 [Visitor Center open May-October]	406-626-5201	na / na

#	Grid	Location	Phone	Acres / Elev.
52	B2	Seeley Lake Ranger D., PO Box 717, Seeley Lake 59868 [Hwy. 83 N, mile marker 18]	406-677-2233	na / na
53	B1	Superior Ranger D., 203 West Riverside, Superior 59872	406-822-4233	na / na
		COE, Omaha District, 215 N. 17th St., Omaha, NE 68102	402-221-4137	na / na
1	A4	Fort Peck Project, Po Box 208, Fort Peck 59223	406-526-3411	na / na
2	A1	COE, Seattle District, PO Box 3755, Seattle, WA 98124	206-764-3442	na / na
1	B2	Libby Dam & Lake Koocanusa, 17115 Highway 37, Libby 59923	406-293-7751	na / na
2	A4	Benton Lake NWR, PO Box 450, Black Eagle 59414 [US 87 N from Gr. Falls 1 mi, L & N on Bootlegger Trail 10 mi]	406-727-7400	12,383 / 3,600
2	A4	Bowdoin NWR, PO Box J, Malta 59538 [7 mi. E of Malta on Old Hwy. 2]	406-654-2863	15,500 / 2,300-2,500
3	B3	Charles M. Russell NWR, PO Box 110, Lewistown 59457	406-538-8706	1,100,000 / 2,210-2,900
4	C3	Halstone NWR, mail c/o CMR NWR, Rapelje [E of Billings & E of CR 306]	406-538-8706	1,900 / 2,500
5	B4	Lake Mason NWR, mail c/o CMR NWR, Roundup [on County road about 15 mi NW of Roundup]	406-538-8706	18,600 / 3,000
6	B4	UL Bend NWR, mail c/o CMR NWR, N of Winnett [about 60 mi N of Winnett]	406-538-8706	50,000 / 2,200-2,700
7	B1	War Horse NWR, mail c/o CMR NWR, near Winnett [about 15 mi NW of Winnett & N of US 87]	406-538-8706	900 / 2,500
8	B1	Lee Metcalf NWR, 3rd & Main St., PO Box 257, Stevensville 59870 [E from US 93 1 mi to SR 269/Main jct. follow s gns]	406-777-5552	2,800 / 3,400
9	A5	Medicine Lake NWR, 223 North Shore Rd., Medicine Lake 59247 [office on refuge, off Hwy 16, 1 mi S/2 mi E of town]	406-789-2305	31,500 / 1,950
10	A5	Medicine Lake WPA's (42 areas), 223 North Shore Rd., Medicine Lake 59247 [Daniels, Sheridan, & Roosevelt Cos.]	406-789-2305	10,000 / 2,000
11	B1	National Bison Range NWR, 132 Bison Range Road, Moiese 59824	406-644-2211	18,500 / 2,500-4,900
12	B1	Ninepipe NWR, c/o NBR, 132 Bison Range Road, Moiese 59824 [located adjacent Hwy. 93 & S of Ronan]	406-644-2211	2,062 / 3,000
13	B1	Pablo NWR, c/o NBR, 132 Bison Range Road, Moiese 59824 [located 2 mi. W of Hwy. 93 near Pablo]	406-644-2211	2,540 / 3,200
14	A1	Northwest Montana WMD, 780 Creston Hatchery Road, Kalispell 59901	406-755-4375	4,458 / 3,200
15	A2	Swan River NWR, 780 Creston Hatchery Rd., Kalispell 59901 [SE of Kalispell on Hwy. 83 near Swan Lake]	406-755-4375	1,568 / 3,200
16	C2	Red Rock Lakes NWR, Monida Star Rt., Box 15, Lima 59739 [on Red Rocks Pass Rd.]	406-276-3347	43,500 / 6,600-9,000
1	C2	Big Hole Nat'l. Battlefield, SH 43, PO Box 237, Wisdom 59761 [W of Wisdom and E of Lost Trail Pass]	406-689-3155	655 / 6,300
2	C4	Bighorn Canyon NRA (MT/WY), Hwy 313, PO Box 458, Fort Smith 59035	406-666-2412	120,000 / 3,640-4,640
3	C4	Custer Battlefield NM, PO Box 39, Crow Agency 59022 [E from I-90 on US 212]	406-638-2621	765 / 3,000
4	A1	Glacier National Park, West Glacier 59936 [off US 2 at West Glacier, follow signs]	406-888-5441	1,013,000 / 3,150-10,500
5	B2	Grant-Kohrs Ranch NHS, 210 Missouri, PO Box 790, Deer Lodge 59722 [exit I-90 at mile marker 184 or 187]	406-846-2070	1,500 / 4,500
1	C4	BLM Montana State Office, 222 N. 32nd Street, PO Box 3388, Billings 59107	406-255-2885	8,000,000 / 2,000-10,500
2	C2	Butte District, 106 N. Parkmont, PO Box 3388, Butte 59702	406-494-5059	1,379,000 / 3,000-10,000
3	C2	Dillon Resource, PO Box 1048, Dillon 59725	406-683-2337	918,172 / na
4	C2	Bear Trap Canyon/Red Mountain SRA, near Ennis	406-683-2337	6,010 / 4,000-5,000
5	C2	Big Sheep Creek SRA, near Lima	406-683-2337	100 / 6,000-7,200
6	C2	Centennial Mountains SRA, near Monida	406-683-2337	50,000 / 6,500-10,000
7	C2	Ruby Reservoir SRA, near Ennis	406-683-2337	10 / 5,400
8	C2	Upper Madison River SRA, near Cameron	406-683-2337	50 / 4,900-6,100
9	B1	Garnet Resource A., 3255 Ft. Missoula Rd., Missoula 59806	406-329-3914	143,856 / 3,300-8,500
10	B2	Garnet Ghost Town SRA, near Potomac	406-329-3914	100 / 7,000
11	B3	Headwaters Resource A., 106 N. Parkmont, PO Box 3388, Butte 59702	406-494-5059	295,351 / 4,000-8,500
12	C2	Big Hole River SRA, near Divide	406-494-5059	200 / 5,000-6,100
13	B2	Holter Lake SRA, near Wolf Creek	406-494-5059	69 / 3,550
14	C2	Humbug Spires SRA, near Divide	406-494-5059	548,773 / 3,000-6,000
15	B2	Sleeping Giant/Holter Lake SRA, near Wolf Creek	406-494-5059	33,000 / 2,400-3,400
16	B2	Lewistown District, 80 Airport Rd., PO Box 1160, Lewistown 59457	406-538-7461	749,633 / 2,400-6,600
17	B3	Great Falls Resource A., 215 1st Ave. N, PO Drawer 2865, Great Falls 59403	406-727-0503	22,000 / 4,600-6,200
18	A2	Rocky Mountain Front ONA, W of Choteau	406-727-0503	1,947 / 3,300-5,680
19	B2	Havre Resource A., West 2nd St., PO Drawer 911, Havre 59501	406-265-5891	94,000 / 2,400-3,000
20	A3	Nez Perce Natl. Historic Trail, S of Chinook	406-265-5891	1,084,690 / 3,300-5,700
21	B3	Judith Resource A., 80 Airport Rd., Lewistown 59457	406-538-7461	25,800 / 3,600-5,700
22	B3	Judith Mountains SRA, NE of Lewistown	406-538-7461	1,019,886 / 2,039-3,000
23	B3	Square Butte SFA, N of Stanford	406-538-7461	3,214,499 / 1,900-3,597
24	B3	Upper Missouri Nat'l Wild & Scenic., begins at, Fort Benton	406-538-7461	1,714,346 / 1,900-3,600
25	A4	Phillips Resource A., 501 S. 2nd St., E, PO Box B, Malta 59538	406-654-1240	na / 2,595
26	B4	Little Rocky Mountains SRA, near Zortman	406-265-5891	42,950 / 2,180-2,900
27	A4	Valley Resource A., RR #1-4775, Glasgow 59230	406-228-4316	427,068 / 3,900-8,000
28	B5	Miles City Dist., PO Box 940, Miles City 59301 [W of Miles City]	406-232-4331	36,600 / 3,900-8,000
29	B5	Big Dry Resource A., Miles City Plaza, Miles City 59301	406-232-7000	3,000 / 3,400
30	B4	Jordan Field Station, PO Box 48, Jordan 59327	406-557-2376	
31	B5	Terry Badlands SRA, near Terry	406-232-7000	
32	C4	Billings Resource A., 810 E. Main St., Billings 59105	406-657-6262	
33	C4	Pryor Mountain Wild Horse Range, near Warren	406-657-6262	1,073,085 / 2,200-4,800
34		South Hills SFA, near Billings	406-657-6262	631 / 2,650
35	B5	Powder River Resource A., Miles City Plaza, Miles City 59301	406-232-7000	na / na
36	B4	Howrey Island SRA, near Hysham	406-444-2535	

Dept. of Fish, Wildlife & Parks (see below for S# and region data), 1420 E. Sixth Ave., Helena 59620

AGENCY/MAP LEGEND . . . INITIALS, MAP SYMBOLS, COLOR CODES

U.S. Forest Service Supervisor & Ranger Dist. Offices NFS (61)
U.S. Army Corps of Engineers Rec. Areas & Offices . COE (31)
USFWS National Wildlife Refuges & Offices . . . . NWR (40)
National Park Service Parks & other NPS Sites . . . . . NPS (7)
Bureau of Land Management Rec. Areas & Offices . . BLM (26)
Bureau of Reclamation Rec. Areas & Reg. Offices . . . BOR (8)
State Parks (also see State Agency notes) . . . . SPS (52)
State Wildlife Areas (also see State Agency notes) . . SWA (19)
Private Preserves, Nature Centers & Tribal Lands . . (15)
The Wild Rivers and Wilderness Areas

★ INFORMATION CHART ★

INFORMATION CHART LEGEND - SYMBOLS & LETTER CODES

- **■** means **YES** & □ means **Yes with disability provisions**
- **sp** means **sp**ring, March through May
- **S** means **S**ummer, June through August
- **F** means **F**all, September through November
- **W** means **W**inter, December through February
- **T** means **T**wo (2) or **T**hree (3) Seasons
- **A** means **A**ll Four (4) Seasons
- **na** means Not Applicable or Not Available

Note: empty or blank spaces in the chart mean **NO**

Note: Refer to yellow block on page 7 (top right) for location name and address abbreviations. If a symbol number has a star ★ that symbol is not shown on the map.

FACILITIES, SERVICES, RECREATION OPPORTUNITIES & CONVENIENCES

S#	MAP	LOCATION NAME (state initials if more than one) with ADDRESS and/or LOCATION DATA	TELEPHONE	ACRES / ELEVATION	INFO OFFICE (IO) / VISITOR CENTER (VC)	IO / VC OPEN SATURDAY / SUNDAY	ENTRY FEE, not camping or permit fee	CONCESSIONAIRE SERVICES AVAILABLE	INTERPRETIVE or EDUCATIONAL DISPLAY	FREE LITERATURE, brochures, maps, etc.	AGENCY GUIDED TOURS, scheduled / by res.	NATURE EDUCATION / STUDY PROGRAMS	WILDFLOWER VIEWING AREA or DRIVE	ARCHAEOLOGICAL / GEOLOGICAL SITES	HISTORIC SITES	INTERPRETIVE TRAILS	WILDLIFE IS ABUNDANT OR COMMON	ENDANGERED SPECIES ARE COMMON	WILDLIFE VIEWING SITES, blinds, signs, etc.	DEVELOPED PICNIC AREAS / PICNIC SITES	DEVELOPED CAMPGROUNDS / CAMPSITES	NO-CHARGE CAMPGROUNDS / CAMPSITES	WILDERNESS AREAS / WILD RIVERS	WALKING / HIKING TRAILS	SWIMMING PERMITTED, at one's own risk	BICYCLING OPPORTUNITIES...areas, trails	HORSEBACK RIDING, w/ your own horse	OFF-ROAD Motorized Vehicle Area / Use OK	FISHING IN SEASON, license / permit reqd.	BOATING FACILITIES, ramps, marinas, etc.	MOTORIZED WATERCRAFT OK, check limits	NON-MOTORIZED WATERCRAFT OK	HUNTING IN SEASON, license / permit reqd.	WINTER SPORTS OPPORTUNITIES	PARK & WALK-IN ONLY AREA	DAY USE ONLY, no overnight	DRINKING WATER	RESTROOMS	S#
1	A1	Big Arm SP, Polson 59620 [on Flathead Lake near Polson, summer call 849-5255]	406-752-5501	55 / 2,917						■										■	■				■				■	■	■	■							1
2	B2	Holter Lake SP, Wolf Creek [on Holter Reservoir near Wolf Creek]	406-454-3441	40 / 3,600																■	■				■		■		■	■	■	■	■						2
3	C2	Lewis & Clark Caverns SP, Three Forks [near Three Forks]	406-287-3541	2,735 / 5,300	■					■				■	■				■	■	■			■			■		■										3
4	A1	Logan SP, W of Kalispell [on Thompson Lake off US 2, W of Kalispell, Summer call 293-7190]	406-752-5501	18 / 3,896						■										■	■				■				■	■	■	■							4
5	A1	Lone Pine SP, 300 Lone Pine Rd., Kalispell 59901	406-755-2706	137 / 2,500	■					■				■					■	■						■	■									■			5
6	B2	Lost Creek SP, near Anaconda	406-542-5500	300 / 6,000										■					■	■	■		■						■										6
7	B2	Placid Lake SP, near Seeley Lake	406-542-5500	32 / 4,100						■										■	■				■				■	■	■	■							7
8	B2	Salmon Lake SP, near Seeley Lake	406-542-5500	42 / 4,000						■										■	■				■				■	■	■	■							8
9	B2	Spring Meadow Lake SP, Country Club Drive, near Helena	406-444-4720	30 / 3,300															■	■					■	■			■			■				■			9
10	B1	Thompson Falls SP, near Thompson Falls [Summer call 827-3732]	406-752-5501	36 / 2,473						■										■	■				■				■	■	■	■							10
11	A1	Wild Horse Island SP, near Polson [located in Flathead Lake]	406-752-5501	2,163 / 2,917						■				■	■				■				■		■				■		■				■	■			11
1	B2	**Dept. of Fish, Wildlife & Parks**, 1420 E. Sixth Ave., Helena 59620	406-444-2535	na / na	■						■	■								■																■		■	1
2	A1	DFWP Region 1 Office, 490 N. Meridan Rd., PO Box 67, Kalispell 59903	406-752-5501	na / na	■																															■			2
3	B1	Alberton WMA, near Alberton	406-755-5505	666 / 2,843																					■		■		■				■						3
4	A1	Flathead Lake WMA, near Lakeside	406-752-5501	136 / 2,917																							■		■			■	■		■				4
5	A1	Kootenai WMA, near Libby	406-755-5505	2,443 / 2,730																							■		■	■	■	■	■						5
6	B1	Ninepipe WMA, near Ronan	406-752-5501	2,983 / 2,890						■									■								■		■	■		■	■						6
7	B1	Pablo WMA, near Polson	406-755-5505	416 / 2,890						■									■								■		■			■	■						7
8	A1	Ray Kuhns WMA, near Whitefish	406-752-5501	1,622 / 2,995											■					■							■		■		■	■	■						8
9	B1	DFWP Region 2 Office, 3201 Spurgin, Missoula 59801	406-542-5500	na / na	■																															■			9
10	B1	Bitterroot WMA, near Hamilton	406-542-5500	2,215 / 3,625																							■						■						10
11	B2	Blackfoot-Clearwater WMA, near Seeley Lake	406-542-5500	49,458 / 2,832															■	■					■		■		■				■						11
12	B2	Nevada Lake WMA, near Helmville	406-542-5500	1,179 / 3,150																					■		■		■	■	■	■	■						12
13	B1	Three Mile WMA, near Stevensville	406-542-5500	6,059 / 4,132																							■						■						13
14	C2	Warm Springs WMA, near Warm Springs	406-542-5500	4,680 / 3,160																					■		■		■	■			■						14
15	C3	DFWP Region 3 Office, 1400 South 19th St., Bozeman 59715	406-994-4042	na / 5,000	■					■										■																■			15
16	C2	Bear Creek WMA, near Cameron	406-994-4042	3,455 / 6,000-8,800																					■		■		■				■						16
17	C2	Blacktail WMA, near Dillon	406-994-4042	17,422 / 6,600-7,800																					■		■		■				■						17
18	C3	Bridger Mountain WMA, near Bozeman	406-994-4042	320 / 6,000																							■		■				■						18
19	C2	Clark Canyon WMA, near Grant	406-994-4042	1,200 / 5,140										■	■												■		■				■						19
20	C3	Dome Mountain WMA, near Gardiner	406-994-4042	4,789 / 5,300-7,500										■											■		■		■	■	■	■	■						20
21	C2	Fleecer Mountain WMA, near Divide	406-994-4042	7,288 / 5,600																							■						■						21
22	C3	Gallatin-Porcupine WMA, near Big Sky	406-994-4042	10,513 / 6,400-8,800																			■		■		■	■	■			■	■						22
23	C2	Mt. Haggin WMA, near Anaconda	406-994-4042	56,138 / 5,500-8,300										■	■				■						■		■		■				■						23
24	C2	Red Rock Lake WMA, near Monida	406-994-4042	26 / 5,995						■									■						■		■		■	■		■	■						24
25	C2	Wall Creek WMA, near Cameron	406-994-4042	7,066 / 5,500-6,600	■																				■	■	■		■				■						25
26	B3	DFWP Region 4 Office, 4600 Giant Springs Rd., PO Box 6610, Great Falls 59405	406-454-3441	na / na	■					■					■				■	■																■			26
27	B2	Beartooth WMA, near Wolf Creek	406-454-3441	31,798 / 4,460																			■				■		■				■		■				27
28	A2	Blackleaf WMA, near Choteau	406-454-3441	8,115 / 4,718															■				■				■		■				■						28
29	B2	Canyon Ferry WMA, near Canyon Ferry	406-454-3441	5,000 / 3,390															■						■		■		■		■	■	■						29
30	A2	Ear Mountain WMA, near Choteau	406-454-3441	3,046 / 4,460																			■				■						■						30
31	B2	Freezeout Lake WMA, near Fairfield	406-454-3441	11,447 / 3,781	■					■									■	■							■					■	■						31
32	B3	Judith River WMA, near Windham	406-454-3441	4,873 / 4,860															■						■		■		■				■						32
33	B2	Pishkun Reservoir, near Choteau	406-454-3441	1,570 / 2,970																■					■		■		■	■	■	■	■						33
34	B2	Sun River WMA, near Augusta	406-454-3441	19,775 / 4,680																			■				■		■				■						34
35	B2	Willow Creek Res., near Augusta	406-454-3441	1,581 / 3,220																■					■		■		■	■	■	■	■						35
36	C4	DFWP Region 5 Office, 2300 Lake Elmo Dr., Billings 59105	406-252-4654	na / na	■															■					■				■	■		■				■			36
37	C3	Big Lake WMA, near Molt	406-252-4654	901 / 3,100															■								■					■	■						37
38	C4	Grant Marsh WMA, near Hardin	406-252-4654	140 / 3,475															■						■		■		■	■	■	■	■						38
39	B3	Haymaker WMA, near Twodot	406-252-4654	1,359 / 4,460																							■						■						39

Montana (continued)

#	Map	Name & Location	Phone	Acres / Elev.
41	C3	Silver Gate WMA, near Silver Gate	406-252-4654	2 / 7,780
42	A4	DFWP Region 6 Office, Rt. #1-4210, Glasgow 59230	406-228-9347	na / 2,298
43	A4	Bowdoin WMA, near Malta	406-228-9347	156 / 2,240
44	B5	Fox Lake WMA, near Lambert	406-228-9347	1,361 / 1,970
45	A3	Fresno Reservoir WMA, near Havre	406-228-9347	2,960 / 2,245
46	A4	Hinsdale WMA, near Hinsdale	406-228-9347	280 / 2,100
47	A4	Milk River WMA, near Malta	406-228-9347	2,241 / 2,360
48	A3	Rookery WMA, near Havre	406-228-9347	2,276 / 3,150
49	B5	DFWP Region 7 Office, RR #1, Box 2004, Miles City 59301	406-232-4365	5 / 2,628
50	B5	Elk Island WMA, 2 mi. SE of Savage	406-232-4365	1,046 / 1,960
51	B4	Isaac Homestead WMA, 4 mi W of Hysham	406-232-4365	1,202 / 3,540
52	B5	Seven Sisters WMA, 10 mi. SW of Sidney	406-232-4365	557 / 1,960
1	B1	Confederated Salish & Kootenai Tribes, Last Chance Gulch and 6th, PO Box 258, Helena 59624	406-675-2700	1,243,970 / 2,800-10,000
2	B2	TNC MT Field Office, PO Box 278, Pablo 59855 [W side of Hwy. 93]	406-443-0303	na / na
3	A2	Pine Butte Swamp Preserve, HC 58, Star Route 34B, Choteau 59422	406-466-5526	20,000 / 4,400-7,000
4	B1	Teller Wildlife Refuge, 1200 Chaffin Rd., Corvallis 59828	406-961-3507	1,300 / 3,460

NEBRASKA NOTES

Summary

There are 30 federal, 81 state, and 8 private recreation areas or local administrative offices covered in this state chapter. Of these, 45 appear in the Information Chart and 74 are covered in the notes. The special indexes feature 3 federally designated wilderness areas and wild rivers, and 2 agency published outdoor maps.

Federal Agencies

U.S. Forest Service

Nebraska is in the Rocky Mountain Region (see Colorado chapter - U.S. Forest Svc., Rocky Mountain Region listing).

For information about recreation opportunities at the Oglala National Grassland, check with the Nebraska National Forest office (S# 1, map A1).

U.S. Army Corps of Engineers (COE)
Missouri River Division Office
PO Box 103, Downtown Station
Omaha, NE 68101-0103   402-221-7284

The Kansas City, Missouri and Omaha, Nebraska District Offices manage COE projects in the lower Missouri River area (see information charts).

National Park Service
Additional NPS Location in Nebraska
The Missouri National Recreation and Niobrara National Scenic Rivers (S# 5, map B5)
c/o Midwest Region, NPS
1709 Jackson Street
Omaha, NE 68102   402-336-3970

Wilderness/Wild River Index

Wilderness Areas
Soldiers Creek Wilderness - 8,100 acres
Nebraska National Forest (S# 1, map A1)

Fort Niobrara Wilderness - 4,635
Fort Niobrara NWR, (S# 3, map A3)

Wild Rivers
Missouri River
Midwest Region, NPS (S# 1, map B5)

Outdoor Map Index

National Park Service (USGS Map)
Scotts Bluff National Monument [1939]
Size: 17x21 inches (43x53 cm)

U.S. Forest Service Map
Nebraska & Samuel R. McKelvie National Forests & Oglala National Grassland (NE-WY)
Scale: 1 inch = 0.5 mile (1 cm = 0.3 km)

Bureau of Reclamation Recreation Areas

Twelve recreation areas are listed here and symbolized on the Nebraska state map.

S#	MAP	LOCATION NAME
1	B3	Arcadia Diversion Dam
2	A1	Box Butte Res.
3	B3	Calamus Lake (Virginia Smith Dam)
4	B3	Davis Creek Dam & Res.
5	C2	Enders Res.
6	C3	Harry Strunk Lake
7	C2	Hugh Butler Lake
8	B1	Lake Minatare
9	A2	Merritt Res.
10	B3	Milburn Diversion Dam
11	B3	Sherman Res.
12	C2	Swanson Lake

State Agencies

NE Game & Parks Commission
Fish & Wildlife
Title 163 - Nebraska Game & Parks Commission, Chapter 4 - State Wildlife Management Area Regulations, describes a multitude of recreation opportunities on Nebraska wildlife management areas. Ask for a copy of the WMA Regulations. Another reference is *Your Nebraska Hunting Lands*. It lists 114 WMAs open to the public. Individual maps with descriptive information are available.

The Fish & Wildlife District Offices are listed in the Information Chart (orange color code). They are local information sources for wildlife management area (WMA) and park information. The magazine *Nebraskaland* is published 10 times each year. It is available by subscription for $12 per year.

WMA NAME & LOCATION

A selection of 62 WMAs exceeding 400 acres in size are listed here with their map symbol numbers and coordinates.

S#	MAP	WMA NAME & LOCATION
7	B3	Acadia Diversion Dam WMA, Comstock
8	A3	American Game Marsh WMA, Johnstown
9	A2	Ballards Marsh WMA, Valentine
10	A2	Big Alkali Lake WMA, Valentine
11	A2	Merritt Reservoir WMA, Valentine
12	B3	Milburn Diversion Dam WMA, Milburn
13	A3	Pine Glen WMA, Bassett
14	B2	Pressey WMA, Oconto
15	A2	Rat and Beaver Lakes WMA, Valentine
16	A2	Schiagel Creek WMA, Valentine
17	A2	Shell Lake WMA, Gordon
18	B3	Sherman Reservoir WMA, Loup City
19	A3	South Twin Lake WMA, Johnstown
20	A3	Thomas Creek WMA, Springview
21	A5	Basswood Ridge WMA, Homer
22	A4	Bazile Creek WMA, Niobrara
23	A4	Bohemia Prairie WMA, Niobrara
24	A4	Buckskin Hills WMA, Newcastle
25	A4	Grove Lake WMA, Royal
26	B4	Long Bow WMA, Genoa
27	B4	Loup Lands WMA (4 tracts), Genoa
28	B4	Oak Valley WMA, Battle Creek
29	B4	Wood Duck WMA, Stanton
30	B4	Yellowbanks WMA, Battle Creek
31	B1	Buffalo Creek WMA, Melbeta
32	B2	Clear Creek WMA, Lewellen
33	A1	Gilbert-Baker WMA, Harrison
34	A1	Metcalf WMA, Hay Springs
35	B1	Nine Mile Creek WMA, Minatare
36	A1	Ponderosa WMA, Crawford
37	A1	Smith Lake WMA, Rushville
38	B5	Alexandria Lakes WMA, Alexandria
39	C4	Arrowhead WMA, Odell
40	B4	Branched Oak Lake WMA, Malcolm
41	B4	Cornhusker WMA, Grand Island
42	C4	Diamond Lake WMA, Odell
43	B4	Jack Sinn Memorial WMA, Ceresco
44	B4	Oak Glen WMA, Garland
45	C5	Osage WMA, Tecumseh
46	C5	Pawnee Prairie WMA, Burchard
47	B4	Pintail WMA, Aurora
48	C4	Sandpiper WMA, Geneva
49	B5	Schilling WMA, Plattsmouth
50	B4	Twin Lakes WMA, Milford
51	C5	Two Oaks WMA, Tecumseh
52	B5	Two Rivers WMA, Valley
53	B5	Wildwood WMA, Agnew
54	B5	Yankee Hill WMA, Denton
55	B3	Bassway Strip WMA, Minden
56	B3	Blue Hole WMA, Elm Creek
57	B3	Cozad WMA, Cozad
58	B3	Dar Strip WMA, Cozad
59	C2	Enders Reservoir WMA, Imperial
60	C3	Limestone Bluffs WMA, Franklin
61	C2	Medicine Creek WMA, Cambridge
62	B2	North River WMA, Hershey
63	B2	Platte WMA, North Platte
64	C3	Quadhamer Lagoon FWA, Hildreth
65	C3	Red Willow Reservoir WMA, McCook
66	C3	Sacramento WMA (satellite areas), Wilcox
67	B3	Sandy Channel WMA, Elm Creek
68	C2	Swanson Reservoir WMA, Trenton

The official Nebraska Dept. of Roads map has symbols for various types of campgrounds, and forests, national parks, and game preserves. Each state park or recreation area is located by map coordinates.

Private Organizations

Tribal Land Areas in Nebraska

Omaha Tribe of the Omaha Indian Reservation - Fishing, hunting, camping.
Omaha Tribal Council (S# 1, map B5)
PO Box 368
Macy, NE 68039   402-837-5391

Santee Sioux Tribe of the Santee Indian Reservation - Fishing, hunting, camping.
Santee Sioux Tribal Council (S# 2, map A4)
Route 2
Niobrara, NE 68760   402-857-3302

Winnebago Tribe of the Winnebago Indian Reservation - Fishing, hunting.
Winnebago Tribal Council (S# 3, map A4)
Winnebago, NE 68071   402-878-2272

ANCA Locations in Nebraska

Chet Ager Nature Center (S# 4, map B5)
2740 A Street
Lincoln, NE 68502   402-471-7895

Fontenelle Forest Nature Center (S# 5, map B5)
1111 Bellevue Blvd. North
Bellevue, NE 68005

Lillian A Rowe Sanctuary (S# 6, map B3)
RR #2, Box 146
Gibbon, NE 68840   308-468-5282

Neale Woods Nature Center (S# 7, map B5)
14323 Edith Marie Ave.
Omaha, NE 68112

Nebraska Chamber of Commerce
1320 Lincoln Mall
PO Box 95128   Phone 402-474-4422
Lincoln, NE 68509   Fax 402-474-2510

NE Game & Parks Commission
Parks Division
A *Nebraska State Parks Guide* (7 state parks, 75 recreation areas) is available free. The guide describes each location, contains a site locator map, and includes information on facilities and activities. There are entry fees charged at some of the areas.

Department of Forestry, Fisheries, & Wildlife
Room 101, Plant Industries Bldg.
Lincoln, NE 68583   402-472-2944
Contact the Department for state forest recreation literature.

Travel & Tourism Division
Dept. of Economic Development
PO Box 94666   1-800-228-4307
Lincoln, NE 68509   1-800-742-7595
in state call

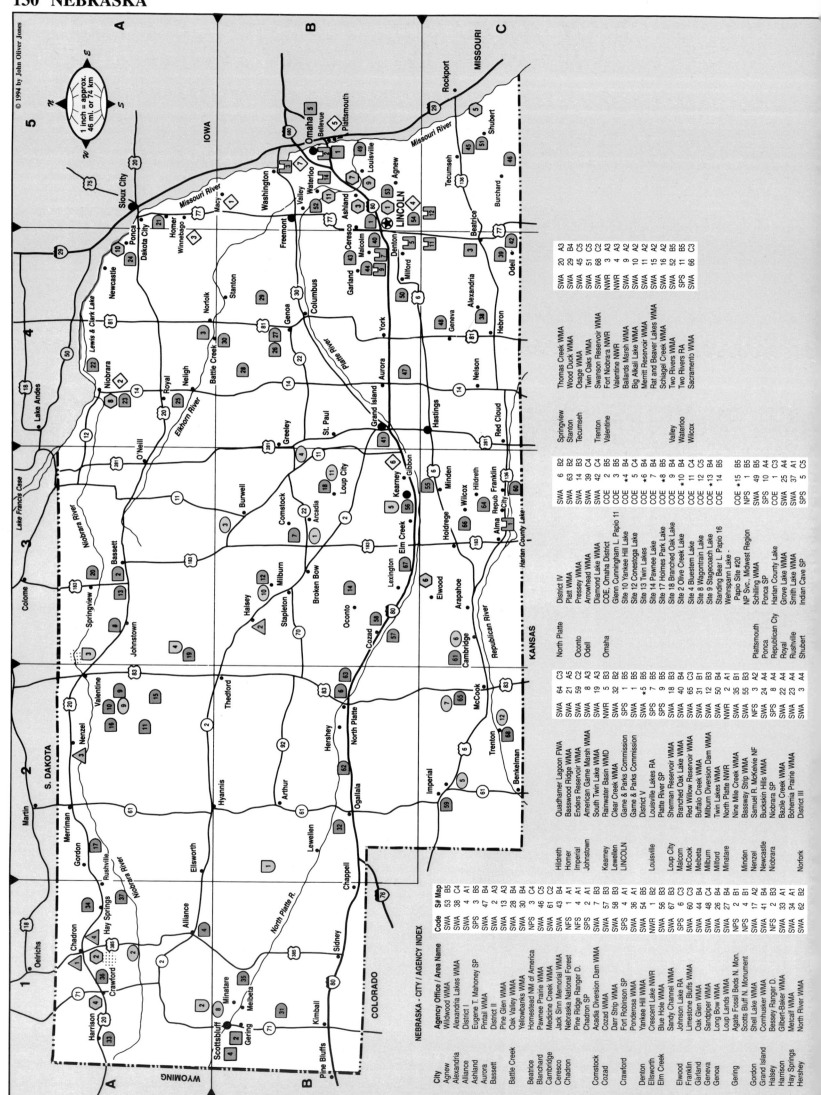

© 1994 by John Oliver Jones

1 inch = approx.
46 mi. or 74 km

★ INFORMATION CHART ★

★ AGENCY/MAP LEGEND - INITIALS, MAP SYMBOLS, COLOR CODES ★

U.S. Forest Service Supervisor & Ranger Dist. Offices . . NFS △ 61
U.S. Army Corps of Engineers Rec. Areas & Offices . . COE ⬡ 31
USFWS National Wildlife Refuges & Offices . . . . NWR ⬠ 40
National Park Service Parks & other NPS Sites . . . . . . NPS ▽ 7
Bureau of Land Management Rec. Areas & Offices . . . BLM ◇ 26
Bureau of Reclamation Rec. Areas & Reg. Offices . . . BOR ⬡ 8
State Parks (also see State Agency notes) . . . . SPS ⬡ 52
State Wildlife Areas (also see State Agency notes) . . . SWA ◇ 19
Private Preserves, Nature Centers & Tribal Lands . . . ⬡ 15
The Wild Rivers 〜 and Wilderness Areas ⬚⬚⬚

INFORMATION CHART LEGEND - SYMBOLS & LETTER CODES

■ means **YES** & □ means **Yes** with disability provisions
sp means **spring**, March through May
S means **Summer**, June through August
F means **Fall**, September through November
W means **Winter**, December through February
T means **Two (2)** or **Three (3)** Seasons
A means **All Four (4)** Seasons
na means **Not** Applicable or Not Available

Note: empty or blank spaces in the chart mean **NO**
Note: *Refer to yellow block on page 7 (top right) for location name and address abbreviations. If a symbol number has a star ★ that symbol is not shown on the map.*

Column headers (top, vertical):
INFO OFFICE (IO) / VISITOR CENTER (VC)
IO / VC OPEN SATURDAY / SUNDAY
ENTRY FEE, not camping or permit fee
INTERPRETIVE or EDUCATIONAL SERVICES / CONCESSIONAIRE SERVICES AVAILABLE
AGENCY LITERATURE AVAILABLE
FREE LITERATURE or brochures, maps, etc.
INTERPRETIVE NATIONAL DISPLAY
WILDFLOWER VIEWING AREA / GEOLOGICAL SITES
NATURE GUIDED TOURS, study / by res.
WILDLIFE EDUCATION / LITERATURE
ARCHAEOLOGICAL / HISTORIC SITES
INTERPRETIVE TRAILS
ENDANGERED SPECIES ARE COMMON
WILDLIFE IS ABUNDANT OR COMMON
DEVELOPED VIEWING SITES, blinds, signs, etc.
WILDLIFE VIEWING AREA COMMON
NO-CHARGE PICNIC AREAS / PICNIC SITES
DEVELOPED CAMPGROUNDS / CAMPSITES
WILDERNESS AREAS / CAMPSITES
WALKING / HIKING TRAILS
SWIMMING PERMITTED, at one's own risk
BICYCLING OPPORTUNITIES, w/ your own horse
HORSEBACK RIDING, "areas, trails
OFF-ROAD Motorized Vehicle Area / Use OK
FISHING OK, w/ license / permit reqd.
BOATING FACILITIES, ramps, marinas, etc.
NON-MOTORIZED WATERCRAFT OK / check limits
MOTORIZED WATERCRAFT OK
HUNTING IN SEASON, license / permit reqd.
WINTER SPORTS OPPORTUNITIES
PARK & WALK-IN SPORTS OPPORTUNITY AREA
DAY USE ONLY, no overnight
DRINKING WATER
RESTROOMS

Section group headers: FACILITIES, SERVICES, RECREATION OPPORTUNITIES & CONVENIENCES

S#	MAP	LOCATION NAME (state initials if more than one) with ADDRESS and/or LOCATION DATA	TELEPHONE	ACRES / ELEVATION
		Nebraska National Forest (Supervisor), 111 North Main, Chadron 69337	308-432-3367	1,000,000 / 3,000-4,700
2	B3	Bessey Ranger D., Halsey 69142	308-533-2257	90,000 / 2,900
3	A2	Samuel R. McKelvie NF, HC 74, Box 10, Nenzel 69219 [19 mi S of Nenzel on Hwy. 16 F]	402-823-4154	116,000 / 2,900
4	A1	Pine Ridge Ranger D., Chadron 69337 [3 mi S of Chadron on Hwy. 385]	308-432-4475	145,000 / 3,600
		COE, Kansas City District, 601 E. 12th St., 716 Federal Bldg., Kansas City, MO 64106	816-426-6816	na / na
1	C3	Harlan County Lake, PO Box 128, Republican Cty 68971	308-799-2105	na / na
2	B5	COE, Omaha District, 215 N. 17th St., Omaha 68102	402-221-4137	na / na
3	B5	Glenn Cunningham Lake Papio 11, 8901 South 154 St., Omaha 68138	402-896-0723	na / na
★4	B4	Site 10 Yankee Hill Lake, 8901 South 154 St., Omaha 68138 [S & W of Lincoln]	402-896-0723	na / na
5	C4	Site 12 Conestoga Lake, 8901 South 154 St., Omaha 68138	402-896-0723	na / na
★6	B4	Site 13 Twin Lakes, 8901 South 154 St., Omaha 68138 [S & W of Lincoln]	402-896-0723	na / na
7	B4	Site 14 Pawnee Lake, 8901 South 154 St., Omaha 68138	402-896-0723	na / na
★8	B5	Site 17 Holmes Park Lake, 8901 South 154 St., Omaha 68138 [S & W of Lincoln]	402-896-0723	na / na
9	B4	Site 18 Branched Oak Lake, 8901 South 154 St., Omaha 68138	402-896-0723	na / na
★10	B4	Site 2 Olive Creek Lake, 8901 South 154 St., Omaha 68139 [S & W of Lincoln]	402-896-0723	na / na
11	C4	Site 4 Bluestem Lake, 8901 South 154 St., Omaha 68138	402-896-0723	na / na
12	C5	Site 8 Wagontrain Lake, 8901 South 154 St., Omaha 68138	402-896-0723	na / na
★13	B4	Site 9 Stagecoach Lake, 8901 South 154 St., Omaha 68138 [S & W of Lincoln]	402-896-0723	na / na
14	B4	Standing Bear Lake - Papio Site 16, 8901 South 154 St., Omaha 68138	402-896-0723	na / na
★15	B5	Wehrspann Lake - Papio Site #20, 8901 South 154 St., Omaha 68138	402-896-0723	na / na
1	B2	**Crescent Lake NWR**, HC 68, Box 21, Ellsworth 69340	308-762-4893	46,000 / 3,770-4,040
2	A1	North Platte NWR (3 units), Box 125 D, Minatare 69356 [7 mi N of Minatare, then NE on Stonegate Rd.]	308-783-2477	5,047 / 4,000-4,200
3	A3	Fort Niobrara NWR, Hidden Timber Route, HC 14, Box 67, Valentine 69201	402-376-3789	19,130 / 2,800
4	A3	Valentine NWR, Hidden Timber Route, HC 14, Box 67, Valentine 69201	402-376-3789	71,000 / 2,000
5	B3	Rainwater Basin WMD, 2610 Ave. "Q", PO Box 1686, Kearney 68847 [1 block N of Hwy 30 (26th St), E edge of town]	308-236-5015	20,000 / 2,000
1	B5	**National Park Service, Midwest Region**, 1709 Jackson Street, Omaha 68102	402-221-3471	na / na
2	B1	Agate Fossil Beds National Monument, PO Box 27, Gering 69341 [34 mi N of Mitchell, NE on Hwy.29]	308-436-4340	3,055 / na
3	C4	Homestead N. Monument of America, Rt. #3, Box 47, Beatrice 68310	402-223-3514	194 / 1,270
4	B1	Scotts Bluff Nat'l. Monument, PO Box 27, Gering 69341 [3 mi W of Gering & NW on Hwy 92]	308-436-4340	2,997 / 4,124-4,649
1	B5	**Game & Parks Commission** (Parks), 2200 N. 33rd St., PO Box 30370, Lincoln 68503	402-471-0641	na / na
2	A1	Chadron SP, Hwy. 385, 9 mi. S of Chadron	308-432-2036	974 / 4,000
3	A1	Eugene T. Mahoney SP, take I-80 exit 426, near Ashland	402-944-2523	479 / 1,150
4	A1	Fort Robinson SP, Hwy. 20, 3 mi. W of Crawford	308-665-2660	22,673 / 3,800
5	C5	Indian Cave SP, on S-64 E, 10 mi. S & 5 mi. E of Brownsville, near Shubert	402-883-2575	3,052 / 1,050
6	C3	Johnson Lake RA, Hwy. 283, 7 mi. S Lexington, near Elwood	308-785-2685	81 / 2,620
7	B5	Louisville Lakes RA, on Hwy. 50, 0.5 mi. NW of Louisville	402-234-6855	192 / 1,020
8	A4	Niobrara SP, on SH N-12, 1.5 mi. SW of Niobrara	402-857-3373	1,640 / 1,470
9	B5	Platte River SP, on S-13 E, 1 mi. S & 2 mi. W of Louisville	402-234-2217	418 / 1,100
10	A4	Ponca SP, on SH N-9, 2 mi. N of Ponca	402-755-2284	859 / 1,250
11	B5	Two Rivers RA, 1 mi. S & 1 mi. W of Venice, near Waterloo	402-359-5165	622 / 1,095
1	B5	**Game & Parks Commission** (Game), 2200 N. 33rd St., PO Box 30370, Lincoln 68503	402-471-0641	na / na
2	A3	District II (WMA S# 7-20), Box 508, Bassett 68714	402-684-2921	na / na
3	A4	District III (WMA S# 21-30), Box 934, Norfolk 68701	402-371-4950	na / na
4	A1	District I (WMA S# 31-37), Box 725, Alliance 68702	308-762-5605	na / na
★5	B5	District V (WMA S# 38-54), 2200 N. 33rd St., PO Box 30370, Lincoln 68503	402-471-0641	na / na
6	B2	District IV (WMA S# 55-68), Rt. #4, Box 36, North Platte 69101	308-532-6225	na / na

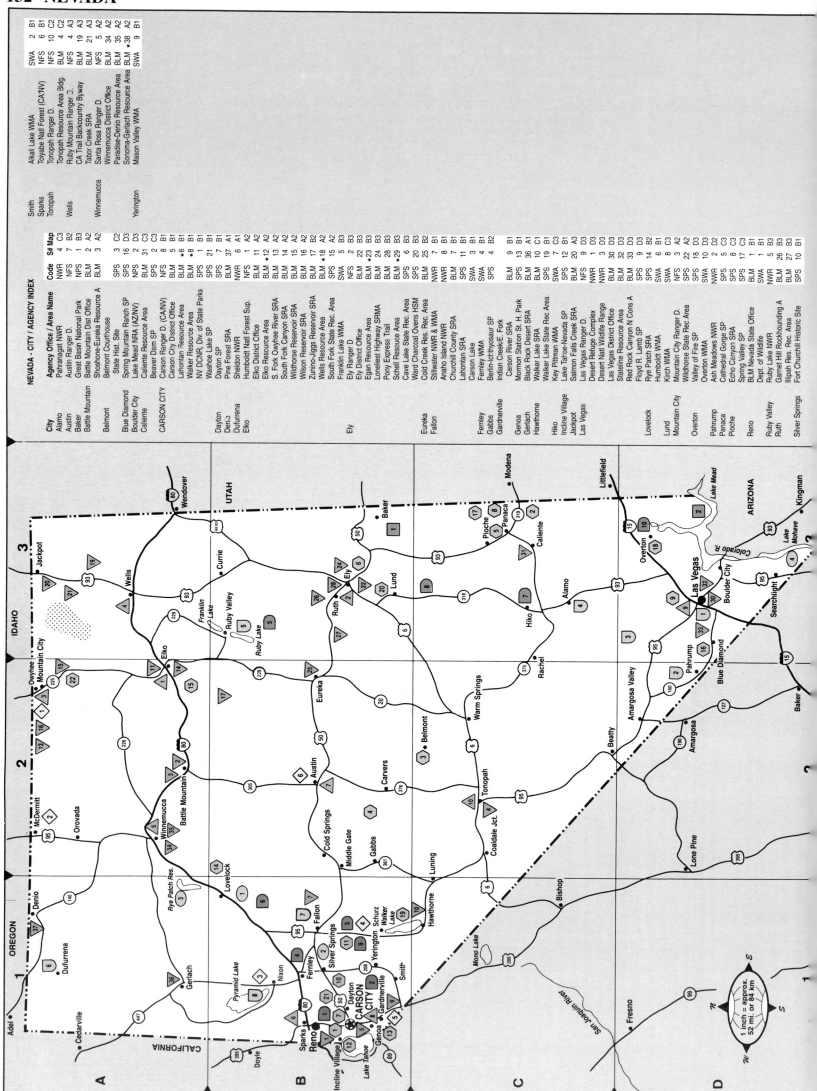

NEVADA NOTES

Summary

There are 63 federal, 35 state, and 7 private recreation areas or local administrative offices covered in this state chapter. Of these, 90 appear in the Information Chart and 15 are covered in the notes. The special indexes feature one federally designated wilderness area, and 83 agency published outdoor maps.

Federal Agencies

U.S. Forest Service

Nevada is in the Intermountain Region (see Utah chapter - U.S. Forest Svc., Intermountain Region listing).

Bureau of Reclamation - USDI

Lower Colorado Region
Nevada Hwy. & Park St.
PO Box 427
Boulder City, NV 89005   702-293-8420
This office administers bureau recreation areas in southern Nevada, all of Arizona except the northeastern portion, and south and southeast California.

Bureau of Reclamation Recreation Areas

Four recreation areas are listed here and symbolized on the Nevada state map. Two others are the Fernley and Stillwater wildlife areas, a state WMA (S# 4, map B1) and a National Wildlife Refuge (S# 7, map B1) respectively.

S#	MAP	LOCATION NAME
1	B1	Humboldt - Toulon Sink
2	B1	Lahontan Res.
3	A1	Rye Patch Res.
4	C3	Sportsman's Park

Wilderness Index

Jarbridge Wilderness - 64,677 acres
Humboldt National Forest Sup. (S# 1, map A2)

National Park Service (USGS Map)

Death Valley Natl. Monument (CA-NV) [1977]
Scale: 1 inch = 4.0 miles (1 cm = 2.5 km)
Size: 24x37 inches (61x94 cm)

U.S. Forest Service Maps

Hoover Wilderness, Toiyabe/Inyo NFs [1987]
Humboldt NF, Ruby Division [1968]
Humboldt NF, Santa Rosa/Humboldt Div [1968]
Humboldt NF, White Pine & Ely RDs [1969]
Toiyabe NF, Austin Ranger District [1987]
Toiyabe NF, Bridgeport Ranger District [1984]
Toiyabe NF, Carson Ranger District [1984]
Toiyabe NF, Las Vegas Ranger Dis [1985]
Toiyabe NF, Tonopah Ranger District [1987]

Bureau of Land Management Maps

See the Nevada BLM intermediate scale map grid covering 68 Nevada BLM intermediate scale maps. An "Order Form #1" available from the Nevada State Office in Reno covers another map series, the 30-minute quad maps (131 maps). The scale is 1 inch = 1 mile. A Land Status Map of Nevada [1971] is available for $5.50. It is a 1:500,000 scale map and 43x64 inches in size.

BLM NEVADA
1:100,000 INTERMEDIATE SCALE MAPS
SURFACE & SURFACE / MINERAL SERIES

120°	119°	118°	117°	116°	115°	114°
Vya 1979	Denio 1979	Quinn River Valley 1979	Bull Run Mountains 1978	Jarbidge Mountains 1979	Jackpot 1978	
High Rock Canyon 1974	Jackson Mountains 1978	Osgood Mountains 1979	Tuscarora 1979	Double Mountains 1978	Wells 1979	
Gerlach 1976	Eugene Mountains 1975	Winnemucca 1978	Battle Mountain 1975	Elko 1976	Wendover 1979	
Kumiva Peak 1974	Lovelock 1978	Fish Creek Mountains 1978	Crescent Valley 1979	Ruby Lake 1978	Currie 1979	
Reno 1975	Carson Sink 1974	Edwards Creek Valley 1978	Simpson Park Mtns. 1979	Newark Lake 1985	Kern Mountains 1976	
Carson City 1975	Fallon 1978	Smith Creek Valley 1975	Summit Mountain 1978	Mount Hamilton 1979	Ely 1977	
Smith Valley 1978	Walker Lake 1978	Ione Valley 1978	Mount Jefferson 1978	Duckwater 1978	Garrison 1979	
Bridgeport 1975	Excelsior Mountains 1973	Tonopah 1978	Warm Springs 1978	Quinn Can. Range 1978	Wilson Cr. Range 1979	
Benton Range 1976	Goldfield 1978	Cactus Flat 1978	Timpahute Range 1977	Callente 1978		
	Last Chance Range 1978	Pahute Mesa 1978	Pahranagat Range 1978	Clover Mountains 1978 T		
	Saline Valley 1976	Beatty 1978	Indian Springs 1979	Overton 1978		
		Death Valley Jct. 1978	Las Vegas 1978	Lake Mead 1978		
			Mesquite Lake 1979	Boulder City 1978		
			Ivanpah 1979	Davis Dam 1979		

Recreation Guide Maps for Carson City, Ely, and Winnemucca Districts are available for $1.50 each. They contain recreation, natural, and cultural features of interest to the public. The Pony Express Trail (Carson City and Ely maps), emigrant trails (Winnemucca map), likely spots to view wild horses, and limited or closed areas to ORV use are shown.

A Rockhounds Map of Nevada shows small samplings of rock and mineral occurrences, and contains a list of the localities, with references listed in parentheses. Reference material is available at large libraries, the University of Nevada, and the Nevada Bureau of Mines. Many mineral locations shown on the map are privately owned, or are claimed by individuals, and some are closed to collecting. Permission should be obtained before collecting. Check with the local BLM office or at a county courthouse for land ownership information.

State Agencies

Dept. of Conservation and Natural Resources (DCNR)

Capitol Complex
123 W. Nye Lane
Carson City, NV 89710   702-687-4360
Parks and Forestry Divisions are under this state agency.

Division of State Parks (S# 1, map B1)

A Nevada State Parks Guide (19 state parks) is available free. The guide describes each area, contains a locator map, and includes information on facilities and activities. There is a daily use fee at some of the parks. There are also fees for camping, firewood, boat launching, and group use.

Division of Forestry

201 S. Fall St.
Carson City, NV 89710   702-687-4353
There is no state forest recreation program in Nevada.

NV Department of Wildlife (S3 1, map B1)

A brochure on wildlife management areas is available.
Licensing and harvest information is published annually.

Commission on Tourism

600 E. William St. #207
Carson City, NV 89710   1-800-638-2328
in state call   702-885-4322
Complete information on Nevada's Tourism Territories, accommodations, campgrounds, special events, ghost towns, and outfitters and guides is available on request. An official road map is also available. The map has symbols for campgrounds, campsites, and winter sports areas. There are different colors for national parks, state parks, recreation areas, wilderness, and scenic areas. A map of historical trails and ghost towns is included.

Private Organizations

Tribal Land Areas in Nevada

Soshone-Paiute Tribes of the Duck Valley Indian Reservation - Fishing, camping.
Soshone-Paiute Business Council (Nevada/Idaho)
(S# 1, map A2)
PO Box 219
Owyhee, NV 89832   702-757-3161

Fort McDermitt Paiute and Shoshone Tribes of the Fort McDermitt Indian Reservation - Camping.
Fort McDermitt Tribal Council (Nevada/Oregon)
(S# 2, map A2)
PO Box 457
McDermitt, NV 89421   702-532-8259

Pyramid Lake Paiute Tribe of the Pyramid Lake Indian Reservation - Fishing, camping, boating.
Pyramid Lake Paiute Tribal Council
(S# 3, map B1)
PO Box 256
Nixon, NV 89424   702-574-0140

Walker River Paiute Tribe of the Walker River Indian Reservation - Fishing, camping, boating.
Walker River Paiute Tribal Council
(S# 4, map B1)
PO Box 220
Schurz, NV 89427   702-773-2306

Washoe Tribe of Nevada and California - Fishing, camping, boating.
Washoe Tribal Council
(S# 5, map B1)
919 Highway 395 South
Gardnerville, NV 89410   702-265-4191

Yomba Shoshone Tribe of the Yomba Indian Reservation - Fishing, camping.
Yomba Tribal Council
(S# 6, map B2)
Route 1, Box 24
Austin, NV 89310   702-964-2463

Nevada Chamber of Commerce

PO Box 3499
Reno, NV 89505   Phone 702-786-3030   Fax 702-329-3499

★ INFORMATION CHART ★

INFORMATION CHART LEGEND - SYMBOLS & LETTER CODES

- ■ means YES & □ means Yes with disability provisions
- sp means spring, March through May
- S means Summer, June through August
- F means Fall, September through November
- W means Winter, December through February
- T means Two (2) or Three (3) Seasons
- A means All Four (4) Seasons
- na means Not Applicable or Not Available

Note: empty or blank spaces in the chart mean NO
* that symbol is not shown on the map.

AGENCY/MAP LEGEND ... INITIALS, MAP SYMBOLS, COLOR CODES

- U.S. Forest Service Supervisor & Ranger Dist. Offices . . NFS
- U.S. Army Corps of Engineers Rec. Areas & Offices . . COE
- USFWS National Wildlife Refuges & Offices . . . . NWR
- National Park Service Parks & other NPS Sites . . . . . . NPS
- Bureau of Land Management Rec. Areas & Offices . . . BLM
- Bureau of Reclamation Rec. Areas & Reg. Offices . . . BOR
- State Parks (also see State Agency notes) . . . . SPS
- State Wildlife Areas (also see State Agency notes) . . . SWA
- Private Preserves, Nature Centers & Tribal Lands . . . .
- The Wild Rivers — and Wilderness Areas

Note: Refer to yellow block on page 7 (top right) for location name and address abbreviations. If a symbol number has a star *

S#	MAP	LOCATION NAME (state initials if more than one) with ADDRESS and/or LOCATION DATA	TELEPHONE	ACRES / ELEVATION
△	A2	Humboldt Nat'l Forest (Sup.), 976 Mountain City Hwy., Elko 89801 [cor Idaho St & Mtn City Hwy across from Airport]	702-738-5171	2,475,000 / 5,000-12,000
2	B3	Ely Ranger D., 350 8th Street, PO Box 539, Ely 89301 [one block N of US 93 on 8th St.]	702-289-3031	1,102,000 / 5,000-12,000
3	A2	Mountain City Ranger D., Mountain City 89831 [on town on Mountain City Hwy.]	702-763-6691	479,000 / 5,000-10,000
4	A3	Ruby Mountain Ranger D., 301 South Humboldt, PO Box 246, Wells 89825 [on Humboldt Ave. N of the Interstate]	702-752-3357	384,000 / 5,000-11,000
5	B1	Santa Rosa Ranger D., 1200 Winnemucca Blvd. East, Winnemucca 89445 [in town go E on Winnemucca]	702-623-5025	268,000 / 5,000-10,000
6	B1	Toiyabe National Forest Sup. (CA/NV), 1200 Franklin Way, Sparks 89431	702-331-6444	3,800,000 / 4,000-12,000
7	B2	Austin Ranger D., Main Street, PO Box 130, Austin 89310	702-964-2671	1,000,000 / 4,000-11,000
8	B1	Carson Ranger D. (CA/NV), 1536 S Carson St., Carson City 89701 [on Hwy. 395 in City. Note: Markville VC in CA]	702-882-2766	380,000 / 5,000-11,000
9	D3	Las Vegas Ranger D., 550 East Charleston, Las Vegas 89104	702-477-7782	300,000 / 3,000-12,000
10	C2	Tonopah Ranger D., 1400 S. Erie Main, PO Box 3940, Tonopah 89049	702-482-6286	1,100,000 / 4,500-11,000
①	D3	Desert Refuge Complex, 1500 North Decatur Blvd., Las Vegas 89108	702-646-3401	1,500,000 / 2,500-10,000
2	D2	Ash Meadows NWR, PO Box 2660, Pahrump 89041 [from town 17.5 mi W on Bell Vista, gravel road R fork to NWR]	702-372-5435	12,736 / 2,200
3	D3	Desert Nat'l Wildlife Range, 1500 N Decatur Blvd., Las Vegas 89108 [23 mi N of Las Vegas. L off Hwy 95, 4 mi]	702-646-3401	1,588,000 / 2,500-10,000
4	C3	Pahranagat NWR, PO Box 510, Alamo 89001 [off US 93 about 90 mi N of Las Vegas, office on refuge]	702-725-3417	5,380 / 3,500
5	B3	Ruby Lake NWR, HC 60, Box 860, Ruby Valley 89833	702-779-2237	37,600 / 6,000
6	A1	Sheldon/Hart Mountain Complex, U.S. PO Bldg., Room 301, PO Box 111, Lakeview, OR 97630	503-947-3315	na / 4,800
7	B1	Sheldon NWR, c/o above Complex, Lakeview, OR 97630, Dufurrena [about 100 mi E of Oregon office off SR 140]	503-947-3315	575,000 / 4,300-7,300
8	B1	Stillwater NWR & WMA, 9604 Auction Rd., PO Box 1236, Fallon 89407 [refuge is 17 mi NE of Fallon]	702-423-5128	140,340 / 3,890
		Anaho Island NWR (no public access), PO Box 1236, Fallon 89407 [located in Pyramid Lake]	702-423-5128	248 / 3,860-4,400
①	B3	Great Basin National Park, Baker 89311	702-234-7331	77,100 / 6,500-13,063
②	D3	Lake Mead NRA (AZ/NV), 601 Nevada Highway, Boulder City 89005	702-293-8906	1,496,000 / na
1	B1	BLM Nevada State Office, 850 Harvard Way, PO Box 12000, Reno 89520	702-785-6586	na / na
2	A2	Battle Mountain District Office, Second & Scott Sts., PO Box 1420, Battle Mountain 89820	702-635-4000	10,400,000 / 2,700-10,150
3	A2	Shoshone-Eureka Resource Area, Second & Scott Sts., PO Box 1420, Battle Mountain 89820	702-635-4000	4,300,000 / 4,500-10,500
4	C2	Tonopah Resource Area Bldg., 102 Old Radar Base, Box 911, Tonopah 89049	702-482-6214	6,100,000 / 2,700-9,560
5	B1	Carson City District Office, 1535 Hot Springs Rd., Suite 300, Carson City 89706	702-885-6000	5,000,000 / 5,000-9,900
*6	B1	Lahontan Resource Area, 1535 Hot Springs Rd., Suite 300, Carson City 89706	702-885-6000	na / na
7	B1	Churchill County SRA, off Hwy. 50, E of Fallon	702-885-6000	10,000 / 5,000
*8	B1	Walker Resource Area, 1535 Hot Springs Rd., Suite 300, Carson City 89706	702-885-6000	na / na
9	B1	Indian Creek/E. Fork Carson River S, off Hwy. 395, S of Gardnerville	702-885-6000	7,000 / 6,000
10	C1	Walker Lake SRA, off Hwy. 95, N of Hawthorne	702-885-6000	50,000 / 5,000
11	A2	Elko District Office, 3900 E. Idaho St., PO Box 831, Elko 89801	702-753-0200	7,200,000 / 4,000-10,000
*12	A2	Elko Resource Area, 3900 E. Idaho St., PO Box 831, Elko 89801	702-753-0200	3,100,000 / 4,500-10,000
13	A2	S. Fork Owyhee River SRA, for access information, request Owyhee River boating guide, Elko	702-753-0200	4,830 / 5,340
14	A2	South Fork Canyon SRA, 10 mi. SW of Elko	702-753-0200	5,040 / 5,500
15	A2	Wildhorse Reservoir SRA, on Hwy. 225, 70 mi. N of Elko	702-753-0200	5,760 / 6,200
16	A2	Wilson Reservoir SRA, on Hwy. 226 about 83 mi. NW of Elko	702-753-0200	5,440 / 5,300
17	A2	Zunino-Jiggs Reservoir SRA, 30 mi. SE of Elko on Hwy. 228, Elko	702-753-0200	800 / 5,600
*18	A2	Wells Resource Area, 3900 E. Idaho St., PO Box 831, Elko 89801	702-753-0200	4,100,000 / 4,000-9,000
19	A3	California Trail Backcountry Byway, Wells [access via Hwy. 93 at two points between Jackpot and Wells]	702-753-0200	na / 5,000-7,000
20	A3	Salmon Falls Creek SRA, 2 mi. S of Jackpot	702-753-0200	2,180 / 5,200
21	A3	Tabor Creek SRA, 25 mi. N of Wells	702-753-0200	250 / 6,000
22	B3	Ely District Office, 702 N. Industrial Way (McGill Hwy.), HC 33, Box 150, Ely 89301	702-289-4865	8,000,000 / 4,000-11,000
*23	B3	Egan Resource Area, 702 N. Industrial Way, HC 33, Box 150, Ely 89301	702-289-4865	3,800,000 / 6,000-10,000
24	B3	Loneliest Highway SRMA (4 areas, ask for map), HC 33, Box 150, Ely 89301	702-289-4865	520 / 6,000-7,300
25	B2	Cold Creek Res. Rec. Area, take Rt. 892 N & E of Eureka	702-289-4865	40 / 6,000
26	B3	Garnet Hill Rockhounding Area, off Hwy. 50 NE of Ruth	702-289-4865	180 / 7,300
27	B3	Illipah Res. Rec. Area, off Hwy. 50 W of Ruth	702-289-4865	300 / 6,800
28	B3	Pony Express Trail (part, 57 mi of the trail), N of Ely	702-289-4865	na / na
*29	B3	Schell Resource Area, 702 N. Industrial Way, HC 33, Box 150, Ely 89301	702-289-4865	4,200,000 / 4,000-11,000

#	Grid	Name	Acreage / Elevation	Phone
31	C3	Caliente Resource Area, PO Box 237, Caliente 89008	na / 2,800-7,762	702-726-3141
32	D3	Stateline Resource Area, 4765 Vegas Drive, PO Box 26569, Las Vegas 89126	3,500,000 / 600-8,087	702-647-5000
33	D3	Red Rock Canyon Nat'l. Cons. Area, 17 mi. W of Las Vegas	83,000 / 3,800-7,39C	702-363-1921
34	A2	Winnemucca District Office, 705 East 4th Street, Winnemucca 89445	8,000,000 / 3,900-9,83C	702-623-1500
35	A2	Paradise-Denio Resource Area, 705 East 4th Street, Winnemucca 89445	3,500,000 / 3,900-8,920	702-623-1500
36	A1	Black Rock Desert SRA (summer access only), near Gerlach	160,000 / 3,900	702-623-1500
37	A1	Pine Forest SFA, near Denio	25,000 / 7,200-9,400	702-623-1500
*38	A2	Sonoma-Gerlach Resource Area, 705 East 4th Street, Winnemucca 89445	4,500,000 / 3,900-9,830	702-623-1500

NV DCNR, Div. of State Parks, 123 W. Nye Lane, Capitol Complex, Carson City 89710

#	Grid	Name	Acreage / Elevation	Phone
1	B1		na / 4,800	702-687-4370
2	C3	Beaver Dam SP, 6 mi. N & 32 mi. E of Caliente	2,233 / 5,400-5,900	702-728-4467
3	C2	Belmont Courthouse State Hist. Site, 45 mi. NE of Tonopah, Belmont	1 / 7,400	702-687-3500
4	B2	Berlin-Ichthyosaur SP, 23 mi. E of Gabbs	1,147 / 7,100	702-964-2440
5	C3	Cathedral Gorge SP, N of Panaca	1,633 / 4,800	702-728-4467
6	B3	Cave Lake State Recreation Area (SR, 8 mi. S & 7 mi. E of Ely	1,240 / 6,600-9,000	702-728-4467
7	B1	Dayton SP, on Hwy. 50 12 mi. E of Carson City, Dayton	152 / 4,320-4,550	702-885-5678
8	C3	Echo Canyon SRA, 18 mi. E of Pioche	920 / 5,200-5,600	702-728-4467
9	D3	Floyd R. Lamb SP, 10 mi. N of Las Vegas	2,041 / 2,500	702-486-5413
10	B1	Fort Churchill Historic State, Monument (HSM), 8 mi. S of Silver Springs	1,232 / 4,200-5,100	702-577-2345
11	B1	Lahontan SRA, Hwy. 50 & 45 mi. SE of Carson City, Fallon	30,362 / 4,100	702-867-3500
12	B1	Lake Tahoe-Nevada SP, on NE shore of Lake Tahoe, Incline Village	14,242 / 6,230-9,200	702-831-0494
13	B1	Mormon Station S:. Historic Park, 12 mi. S of Carson City, Genoa	2 / 5,000	702-687-4379
14	B2	Rye Patch SRA, 22 mi. E of Lovelock	20,241 / 3,800	702-867-3500
15	A2	South Fork State Recreation Area, 16 mi. SW of Elko, Elko	3,924 / 5,300	702-744-4346
16	D3	Spring Mountain Ranch SP, 15 mi. W of Las Vegas, Blue Diamond	17,600 / 3,700	702-875-4141
17	C3	Spring Valley SP, 18 mi. E of Pioche	1,230 / 5,700-6,500	702-962-5102
18	D3	Valley of Fire SP, 55 mi. NE of Las Vegas, Overton	34,880 / 2,100-3,000	702-397-2088
19	B1	Walker Lake State Recreation Area, 11 mi. N of Hawthorne	280 / 4,000	702-867-3500
20	B3	Ward Charcoal Owens HSM, 16 mi. S of Ely	680 / 7,000	702-728-4467
21	B1	Washoe Lake SP, S of Reno on US 395 & 10 mi. N of Carson City	7,778 / 5,000	702-687-4319
22	A2	Wildhorse State Recreation Area, 67 mi. N of Elko, Mountain City	na / 4,395	702-758-6493

Dept. of Wildlife, 1100 Valley Rd., PO Box 10678, Reno 89520

#	Grid	Name	Acreage / Elevation	Phone
1	B1			
2	B1	Alkali Lake WMA, 9 mi. N of Smith	3,440 / 4,560	702-463-2741
3	B1	Carson Lake (Greenhead Hunt Club), 10 mi. S of Fallon	13,000 / 3,910	702-423-3171
4	B1	Fernley WMA, 7 mi. E of Fernley	13,000 / 4,100	702-463-2741
5	B3	Franklin Lake WMA, 70 mi. SE of Elko	3,340 / 5,000	702-738-5332
6	B1	Humboldt WMA, 15 mi. S of Lovelock	36,400 / 3,890	702-463-2741
7	C3	Key Pittman WMA, Hiko	1,330 / 3,800	702-725-3521
8	C3	Kirch WMA, 28 mi. S of Lund	15,500 / 5,200	702-238-5378
9	B1	Mason Valley WMA, 8 mi. NE of Yerington	12,030 / 4,500	702-463-2741
10	D3	Overton WMA, 1 mi. E of Overton	12,990 / 1,150	702-397-2142

NEW HAMPSHIRE NOTES

Summary

There are 16 federal, 64 state, and 31 private recreation areas or local administrative offices covered in this state chapter. Of these, 84 appear in the Information Chart and 27 are covered in the notes. The special indexes feature 4 federally designated wilderness areas and a wild river, and the White Mountain National Forest map.

Federal Agencies

U.S. Forest Service

New Hampshire is in the Eastern Region (see Wisconsin chapter - U.S. Forest Svc., Eastern Region listing).

Wilderness Areas

White Mountain National Forest (S# 1, map D3)
Great Gulf Wilderness - 5,552 acres
Pemigewasset Wilderness - 45,000 acres
Presidential Range-Dry River Wilderness - 27,380 acres
Sandwich Range Wilderness - 25,000 acres

Wild Rivers

Wildcat Creek
Town of Jackson, PO Box 268, Jackson NH 03846 and White Mountain National Forest (S# 1, map D3)

Outdoor Map Index

U.S. Forest Service Map
White Mountain National Forest [1989]
Scale: 1 inch = 4.0 miles (1 cm = 2.5 km)
Size: 35x36 inches (89x91 cm)

State Agencies

Dept. of Resources and Economic Development
172 Pembroke Rd.
PO Box 856
Concord, NH 03302-0856
This department is the parent agency for divisions managing New Hampshire's forests and parks.

NH Division of Parks & Recreation (S# 1, map E3) 603-271-2214
A New Hampshire State Parks Guide (47 state parks) is available free. The guide describes each area, contains a locator map, and includes information on facilities and activities. There is a daily use fee at some of the parks.

NH Division of Forests & Lands
Box 856, Prescott Park
105 Loudon Rd.
Concord, NH 03301
There is no state forest recreation program in New Hampshire.

NH Fish & Game Department (S# 1, map E3) 603-271-2666
A basic reference is the brochure listing wildlife management areas. A locator map is included. The New Hampshire Natural Resources magazine and a monthly publication Field Notes are available by subscription for $6 per year from the Department.

Office of Vacation Travel
Box 856
Concord, NH 03301
A New Hampshire's Guidebook, a comprehensive travel planner, is available on request. A variety of public and

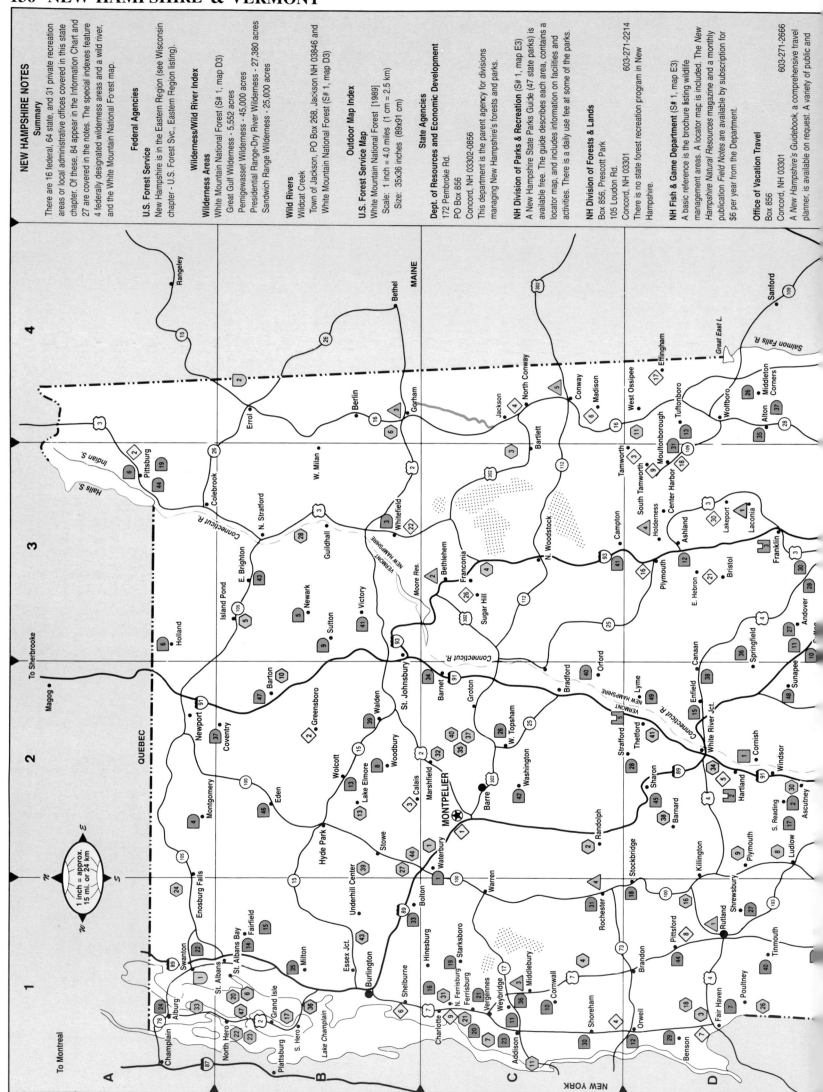

private recreation attractions are described and located by coordinates on small regional maps. A more detailed road map, using the same coordinates, is available from this office. The road map has symbols for campgrounds, campsites, and winter sports areas.

Private Organizations

Audubon Society of New Hampshire (ASNH)

A free fold-out *Guide to ASNH Wildlife Sanctuaries* is available and contains recreation details. The sanctuaries which do not contain "critical habitat" are featured on the Guide map and listed here. The two staffed facilities are Silk Farm Nature Center (ASNH headquarters) in Concord (see Information Chart S# 7, map E3), and Paradise Point Nature Center

North Shore Rd.
East Hebron, NH 03232
603-744-3516

ASNH SANCTUARY & LOCATION

S#	MAP	Sanctuary & Location
8	E3	Abe Emerson Marsh, Manchester
9	D3	Alice Bemis Thompson, South Tamworth
10	E4	Bellamy River, Dover
11	F3	Betsy Fosket, Rindge
12	E4	Brookside, Hampton
13	E3	Deering, Hillsboro
14	E3	DePierrefeur-Willard Pond, Hancock Village
15	E4	Hampton Saltmarshes, Hampton Falls
16	D3	Hebron Marsh, Plymouth
17	D4	Hoyt, Effingham
18	D3	Markus, Moultonborough
19	E2	Meetinghouse Pond, Marlborough
20	E2	Nye Meadow Easement, Munsonville
21	D3	Paradise Point, Bristol
22	B3	Pondicherry, Whitefield
23	E3	Poneman Bog, Amherst
24	D3	Proctor, Center Harbor
25	E3	Samuel Myron Chase, Hopkinton
26	C3	Scotland Brook, Sugar Hill
27	D3	Smith Pond Bog, Hopkinton Village
28	E2	Stoney Brook, Newbury Harbor
29	E2	Sucker Brook Cove, Nelson Center

ANCA Location in New Hampshire

(Association of Nature Center Administrators)
John R. Forbes Nature Center (S# 30, map D3)
Ragged Island
Lakeport, NH 03246
603-253-7685

Business & Industry Assn. of NH

(State Chamber of Commerce)
122 North Main St.
Concord, NH 03301
603-224-5388

NEW HAMPSHIRE - CITY / AGENCY INDEX

City	Agency Office / Area Name	Code	S#	Map
Allenstown	Hall Mountain Marsh WMA	SWA	20	D3
Alton	Hayes Marsh WMA	SWA	22	E3
Alton	Marks Wildlife Area	SWA	35	D4
Amherst	Merrymeeting Marsh WMA	SWA	37	D4
Andover	Ponemah Bog	INA	23	E3
Andover	Kearsarge Wildlife Area	SWA	27	D3
Antrim	Hosmer WMA	SWA	25	E3
Ashland	Church Hill Wildlife Area	SWA	12	D3
Bartlett	Crawford Notch SP	NFS	5	C3
Bethlehem	Ammonoosuc Ranger D.	NFS	3	C3
Boscawen	Hirst Wildlife Area	SWA	23	E3
Bristol	Paradise Point	INA	41	D3
Campton	Rowbarwood Marsh WMA	SWA	44	D2
Canaan	Myrl Webster Wildlife Area	SWA	38	D2
Charlestown	Proctor	INA	24	E2
Chesterfield	Spaulding WMA	SWA	45	E2
CONCORD	Pisgah SP	SPS	10	E4
	NH Div. of Parks & Rec	SPS	1	
	Fish & Game Department	SWA	1	
	Audubon Society of NH & Silk Farm Sanctuary	INA	7	E3
Contoocook	TNC NH Field Office	TNC	1	
Conway	Saco Ranger D.	NFS	4	
Cornish	Saint-Gaudens N. Hist. Site	NPS	5	C4
Deerfield	Dole's Marsh WMA	SWA	14	D2
	Lamontagne WMA	SWA	32	E4
Derry	Moose Brook SP	SPS	6	
	Ballard Marsh WMA	SWA	4	
Dover	Bellamy River	INA	10	E4
Dublin	Ryan WMA	SWA	42	E2
Dunbarton	Stark Pond WMA	SWA	46	E3
Durham	Adams Point WMA	SWA	2	E4
Effingham	Hoyt	INA	17	D4
Enfield	Enfield WMA	SWA	15	D2
Errol	Lake Umbagog NWR (ME-NH)	NWR	2	
Franconia	Franconia Notch SP	SPS	4	C3
Franklin	Blackwater Dam	COE	1	D2
	Franklin Falls Dam	COE	3	D3
Gorham	Androscoggin Ranger D.	NFS	3	B4
Greenfield	Greenfield SP	SPS	6	E3
Hampton	Brookside	INA	12	E4
Hampton Falls	Hampton Saltmarshes	INA	15	E4
Hancock	Carpenter's Marsh WMA	SWA	16	E3
	Eva's Marsh WMA	SWA	13	E3
Hancock Village	DePierrefeur-Willard Pond	INA	14	E3
Hillsboro	Farrar Marsh WMA	SWA	18	E3
Holderness	Deering	INA	13	E3
Hooksett	Pemigewasset Ranger D.	NFS	2	
	Bear Brook SP	SPS	2	E3
Hopkinton	Stumpfield Marsh WMA	SWA	47	E3
	Samuel Myron Chase	INA	25	E3
Hopkinton Village	Smith Pond Bog	INA	27	E3
Keene	Otter Brook Lake	COE	5	E2
	Surry Mountain Lake	COE	6	E2
Laconia	White Mtn Natl. Forest	NFS	1	D3
Londonderry	Little Cohas Marsh WMA	SWA	34	F3
Lyme	W Branch Pine Barrens Pre	TNC	1	C2
Madison	Abe Emerson Marsh	INA	8	D3
Manchester	Meetinghouse Pond	INA	19	E2
Marlborough	Markus	INA	18	D3
Marlow	Nye Meadow Easement	INA	29	E2
Middleton	Sucker Brook Cove	INA	28	E2
Moultonborough	Mt. Sunapee SP	SPS	7	D2
Munsonville	Stoney Brook	SPS	9	E2
Nelson Center	Sargent WMA	SWA	43	F3
Newbury	Jones Brook Wildlife Area	SWA	26	D4
Newton	Kona Wildlife Area	SWA	31	D3
North Conway	Markus	INA	18	D3
Northwood	Nye Meadow Easement	INA	29	E2
Nottingham	Sucker Brook Cove	INA	29	E2
Orford	Peaked Mountain Preserve	TNC	2	E4
Peterborough	Woodman Marsh WMA	SWA	50	E4
	Burnhams Marsh WMA	SWA	40	C2
Pittsburg	Reed's Marsh WMA	SWA	2	E3
	Edward Macdowell Lake	COE	4	E3
Plymouth	Casalis Marsh WMA	SWA	6	A3
	Brown Lots WMA	SWA	19	A3
Portsmouth	Gray WMA	SWA	11	D3
Raymond	Scotts Bog WMA	TNC	2	A3
Richmond	Fourth Connecticut Lake Pre	TNC		
Rindge	Great Bay NWR	NWR	1	
Rye	Pawtuckaway SP	SPS	9	E4
Seabrook	Barden WMA	SWA	11	F2
South Tamworth	Betsy Fosket	INA		
Springfield	Odiorne Point SP	SPS	4	
Sugar Hill	Hampton Salt Marsh Cons. Area	SWA	21	E4
Sutton	Alice Bemis Thompson	INA		
Tamworth	McDaniels Marsh WMA	SWA	36	D2
Tuftonboro	Scotland Brook	INA	26	C3
Unity	Cascade Marsh WMA	SWA	10	D3
Weare	Chadwick Meadows WMA	SWA	11	D3
Webster	Frank Bolles Nature Reserve	TNC	3	
West Ossipee	Copps Pond WMA	SWA	13	D3
Westmoreland	Gallop Marsh	INA	18	E2
Whitefield	Perkins Pond WMA	SWA	28	B3
	Kimball Lot WMA	SWA	30	D3
	Knights Meadow Marsh	INA	16	D3
	Leonard Wildlife Area	SWA	8	D2
West Ossipee	Stumpfield Marsh WMA	SPS	11	D4
Westmoreland	Samuel Myron Chase	TNC	5	E2
Whitefield	Airport Marsh WMA	SWA	3	B3
Pondicherry		INA	22	B3

VERMONT - CITY / AGENCY INDEX

City	Agency Office / Area Name	Code	S#	Map
Addison	Dead Creek WMA	SWA	11	D1
	McCuen Slang WMA	SWA	23	C1
Alburg	Mud Creek WMA	SWA	24	A1
Ascutney	Wilgus SP	SPS	38	D2
Barnard	Silver Lake SP	SPS	34	C2
Barton	Crystal Lake SP	SPS	5	B2
Bennington	Willoughby Falls WMA	SWA	47	B2
Benson	Woodford SP	SPS	46	E1
Bolton	Pond Woods WMA	SWA	29	D1
Brandon	Shaw Mountain Natural Area	TNC	7	D1
Branbury	Robbins Mountain WMA	SWA	33	B1
Brattleboro	Branbury SP	SPS	12	E2
Brattleboro	Dutton Pines SP	SPS	15	E2
Calais	Fort Dummer SP	SPS	17	C2
Charlotte	Williams Woods	TNC	3	
Cornwall	Cornwall Swamp WMA	SWA	9	C1
Coventry	South Bay WMA	SWA	37	B2
E. Brighton	Wenlock WMA	SWA	43	B3
East Dorset	Emerald Lake SP	SPS	14	E1
East Thetford	Union Village Dam	COE	2	D2
Eden	Wild Branch WMA	SWA	46	B2
Enosburg Falls	Bird Mountain WMA	SWA	24	A1
Fair Haven	Lake Carmi SP	SPS	18	D1
Fairfield	Bomoseen SP	SPS	18	D1
Ferrisburg	Half Moon SP	SPS	15	D1
	Elm Brook WMA	SWA	21	C1
Grand Isle	Fairfield Swamp WMA	SWA	20	C1
	Kingsland Bay SP	SPS	47	B1
Greensboro	Little Otter Creek WMA	SWA	38	F1
Groton	Lower Otter Creek WMA	SWA	19	C1
Guildhall	Maidstone SP	SPS	39	B2
Hartland	Eshqua Bog	TNC	5	D2
Hinesburg	Fred Johnson WMA	SWA	10	C1
Holland	Bill Sladyk WMA	SWA	11	A3
Island Pond	Brighton SP	SPS	13	B3
Jamaica	Ball Mountain Lake	COE	1	E1
Killington	Gifford Woods SP	SPS	19	D1
Lake Elmore	Elmore SP	SPS	16	C2
Ludlow	Camp Plymouth SP	SPS	33	D2
Manchester	Manchester RD	NFS	2	E1
	& White Rocks NRA	NFS	32	C2
Marshfield	Middlebury Ranger D.	NFS	3	C1
Middlebury	Sand Bar SP	SPS	36	B1
Milton	Sandbar WMA	SWA	4	A2
Montgomery	Averys Gore (West) WMA	TNC	1	C2
MONTPELIER	TNC Vermont Field Office	SPS	31	C1
Mount Tabor	Otter Creek WMA	SWA	5	B3
N. Ferrisburg	Mt. Philo SP	COE	2	D2
Newark	Bald Hill	SPS	22	B1
North Hartland	North Hartland SP	SPS	23	D1
	Knight Island SP	SPS	33	A1
North Hero	North Hero SP	SWA	12	C1
Orwell	East Creek WMA	TNC	44	C1
	East Creek Natural Area	SWA	8	D1
Pittsford	Whipple Hollow Preserve	TNC	2	D2
Plymouth	Sugar Hollow Preserve	SPS	26	D1
Poultney	Coolidge SP	SPS	7	D1
	Lake St. Catherine SP	SWA	17	D2
Randolph	Allis SP on VT Rt.65	NFS	4	C1
Reading	Bird Mountain WMA	SWA	31	C1
Rochester	Knapp Brook WMA			
	Riley Bostwick WMA			
Rutland	Green Mtn. & Finger Lakes Natl Forest Sup.	NFS	1	D1
S. Reading	Arthur Davis WMA	SWA	25	E1
Shaftsbury	Lake Shaftsbury SP	SPS	45	D2
Sharon	White River WMA	SWA	30	C1
Shelburne	Laplatte River Marsh	TNC	27	B1
Shoreham	Richville WMA	SWA	41	C1
Shrewsbury	Plymsbury WMA	SWA	20	B1
Springfield	North Springfield Lake	COE	3	D2
St. Albans	Kamp Kill Kare SP	SPS	9	B1
St. Albans Bay	Burton Island SP	SWA	6	B1
Stamford	Woods Island SP	SWA	38	F1
Starksboro	Stamford Meadows WMA	SWA	19	C1
Stockbridge	Lewis Creek WMA	SWA	14	B1
Stowe	Les Newell WMA	SWA	39	B2
Stratford	Smugglers Notch SP	SPS	28	B2
Sutton	Podunk WMA	SPS	1	D2
Swanton	Calendar Brook WMA	NWR	1	A1
	Missisquoi NWR	SPS	41	B2
Thetford Hill	Maquam Bay WMA	SWA	40	A1
Tinmouth	Thetford Hill SP	SWA	4	D1
Townshend	Tinmouth Channel WMA	SPS	43	E2
	Townshend Lake	COE	4	E1
Underhill Center	Underhill SP	SPS	43	B1
Vergennes	Button Bay SP	SPS	11	C1
Vernon	DAR SP	SWA	13	B2
	Roaring Brook WMA	SPS	32	F2
Victory	Victory Bog WMA	SWA	41	B3
W. Topsham	Pine Mountain WMA	SWA	26	C2
Walden	Steam Mill Brook WMA	SWA	39	B2
Washington	Washington WMA	SWA	42	C2
Waterbury	Dept. Forests, Parks & Rec.	SPS	1	
	Little River SP	SPS	27	B2
Waterbury Center	SP	SWA	44	B2
	Fish & Wildlife Dept.	SWA	1	
Weybridge	Snake Mountain WMA	SWA	36	C1
White River Jct.	Quechee Gorge SP	SWA	34	D2
Whitingham	Atherton Meadow WMA	SPS	29	E1
Wilmington	Molly Stark SP	SWA	30	D2
Windsor	Mt. Ascutney SP	SPS	5	
Wolcott	East Hill WMA	SWA	13	B2
Woodbury	Buck Lake WMA	SPS	8	B2

© 1994 by John Oliver Jones

VERMONT NOTES

Summary

There are 11 federal, 96 state, and 10 private recreation areas or local administrative offices covered in this state chapter. Of these, 67 appear in the Information Chart and 50 are covered in the notes. The special indexes feature 6 federally designated wilderness areas and wild rivers, and the Green Mountain National Forest map.

Federal Agencies

U.S. Forest Service

Vermont is in the Eastern Region (see Wisconsin chapter - U.S. Forest Svc., Eastern Region listing).

National Park Service Location in Vermont

Marsh-Billings NHP   617-223-5200

New NPS location established August 26, 1992. Phone number is the NPS regional office in Boston, MA.

State Agencies

Agency of Natural Resources

103 South Main St.
Waterbury, VT 05677   802-244-7347

Parent agency for the Departments of Fish & Wildlife and Forests, Parks, and Recreation.

Dept. of Forests, Parks, & Recreation

A directory to Vermont's State Parks (45 parks) and Forest Recreation Areas (5 areas) is available. There are written directions and a description of the activities and facilities and a locator map is included. There are day-use fees and camping fees.

Dept. of Fish & Wildlife

Licensing and game harvest information is published annually. The publication *Vermont Guide to Hunting* is a basic reference to 46 of 71 Vermont WMAs. Those 46 are noted here and their symbol numbers appear on the Guide map.

Wilderness Index

Green Mountain (& Finger Lakes) National Forest Sup. (S# 1, map D1)

Big Branch Wilderness - 6,720 acres
Breadloaf Wilderness - 21,480 acres
Bristol Cliffs Wilderness - 3,738 acres
George D. Aiken Wilderness - 5,060 acres
Lye Brook Wilderness - 15,530 acres
Peru Peak Wilderness - 6,920 acres

Outdoor Map Index

U.S. Forest Service Map

Green Mountain National Forest [1982]
Scale: 1 inch = 4.0 miles (1 cm = 2.5 km)
Size: 20x32 inches (51x81 cm)

Private Organizations

TNC-Vermont Field Office   802-229-4425

Montpelier, VT 05602

The Vermont chapter manages 19 preserves. Whenever possible, preserves are open to visitation. However, because some areas are ecologically fragile, there may be limitations on public use. A project directory is available.

Vermont Chamber of Commerce

PO Box 37   Phone 802-223-3443
Montpelier, VT 05601   Fax 802-229-4581

Vermont Travel Division   802-828-3236

134 State St.
Montpelier, VT 05602

A Vacation Guide provides information on Vermont's attractions and events. There are other publications on private accommodations, scenic areas, campgrounds, and historic sites. An official road map is also available.

WMA NAME & LOCATION (Index)

S#	MAP	WMA NAME & LOCATION
2	D2	Arthur Davis WMA, Reading
3	F1	Atherton Meadow WMA, Whitingham
4	A2	Averys Gore (West) WMA, Montgomery
5	B3	Bald Hill, Newark
6	A3	Bill Sladyk WMA, Holland
7	D1	Bird Mountain WMA, Poultney
8	B2	Buck Lake WMA, Woodbury
9	B3	Calendar Brook WMA, Sutton
10	C1	Cornwall Swamp WMA, Cornwall
11	C1	Dead Creek WMA, Addison
12	D1	East Creek WMA, Orwell
13	B2	East Hill WMA, Wolcott
14	B1	Elm Brook WMA, Fairfield
15	B1	Fairfield Swamp WMA, Fairfield
16	C1	Fred Johnson WMA, Hinesburg
17	D2	Knapp Brook WMA, Reading
18	D1	Les Newell WMA, Stockbridge
19	C1	Lewis Creek WMA, Starksboro
20	C1	Little Otter Creek WMA, Ferrisburg
21	C1	Lower Otter Creek WMA, Ferrisburg
22	A1	Maquam Bay WMA, Swanton
23	C1	McCuen Slang WMA, Addison
24	A1	Mud Creek WMA, Alburg
25	D1	Otter Creek WMA, Mount Tabor
26	C2	Pine Mountain WMA, W. Topsham
27	D1	Plymsbury WMA, Shrewsbury
28	D2	Podunk WMA, Stratford
29	D1	Pond Woods WMA, Benson
30	C1	Richville WMA, Shoreham
31	C1	Riley Bostwick WMA, Rochester
32	F2	Roaring Brock WMA, Vernon
33	B1	Robbins Mountain WMA, Bolton
34	C2	Roy Mountain WMA, Barnet
35	B1	Sandbar WMA, Milton
36	C1	Snake Mountain WMA, Weybridge
37	B2	South Bay WMA, Coventry
38	F1	Stamford Meadows WMA, Stamford
39	B2	Steam Mill Brook WMA, Walden
40	D1	Tinmouth Channel WMA, Tinmouth
41	B3	Victory Bog WMA, Victory
42	C2	Washington WMA, Washington
43	B3	Wenlock WMA, E. Brighton
44	D1	Whipple Hollow WMA, Pittsford
45	D2	White River WMA, Sharon
46	B2	Wild Branch WMA, Eden
47	B2	Willoughby Falls WMA, Barton

★ INFORMATION CHART ★

AGENCY/MAP LEGEND . . . INITIALS, MAP SYMBOLS, COLOR CODES

U.S. Forest Service Supervisor & Ranger Dist. Offices . . NFS △ 61
U.S. Army Corps of Engineers Rec. Areas & Offices . . COE ⬡ 31
USFWS National Wildlife Refuges & Offices . . . . NWR ◇ 40
National Park Service Parks & other NPS Sites . . . . . . NPS ▽ 7
Bureau of Land Management Rec. Areas & Offices . . . . BLM ⬠ 26
Bureau of Reclamation Rec. Areas & Reg. Offices . . . . BOR ◯ 8
State Parks (also see State Agency notes) . . . . SPS ⬡ 52
State Wildlife Areas (also see State Agency notes) . . . . SWA ◯ 19
Private Preserves, Nature Centers & Tribal Lands . . . . . ▦
The Wild Rivers ⌇ and Wilderness Areas ▨

Note: *Refer to page 7 (top right) for location name and address abbreviations.*

INFORMATION CHART LEGEND - SYMBOLS & LETTER CODES

■ means **YES** & □ means **Yes with disability provisions**
sp means **spring**, March through May
S means **Summer**, June through August
F means **Fall**, September through November
W means **Winter**, December through February
T means **Two** (2) or **Three** (3) Seasons
A means **All Four** (4) Seasons
na means **Not Applicable or Not Available**

Note: empty or blank spaces in the chart mean **NO**
* that symbol number is not shown on the map.

Note: If a symbol number has a star ★

FACILITIES, SERVICES, RECREATION OPPORTUNITIES & CONVENIENCES

S#	MAP	LOCATION NAME (state initials if more than one) with ADDRESS and/or LOCATION DATA	TELEPHONE	ACRES / ELEVATION	S#

NEW HAMPSHIRE

S#	MAP	LOCATION NAME	TELEPHONE	ACRES / ELEVATION
△	D3	**White Mountain National Forest** (Supervisor), 719 Main St., PO Box 638, Laconia 03247	603-528-8721	769,000 / 800-6,288
2	C3	Ammonoosuc Ranger D., Trudeau Rd., Box 239, Bethlehem 03574	603-869-2626	111,000 / na
3	B4	Androscoggin Ranger D., 80 Glen Rd., Gorham 03581	603-466-2713	125,000 / na
4	D3	Pemigewasset Ranger D., Hwy. Rt. 175, Holderness 03264	603-536-1310	228,500 / na
5	C4	Saco Ranger D., Kancamagus Hwy., RFD #1, Box 94, Conway 03818	603-447-5448	202,000 / na
⬡		**COE, New England District**, 424 Trapelo Road, Waltham, MA 02254	617-647-8107	na / na
1	E3	Blackwater Dam, PO Box 340, Franklin 03235	603-934-2116	na / na
2	E3	Edward Macdowell Lake, 75 Wilder St., Peterborough 03458	603-924-3431	na / na
3	D3	Franklin Falls Dam, PO Box 340, Franklin 03235	603-934-2116	na / na
4	E3	Hopkinton-Everett Lakes, 2097 Maple Street, Contoocook 03229	603-746-3601	na / na
5	E2	Otter Brook Lake, RFD #4, Keene 03431	603-352-4130	na / na
6	E2	Surry Mountain Lake, RFD #4, Keene 03431	603-352-2447	1,054 / 100
◇1	E4	**Great Bay NWR** (new), 601 Spaulding, Suite 17, Portsmouth 03801	603-431-7511	150 / 1,200-2,400
2	B4	Lake Umbagog NWR (ME-NH), PO Box 280, Errol 03579 [new refuge, E side of Hwy 16, 5 mi N of Errol]	603-482-3415	3,000 / 120
		Great Meadows NWR, Weir Hill Road, Sudbury, MA 01776	508-443-4661	
3	E3	John Hay NWR, c/o Great Meadows NWR, Sudbury, MA 01776, near Newbury [not presently open to the public]	508-443-4661	164 / 1,200
4	E3	Wapack NWR, c/o Great Meadows NWR, Sudbury, MA 01776, near Peterborough	508-443-4661	1,672 / 1,200-2,278
▽1	D2	**Saint-Gaudens Nat'l HS**, RR #3, Box 73, Cornish 03745 [from W. Lebanon, NH I-89 exit 20, go S 12 mi on Rt. 12A]	603-675-2175	148 / 1,000
1	E3	NH Div. of Parks & Recreation, 172 Pembroke Road, PO Box 856, Concord 03302	603-271-3254	na / na

Grid	No.	Name / Location	Acres	Phone
C3	4	Franconia Notch SP, adjacent White Mtn. NF, off I-93 near Franconia	6,000 / 4,200	603-823-5563
E3	5	Greenfield SP, on SR 136, 1 mi. W of Greenfield	400 / na	603-547-3497
B4	6	Moose Brook SP, off Rt. #2, 2 mi. W of Gorham	100 / na	603-466-3860
E2	7	Mt. Sunapee SP, on SR 103, 3 mi. W of Newbury	3,000 / 2,800	603-763-2356
E4	8	Odiorne Point SP, on Rt. 1A, Rye	140 / na	603-436-7406
E4	9	Pawtuckaway SP, W of SR 156, 3.5 mi. NE of Raymond	6,000 / 1,000	603-895-3031
E2	10	Pisgah SP, off SR 63, 2 mi. E of Chesterfield	13,000 / na	603-239-8153
D4	11	White Lake SP, on SR 16, 0.5 mi. N of West Ossipee	700 / na	603-323-7350
E3	1	**Fish & Game Department.** 2 Hazen Drive, Concord 03301	na / na	603-271-2461
E4	2	Adams Point WMA, Durham	82 / na	603-271-2461
B3	3	Airport Marsh WMA, (leased area), Whitefield	25 / na	603-271-2461
E3	4	Ballard Marsh WMA (owned by DRED & managed by F&G), Derry	121 / na	603-271-2461
F2	5	Barden WMA, Richmond	125 / na	603-271-2461
A3	6	Brown Lots WMA, Black Lake Rd., Pittsburg	803 / na	603-271-2461
E4	7	Burnhams Marsh WMA (owned by DRED & managed by F&G), Nottingham	30 / na	603-271-2461
E3	8	Carpenter's Marsh WMA, Hancock	290 / na	603-271-2461
E3	9	Casalis Marsh WMA, Peterborough	10 / na	603-271-2461
D3	10	Cascade Marsh WMA, Sutton	250 / na	603-271-2461
D3	11	Chadwick Meadows WMA, Sutton	100 / na	603-271-2461
D3	12	Church Hill Wildlife Area, near Ashland	500 / na	603-271-2461
D4	13	Copps Pond WMA, near Rt. 109-A, Tuftonboro	208 / na	603-271-2461
E4	14	Dole's Marsh WMA, Deerfield	25 / na	603-271-2461
D2	15	Enfield WMA, near I-89 exit 14, Enfield	2,600 / na	603-271-2461
E3	16	Eva's Marsh WMA, Hancock	77 / na	603-271-2461
E3	17	Farrar Marsh WMA, Hillsboro	297 / na	603-271-2461
E2	18	Gallop Marsh, near Lempster & Unity	19 / na	603-271-2461
A3	19	Gray WMA, near Pittsburg	196 / na	603-271-2461
E3	20	Hall Mountain Marsh WMA (owned by DRED & managed by F&G), near Hooksett & Allenstown	60 / na	603-271-2461
E4	21	Hampton Salt Marsh Cons. Area, near Hampton & Seabrook	246 / na	603-271-2461
E3	22	Hayes Marsh WMA (owned by DRED & managed by F&G), Allenstown	60 / na	603-271-2461
D3	23	Hirst Wildlife Area, Boscawen	135 / na	603-271-2461
D3	24	Hoit Road Marsh WMA, exit 17 off I-93, Loudon & Concord	191 / na	603-271-2461
D3	25	Hosmer WMA, Antrim	74 / na	603-271-2461
D4	26	Jones Brook Wildlife Area, 2.5 mi. N of Middleton Corners	1,079 / na	603-271-2461
D3	27	Kearsarge Wildlife Area, Andover	1,050 / na	603-271-2461
D3	28	Kimball Lot WMA, Webster	18 / na	603-271-2461
E2	29	Kinson Lot WMA, 0.2 mi. S of Marlow Village, Marlow	8 / na	603-271-2461
E3	30	Knights Meadow Marsh (part of Leonards WMA), W of Winnipocket Lake near Webster	75 / na	603-271-2461
D3	31	Kona Wildlife Area. 3 mi. from Rt. 25, Moultonborough	315 / na	603-271-2461
E4	32	Lamontagne WMA, Deerfield	337 / na	603-271-2461
D3	33	Leonard Wildlife Area, Webster	885 / na	603-271-2461
F3	34	Little Cohas Marsh WMA, Londonderry	3 / na	603-271-2461
D4	35	Marks Wildlife Area Alton	286 / na	603-271-2461
D3	36	McDaniels Marsh WMA, near Grafton & Springfield	300 / na	603-271-2461
D4	37	Merrymeeting Marsh WMA, New Durham & Alton	722 / na	603-271-2461
D2	38	Myrl Webster Wildlife Area, 0.5 mi. W of West Canaan, Canaan	91 / na	603-271-2461
D3	39	Perkins Pond WMA, 1.8 mi. from South Weare, Weare	307 / na	603-271-2461
C2	40	Reed's Marsh WMA, Orford	64 / na	603-271-2461
C3	41	Rowbartwood Marsh WMA, 1.5 mi. W of exit 27 off I-93, Campton	60 / na	603-271-2461
E2	42	Ryan WMA, 4 mi. W of Dublin	46 / na	603-271-2461
E4	43	Sargent WMA, Newton	356 / na	603-271-2461
A3	44	Scotts Bog WMA (leased from Champion, Pittsburg)	98 / na	603-271-2461
E2	45	Spaulding WMA, Charlestown	57 / na	603-271-2461
D3	46	Stark Pond WMA, Northwood	92 / na	603-271-2461
E3	47	Stumpfield Marsh WMA (owned by US Army Corps of Engrs.), Hopkinton	95 / na	603-271-2461
D2	48	Wendell Marsh WMA, Rt. 11, 1 mi. W of Sunapee	42 / na	603-271-2461
D2	49	Wilder Management Area, 1.5 mi. S of E. Thetford VT bridge, Lyme	40 / na	603-271-2461
E4	50	Woodman Marsh WMA, Northwood	20 / na	603-271-2461
E3	1	**TNC New Hampshire Field Office.** 2 1/2 Beacon St., Suite 6, Concord 03301	na / na	603-224-5853
A3	2	Fourth Connecticut Lake Preserve, contact Field Office, near Pittsburg	78 / 2,600	603-224-5853
D3	3	Frank Bolles Nature Reserve, contact Field Office, near Tamworth	247 / 600	603-224-5853
C4	4	Peaked Mountain Preserve, contact Field Office, near North Conway	2,822 / 800-2,400	603-224-5853
E2	5	Warwick Preserve, contact Field Office, near Westmoreland	40 / 800	603-224-5853
C4	6	West Branch Pine Barrens Preserve, contact Field Office, near Madison	341 / 500	603-224-5853

★ INFORMATION CHART ★

AGENCY/MAP LEGEND . . . INITIALS, MAP SYMBOLS, COLOR CODES

U.S. Forest Service Supervisor & Ranger Dist. Offices NFS
U.S. Army Corps of Engineers Rec. Areas & Offices . COE
USFWS National Wildlife Refuges & Offices . . . . . . NWR
National Park Service Parks & other NPS Sites . . . . NPS
Bureau of Land Management Rec. Areas & Offices . . BLM
Bureau of Reclamation Rec. Areas & Reg. Offices . . BOR
State Parks (also see State Agency notes) . . . . SPS
State Wildlife Areas (also see State Agency notes) . . SWA
Private Preserves, Nature Centers & Tribal Lands . .
The Wild Rivers and Wilderness Areas
Note: Refer to yellow block on page 7 for location name and address abbreviations.

INFORMATION CHART LEGEND - SYMBOLS & LETTER CODES

■ means **YES** & □ means **Yes with disability provisions**
sp means **spring**, March through May
S means **Summer**, June through August
F means **Fall**, September through November
W means **Winter**, December through February
T means **Two (2) or Three (3) Seasons**
A means **All Four (4) Seasons**
na means **Not Applicable or Not Available**
Note: empty or blank spaces in the chart mean **NO**
If a symbol number has a star ★ that symbol is not shown on the map.

FACILITIES, SERVICES, RECREATION OPPORTUNITIES & CONVENIENCES

Column categories (left to right): INFO OFFICE (IO) / VISITOR CENTER (VC); IO / VC OPEN SATURDAY / SUNDAY; ENTRY FEE not camping or permit fee; CONCESSIONAIRE SERVICES; FREE LITERATURE maps, etc.; INTERPRETIVE / EDUCATIONAL SERVICES; NATURE EDUCATION / STUDY PROGRAMS; AGENCY LITERATURE brochures, maps, etc.; GUIDED TOURS scheduled / by res.; WILDFLOWER VIEWING AREA or DRIVE; HISTORIC SITES; ARCHAEOLOGICAL / GEOLOGICAL SITES; INTERPRETIVE TRAILS; WILDLIFE IS ABUNDANT OR COMMON; ENDANGERED SPECIES ARE COMMON; WILDLIFE VIEWING SITES blinds signs, etc.; DEVELOPED PICNIC AREAS; NO-CHARGE CAMPGROUNDS / PICNIC SITES; DEVELOPED CAMPGROUNDS / CAMPSITES; WILDERNESS AREAS / WILD RIVERS; WALKING / HIKING TRAILS; SWIMMING PERMITTED; BICYCLING PERMITTED; HORSEBACK RIDING w/ your own horse; OFF-ROAD MOTORIZED Vehicle Area; FISHING IN SEASON / license req'd.; BOATING FACILITIES ramps, marinas etc.; MOTORIZED WATERCRAFT OK / permit req'd.; NON-MOTORIZED WATERCRAFT OK, check limits; HUNTING IN SEASON / license req'd.; WINTER SPORTS OPPORTUNITIES OK; PARK & WALK-IN AREA; DAY USE ONLY, no overnight; DRINKING WATER; RESTROOMS

S#	MAP	LOCATION NAME (state initials if more than one) with ADDRESS and/or LOCATION DATA	TELEPHONE	ACRES / ELEVATION
7	E3	Audubon Society of NH & Silk Farm Sanctuary (ASNH), 3 Silk Farm Rd., PO Box 528-B, Concord 03302, [see notes]	603-224-9909	15 / na
		VERMONT		
		Green Mountain & Finger Lakes National Forests, FOB, 231 N. Main St., Rutland 05701	802-747-6700	40,000 / 600-4,000
1	D1	Manchester Ranger D. & White Rocks, Box 1940, Manchester 05255	802-362-2307	199,591 / 800-3,900
2	E1	Middlebury Ranger D., RD #4, Box 1260, Middlebury 05753	802-388-4362	70,000 / 600-3,800
3	C1	Rochester Ranger D., RD #1, Box 108, Rochester 05767	802-767-4777	70,000 / 900-4,000
4	C1	**COE, New England District**		
1	E1	Ball Mountain Lake, RR #1, Box 372, Jamaica 05343	617-647-8107	na / na
2	D2	North Hartland Lake, PO Box 55, North Hartland 05052	802-874-4881	na / na
3	D2	North Springfield Lake, 98 Reservoir Road, Springfield 05156	802-295-2855	na / na
			802-886-2775	na / na
4	E2	Townshend Lake, PO Box 176, Townshend 05353	802-365-7703	na / na
5	D2	Union Village Dam, RFD, East Thetford 05043	802-649-1606	na / na
1	A1	**Missisquoi NWR**, Rt. 78, PO Box 163, Swanton 05488	802-868-4781	5,831 / na
2	C2	**Dept. Forests, Parks & Recreation**, 103 S. Main St., Waterbury 05676	802-244-8711	na / na
		Allis SP on VT Rt.65 (12 mi. N & 1.5 mi. E of Randolph), RFD #2, Box 192, Randolph 05060	802-276-3175	487 / 1,900
3	D1	Bomoseen SP (4 mi. N of Hydeville), RFD #1, Box 2620, Fair Haven 05743	802-265-4242	2,840 / 450
4	C3	Branbury SP (11 mi. S of Middlebury), RFD #2, Box 2421, Brandon 05733	802-247-5925	96 / 580
5	D2	Brighton SP, 2 mi. E & .75 mi. S of Island Pond 05846	802-723-4360	152 / 1,190
6	B3	Burton Island SP (take ferry from Kamp Kill Kare SP), Box 123, St. Albans Bay 05481	802-524-6353	243 / 110
7	C1	Button Bay SP, 0.5 mi. S & 6.5 mi. W of Vergennes, RFD #3, Box 570, Vergennes 05491	802-475-2377	236 / 130
8	D2	Camp Plymouth SP (1 mi. E & 1 mi. N of Tyson), RD #1, Box 489, Ludlow 05149	802-228-2025	300 / 1,100
9	D2	Coolidge SP, HCR 70, Box 105, Plymouth 05056	802-672-3612	16,165 / 1,600
10	B2	Crystal Lake SP, N end Crystal Lake in Barton Vil., Barton 05822	802-525-6205	16 / 950
11	C1	DAR SP (13 mi. SW of Vergennes), RFD #3, Box 2145, Vergennes 05491	802-759-2354	95 / 130
12	E2	Dutton Pines SP (5 mi. N of Brattleboro), Brattelboro	802-244-8711	13 / 400
13	B2	Elmore SP (5 mi. S of Morrisville), Box 93, Lake Elmore 05657	802-888-2982	750 / 1,200
14	E1	Emerald Lake SP (in North Dorset on US 7), RD, Box 485, East Dorset 05253	802-362-1655	910 / 800
15	E2	Fort Dummer SP (near Brattleboro), RR #6, Box 11, Brattleboro 05301	802-254-2610	217 / 650
16	D1	Gifford Woods SP, VT Route 100, Killington 05751	802-775-5354	114 / 1,400
17	B3	Grand Isle SP (1 mi. S of Grand Isle), 36 E. Shore Rd., Grand Isle 05458	802-372-4300	226 / 150
18	D1	Half Moon SP, 2 mi. N, 2 W & 1.5 S of Hubbardton, RFD #1, Box 2730, Fair Haven 05743	802-273-2848	2,840 / 630
19	E2	Jamaica SP (0.5 mi. N of Jamaica), Box 45, Jamaica 05343	802-874-4600	760 / 700
20	B3	Kamp Kill Kare SP (8 mi. W of St. Albans Bay), Box 123, St. Albans 05481	802-524-6021	18 / 120
21	B3	Kingsland Bay SP, 1 mi. W & 3.5 mi. N of Ferrisburg, Ferrisburg 05456	802-877-3445	130 / 130
22	B1	Knight Island SP (park at Tudhope Marine), North Hero	802-524-6353	190 / 120
23	B1	Knight Point SP (2 mi. S of North Hero), RD #1, Box 21, North Hero 05481	802-372-8389	54 / 120
24	A1	Lake Carmi SP (3 mi. W & 3 mi. N Enosburg Falls), RR #1, Box 1710, Enosburg Falls 05450	802-933-8383	590 / 450
25	E1	Lake Shaftsbury SP (10.5 mi. N of Bennington), RFD #1, Box 266, Shaftsbury 05262	802-375-9978	101 / 900
26	D1	Lake St. Catherine SP (3 mi. S of Poultney), RD #2, Box 230, Poultney 05764	802-287-9158	130 / 500
27	B3	Little River SP (NW Waterbury on Little R. Rd.), RFD #1, Box 1150, Waterbury 05676	802-244-7103	12,000 / 650
28	B3	Maidstone SP, 5 mi. SW of VT Rt. 102, between Bloomfield and Guildhall	802-676-3930	470 / 1,330
29	D1	Molly Stark SP (15 mi. W of Brattleboro), Wilmington 05363	802-464-5460	170 / 1,800
30	D2	Mt. Ascutney SP (1 mi. NW on VT Hwy. 44A), HCR 71, Box 186, Windsor 05089	802-674-2060	1,984 / 3,144
31	C1	Mt. Philo SP, 6 mi N, 1 E from Jct. Hwy 22A-US 7, RD #1, Box 1049, N. Ferrisburg 05473	802-425-2390	648 / 970
32	C2	New Discovery SP, VT Rt. 232, Marshfield	802-584-3820	26,130 / 1,500
33	A1	North Hero SP (near Alburg), RR, Box 259, North Hero 05474	802-372-8727	399 / 110
34	D2	Quechee Gorge SP (3 mi. W of Jct. I-89 & US 4), 190 Dewey Mills Rd., White River Jct. 05001	802-295-2990	612 / 600
35	C2	Ricker Pond SP (within Groton State Forest), VT Rt. 232, Groton	802-584-3821	26,130 / 1,000
36	B1	Sand Bar SP (7 mi. E of South Hero), U.S. Rt. 2, Milton 05468	802-893-2825	20 / 105

39	B2	Smugglers Notch SP (10 mi. NW of Stowe), RR #1, Box 2040, Stowe 05672	802-253-4014	50 / 1,000	39
40	C2	Stillwater SP (within Groton SF), off VT Rt. 232, Groton	802-584-3823	26,130 / 1,100	40
41	D2	Thetford Hill SP (2.5 mi. S of Thetford Hill), Box 132, Thetford Hill 05074	802-785-2266	262 / 700	41
42	E2	Townshend SP (5 mi. N of Newfane), Rt. #1, Box 2650, Townshend 05353	802-365-7500	856 / 600	42
43	B1	Underhill SP (17 mi. E of Essex Jct.), Underhill Center 05490	802-899-3022	150 / 2,400	43
44	B2	Waterbury Center SP (S of Waterbury Ctr. Village), RFD #1, Box 1150, Waterbury 05676	802-244-7103	100 / 650	44
45	E2	Wilgus SP (1.5 mi. S of Ascutney), Box 196, Ascutney 05030	802-674-5422	100 / 320	45
46	E1	Woodford SP (10 mi. E of Bennington), HCR 65, Box 0928, Bennington 05201	802-447-7169	400 / 2,400	46
47	B1	Woods Island SP (2 mi. N Burton Is., boat access), c/o Burton Island SP, Box 123, St. Albans Bay 05481	802-524-6353	125 / 120	47
1	C2	Fish & Wildlife Dept., 103 S. Main St., Waterbury 05676 [see notes for WMAs]	802-244-7331	na / na	1
2	C2	TNC Vermont Field Office, 27 State Street, Montpelier 05602	802-229-4425	na / na	2
3	B2	Barr Hill Preserve, contact Field Office, N of Greensboro	802-229-4425	256 / na	3
4	C1	Chickering Bog, contact Field Office, off Lightning Ridge Rd., Calais	802-229-4425	131 / na	4
		East Creek Natural Area, contact Field Office, on Rt.73, 3 mi. E of Orwell	802-229-4425	610 / na	
5	D2	Eshqua Bog, contact Field Office, on Garvin Hill Rd. near Woodstock, Hartland	802-229-4425	40 / na	5
6	B1	Laplatte River Marsh, contact Field Office, on Shelburne Bay, Shelburne	802-229-4425	206 / na	6
7	D1	Shaw Mountain Natural Area, contact Field Office, SE of Benson	802-229-4425	275 / na	7
8	D1	Sugar Hollow Preserve, contact Field Office, Sugar Hollow Rd., Pittsford	802-229-4425	261 / na	8
9	C1	Williams Woods, contact Field Office, on Greenbush Rd., Charlotte	802-229-4425	63 / na	9

NEW JERSEY NOTES

Summary

There are 10 federal, 60 state, and 19 private recreation areas or local administrative offices covered in this state chapter. Of these, 55 appear in the Information Chart and 34 are covered in the notes. The special indexes feature 2 federally designated wilderness areas and a wild river.

Federal Agency

National Park Service

Additional NPS Locations in New Jersey
Edison National Historic Site (21 acres)
(S# 3, map B3)
Main St. and Lakeside Ave.
West Orange, NJ 07052   201-736-0550

Egg Harbor National Scenic and Recreation River
No office, new NPS site approved October 27, 1992.

Wilderness/Wild River Index

Wilderness Areas
Brigantine Wilderness - 6,681 acres
Edwin B. Forsythe NWR (S# 1, map E2)
Great Swamp Wilderness - 3,660 acres
Great Swamp NWR (S# 2, map B2)

Wild Rivers
Delaware (Middle) River, New Jersey and Pennsylvania
Delaware Water Gap NRA, Bushkill, PA 18324
Phone 717-588-2435 (S# 2, map B5 in PA)

State Agencies

The NJ Pinelands Commission
PO Box 7
New Lisbon, NJ 08064   609-894-9342

A variety of brochures are available about recreation opportunities within the "Pinelands Reserve," a hugh area covering most of the southern half of New Jersey. In 1978 the Pinelands was designated by the United States Congress as the nation's first National Reserve. The NJ Pinelands Commission cooperates with local and state agencies in preserving the area.

Department of Environmental Protection
401 East State St., CN 402
Trenton, NJ 08625-0402   609-292-2885
The parent agency for the Fish, Game and Wildlife and parks, and Forestry Divisions.

Division of Parks & Forestry
A New Jersey State Parks Guide has information on 35 state parks, 11 state forests, 5 recreation areas, 38 natural areas, 24 historic sites, and 4 state marinas. The guide describes facilities, water activities, other recreational opportunities, and winter activities available at each area. It contains a small locator map for each of five recreation regions. There is a camping fee.

Liberty State Park (S# 12, map B3), with ferry service to the Statue of Liberty and Ellis Island, features a world-class interactive science education center. The Liberty Science Center devotes one whole floor to the environment, includes a 170 foot observation tower, and the largest OMNIMAX® theater in the nation. For visitor information contact:
Liberty Science Center
Liberty State Park
251 Phillip Street
Jersey City, NJ 07304-4629   201-200-1000

Selected New Jersey Parks are listed here and their locations shown on the Guide map.

S#	MAP	PARK NAME & LOCATION
2	C3	Allaire SP, Farmingdale
3	B2	Allamuchy Mt. SP, Hackettstown
4	F2	Cape May Point SP, Cape May Point
5	C3	Cheesequake SP, Matawan
6	B2	Delaware & Raritan Canal SP, Belle Mead
7	D1	Fort Mott SP, Salem
8	B2	Hacklebarney Park, Long Valley

S#	MAP	PARK NAME & LOCATION
9	A2	High Point SP, Sussex
10	A2	Hopatcong SP, Landing
11	D3	Island Beach Park, Seaside Park
12	B3	Liberty SP, Jersey City
13	D1	Parvin Park SP, Elmer
14	D2	Rancocas SP, New Lisbon
15	B2	Round Valley SP, Lebanon
16	B2	Spruce Run SP, Clinton
17	A2	Swartswood SP, Newton
18	B2	Voorhees SP, Glen Gardner
19	C2	Washington Crossing SP, Titusville
20	A2	Wayawanda Park SP, Highland Lakes

Division of Fish, Game & Wildlife (DFGW)
A Guide to New Jersey's Wildlife Management Areas is available for $7.50. It includes area details and maps for 64 locations. Information Chart WMA data were compiled from a Guide copy furnished by the agency. The agency quarterly newsletter is available free at license agents.

Division of Travel & Tourism
One W. State St., CN 826
Trenton, NJ 08625
in state call   1-800-537-7397
                       609-292-2470

Private Organizations

ANCA Locations in New Jersey
Annie M Carter Nature Center (S# 10, map D2)
RD #4
Hammonton, NJ 08037   609-561-0024

Great Swamp Outdoor Education Center
(S# 11, map B2)
Box 1259R
Morristown, NJ 07960   201-829-0474

John J. Crowley Nature Center (S# 12, map A3)
Rifle camp Road
Paterson, NJ 07503   201-523-0024

Nature Center (S# 13, map F2)
Lighthouse Ave. Box 107
Cape May Point, NJ 08212   609-884-2159

Owl Haven Nature Center (S# 14, map C3)
PO Box 26
Tennent, NJ 07763-0026   201-780-7007

Paws Farm Nature Center (S# 15, map D2)
1105 Hainesport Road
Mount Laurel, NJ 08054   609-778-8795

Tenafly Nature Center (S# 16, map A3)
313 Hudson Ave.
Tenafly, NJ 07670   201-568-6093

Trailside Nature/Science Center (S# 17, map B3)
Coles Ave. & New Providence Road
Mountainside, NJ 07092   201-232-5930

Wildlife Center (S# 18, map A3)
Crescent Ave.
Wyckoff, NJ 07481   201-891-5571

New Jersey Chamber of Commerce
50 West State St., # 1110
Trenton, NJ 08608   609-989-7888

NEW JERSEY - CITY / AGENCY INDEX

City	Agency Office / Area Name	Code	S#	Map
Barnegat	Edwin B. Forsythe (Barnegat) NWR	NWR	2	D3
Basking Ridge	Great Swamp NWR	NWR	4	B2
Belle Mead	Delaware & Raritan Canal SP	SPS	6	B2
Bernardsville	Scherman-Hoffman San (NJAS)	INA	6	B2
Branchville	Flatbrook-Roy WMA	SWA	13	A2
Canton	Mad Horse Creek WMA	SWA	21	E1
Cape May	Cape May NWR	NWR	1	F2
	Bennett Bogs Preserve	TNC	8	F2
	Wm. D. & Jane C. Blair, Jr.	TNC	9	F2
Cape May Point	Cape May Point SP	SPS	9	F2
	Cape May Bird Observatory	INA	2	F2
Cedarville	Nantuxent WMA	SWA	26	E1
Chester	Black River WMA	SWA	6	B2
Clinton	Spruce Run SP	SPS	16	B2
Colliers Mills	Colliers Mills WMA	SWA	8	C2
Dennisville	Dennis Creek WMA	SWA	5	E2
Dover	Berkshire Valley WMA	SWA	11	B2
Elmer	Parvin Park SP	SPS	13	D1
Fairton	Clarks Pond WMA	SWA	10	E1
	Dix WMA	SWA	1	B3
Farmingdale	Allaire SP	SPS	1	B3
Fort Hancock	Gateway NRA (Sandy Hook)	NPS	1	B3
Fortescue	Fortescue WMA	SWA	14	E1
Franklin	Hamburg Mt. WMA	SWA	17	A2
Franklin Lakes	New Jersey Audubon Society	INA	3	A3
Freehold	Turkey Swamp WMA	SWA	32	C3
Glen Gardner	Voorhees SP	SPS	18	B2
Hackettstown	Allamuchy Mt. SP	SPS	3	B2
Heislerville	Heislerville WMA	SWA	18	E2
High Bridge	Ken Lockwood Gorge WMA	SWA	19	B2
Highland Lakes	Wawayanda Park SP	SPS	20	A2
Jersey City	Liberty SP	SPS	12	B3
Lakehurst	Manchester WMA	SWA	23	C3
Landing	Hopatcong SP	SPS	10	A2
Lebanon	Round Valley SP	SPS	15	B2
Linvale	Amwell WMA	SWA	2	C2
Long Valley	Hacklebarney Park	SPS	8	B2
Manahawkin	Manahawkin WMA	SWA	22	D3
Matawan	Stafford Forge WMA	SWA	30	D3
Medford	Cheesequake SP	SPS	5	C3
Millville	Medford WMA	SWA	25	D2
	Edward G. Bevan WMA	SWA	11	E2
	Peaslee WMA	SWA	27	E2
Morristown	Morristown Natl Hist Park	NPS	4	C2
Mt. Holly	Owl Haven Nature Center	INA	5	D2
	Rancocas Nature Center	INA	4	C2
New Greta	Swan Bay WMA	SWA	31	D2
New Lisbon	Rancocas SP	SPS	14	D2
Newton	Swartswood SP	SPS	17	A2
Ocean City	Whittingham WMA	SWA	36	A2
Oceanville	Marmora WMA	SWA	24	E2
	Edwin B. Forsythe (Brigantine) NWR	NWR	3	E2
Oxford	Pequest WMA	SWA	28	B2
Port Norris	Egg Island WMA	SWA	12	E1
Port Republic	Port Republic WMA	SWA	29	D2
Pottersville	TNC New Jersey Field Off	TNC	7	B2
Salem	Supawna Meadows NWR	NWR	5	D1
Seaside Park	Fort Mott SP	SPS	7	D1
South Dennis	Island Beach Park	SPS	11	D3
Sussex	Beaver Swamp WMA	SWA	4	B2
	Wallkill River NWR	NWR	6	A2
Titusville	High Point SP	SPS	19	C2
TRENTON	Washington Crossing SP	SWA	1	C2
	DEP, Div. Parks & Forestry			
	DEP, Div. of Fish, Game & Wildlife			
Tuckahoe	Assunpink WMA	SWA	1	C2
Tuckerton	Lester G. MacNamara WMA	SWA	3	C2
Warren Grove	Great Bay WMA	SWA	20	D3
West Milford	Greenwood Forest WMA	SWA	15	D3
Williamstown	Wanaque WMA	SWA	33	A2
	Whiting WMA	SWA	16	D3
	Winslow WMA	SWA	34	A3
		SWA	35	D3
		SWA	37	D2

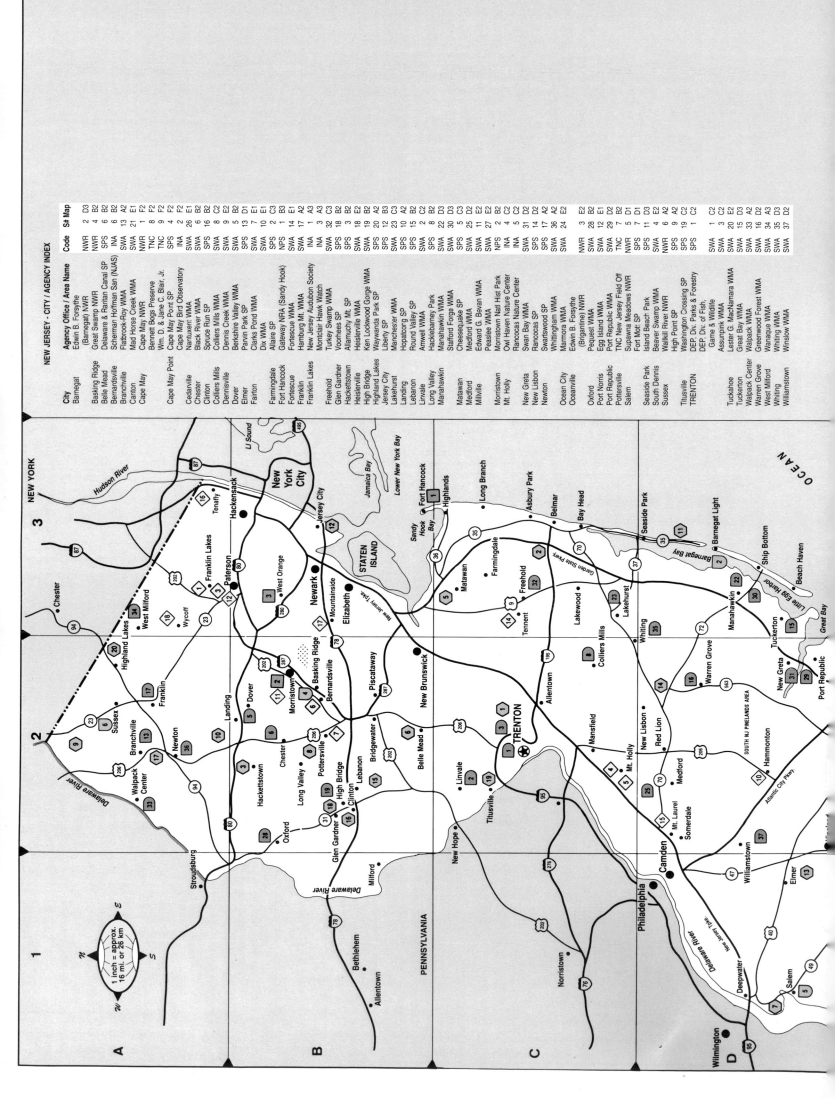

© 1994 by John Oliver Jones

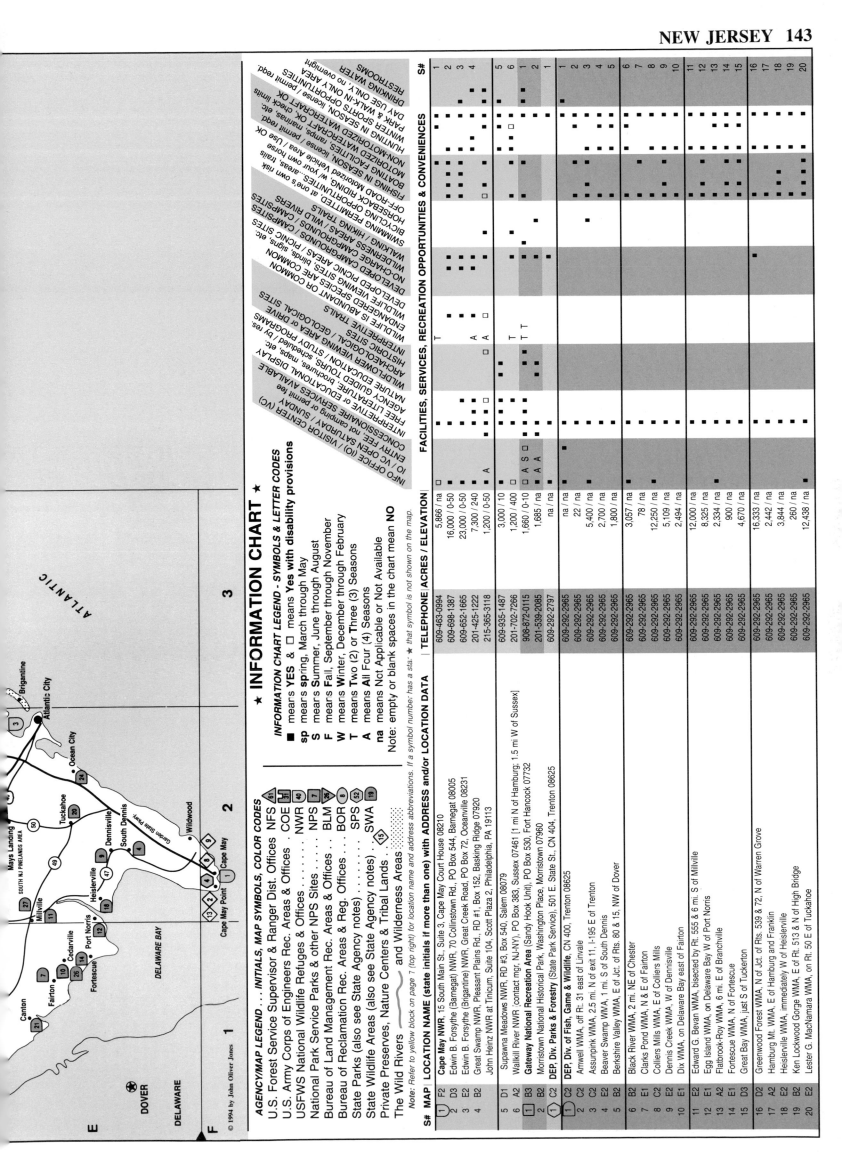

★ INFORMATION CHART ★

INFORMATION CHART LEGEND - SYMBOLS & LETTER CODES

■ means YES & □ means Yes with disability provisions

sp means spring, March through May
S means Summer, June through August
F means Fall, September through November
W means Winter, December through February
T means Two (2) or Three (3) Seasons
A means All Four (4) Seasons
na means Not Applicable or Not Available

Note: empty or blank spaces in the chart mean NO

AGENCY/MAP LEGEND ... INITIALS, MAP SYMBOLS, COLOR CODES

U.S. Forest Service Supervisor & Ranger Dist. Offices . . NFS
U.S. Army Corps of Engineers Rec. Areas & Offices . . COE
USFWS National Wildlife Refuges & Offices . . . . NWR
National Park Service Parks & other NPS Sites . . . . . NPS
Bureau of Land Management Rec. Areas & Offices . . . BLM
Bureau of Reclamation Rec. Areas & Reg. Offices . . . BOR
State Parks (also see State Agency notes) . . . . SPS
State Wildlife Areas (also see State Agency notes) . . . SWA
Private Preserves, Nature Centers & Tribal Lands . . .
The Wild Rivers ~~~~ and Wilderness Areas

Note: Refer to yellow block on page 7 (top right) for location name and address abbreviations. If a symbol number has a star ★ — that symbol is not shown on the map.

INFO OFFICE (IO) / VISITOR CENTER (VC)
IO / VC OPEN SATURDAY / SUNDAY
ENTRY FEE, not camping or permit fee
INTERPRETIVE or EDUCATIONAL SERVICES AVAILABLE
CONCESSIONAIRE / AGENCY LITERATURE, maps, etc.
FREE LITERATURE / brochures, scheduled / by res.
NATURE GUIDED TOURS / STUDY PROGRAMS
WILDLIFE EDUCATION / INTERPRETIVE DISPLAY
ARCHAEOLOGICAL / GEOLOGICAL SITES
HISTORIC SITES
INTERPRETIVE TRAILS
WILDLIFE VIEWING AREA or DRIVE
ENDANGERED SPECIES ARE COMMON
WILDLIFE VIEWING SITES, birds, signs, etc.
DEVELOPED PICNIC AREAS / PICNIC SITES
NO-CHARGE CAMPGROUNDS / CAMPSITES
WALKING / WILDERNESS AREAS / HIKING TRAILS
SWIMMING PERMITTED
BICYCLING OPPORTUNITIES
HORSEBACK RIDING w/ your own horse
OFF-ROAD MOTORIZED VEHICLE Area / Use OK
FISHING OPPORTUNITIES, at one's own risk
BOATING IN SEASON, license / permit req'd.
NON-MOTORIZED WATERCRAFT OK
MOTORIZED WATERCRAFT OK / check limits
HUNTING IN SEASON, license / permit req'd.
WINTER SPORTS OPPORTUNITIES OK
PARK & WALK-IN USE ONLY AREA
DAY USE ONLY, no overnight
DRINKING WATER
RESTROOMS

FACILITIES, SERVICES, RECREATION OPPORTUNITIES & CONVENIENCES

S#	MAP	LOCATION NAME (state initials if more than one) with ADDRESS and/or LOCATION DATA	TELEPHONE / ACRES / ELEVATION
1	F2	**Cape May NWR**, 15 South Main St., Suite 3, Cape May Court House 08210	609-463-0994 / 5,866 / na
2	D3	Edwin B. Forsythe (Barnegat) NWR, 70 Collinstown Rd., PO Box 544, Barnegat 08005	609-698-1387 / 16,000 / 0-50
3	E2	Edwin B. Forsythe (Brigantine) NWR, Great Creek Road, PO Box 72, Oceanville 08231	609-652-1665 / 23,000 / 0-50
4	B2	Great Swamp NWR, Pleasant Plains Rd., RD #1, Box 152, Basking Ridge 07920	201-425-1222 / 7,300 / 240
		John Heinz NWR at Tinicum, Suite 104, Scott Plaza 2, Philadelphia, PA 19113	215-365-3118 / 1,200 / 0-50
5	D1	Supawna Meadows NWR, RD #3, Box 540, Salem 08079	609-935-1487 / 3,000 / 10
6	A2	Wallkill River NWR (contact mgr. NJ-NY), PO Box 383, Sussex 07461 [1 mi N of Hamburg; 1.5 mi W of Sussex]	201-702-7266 / 1,200 / 400
1	B3	**Gateway National Recreation Area** (Sandy Hook Unit), PO Box 530, Fort Hancock 07732	908-872-0115 / 1,660 / 0-10
2	B2	Morristown National Historical Park, Washington Place, Morristown 07960	201-539-2085 / 1,685 / na
1	C2	**DEP, Div. Parks & Forestry** (State Park Service), 501 E. State St., CN 404, Trenton 08625	609-292-2797 / na / na
1	C2	**DEP, Div. of Fish, Game & Wildlife**, CN 400, Trenton 08625	609-292-2965 / na / na
2	C2	Amwell WMA, off Rt. 31 east of Linvale	609-292-2965 / 22 / na
3	C2	Assunpink WMA, 2.5 mi. N of exit 11, I-195 E of Trenton	609-292-2965 / 5,400 / na
4	E2	Beaver Swamp WMA, 1 mi. S of South Dennis	609-292-2965 / 2,700 / na
5	C2	Berkshire Valley WMA, E of Jct. of Rts. 80 & 15, NW of Dover	609-292-2965 / 1,800 / na
6	B2	Black River WMA, 2 mi. NE of Chester	609-292-2965 / 3,057 / na
7	E1	Clarks Pond WMA, N & E of Fairton	609-292-2965 / 78 / na
8	C2	Colliers Mills WMA, E of Colliers Mills	609-292-2965 / 12,250 / na
9	E1	Dennis Creek WMA, W of Dennisville	609-292-2965 / 5,109 / na
10	E1	Dix WMA, on Delaware Bay east of Fairton	609-292-2965 / 2,494 / na
11	E2	Edward G. Bevan WMA, bisected by Rt. 555 & 6 mi. S of Millville	609-292-2965 / 12,000 / na
12	E1	Egg Island WMA, on Delaware Bay W of Port Norris	609-292-2965 / 8,325 / na
13	A2	Flatbrook-Roy WMA, 6 mi. E of Branchville	609-292-2965 / 2,334 / na
14	E1	Fortescue WMA, N of Fortescue	609-292-2965 / 900 / na
15	D3	Great Bay WMA, just S of Tuckerton	609-292-2965 / 4,670 / na
16	D2	Greenwood Forest WMA, N of Jct. of Rts. 539 & 72, N of Warren Grove	609-292-2965 / 16,333 / na
17	A2	Hamburg Mt. WMA, E of Hamburg and Franklin	609-292-2965 / 2,442 / na
18	E2	Heislerville WMA, immediately W of Heislerville	609-292-2965 / 3,844 / na
19	B2	Ken Lockwood Gorge WMA, E of Rt. 513 & N of High Bridge	609-292-2965 / 260 / na
20	E2	Lester G. MacNamara WMA, on Rt. 50 E of Tuckahoe	609-292-2965 / 12,438 / na

(Map area, left)

ATLANTIC

DOVER

DELAWARE

DELAWARE BAY

Mays Landing
SOUTH NJ PINELANDS AREA
Tuckahoe
South Dennis
Dennisville
Heislerville
Millville
Cedarville
Port Norris
Fortescue
Canton
Fairton
Cape May Point
Cape May
Wildwood
Ocean City
Atlantic City
Brigantine

Garden State Pkwy.

1 2 3

E F

★ INFORMATION CHART ★

AGENCY/MAP LEGEND . . . INITIALS, MAP SYMBOLS, COLOR CODES

U.S. Forest Service Supervisor & Ranger Dist. Offices . NFS ⬡61
U.S. Army Corps of Engineers Rec. Areas & Offices . . COE ⬡31
USFWS National Wildlife Refuges & Offices . . . . NWR ⬡40
National Park Service Parks & other NPS Sites . . . . . NPS ⬡7
Bureau of Land Management Rec. Areas & Offices . . . BLM ⬡26
Bureau of Reclamation Rec. Areas & Reg. Offices . . . BOR ⬡8
State Parks (also see State Agency notes) . . . . SPS ⬡52
State Wildlife Areas (also see State Agency notes) . . SWA ⬡19
Private Preserves, Nature Centers & Tribal Lands . . . ⬡15
The Wild Rivers ⌒ and Wilderness Areas

Note: Refer to yellow block on page 1 (top right) for location name and address abbreviations. If a symbol number has a star ★, that location is not shown on the map.

INFORMATION CHART LEGEND - SYMBOLS & LETTER CODES

■ means YES & □ means Yes with disability provisions
sp means spring, March through May
S means Summer, June through August
F means Fall, September through November
W means Winter, December through February
T means Two (2) or Three (3) Seasons
A means All Four (4) Seasons
na means Not Applicable or Not Available

Note: empty or blank spaces in the chart mean NO

NEW JERSEY

S#	MAP	LOCATION NAME (state initials if more than one) with ADDRESS and/or LOCATION DATA	TELEPHONE	ACRES / ELEVATION
21	E1	Mad Horse Creek WMA, in Salem County S of Canton	609-292-2965	5,826 / na
22	D3	Manahawkin WMA, N of Rt. 72 & E of Manahawkin	609-292-2965	965 / na
23	C3	Manchester WMA, on Bakersville Rd. E of Lakehurst	609-292-2965	2,376 / na
24	E2	Marmora WMA, coastal wetlands Cape May Co. S of Ocean City	609-292-2965	6,485 / na
25	D2	Medford WMA, on Brace Rd. off Rt. 541 N of Medford	609-292-2965	214 / na
26	E1	Nantuxent WMA, 4 mi. W of Cedarville	609-292-2965	916 / na
27	E2	Peaslee WMA, 7 mi. E. Millville	609-292-2965	14,200 / na
28	B2	Pequest WMA, Warren Co. N of Oxford	609-292-2965	1,612 / na
29	D2	Port Republic WMA, W of Garden St. Pkwy. & N of Port Republic	609-292-2965	755 / na
30	D3	Stafford Forge WMA, on Garden St. Pkwy. S of Manahawkin	609-292-2965	2,788 / na
31	D2	Swan Bay WMA, on Rt. 542 SW of New Greta	609-292-2965	1,078 / na
32	C3	Turkey Swamp WMA (many parcels), 6 mi. S of Freehold	609-292-2965	2,211 / na
33	A3	Walpack WMA, 5 mi. W of Walpack Center	609-292-2965	387 / na
34	A3	Wanaque WMA, NE of West Milford	609-292-2965	2,277 / na
35	D3	Whiting WMA, SE of Whiting	609-292-2965	1,200 / na
36	A2	Whittingham WMA, W of Rt. 206 S of Newton	609-292-2965	1,514 / na
37	D2	Winslow WMA, S of Rt. 720 & SE of Williamstown	609-292-2965	6,566 / na
1	A3	New Jersey Audubon Society (NJAS) & Lorrimer Nature Center, 790 Ewing Ave., Franklin Lakes 07417	201-891-2185	35 / 400-500
2	F2	Cape May Bird Observatory, c/o NJAS, 707 East Lake Dr., PO Box 3, Cape May Point 08212	609-884-2736	1 / 20
3	A3	Montclair Hawk Watch, c/o NJAS, PO Box 125, Franklin Lakes 07417	201-891-1211	2 / 500
4	C2	Owl Haven Nature Center (NJAS), Englishtown-Freehold Rd., Mt. Holly 08060	201-780-7007	1,500 / 100
5	C2	Rancocas Nature Center (NJAS), Rancocas Mt. Holly Rd. (Rancocas State Park), Mt. Holly 08060	609-261-2495	120 / 40
6	B2	Scherman Hoffman Sanctuary (NJAS), 11 Hardscrabble Rd., Bernardsville 07924	201-766-5787	263 / na
7	B2	TNC New Jersey Field Office, 17 Fairmount Road, PO Box 181, Pottersville 07979	908-439-3007	na / na
8	F2	Bennett Bogs Preserve, contact Field Office, near Cape May	908-439-3007	25 / 10
9	F2	Wm. D. & Jane C. Blair, Jr., Cape May Migratory Bird Refuge, contact Field Office, Cape May		187 / na

NEW JERSEY CITY/AGENCY INDEX

City	Agency Office / Area Name	Code	S# Map
	Ghost Ranch Living Museum	NFS	2a A2
Abiquiu	Abiquiu Dam	COE	2 C2
	Lincoln Nat'l. Forest Sup.	NFS	24 C2
Alamogordo	Three Rivers Petroglyphs SRA	BLM	17 C2
	Oliver Lee Memorial SP	SPS	13 C2
	U.S. Forest Svc., SW Reg.	NFS	1 B2
Albuquerque	Cibola Nat'l. Forest Sup.	NFS	9 B2
	COE, Albuquerque District	COE	1 B2
	USFWS Region 2	NWR	1 B2
	Rio Puerco Resource Area	BLM	6 B2
	Rio Grande Nature Ctr SP	SPS	14 B2
	Northwest Area Office	TNC	3 B1
Amalia	Rio de los Pinos Wildlife & Fishing Area	SWA	18 A2
Bernalillo	Coronado SP	COE	6 B2
Blanco	Jemez Canyon Dam	BLM	6 A1
	Jicarilla Ranger D.	NFS	5 A1
Bloomfield	Simon Canyon SRA	BLM	5 A1
Caballo	Chaco Culture Nat'l Hist Park	NPS	4 A1
	Angel Peak SRA	BLM	4 A1
	Caballo Lake SP	SPS	4 C2
Canjilon	Canjilon RD	NFS	4 A2
Capulin	Bonito Lake	SWA	20 C2
	Capulin Volcano Natl Mon	NPS	3 A3

NEW MEXICO - CITY / AGENCY INDEX

City	Agency Office / Area Name	Code	S#	Map
Carlsbad	Guadalupe Ranger D.	NFS	26	D3
	Carlsbad Caverns Natl Park	NPS	4	D3
	Brantley Wildlife Area	BLM	21	D3
	Rattlesnake Springs Pre	SWA	21	C3
Carrizozo	Valley of Fires Rec Area	BLM	25	C2
Chama	Rio Chama River SRA	BLM	9	A2
	Edward Sargeant Wildlife A	SWA	14	A2
	W.A. Humphries Wildlife A	SWA	19	A2
Cimarron	Colin Neblett Wildlife Area	SWA	8	A2
	E.S. Barker Wildlife Area	SWA	8	A2
Clayton	Kiowa National Grasslands	NFS	10	A3
Cloudcroft	Cloudcroft Ranger D.	NFS	25	C2
Conchas	Conchas Lake	COE	4	B3
Cowles	Bert Clancy Fishing & Wildlife Area	SWA	6	B2
Coyote	Coyote Ranger D.	NFS	30	A2
Cuba	Cuba Ranger D.	NFS	31	A2
Datil	Datil Well SRA	BLM	19	C1
El Rito	El Rito Ranger D.	NFS	5	A2
El Vado	Rio Chama Wildlife & Fishing Area	SWA	17	A2
Elephant Butte	Elephant Butte Lake SP	SPS	8	C2
Espanola	Espanola Ranger D.	NFS	32	A2
Farmington	Farmington District Office	BLM	3	A1
Faywood	Jackson Lake Wildlife Area	SWA	15	A1
Gila Hot Springs	City of Rocks SP	SPS	5	C1
	Heart Bar Wildlife Area	SWA	24	C1

NEW MEXICO

S#	MAP	LOCATION NAME with ADDRESS and/or LOCATION DATA		Code	S#	Map
Glenwood	Glenwood Ranger D.		SWA	25	C1
Grants	Mount Taylor Ranger D.		NFS	17	C1
Guadalupita	Coyote Creek SP		BLM	12	B1
Holman AFB	Murphy Lake SP		SPS	7	A2
	White Sands Natl Monument		SPS	11	A2
Jemez Springs	Jemez Ranger D.		NFS	8	C2
Las Cruces	Las Cruces District Office		NFS	33	B2
	Caballo Resource Area		BLM	13	D2
	Mimbres Resource Area		BLM	*14	D2
	Organ Mountain SRA		BLM	*15	D2
	Southwest Area Office		SWA	8	A2
	Dripping Springs Preserve		NFS	16	D2
	Las Vegas NWR		TNC	4	D2
Las Vegas	McAllister Lake		NWR	5	B3
	Fort Stanton SRA		SWA	11	B3
Lincoln	Lincoln		BLM	23	C2
Logan	Ute Lake SP		SPS	16	B3
Los Alamos	Bandelier Natl. Monument		NPS	18	C1
Luna	Luna Ranger D.		NFS	11	C1
Magdalena	Magdalena Ranger D.		NFS	6	A3
Maxwell	Maxwell NWR		NWR	6	A3
Mayhill	Mayhill Ranger D.		NFS	27	C2
Mimbres	Mimbres Ranger D.		NFS	34	B2
Mountainair	Bear Canyon Reservoir		SWA	22	C1
	Mountainair Ranger D.		NFS	13	B2
	Manzano Mtns. SP		SPS	12	A1
Navajo Dam	Navajo Lake SP		NFS	35	B2
Pecos	Pecos Ranger D.		SPS	12	A1

NEW MEXICO (continued)

S#	City	Location	Code	S#	Map
1	Santa Rosa	Santa Rosa Dam & Lake	COE	7	B3
2		Two Rivers Dam & Res	COE	8	C3
3	Silver City	Gila National Forest Sup	NFS	15	C1
		Silver City Ranger D.	SPS	22	C1
		Wilderness RD &			
4		Gila Cliff Dwellings NM	NFS	23	C1
5		Gila Cliff Dwellings NM	NPS	7	C1
6		Bill Evans Lake	SWA	23	C1
	Socorro	Bosque del Apache NWR	NWR	3	C2
		Sevilleta NWR (permit only)	NWR	4	B2
		Socorro Resource Area	SWA	12	B2
	Springer	Springer Lake	SWA	15	A3
	Taos	Sugarite Canyon SP	SWA	2	A2
	Tijeras	Northeast Area Office	NFS	21	C1
	Tres Piedras	Reserve Ranger D.	BLM	20	C3
	Truth or Consequences	Bitter Lake NWR	NWR	2	C3
		Roswell District Office	BLM	22	C3
	Tucumcari	Roswell Resource Area	SWA	3	C3
	Ute Park	Mescalero Sand SRA	NFS	9	A2
	Velarde	Bottomless Lakes SP	SPS	29	B2
	Wagon Mound	Smokey Bear Ranger D.	NPS	1	B1
		Heron Lake SP	BLM	11	A2
		Santa Fe Natl. Forest Sup.	SPS	1	A2
		Natl. Park Svc., SW Region	SWA	1	A2
		Santa Cruz Lake SRA	SWA	13	B2
		EMNRD-State Pks & Rec Div	SPS	1	B2
		Dept. NM Game & Fish	TNC	2	A1
		TNC New Mexico Field Off	NAS	1	B2
		Randall Davey Audubon Ctr			

Galisteo Dam	COE	3	B2
Camino Real Ranger D.	NFS	5	B2
Bluewater Lake SP	SPS	20	B1
Questa Ranger D.	NFS	7	A2
Urraca Wildlife Area	BLM	12	A2
El Morro Natl. Monument	NPS	6	B1
Ramah Lake	SWA	16	B1
Sugarite Canyon SRA	SWA	2	A3
Carson Natl Forest Sup	NFS	21	C1
Taos Resource Area	BLM	8	C2
Orilla Verde Rec. Area	BLM	14	A2
Sandia Ranger D.	NFS	8	A2
Black Range Ranger D.	NFS	16	C1
Ladd S. Gordon Wildlife A	SWA	10	B3
Cimarron Canyon SP	SPS	5	A2
Rio Grande Racecourse SRA	BLM	10	A2
Charette Lakes	SWA	7	A3

S#	MAP	LOCATION NAME
1	D3	Avalon Res.
2	C3	Brantley
3	C1	Caballo Res.
4	A2	Elephant Butte Res.
5	A2	El Vado Res.
6	A2	Heron Res.
7	B3	Lake Sumner
8	D2	Leasburg Diversion Dam
9	A2	Nambe Falls Res.
10	A3	Reservoir No. 13
11	A3	Stubblefield & Res. No. 2

Wilderness/Wild River Index

Wilderness Areas

Carson National Forest (S# 2, map A2)
Cruces Basin Wilderness - 18,000 acres
Latir Peak Wilderness - 20,000 acres
Wheeler Peak Wilderness - 19,661 acres
Carson National Forest (S# 2, map A2), and
Santa Fe National Forest (S# 29, map B2)
Chama River Canyon Wilderness - 50,300 acres
Pecos Wilderness - 223,333 acres
Cibola National Forest (S# 9, map B2)
Apache Kid Wilderness - 44,650 acres
Manzano Mountain Wilderness - 36,785 acres
Sandia Mountain Wilderness - 37,906 acres
Withington Wilderness - 19,000 acres
Gila National Forest (S# 15, map C1)
Aldo Leopold Wilderness - 202,016 acres
Blue Range Wilderness - 30,000 acres
Gila Wilderness - 557,873 acres
Lincoln National Forest (S# 24, map C2)
Capitan Mountains Wilderness - 34,513 acres
White Mountains Wilderness - 48,366 acres
Santa Fe National Forest (S# 29, map B2)
Dome Wilderness - 5,200 acres
San Pedro Peaks Wilderness - 41,132 acres
Bitter Lake NWR (S# 2, map C3)
Salt Creek Wilderness - 9,621 acres
Bosque del Apache NWR (S# 3, C2)
Bosque del Apache Wilderness
Chupadera Unit - 5,289 acres
Indian Wells Unit - 5,139 acres
San Pasqual Unit - 19,859 acres
Bandelier Natl. Monument (S# 2, map C3)
Bandelier Wilderness - 23,267 acres
Carlsbad Caverns Natl. Park (S# 4, D3)
Carlsbad Wilderness - 33,125 acres
BLM Albuquerque District Office (S# 2, map B2)
Bisti Wilderness - 3,968 acres
De-na-zin Wilderness - 23,872 acres

Wild Rivers

Jemez River, East Fork and Pecos River
Santa Fe National Forest (S# 29, map B2)
Rio Chama and Rio Grande
Carson National Forest (S# 2, map A2)
BLM Albuquerque District Office (S# 2, map B2)

New Mexico Notes continue on page 148 -

NEW MEXICO NOTES

Summary

There are 103 federal, 44 state, and 24 private recreation areas or local administrative offices covered in this state chapter. Of these, 109 appear in the Information Chart and 62 are covered in the notes. The special indexes feature 25 federally designated wilderness areas and wild rivers, and 107 agency published outdoor maps.

Federal Agencies

U.S. Forest Service

Ghost Ranch Museum and Visitor Center managed by the Canjilon Ranger District (see S# 4) of the Carson NF serves as an environmental learning center for adults and school groups. Wildlife conservation and management, interpretation of cultural and local history, and wild animals are featured in their educational programs.

National Park Service & U.S. Forest Service

Gila Cliff Dwellings Visitor Center and National Monument is a NPS site (see S# 7) managed by the Gila National Forest Wilderness Ranger District office (see S# 23) through an inter-agency agreement. Outdoor exhibits interpret the geology and flora. An interpretive trail, the cliff dwellings, and other recreation opportunities are available here.

Additional NPS Locations in New Mexico

Aztec Ruins National Monument (319 acres)
(S# 9, map A1)
PO Box 640
Aztec, NM 87410   505-334-6174

El Malpais National Monument (114,335 acres)
(S# 10, map B1, now open to visitors)
PO Box 939
Grants, NM 87020   505-285-5406

Fort Union National Monument (721 acres)
(S# 11, map A3)
Watrous, NM 87753   505-425-8025

Pecos National Historical Park (365 acres)
(S# 12, map B2)
PO Drawer 418
Pecos, NM 87552   505-756-6414

Petroglyph National Monument (5,208 acres)
(S# 13, map B2)
PO Box 1293
Albuquerque, NM 87103   505-988-6012

Salinas Pueblo Missions NM (1,077 acres)
(S# 14, map B2)
Box 496
Mountainair, NM 87036   505-847-2585

Zuni-Cibola National Historical Park (800 acres)
(S# 15, map B2)
c/o SW Region, NPS
PO Box 728
Santa Fe, NM 87504   505-988-6340

Bureau of Reclamation Recreation Areas

Eleven recreation areas are listed here and symbolized on the New Mexico state map.

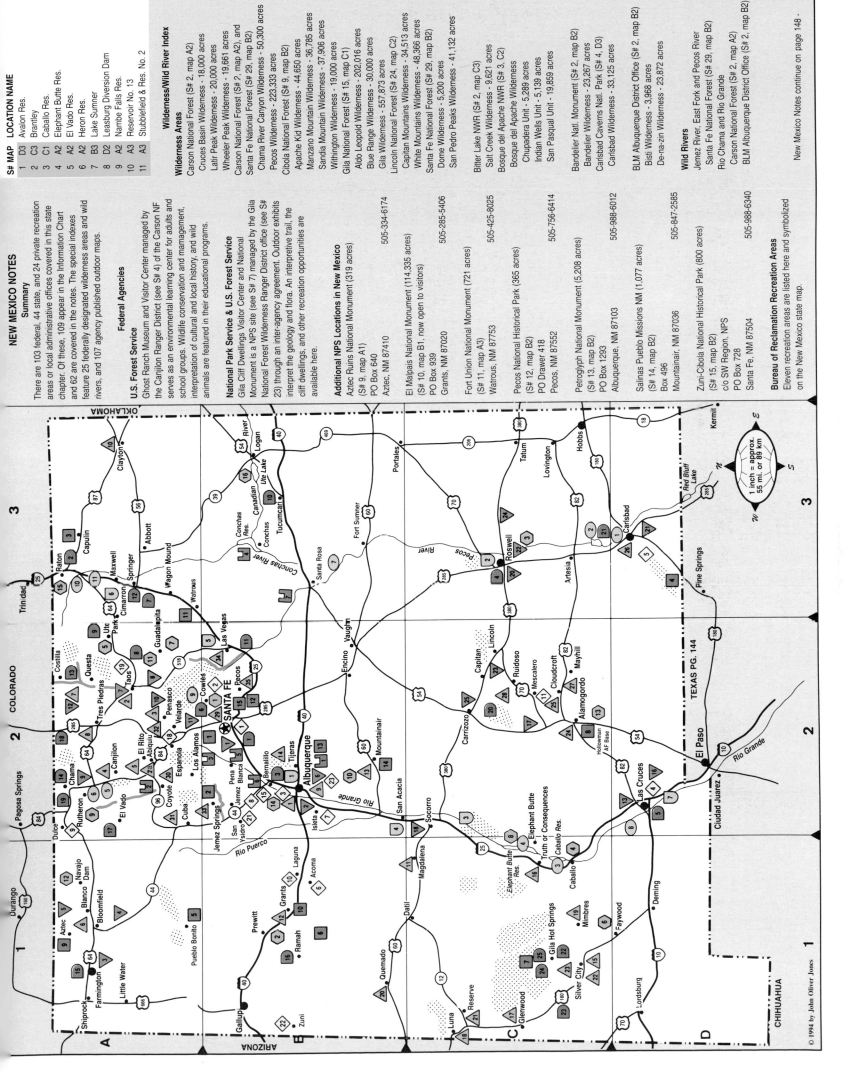

© 1994 by John Oliver Jones

★ INFORMATION CHART ★

AGENCY/MAP LEGEND . . . INITIALS, MAP SYMBOLS, COLOR CODES

U.S. Forest Service Supervisor & Ranger Dist. Offices	NFS
U.S. Army Corps of Engineers Rec. Areas & Offices	COE
USFWS National Wildlife Refuges & Offices	NWR
National Park Service Parks & other NPS Sites	NPS
Bureau of Land Management Rec. Areas & Offices	BLM
Bureau of Reclamation Rec. Areas & Reg. Offices	BOR
State Parks (also see State Agency notes)	SPS
State Wildlife Areas (also see State Agency notes)	SWA
Private Preserves, Nature Centers & Tribal Lands	

The Wild Rivers ~~~ and Wilderness Areas

INFORMATION CHART LEGEND - SYMBOLS & LETTER CODES

- ■ means YES, □ means Yes with disability provisions
- sp means spring, March through May
- S means Summer, June through August
- F means Fall, September through November
- W means Winter, December through February
- T means Two (2) or Three (3) Seasons
- A means All Four (4) Seasons
- na means Not Applicable or Not Available

Note: empty or blank spaces in the chart mean NO

* that symbol number is not shown on the map.

Note: Refer to yellow block on page 7 (top right) for location name and address abbreviations.

S#	MAP	LOCATION NAME (state initials if more than one) with ADDRESS and/or LOCATION DATA	TELEPHONE	ACRES / ELEVATION
1	B2	**U.S.F.S., SW Reg.**, FOB, PA Office, 5th floor, 517 Gold Ave. SW, Albuquerque 87102 [between 5th & 6th Sts]	505-842-3292	21,000,000 / 1,300-13,000
2	A2	Carson National Forest Sup., 208 Cruz Alta Road, PO Box 558, Taos 87571	505-758-6300	1,500,000 / 6,500-13,161
2a	A2	Ghost Ranch Living Museum, US Hwy. 84, Abiquiu 87510	505-685-4312	4 / na
3	A2	Camino Real Ranger D., PO Box 68, Penasco 87553 [off SH 75]	505-587-2255	na / na
4	A2	Canjilon RD., SH 115, PO Box 488, Canjilon 87515	505-684-2486	na / na
5	A2	El Rito Ranger D., off SH 554, PO Box 56, El Rito 87530	505-581-4554	na / na
6	A1	Jicarilla Ranger D., Gobernador Route, Blanco 87412	505-334-2876	na / na
7	A2	Questa Ranger D., PO Box 110, Questa 87556 [off SH 38]	505-586-0520	na / na
8	A2	Tres Piedras Ranger D., Hwy. 64, PO Box 728, Tres Piedras 87577	505-758-8678	na / na
9	B2	Cibola Natl. Forest Sup., 2113 Osuna Rd. NE, #A, Albuquerque 87113	505-761-4650	1,886,000 / 2,000-11,300
10	A3	Kiowa National Grasslands, 16 North Second Street, Clayton 88415	505-374-9652	136,500 / 4,500-6,300
11	C1	Magdalena Ranger D., Hwy.60, Box 45, Magdalena 87825	505-854-2381	797,500 / 5,850-10,780
12	B1	Mount Taylor Ranger D., 1800 Lobo Canyon Road, Grants 87020	505-287-8833	517,500 / 6,960-11,301
13	C1	Mountainair Ranger D., off Hwy. 60, PO Box E, Mountainair 87036	505-847-2990	204,500 / 6,600-9,500
14	B2	Sandia Ranger D., 11776 Hwy. 14 South, Tijeras 87059	505-281-3304	102,000 / 5,400-10,680
15	C1	Gila National Forest Sup., 2610 N. Silver St., Silver City 88061	505-388-8201	3,300,000 / 4,000-11,000
16	C1	Black Range Ranger D., 1804 Date St., Box 431, Truth or Consequences 87901	505-894-6677	na / na
17	C1	Glenwood Ranger D., Hwy. 180, Box 8, Glenwood 88039	505-539-2481	na / na
18	C1	Luna Ranger D., Hwy. 180, Box 91, Luna 87824	505-547-2612	na / na
19	C1	Mimbres Ranger D., Hwy. 35, Box 79, Mimbres 88049	505-536-2250	na / na
20	B1	Quemado Ranger D., Hwy. 60, Box 158, Quemado 87829	505-773-4678	na / na
21	C1	Reserve Ranger D., Hwy. 12, Box 170, Reserve 87830	505-533-6231	na / na
22	C1	Silver City Ranger D., 2915 Hwy. 180 East, Silver City 88061	505-538-2771	na / na
23	C1	Wilderness RD & Gila Cliff Dwelling., Rt. #11, Box 100, Silver City 88061 [VC at N end of city, end of Hwy 15]	505-536-9461	1,132,122 / 350-11,580
24	C2	Lincoln Natl. Forest Sup., FOB, 1101 New York Ave., Alamogordo 88310	505-437-6030	1,567,000 / 7,100
25	C2	Cloudcroft Ranger D., PO Box 288, Cloudcroft 88317	505-682-2551	209,570 / 4,200-9,500
26	D3	Guadalupe Ranger D., FOB, Room 159, Carlsbad 88220	505-885-4181	285,000 / 350-6,500
27	C2	Mayhill Ranger D., PO Box 5, Mayhill 88339	505-687-3411	273,200 / 5,990-9,360
28	C2	Smokey Bear Ranger D., 901 Mechem Drive, Ruidoso 88345	505-257-4095	364,352 / 5,400-11,580
29	C2	Santa Fe Natl. Forest Sup., 1220 St. Francis Drive, PO Box 1689, Santa Fe 87504	505-988-6940	1,567,000 / 7,100
30	A2	Coyote Ranger D., Coyote 87012	505-638-5526	265,000 / 6,700
31	A2	Cuba Ranger D., PO Box 130, Cuba 87013	505-289-3264	275,000 / 6,900
32	B3	Espanola Ranger D., PO Box R, Espanola 87532	505-753-7331	175,000 / 5,700
33	B2	Jemez Ranger D., Jemez Springs 87025	505-829-3535	275,000 / 7,100
34	B2	Las Vegas Ranger D., 1926 N. Seventh Street, Las Vegas 87701	505-425-3534	180,000 / 6,500
35	B2	Pecos Ranger D., PO Drawer 3, Pecos 87552	505-757-6121	397,000 / 7,100
		COE, Albuquerque District, PO Box 1580, Albuquerque 87103	505-766-2724	
1	A2	Abiquiu Dam, Drawer D., Abiquiu 87510	505-685-4371	na / na
2	A2	Cochiti Lake, 82 Dam Crest Rd., Pena Blanca 87041	505-242-8302	na / na
3	B3	Conchas Lake, Conchas Dam, Conchas 88416	505-868-2221	na / na
4	B2	Galisteo Dam, 82 Dam Crest Rd., Pena Blanca 87041	505-242-8302	na / na
5	B2	Jemez Canyon Dam, PO Box 337, Bernalillo 87004	505-242-8302	na / na
6	B3	Santa Rosa Dam & Lake, PO Box 345, Santa Rosa 88435	505-472-3115	na / na
7	B3	Two Rivers Dam & Reservoir, PO Box 345, Santa Rosa 88435	505-472-3115	na / na
8	C3		505-766-3940	na / na
		USFWS Region 2, 500 Gold Ave., SW, PO Box 1306, Albuquerque 87103 [states of AZ, NM, OK, TX]		
1	C3	Bitter Lake NWR, PO Box 7, Roswell 88202 [11 mi. NE of Roswell]	505-622-6755	24,500 / 3,500
2	C2	Bosque del Apache NWR, PO Box 1246, Socorro 87801 [exit 139 off I-25 in San Antonio, then 8 mi S on NM Hwy 1]	505-835-1828	57,200 / 4,500
3	B2	Las Vegas NWR, (entry by permit), PO Box 1248, Socorro 87801 [Research Natural Area closed to the public]	505-864-4021	228,000 / 4,400-8,100
4	B2	Sevilleta NWR, Rt. #1, Box 399, Las Vegas 87701	505-425-3581	8,672 / 6,500

Grid	No.	Name / Location	Phone	Acres / Elevation
B2	2	Bandelier Nat'l. Monument, HCR-1, Box 1-13, Los Alamos 87544	505-672-3861	36,971 / 5,400-10,200
A3	3	Capulin Volcano National Monument, PO Box 40, Capulin 88414	505-278-2201	790 / 7,889-8,182
D3	4	Carlsbad Caverns National Park, 3225 National Parks Hwy., Carlsbad 88220	505-785-2232	46,755 / 3,600-6,300
A1	5	Chaco Culture National Historical Park (at Pueblo Bonito), Star Rt. #4, Box 6500, Bloomfield 87413	505-786-7014	33,974 / 6,200-6,700
B1	6	El Morro Nat'l. Monument, Rt. #2, Box 43, Ramah 87321	505-783-4226	1,279 / 7,219
C1	7	Gila Cliff Dwellings NM (managed by Gila Nat'l. Forest), Route 11, Box 100, Silver City 88061	505-536-9461	533 / 6,000
C2	8	White Sands National Monument, PO Box 1086, Holman AFB 88330	505-479-6124	143,733 / 3,800-4,100
B1	1	**BLM New Mexico State Office**, 1474 Rodeo Drive, Santa Fe 87505	505-988-6227	na / na
B2	2	Albuquerque District Office, 435 Montano Road, NE, Albuquerque 87107	505-761-8700	na / na
A1	3	Farmington District Office, 1235 La Plata Highway, Farmington 87401	505-327-5344	na / na
A1	4	Angel Peak SRA, South on SR 44 near Bloomfield	505-327-5344	10,000 / 6,000-6,500
A1	5	Simon Canyon SRA, 3 mi. W of Navajo Dam, on N bank of San Juan River NE of Blanco	505-327-5344	3,800 / 5,700-6,500
B2	6	Rio Puerco Resource Area, 435 Montano Road, NE, Albuquerque 87107	505-761-8700	na / na
A2	7	Taos Resource Area, 224 Cruz Alta Rd., Taos 87571	505-758-8851	na / na
C2	8	Orilla Verde Recreation Area, along St. Hwy. 570, 10 mi. S of Taos	505-758-8851	2,840 / 6,100
A2	9	Rio Chama River SRA (recorded info, call 505-758-8148), 20 mi. S of Chama	505-758-8851	10,000 / na
A2	10	Rio Grande Racecourse SRA, 20 mi. S of Taos along Rio Grande, & S Hwy. 68 between Pilar & Velarde	505-758-8851	2,020 / 6,000
B2	11	Santa Cruz Lake SRA, on St. Hwy. 596, 25 mi. N of Santa Fe	505-758-8851	2,543 / 6,300
A2	12	Wild Rivers Recreation Area SRA, on SR 378, 14 mi. NW of Questa	505-758-8851	20,300 / 6,800-7,500
D2	13	Las Cruces District: Office, 1800 Marquess Street, Las Cruces 88005	505-525-8228	na / na
D2	*14	Caballo Resource Area, 1800 Marquess Street, Las Cruces 88005	505-525-8228	na / na
D2	*15	Mimbres Resource Area, 1800 Marquess Street, Las Cruces 88005	505-525-8228	na / na
D2	16	Organ Mountain SRA, about 10 mi. E of Las Cruces	505-522-1219	60,000 / 3,900-8,900
C2	17	Three Rivers Petroglyphs SRA, Hwy. 54, 25 mi. N of Alamogordo	505-525-8228	960 / 4,000
C2	18	Socorro Resource Area, 198 Neel Ave., NW, Socorro 87801	505-835-0400	na / na
C1	19	Datil Well SRA, about 60 mi. W of Socorro, S of Hwy. 60 near Datil	505-835-0412	na / 6,000
C2	20	Roswell District Office, 1717 W. 2nd St., Roswell 88202	505-622-9042	na / na
D3	21	Carlsbad Resource Area, 101 E. Mermod, Carlsbad 88220	505-887-6544	na / na
C2	22	Roswell Resource Area, 5th & Richardson, FOB #216, Roswell 88201	505-624-1790	na / na
C2	23	Fort Stanton SRA, 5 mi. W of Lincoln	505-624-1790	23,000 / 6,000
C3	24	Mescalero Sand SRA, off Hwy. 380, 33 mi. E of Roswell	505-624-1790	6,300 / 1,225
C2	25	Valley of Fires Recreation Area, 4 mi. W of Carrizozo	505-827-7465	463 / 5,000
B2	1	**EMNRD-State Parks & Recreation Div.**, 408 Galisteo, PO Box 1147, Santa Fe 87504	505-827-7465	7,000 / na
B1	2	Bluewater Lake SP, PO Box 3419, Prewitt 87045	505-876-2391	3,000 / 7,402
C3	3	Bottomless Lakes SP, Auto Route E, PO Box 1200, Roswell 88201	505-624-6058	1,400 / 3,470
D2	4	Caballo Lake SP, PO Box 32, Caballo 87931	505-743-3942	5,326 / 4,100
A2	5	Cimarron Canyon SP, PO Box 147, Ute Park 87749	505-377-6271	33,000 / 8,000
C1	6	City of Rocks SP, PO Box 50, Faywood 88034	505-536-2800	680 / 5,200
A2	7	Coyote Creek SP, PO Box 291, Guadalupita 87722	505-387-2328	80 / 7,700
C2	8	Elephant Butte Lake SP, PO Box 13, Elephant Butte 87935	505-744-5421	24,520 / 4,702
A2	9	Heron Lake SP, PO Box 31, Rutheron 87563	505-588-7470	4,107 / 7,200
B2	10	Manzano Mtns. SP, Rt. #2, Box 52, Mountainair 87036	505-847-2820	170 / 7,650
B2	11	Murphy Lake SP, PO Box 291, Guadalupita 87722	505-387-2328	18 / 7,840
A2	12	Navajo Lake SP, PO Box 6429, Navajo Dam 87419	505-632-2278	21,841 / 6,100
C2	13	Oliver Lee Memorial SP, HC-63, PO Box 1558, Alamogordo 88310	505-437-8284	180 / 4,500
B2	14	Rio Grande Nature Center SP, 2901 Candelaria, NW, Albuquerque 87107	505-344-7240	3,000 / 7,400
A3	15	Sugarite Canyon SP, HCR, Raton 87740	505-445-5607	3,600 / 8,200
B3	16	Ute Lake SP, PO Box 52, Logan 88426	505-487-2284	1,524 / 3,895
B2	1	**Dept. of Game & Fish**, 104 Galisteo St., Santa Fe 87503 [State Capitol, Villagra Bldg.]	505-827-7911	na / na
A3	2	Northeast Area Office (S# 6-13), York Canyon Rd., PO Box 1145, Raton 87740	505-445-2311	na / na
B1	3	Northwest Area Office (S# 14-19), 3841 Midway Place NE, Albuquerque 87109	505-841-8881	na / na
C3	4	Southeast Area Office (S# 20-21), 1912 W. Second St., Roswell 88201	505-624-6135	na / na
D2	5	Southwest Area Office (S# 22-25), 401 N. 17th St., Suite 4, Las Cruces 88005	505-524-6090	na / na
B2	1	**Randall Davey Audubon Center**, PO Box 9314, Santa Fe 87504 [at end of Upper Canyon Rd.]	505-983-4609	135 / 7,500
B2	2	**TNC New Mexico Field Office**, 107 Cienega Street, Santa Fe 87501	505-988-3867	na / na
B2	3	Corrales Bosque Preserve, contact Field Office, N of Albuquerque	505-988-3867	662 / 5,000
D2	4	Dripping Springs Preserve, PO Box 3103, Las Cruces 88003	505-522-1219	2,852 / 5,900
D3	5	Rattlesnake Springs Preserve, contact Field Office, SW of Carlsbad	505-988-3867	9 / 3,650

continued from page 144 -

Outdoor Map Index

National Park Service (USGS Map)

Bandelier National Monument [1953]
Scale: 1 inch = 0.4 mile (1 cm = 0.3 km)
Size: 42x53 inches (106x134 cm)

U.S. Forest Service Maps

The regional office in Albuquerque offers a series of topographic and planimetric maps at a scale of 2.64 inches = 1 mile. They cover approximately 6.5x8.5 miles. There are 91 maps in this series for the Santa Fe National Forest alone, and a total of 1,040 are available. They are printed in black-and-white.

There is a Travel Map for the Lincoln National Forest with ORV information, directions, tips, restrictions, and regulations. Wilderness maps printed on water-resistant paper have an asterisk (*) after the map name.

Aldo Leopold Wilderness *
Scale: 1 inch = 1.0 mile (1 cm = 0.6 km)
Apache Kid Wilderness
Scale: 1 inch = 2.7 miles (1 cm = 1.7 km)
Black Kettle Nat'l. Grassland
Carson National Forest
Scale: 1 inch = 2.0 miles (1 cm = 1.3 km)
Cibola National Forest, Sandia RD
Scale: 1 inch = 2.0 miles (1 cm = 1.3 km)
Cibola National Forest, Magdalena RD
Scale: 1 inch = 2.0 miles (1 cm = 1.3 km)

Cibola National Forest, Mountainair RD
Scale: 1 inch = 2.0 miles (1 cm = 1.3 km)
Cibola National Forest, Mt. Taylor RD
(black-and-white map available)
Scale: 1 inch = 2.0 miles (1 cm = 1.3 km)
Gila National Forest
Scale: 1 inch = 2.0 miles (1 cm = 1.3 km)
Gila Wilderness *
Scale: 1 inch = 1.0 mile (1 cm = 0.6 km)
Kiowa & Rita Blanca Natl. Grasslands
Scale: 1 inch = 2.0 miles (1 cm = 1.3 km)
Lincoln National Forest
Scale: 1 inch = 2.0 miles (1 cm = 1.3 km)
Lincoln NF Travel / ORV Guide ($1)
Lincoln NF, Guadalupe Ranger D.
Scale: 1 inch = 2.0 miles (1 cm = 1.3 km)
Manzano Mountain Wilderness *
Scale: 1 inch = 2.7 miles (1 cm = 1.7 km)
Pecos Wilderness
Scale: 1 inch = 2.7 miles (1 cm = 1.7 km)
Rio Chama River Running
Scale: 1 inch = 2.7 miles (1 cm = 1.7 km)
San Pedro Parks Wilderness
Scale: 1 inch = 2.7 miles (1 cm = 1.7 km)
Sandia Wilderness
Scale: 1 inch = 2.7 miles (1 cm = 1.7 km)
Santa Fe National Forest
Scale: 1 inch = 2.0 miles (1 cm = 1.3 km)
Wheeler/Latir Wilderness

Wheeler Peak Wilderness *
Scale: 1 inch = 2.7 miles (1 cm = 1.7 km)
White Mountain Wilderness *
Scale: 1 inch = 2.7 miles (1 cm = 1.7 km)
Withington Wilderness
Scale: 1 inch = 2.7 miles (1 cm = 1.7 km)

Bureau of Land Management Maps

See the New Mexico BLM intermediate scale map grid. Surface type intermediate maps in the grid include topography. The grid does not include the five maps covering parts of Oklahoma. These are the McAlester, Eufaula, Fort Smith, Mena, and Ada maps.

The BLM State Office (S# 1) in Santa Fe has a variety of maps available covering New Mexico and portions of Texas, Oklahoma and Arizona. Texas maps include Status and Planimetric Plats. Special maps include an Oklahoma (black-and-white) and a New Mexico (color) map. They are printed in 1:500,000 scale. The New Mexico map is also available in 1:1,000,000 scale.

State Agencies

Energy, Minerals, and Natural Resources Department

2040 Pacheco St.
Santa Fe, NM 87505   505-827-5950
Parent agency for Forestry and the Parks and Recreation Divisions.

State Parks & Recreation Division

A New Mexico State Parks Guide (37 state parks) is available free. The guide describes each area, contains a locator map, and includes information on facilities and activities.

Forestry & Resources Conservation Division

PO Box 1948
Santa Fe, NM 87504   505-827-5830
There is no state forest recreation program in New Mexico.

NM Dept. of Game & Fish (S# 1, map B2)

A special issue of New Mexico Wildlife magazine features information on 66 DGF properties, has a locator map for the areas, and describes recreational opportunities. Availability of this January-February 1989 issue of the magazine is limited, viewing may be restricted to a DGF office or public library. A bi-monthly magazine, New Mexico Wildlife is available by subscription for $10 per year.

The HQ and Area offices are listed in the Information Chart. A selection of Game & Fish managed properties are listed here and shown on the Guide map.

S#	MAP	AREA NAME & LOCATION
6	B2	Bert Clancy Fishing & Wildlife Area, Cowles
7	A3	Charette Lakes, Wagon Mound
8	A2	Colin Neblett Wildlife Area, Cimarron
9	A2	E.S. Barker Wildlife Area, Cimarron
10	B3	Ladd S. Gordon Wildlife Area, Tucumcari
11	B3	McAllister Lake, Las Vegas
12	A2	Springer Lake, Springer

S#	MAP	NAME & LOCATION
13	A2	Urraca Wildlife Area, Questa
14	A2	Edward Sargeant Wildlife Area, Chama
15	A1	Jackson Lake Wildlife Area, Farmington
16	B1	Ramah Lake. Ramah
17	A2	Rio Chama Wildlife & Fishing Area, El Vado
18	A2	Rio De los Pinos Wildlife & Fish, Chama
19	A2	W.A. Humphries Wildlife Area, Chama
20	C2	Bonito Lake, Capitan
21	C3	Brantley Wildlife Area, Carlsbad
22	C1	Bear Canyon Reservoir, Mimbres
23	C1	Bill Evans Lake, Silver City
24	C1	Heart Bar Wildlife Area, Gila Hot Springs
25	C1	Lake Roberts, Gila Hot Springs

Tourism and Travel Division

Economic Development & Tourism Dept.
Joseph M. Montoya Bldg.
1100 St. Francis Drive, PO Box 20003
Santa Fe, NM 87503   1-800-545-2040
in state call   505-827-0291

A free joint-agency NM State & Federal Natural Resource Recreation Map is available. It is color-coded to show land by agency ownership. Selected recreation areas are listed with their map coordinates.

Private Organizations

Tribal Land Areas in New Mexico

Acoma Pueblo - Hunting, touring.
Acoma Pueblo (S# 6, map B1)
PO Box 309
Acoma, NM 87034   505-552-6606

Isleta Pueblo - Fishing, camping, touring.
Isleta Pueblo (S# 7, map B2)
PO Box 317
Isleta, NM 87022   505-869-3111

Jemez Pueblo - Fishing, hunting.
Jemez Pueblo (S# 8, map B2)
PO Box 78
Jemez Pueblo, NM 87024   505-834-7359

Jicarilla Apache Tribe of the Jicarilla Apache Indian Reservation - Fishing, hunting, camping, boating, touring.
Jicarilla Apache Tribal Council (S# 9, map A2)
PO Box 147
Deluce, NM 87528   505-759-3242

Laguna Pueblo - Hunting.
Laguna Pueblo (S# 10, map B1)
PO Box 194
Laguna, NM 87026   505-552-6654

Mescalero Apache Tribe of the Mescalero Indian Reservation - Fishing, hunting, camping, boating, hiking, touring.
Mescalero Apache Tribal Council (S# 11, map C2)
PO Box 176
Mescalero, NM 87340   505-671-4495

Nambe Pueblo - Fishing, camping, boating.
Nambe Pueblo (S# *12, map B2)

Route 1, Box 117-BB
Santa Fe, NM 87501   505-455-7752

Picuris Pueblo - Fishing, camping.
Picuris Pueblo (S# *13, map A2)
PO Box 127
Penasco, NM 87553   505-587-2519

Pojoaque Pueblo - Camping.
Pojoaque Pueblo (S# *14, map B2)
Route 11, Box 71
Santa Fe, NM 87501   505-455-2278

Sandia Pueblo - Fishing.
Sandia Pueblo (S# 15, map B2)
PO Box 6008
Bernalillo, NM 87004   505-867-3317

San Ildefonso Pueblo - Fishing, hunting, camping, hiking.
San Ildefonso Pueblo (S# *16, map B2)
Route 5, Box 315A
Santa Fe, NM 87501   505-455-2273

San Juan Pueblo - Fishing.
San Juan Pueblo (S# *17, map A2)
PO Box 1099
San Juan Pueblo, NM 87566   505-852-4400

Santa Clara Pueblo - Fishing, camping, touring.
Santa Clara Pueblo (S# 18, map A2)
PO Box 580
Espanola, NM 87532   505-753-7316

Taos Pueblo - Touring.
Taos Pueblo (S# 19, map A2)
PO Box 1846
Taos, NM 87571   505-758-9593

Tesuque Pueblo - Camping, hiking.
Tesuque Pueblo (S# *20, map B2)
Route 11, Box 1
Santa Fe, NM 87501   505-983-2667

Zia Pueblo - Fishing.
Zia Pueblo (S# 21, map B2)
General Delivery
San Ysidro, NM 87053   505-867-3304

Zuni Tribe of the Zuni Indian Reservation - Fishing, hunting, camping, biking, hiking.
Zuni Tribal Council (New Mexico/Arizona)
(S# 22, map B1)
PO Box 339
Zuni, NM 87327   505-782-4481

ANCA Location in New Mexico

Rio Grand Nature Center (S# 23, map C2)
2901 Candelaria Road West
Albuquerque, NM 87112   505-344-7240

Assn. of Comm. & Industry of NM

(State Chamber of Commerce)
2309 Renard Pl. SE, #402
Albuquerque, NM 87106-4259   Phone 505-842-0644
Fax 505-842-0734

BLM NEW MEXICO
1:100,000 INTERMEDIATE SCALE MAPS
SURFACE & SURFACE / MINERAL SERIES

Longitude: 110° 109° 108° 107° 106° 105° 104° 103°
Latitude: 37° 36° 35° 34° 33° 32° 31°

110°–109°	109°–108°	108°–107°	107°–106°	106°–105°	105°–104°	104°–103°
	Farmington	Navajo Reservoir	Chama	Wheeler Peak	Raton	Capulin Mountains
	Toadlena	Chaco Canyon	Abiquiu	Taos	Springer	Clayton
Sanders	Gallup	Chaco Mesa	Los Alamos	Santa Fe	Roy	Mosquero
	Zuni	Grants	Albuquerque	Villanueva	Conchas Lake	Tucumcari
	Fence Lake	Acoma Pueblo	Belen	Vaughn	Santa Rosa	The Caprock
	Quemado	Magdalena	Socorro	Corona	Fort Sumner	Clovis
	Tularosa Mountains	San Mateo Mountains	Oscura Mountains	Carrizozo	Salt Creek	Elida
Clifton	Mogollon Mountains	Truth or Consequences	Tularosa	Ruidoso	Roswell	Tatum
Safford	Silver City	Hatch	White Sands	Alamogordo	Artesia	Hobbs
	Lordsburg	Deming	Las Cruces	Crow Flats	Carlsbad	Jal
Chiricahua Peak	Animas	Columbus	El Paso			
Douglas	Alamo Hueco Mountains					

NEW YORK NOTES

Summary

There are 31 federal, 106 state, and 44 private recreation areas or local administrative offices covered in this state chapter. Of these, 139 appear in the Information Chart and 42 are covered in the notes The special indexes feature a federally designated wilderness area and a wild river.

Federal Agencies

U.S. Forest Service
New York is in the Eastern Region (see Wisconsin chapter - U.S. Forest Svc., Eastern Region listing).

U.S. Army Corps of Engineers (COE)
North Atlantic Division Office
90 Church Street
New York, NY 10007-9998   212-264-7535

The Baltimore, Maryland, Norfolk, Virginia, and Philadelphia, Pennsylvania District Offices manage COE projects in the central Atlantic states area (see information charts).

National Park Service
Additional NPS Locations in New York
Castle Clinton National Monument (1 acre)
Manhattan Sites (Battery Park) (S# 5, F2)
National Park Service
26 Wall Street
New York, NY 10005   212-344-7220

Eleanor Roosevelt National Historic Site (181 acres)
(S# 6, D5)
519 Albany Post Road
Hyde Park, NY 12538   914-229-9115

Federal Hall National Memorial (0.45 acre)
Manhattan Sites (S# ★7, F2)
National Park Service
26 Wall Street
New York, NY 10005   212-264-8711

Fort Stanwix National Monument (16 acres)
112 E. Park Street (S# 8, C4)
Rome, NY 13440   315-336-2090

General Grant National Memorial (0.76 acre)
122nd St. & Riverside Drive (S# 9, F2)
New York, NY 10027   212-666-1640

Hamilton Grange National Memorial (0.11 acre)
287 Convent Ave. (S# ★10, F2)
New York, NY 10031   212-283-5154

Home of Franklin D. Roosevelt NHS (290 acres)
519 Albany Post Road (S# 11, D5)
Hyde Park, NY 12538   914-229-9115

Martin Van Buren National Historic Site (40 acres)
PO Box 545 (S# 12, C5)
Kinderhook, NY 12106   518-758-9689

Sagamore Hill National Historic Site (83 acres)
20 Sagamore Hill Roa (S# 13, F2)
Oyster Bay, NY 11771   516-922-4788

Saint Paul's Church National Historic Site (6 acres)
897 South Columbus Ave. (S# 14, F2)
Mount Vernon, NY 10550   914-667-4116

Statue of Liberty National Monument (58 acres)
Liberty Island (S# 15, F2)
New York, NY 10004   212-363-5804

Theodore Roosevelt Birthplace NHS (0.11 acre)
28 E. 20th Street (S# 16, F2)
New York, NY 10003   212-260-1616

Theodore Roosevelt Inaugural NHS (1 acre)
641 Delaware Avenue (S# 17, C1)
Buffalo, NY 14202   716-884-0094

Vanderbilt Mansion NHS (212 acres)
519 Albany Post Road (S# 18, D5)
Hyde Park, NY 12538   914-229-9115

Women's Rights National Historical Park (6 acres)
PO Box 70 (S# 19, C3)
Seneca Falls, NY 13148   315-568-2991

Wilderness/Wild River Index

Wilderness Areas
Fire Island Wilderness - 1,363 acres
Fire Island National Seashore (S# 1, map F3)

Wild Rivers
Delaware (Upper) River
Upper Delaware Scenic & Rec. River (S# 4, map D4)

State Agencies

Adirondack Park Agency
PO Box 99
Ray Brook, NY 12977   518-891-4050

Adirondack Park encompasses more than 6 million acres. It is located north of the Mohawk River and west of Lake Champlain...roughly between Albany, Plattsburgh, and Watertown (map segments A4 and 5, and B4 and 5). More than half of the acres are privately owned.

Within the borders of the park area are towns and villages (the largest is Saranac Lake, Pop. 6,000), businesses and resorts, private homes, state parks, forests, wildlife management areas, preserves, and sanctuaries. Contact the commission at park HQ or the two Visitor Centers for recreation and/or current land status information. Park VCs are open 9 a.m. to 7 p.m. May 1 through September 30, and 9 a.m. through 5 p.m. October 1 through April 30.

Adirondack Park Paul Smiths Visitor Interpretive Center
Box 3000
Paul Smiths, NY 12970   518-327-3000
Located on Rt. 30, one mile north of Rt. 86 intersection (formerly Rt. 192), and a half hour from Lake Placid and Malone.

Adirondack Park Newcomb Visitor Interpretive Center
Location: On Rt. 28N, 14 miles east of Long Lake and a half hour from Blue Mountain Lake and Northway (Rt. 87, exit 29).

Catskill Park
The Catskill Park (map D4 and 5) was established by the state leg slature in 1904 and includes parts of Delaware, Greene, Sullivan, and Ulster counties. About a third of the land within park borders is state owned (705,000 acres) and the balance is privately owned.

The state land is classified as "forever wild" forest preserve and provides a variety of recreation opportunities. For details and a comprehensive map of the Catskill Park and surrounding area, contact The Catskill Center (for Conservation and Development, Inc.), Arkville, NY 12406. The phone number is (914) 586-2611. The Center offers memberships and a variety of publications about the park and activities, including their newsletter titled Catskill Center News.

NY Dept of Environmental Conservation (DEC)
Public Affairs
50 Wolf Road
Albany, NY 12233   518-457-2390
Parent agency for the following three Divisions.

Division of Marine Resources
same address as above   516-751-7900

Division of Fish & Wildlife
Bureau of Wildlife (S# 1, map C5)
A brochure/map (Big Game Guide) is available that describes: and locates many of the Wildlife Management Areas (WMA) owned by the state, and cooperative areas leased under the Fish and Wildlife Management Act (FWMA)' or hunting and/or fishing.

Division of Lands & Forests
Dept. of Environmental Conservation
50 Wolf Rd.
Albany, NY 12233   518-457-2475
Contact the Division for state forest recreation literature.

Office of Parks, Recreation & Historic Preservation
Empire State Plaza
Agency Building 1
Albany, NY 12238   518-474-0456

A New York State Parks Guide (150 state parks) is available free. The guide describes each area, contains a locator map, and includes information on facilities and activities. Selected parks are covered in the New York Information Chart.

Outfitter & Guide Licensing
New York Outdoor Guides Association
PO Box 855
Saranac Lake, NY 12983   518-891-1176
The New York Guides Association has more than 300 outdoorsmen who have met New York State licensing requirements. The guides association published A Guide to the Outdoor Guides of New York State, listing guides and their specialties.

Division of Tourism
One Commerce Plaza
Albany, NY 12245   1-800-225-5697

A state Travel Guide and a Camping and Outdoor Adventures Guide is available free from this office. Comprehensive information on state and private accommodations, campgrounds, and special events is included. An official road map is also available. The map has symbols for state and private campgrounds, state parks and recreation areas, and winter sports areas. Scenic roads and trails are also marked.

Private Organizations

TNC New York Field Office
1736 Western Avenue
Albany, NY 12203   518-869-6959

There are six TNC Chapter Offices and selected preserves listed in the Information Chart. Contact those offices about preserve tours and additional TNC preserves in New York.

Tribal Land Area in New York
Seneca Nation of New York - Fishing, camping, boating.
Seneca Nation (S# 28, map D1)
PO Box 231
Salamanca, NY 14779   716-945-1790
and
Seneca Indians Council of Chiefs
7027 Meadville Road
Basom, NY 14013

ANCA Locations in New York
Beaver Lake Nature Center (S# 29, map C3)
East Mud Lake road
Baldwinsville, NY 13027   315-638-2519

Beaver Meadow Audubon Center (S# 30, map C2)
1610 Welch Road
North Java, NY 14113-9713   716-457-3228

Cayuga Nature Center (S# 31, map C3)
1420 taughannock Blvd.
Ithaca, NY 14850   607-273-6260

Cumming Nature Center (S# 32, map C2)
6472 Gulick Road
Naples, NY 14512   716-374-6160

Constitution Marsh Sanctuary (S# 33, map D5)
RR #2, Route 9D
Garrison, NY 10524   914-265-2601

Finch Hollow Nature Center (S# 34, map D3)
1428 Oakdale Road
Johnson City, NY 13790   607-729-4231

Great Neck Outdoor Education Center (S# 35, map F2)
345 Lakeville Road
Great Neck, NY 11020   516-773-1463

Greenburgh Nature Center (S# 36, map F2)
Dromore Road
Scarsdale, NY 10583   914-723-3470

Jamestown Audubon Nature Center (S# 37, map D1)
1600 Riverside Road
Jamestown, NY 14701   716-569-2345

Minna Anthony Common Nature Center (S# 38, map A4)
RD #1, Box W 437
Alexandria Bay, NY 13607   315-482-2479

New York Zoological Park (S# 39, map F2)
185th St. & Southern Blvd.
Bronx, NY 10460   212-220-5100

Rockland Lake Nature Center (S# 40, map E2)
Palisades Interstate Park Commission
Bear Mountain, NY 10911   914-268-2503

Rye Nature Center (S# 41, map F2)
PO Box 435
Rye, NY 10580-0435   914-967-5150

Tanglewood Comminity Nature Center (S# 42, map D3)
PO Box 117
Elmira, NY 14902-0117   607-732-6060

No State Chamber of Commerce in New York
There are local Chamber of Commerce Offices located in cities and towns throughout the state.

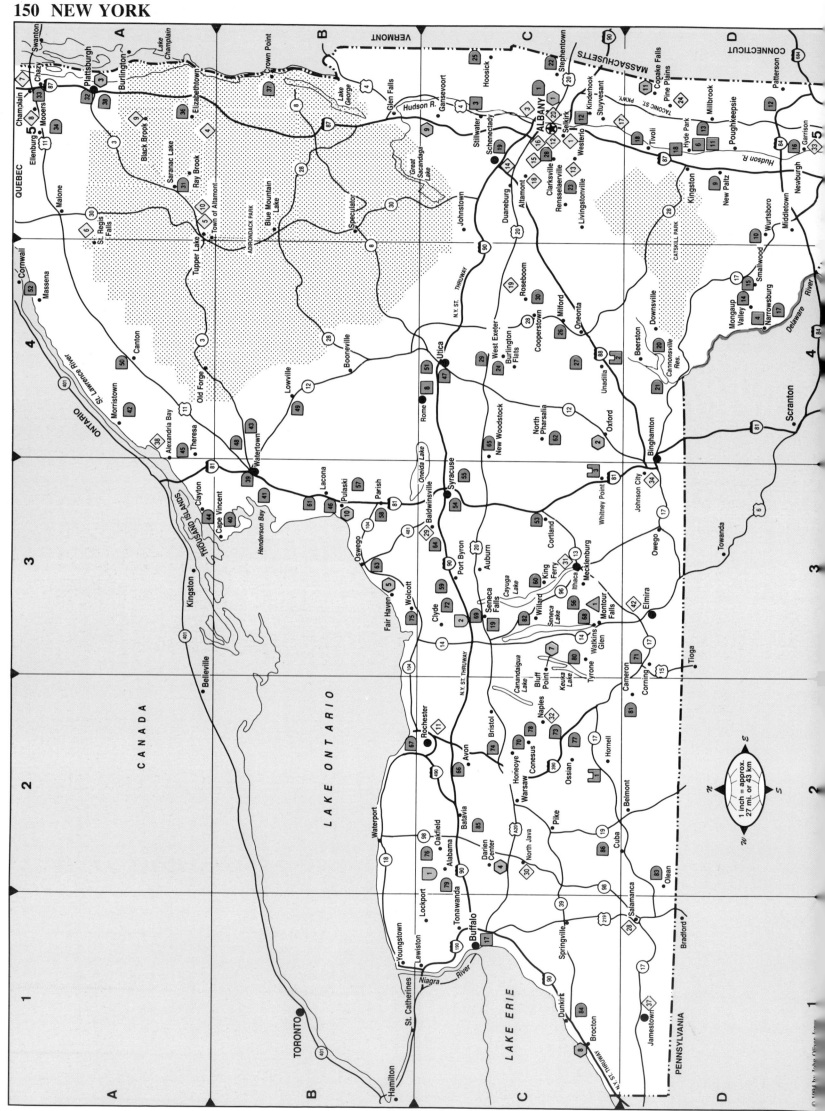

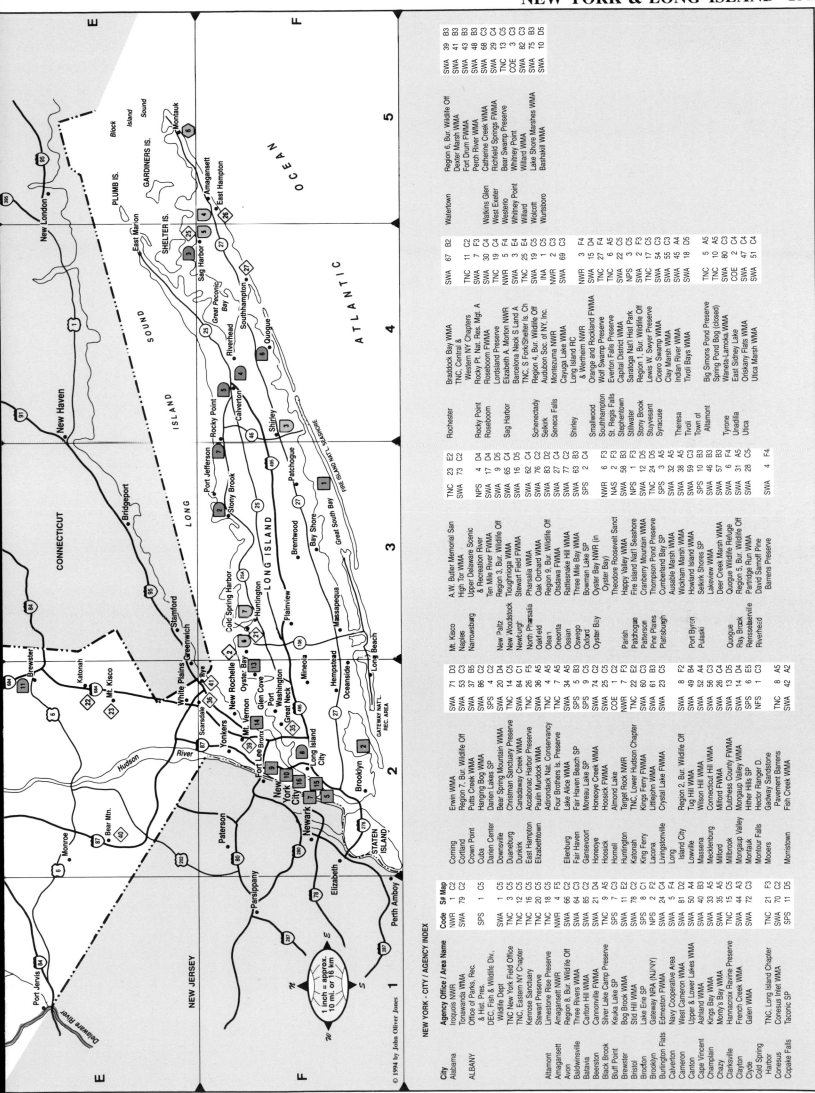

© 1994 by John Oliver Jones

1 inch = approx. 10 mi. or 16 km

★ INFORMATION CHART ★

S#	MAP	LOCATION NAME (state initials if more than one) with ADDRESS and/or LOCATION DATA	TELEPHONE	ACRES / ELEVATION
	C3	**Green Mountain & Finger Lakes Nat'l Forests.** FOB, 231 N. Main St., Rutland, VT 05701	802-747-6700	40,000 / 600-4,000
1	C3	Hector Ranger E.., PO Box W, Montour Falls 14865	607-594-2750	13,232 / 1,100-1,500
		COE, Baltimore District, PO Box 1715, Baltimore, MD 21203	410-962-3693	na / na
1	C2	Almond Lake, PO Box 400, Hornell 14843	607-324-6531	na / na
2	C4	East Sidney Lake, PO Box 233, Unadilla 13849	607-829-6006	na / na
3	C3	Whitney Point, PO Box 706, Whitney Point 13862	607-692-3165	na / na
	C2	**Iroquois NWR**, 1101 Casey Road, PO Box 517, Alabama 14003 [1 mi N of town, 16 mi NW of Batavia off Rt 63]	716-948-5445	10,818 / 610-650
2	C3	Montezuma NWR, 3395 Route 5/20 East, Seneca Falls 13148	315-568-5987	6,432 / 385-400
3	F4	Long Island RC & Wertheim NWR, Smith Rd., PO Box 21, Shirley 11967	516-286-0485	2,400 / 5
4	F5	Amagansett NWR, Atlantic Ave., Amagansett	516-286-0485	2 / 0
5	F4	Elizabeth A. Morton NWR, Noyac Rd., Sag Harbor 11963	516-286-0485	180 / 20
6	F3	Oyster Bay NWR (in Oyster Bay), Oyster Bay	516-286-0485	3,200 / 0
7	F3	Target Rock NWR, Target Rock Rd., Huntington 11743	516-271-2409	80 / 10
1	F3	**Fire Island National Seashore**, 120 Laurel Street, Patchogue 11772	516-289-4810	19,578 / na
2	F2	Gateway National Recreation Area (NJ/NY), Floyd Bennett Field, Bldg. 69, Brooklyn 11234	718-338-3688	26,310 / na
3	C5	Saratoga Nat'l. Historical Park, 648 Route 32, Stillwater 12170	518-664-9821	3,406 / 400
4	D4	Upper Delaware Scenic & Recreation River (NY/NJ/PA), PO Box C, Narrowsburg 12764	717-729-7134	53,000 / na
		Office of Parks, Rec. & Hist. Preservation, Empire State Plaza, Agency Bldg. 1, Albany 12238	518-474-0456	na / na
2	C4	Bowman Lake SP, Star Rt. off Rt. 220, 8 mi. NW of Oxford 13830	607-334-2718	653 / 1,600-1,800
3	A5	Cumberland Bay SP, 1 mi. E of Plattsburgh 12901	518-563-5240	319 / 100
4	C2	Darien Lakes SP, 10289 Harlow Rd., 8 mi. S of NYS Thruway exit 48A, Darien Center 14040	716-547-9242	1,845 / 1,000
5	B3	Fair Haven Beach SP, Rt. #104A, Fair Haven 13064	315-947-5205	870 / 250-360
6	E5	Hither Hills SP, Rt. #1, Box 85A, Old Montauk Hwy., Montauk 11954	516-668-2554	1,755 / na
7	C3	Keuka Lake SP, 6 mi. SW of Penn Yan, 3370 Pepper Rd., Bluff Point 14478	315-536-3666	620 / 720-1,200
8	C1	Lake Erie SP, RD, Rt. #5 (W of Dunkirk), Brocton 14716 [closed, substitute Allegany SP]	716-792-9214	355 / 574-646
9	C5	Moreau Lake SP, 635 Old Saratoga Rd., Gansevoort 12831	518-793-0511	900 / na
10	B3	Selkirk Shores SP, RD, Rt. #3, Pulaski 13142	315-298-5737	980 / 246-290
11	D5	Taconic SP, Copake Falls 12517	518-329-3993	5,000 / 490-2,300
		DEC, Fish & Wildlife Div., Wildlife, 50 Wolf Road, Albany 12233	518-474-2121	na / na
2	F3	Region 1, Bur. Wildlife Office, Bldg. 40, SUNY, Stony Brook 11790	516-751-7030	na / na
3	E4	Barcelona Neck State Land Area, near Sag Harbor	516-751-7030	500 / 50
4	F4	David Sarnoff Pine Barrens Preserve, near Riverhead	516-751-7030	2,000 / 50
5	F4	Navy Cooperative Area, near Calverton	516-751-7030	4,000 / 50
6	F4	Quogue Wildlife Refuge. Box 492, Quogue 11959	516-653-4771	200 / 30
7	F3	Rocky Point Natural Resources MA, near Rocky Point	516-751-7030	5,000 / 50
8	F2	Region 2, Bur. Wildlife Office, Hunter Pt. Plaza, 4740 21st St., Long Island City 11101	718-482-4922	na / na
9	D5	Region 3, Bur. Wildlife Office, 21 So. Putt Corners Rd., New Paltz 12561	914-255-5453	na / na
10	D5	Bashakill WMA, in Orange & Sullivan Cos. near Wurtsboro	914-255-5453	2,600 / 500
11	E2	Bog Brook WMA, in Putnam County near Brewster	914-255-5453	na / na
12	E2	Cranberry Mountain FWMA, in Putnam County near Patterson	914-255-5453	500 / 1,000
13	D5	Dutchess County FWMA, in Dutchess County near Millbrook	914-255-5453	3,000 / 900
14	D5	Mongaup Valley WMA, in Sullivan County near Mongaup Valley	914-255-5453	6,500 / na
15	D4	Orange and Rockland FWMA, in Sullivan County near Smallwood	914-255-5453	12,000 / na
16	E2	Stewart Field FWMA, in Orange County near Newburgh	914-255-5453	7,000 / 500
17	D4	Ten Mile River FWMA, in Sullivan County near Narrowsburg	914-255-5453	10,000 / na
18	D5	Tivoli Bays WMA, in Dutchess County near Tivoli	914-255-5453	1,500 / 0-200
19	C5	Region 4, Bur. Wildlife Office, 2176 Guilderland Ave. Rd., Schenectady 12306	518-382-0680	na / na
20	D4	Bear Spring Mountain WMA, Field HQ., Rt. #206, Downsville 13755	607-652-7364	7,000 / 1,400-2,400
21	D4	Cannonville FWMA, Water Supply Police, Beerston	607-652-7364	na / na

#	Grid	Site	Phone	Acreage
23	C5	Crystal Lake FWMA, just N of Livingstonville	607-652-7364	10,000 / na
24	C4	Edmeston FWMA, near Burlington Flats	607-652-7364	10,000 / na
25	C5	Hoosick FWMA, near Hoosick	518-382-0680	11,000 / na
26	C4	Milford FWMA, near Milford	607-652-7364	10,000 / na
27	C4	Otsdawa FWMA, W of Oneonta, near Oneonta	607-652-7364	na / na
28	C5	Partridge Run WMA, near Rensselaerville	607-652-7364	5,400 / 2,000
29	C4	Richfield Springs FWMA, near West Exeter	607-652-7364	12,000 / na
30	C4	Roseboom FWMA, near Roseboom	607-652-7364	10,000 / na
31	A5	Region 5, Bur. Wildlife Office, Route 86, Ray Brook 12977	518-891-1370	na / na
32	A5	Ausable Marsh WMA, Lake Champlain near Plattsburgh	518-891-1370	10 / na
33	A5	Kings Bay WMA, Clinton County, E of Champlain	518-891-1370	100 / na
34	A5	Lake Alice WMA, Clinton County, E of Ellenburg	518-891-1370	na / na
35	A5	Monty's Bay WMA, Lake Shore Rd. near Chazy	518-891-1370	100 / na
36	B5	Paulin Murdock WMA, Wadhams Road, near Elizabethtown	518-891-1370	500 / na
37	B5	Putts Creek WMA, Lake Champlain near Crown Point	518-891-1370	100 / na
38	A5	Wickham Marsh WMA, Essex County, S of Plattsburgh	518-891-1370	na / na
39	B3	Region 6, Bur. Wildife Office, State Office Bldg., 317 Washington Street, Watertown 13601	315-785-2261	na / na
40	B3	Ashland WMA, E of Cape Vincent	315-785-2261	2,040 / 320
41	B3	Dexter Marsh WMA, W of Watertown	315-785-2261	1,340 / 250
42	A2	Fish Creek WMA, SE of Morristown	315-785-2261	4,400 / 350
43	B3	Fort Drum FWMA, E of Watertown	315-785-2261	82,000 / 370
44	A3	French Creek WMA, S of Clayton	315-785-2261	2,270 / 250
45	A4	Indian River WMA, N of Theresa	315-785-2261	970 / 320
46	B3	Lakeview WMA (adjacent Southwick's Beach SP), N of Pulaski	315-785-2261	3,460 / 250
47	C4	Oriskany Flats WMA, W of Utica	315-785-2261	460 / 400
48	B3	Perch River WMA, NE of Watertown	315-785-2261	7,800 / 350
49	B4	Tug Hill WMA, SW of Lowville	315-785-2261	5,110 / 1,900
50	A4	Upper & Lower Lakes WMA (near Indian Creek Nature Center), W of Canton	315-785-2261	8,780 / 310
51	C4	Utica Marsh WMA, Utica	315-785-2261	213 / 400
52	A4	Wilson Hill WMA, N of Massena	315-785-2261	3,400 / 250
53	C3	Region 7, Bur. Wildlife Office, Fisher Ave., PO Box 5170, Cortland 13045	607-753-3095	na / na
54	C3	Cicero Swamp WMA, near Syracuse	607-753-3095	3,961 / 400
55	C3	Clay Marsh WMA, near Syracuse	607-753-3095	1,474 / 380
56	C3	Connecticut Hill WMA, near Mecklenburg	607-753-3095	11,012 / 1,200-2,100
57	B3	Deer Creek Marsh WMA, Pulaski	607-753-3095	1,195 / 250
58	B3	Happy Valley WMA, near Parish	607-753-3095	8,755 / 700
59	C3	Howland Island WMA, near Port Byron	607-753-3095	3,600 / 400
60	C3	Kings Ferry FWMA (VC ph. Oct/Jan only, 315-364-7777), King Ferry	607-753-3095	12,000 / 1,000
61	C3	Littlejohn WMA, near Lacona	607-753-3095	8,029 / 1,400
62	C4	Pharsalia WMA, North Pharsalia	607-753-3095	4,700 / 1,800
63	B3	Three Mile Bay WMA, near Oswego	607-753-3095	3,695 / 400
64	C3	Three Rivers WMA, near Baldwinsville	607-753-3095	3,655 / 400
65	C4	Tioughnioga WMA, New Woodstock	607-753-3095	3,605 / 1,600-2,000
66	C2	Region 8, Bur. Wilcife Office, 6274 E. Avon-Lima Rd., Avon 14414	716-226-2466	80 / 850
67	B2	Braddock Bay WMA, N of lake Ontario Parkway, near Rochester	716-226-2466	2,400 / 250
68	C3	Catherine Creek WMA, E of NY Rt. #14, near Watkins Glen	716-226-2466	660 / 450
69	C3	Cayuga Lake WMA, off NY Rt. #89, near Seneca Falls	716-226-2466	220 / 380
70	C2	Conesus Inlet WMA, E of NY Rt. 256, near Conesus	716-226-2466	1,120 / 900
71	D3	Erwin WMA, near Corning	716-226-2466	2,490 / 1,600
72	C3	Galen WMA, River Road, near Clyde	716-226-2466	710 / 400
73	C2	High Tor WMA, near Naples	716-226-2466	6,110 / 1,200
74	C2	Honeoye Creek WMA, N of Honeoye	716-226-2466	717 / 800
75	B3	Lake Shore Marshes WMA, near Wolcott	716-226-2466	6,130 / 300
76	C2	Oak Orchard WMA, near Oakfield	716-226-2466	2,550 / 600
77	C2	Rattlesnake Hill WMA, near Ossian	716-226-2466	5,150 / 1,900
78	C3	Stid Hill WMA, E of NY Rt. #64, near Bristol	716-226-2466	740 / 1,400
79	C2	Tonawanda WMA, off NY Rt. 77, near Alabama	716-226-2466	5,600 / 600
80	C3	Waneta-Lamoka WMA, County Rd. 23, near Tyrone	716-226-2466	160 / 1,100
81	D2	West Cameron WMA, off Angel Rd., near Cameron	716-226-2466	170 / 1,700
82	C3	Willard WMA, off County Rd. 131, near Willard	716-226-2466	158 / 600
83	D2	Region 9, Bur. Wildlife Office, 128 South St., Olean 14760	716-372-0645	na / na
84	C1	Canadaway Creek WMA, Chautauqua Co. 7 mi. S of Dunkirk	716-372-0645	2,180 / 1,250-1,900
85	C2	Carlton Hill WMA, about 10 mi. S of Batavia	716-372-0645	2,700 / 1,400-1,600
86	C2	Hanging Bog WMA, about 7 mi. N of Cuba	716-372-0645	4,571 / 1,800-2,000
1	C5	The Audubon Soc. of NY State, Inc., Hollyhock Hollow Sanctuary, Rt. 2, Box 131 Rarick Rd., Selkirk 12158	518-767-9051	140 / 300-400

★ INFORMATION CHART ★

INFORMATION CHART LEGEND - SYMBOLS & LETTER CODES

■ means YES & □ means Yes with disability provisions
sp means spring, March through May
S means Summer, June through August
F means Fall, September through November
W means Winter, December through February
T means Two (2) or Three (3) Seasons
A means All Four (4) Seasons
na means Not Applicable or Not Available
Note: empty or blank spaces in the chart mean NO

AGENCY/MAP LEGEND... INITIALS, MAP SYMBOLS, COLOR CODES

U.S. Forest Service Supervisor & Ranger Dist. Offices . NFS
U.S. Army Corps of Engineers Rec. Areas & Offices . COE
USFWS National Wildlife Refuges & Offices . . . . NWR
National Park Service Parks & other NPS Sites . . . . . . NPS
Bureau of Land Management Rec. Areas & Offices . . . BLM
Bureau of Reclamation Rec. Areas & Reg. Offices . . . BOR
State Parks (also see State Agency notes) . . . . SPS
State Wildlife Areas (also see State Agency notes) . . . SWA
Private Preserves, Nature Centers & Tribal Lands . .
The Wild Rivers ~~~~ and Wilderness Areas

Note: Refer to yellow block on page 7 (top right) for location name and address abbreviations. If a symbol number has a star ★ that symbol is not shown on the map.

S#	MAP	LOCATION NAME (state initials if more than one) with ADDRESS and/or LOCATION DATA	TELEPHONE	ACRES / ELEVATION	S#
2	F3	**Theodore Roosevelt Sanctuary,** 134 Cove Road, Oyster Bay 11771	516-922-3200	12 / na	2
3	C5	**TNC New York Field Office,** 1736 Western Avenue, Albany 12203 [contact Chapter offices for preserve details]	518-869-6959	na / na	3
4	A5	Adirondack Nature Conservancy, PO Box 188, Elizabethtown 12932	518-873-2610	na / na	4
5	A5	Big Simons Pond Preserve, contact Adirondack NC Office, 3 mi. S of Tupper Lake in, Town of Altamont	518-873-2610	5 / na	5
6	A5	Everton Falls Preserve, contact Adirondack Cons. Office, 7 mi. E of St. Regis Falls	518-873-2610	530 / na	6
7	A5	Four Brothers Is. Pres (closed), c/o Manager, Discovery Farm, Elizabethtown 12932 [N end L Chmplain]	518-873-2052	17 / na	7
8	A5	Gadway Sandstone Pavement Barrens, contact Adirondack Cons. Office, 3.5 mi. W of Mooers	518-873-2610	520 / na	8
9	A5	Silver Lake Camp Preserve, contact Adirondack Cons. Office, near Black Brook	518-873-2610	63 / 1,400	9
10	A5	Spring Pond Bog (closed), contact Adirondack Cons. Office, Town of Altamont	518-873-2610	4,274 / na	10
11	C2	TNC, Central & Western NY Chapters, 315 Alexander St., Rochester 14604	716-546-8030	na / na	11
12	C5	TNC, Eastern NY Chapter, 1736 Western Ave., Albany 12203	518-869-0453	na / na	12
13	C5	Bear Swamp Preserve, contact Chapter Office, Westerlo	518-869-0453	310 / 400	13
14	C5	Christman Sanctuary Preserve, contact Chapter Office, SE of Duaneburg	518-869-0453	97 / 300	14
15	C5	Hannacroix Ravine Preserve, contact Chapter Office, near Clarksville	518-869-0453	323 / 400	15
16	C5	Kenrose Sanctuary, contact Chapter Office, W of Albany	518-869-0453	360 / na	16
17	C5	Lewis W. Swyer Preserve (contact Chapter Office), Mill Cr. Marsh on Hudson R., Stuyvesant	518-869-0453	98 / na	17
18	C5	Limestone Rise Preserve, contact Chapter Office, near Altamont	518-869-0453	62 / 300	18
19	C4	Lordsland Preserve, contact Chapter Office, near Roseboom	518-869-0453	80 / na	19
20	C5	Stewart Preserve, contact Chapter Office, in Rensselaer Co. E of Albany	518-869-0453	123 / 400	20
21	F3	TNC, Long Island Chapter, 250 Lawrence Hill Rd., Cold Spring Harbor 11724	516-367-3225	na / na	21
22	E2	TNC, Lower Hudson Chapter, 223 Katonah Ave., Katonah 10536	914-232-9431	na / na	22
23	E2	A.W. Butler Memorial Sanctuary, contact Chapter Office, near Mt. Kisco	914-232-9431	358 / 200	23
24	D5	Thompson Pond Preserve, contact Chapter Office, S of Pine Plains	914-232-9431	466 / 500	24
25	E4	TNC, South Fork/Shelter Is. Chapter, PO Box 2694, Sag Harbor 11963	516-725-2936	na / na	25
26	F5	Accabonac Harbor Preserve, contact Chapter Office, near East Hampton	516-725-2936	90 / na	26
27	F4	Wolf Swamp Preserve, contact Chapter Office, near Southhampton	516-725-2936	20 / na	27

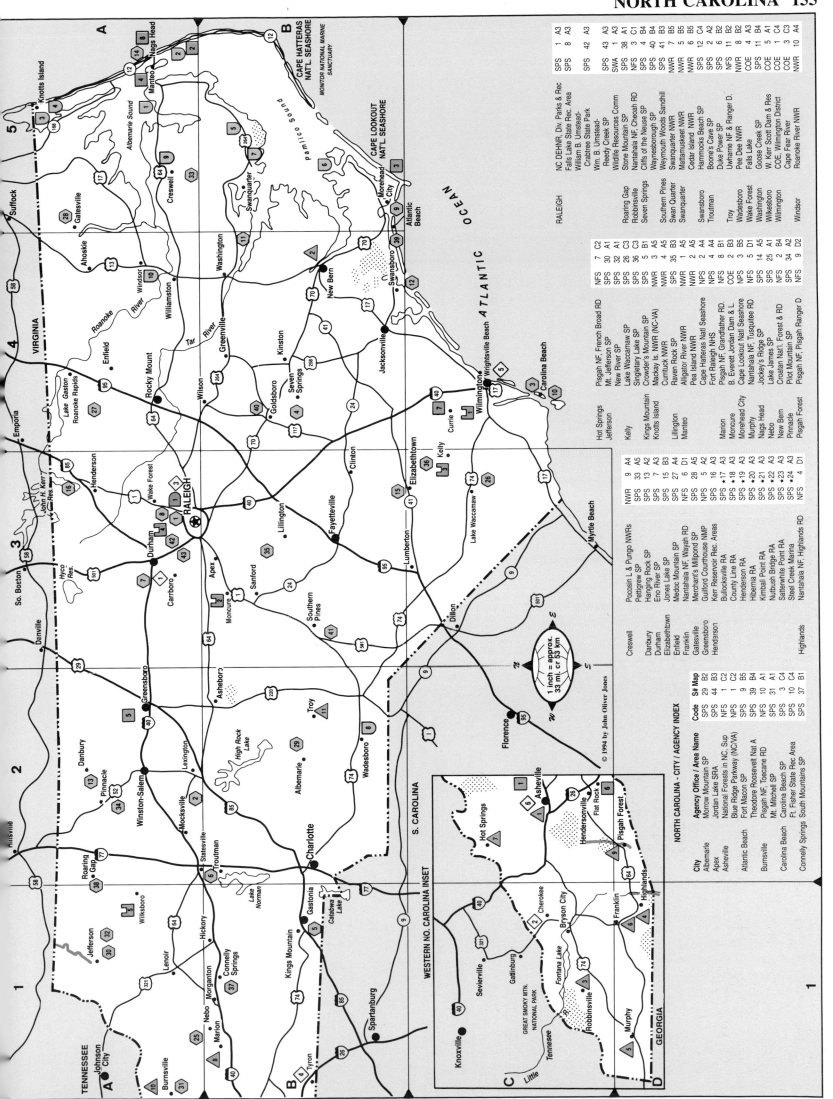

NORTH CAROLINA NOTES

Summary

There are 37 federal, 49 state, and 7 private recreation areas or local administrative offices covered in this state chapter. Of these, 76 appear in the Information Chart and 17 are covered in the notes. The special indexes feature 15 federally designated wilderness areas and wild rivers, and 16 agency published outdoor maps.

Federal Agencies

U.S. Forest Service

North Carolina is in the Southern Region (see Georgia chapter - U.S. Forest Svc., Southern Region listing).

The Cradle of Forestry Visitor Center includes historic buildings and interpretive trails. These facilities are the site of the first forestry school and the first scientific forestry practiced in the United States. They tell the story of Gilford Pinchot the first professional forester. Contact the Pisgah National Forest, Pisgah Ranger District (S# 9, map D2) for information.

National Park Service

Great Smoky Mtn. Nat'l. Park see Tennessee chapter.

Additional NPS Locations in North Carolina

Carl Sandburg Home National Historic Site (264 acres)
1928 Little River Road (S# 6, map C2)
Flat Rock, NC 28731   704-693-4178

Moores Creek National Battlefield (87 acres)
PO Box 69 (S# 7, map C4)
Currie, NC 28435   919-283-5591

Wright Brothers National Memorial (431 acres)
c/o Cape Hatteras National Seashore (S# 8, map A5)
Seashore Route 1, Box 675
Manteo, NC 27954   919-473-2111

New River, South Fork
Stone Mountain State Park (S# 38, map A1)

Outdoor Map Index

National Park Service (USGS Maps)

Great Smoky Mountains NP East [1931]
  Scale: 1 inch = 1.0 mile (1 cm = 0.6 km)
Great Smoky Mountains NP (NC-TN) [1972]
  Scale: 1 inch = 2.0 miles (1 cm = 1.3 km)
Great Smoky Mountains NP West [1931]
  Scale: 1 inch = 1.0 mile (1 cm = 0.6 km)

U.S. Forest Service Maps

Appalachian Trail, Pisgah/Cherokee NF [1974]
Appalachian Trail, Nantahala NF
Birkhead Mtn. Wil., Uwharrie NF [1987]
Chattooga National Wild & Scenic R. [1981]
Croatan National Forest [1984]
Joyce Kilmer-Slickrock & Citico Cr. Wilderness [1988]
Linville Gorge Wilderness, Pisgah NF [1987]
Nantahala National Forest [1986]
Pisgah National Forest [1984]
Pisgah NF, Pisgah Ranger District [1986]
Southern Nantahala Wilderness & Standing
  Indian Basin [1988]
Shining Rock-Middle Prong Wilderness [1988]
Uwharrie National Forest [1985]

State Agencies

Dept. of Environmental Health, & Natural Resources
PO Box 27687
Raleigh, NC 27611   919-733-4984
This is the parent agency for the following three Divisions and the NC Wildlife Resources Commission.

Division of Parks & Recreation
A North Carolina State Parks Guide (37 state parks) is available free. The guide describes each area, contains a

locator map, and includes specific information on facilities and activities.

Division of Forest Resources
PO Box 27687
Raleigh, NC 27611-7687   919-733-2162
Contact the Division for state forest recreation literature.

Division of Marine Fisheries
PO Box 769
Morehead City, NC 28557   919-726-7021
Contact the Division for marine fisheries information.

NC Wildlife Resources Commission (WRC)
The WRC headquarters in Raleigh is the only agency office in North Carolina. It owns or manages 2 million acres of Game Lands (90 locations) for hunting and fishing, where appropriate. Game Lands are not listed in the Guide. They are described in depth in a booklet titled *Hunting & Fishing Maps for North Carolina Game Lands*. The booklet contains local area maps, game species information by area, and camping information. It is revised every year. An annual $10 permit is required to use North Carolina's Game Lands.

A monthly magazine, *Wildlife in North Carolina*, is available by subscription for $7.50 per year and on the newsstands for $1.50 per copy.

Division of Travel & Tourism
430 N. Salisbury St.
Raleigh, NC 27611

Private Organizations

The Nature Conservancy owns and manages a number of preserves in North Carolina. Many are open to the public from April through October, through the chapter's extensive guided field-trip program. Contact this office for tour details and Chapter membership information.

Tribal Land Area in North Carolina
Eastern Band of Cherokee Indians of the Cherokee Indian Reservation - Fishing, camping, biking, boating, hiking, touring.

Eastern Band of Cherokee Indians Tribal Council
(S# 2, map C1)
PO Box 455
Cherokee, NC 28719   704-497-2771

ANCA Locations in North Carolina
Durant Nature Park (S# 3, map A3)
PO Box 590
Raleigh, NC 27602-0590   919-755-6640

Foothills Equestrian Nature Center
(S# 4, map B1)
500 Hunting Country Drive
Tryon, NC 28782

NC Coastal Islands Sanctuary (S# 5, map C4)
PO Box 5223
Wrightsville Beach, NC 28480

Western NC Nature Center (S# 6, map C2)
75 Gashes Creek Rd.
Asheville, NC 28805   1-800-847-4862

NC Assoc. of C of C Executives
(State Chamber of Commerce)
PO Box 1001
Raleigh, NC 27602
                        Phone 919-828-0758
                        Fax 919-821-4992

TNC North Carolina Chapter (S# 1, map A3)
Carr Mill Mall, Suite 223
Carrboro, NC 27510   919-967-7007

Federal Agencies

USDC, Natl. Oceanic & Atmospheric Admin. (NOAA)
The Monitor National Marine Sanctuary (USS Monitor site) is located about 16 miles south-southeast of Cape Hatteras, North Carolina. For information contact:
Monitor National Marine Sanctuary
NOAA Atlantic Marine Center
439 West York St.
Norfolk, VA 23510   804-441-6469

Wilderness/Wild River Index

Wilderness Areas
Croatan Natl. Forest & RD (S# 2, map B4)
Catfish Lake South Wilderness - 7,600 acres
Pocosin Wilderness - 11,000 acres
Pond Pine Wilderness - 1,860 acres
Sheep Ridge Wilderness - 9,540 acres
Nantahala NF, Highlands RD (S# 4, map D1)
Ellicott Rock Wilderness - 4,022 acres
Southern Nantahala Wilderness - 10,900 acres
Nantahala NF, Wayah RD (S# 6, map D1)
Joyce Kilmer-Slickrock Wilderness - 13,181 acres
Pisgah NF, Grandfather RD (S# 8, map B1)
Linville Gorge Wilderness - 10,975 acres
Pisgah NF, Pisgah RD (S# 9, map D2)
Middle Prong Wilderness - 7,900 acres
Shining Rock Wilderness - 18,450 acres
Uwharrie NF & RD (S# 11, map B2)
Birkhead Mountains Wilderness - 4,790 acres
Swanquarter NWR (S# 8, map B5)
Swanquarter Wilderness - 8,785 acres

Wild Rivers
Chattooga Wild River - also see GA and SC
Nantahala NF, Highlands RD (S# 4, map D1)
Horsepasture Wild River
Nantahala NF, Highlands RD (S# 4, map D1)

★ INFORMATION CHART ★

INFORMATION CHART LEGEND - SYMBOLS & LETTER CODES

■ means **YES** & □ means **Yes with disability provisions**
sp means **spring**, March through May
S means **Summer**, June through August
F means **Fall**, September through November
W means **Winter**, December through February
T means **Two (2) or Three (3) Seasons**
A means **All Four (4) Seasons**
na means **Not Applicable or Not Available**

Note: empty or blank spaces in the chart mean **NO**

that symbol is not shown on the map.

AGENCY/MAP LEGEND . . . INITIALS, MAP SYMBOLS, COLOR CODES

U.S. Forest Service Supervisor & Ranger Dist. Offices NFS
U.S. Army Corps of Engineers Rec. Areas & Offices . COE
USFWS National Wildlife Refuges & Offices . . . . NWR
National Park Service Parks & other NPS Sites . . . . . NPS
Bureau of Land Management Rec. Areas & Offices . . BLM
Bureau of Reclamation Rec. Areas & Reg. Offices . . BOR
State Parks (also see State Agency notes) . . . . SPS
State Wildlife Areas (also see State Agency notes) . SWA
Private Preserves, Nature Centers & Tribal Lands . .
The Wild Rivers ～ and Wilderness Areas

Note: Refer to yellow block on page 7 (top right) for location name and address abbreviations.

S#	MAP	LOCATION NAME (state initials if more than one) with ADDRESS and/or LOCATION DATA	TELEPHONE	ACRES / ELEVATION
1	C2	National Forests in No. Carolina, South Post & Otis Streets, PO Box 2750, Asheville 28802	704-257-4203	1,237,000 / 0-6,000
2	B4	Croatan Nat'l Forest & RD, 141 E Fisher Ave, New Bern 28560 [E side of US Hwy 70, 10.5 mi SE of town]	919-638-5628	157,829 / 0-30
3	C1	Nantahala NF, Cheoah RD, Rt. #1, Box 16-A, Robbinsville 28771 [2 mi NW of town on Massey Branch Rd.]	704-479-6431	120,000 / 3,200
4	D1	Nantahala NF, Highlands Ranger D., 210 Flat Mountain Rd., Rt. #1, Box 247, Highlands 28741	704-526-3765	112,000 / 2,400-5,280
5	D1	Nantahala NF, Tusquitee RD, 201 Woodland Drive, Murphy 28906 [2 blocks S of Hwy 65 at McDonalds]	704-837-5152	159,000 / 1,100-5,400
6	D1	Nantahala NF, Wayah Ranger D., 8 Sloan Road, Franklin 28734	704-524-6441	133,939 / 1,700-5,500
7	C2	Pisgah NF, French Broad Ranger D., PO Box 128, Hot Springs 28743	704-622-3202	82,000 / 1,000-5,000
8	B1	Pisgah NF, Grandfather Ranger D., PO Box 519, Marion 28752 [in town, corner of Logan & W Court Sts.]	704-652-2144	187,000 / 1,100-5,000
9	D2	Pisgah NF, Pisgah Ranger D., 1001 Pisgah Highway, Pisgah Forest 28768	704-877-3350	155,500 / 2,200-6,000
10	A1	Pisgah NF, Toecane Ranger D., PO Box 128, Burnsville 28714	704-682-6146	80,000 / 3,000-6,000
11	B2	Uwharrie Nat'l Forest & RD, Rt. #3, Box 470, Troy 27371 [50 mi S of Greensboro, 70 mi E of Charlotte]	919-576-6391	46,977 / 290-1,010

COE, Wilmington District, PO Box 1890, Wilmington 28402

#	Grid	Name / Location	Acres / Capacity	Phone
1	C4	COE, Wilmington District, PO Box 1890, Wilmington 28402	na / na	919-251-4827
2	B3	B. Everett Jordan Dam & Lake, PO Box 144, Moncure 27559	na / na	919-542-4501
3	C3	Cape Fear River (3 Locks & Dams), PO Box 1890, Wilmington 28402	na / na	919-251-4829
4	A3	Falls Lake, 11405 Falls Of Neuse River, Wake Forest 27587	na / na	919-846-9332
5	A1	W. Kerr Scott Dam & Reservoir, PO Box 182, Wilkesboro 28697	na / na	919-921-3750

Alligator River NWR, 708 N. Hwy. 64, PO Box 1969, Manteo 27954

#	Grid	Name / Location	Acres / Capacity	Phone
1	A5	Alligator River NWR, 708 N. Hwy. 64, PO Box 1969, Manteo 27954	151,000 / na	919-473-1131
2	A5	Pea Island NWR (part of Hatteras Is, PO Box 1969, Manteo 27954	5,915 / na	919-987-2394
3	A5	Mackay Island NWR (NC-VA), State Rt. 615, PO Box 39, Knotts Island 27950	8,000 / na	919-429-3100
4	A5	Currituck NWR, State Rt. 615, PO Box 39, Knotts Island 27950	1,787 / na	919-429-3100
5	B5	Mattamuskeet NWR, Rt. #1, Box N-2, Swanquarter 27885 [10 mi E of Swanquarter off Hwy. 94, follow signs]	50,000 / 0-6	919-926-4021
6	B5	Cedar Island NWR, Rt. #1, Box N-2, Swanquarter 27885 [10 mi N of Sea Level off Hwy 52]	14,411 / 0-3	919-926-4021
7	B5	Swanquarter NWR, Rt. #1, Box N-2, Swan Quarter 27885	16,200 / 0-3	919-926-4021
8	B2	Pee Dee NWR, Rt. #1, Box 92, Wadesboro 28170 [8 mi N of Wadesboro on US Hwy 52]	8,443 / 200	704-694-4424
9	A4	Pocosin Lakes & Pungo NWRs, Rt. #1, Box 195-B, Creswell 27928	111,000 / 15	919-797-4431
10	A4	Roanoke River NWR, 102 Dundee St., Box 430, Windsor 27983	na / na	919-794-5326

Blue Ridge Parkway (NC/VA), 200 BB&T Bldg., 1 Pack Square, Asheville 28801 [470 mi. long]

#	Grid	Name / Location	Acres / Capacity	Phone
1	C2	Blue Ridge Parkway (NC/VA), 200 BB&T Bldg., 1 Pack Square, Asheville 28801 [470 mi. long]	82,110 / 650-6,200	704-259-0779
2	A4	Cape Hatteras National Seashore, Rt. #1, Box 675, Manteo 27954	30,320 / 0-40	919-995-4474
3	B5	Cape Lookout Nat'l. Seashore, 3601 Bridges St., Suite F, Morehead City 28557	28,415 / 10	919-728-2250
4	A4	Fort Raleigh NHS c/o Cape Hatteras, Rt. #1, Box 675, Manteo 27954	157 / 15	919-473-5772
5	A2	Guilford Cthse NMP, 2332 New Garden Rd, PO Box 9806, Greensboro 27429 [0.2 mi E of US 220 on New Garden Rd]	220 / 890	919-288-1776

NC DEHNR, Div. Parks & Recreation, 512 N. Salisbury St., PO Box 27687, Raleigh 27611

#	Grid	Name / Location	Acres / Capacity	Phone
1	A3	Boone's Cave SP, 14 mi. W of Lexington, W. Dist. Office, Rt. #2, Box 224, Troutman 28166	110 / na	919-733-4181
2	A2	Carolina Beach SP, 10 mi. S off Hwy.421, PO Box 475, Carolina Beach 28428	1,720 / na	704-528-6514
3	C4	Cliffs of the Neuse SP, 14 mi. SE of Goldsboro on SR 111, Rt. #2, Box 50, Seven Springs 28578	750 / na	919-458-8206
4	B4	Crowder's Mountain SP, 6 mi. W of Gastonia on SR 1125, Rt. #1, Box 159, Kings Mountain 28086	2,586 / 1,705	704-867-1181
5	B1	(Crowder's Mountain SP)		
6	B2	Duke Power SP, 1C mi. S of Statesville on SR 1330, Rt. #2, Box 224M, Troutman 28166	1,458 / na	704-528-6350
7	A3	Eno River SP, 3 mi NW off SR 1569, Rt. #2, Box 436-C, Durham 27705	2,141 / na	919-383-1686
8	A3	Falls Lake State Rec. Area, 12700 Bayleaf Road, Raleigh 27614	12,500 / na	919-676-1027
9	A3	Fort Macon SP, 2 mi. E on SR 1190, PO Box 127, Atlantic Beach 28512	389 / na	919-726-3775
10	C4	Ft. Fisher State Recreation Area, 5 mi. S off Hwy.421, PO Box 475, Carolina Beach 28428	287 / na	919-458-8206
11	B4	Goose Creek SP, 10 mi. E. off SR 1334, Rt. #2, Box 372, Washington 27889	1,327 / na	919-923-2191
12	C4	Hammocks Beach SP, 4.5 mi. W off NC 24, 1400 Hammocks Beach Rd., Swansboro 28584	736 / na	919-326-4881
13	B4	Hanging Rock SP, 5 mi. W off SR 1101, PO Box 186, Danbury 27016	6,194 / na	919-593-8480
14	A5	Jockey's Ridge SP, U.S. 158 Bypass in Nags Head, PO Box 592, Nags Head 27959	413 / na	919-441-7132
15	B3	Jones Lake SP, 4 mi. N on NC 242, Rt. #2, Box 945, Elizabethtown 28337	2,208 / na	919-588-4550
16	A3	Kerr Reservoir Rec. Areas (RAs), 11 mi. N off US 85 to SR 1319, Rt. #3, Box 800, Henderson 27536	106,860 / na	919-438-7791
*17	A3	Bullocksville RA, c/o Kerr Reservoir, Henderson	455 / na	919-438-7791
*18	A3	County Line RA, c/o Kerr Reservoir, Henderson	285 / na	919-438-7791
*19	A3	Henderson RA, c/o Kerr Reservoir, Henderson	329 / na	919-438-7791
*20	A3	Hibernia RA, c/o Kerr Reservoir, Henderson	446 / na	919-438-7791
*21	A3	Kimball Point RA, c/o Kerr Reservoir, Henderson	93 / na	919-438-7791
*22	A3	Nutbush Bridge RA, c/o Kerr Reservoir, Henderson	363 / na	919-438-7791
*23	A3	Satterwhite Point RA, c/o Kerr Reservoir, Henderson	282 / na	919-438-7791
*24	A3	Steel Creek Marina, c/o Kerr Reservoir, Henderson	375 / na	919-438-7791
25	A1	Lake James SP, 5 mi. NE of Marion on Hwy. 126, PO Box 340, Nebo 28761	585 / 1,995-2,300	704-652-5047
26	C3	Lake Waccamaw SP, 6 mi. S of L. Waccamaw off US 74/76, Rt. #1, Box 63, Kelly 28448	10,670 / na	919-669-2928
27	A4	Medoc Mountain SP, 15mi SW of Roanoke Rpds. off NC 561, Rt. #3, Box 219-G, Enfield 27823	2,287 / na	919-445-2280
28	A5	Merchant's Millpond SP, 6 mi. NE on SR 1403, Rt. #1, Box 141A, Gatesville 27938	2,918 / na	919-357-1191
29	A2	Morrow Mountain SP, 5 mi. E. on Morrow Mountain Rd., Rt. #5, Box 430, Albemarle 28001	4,693 / 936	704-982-4402
30	A1	Mt. Jefferson SP, 1.5 mi. S on US 221, PO Box 48, Jefferson 28640	489 / 4,864	919-246-9653
31	A3	Mt. Mitchell SP, 30 mi. NE of Asheville off BR Pkwy., Rt. #5, Box 700, Burnsville 28714	1,667 / 6,684	704-675-4611
32	A1	New River SP, 8 mi. SE off NC 88 on SR 1588, PO Box 48, Jefferson 28640	1,089 / na	919-982-2587
33	A5	Pettigrew SP, 9 mi. S off US 64 on SR 1166, Rt. #1, Box 336, Creswell 27928	17,743 / na	919-797-4475
34	A2	Pilot Mountain SP, 24 mi. N of Winston-Salem off US 52, Rt. #1, Box 21, Pinnacle 27042	3,703 / 2,420	919-325-2355
35	B3	Raven Rock SP, 6 mi. W off US 421 on SR 1314, Rt. #3, Box 1005, Lillington 27546	2,990 / na	919-893-4888
36	C3	Singletary Lake SF, 12 mi. SE of Elizabethtown on NC 53, Rt. #1, Box 63, Kelly 28448	1,221 / na	919-669-2928
37	A1	South Mountains SP, 18 mi. S of Morganton on SR 1904, Rt. #1, Box 206, Connelly Springs 28612	7,226 / 1,200-2,900	704-433-4772
38	A5	Stone Mountain SP, 7 mi. side off US 21 on SR 1002, Star Rt. #1, Roaring Gap 28668	13,434 / 1,600-3,200	919-957-8185
39	B4	Theodore Roosevelt Natural Area, 7 mi. W on SR 1201, PO Box 127, Atlantic Beach 28512	265 / na	919-726-3775
40	B4	Waynesborough SP, off U.S. 117 Bypass in Goldsboro, Rt. #2, Box 50, Seven Springs 28578	142 / na	919-778-6234
41	B3	Weymouth Woods Sandhill Nature Pre., 2 mi. S on SR 2074, 400 N. Ft. Bragg Rd., Southern Pines 28387	676 / na	919-692-2167
42	A3	William B. Umstead SP, 10 mi. W on US 70, Rt. #8, Box 130, Raleigh 27612	5,337 / na	919-787-3033
43	A3	William B. Umstead-Reedy Creek SP, 11 mi. W on I-40, Rt. #8, Box 130, Raleigh 27612	5,337 / na	919-467-7259
44	A3	Jordan Lake SRA, Rt. #2, Box 159, Apex 27502 [21 mi. SW of Raleigh off NC 64]	14,310 / na	919-362-0586

Wildlife Resources Commission, Archdale Bldg., 512 N Salisbury St., Raleigh 27611

#	Grid	Name / Location	Acres / Capacity	Phone
1	A3	Wildlife Resources Commission, Archdale Bldg., 512 N Salisbury St., Raleigh 27611	na / na	919-733-3391

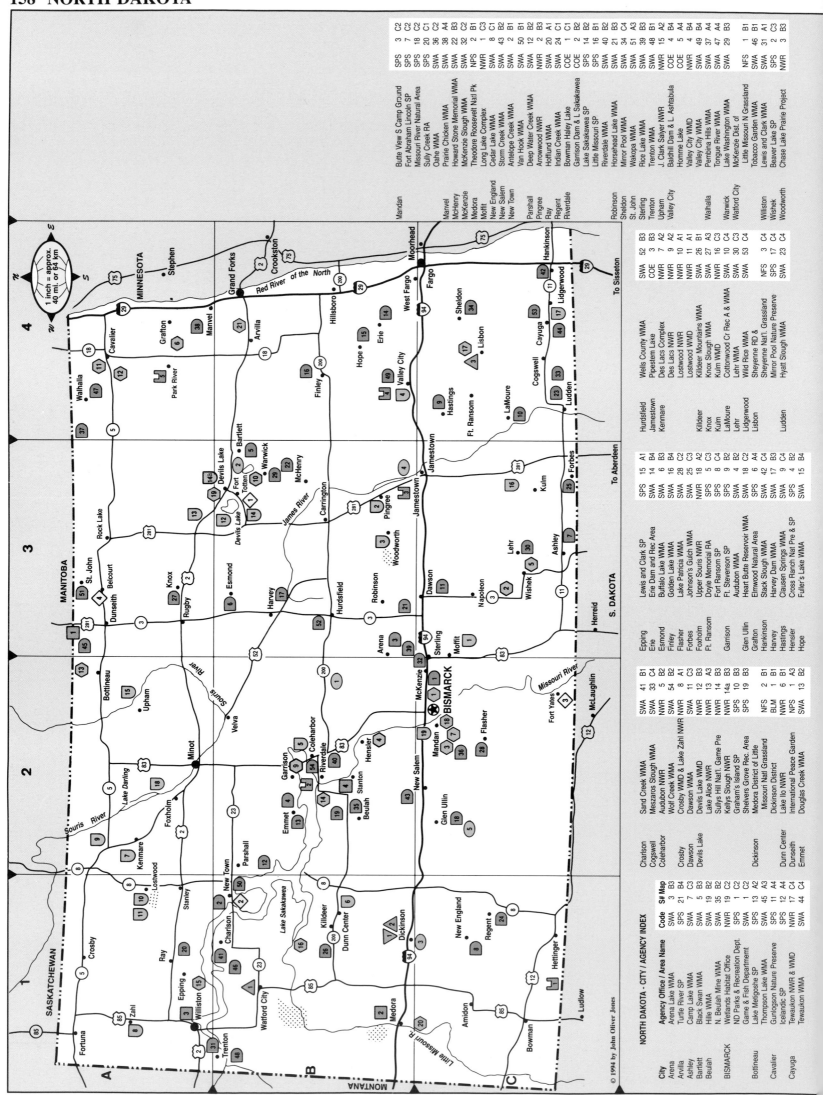

NORTH DAKOTA NOTES

Summary

There are 38 federal, 77 state, and 5 private recreation areas or local administrative offices covered in this chapter. Of these, 53 appear in the Information Chart and 67 are covered in the notes. The special indexes feature 3 federally designated wilderness areas, 56 agency published outdoor maps, and another 56 BLM intermediate scale maps covering South Dakota.

Federal Agencies

U.S. Forest Service

North Dakota is in the Northern Region (see Montana chapter - U.S. Forest Svc., Northern Region listing).

National Park Service

Additional NPS Locations in North Dakota

Fort Union Trading Post NHS (442 acres)
Buford Route (S# 3, map A1)
Williston, ND 58571   701-572-9083

Knife River Indian Village NHS (1,293 acres)
RR 1, Box 168 (S# 4, map B2)
Stanton, ND 58571   701-745-3300

Bureau of Reclamation Recreation Areas

Five recreation areas are listed here and symbolized on the North Dakota state map.

S#	MAP	LOCATION NAME
1	B2	Chain of Lakes
2	B3	Devils and Stump Lakes
3	C1	Edward A. Patterson Lake
4	B3	Jamestown Res.
5	C2	Lake Tschida

Wilderness Index

Chase Lake Wilderness - 4,155 acres
Chase Lake (USFWS) Prairie Project (S# 2, map B3)
Lostwood Wilderness - 5,577 acres
Lostwood NWR (S# 10, map A1)
Theodore Roosevelt Wilderness - 29,920 acres
Theodore Roosevelt National Park (S# 2, map B1)

Outdoor Map Index

National Park Service (USGS Maps)

Theodore Roosevelt Natl. Park North [1974]
Scale: 1 inch = 0.4 mile (1 cm = 0.3 km)
Size: 27x36 inches (68x91 cm)
Theodore Roosevelt Natl. Park South [1974]
Scale: 1 inch = 0.4 mile (1 cm = 0.3 km)
Size: 38x46 inches (96x116 cm)

U.S. Forest Service Maps

Custer NF, Little Missouri Natl. Grassland [1986]
Custer, Grand & Cedar River Nat. Grasslands [1981]
Scale: 1 inch = 0.5 mile (1 cm = 0.3 km)

Bureau of Land Management Maps

The BLM map grid (right) includes the North and South Dakota intermediate scale maps.

State Agencies

ND Parks & Recreation Department (S# 1, C2)
A North Dakota State Parks Outdoor Adventure Guide is available free. The guide includes information on facilities and activities. There is an overnight fee at most parks.

State Forest Service

Molberg Forestry Center
First & Brander
Bottineau, ND 58318   701-228-2277
Contact the Center for state forest recreation literature.

ND Game & Fish Department (S# 1, C2)

Licensing and harvest information is published annually. A magazine published 10 times per year, North Dakota Outdoors, is available by subscription for $7 per year and on newsstands. A brochure describing 144 wildlife management areas open to the public is available.

Selected larger North Dakota WMAs are listed here, and their locations shown on the Guide map.

S#	MAP	WMA NAME & LOCATION
2	B1	Antelope Creek WMA, New Town
3	B3	Arena Lake WMA, Arena
4	B2	Audubon WMA, Garrison
5	B3	Black Swan WMA, Bartlett
6	B3	Buffalo Lake WMA, Esmond
7	C3	Camp Lake WMA, Ashley
8	C1	Cedar Lake WMA, New England
9	C4	Clausen Springs WMA, Hastings
10	C4	Cottonwood Cr. Rec. Area & WMA, LaMoure
11	C3	Dawson WMA, Dawson
12	B2	Deep Water Creek WMA, Parshall
13	B2	Douglas Creek WMA, Emmet
14	B4	Erie Dam and Recreation Area, Erie
15	B4	Fuller's Lake WMA, Hope
16	B4	Golden Lake WMA, Finley
17	B3	Harvey Dam WMA, Harvey
18	C2	Heart Butte Reservoir WMA, Glen Ullin
19	B2	Hille WMA, Beulah
20	A1	Hofflund WMA, Ray
21	B3	Horsehead Lake WMA, Robinson
22	B3	Howard Stone Memorial WMA, McHenry
23	C4	Hyatt Slough WMA, Ludden
24	C1	Indian Creek WMA, Regent
25	C3	Johnson's Gulch WMA, Forbes
26	B1	Killdeer Mountains WMA, Killdeer
27	A3	Knox Slough WMA, Knox
28	B3	Lake Patricia WMA, Flasher
29	B3	Lake Washington WMA, Warwick
30	C3	Lehr WMA, Lehr
31	A1	Lewis and Clark WMA, Williston
32	C2	McKenzie Slough WMA, McKenzie
33	C4	Meszaros Slough WMA, Cogswell
34	C4	Mirror Pool WMA, Sheldon
35	B2	N. Beulah Mine WMA, Beulah
36	C2	Oahe WMA, Mandan
37	A4	Pembina Hills WMA (several tracts), Walhalla
38	A4	Prairie Chicken WMA (several areas), Manvel
39	B3	Rice Lake WMA, Sterling
40	B2	Riverdale WMA, Riverdale
41	B1	Sand Creek WMA, Charlson
42	C4	Stack Slough WMA, Hankinson
43	B2	Storm Creek WMA, New Salem
44	C4	Tewaukon WMA, Cayuga
45	A3	Thompson Lake WMA, Bottineau
46	B1	Tobacco Garden WMA, Watford City
47	A4	Tongue River WMA, Walhalla
48	B1	Trenton WMA, Trenton
49	B4	Valley City WMA, Valley City
50	B1	Van Hook WMA, New Town
51	A3	Wakopa WMA, St. John
52	B3	Wells County WMA, Hurdsfield
53	C4	Wild Rice WMA, Lidgerwood
54	B2	Wolf Creek WMA, Colehartor

ND Tourism Promotion

Liberty Memorial Bldg.
Capitol Grounds
Bismarck, ND 58505   1-800-437-2077
in state toll free   1-800-472-2100
A Visitors Planning Guide is available from this office. It contains an extensive list of public and private accommodations and attractions. Special hunting or fishing packets are available. The official ND State Highway Dept. map has symbols for state, city, and national parks, ski areas, and dams. The Lewis & Clark Trail is also indicated.

Private Organizations

Tribal Land Areas in North Dakota

Devils Lake Sioux Tribe of the Devils Lake (Fort Totten) Indian Reservation - Fishing, hunting, camping, boating.
Devils Lake Sioux Tribal Council (S# 1, map B3)
Sioux Community Center
Fort Totten, ND 58335   701-766-4221

Three Affiliated Tribes of the Fort Berthold Indian Reservation - Fishing, hunting, camping, boating, touring.
Fort Berthold Tribal Business Council (S# 2, map B1)
PO Box 220
New Town, ND 58763   701-627-4781

Standing Rock Sioux Tribe of the Standing Rock Indian Reservation - Fishing, hunting, camping, boating.
Standing Rock Sioux Tribal Council (S# 3, map C2)
Fort Yates, ND 58538   701-854-7231

Turtle Mountain Band of Chippewa Indians of North Dakota - Fishing, hunting, camping, boating.
Turtle Mountain Tribal Council (S# 4, map A3)
Belcourt, ND 58316   701-477-6451

Greater North Dakota Assn.

(State Chamber of Commerce)
808 3rd Ave. South
PO Box 2467
Fargo, ND 58108   701-237-9463

NORTH DAKOTA map grid (quadrangle names): Plentywood, Crosby, Kenmare, Mohall, Bottineau, Rock Lake, Langdon, Cavalier, Crookston, Ada; Culbertson, Williston, Stanley, Minot, Velva, Leeds, Devil's Lake, Grafton; Sidney, Watford City, Parshall, Garrison, Drake, New Rockford, Stump Lake, Grand Forks; Glendive, Grassy Butte, Killdeer, Hazen, McClusky, Carrington, Coopers Town, Hillsboro; Belfield, Dickinson, Glen Ullin, Bismarck, Steele, Jamestown, Caselton, Fargo; Wibaux, Bowman, Mott, Elgin, Linton, Wahek, LaMoure, Lisbon, Wahpeton; Baker.

Longitude markers: 105°, 104°, 103°, 102°, 101°, 100°, 99°, 98°, 97°, 96°. Latitude markers: 49°, 48°, 47°, 46°.

SOUTH DAKOTA map grid (quadrangle names): Ekalaka, Camp Crook, Lemmon, McIntosh, Mobridge, Eureka, Sisseton; Alzada, Redig, Faith, Timber Lake, LaPlant, Gettysburg, Aberdeen, Webster; Devils Tower, Belle Fourche, Camp Creek, Cherry Creek, Onida, Highmore, Redfield, Milbank; Sundance, Rapid City, New Underwood, Philip, Big Bend Dam, Huron, Watertown, Clear Lake; Mount Rushmore, Wall, Pierre, White River, Chamberlain, Mitchell Lake, Brookings; Newcastle, Kadoka, Martin, Winner, Salem, DeSmet; Lance Creek, Hot Springs, Pine Ridge, Mission, Freeman, Sioux Falls, Rock Rapids; Lusk, Crawford, Gordon, Cody, Valentine, Ainsworth, Atkinson, Yankton, Sioux City North.

Latitude markers: 46°, 45°, 44°, 43°.

BLM NORTH & SOUTH DAKOTA
1:100,000 INTERMEDIATE SCALE MAPS
SURFACE & SURFACE / MINERAL SERIES
/ Base Map Not Available

★ INFORMATION CHART ★

AGENCY/MAP LEGEND . . . INITIALS, MAP SYMBOLS, COLOR CODES

- U.S. Forest Service Supervisor & Ranger Dist. Offices NFS [61]
- U.S. Army Corps of Engineers Rec. Areas & Offices . COE [31]
- USFWS National Wildlife Refuges & Offices . . . . . NWR [40]
- National Park Service Parks & other NPS Sites . . . . NPS [7]
- Bureau of Land Management Rec. Areas & Offices . BLM [29]
- Bureau of Reclamation Rec. Areas & Reg. Offices . BOR [8]
- State Parks (also see State Agency notes) . . . . SPS [52]
- State Wildlife Areas (also see State Agency notes) . . SWA [19]
- Private Preserves, Nature Centers & Tribal Lands
- The Wild Rivers ~ and Wilderness Areas [15]

Note: Refer to yellow block on page 7 (top right) for location name and address abbreviations.

INFORMATION CHART LEGEND - SYMBOLS & LETTER CODES

- ■ means YES & □ means Yes with disability provisions
- **sp** means spring, March through May
- **S** means Summer, June through August
- **F** means Fall, September through November
- **W** means Winter, December through February
- **T** means Two (2) or Three (3) Seasons
- **A** means All Four (4) Seasons
- **na** means Not Applicable or Not Available
- Note: empty or blank spaces in the chart mean **NO**
- Note: ★ that symbol is not shown on the map.

Column groups across the chart: **FACILITIES, SERVICES, RECREATION OPPORTUNITIES & CONVENIENCES**

S#	MAP	LOCATION NAME (state initials if more than one) with ADDRESS and/or LOCATION DATA	TELEPHONE	ACRES / ELEVATION
		Custer National Forest (MT-ND-SD), 2602 First Ave. N., PO Box 2556, Billings, MT 59103	406-657-6361	2,446,130 / 1,000-12,800
1	B1	McKenzie Dist. of Little Missouri Nat'l Grassland, Star Rt. #2, Box 8, Watford City 58854	701-842-2393	503,000 / 2,000-3,000
2	B1	Medora District of Little Missouri Nat'l Grassland, Rt. #3, Box 131-B, Dickinson 58601	701-225-5151	524,000 / 2,200-3,500
3	C4	Sheyenne RD (Sheyenne Nat'l. Grassl, Box 946, Lisbon 58054	701-683-4342	70,000 / 1,000-1,100
		COE, Omaha District, 215 N. 17th St., Omaha, NE 68102	402-221-4137	na / na
1	C1	Bowman Haley Lake, PO Box 527, Riverdale 58565 [SW of Bowman]	701-654-7411	na / na
2	B2	Garrison Dam & Lake Sakakawea, PO Box 527, Riverdale 58565	701-654-7411	na / na
3	B3	Pipestem Lake, PO Box 1752, Jamestown 58402	701-252-7666	na / na
		COE, St. Paul District, 180 E. Kellog Blvd., Rm. 1421, St. Paul, MN 55101	612-220-0325	na / na
4	B4	Baldhill Dam & Lake Ashtabula, 2630 114th Ave. SE, Valley City 58072	701-845-2970	na / na
5	A4	Homme Lake, 2630 114th Ave. SE, Valley City 58072 [NW of Park River]	701-845-2970	na / na
1		**Long Lake Complex**, RR #1, Box 23, Moffit 58560 [12 mi S on Hwy 83 from I-94 Sterling exit, E for 2.5 mi, N 0.5 mi]	701-387-4397	22,300 / 1,720
2	C3	Arrowwood NWR, 7745 11th St., SE, Pingree 58476	701-285-3341	14,934 / 1,428-1,460
3	B3	Chase Lake Prairie Project, RR #1, Box 144, Woodworth 58496 [a 5.5 million acre multi-agency project]	701-752-4218	na / 1,877
4	B4	Valley City WMD, 11515 River Rd., Valley City 58072 [exit I-94 at mile marker 292]	701-845-3466	18,400 / na
5	B2	Audubon NWR, RR #1, Coleharbor 58531	701-442-5474	14,500 / 1,500
6	B1	Lake Ilo NWR, PO Box 127, Dunn Center 58626 [1 mi W of Dunn Center on Hwy 200, office at refuge]	701-548-8110	4,030 / 2,180-2,290
7	A2	Des Lacs Complex, PO Box 578, Kenmare 58746 [1 mi W of Kenmare on CR 1A]	701-385-4046	80,000 / 2,000-2,500
8	A1	Crosby WMD (92 WPAs) & Lake Zahl NW, PO Box 148, Crosby 58730	701-965-6488	20,800 / 1,800
9	A2	Des Lacs NWR, PO Box 578, Kenmare 58746	701-385-4046	19,544 / 1,780-1,980
10	A1	Lostwood NWR, RR #2, Box 98, Kenmare 58746	701-848-2722	26,900 / 2,200-2,400
11	A1	Lostwood WMD, RR #2, Box 98, Kenmare 58746 [20 mi. N of Stanley on Hwy. 8]	701-848-2466	11,902 / 2,500
12	A3	Devils Lake WMD, PO Box 908, Devils Lake 58301	701-662-8611	41,700 / 1,400
13	A3	Lake Alice NWR, PO Box 908, Devils Lake 58301	701-662-8611	11,300 / 1,400
14	B3	Sullys Hill Nat'l. Game Preserve, PO Box 908, Devils Lake 58301	701-662-8611	1,600 / 1,440-1,735
14a	B3	Kellys Slough NWR, PO Box 908, Devils Lake 58301	701-662-8611	na / na
15	A2	J. Clark Salyer NWR, Box 66, Upham 58789 [2 mi N of Upham on Hwy 14]	701-768-2548	58,700 / 1,430
16	C3	Kulm WMD, PO Box E, Kulm 58456	701-647-2866	42,645 / 2,028
17	C4	Tewaukon NWR & WMD, RR #1, Box 75, Cayuga 58013	701-724-3598	20,420 / na
18	A2	Upper Souris NWR, RR #1, Foxholm 58738	701-468-5467	32,092 / 1,700
19	C2	Wetlands Habitat Office (N. Dakota), 1500 East Capitol Ave., Bismarck 58501	701-250-4418	na / na
1	A3	**International Peace Garden**, RR #1, Box 116, Dunseith 58329 [13 mi N of Dunseith]	701-263-4390	2,339 / 2,300
2	B1	Theodore Roosevelt National Park, RR #1, Box 7, Medora 58645	701-623-4466	70,446 / 2,250-2,870
		BLM Montana State Office, 222 N. 32nd Street, PO Box 36800, Billings, MT 59107	406-255-2885	8,000,000 / 2,000-10,500
1	B1	Dickinson District, 2933 3rd Ave. West, Dickinson 58601	701-225-9148	67,000 / 1,800-3,200
		ND Parks & Recreation Dept., Pinehurst Office Park, 1424 W. Century Ave., Suite 202, Bismarck 58501	701-244-4887	na / na
1	C2	Beaver Lake SP (17 mi. SE of Napoleon), Rt. #1, Box 216, Wishek 58495	701-452-2752	93 / na
2	C3	Butte View St. Camp Ground (3 mi. E of Bowan), c/o Ft. Lincoln SP, Rt. #2, Box 139, Mandan 58554	701-663-9571	20 / na
3	B2	Cross Ranch Nature Preserve & SP, HC 2, Box 152, Hensler 58530	701-794-3731	560 / na
4	B2	Cross Ranch Nature Preserve & SP, HC 2, Box 152, Hensler 58530	701-973-4331	21 / na
5	C3	Doyle Memorial RA, c/o Ft. Ransom, Rt. #1, Box 20A, Ft. Ransom 58033 [SE of Wishek on Green Lake]	701-352-0152	5 / 820
6	A4	Elmwood Natural Area, near Grafton	701-663-9571	1,006 / 1,850
7	C2	Fort Abraham Lincoln SP (4 mi. S of Mandan), Rt. #2, Box 139, Mandan 58554	701-973-4331	887 / na
8	C4	Fort Ransom SP (2 mi. N of Ft. Ransom), RR #1, Box 20A, Ft. Ransom 58033	701-337-5576	438 / 1,850-1,900
9	B2	Ft. Stevenson SP (3 mi. S of Garrison), Rt. #1, Box 13A, Garrison 58540	701-766-4015	1,200 / na
10	B3	Graham's Island SP (14 mi. SW of Devils Lake), Rt. #1, Box 165, Devils Lake 58301	701-265-4561	95 / 945-990
11	A4	Gunlogson Nature Preserve, near Cavalier	701-265-4561	884 / 970
12	A4	Icelandic SP (4 mi. W of Cavalier), HCR 3, Box 64A, Cavalier 58220	701-263-4651	1,141 / 2,150
13	A4	Lake Metigoshe SP (14 mi. NE of Bottineau), Rt. #1, Box 359, Bottineau 58318	701-487-3315	822 / 1,850-1,900
14	B3	Lake Sakakawea SP (1 mi. N of Pick City), PO Box 832, Riverdale 58565	701-859-9071	490 / 1,850-1,900
15	B2	Lewis and Clark SP (19 mi. SE of Williston), Rt. #1, Box 13A, Epping 58843		

17	C4	Mirror Pool Nature Preserve, near Lisbon	701-683-4900
18	C2	Missouri River Natural Area, c/o ND Parks & RD in Bismarck, near Mandan	701-224-4887
19	B3	Shelvers Grove Rec. Area, Rt. #1, Box 165, Devils Lake 58301	701-662-7106
20	C1	Sully Creek RA (2.5 mi. S of Medora), c/o Ft. Lincoln SP, Rt. #2, Box 139, Mandan 58554	701-662-9571
21	B4	Turtle River SP (22 mi. W of Grand Forks), Box 913, Arvilla 58214	701-594-4445
1	C2	Game & Fish Departmemt, 100 N. Bismarck Expressway, Bismarck 58501	701-221-6300

420 / 970-1,070
157 / na
20 / 1,423-1,460
80 / na
682 / na
na / na

OHIO NOTES

Summary

There are 45 federal, 76 state, and 22 private recreation areas or local administrative offices covered in this state chapter. Of these, 120 appear in the Information Chart and 23 are covered in the notes. The special indexes feature 3 federally designated wilderness areas and wild rivers, and one agency published outdoor map.

Federal Agencies

U.S. Forest Service

Ohio is in the Eastern Region (see Wisconsin chapter - U.S. Forest Svc., Eastern Region listing).

U.S. Army Corps of Engineers (COE)

Ohio River Division Office
PO Box 1159
Cincinnati, OH 45210-1159   513-684-3192

The Huntington, W. Virginia, Louisville, Kentucky, Nashville, Tennessee, and Pittsburgh, Pennsylvania District Offices manage COE projects in the Ohio River area (see information charts).

National Park Service

Additional NPS Locations in Ohio
Dayton Aviation National Historica Park (S# 3, map C1)
No office, new location established October 16, 1992.

James A. Garfield National Historic Site (8 acres)
8095 Mentor Avenue (S# 4, map A3)
Mentor, OH 44060   216-255-8722

Perry's Victory and International Peace Memorial
(25 acres) (S# 5, map A2)
PO Box 549
Put-in-Bay, OH 43456   419-285-2184

William Howard Taft National Historic Site (3 acres)
2038 Auburn Ave. (S# 6, map D1)
Cincinnati, OH 45219   513-684-3262

Wilderness/Wild River Index

Wilderness Areas

West Sister Island Wilderness - 77 acres (closed)
West Sister Island NWR (S# 3, map A2)

Wild Rivers

Little Beaver Creek and
Little Miami River
Ohio DNR, Div. of Natural Resources
(see State Agencies)

Outdoor Map Index

U.S. Forest Service Map

Wayne National Forest [1975]
Scale: 1 inch = 4.0 miles (1 cm = 2.5 km)
Size: 28x35 inches (71x89 cm)

State Agencies

Ohio Department of Natural Resources (DNR)

Fountain Square
Columbus, OH 43224   614-265-6565
The following four divisions operate under this Department.

Division of Natural Areas and Preserves

Fountain Square (see above address)   614-265-6453
Contact the Division for information on natural areas and preserves.

Division of Forestry

Fountain Square (see above address)   614-265-6690
Contact the Division for state forest recreation literature.

Division of Parks & Recreation (S# 1, map C2)

TDD telephone number: 614-265-6994   614-265-6565
An Ohio State Parks Directory (72 state parks) is available free. The Directory describes each area. contains a locator map, and includes information on facilities and activities. There are 57 parks that offer camping.

Division of Wildlife (S# 1, map C2)

This division has a publications list with the information categorized as leaflets and reports; life histories of birds, fish, and wildlife; and public hunting and fishing maps. There is a nominal charge for some of the items. Licensing and harvest information is published annually. A quarterly magazine, Wild Ohio, is available free.

A fold-out brochure, Ohio Public Hunting & Fishing Areas, contains information on and directions to 365 sites. Fifty-six of the larger areas are shown on the Guide map and covered in the Ohio Information Chart.

Department of Development

Division of Travel and Tourism
PO Box 1001
Columbus, OH 43266   1-800-282-5393

A traveler's guide to Ohio is available with information on accommodations and special events. An official road map is also available. The map has symbols for state forests, parks or reserves, camping, national parks and tourist information centers. Scenic highways are also marked.

Private Organizations

ANCA Locations in Ohio

Brecksville Nature Center (S# 7, map A3)
9305 Brecksville Road
Brecksville, OH 44141   216-526-1012

Brukner Nature Center (S# 8, map C1)
5995 Horseshoe Benc Road
Troy, OH 45373   513-698-6493

Cincinnati Nature Center (S# 9, map D1)
4949 Tealtown Road
Milford, OH 45150   513-831-1711

Cincinnati Zoo & Botanical Garden (S# 10, map D1)
3400 Vine St.
Cincinnati, OH 45220   513-281-4701

Ford Nature Center/Mill Creek Park (S# 11, map B4)
Dist. 840 Old Furnace Road
Youngstown, OH 44511   216-740-7107

Garfield Park Nature Center (S# 12, map A3)
11350 Broadway
Garfield Heights, OH 44125   216-341-3152

Germantown Reserve/Nature Center (S# 13, map C1)
1375 East Siebenthaler Ave.
Dayton, OH 45414   513-278-8231

Glen Helen Nature Preserve (S# 14, map C1)
405 Corry St.
Yellow Springs, OH 45387   513-767-7376

Gorman Nature Center (S# 15, map B2)
2295 Lexington Ave.
Mansfield, OH 44907   419-884-3764

Hueston Woods Nature Center (S# 16, map C1)
Route 1
College Corner, OH 45003   513-523-6347

Lake Erie Nature/Science Center (S# 17, map A3)
28728 Wolf Road
Bay Village, OH 44140   216-871-2900

Rocky River Nature Center (S# 18, map A3)
Valley Parkway
Rocky River, OH 44070   216-734-6660

Sanctuary Marsh Nature Center (S# 19, map A3)
3037 Som Center Road
Willoughby Hills, OH 44094   216-526-1012

Secor Metropark Nature Center (S# 20, map A1)
Route 1, Box 183
Berkey, OH 43504   419-829-2761

Shaker Lakes Nature Center (S# 21, map A3)
2600 South Park Blvd.
Cleveland, OH 44120   216-321-5935

Ohio Chamber of Commerce

35 E. Gay St., 2nd Floor
Columbus, OH 43215   614-228-4201

Ohio City / Agency Index continued on page 162

Index continued from page 161

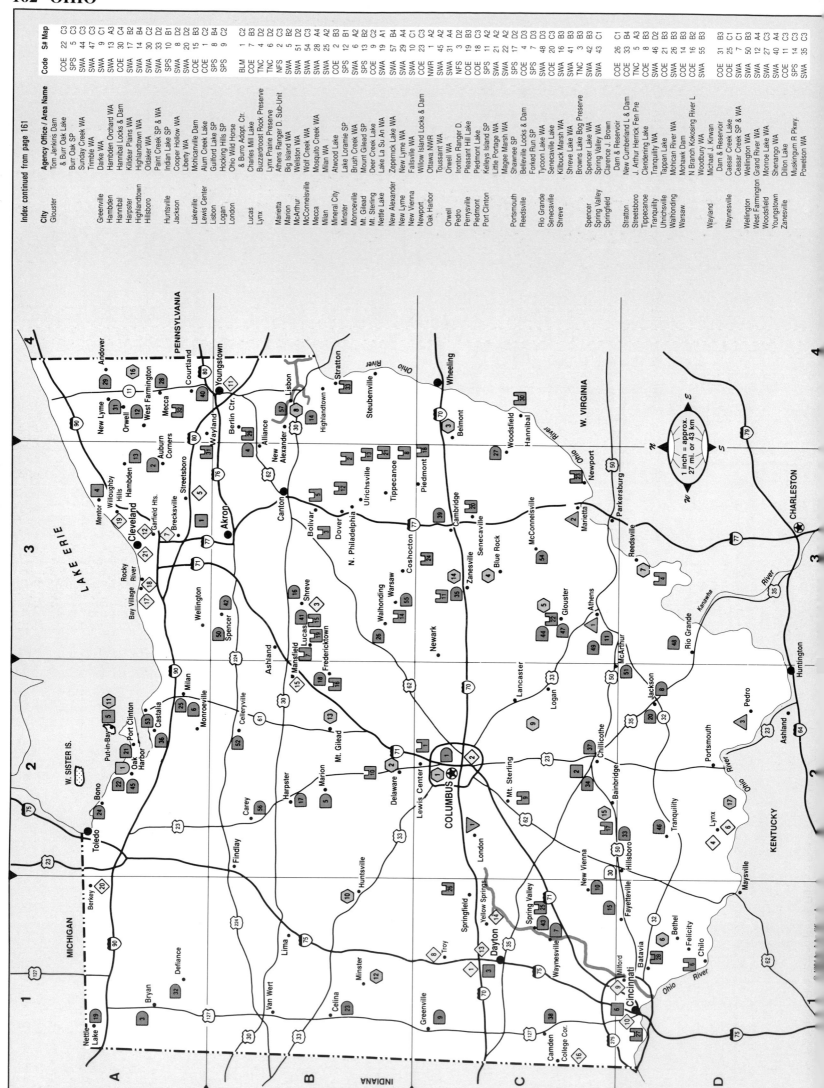

U.S. Forest Service Supervisor & Ranger Dist. Offices NFS [61]
U.S. Army Corps of Engineers Rec. Areas & Offices . . COE [31]
USFWS National Wildlife Refuges & Offices . . . . NWR [40]
National Park Service Parks & other NPS Sites . . . . . NPS [7]
Bureau of Land Management Rec. Areas & Offices . . . BLM [26]
Bureau of Reclamation Rec. Areas & Reg. Offices . . . BOR [8]
State Parks (also see State Agency notes) . . . . SPS [52]
State Wildlife Areas (also see State Agency notes) . . SWA [19]
Private Preserves, Nature Centers & Tribal Lands . . [15]
The Wild Rivers —— and **Wilderness Areas**

Note: Refer to yellow block on page 7 (top right) for location name and address abbreviations.

INFORMATION CHART LEGEND - SYMBOLS & LETTER CODES
■ means **YES** & □ means **Yes with disability provisions**
sp means **spring**, March through May
S means **Summer**, June through August
F means **Fall**, September through November
W means **Winter**, December through February
T means **Two** (2) or **Three** (3) Seasons
A means **All Four** (4) Seasons
na means **Not Applicable or Not Available**
Note: empty or blank spaces in the chart mean **NO**
(If a symbol number has a star ★ that symbol is not shown on the map.)

FACILITIES, SERVICES, RECREATION OPPORTUNITIES & CONVENIENCES

S#	MAP	LOCATION NAME (state initials if more than one) with ADDRESS and/or LOCATION DATA	TELEPHONE	ACRES / ELEVATION
		Wayne-Hoosier Nat'l. Forests Sup., 811 Constitution Ave., Bedford, IN 47421	812-275-5987	413,798 / na
1	C3	Athens Ranger D., 219 Columbus Rd., Athens 45701	614-592-6644	113,823 / na
2	C3	Athens Ranger D. Sub-Unit, Rt. #1 Box 132, Marietta 45750	614-373-9055	na / na
3	D2	Ironton Ranger D., RR #2, Box 203, Pedro 45659	614-533-0383	86,074 / na
		COE, Huntington District, 502 8th St., Huntington, WV 25701	304-529-5607	na / na
1	C2	Alum Creek Lake, PO Box 31, Lewis Center 43035	614-548-6151	na / na
2	B3	Atwood Lake, RFD #1, Box 417, Mineral City 44656	216-343-5611	na / na
3	B3	Beach City Lake, Rt. #1, Box 103, Beach City 44608	216-878-7391	na / na
4	D3	Belleville Locks & Dam (Ohio River), Rt. #1, Box 13A, Reedsville 45772	304-863-6331	na / na
5	B3	Bolivar Dam, 1201 Boivar Dam Road, Bolivar 44612	216-874-2121	na / na
6	D1	Capt Anthony Meldahl Locks & Dam, 2443 US Hwy. 52, Felicity 45120	513-876-2921	na / na
7	B3	Charles Mill Lake, 22C3 SR 603, Lucas 44843	419-368-4334	na / na
8	B3	Clendening Lake, PO Box 116, Tippecanoe 44699	614-658-3743	na / na
9	C2	Deer Creek Lake, 21879 Deer Creek Rd., Mt. Sterling 43143	614-869-2243	na / na
10	B2	Delaware Lake, 3920 US Hwy. 23 North, Delaware 43015	614-363-4011	na / na
11	C3	Dillon Lake, 4969 Dillon Dam Rd., Zanesville 43701	614-454-2225	na / na
12	B3	Dover Dam, RR #3, Box 55, Dover 44622	216-343-5725	na / na
13	B3	Leesville Lake, 5037 Deer Road SW, Bowerston 44695	614-269-2131	na / na
14	B3	Mohawk Dam, 36007 SR 715, Warsaw 43844	614-824-4343	na / na
15	B3	Mohicanville Dam, 2297 County Road 175, Lakeville 44638	419-368-4712	na / na
16	B2	North Branch Kokosing River Lake, 36007 SR 715, Warsaw 43844	614-824-4343	na / na
17	C2	Paint Creek Lake, 504 Reservior Road, Bainbridge 45612	513-365-1470	na / na
18	B3	Piedmont Lake, Rt. #1, Piedmont 43983	614-966-4440	na / na
19	B3	Pleasant Hill Lake, 1(041 County Road 3006, Perrysville 44864	419-938-5785	na / na
20	C3	Senecaville Lake, 57005 Senecaville Drive, Senecaville 43780	614-685-5565	na / na
21	B3	Tappan Lake, 86801 Eslick Rd., Uhrichsville 44683	614-269-2681	na / na
22	C3	Tom Jenkins Dam & Burr Oak Lake, 23560 Jenkins Dam Road, Glouster 45732	614-767-3527	na / na
23	C3	Willow Island Locks & Dam (Ohio Riv, Route 1, Newport 45768	614-374-8710	na / na
24	C3	Wills Creek Lake, 49320 CR 497, Coshocton 43812	614-829-2425	na / na
		COE, Louisville District, PO Box 59, Louisville, KY 40201	502-582-6292	na / na
25	C1	Caesar Creek Lake, 4020 N. Clarksville Rd., Waynesville 45068	513-897-1050	na / na
26	C1	Clarence J. Brown Dam & Reservoir, 2630 Croft Rd., Springfield 45503	513-325-2411	na / na
27	D1	West Fork Mill Creek Lake, 10558 Mckelvey Road, Cincinnati 45240	513-897-1050	na / na
28	D1	William H. Harsha Lake, 2185 Sade Road, Batavia 45103	513-797-6081	na / na
		COE, Pittsburgh District, 1000 Liberty Ave., Pittsburgh, PA 15222	412-644-4191	na / na
29	B4	Berlin Lake, 7400 Bedell Road, Berlin Center 44401	216-547-3781	na / na
30	C4	Hannibal Locks & Dam (Ohio River), PO Box 8, Hannibal 43931	614-483-2305	na / na
31	B3	Michael J. Kirwan Dam & Reservoir, PO Box 58, Wayland 44285	216-359-2622	na / na
32	A4	Mosquito Creek Lake, 2961B Warren-Mead Rd., Cortland 44410	216-637-1961	na / na
33	B4	New Cumberland Locks & Dam (Ohio Ri, PO Box 158, Stratton 43961	614-537-2571	na / na
1	A2	**Ottawa NWR**, 14000 W. State Route 2, Oak Harbor 43449 [see USFWS chapter note]	419-898-0014	5,790 / 580
1	A3	**Cuyahoga Valley Natl. Rec. Area**, 15610 Vaughn Road, Brecksville 44141	216-650-4636	32,460 / 660-1,160
2		Mound City Group Natl. Monument, 16062 State Route 104, Chillicothe 45601	614-774-1125	270 / 650
1		**BLM - Ohio Wild Horse & Burro Adopt. Ctr.**, 4420 State Rd., London 43140 [4 mi. E of London on Hwy. 66E]	614-852-0095	na / na
1	C2	**OH DNR, Div. Parks & Recreation**, 1952 Belcher Dr., Bldg. C-1, Columbus 43224	614-265-7000	na / na
2	B2	Alum Creek SP, 3615 S. Old State Rd., Delaware 43015	614-548-4631	8,600 / na
3	C4	Barkcamp SP, 65330 Barkcamp Park Fd., Belmont 43718	614-484-4064	1,232 / na
4	C3	Blue Rock SP, 7924 Cutler Lake Rd., Blue Rock 43720	614-674-4794	350 / na
5	C3	Burr Oak SP, Rt. #2, Box 286, Glouster 45732	614-767-2112	3,256 / na
6	D1	East Fork SP, Box 119, Bethel 45106	513-734-4323	10,580 / na

★ INFORMATION CHART ★

INFORMATION CHART LEGEND - SYMBOLS & LETTER CODES

- ■ means **YES** & □ means **Yes** with disability provisions
- **sp** means **spring**, March through May
- **S** means **Summer**, June through August
- **F** means **Fall**, September through November
- **W** means **Winter**, December through February
- **T** means **Two** (2) or **Three** (3) Seasons
- **A** means **All Four** (4) Seasons
- **na** means Not Applicable or Not Available

Note: empty or blank spaces in the chart mean **NO**

Note: Refer to yellow block on page 7 (top right) for location name and address abbreviations. If a symbol number has a star ★ that symbol is not shown on the map.

AGENCY/MAP LEGEND . . . INITIALS, MAP SYMBOLS, COLOR CODES

- U.S. Forest Service Supervisor & Ranger Dist. Offices . . NFS ⬟61
- U.S. Army Corps of Engineers Rec. Areas & Offices . . COE ⬟31
- USFWS National Wildlife Refuges & Offices . . . . NWR ⬟40
- National Park Service Parks & other NPS Sites . . . . . . NPS ⬟7
- Bureau of Land Management Rec. Areas & Offices . . . BLM ⬟26
- Bureau of Reclamation Rec. Areas & Reg. Offices . . . BOR ⬟8
- State Parks (also see State Agency notes) . . . . SPS ⬟52
- State Wildlife Areas (also see State Agency notes) . . SWA ⬟19
- Private Preserves, Nature Centers & Tribal Lands .
- The Wild Rivers ⁓ and Wilderness Areas ⬟15

S#	MAP	LOCATION NAME (state initials if more than one) with ADDRESS and/or LOCATION DATA	TELEPHONE	ACRES / ELEVATION	S#
7	D3	Forked Run SP, PO Box 127, Reedsville 45772	614-378-6206	817 / na	7
8	B4	Guilford Lake SP, 6835 E Lake Rd., Lisbon 44432	216-222-1712	488 / na	8
9	C2	Hocking Hills SP, 20160 SR 664, Logan 43138	614-385-6841	2,348 / na	9
10	B1	Indian Lake SP, 7490 Edgewater Ave., Huntsville 43324	513-843-2098	6,448 / na	10
11	A2	Kelleys Island SP, 4049 E Moores Dock Rd., Port Clinton 43452	419-746-2546	661 / na	11
12	B1	Lake Loramie SP, 11221 SR 362, Minster 45865	513-295-2011	2,055 / na	12
13	B2	Mount Gilead SP, 4119 SR 95, Mt. Gilead 43338	419-946-1961	172 / na	13
14	C3	Muskingum R Pkwy., PO Box 2806, Zanesville 43701	614-452-3820	120 / na	14
15	C2	Paint Creek SP, 14265 US Hwy. 50, Bainbridge 45612	513-365-1401	10,200 / na	15
16	A4	Pymatuning SP (cabin res. call 293-, PO Box 1000, Andover 44003	216-293-6030	17,500 / na	16
17	D2	Shawnee SP, Star Route, Box 68, Portsmouth 45662	614-858-4561	1,168 / na	17
1	C2	**DNR, Division of Wildlife,** 1840 Belcher Rd., Bldg. G, Columbus 43224	614-265-6305	na / na	1
2	A3	Auburn Marsh WA, N off U.S. 422 at, Auburn Corners	216-644-2293	461 / 1,240	2
3	A1	Beaver Creek WA, on Twp. Rd. 41, 4 mi. N of Bryan	419-424-5000	150 / na	3
4	B3	Berlin Lake WA, N of Alliance	216-644-2293	8,518 / 1,040	4
5	B2	Big Island WA, 5 mi. W of Marion	614-481-6300	1,904 / na	5
6	A2	Brush Creek WA, E of Monroeville	216-644-2293	2,546 / 800-1,200	6
7	C1	Ceasar Creek SP & Wildlife Area, SR 73, 4.5 mi. E of Waynesville	513-372-9261	9,390 / na	7
8	D2	Cooper Hollow WA, 11 mi. SE of Jackson	614-594-2211	4,775 / na	8
9	C1	Darke WA, on SR 36, 6 mi. E of Greenville	513-372-9261	317 / na	9
10	C1	Fallsville WA, on SR 73, 3 mi. SE of New Vienna	513-372-9261	1,212 / na	10
11	C3	Fox Lake WA, on Baker Rd. W of Athens	614-594-2211	421 / na	11
12	A4	Grand River WA, 1 mi. N of SR 88 & 534 near West Farmington	216-889-3280	6,296 / 820	12
13	A3	Hambden Orchard WA, 3 mi. S of Hambden	216-644-2293	841 / 1,240	13
14	B4	Highlandtown WA, NW of Highlandtown	216-679-2201	2,206 / 1,070	14
15	D1	Indian Creek WA, 1 mi. E of Fayetteville	513-372-9261	1,691 / na	15
16	B3	Killbuck Marsh WA, E of Shreve	216-567-3390	5,306 / 900	16
17	B2	Killdear Plains WA, S of SR 294, 2 mi. SW of Harpster	614-424-5000	8,626 / na	17
18	B2	Kokosing Lake WA, 3 mi. NW of Fredericktown	614-481-6300	1,354 / na	18
19	A1	Lake La Su An WA, 3 mi. N of US 20 near Nettle Lake	419-424-5000	1,161 / na	19
20	D2	Liberty WA, 8 mi. NW of Jackson	614-594-2211	145 / na	20
21	A2	Little Portage WA, off SR 53 on Co. Rd. 12, 5 mi. W of Port Clinton	419-424-5000	357 / na	21
22	A2	Magee Marsh WA, 17 mi. W of Port Clinton	419-898-0960	1,821 / na	22
23	B1	Mercer WA, US 127 & SR 703, S of Celina	513-372-9261	358 / na	23
24	A2	Metzger Marsh WA, on SR 2, 1 mi. E of Bono	419-424-5000	558 / na	24
25	A2	Milan WA, on SR 113, 3 mi. W of Milan	419-424-5000	296 / na	25
26	B3	Mohican River WA, 4 mi. NW of Walhonding	614-594-2211	409 / na	26
27	C3	Monroe Lake WA, 5 mi. N of Woodsfield	614-594-2211	1,333 / na	27
28	A4	Mosquito Creek WA, near Mecca	216-685-4776	9,515 / 910	28
29	A4	New Lyme WA, 1 mi. E of New Lyme	216-644-2293	5,295 / 940	29
30	C2	Oldaker WA, 6 mi. W of Hillsboro	513-372-9261	140 / na	30
31	A4	Orwell WA, 2 mi. N of Orwell	216-644-2293	197 / 930	31
32	A1	Oxbow Lake WA, on SR 15, 8 mi. NW of Defiance	419-424-5000	416 / na	32
33	D2	Paint Creek SP & WA, 17 mi. E of Hillsboro	513-372-9261	11,969 / na	33
34	C2	Pleasant Valley WA, 3 mi. NW of Chillicothe	614-481-6300	1,465 / na	34
35	C3	Powelson WA, 7 mi. N of Zanesville	614-594-2211	2,774 / na	35
36	A2	Resthaven WA, off SR 269, Castalia 44824	419-424-5000	2,275 / na	36
37	D2	Ross Lake WA, 3.5 mi. E of Chillicothe	614-594-2211	1,112 / na	37
38	C1	Rush Run WA, 4 mi. SE of Camden	513-372-9261	1,174 / na	38

Ohio (continued)

S#	MAP	Name & Location	Phone	Acres / na
41	B3	Shreve Lake WA, 1 mi. W of Shreve	216-644-2293	228 / 98C
42	B3	Spencer Lake WA, 2 mi. E of Spencer	216-648-2621	618 / 85C
43	C1	Spring Valley WA, 2 mi. S of Spring Valley	513-372-9261	841 / na
44	C3	Sunday Creek WA, near Glouster	614-594-2211	17,967 / na
45	A2	Toussaint WA, 2 mi. S of SR 2 on 19 toward, Oak Harbor	419-424-5000	236 / na
46	D2	Tranquility WA, NE of Tranquility	513-372-9261	3,820 / na
47	C3	Trimble WA, W of Glouster	614-594-2211	2,096 / na
48	D3	Tycoon Lake WA, NE of Rio Grande	614-594-2211	767 / na
49	C3	Waterloo WA, 10 mi. W of Athens	614-594-2211	1,361 / na
50	B3	Wellington WA, 3 mi. S of Wellington	216-644-2293	2,011 / 910
51	D2	Wellston WA, 4 mi. S of McArthur	614-594-2211	1,298 / na
52	B2	Willard Marsh WA, 1.5 mi. W of Celeryville	419-424-5000	1,676 / na
53	A2	Willow Point WA, 5 mi. NW of Castaia	419-424-5000	621 / na
54	C3	Wolf Creek WA, 7 mi. SW of McConnelsville	614-594-2211	3,703 / na
55	B3	Woodbury WA, 4 mi. S of Warsaw	614-594-2211	7,882 / na
56	B2	Wyandot WA, 1 mi. S of Carey	419-424-5000	339 / na
57	B4	Zepernick Lake WA, 2 mi. E of New Alexander	216-544-2293	518 / 1,240
1	C1	Aullwood Audubon Center & Farm, 1000 Aullwood Road, Dayton 45414	513-390-7360	200 / 936
2	C2	TNC Ohio Field Office, 1504 West 1st Avenue, Columbus 43212	614-486-4194	na / na
3	B3	Browns Lake Bog Preserve, contact Field Office, near Shreve	614-486-4194	80 / 940-980
4	D2	Buzzardroost Rock Preserve, contact Field Office, near Lynx	614-486-4194	526 / 800-1,000
5	A3	J. Arthur Herrick Fen Preserve, contact Field Office, near Streetsboro	614-486-4194	126 / 1,030-1,080
6	D2	Lynx Prairie Preserve, contact Field Office, near Lynx	614-486-4194	200 / 760-860

OKLAHOMA NOTES

Summary

There are 50 federal, 62 state, and 14 private recreation areas or local administrative offices covered in this state chapter. Of these, 51 appear in the Information Chart and 75 are covered in the notes. The special indexes feature 2 federally designated wilderness areas and wild rivers, and one agency published outdoor maps.

Federal Agencies

U.S. Forest Service

Eastern Oklahoma is in the Southern Region, see Georgia chapter - U.S. Forest Service. Western Oklahoma is in the Southwestern Region (see New Mexico chapter.

Bureau of Reclamation Recreation Areas

Seven recreation areas are listed here and symbolized on the Oklahoma state map.

S#	MAP	LOCATION NAME
1	B3	Altus Res.
2	B4	Chickasaw Natl. Recreation Area
3	B4	Fort Cobb Res.
4	B3	Foss Res.
5	B4	Lake Thunderbird
6	C5	McGee Creek Dam
7	B3	Tom Steed Res.

Wilderness Index

Wichita Mountains NWR (S# 7, map B3)
Wichita Mountains Wilderness,
Charon Gardens Unit - 5,723 acres, and
North Mountain Unit - 2,847 acres

Outdoor Map Index

U.S. Forest Service Map

Ouachita National Forest [1987]

State Agencies

OK Tourism, Division of State Parks

An Oklahoma State Parks Guide (32 state parks) is available free. The guide describes each area, contains a locator map, and includes information on facilities and activities. There is no entry fee for most parks. Selected state parks with their map symbol numbers and coordinates, the park name and location are listed here.

S#	MAP	NAME & LOCATION
2	B5	Arrowhead SP, Canadian
3	A2	Beavers Bend SP, Beaver
4	B5	Greenleaf SP, Braggs
5	C5	Hochatown SP, Broken Bow
6	C4	Lake Murray SP, Ardmore
7	B4	Little River SP, Norman
8	B3	Quartz Mountain SP, Lone Wolf
9	B3	Red Rock Canyon SP, Hinton
10	B5	Robbers Cave SP, Wilburton
11	A5	Sequoyah SP, Wagoner

Department of Agriculture

Forestry Division
2800 N. Lincoln Blvd.
Oklahoma City, OK 73105   405-521-3864
There is no state forest recreation program in Oklahoma.

OK Department of Wildlife Conservation

An extensive list of publications is available on request. The hunting regulations contain a list of lands open to the public for hunting. The name and location of selected WMAs, their map symbol numbers and coordinates, are listed here.

S#	MAP	NAME & LOCATION
2	B3	Altus-Lugert WMA, Granite
3	E4	Arbuckle WMA, Atoka
4	E4	Atoka WMA, Atoka
5	B2	Black Kettle (112 units), Cheyenne
6	C4	Blue River WMA, Tishomingo
7	B5	Bolen Hollow WMA, Hartshorne
8	C5	Broken Bow WMA, Broken Bow
9	A3	Canton WMA, Canton
10	A5	Chouteau WMA, Wagoner
11	B5	Cookson WMA, Cookson
12	A4	Copan WMA, Copan
13	A2	Ellis WMA, Arnett
14	B5	Eufaula WMA (5 areas), Muskogee
15	C4	Fobb Bottom WMA (several areas), Ardmore
16	B2	Fort Cobb WMA, Fort Cobb
17	A5	Fort Gibson WMA (many areas), Wagoner
18	A2	Fort Supply WMA (many areas), Fort Supply
19	B5	Gruber/Cherokee WMA, Muskogee
20	A4	Heyburn WMA, Bristow
21	C4	Hickory Creek WMA, Marietta
22	C5	Hugo WMA, Hugo
23	A4	Hula WMA, Bartlesville-
24	A4	Kaw WMA, Ponca City
25	A4	Keystone WMA, Foraker
26	A1	Lake Etling WMA, Guymon
27	B4	Lexington WMA, Lexington
28	C4	Love Valley WMA, Thackerville
29	B5	McGee Creek WMA, Stringtown
30	B3	Mountain Park WMA, Roosevelt
31	B4	Okmulgee WMA, Okmulgee
32	A5	Oologah WMA, Nowata
33	A2	Optima WMA, Hardesty
34	A4	Osage WMA, Foraker
35	B5	Ouachita WMA, Talihina
36	C5	Pine Creek WMA, Wright City
37	B5	Pushmataha WMA, Clayton
38	A1	Rita Blanca WMA, Boise City
39	B5	Robbers Cave WMA, Wilburton
40	B5	Robert S. Kerr WMA (several areas), Vian
41	A5	Spavinaw WMA, Spavinaw
42	B5	Tenkiller WMA (several areas), Braggs
43	C5	Tiak WMA (several areas), Haworth
44	C4	Tishomingo WMA, Tishomingo
45	B3	Washita WMA, Clinton
46	C4	Washita Arm WMA, Tishomingo
47	C3	Waurika WMA, Waurika
48	B5	Webbers Falls WMA, Muskogee
49	B5	Wister WMA, Heavener

Tourism & Recreation Department

500 Will Rogers Bldg.
Oklahoma City, OK 73105   405-521-2464

A variety of vacation, attraction, and special events literature is available. The Oklahoma Vacation Guide provides information on accommodations, all types of recreational areas, campgrounds, and tours. An official road map is also available with symbols for public launching boat ramps, recreational areas, state parks, public hunting areas, and national wildlife refuges. Forest, preserve, and wilderness areas are shown in green.

Private Organizations

ANCA Locations in Oklahoma

Martin Park Nature Center (S# 9, map B4)
5000 West Memorial Road
Oklahoma City, OK 73142   405-755-0676

Oxley Nature Center (S# 10, map A5)
5701 East 36th Street North
Tulsa, OK 74115   918-832-8112

Three Forks Nature Center (S# 11, map A5)
Route 1, Box 2100
Hulbert, OK 74441   918-772-2108

Travertine Nature Center (S# 12, map B4)
PO Box 201
Sulphur, OK 73086-0201   405-622-3165

Tucker Tower Nature Center (S# 13, map C4)
PO Box 1649
Ardmore, OK 73402-1649   405-223-2109

Tribal Land Areas in Oklahoma

Cherokee Nation of Oklahoma - Touring.
Cherokee Nation of Oklahoma (S# 7, map A5)
PO Box 948
Tahlequah, OK 74465   918-456-0671

Citizens Band Potawatomi Indian Tribe of Oklahoma - Camping, touring.
Citizens Band Potawatomi Business Committee
(S# 8, map B4)
901 S. Gordon Cooper Drive
Shawnee, OK 74801   405-275-3121

Oklahoma Chamber of Commerce

4020 N. Lincoln Blvd.
Oklahoma City, OK 73105   Phone 405-424-4003   Fax 405-424-3137

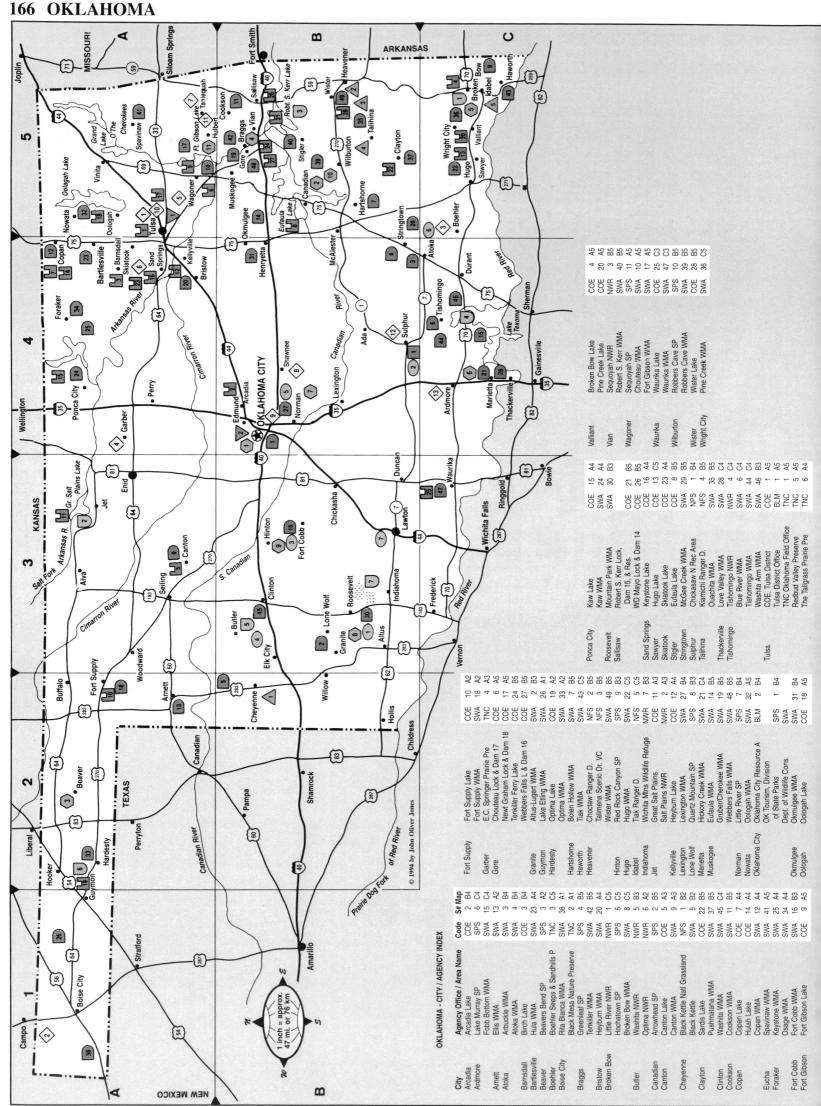

OKLAHOMA - CITY / AGENCY INDEX

© 1994 by John Oliver Jones

1 inch = approx.
47 mi. or 76 km

Legend

U.S. Forest Service Supervisor & Ranger Dist. Offices . . NFS (61)
U.S. Army Corps of Engineers Rec. Areas & Offices . . COE (31)
USFWS National Wildlife Refuges & Offices . . . . NWR (40)
National Park Service Parks & other NPS Sites . . . . . . NPS (7)
Bureau of Land Management Rec. Areas & Offices . . . BLM (26)
Bureau of Reclamation Rec. Areas & Reg. Offices . . . BOR (8)
State Parks (also see State Agency notes) . . . . SPS (52)
State Wildlife Areas (also see State Agency notes) . . SWA (19)
Private Preserves, Nature Centers & Tribal Lands
The Wild Rivers ~~~ and Wilderness Areas ▒▒▒

INFORMATION CHART LEGEND - SYMBOLS & LETTER CODES
- ■ means **YES** & □ means **Yes with disability provisions**
- **sp** means spring, March through May
- **S** means Summer, June through August
- **F** means Fall, September through November
- **W** means Winter, December through February
- **T** means Two (2) or Three (3) Seasons
- **A** means All Four (4) Seasons
- **na** means Not Applicable or Not Available
- Note: empty or blank spaces in the chart mean **NO**

Column category groups (left to right): INFO OFFICE (IO) / VISITOR CENTER (VC); FACILITIES, SERVICES, RECREATION OPPORTUNITIES & CONVENIENCES.

Note: Refer to yellow block on page 1 (top right) for location name and address abbreviations. If a symbol number has a star ★ that symbol is not shown on the map.

Location Data

S#	MAP	LOCATION NAME (state initials if more than one) with ADDRESS and/or LOCATION DATA	TELEPHONE	ACRES / ELEVATION
		Cibola Nat'l. Forest Sup., 2113 Osuna Rd. NE. #A, Albuquerque, NM 87113	505-761-4650	1,886,000 / 2,000-11,300
1	B2	Black Kettle National Grasslands, Rt. #1, Box 55B, Cheyenne 73628	405-497-2143	33,000 / 2,000-2,900
2	B5	Ouachita National Forest Sup., PO Box 1270, Hot Springs, AR 71902	501-321-5202	1,613,120 / 540-2,660
3	B5	Choctaw Ranger D. (see chapter note), HC 64, Box 3467, Heavener 74937 [1 mi S of Heavener, W side of Hwy. 259]	918-653-2991	97,400 / 540-2,666
		Talimena Scenic Drive VC, c/o Choctaw RD, HC 64, Box 3467, Heavener 74937 [at Hwy 1 & 271 intersection]	918-653-2991	2 / 1,300
4	B5	Kiamichi Ranger D., PO Box 577, Talihina 74571 [0.5 mi E of Talihina on Hwy 63]	918-567-2326	110,000 / 500-2,034
5	C5	Tiak Ranger D., 201 N. Central, PO Box 389, Idabel 74745	405-286-6564	43,000 / 520
		COE, Tulsa District, PO Box 61, Tulsa 74121	918-581-7349	
1	A5	Arcadia Lake, PO Box 192, Arcadia 73007	405-396-8026	na / na
2	B4	Birch Lake, RR #1, Box 721, Barnsdall 74002	405-847-2001	na / na
3	B4	Broken Bow Lake, Route 1, Box 400, Valliant 74764	405-933-4239	na / na
4	A5	Canton Lake, PO Box 69, Canton 73724	405-886-2989	na / na
5	A3	Chouteau Lock & Dam 17, Route 2, Box 21, Gore 74435	918-489-5541	na / na
6	A5	Copan Lake, Route 1, Box 260, Copan 74022	918-532-4334	na / na
7	A4	Eufaula Lake, Route 4, Box 5500, Stigler 74462	918-484-5135	na / na
8	B5	Fort Gibson Lake, PO Box 370, Fort Gibson 74434	918-682-4314	na / na
9	A5	Fort Supply Lake, PO Box 248, Fort Supply 73841	405-766-2701	na / na
10	A2	Great Salt Plains, Route 1, Box 27, Jet 73749	405-626-4741	na / na
11	A2	Heyburn Lake, Route 2, Box 140, Kellyville 74039	918-247-6391	na / na
12	A3	Hugo Lake, PO Box 99, Sawyer 74756	405-326-3345	na / na
13	C5	Hulah Lake, Route 1, Box 260, Copan 74022	918-532-4334	na / na
14	A4	Kaw Lake, RR #2, Box 500, Ponca City 74601	405-762-5611	na / na
15	A4	Keystone Lake, Route 1, Box 100, Sand Springs 74063	918-865-2621	na / na
16	A4	Newt Graham Lock & Dam 18, Route 2, Box 21, Gore 74435	918-489-5541	na / na
17	A5	Oologah Lake, Route 1, Box 1610, Oologah 74053	918-443-2250	na / na
18	A5	Optima Lake, PO Box 30, Hardesty 73944	405-888-4226	na / na
19	A2	Pine Creek Lake, Route 1, Box 400, Valliant 74764	405-933-4239	na / na
20	A2	Robert S. Kerr Lock, Dam 15, & Res., HC 61, Box 238, Sallisaw 74955	918-775-4474	na / na
21	B5	Sardis Lake, PO Box 129, Clayton 74536	918-569-4131	na / na
22	A2	Skiatook Lake, HC 57, Box 135, Skiatook 74070	918-396-3170	na / na
23	A4	Tenkiller Ferry Lake, Route 1, Box 259, Gore 74435	918-487-5252	na / na
24	B5	Waurika Lake, PO Box 29, Waurika 73573	405-963-2111	na / na
25	C3	WD Mayo Lock & Dam 14, HC 61, Box 238, Sallisaw 74955	918-775-4474	na / na
26	A4	Webbers Falls Lock & Dam 16, Route 2, Box 21, Gore 74435	918-489-5541	na / na
27	A4	Wister Lake, Route 2, Box 7B, Wister 74966	918-655-7206	na / na
28	B5			
1	C5	**Little River NWR**, 635 S Park St (office), PO Box 340, Broken Bow 74728 [4.5 mi W from town on US 70 to NWR]	405-584-6211	11,237 / 320-370
2	A3	Salt Plains NWR, Rt. #1, Box 76, Jet 73749 [2 mi S, 1 mi W of jct. SRs 11 & 38]	405-626-4794	32,030 / 1,125-1,165
3	B5	Sequoyah NWR, Rt. #1, Box 18A, Vian 74962 [3 mi. S of Vian]	918-773-5251	20,800 / 460-500
4	C4	Tishomingo NWR, Rt. #1, Box 151, Tishomingo 73460	405-371-2402	16,464 / 620-680
5	B3	Washita NWR, Rt. #1, Box 68, Butler 73625 [15 mi N of Elk City on Hwy, 34, then 6 mi E on Hwy. 33]	405-664-2205	8,200 / 1,650
6	A2	Optima NWR, Rt. #1, Box 68, Butler 73625 [near Guymon]	405-664-2205	4,330 / 2,770
7	B3	Wichita Mountains Wildlife Refuge. Rt. #1, Box 448, Indiahoma 73552 [Hwy. 62 to Indiahoma & follow signs]	405-429-3222	59,020 / 1,350-2,479
1	B4	**Chickasaw National Recreation Area**, PO Box 201, Sulphur 73086	405-622-3165	9,522 / 1,000
		BLM New Mexico State Office, 1474 Rodeo Drive, Santa Fe, NM 87505	505-988-6227	na / na
1	B4	Tulsa District Office, 9522-H East 47th Place, Tulsa 74145	918-561-6480	na / na
2	B4	Oklahoma City Resource Area, 200 NW Fifth, RM. 548, Oklahoma City 73102	405-231-5491	na / na
		OK Tourism, Div. of State Parks, 500 Will Rogers Bldg., 2424 N. Lincoln, Oklahoma City 73105	405-521-3411	na / na
1	B3	**Dept. of Wildlife Conservation**, 1801 N. Lincoln, PO Box 53465, Oklahoma City 73105 [see notes]	405-521-2739	na / na
1	A5	**TNC Oklahoma Field Office**, 320 South Boston, Suite 1222, Tulsa 74103	918-585-1117	na / na
2	A1	Black Mesa Nature Preserve, contact Black Mesa State Park, NW of Boise City	405-426-2222	1,500 / 4,000

AGENCY/MAP LEGEND . . . INITIALS, MAP SYMBOLS, COLOR CODES

U.S. Forest Service Supervisor & Ranger Dist. Offices NFS
U.S. Army Corps of Engineers Rec. Areas & Offices . COE
USFWS National Wildlife Refuges & Offices . . . . NWR
National Park Service Parks & other NPS Sites . . . . . NPS
Bureau of Land Management Rec. Areas & Offices . . BLM
Bureau of Reclamation Rec. Areas & Reg. Offices . . . BOR
State Parks (also see State Agency notes) . . . . SPS
State Wildlife Areas (also see State Agency notes) . . SWA
Private Preserves, Nature Centers & Tribal Lands . .
The Wild Rivers and Wilderness Areas

★ INFORMATION CHART ★

INFORMATION CHART LEGEND - SYMBOLS & LETTER CODES

- ■ means **YES** & □ means **Yes with disability provisions**
- **sp** means **sp**ring, March through May
- **S** means **S**ummer, June through August
- **F** means **F**all, September through November
- **W** means **W**inter, December through February
- **T** means **T**wo (2) or Three (3) Seasons
- **A** means **A**ll Four (4) Seasons
- **na** means Not Applicable or Not Available

Note: empty or blank spaces in the chart mean **NO**

Note: Refer to yellow block on page 7 (top right) for location name and address abbreviations. If a symbol number has a star ★ that symbol is not shown on the map.

S#	MAP	LOCATION NAME (state initials if more than one) with ADDRESS and/or LOCATION DATA	TELEPHONE	ACRES / ELEVATION	INFO OFFICE (IO) / VISITOR CENTER (VC)	IO / VC OPEN SATURDAY / SUNDAY	ENTRY FEE, not camping or permit fee	CONCESSIONAIRE SERVICES AVAILABLE	INTERPRETIVE or EDUCATIONAL DISPLAY	FREE LITERATURE, brochures, maps, etc.	AGENCY GUIDED TOURS, scheduled / by res.	NATURE EDUCATION / STUDY PROGRAMS	WILDFLOWER VIEWING AREA or DRIVE	ARCHAEOLOGICAL / GEOLOGICAL SITES	HISTORIC SITES	INTERPRETIVE TRAILS	WILDLIFE IS ABUNDANT OR COMMON	ENDANGERED SPECIES ARE COMMON	WILDLIFE VIEWING SITES, blinds, signs, etc.	DEVELOPED PICNIC AREAS / PICNIC SITES	DEVELOPED CAMPGROUNDS / CAMPSITES	NO-CHARGE CAMPGROUNDS / CAMPSITES	WILDERNESS AREAS / WILD RIVERS	WALKING / HIKING TRAILS	SWIMMING PERMITTED, at one's own risk	BICYCLING OPPORTUNITIES...areas, trails	HORSEBACK RIDING, w/ your own horse	OFF-ROAD Motorized Vehicle Area / Use OK	FISHING IN SEASON, license / permit reqd.	BOATING FACILITIES, ramps, marinas, etc.	MOTORIZED WATERCRAFT OK, check limits	NON-MOTORIZED WATERCRAFT OK	HUNTING IN SEASON, license / permit reqd.	WINTER SPORTS OPPORTUNITIES	PARK & WALK-IN ONLY AREA	DAY USE ONLY, no overnight	DRINKING WATER	RESTROOMS	S#
3	C5	Boehler Seeps & Sandhills Preserve, contact Field Office, near Boehler	918-585-1117	77 / 550																															■	■			3
4	A3	E.C. Springer Prairie Preserve, contact Field Office, near Garber	918-585-1117	40 / 1,100																															■	■			4
5	A5	Redbud Valley Preserve, Oxley Nature Center, near Tulsa	918-832-8117	82 / 650						■														■											■	■			5
6	A4	The Tallgrass Prairie Preserve, contact Field Office, NW of Tulsa	918-585-1117	na / na	■					■					■					■																■			6

OREGON - CITY / AGENCY INDEX

City	Agency Office / Area Name	Code	S#	Map
Alsea	Alsea Ranger D.	NFS	44	B1
Ashland	Ashland Ranger District	NFS	34	D2
	Hyatt-Howard Prairie L. SRA	BLM	25	D2
Baker City	Wallowa-Whitman N Forest	NFS	58	B4
	Baker Ranger D.	NFS	59	B4
	Baker Resource Area	BLM	51	B4
Bandon	Bandon Marsh NWR	NWR	11	C1
	Bullards Beach SP	SPS	2	C1
Bend	Deschutes Nat'l. Forest	NFS	2	C3
	Bend Ranger D.	NFS	3	C3
	Fort Rock Ranger D.	NFS	5	C3
	Region 3, Central	SWA	4	D3
Biggs	Deschutes River SRA	BLM	34	A3
Blue River	Blue River Ranger D.	NFS	67	B2
Bly	Bly Ranger District	NFS	8	D3
Boardman	Willow Creek Wildlife Area	SWA	21	A3
Brookings	Chetco Ranger D.	NFS	38	D1
Butte Falls	Butte Falls Ranger District	NFS	35	D2
Cascade Locks	Bonneville Lock, Dam & L.	COE	3	A2
Cave Junction	Illinois Valley Ranger D.	NFS	41	D1
	Oregon Caves National Mon.	NPS	3	D1
Central Point	Denman Wildlife Area	SWA	11	D2
Chemult	Chemult Ranger D.	NFS	75	C2
Chiloquin	Chiloquin Ranger D.	NFS	76	D2
Clackamas	Region 7, Columbia	SWA	8	B2
Coos Bay	Coos Bay Shorelands SRA	BLM	7	C1
	Sunset Bay SP	SPS	9	C1
Corbett	Memaloose SP	SPS	6	A3
Corvallis	Siuslaw Nat'l. Forest	NFS	43	B2
	William L. Finley NWR & W. Oregon RC	NWR	8	B2
	Region 1, Northwest	SWA	2	B2
Cottage Grove	Cottage Grove Ranger D.	NFS	54	C2
Crater Lake	Crater Lake National Park	NPS	1	C2
Crescent	Crescent Ranger D.	NFS	4	C2
Culver	The Cove Palisades SP	SPS	10	B3
Dallas	Baskett Slough NWR	NWR	10	B1
Dayville	Murderers Creek Wildlife A	SWA	19	B3
Dufur	Barlow Ranger D.	NFS	18	A3
Enterprise	Eagle Cap Ranger D.	NFS	60	A5
	Hells Canyon National Recreation Area HQ & VC	NFS	60	A5
	Wallowa Valley Ranger	NFS	65	A5
	Wenaha Wildlife Area	SWA	20	A5
Estacada	Clackamas RD & Ripplebrook RS	NFS	20	B2
	Estacada Ranger D.	NFS	23	B2
Eugene	Willamette National Forest	NFS	66	B2
	Eugene District Office	BLM	13	B2
	Coast Range Resource Area	BLM	★14	B2
	McKenzie Resource Area	BLM	★15	B2
	South Valley Resource Area	BLM	★17	B2
	Fern Ridge Wildlife Area	SWA	10	C2
Florence	Jessie M. Honeyman SP	SPS	4	C1
Frenchglen	Steens Mountain SRA	BLM	4	C4
Glide	North Umpqua Ranger D.	NFS	56	C2
Gold Beach	Gold Beach Ranger D.	NFS	40	D1
Grants Pass	Siskiyou National Forest	NFS	37	D1
	Galice Ranger D.	NFS	39	D1
Gresham	Mt. Hood National Forest	NFS	17	A2
Halfway	Pine Ranger D.	NFS	63	B5
Hammond	Fort Stevens SP	SPS	3	A1
Hebo	Hebo Ranger D.	NFS	46	B1
Heppner	Heppner Ranger D.	NFS	51	B3
Hines	Burns Ranger D.	NFS	14	C4
	Snow Mountain Ranger D.	NFS	31	C4
	Burns District Office	BLM	2	C4
	Andrews Resource Area	BLM	3	C4
	Three Rivers Resource Area	BLM	★5	C4
	Region 5, Southeast	SWA	6	C4
Hood River	Columbia River Gorge NSA	NFS	22	A2
Idleyld Park	Diamond Lake Ranger D.	NFS	55	C2
Jacksonville	Applegate Ranger District	NFS	33	D2
Jefferson	Ankeny NWR	NWR	9	B2
John Day	Malheur Nat'l. Forest Sup.	NFS	12	B4
	Bear Valley Ranger D.	NFS	13	B4
	Long Creek Ranger D.	NFS	15	B4
	John Day Fossil Beds National Monument	NPS	2	B3
Joseph	Wallowa Lake SP	SPS	11	B5
Keno	Klamath River SRA	BLM	20	D2
Klamath Falls	Winema Nat'l. Forest Sup.	NFS	74	D2
	Klamath Ranger D.	NFS	77	D2
	Klamath Falls Resource A	BLM	19	D2
	Klamath Wildlife Area	SWA	12	D2
La Grande	La Grande Ranger D.	NFS	62	B4
	Region 4, Northeast	SWA	5	A4
	Ladd Marsh Wildlife Area	SWA	18	B4
Lakeview	Fremont Nat'l. Forest Sup.	NFS	7	D3
	Lakeview Ranger D.	NFS	9	D3
	Sheldon/Hart Mtn. Complex	NWR	3	D3
	Hart Mountain NWR	NWR	4	D3
	Lakeview District Office	BLM	18	D3
	Lakeview Resource Area	BLM	21	D3
Lowell	Lowell Ranger D.	NFS	69	C2
	Blue River Lake	COE	2	B2
	Cottage Grove Lake	COE	4	C2
	Cougar Lake	COE	5	B2
	Detroit Lake	COE	6	B2
	Dexter Lake	COE	7	C2
	Dorena Lake	COE	8	C2
	Fall Creek Lake	COE	9	C2
	Fern Ridge Lake	COE	10	B2
	Foster Lake	COE	11	B2
	Green Peter Lake	COE	12	B2
	Hills Creek	COE	13	C2
	Lookout Point Lake	COE	15	C2
Mapleton	Mapleton Ranger D.	NFS	47	B1
Marcola	Shotgun SRMA	BLM	16	B2
Maupin	Bear Springs Ranger D.	NFS	19	B3
McKenzie Bridge	McKenzie Ranger D.	NFS	70	B2
Medford	Rogue River National Forest	NFS	32	D2
	Medford District Office	BLM	23	D2
	Ashland Resource Area	BLM	★24	D2
	Butte Falls Resource Area	BLM	★26	D2
	Glendale Resource Area	BLM	★27	D2
	Grants Pass Resource Area	BLM	★28	D2
	Rogue River SRA	BLM	29	D1
Mill City	Detroit Ranger D.	NFS	68	B2
	Fishermen's Bend Rec. Site	BLM	46	B2
Monmouth	E.E. Wilson Wildlife Area	SWA	9	B2
Mt. Hood-Parkside	Hood River Ranger D.	NFS	24	A2
Nehalem	Nehalem Bay SP	SPS	7	A1
Newport	Oregon Coastal Refuges	NWR	13	B1
	Yaquina Head Outstanding Natural Area	BLM	49	B1
	Region 6, Marine	SWA	7	B1
North Bend	Coos Bay District Office	BLM	6	C1
	Myrtlewood Resource Area	BLM	10	C1
	Tioga Resource Area	BLM	11	C1
	Umpqua Resource Area	BLM	12	C1
North Powder	Elkhorn Wildlife Area	SWA	16	B4
Oakridge	Rigdon Ranger D.	NFS	72	C2
Paisley	Paisley Ranger D.	NFS	10	D3
Paulina	Paulina Ranger D.	NFS	29	C3
Pendleton	Umatilla National Forest	NFS	50	A4
Plush	Warner Wetlands SRA	BLM	22	D3
Portland	U.S. Forest Svc., Pacific NW Region	NFS	1	A2
	COE, Portland District	COE	1	A2
	USFWS Region 1	NWR	1	A2
	BLM Oregon/Washington States Office	BLM	1	A2
	Dept. of Fish & Wildlife	SWA	1	A2
	Sauvie Island Wildlife Area	SWA	24	A2
Powers	Powers Ranger D.	NFS	42	C1
Prairie City	Prairie City Ranger D.	NFS	16	B4
Princeton	Malheur NWR	NWR	2	C4
Prineville	Ochoco Nat'l. Forest Sup.	NFS	26	B3
	Big Summit Ranger D.	NFS	27	B3
	Crooked River National Grassland	NFS	28	B3
	Prineville Ranger D.	NFS	30	B3
	Prineville District Office	BLM	30	B3
	Central Oregon Resource A	BLM	★31	B3
	Deschutes Resource Area	BLM	★33	B3
	Lower Crooked Wild & Scenic River	BLM	35	B3
Prospect	Prospect Ranger District	NFS	36	D2
Quinton	John Day River SRA	BLM	32	A3
Reedsport	Oregon Dunes NRA	NFS	48	C1
	Dean Creek Elk Viewing Area SRA	BLM	8	C1
	Loon Lake SRA	BLM	9	C1
Roseburg	Umpqua Nat'l. Forest Sup.	NFS	53	C1
	Roseburg District Office	BLM	36	C1
	Dillard Resource Area	BLM	★37	C1
	Drain Resource Area	BLM	★38	C1
	North Umpqua Resource A	BLM	★39	C1
	South Umpqua Resource A	BLM	★40	C1
	Region 2, Southwest	SWA	3	C1
Salem	Salem District Office	BLM	41	B2
	Alsea Resource Area	BLM	★42	B2
	Clackamas Resource Area	BLM	★43	B2
	Santiam Resource Area	BLM	★45	B2
	Yamhill Resource Area	BLM	★48	B2
	OR State Parks & Rec. Dept.	SPS	1	B2
Seaside	Jewell Meadows Wildlife A	SWA	23	A1
Silver Lake	Silver Lake Ranger D.	NFS	11	C3
Sisters	Sisters Ranger D.	NFS	6	B2
Sublimity	Silver Falls SP	SPS	8	B2
Summer Lake	Summer Lake Wildlife Area	SWA	22	C3
Sweet Home	Sweet Home Ranger D.	NFS	73	B2
The Dalles	John Day Lock & Dam, Lake Umatilla	COE	14	A3
	Willow Creek	COE	18	B4
	Lower Deschutes Wildlife A	SWA	13	A3
Tillamook	Cape Meares NWR	NWR	12	A1
	Tillamook Resource Area-Nestucca River	BLM	★47	B2
Tiller	Tiller Ranger D.	NFS	57	C2
Trail	Lost Creek Lake	COE	16	C2
	Joseph H. Stewart SP	SPS	5	D2
Troutdale	Columbia Gorge Ranger D.	NFS	21	A2
Tulelake, CA	Bear Valley NWR	NWR	14	D2
	Klamath Marsh NWR	NWR	15	C2
	Upper Klamath NWR	NWR	16	D2
Tygh Valley	White River Wildlife Area	SWA	14	B3
Ukiah	North Fork John Day RD	NFS	52	B4
	Bridge Creek Wildlife Area	SWA	15	B4
Umatilla	Umatilla NWR (OR/WA)	NWR	5	A3
	Cold Springs NWR	NWR	6	A4
	McKay Creek NWR	NWR	7	A4
	Irrigon Wildlife Area	SWA	17	A4
Unity	Unity Ranger D.	NFS	64	B4
Vale	Vale District Office	BLM	50	C5
	Jordan Resource Area	BLM	52	C5
	Malheur Resource Area	BLM	53	C5
Waldport	Waldport Ranger D.	NFS	49	B1
Welches	Wildwood SRA	BLM	44	B2
West Linn	Willamette Falls Locks	COE	17	B2
Westfir	Oakridge Ranger D.	NFS	71	C2
Yachats	Cape Perpetua VC	NFS	45	B1
Zigzag	Zigzag Ranger D.	NFS	25	B2

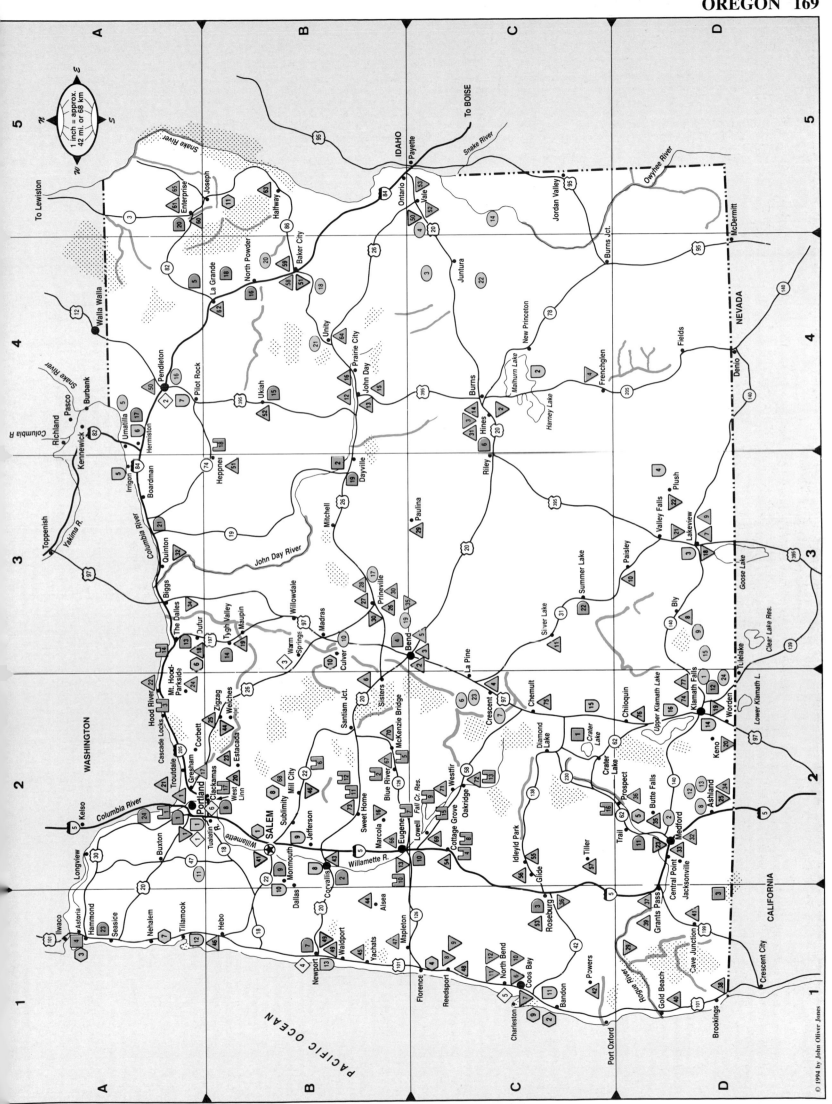

OREGON NOTES

Summary

There are 200 federal, 37 state, and 6 private recreation areas or local administrative offices covered in this chapter. Of these, 186 appear in the Information Chart and 57 are covered in the notes. The special indexes feature 86 federally designated wilderness areas and wild rivers, and 113 agency published outdoor maps.

Federal Agencies

U.S. Forest Service

Hells Canyon NRA (S# 61, map A5) covers a three state area. There are Visitor Centers (offices) at Riggins, Idaho (Idaho S# 63, map C1), and Clarkston, Washington (Washington S# 37, map C5). See those state maps and charts for details.

The Hells Canyon Visitors Center in Oregon features exhibits about natural and cultural resources. The building is also home to the Wallowa-Whitman National Forest Eagle Cap and Wallowa Mountain Ranger District and Visitors Center offices.

Cape Perpetua Visitors Center (S# 45, map B1) in the Siuslaw National Forest. A film, "Forces of Nature," describes the influence of weather and other natural forces upon the land and forest. Exhibits explain climate, geology, plant life, and the ocean...especially tidal areas.

Oregon Dunes NRA Visitors Center (S# 48, map C1). Exhibits interpret dune ecology and management, outdoor recreation opportunities, marine life, and history of the Oregon Coast. VC phone is 503-547-3289.

Lava Lands Visitors Center
1230 SE Third St., #A-262   503-593-2421
Bend, OR 97049
Exhibits and interpretive trails tell the story of loacl volcanic activity. Lava Lands VC is in the Fort Rock Ranger District (S# 5, map C3) of the Deschutes NF.

Timberline Lodge Visitors Center. The Lodge was dedicated by President Franklin D. Roosevelt in 1937 and is an example of "WPA" craftsmanship. It is located in Zigzag, OR and managed by the Zigzag Ranger District (S# 25, map B2) of the Mt. Hood NF.

Multnomah Falls Visitors Center is located in the historic Multnomah Lodge at the base of a series of spectacular waterfalls. Columbia Gorge National Scenic Area history and features are interpreted and information on trails and recreation opportunities is available. The Center is managed by the Columbia Gorge Ranger District (S# 21, map A2) of the Mt. Hood NF.

U.S. Army Corps of Engineers

North Pacific Division Office
PO Box 2870
Portland, OR 97208-2870   503-326-4087

The Alaska, Portland, Oregon, Seattle and Walla Walla, Washington District Offices manage COE projects in the north Pacific states area (see information charts).

USFWS National Wildlife Refuges

Access and recreational opportunities on Oregon's Coastal Wildlife Refuges are limited. Inquire for specific information at the W.L. Finley NWR. Ask about a new brochure describing Oregon's Coastal Refuges.

The Umatilla NWR administers three Columbia River island units described in the Washington chapter.

The Bear Valley, Klamath Forest, and Upper Klamath NWRs are managed from the Klamath Basin Refuges office in Tulelake, California.

National Park Service

Additional NPS Location in Oregon

Fort Clatsop National Memorial (125 acres)
(S# 4, map A1)
Route 3, Box 604-FC
Astoria, OR 97103   503-861-2471

Bureau of Land Management

National Historic Oregon Trail Interpretive Center
PO Box 987
Baker City, OR 97814   503-523-9170

The Oregon National Historic Trail Interpretive Center is the first national facility commemorating the Oregon Trail. Location is on Hwy. 86, approximately 3 miles east of Baker City and the I-84 exit. The Center is open daily from 9 a.m. to 4 p.m. except Christmas and New Year holidays.

Situated in a park-like setting on 510 acres, the Center features state-of-the-art indoor and outdoor exhibits and an interpretive trail.

Bureau of Reclamation Recreation Areas

Twenty-four recreation areas are listed here and symbolized on the Oregon state map.

S#	MAP	LOCATION NAME
1	D2	"A" Canal Trail
2	D2	Agate Res.
3	C4	Beulah Res.
4	C5	Bully Creek Res.
5	A4	Cold Springs Res.
6	C2	Crane Prairie Res.
7	C2	Crescent Lake
8	D2	Emigrant Lake
9	D3	Gerber Res.
10	B3	Haystack Res.
11	A2	Henry Hagg Lake
12	D2	Howard Prairie Lake
13	D2	Hyatt Res.
14	C5	Lake Owyhee
15	D3	Malone Diversion Dam
16	A4	McKay Res.
17	B3	Ochoco Res.
18	B4	Phillips Lake
19	B3	Prineville Res.
20	B4	Thief Valley Res.
21	B4	Unity Res.
22	C4	Warm Springs Res.
23	C2	Wickiup Res.
24	D2	Wilson Res.

Wilderness/Wild River Index

In this index more than one agency office may manage a listing wild river or wilderness), or a single office may be in charge of several listings. The index structure varies to reflect these variations and office names are followed by S# and map coordinate information in parentheses.

Wilderness Areas

Deschutes (S# 2, map C3) and Willamette National Forests (S# 66, map B2)
Diamond Peak Wilderness - 52,337 acres
Mount Washington Wilderness - 52,516 acres
Three Sisters Wilderness - 285,202 acres
Deschutes (S# 2, map C3), Mt. Hood (S# 17, map A2), and Willamette National Forests (S# 66, map B2)
Mt. Jefferson Wilderness - 107,008 acres
Fremont National Forest (S# 7, map D3)
Gearhart Mountain Wilderness - 22,809 acres
Malheur National Forest (S# 12, map B4)
Strawberry Mountain Wilderness - 68,700 acres
Malheur (S# 12, map B4) and Wallowa-Whitman National Forests (S# 58, map B4)
Monument Rock Wilderness - 19,800 acres
Mt. Hood National Forest (S# 17, map A2)
Badger Creek Wilderness - 24,000 acres
Columbia Wilderness - 39,000 acres
Mt. Hood Wilderness - 46,520 acres
Salmon-Huckleberry Wilderness - 44,560 acres
Mt. Hood (S# 17, map A2) and Willamette National Forests (S# 66, map B2)
Bull of the Woods Wilderness - 34,900 acres
Ochoco National Forest (S# 26, map B3)
Black Canyon Wilderness - 13,400 acres
Bridge Creek Wilderness - 5,400 acres
Mill Creek Wilderness - 17,400 acres
Rogue River (S# 32, map D2) and Siskiyou National Forests (S# 37, map D1)
Red Buttes - 3,750 acres
Rogue River (S# 32, map D2) and Umpqua National Forests (S# 53, map C1)
Rogue-Umpqua Divide Wilderness - 33,200 acres
Rogue River (S# 32, map D2) and Winema National Forests (S# 74, map D2)
Sky Lakes Wilderness - 116,300 acres
Siskiyou National Forest (S# 37, map D1)
Grassy Knob Wilderness - 17,200 acres
Kalmiopsis Wilderness - 179,700 acres
Wild Rogue Wilderness - 25,658 acres
Siuslaw National Forest (S# 43, map B2)
Cummins Creek Wilderness - 9,300 acres
Drift Creek Wilderness - 5,800 acres
Rock Creek Wilderness - 7,400 acres
Umatilla National Forest (S# 50, map A4)
North Fork Umatilla Wilderness - 20,200 acres
Wenaha-Tucannon Wilderness - 66,375 acres
Umatilla (S# 50, map A4) and Wallowa-Whitman National Forests (S# 58, map B4)
North Fork John Day Wilderness - 121,400 acres
Umpqua National Forest (S# 53, map C1)
Boulder Creek Wilderness - 19,100 acres
Umpqua (S# 53, map C1), Willamette (S# 66, map B2), and Winema National Forests (S# 74, map D2)
Mount Thielsen Wilderness - 55,100 acres
Wallowa-Whitman National Forest (S# 58, map B4)
Eagle Cap Wilderness - 358,461 acres

Hells Canyon Wilderness - 130,095 acres
Willamette National Forest (S# 66, map B2)
Menagerie Wilderness - 4,725 acres
Middle Santiam Wilderness - 7,500 acres
Waldo Lake Wilderness - 39,200 acres
Winema National Forest (S# 74, map D2)
Mountain Lake Wilderness - 23,071 acres

William L. Finley NWR (S# 11, map B2) for information about these areas:
Oregon Islands Wilderness - 480 acres
Three Arch Rocks Wilderness - 15 acres

BLM Vale District Office (S# 50, map C5)
Hells Canyon Wilderness - 1,038 acres
BLM Coos Bay District Office (S# 8, map C1)
Oregon Islands Wilderness - 5 acres
BLM Salem District Office (S# 41, map B2)
Table Rock Wilderness - 5,500 acres
BLM Medford District Office (S# 23, map D2)
Wild Rogue Wilderness - 10,000 acres

Wild Rivers

Big Marsh Creek, also
Crescent Creek
Deschutes National Forest (S# 2, map C3)
Chetco River
Siskiyou National Forest (S# 37, map D1)
Clackamas River
Mount Hood National Forest (S# 17, map A2)
Crooked River, also
Crooked River, North Fork
Ochoco National Forest (S# 26, map B3), also
BLM Prineville District Office (S# 30, map B3)
Deschutes River
Deschutes National Forest (S# 2, map C3), also
BLM Prineville District Office (S# 30, map B3)
BLM Burns District Office (S# 2, map C4)
Eagle Creek
Wallowa-Whitman National Forest (S# 58, map B4)
Elk River
Siskiyou National Forest (S# 37, map D1), also
Oregon State Parks & Rec. Dept. (S# 1, map B2)
Grande Ronde River
Umatilla National Forest (S# 50, map A4), also
Wallowa-Whitman National Forest (S# 58, map B4), and BLM Vale District Office (S# 50, map C5)
Illinois River
Siskiyou National Forest (S# 37, map D1)
Imnaha River
Wallowa-Whitman National Forest (S# 58, map B4)
John Day River, also
John Day River, South Fork
BLM Prineville District Office (S# 30, map B3)
John Day River, North Fork
Umatilla National Forest (S# 50, map A4), also
Wallowa-Whitman National Forest (S# 58, map B4)
Joseph Creek
Wallowa-Whitman National Forest (S# 58, map B4)
Klickitat River
Columbia River Gorge NSA (see USFS S# 22, map A2)
Little Deschutes River
Deschutes National Forest (S# 2, map C3)
Lostine River

Wallowa-Whitman National Forest (S# 58, map B4)
Malheur River, also
Malheur River, North Fork
Malheur National Forest (S# 12, map B4)
McKenzie River
Willamette National Forest (S# 66, map B2)
Metolius River
Deschutes National Forest (S# 2, map C3)
Minam River, also
North Powder
Wallowa-Whitman National Forest (S# 58, map B4)
Owyhee River, also
Owahee River, North Fork, and
Owahee River, West Little, and
Powder River
BLM Vale District Office (S# 50, map C5)
Quartzville Creek
BLM Salem District Office (S# 41, map B2)
Roaring River
Mount Hood National Forest (S# 17, map A2)
Rogue River
Siskiyou National Forest (S# 37, map D1), also
BLM Medford District Office (S# 23, map D2)
Rogue River, Upper
Rogue River National Forest (S# 32, map D2)
Salmon River, Oregon, and
Sandy River
Mount Hood National Forest (S# 17, map A2), also
BLM Salem District Office (S# 41, map B2)
Smith River, North Fork
Siskiyou National Forest (S# 37, map D1')
Snake River
Hells Canyon Natl. Recreation Area (S# 61, map E5)
Sprague River, North Fork
Fremont National Forest (S# 7, map D3)
Squaw Creek
Deschutes National Forest (S# 2, map C3)
Sycan River
Fremont National Forest (S# 7, map D3;
Winema National Forest (S# 74, map D2)
Umpqua River, North
Umpqua National Forest (S# 53, map C1)
BLM Roseburg District Office (S# 36, map C1)
Wenaha River
Umatilla National Forest (S# 50, map A4)
White River
Mount Hood National Forest (S# 17, map A2), also
BLM Prineville District Office (S# 30, map B3)
White Salmon River
Columbia River Gorge NSA (see USFS S# 22, map A2)
Willamette River, North Fork of Middle Fcrk
Willamette National Forest (S# 66, map B2)

Outdoor Map Index

National Park Service (USGS Map)

Crater Lake National Park [1956]
Scale: 1 inch = 1.0 mile (1 cm = 0.6 km)
Size: 25x35 inches (63x89 cm)

U.S. Forest Service Maps

The USFS regional office is in Portland. Forest maps in this region do not all contain a quad map index.

Boulder Cr. & Mt. Thielsen Wilderness [1987]
Scale: 1 inch = 1.0 mile (1 cm = 0.6 km)

BLM OREGON
1:100,000 INTERMEDIATE SCALE MAPS
SURFACE & SURFACE / MINERAL SERIES

Astoria	Nehalem River	Pendleton	Hermiston	Goldendale	Hood River	Vancouver			
Waldport	Yamhill River	Oregon City	Condon	Heppner	LaGrande	Enterprise	Wallowa	Grangeville	
Reedsport	Corvallis	North Santiam River	Mount Hood	Stephenson Mountain	Bates	Riggins			
Coos Bay	Eugene	McKenzie River	Madras	Monument	John Day	Baker	McCall		
Port Orford	Cottage Grove	Oakridge	Bend	Prineville	Dayville	Brogan	Weiser		
Gold Beach	Roseburg	Diamond Lake	LaPine	Brothers	Burns	Vale	Boise		
Canyonville	Crater Lake	Crescent	Christmas Valley	Harney Lake	Malheur Lake	Mahogany Mountain			
Grants Pass	Medford	Williamson River	Lake Albert	Blue Joint Lake	Steens Mountain	Jordan Valley			
Klamath Falls	Lakeview	Adel	Alvord Lake	LaRosa Canyon					

Columbia River Gorge NSA

Deschutes National Forest [1985]
Scale: 1 inch = 2.0 miles (1 cm = 1.3 km)

Diamond Peak Wilderness [1982]

Eagle Cap Wilderness [1982]
Scale: 1 inch = 1.0 mile (1 cm = 0.6 km)

Forest Trails of the Columbia Gorge [1978]
Scale: 1 inch = 1.0 mile (1 cm = 0.6 km)

Fremont National Forest [1987]
Scale: 1 inch = 2.0 miles (1 cm = 1.3 km)

Gearhart Mountain Wilderness [1982]
Scale: 1 inch = 1.0 mile (1 cm = 0.6 km)

Hells Canyon NRA [1987]
Scale: 1 inch = 1.0 mile (1 cm = 0.6 km)

Kalmiopsis / Wild Rogue Wilderness [1980]
Scale: 1 inch = 1.0 mile (1 cm = 0.6 km)

Malheur National Forest [1987]
Scale: 1 inch = 2.0 miles (1 cm = 1.3 km)

Mountain Lakes Wilderness [1976]
Scale: 1 inch = 0.5 mile (1 cm = 0.3 km)

Mt. Hood Wilderness [1984]

Mt. Jefferson Wilderness [1979]

Mt. Washington Wilderness [198C]
Scale: 1 inch = 0.5 mile (1 cm = 0.3 km)

Mt. Hood National Forest [1987]
Scale: 1 inch = 2.0 miles (1 cm = 1.3 km)

Ochoco National Forest [1986]
Scale: 1 inch = 2.0 miles (1 cm = 1.3 km)

Oregon Dunes Natl. Recreation Area [1982]
Scale: 1 inch = 1.0 mile (1 cm = 0.6 km)

Pacific Crest Trail - Central [1985]
Scale: 1 inch = 1.0 mile (1 cm = 0.6 km)

Pacific Crest Trail - North [1985]
Scale: 1 inch = 1.0 mile (1 cm = 0.6 km)

Pacific Crest Trail - South [1985]
Scale: 1 inch = 1.0 mile (1 cm = 0.6 km)

Red Buttes Wilderness [1985]

Rouge River National Forest [1987]
Scale: 1 inch = 2.0 miles (1 cm = 1.3 km)

Siskiyou National Forest [1986]
Scale: 1 inch = 2.0 miles (1 cm = 1.3 km)

Siuslaw National Forest [1982]
Scale: 1 inch = 2.0 miles (1 cm = 1.3 km)

Sky Lakes Wilderness [1986]
Scale: 1 inch = 1.0 mile (1 cm = 0.6 km)

Strawberry Mountain Wilderness [1976]
Scale: 1 inch = 0.7 mile (1 cm = 0.4 km)

The Wild & Scenic Rogue River [1979]
Scale: 1 inch = 1.0 mile (1 cm = 0.6 km)

The Wild & Scenic Snake River [1985]
Scale: 1 inch = 0.5 mile (1 cm = 0.3 km)

Three Sisters Wilderness [1982]
Scale: 1 inch = 1.0 mile (1 cm = 0.6 km)

Umatilla National Forest [1987]
Scale: 1 inch = 2.0 miles (1 cm = 1.3 km)

Umpqua National Forest [1986]
Scale: 1 inch = 2.0 miles (1 cm = 1.3 km)

Waldo Lake Wilderness & Recreation Area [1987]
Scale: 1 inch = 1.0 mile (1 cm = 0.6 km)

Wallowa-Whitman National Forest North [1985]
Scale: 1 inch = 2.0 miles (1 cm = 1.3 km)

Wallowa-Whitman National Forest South [1985]
Scale: 1 inch = 2.0 miles (1 cm = 1.3 km)

Wenaha-Tucannon Wilderness [1980]
Scale: 1 inch = 1.0 mile (1 cm = 0.6 km)

Willamette National Forest [1984]
Scale: 1 inch = 1.0 mile (1 cm = 0.6 km)

Winema National Forest [1986]
Scale: 1 inch = 2.0 miles (1 cm = 1.3 km)

Bureau of Land Management Maps

The Oregon/Washington State Office is in Portland (BLM S# 1). The BLM intermediate scale maps are indicated on the grid (right) and are available in surface and mineral editions.

Special purpose BLM maps are as follows: The Oregon BLM Resource (recreation) Map in 1:1,000,000 scale. A State of Oregon - Major Federal and State Lands Map in 1:500,000 scale available for $5 folded. Add $3 if you wish the map shipped in a mailing tube (flat). Another map in the same sacle is the Western Oregon Special Management Area Map.

A Steens Mountain Recreation Map has a 1 inch = 2.5 miles scale. Four other maps, all in 1:100,000 scale are: Lower Deschutes River, Lower John Day River, Upper John Day River, Central Oregon Public Lands.

State Agencies

OR State Parks & Recreation Dept. (S# 1, map C1)

An *Oregon State Parks Guide* (225 state parks) is available free. The guide describes each area, contains a locator map, includes information on facilities and activities, and lists special facilities and unique features. Individual brochures are available for many of the parks. Fees vary from park to park.

Other general publications include *Oregon's Recreation Trails*, *Oregon Coast Trail Guide*, and *Mountain Bike Guide to Oregon*.

Oregon Department of Forestry

2600 State St.
Salem, OF 97310   503-378-2511

Contact the Department about state forest recreation literature.

OR Dept. Fish & Wildlife (S# 1, map A2)

Guide Information Chart coverage is limited to agency headquarters and seven regional office locations. Individual brochures are available for many wildlife management areas. A 17-page loose-leaf *Wildlife Management Area Highlights* paper describes WA locaticrs. The symbols of those listed here (S# 9-24) are shown on the map.

S#	MAP	WILDLIFE AREA NAME & LOCATION
9	B2	E.E. Wilson Wildlife Area, Monmouth
10	C2	Fern Ridge Wildlife Area, Eugene
11	D2	Denman Wildlife Area, Central Point
12	D2	Klamath Wildlife Area, Klamath Falls
13	A3	Lower Deschutes Wildlife Area, The Dalles
14	B3	White River Wildlife Area, Tygh Valley
15	B4	Bridge Creek Wildlife Area, Ukiah
16	B4	Elkhorn Wildlife Area, North Powder
17	A4	Irrigon Wildlife Area, Umatilla
18	B4	Ladd Marsh Wildlife Area, La Grande
19	B3	Murderers Creek Wildlife Area, Dayville
20	A5	Wenaha Wildlife Area, Enterprise
21	A3	Willow Creek Wildlife Area, Boardman
22	C3	Summer Lake Wildlife Area, Summer Lake
23	A1	Jewell Meadows Wildlife Area, Seaside
24	A2	Sauvie Island Wildlife Area, Portland

Oregon Tourism Division

595 Cottage St., NE
Salem, OF 97310
in state   1-800-547-7842
                                  1-800-543-8888

Private Organizations

TNC Oregon Field Office (S# 1, map A2)
1205 NW 25th Ave.
Portland, OR 97210   503-228-9561

For membership, preserve, and guided tour information contact the field office.

Tribal Land Area in Oregon

Confederated Tribes of the Umatilla Indian Reservation - Fishing, hunting, camping.
Umatilla Board of Trustees (S# 2, map A4)
PO Box 638
Pendleton, OR 97801   503-276-3165

Confederated Tribes of the Warm Springs Indian Reservation - Fishing, camping, biking, boating, hiking, touring.
Warm Springs Tribal Council (S# 3, map B3)
PO Box C
Warm Springs, OR 97761   503-553-1161

ANCA Locations in Oregon

Hatfield Marine Science Center (S# 4, map B1)
2030 Marine Science Drive
Newport, OR 97365   503-867-3011

South Slough Estuarine Reserve (S# 5, map C1)
PO Box 5417
Charleston, OR 97420   503-888-5558

The Wetlands Conservancy (S# 6, map B2)
PO Box 1195
Tualatin, OR 97062   503-691-1394

No State Chamber of Commerce in Oregon

There are local Chamber of Commerce offices throughout the state.

★ INFORMATION CHART ★

INFORMATION CHART LEGEND - SYMBOLS & LETTER CODES

- ■ means YES & □ means Yes with disability provisions
- **sp** means spring, March through May
- **S** means Summer, June through August
- **F** means Fall, September through November
- **W** means Winter, December through February
- **T** means Two (2) or Three (3) Seasons
- **A** means All Four (4) Seasons
- **na** means Not Applicable or Not Available

Note: empty or blank spaces in the chart mean **NO**
★ that symbol is not shown on the map.

AGENCY/MAP LEGEND . . . INITIALS, MAP SYMBOLS, COLOR CODES

- U.S. Forest Service Supervisor & Ranger Dist. Offices NFS
- U.S. Army Corps of Engineers Rec. Areas & Offices . COE
- USFWS National Wildlife Refuges & Offices . . . . NWR
- National Park Service Parks & other NPS Sites . . . . . NPS
- Bureau of Land Management Rec. Areas & Offices . . . BLM
- Bureau of Reclamation Rec. Areas & Reg. Offices . . . BOR
- State Parks (also see State Agency notes) . . . . SPS
- State Wildlife Areas (also see State Agency notes) . . SWA
- Private Preserves, Nature Centers & Tribal Lands . .
- The Wild Rivers   and Wilderness Areas

Note: Refer to yellow block on page 7 (top right) for location name and address abbreviations. If a symbol number has a star ★ that symbol is not shown on the map.

Column headers (FACILITIES, SERVICES, RECREATION OPPORTUNITIES & CONVENIENCES) and legend detail include: DRINKING WATER / RESTROOMS; DAY USE ONLY, no overnight; PARK & WALK-IN SPORTS ONLY AREA; WINTER SPORTS OK; NON-MOTORIZED WATERCRAFT OK; MOTORIZED WATERCRAFT OK / check limits; BOATING FACILITIES ramps, marinas, etc.; FISHING / license / permit req'd; HUNTING IN SEASON license / permit req'd; HORSEBACK RIDING w/ your own horse, at one's own risk; OFF-ROAD Motorized Vehicle Area / Use OK; BICYCLING OPPORTUNITIES / areas, trails; WALKING / HIKING TRAILS; WILDERNESS AREAS / WILD RIVERS; SWIMMING PERMITTED; DEVELOPED CAMPGROUNDS / CAMPSITES; NO-CHARGE CAMPGROUNDS / CAMPSITES; DEVELOPED PICNIC AREAS / PICNIC SITES; COMMON SPECIES ARE COMMON; WILDLIFE VIEWING SITES, birds, etc.; ENDANGERED SPECIES IS ABUNDANT OR COMMON; WILDLIFE IS ABUNDANT OR COMMON; INTERPRETIVE SITES / GEOLOGICAL SITES; HISTORIC SITE; ARCHAEOLOGICAL SITES; NATURE STUDY PROGRAMS; WILDFLOWER VIEWING AREA or DRIVE; NATURE GUIDED TOURS, scheduled / by res.; INTERPRETIVE EDUCATION LITERATURE, brochures, maps, etc.; FREE LITERATURE OR EDUCATIONAL DISPLAY; AGENCY SERVICES AVAILABLE; CONCESSIONAIRE SERVICES; ENTRY FEE, not camping or permit fee; IO / VC OPEN SATURDAY / SUNDAY; INFO OFFICE (IO) / VISITOR CENTER (VC).

S#	MAP	LOCATION NAME (state initials if more than one) with ADDRESS and/or LOCATION DATA	TELEPHONE	ACRES / ELEVATION
1	A2	U.S. Forest Svc., Pacific NW Region, 333 SW First St., PO Box 3623, Portland 97208	503-326-2877	na / na
2	C3	Deschutes Nat'l. Forest Sup., 1645 Hwy. 20 East, Bend 97701	503-388-2715	1,620,900 / 1,900-10,400
3	C3	Bend Ranger D., 1645 Hwy. 20 East, Bend 97701	503-388-5664	390,600 / 3,800-10,400
4	C2	Crescent Ranger D., PO Box 208, Crescent 97733	503-433-2234	326,100 / 4,400-8,700
5	C3	Fort Rock Ranger D., 1645 Hwy. 20 East, Bend 97701	503-388-5664	587,300 / 3,800-8,000
6	B2	Sisters Ranger D., PO Box 248, Sisters 97759	503-549-2111	316,400 / 1,900-10,400
7	D3	Fremont Nat'l. Forest Sup., 524 North G Street, Lakeview 97630	503-947-2151	na / na
8	D3	Bly Ranger District, Hwy. 140, Bly 97622 [between Lakeview & Klamath Falls off Hwy 140]	503-353-2427	340,000 / 4,500-8,300
9	D3	Lakeview Nat'l. Forest D., HC-64, Box 60, Lakeview 97630	503-947-3334	320,000 / 5,000-8,300
10	D3	Paisley Ranger D., 303 Hwy. 31, Paisley 97636	503-943-3131	330,000 / 4,369-8,134
11	C3	Silver Lake Ranger D., PO Box 129, Silver Lake 97638	503-576-2107	303,000 / 4,300
12	B4	Malheur Nat'l. Forest Sup., 139 NE Dayton St., John Day 97845	503-575-1731	1,000,460 / 3,500-9,100
13	B4	Bear Valley Ranger D., 528 E. Main St., John Day 97845	503-575-2110	368,000 / 3,000-8,000
14	C4	Burns Ranger D., 12870 Hwy 20, Star Rt. #4, Hines 97738	503-573-7292	420,000 / 4,400-7,163
15	B4	Long Creek Ranger D., 528 E. Main St., John Day 97845	503-575-2110	333,671 / 3,300-8,131
16	B4	Prairie City Ranger D., 327 W. Front St, Prairie City 97869	503-820-3311	388,000 / 3,500-9,038
17	A3	Mt. Hood National Forest Sup., 2955 NW Division, Gresham 97030	503-666-0771	1,108,727 / 300-11,245
18	A3	Barlow Ranger D., PO Box 67, Dufur 97021	503-467-2291	na / na
19	B3	Bear Springs Ranger D., Rt. #1, Box 222, Maupin 97037	503-328-6211	na / na
20	B2	Clackamas Ranger D. & Ripplebrook R, 61431 East Hwy. 224, Estacada 97023	503-630-4256	na / na
21	A2	Columbia Gorge Ranger D., 31520 SE Woodard Rd., Troutdale 97060	503-695-2276	237,089 / na
22	A2	Columbia River Gorge NSA, Waucoma Center, Suite 200, 902 Wasco Ave., Hood River 97060	503-386-2333	265,000 / 0-4,000
23	A2	Estacada Ranger D., 595 NW Industrial Way, Estacada 97023	503-630-6861	na / na
24	A2	Hood River Ranger D., 6780 Highway 35, Mt. Hood-Parkside 97041	503-666-0701	na / na
25	B2	Zigzag Ranger D., 70220 East Hwy. 26, Zigzag 97049	503-666-0704	na / na
26	B3	Ochoco Nat'l. Forest Sup., FOB, 300 E Third, PO Box 490, Prineville 97754	503-447-6247	959,317 / 2,900-7,163
27	B3	Big Summit Ranger D., 348855 Ochoco Ranger Station, Prineville 97754	503-447-9645	215,063 / na
28	B3	Crooked River National Grassland, 155 N. Court, Prineville 97754	503-447-9640	111,379 / na
29	C3	Paulina Ranger D., 171500 Beaver Creek Rd, HC-68, Box 6015, Paulina 97751	503-477-3713	260,259 / na
30	B3	Prineville Ranger D., 155 N. Court, Prineville 97754	503-447-9641	162,427 / na
31	C4	Snow Mountain Ranger D., HC-74, Box 12870, Hines 97738	503-573-7292	237,089 / na
32	D2	Rogue River National Forest, 333 West 8th Street, PO Box 520, Medford 97501	503-776-3600	628,780 / 1,524-9,500
33	D2	Applegate District, 6941 Upper Applegate Rd., Jacksonville 97530	503-899-1812	219,000 / 1,524-7,420
34	D2	Ashland Ranger District, 645 Washington St., Ashland 97520	503-482-3333	80,000 / 2,000-7,500
35	D2	Butte Falls Ranger District, 720 Laurel Ave., Butte Falls 97522	503-865-3581	136,168 / 3,500-9,500
36	D2	Prospect Ranger District, 47201 Hwy. 62, Prospect 97536	503-560-3623	na / na
37	D1	Siskiyou Nat'l. Forest, 200 NE Greenfield Rd., PO Box 440, Grants Pass 97526 [N I-5 exit next to State Police]	503-471-6500	1,163,944 / 81-7,055
38	D1	Chetco Ranger D., 555 5th Street, Brookings 97415	503-469-2196	127,431 / na
39	D1	Galice Ranger D., 1465 NE 7th St., PO Box 1131, Grants Pass 97526	503-476-3830	126,294 / na
40	D1	Gold Beach Ranger D., 1225 South Ellensburg, PO Box 7, Gold Beach 97444	503-247-6651	150,759 / na
41	D1	Illinois Valley Ranger D., 26568 Redwood Highway, Cave Junction 97523	503-592-2166	102,107 / na
42	C1	Powers Ranger D., Powers 97466	503-439-3011	109,122 / na
43	B2	Siuslaw Nat'l. Forest Sup., 4077 Research Way, PO Box 1148, Corvallis 97339	503-757-4480	621,000 / 0-4,100
44	B1	Alsea Ranger D., 18591 Alsea Highway, Alsea 97324	503-487-5811	111,100 / 200-4,100
45	B1	Cape Perpetua Visitors Center, Hwy. 101 South, PO Box 274, Yachats 97498	503-547-3289	2,700 / 0-800
46	B1	Hebo Ranger D., PO Box 324, Hebo 97122	503-392-3161	150,000 / 0-3,200
47	B1	Mapleton Ranger D., 10692 Hwy. 26, Mapleton 97453	503-268-4473	190,000 / 0-2,600
48	C1	Oregon Dunes National Recreation Ar, 855 Highway Ave., Reedsport 97467	503-271-3611	32,000 / 0-500
49	B1	Waldport Ranger D., 1049 SW Pacific Hwy., PO Box 400, Waldport 97394	503-563-3211	140,000 / 0-2,400
50	A1	Umatilla National Forest Sup., 2517 SW Hailey Ave., Pendleton 97801	503-278-3716	1,402,467 / 1,900-8,000

#	Grid	Name / Address	Phone	Acreage / Elevation
52	B4	North Fork John Day Ranger D., PO Box 158, Ukiah 97880	503-427-3231	465,275 / 3,100-8,000
53	C1	Umpqua Nat'l. Forest Sup., 2900 Stewart Parkway, PO Box 1008, Roseburg 97470	503-672-6601	1,029,309 / 800-9,180
54	C2	Cottage Grove Ranger D., 78405 Cedar Parks Rd., PO Box 38, Cottage Grove 97424	503-942-5591	91,000 / 1,500-6,000
55	C2	Diamond Lake Ranger D., HC-60, Box 101, Idleyld Park 97447	503-498-2531	300,000 / 1,600-9,180
56	C2	North Umpqua Ranger D., 18782 N. Umpqua Hwy., Glide 97443	503-496-3532	275,000 / 800-6,000
57	C2	Tiller Ranger D., 27812 Tiller Trail Hwy., Tiller 97484	503-825-3201	365,000 / 1,000-6,000
58	B4	Wallowa-Whitman Nat'l. Forest Sup., 1550 Dewey Ave., PO Box 907, Baker City 97814	503-523-6391	2,396,049 / 900-9,393
59	B4	Baker Ranger D., 3165 Tenth St., Baker City 97814	503-523-4476	na / 3,000-8,900
60	A5	Eagle Cap Ranger D., 88401 Hwy. 82, Enterprise 97828 [off Hwy. 82]	503-426-4978	na / 5,000-9,845
61	A5	Hells Canyon NRA HQ & VC, 88401 Hwy. 82, Enterprise 97828 [Wallowa Mtn/Hells Canyon VC is off Hwy. 82]	503-426-4978	652,488 / 900-9,393
62	B4	La Grande Ranger D., 3502 Highway 30, La Grande 97850	503-963-7186	
63	B5	Pine Ranger D., General Delivery, Halfway 97834 [off Hwy. 60]	503-742-7511	
64	B5	Unity Ranger D., Hwy. 26 in town, PO Box 38, Unity 97884	503-446-3351	
65	A5	Wallowa Valley Ranger D., 88401 Hwy. 82, Enterprise 97828 [off Hwy. 82]	503-426-4978	
66	B2	Willamette National Forest Sup., 211 E. 7th, PO Box 10607, Eugene 97440	503-465-6521	1,700,000 / 400-10,000
67	B2	Blue River Ranger D., Blue River 97413 [off Hwy. 126]	503-822-3317	
68	B2	Detroit Ranger D., HC-73, Box 320, Mill City 97360 [on Hwy. 22]	503-854-3366	
69	C2	Lowell Ranger D., Lowell 97452 [off Hwy. 58]	503-937-2129	
70	B2	McKenzie Ranger D., McKenzie Bridge 97413 [on Hwy. 126]	503-822-3381	
71	B2	Oakridge Ranger D., 46375 Hwy. 58, Westfir 97492	503-782-2291	na / na
72	B2	Rigdon Ranger D., 49098 Salmon Creek Rd., Hwy. 58, Oakridge 97463	503-782-2283	na / na
73	B2	Sweet Home Ranger D., 3225 Hwy. 20, Sweet Home 97386	503-367-5168	na / na
74	D2	Winema Nat'l Forest, 2819 Dahlia Street, Klamath Falls 97601 [take Campus Dr. E off US 97 1 block and N on Dahlia]	503-883-6714	1,038,986 / 4,100-9,180
75	C2	Chemult Ranger D., PO Box 150, Chemult 97731	503-365-7001	389,645 / 4,500-9,180
76	D2	Chiloquin Ranger D., PO Box 357, Chiloquin 97624 [W side of US 97 near Chiloquin exit]	503-783-4001	460,656 / 4,100-7,000
77	D2	Klamath Ranger D., 1936 California Ave. Klamath Falls 97601 [W side of US 97 at Oregon Ave, N end of town]	503-885-3400	188,685 / 4,100-8,000

COE, Portland District

#	Grid	Name / Address	Phone	Acreage / Elevation
1	A2	COE, Portland District, PO Box 2946 Portland 97208	503-326-6075	
2	B2	Blue River Lake, Willamette Valley Project, Lowell 97452	503-937-2131	na / na
3	A2	Bonneville Lock, Dam & Lake, Bonneville Lock & Dam, Cascade Locks 97014	503-374-8442	na / na
4	C2	Cottage Grove Lake, Willamette Valley Project, Lowell 97452	503-937-2131	na / na
5	B2	Cougar Lake, Willamette Valley Project, Lowell 97452	503-937-2131	na / na
6	B2	Detroit Lake, Willamette Valley Project, Lowell 97452	503-937-2131	na / na
7	C2	Dexter Lake, Willamette Valley Project, Lowell 97452	503-937-2131	na / na
8	C2	Dorena Lake, Willamette Valley Project, Lowell 97452	503-937-2131	na / na
9	C2	Fall Creek Lake, Willamette Valley Project, Lowell 97452	503-937-2131	na / na
10	B2	Fern Ridge Lake, Willamette Valley Project, Lowell 97452	503-937-2131	na / na
11	B2	Foster Lake, Willamette Valley Project, Lowell 97452	503-937-2131	na / na
12	B2	Green Peter Lake, Willamette Valley Project, Lowell 97452	503-937-2131	na / na
13	C2	Hills Creek, Willamette Valley Project, Lowell 97452	503-937-2131	na / na
14	A3	John Day Lock & Dam, Lake Umatilla PO Box 564, The Dalles 97058	503-296-1181	na / na
15	B2	Lookout Point Lake, Willamette Valley Project, Lowell 97452	503-937-2131	na / na
16	B2	Lost Creek Lake, 100 Cole M. Rivers Dr., Trail 97541	503-878-2255	na / na
17	B4	Willamette Falls Locks, US Army Corps of Engineers, West Linn 97068	503-656-4481	na / na
18	B4	Willow Creek, PO Box 564, The Dalles 97058	503-296-1181	na / na

USFWS Region 1

#	Grid	Name / Address	Phone	Acreage / Elevation
1	A2	USFWS Region 1, 911 NE 11th Ave., Portland 97232 [states of CA, ID, HI, NV, OR, WA]	503-231-6121	
2	C4	Malheur NWR, HC 72, Box 245, Princeton 97721	503-493-2612	185,000 / 4,000
3	D3	Sheldon/Hart Mountain Complex, U.S. PO Bldg., Room 301, Lakeview 97630	503-947-3315	na / 4,800
4	D3	Hart Mountain NWR, U.S. PO Bldg., Room 308, PO Box 111, Lakeview 97630 [27 mi. E of Plush, NWR office in town]	503-947-3315	275,000 / 4,500-8,065
5	A3	Umatilla NWR (ORWA), PO Bldg., 6th & I Sts., PO Box 239, Umatilla 97882 [4 mi. W of Irrigon]	503-922-3232	22,857 / 300
6	A4	Cold Springs NWR, PO Box 239, Umatilla 97882 [7 mi. E of Hermiston]	503-922-3232	3,117 / 500
7	A4	McKay Creek NWR, PO Box 239, Umatilla 97882 [6 mi. S of Pendleton]	503-922-3232	1,837 / 650
8	B2	William L. Finley NWR, W Oregon Refuges, 26208 Finley Refuge Road, Corvallis 97333	503-757-7236	5,235 / 400
9	B2	Ankeny NWR, 2301 Wintel Road, Jefferson 97352	503-757-7236	2,796 / 400
10	B1	Baskett Slough NWR, 10995 Highway 22, Dallas 97338 [go W 1.5 mi on 22 from Hwy 22 & 99w jct to "info" turnout]	503-623-2749	2,492 / 200
11	C1	Bandon Marsh NWR, near Bandon	503-757-7236	289 / 0
12	A1	Cape Meares NWR, near Tillamook	503-757-7236	138 / 0-150
13	B1	Oregon Coastal Refuges, 2030 S. Marine Scenic Dr., Newport 97365 [coastal refuges are not open to the public]	503-867-4550	na / na
14	D2	Klamath Basin Refuges Office, VC & Tule Lake NWR, Rt. #1, Box 74, Tulelake, CA 96134 [NW of Worden]	916-667-2231	39,100 / 4,100
15	C2	Bear Valley NWR, c/o Klamath Basin RO, Rt. #1, Box 74, Tulelake, CA 96134	916-667-2231	4,200 / 4,200-5,000
15	C2	Klamath Marsh NWR, c/o Klamath Basin RO, Rt. #1, Box 74, Tulelake, CA 96134 [Sand Creek, N of Chiloquin]	916-667-2231	37,600 / 4,200-5,100
16	C2	Upper Klamath NWR, c/o Klamath Basin RO, Rt. #1, Box 74, Tulelake, CA 96134 [N of Klamath Falls]	916-667-2231	14,900 / 4,100-4,400

Crater Lake National Park

#	Grid	Name / Address	Phone	Acreage / Elevation
1	C2	Crater Lake National Park, PO Box 7, Crater Lake 97604	503-594-2211	183,224 / 5,000-9,000
2	B3	John Day Fossil Beds Nat'l. Monument, 420 W. Main Street, John Day 97845 [near Dayville]	503-575-0721	14,014 / 2,000-4,000
3	D1	Oregon Caves National Monument, 19000 Caves Highway, Cave Junction 97523 [SW of Cave Junction]	503-592-2100	488 / 3,800-5,400

★ INFORMATION CHART ★

INFORMATION CHART LEGEND - SYMBOLS & LETTER CODES
■ means YES & □ means Yes with disability provisions
sp means spring, March through May
S means Summer, June through August
F means Fall, September through November
W means Winter, December through February
T means Two (2) or Three (3) Seasons
A means All Four (4) Seasons
na means Not Applicable or Not Available
Note: empty or blank spaces in the chart mean NO
Note: that symbol is not shown on the map.

AGENCY/MAP LEGEND . . . INITIALS, MAP SYMBOLS, COLOR CODES

U.S. Forest Service Supervisor & Ranger Dist. Offices . NFS [61]
U.S. Army Corps of Engineers Rec. Areas & Offices . COE [31]
USFWS National Wildlife Refuges & Offices .... NWR [40]
National Park Service Parks & other NPS Sites ..... NPS [7]
Bureau of Land Management Rec. Areas & Offices .. BLM [26]
Bureau of Reclamation Rec. Areas & Reg. Offices ... BOR (8)
State Parks (also see State Agency notes) .... SPS (52)
State Wildlife Areas (also see State Agency notes) . SWA (19)
Private Preserves, Nature Centers & Tribal Lands
The Wild Rivers ——— and Wilderness Areas
Note: Refer to yellow block on page 7 (top right) for location name and address abbreviations.

Column group: FACILITIES, SERVICES, RECREATION OPPORTUNITIES & CONVENIENCES

S#	MAP	LOCATION NAME (state initials if more than one) with ADDRESS and/or LOCATION DATA	TELEPHONE	ACRES / ELEVATION
1	A2	BLM Oregon/Washington States Office, 1300 NE 44th St., PO Box 2965, Portland 97208	503-280-7001	16,000,000 / na
2	C4	Burns District Office HC 74, Hwy, 20 W, Hines 97738	503-573-5241	3,376,357 / 3,400-9,733
3	C4	Andrews Resource Area, HC 74, Hwy, 20 W, Hines 97738	503-573-5241	1,666,439 / 3,900-9,733
4	C4	Steens Mountain SRA, near Frenchglen	503-573-5241	161,500 / 4,071-9,733
*5	C4	Three Rivers Resource Area, HC 74, Hwy, 20 W, Hines 97738	503-573-5241	1,709,918 / 3,400-6,510
6	C1	Coos Bay District Office, 1300 Airport Lane, North Bend 97459	503-756-0100	326,000 / 0-1,500
7	C1	Coos Bay Shorelands SRA, near Coos Bay	503-756-0100	1,600 / 50
8	C1	Dean Creek Elk Viewing Area SRA, near Reedsport	503-756-0100	923 / 50
9	C1	Loon Lake SRA, near Reedsport	503-756-0100	80 / 50
10	C1	Myrtlewood Resource Area, 1300 Airport Land, North Bend 97459	503-756-0100	105,000 / 500
11	C1	Tioga Resource Area, 1300 Airport Lane, North Bend 97459	503-756-0100	100,000 / 500
12	C1	Umpqua Resource Area, 1300 Airport Lane, North Bend 97459	503-756-0100	121,000 / 500
13	B2	Eugene District Office, 2890 Chad Dr., PO Box 10226, Eugene 97401	503-683-6600	316,000 / 0-4,750
*14	B2	Coast Range Resource Area, 2890 Chad Dr., PO Box 10226, Eugene 97401	503-683-6600	114,661 / 0-2,600
*15	B2	McKenzie Resource Area, 2890 Chad Dr., PO Box 10226, Eugene 97401	503-683-6600	93,540 / 200-3,300
16	B2	Shotgun SRMA, 5 mi. NE of Marcola	503-683-6600	260 / 800
*17	B2	South Valley Resource Area. 2890 Chad Dr., PO Box 10226, Eugene 97401	503-683-6600	108,408 / 240-4,750
18	D3	Lakeview District Office, 1000 Ninth Street South, PO Box 151, Lakeview 97630	503-947-2177	3,386,000 / 4,000-9,000
19	D2	Klamath Falls Resource Area, 2795 Anderson Ave., Suite 25. Klamath Falls 97603	503-883-6916	212,000 / 4,000-9,000
20	D2	Klamath River SRA, S of Keno	503-883-6916	5,700 / 3,000-4,000
21	D3	Lakeview Resource Area, 1000 Ninth Street South, PO Box 151, Lakeview 97630	503-947-2177	3,174,000 / 4,000-9,000
22	D3	Warner Wetlands SRA, W of Plush	503-947-2177	51,000 / 4,500
23	D2	Medford District Office, 3040 Biddle Road, Medford 97504	503-770-2200	866,300 / 700-7,000
*24	D2	Ashland Resource Area, 3040 Biddle Road, Medford 97504	503-770-2200	250,000 / 1,000-5,000
25	D1	Hyatt-Howard Prairie Lake SRA, E of Ashland	503-770-2200	17,000 / 5,200
*26	D2	Butte Falls Resource Area, 3040 Biddle Road, Medford 97504	503-770-2200	220,000 / 800-5,000
*27	D2	Glendale Resource Area, 3040 Biddle Road, Medford 97504	503-770-2200	167,000 / 1,000-5,265
*28	D2	Grants Pass Resource Area, 3040 Biddle Road, Medford 97504	503-770-2200	200,000 / 500-5,500
29	D1	Rogue River SRA, c/o BLM, 3040 Biddle Road (Rand VC Ph. 503-479-3735), Medford 97504	503-770-2200	14,000 / 500-1,100
30	B3	Prineville District Office, 185 E. 4ht St., PO Box 550, Prineville 97754	503-447-4115	2,000,000 / 3,100
*31	B3	Central Oregon Resource Area, 185 E. 4th St.. PO Box 550, Prineville 97754	503-447-4115	1,000,000 / 3,100
32	A3	John Day River SRA, along John Day River S from, Quinton	503-447-4115	48,000 / 1,500
*33	B3	Deschutes Resource Area, 185 E. 4th St., PO Box 550, Prineville 97754	503-447-4115	na / 100-6,000
34	A3	Deschutes River SRA, along the Deschutes River S from, Biggs	503-447-4115	32,000 / 100-1,000
35	B3	Lower Crooked Wild & Scenic R (Chimney Rock Segment), Prineville [S from Prineville along Crooked R & SR 27]	503-447-4115	15,000 / 3,000-3,200
36	C1	Roseburg District Office, 777 NW Garden Valley Blvd., Roseburg 97470	503-440-4930	419,000 / 570-1,500
*37	C1	Dillard Resource Area, 777 NW Garden Valley Blvd., Roseburg 97470	503-440-4930	na / na
*38	C1	Drain Resource Area, 777 NW Garden Valley Blvd., Roseburg 97470	503-440-4930	na / na
39	C1	North Umpqua Resource Area, 777 NW Garden Valley Blvd., Roseburg 97470	503-440-4930	na / na
*40	C1	South Umpqua Resource Area, 777 NW Garden Valley Blvd., Roseburg 97470	503-440-4930	na / na
41	B2	Salem District Office, 1717 Fabry Road, SE, Salem 97306	503-375-5646	397,172 / na
*42	B2	Alsea Resource Area, 1717 Fabry Road, SE, Salem 97306	503-375-5646	80,000 / 0-4,000
*43	B2	Clackamas Resource Area, 1717 Fabry Road, SE, Salem 97306	503-375-5646	72,000 / 100-4,500
44	B2	Wildwood SRA, Hwy, 26 near Welches	503-375-5644	280 / 1,200
*45	B2	Santiam Resource Area, 1717 Fabry Road, SE, Salem 97306	503-375-5644	88,000 / 1,000-4,400
46	B2	Fishermen's Bend Rec. Site, 27300 N Santiam Hwy., PO Box 785, Mill City 97360	503-897-2406	152 / 800
*47	B2	Tillamook Res. Area-Nestucca River, 4610 Third, Tillamook 97141	503-842-7546	100 / 3,100
*48	B2	Yamhill Resource Area, 1717 Fabry Road, SE, Salem 97306	503-867-4851	86,000 / 0-3,500
49	B1	Yaquina Head Outstanding Nat. Area, PO Box 936, Newport 97365	503-473-3144	100 / 0-400
50	C5	Vale District Office, 100 Oregon Street Vale 97918	503-473-3144	5,100,000 / 2,000-6,000

Oregon Listings (Information Chart)

S#	MAP	Park Name & Address	Phone	Acres / Units
52	C5	Jordan Resource Area, 100 Oregon Street, Vale 97918	503-473-3144	na / na
53	C5	Malheur Resource Area, 100 Oregon Street, Vale 97918	503-473-3144	na / na
(1)	B2	**OR State Parks & Recreation Dept.** 525 Trade St. SE, Number 301, Salem 97310	503-378-8605	na / na
2	C1	Bullards Beach SP, PO Box 25, 2 mi N of Bandon 97411	503-347-2209	1,289 / 10
3	A1	Fort Stevens SP, 10 mi. W of Astoria, Hammond 97121	503-861-1671	3,760 / 20
4	C1	Jessie M. Honeyman SP, 3 mi. S of Florence	503-997-3641	522 / 72
5	D2	Joseph H. Stewart SP (35 mi. N of Medford), 35251 Hwy. 62, Trail 97541	503-560-3334	1,000 / 2,000
6	A3	Memaloose SP, c/o Rooster Rock SP, PO Box 100, Corbett 97019 [I-84 westbound access only, 11 mi W of The Dalles]	503-478-3008	340 / 500
7	A1	Nehalem Bay SP, SP is 3 mi. S of Manzanita Jct., 8300 R 3rd St., Nehalem 97131	503-368-5943	890 / 10
8	B2	Silver Falls SP, 26 mi. E of Salem, 20024 Silver Falls Hwy. SE, Sublimity 97385	503-873-8681	8,706 / 1,200-1,600
9	C1	Sunset Bay SP, 10965 Cape Argo Hwy., 12 mi. SW of Coos Bay 97420	503-888-4902	395 / 20
10	B3	The Cove Palisades SP, 15 mi. SW of Madras, Rt. #1, Box 60 CP, Culver 97734	503-546-3412	4,129 / 2,000
11	B5	Wallowa Lake SP, Rt. #1, Box 323, 6 mi. S of Joseph 97846	503-432-4185	170 / 4,430
(1)	A2	**Dept. of Fish & Wildlife,** 2501 SW First St., PO Box 59, Portland 97207	503-229-5403	na / na
2	B2	Region 1, Northwest (S# 9-10), 170 NW Van Denberg Ave., Corvallis 97330	503-757-4186	na / na
3	C1	Region 2, Southwest (S# 11), 4192 N. Umpqua Hwy., Roseburg 97470	503-440-3353	na / na
4	D3	Region 3, Central (S# 12-14), 61374 Parrell Rd., Bend 97702	503-388-6363	na / na
5	A4	Region 4, Northeast (S# 15-21), 107 20th St., La Grande 97850	503-963-2138	na / na
6	C4	Region 5, Southeast (S# 22), 237 S. Hines Rd., Box 8, Hines 97738	503-573-6582	na / na
7	B1	Region 6, Marine, Bldg. 3, Marine Science Dr., Newport 97365	503-867-4741	na / na
8	B2	Region 7, Columbia (S# 23-24), 17330 SE Evelyn St., Clackamas 97015	503-657-2008	na / na

PENNSYLVANIA NOTES

Summary

There are 65 federal, 32 state, and 16 private recreation areas or local administrative offices covered in this state chapter. Of these, 86 appear in the Information Chart and 27 are covered in the notes. The special indexes feature 3 federally designated wilderness areas and wild rivers, and one agency published outdoor map.

Federal Agencies

U.S. Forest Service

Pennsylvania is in the Eastern Region (see Wisconsin chapter - U.S. Forest Svc... Eastern Region listing).

Grey Towers National Historic Landmark, Milford (see map B5). Grey Towers was the country home of Gifford Pinchot, the first Chief of the USFS and a two-term Governor of Pennsylvania. House and garden interpretive tours are available on the hour. For directions contact:

Pinchot Institute
PO Box 188
Milford PA, 18337   717-296-6401

USFWS National Wildlife Refuges

The John Heinz NWR and Tinicum National Environmental Center main entrance is at Lindbergh Blvd. and 86th Street in southwest Philadelphia. The Center is open from 8:30 a.m. to 4 p.m. daily.

National Park Service

The National Park regional (administrative) office in Philadelphia is not included in the Information Chart as there are no visitor facilities.

Additional NPS Locations in Pennsylvania

Edgar Allen Poe National Historic Site (0.52 acre)
(S# 9, map C5)
532 N. Seventh Street
Philadelphia, PA   215-597-7120
Note: Contact is Independence NHP (see below).

Eisenhower National Historic Site (690 acres)
(S# 10, map C3)
Gettysburg, PA 17325   717-334-1124

Independence National Historical Park (45 acres)
(S# 11, map C5)
313 Walnut Street
Philadelphia, PA 19106   215-597-7120

Steamtown National Historic Site (44 acres)
(S# 12, map A4)
150 South Eashington Ave.
Scranton, PA 18503   717-961-2033

Thaddeus Kosciuszko National Memorial (0.02 acre)
(S# 13, map C5)
301 Pine Street
Philadelphia, PA
c/o Independence NHP (see above)   215-597-7120

Wilderness/Wild River Index

Wilderness Areas

Allegheny National Forest (S# 1, map A2)
Allegheny Islands Wilderness - 368 acres
Hickory Creek Wilderness - 9,337 acres

Wild Rivers

Delaware (Middle) Natl. Scenic River
Delaware Watergap NRA (S# 2, map B5)

Outdoor Map Index

U.S. Forest Service Map

Allegheny National Forest [1981]
Scale: 1 inch = 2.0 miles (1 cm = 1.3 km)
Size: 30x34 inches (76x86 cm)

State Agencies

Department of Environmental Resources (DER)
Public Liason Office, 9th Floor
Fulton Building
PO Box 2063
Harrisburg, PA 17120   717-783-8303
Parent agency for the Bureau of State Parks and Bureau of Forestry in Pennsylvania.

Bureau of State Parks (S# 1, map C3)
A Pennsylvania Recreational Guide provides information on 114 state parks. It features a bar chart that provides facilities and activities information. Various special activity brochures are available from the Bureau. Selected parks are listed here and shown on the Pennsylvania map.

S#	MAP	Park Name & Address
2	C3	Caledonia SP, Fayetteville
3	B2	Cook Forest SP, Cooksburg
4	C4	French Creek SP, Elverson
5	B3	Kettle Creek SP, Renovo
6	B4	Locust Lake SP, Barnesville
7	C1	Ohiopyle SP, Ohiopyle
8	C3	Pine Grove Furnace SP, Gardners
9	B5	Promised Land SP, Greentown
10	C1	Raccoon Creek SP, Hookstown
11	B4	Ricketts Glen SP, Benton

Bureau of Forestry
PO Box 1467
Harrisburg, PA 17105-2703   717-787-2703
Contact the Bureau for state forest recreation literature.

Pennsylvania Game Commission
Guide coverage is limited to the Regional Office locations. Descriptive information about Pennsylvania's 283 Game Lands and a one-page map list/order form are available. A monthly magazine, Pennsylvania Game News, is available by subscription for $9 per year and at newsstands for $1.50 per copy.

Pennsylvania Fish Commission (PFC)
A round turquoise symbol and Information Chart color code identify PFC offices, and Fish Culture Stations with visitor centers. The PFC publishes books, pamphlets, and brochures on a variety of subjects including public fishing waters, boating access and fishing rules and regulations; and two magazines. A free Publications List is available on request.

The Pennsylvania Angler magazine is published monthly, and Boat Pennsylvania is a quarterly. They are available at agency offices for $1.50 per issue. You may subscribe through the headquarters office care of the Angler and/or Boat Circulation Department for $9 and $6 per year respectively.

Dept. of Commerce
Tourist Information
433 Forum Bldg.
Harrisburg, PA 17120   1-800-847-4872

Private Organizations

ANCA Locations in Pennsylvania

Asbury Woods Nature Center (S# 9, map A1)
4105 Asbury Road
Erie, PA 16506   814-838-4050

Briar Bush Nature Center (S# 10, map C5)
1212 Edge Hill Road
Abington, PA 19001   215-887-6603

Frick Nature Center (S# 11, map C1)
2005 Beachwood Blvd.
Pittsburgh, PA15217   412-422-6538

Peace Valley Nature Center (S# 12, map C5A1)
170 Chapman Road
Doylestown, PA 18901   215-345-7860

Philadelphia Zoological Garden (S# 13, map C5)
34th St. & Girard Ave.
Philadelphia, PA 19104   215-243-1100

Reading Nature Center (S# 14, map C4)
c/o 3rd & Spruce Recreation Center
Reading, PA 19601   215-320-6021

Silver Lake Nature Center (S# 15, map C5)
1306 Bath Road
Bristol, PA 19007   215-785-1177

Pennsylvania Bus. & Industry
(State Chamber of Commerce)
417 Walnut St.
Harrisburg, PA 17101   Phone 717-255-3252
Fax 717-255-3298

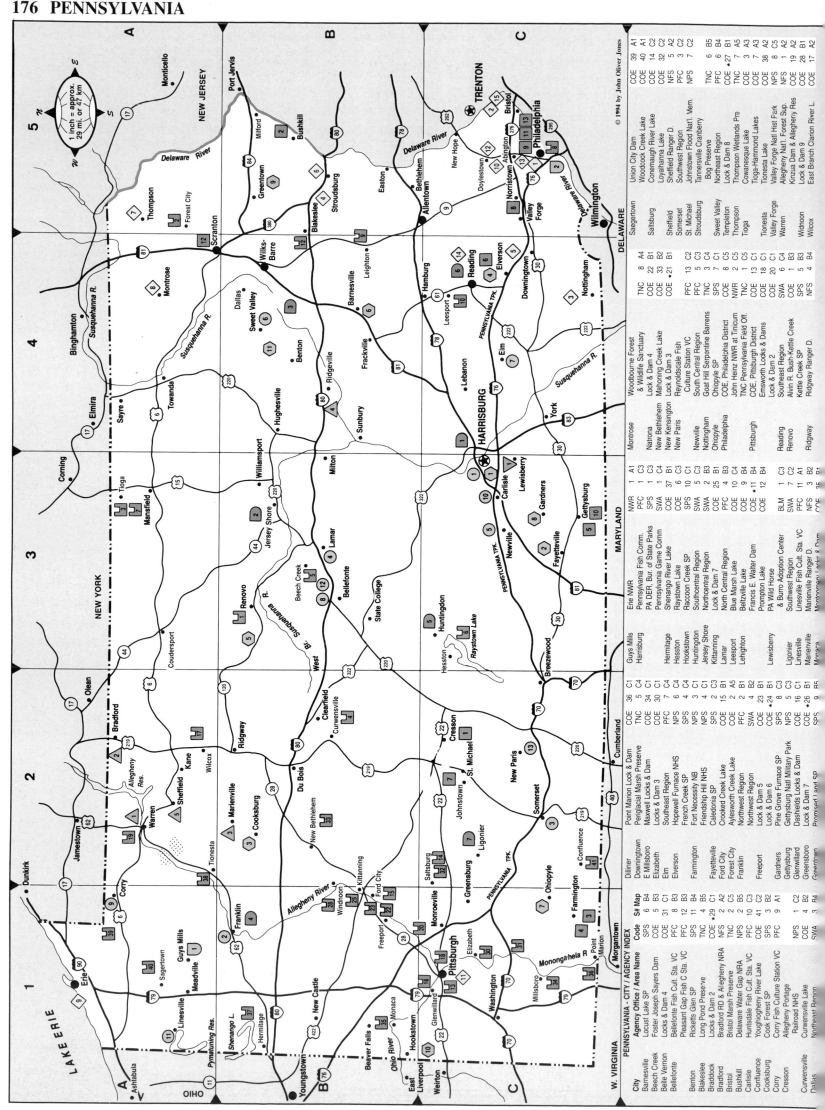

© 1994 by John Oliver Jones

AGENCY/MAP LEGEND — INITIALS, MAP SYMBOLS, COLOR CODES

- U.S. Forest Service Supervisor & Ranger Dist. Offices . . NFS [61]
- U.S. Army Corps of Engineers Rec. Areas & Offices . . . COE [31]
- USFWS National Wildlife Refuges & Offices . . . . NWR [40]
- National Park Service Parks & other NPS Sites . . . . . NPS [7]
- Bureau of Land Management Rec. Areas & Offices . . . . BLM [76]
- Pennsylvania Fish Commission Sites . . . . [16]
- State Parks (also see State Agency notes) . . . . SPS [52]
- State Wildlife Areas (also see State Agency notes) . . . SWA [19]
- Private Preserves, Nature Centers & Tribal Lands
- The Wild Rivers ~~~ and Wilderness Areas

★ INFORMATION CHART ★

INFORMATION CHART LEGEND - SYMBOLS & LETTER CODES

- ■ means **YES** & □ means **Yes with disability provisions**
- **sp** means **spring**, March through May
- **S** means **Summer**, June through August
- **F** means **Fall**, September through November
- **W** means **Winter**, December through February
- **T** means **Two (2) or Three (3) Seasons**
- **A** means **All Four (4) Seasons**
- **na** means **Not Applicable or Not Available**
- Note: empty or blank spaces in the chart mean **NO**
- Note: Refer to yellow block on page 7 (top right) for location name and address abbreviations. If a symbol number has a star ★ that symbol is not shown on the map.

S#	MAP	LOCATION NAME (state initials if more than one) with ADDRESS and/or LOCATION DATA	TELEPHONE	ACRES / ELEVATION
1	A2	Allegheny Nat'l Forest Sup., Spircon Bldg., Box 847, Warren 16365	814-723-5150	520,000 / 1,300
2	A2	Bradford Ranger D. & Allegheny NRA, Routes 59 & 321, Bradford 16701	814-362-4613	na / na
3	B2	Marienville Ranger D., Route 66, Marienville 16239	814-927-6628	na / na
4	B4	Ridgway Ranger D., Route 948, Ridgway 15853	814-776-6172	na / na
5	A2	Sheffield Ranger D., Route 6, Sheffield 16347	814-968-3232	na / na
		COE, Baltimore District, PO Box 1715, Baltimore, MD 21203	410-962-3693	na / na
1	B3	Alvin R. Bush - Kettle Creek, Star Route, Renovo 17764	717-923-1800	na / na
2	A5	Aylesworth Creek Lake, PO Box 143 Forest City 18421	717-679-2381	na / na
3	A3	Cowanesque Lake, RD 1, Box 65, Tioga 16946	717-835-5281	na / na
4	B2	Curwensville Lake, PO Box 128, Curwensville 16833	814-236-2000	na / na
5	B3	Foster Joseph Sayers Dam, PO Box 227, Beech Creek 16822	717-962-2500	na / na
6	C3	Raystown Lake, RD 1, Box 222, Hesston 16647	814-658-3405	na / na
7	A3	Tioga-Hammond Lakes, RD 1, Box 65, Tioga 16946	717-835-5281	na / na
8	C5	COE, Philadelphia District, U.S. Custom House, 2nd & Chestnut St., Philadelphia 19106	215-597-4741	na / na
9	B4	Beltzville Lake, Beltzville Dam Rd 4, Lehighton 18235	215-377-0438	na / na
10	C4	Blue Marsh Lake, Blue Marsh Lake, Leesport 19533	215-376-6337	na / na
*11	B4	Francis E. Walter Dam, Beltzville Dam Rd 4, Lehighton 18235	215-377-0438	na / na
12	B4	Prompton Lake, Lehighton 18235	215-377-0438	na / na
13	C1	COE, Pittsburgh District, 1000 Liberty Ave., Pittsburgh 15222	412-644-4191	na / na
14	C2	Conemaugh River Lake, RD 1, Box 702, Saltsburg 15681	412-459-7240	na / na
15	C1	Crooked Creek Lake, RD 3, Box 323A, Ford City 16226	412-763-3161	na / na
16	B1	Dashields Locks & Dam (Ohio River), PO Box 475, Glenwillard 15046	412-457-8430	na / na
17	A2	East Branch Clarion River Lake, RD 1, Wilcox 15870	814-965-2065	na / na
18	C1	Emsworth Locks & Dams (Ohio River), Pittsburgh 15202	412-766-6213	na / na
19	A2	Kinzua Dam & Allegheny Reservoir, PO Box 983, Warren 16365	814-726-0661	na / na
20	C1	Lock & Dam 2 (Allegheny River), 7451 Lock Way West, Pittsburgh 15206	412-661-2217	na / na
*21	B1	Lock & Dam 3 (Allegheny River), PO Box 208, New Kensington 15068	412-828-3550	na / na
22	B1	Lock & Dam 4 (Allegheny River), Natrona 15065	412-224-2666	na / na
23	B1	Lock & Dam 5 (Allegheny River), 830 River Road, Freeport 16229	412-295-2261	na / na
*24	B1	Lock & Dam 6 (Allegheny River), 1258 River Road, Freeport 16229	412-295-3775	na / na
25	B1	Lock & Dam 7 (Allegheny River), PO Box 874, Kittanning 16201	412-543-2551	na / na
*26	B1	Lock & Dam 7 (Monongahela River), PO Box 87, Greensboro 15338	412-943-3112	na / na
*27	B1	Lock & Dam 8 (Allegheny River), RD 1, Templeton 16259	412-548-5119	na / na
28	B1	Lock & Dam 9 (Allegheny River), Box 161, Widnoon 16261	412-868-2486	na / na
*29	C1	Locks & Dam 2 (Monongahela River), 11th Street, Braddock 15104	412-271-1272	na / na
30	C1	Locks & Dam 3 (Monongahela River), PO Box 455, Elizabeth 15037	412-384-4532	na / na
31	B1	Locks & Dam 4 (Monongahela River), RD 5, Box 25G, Belle Vernon 15012	412-684-8442	na / na
32	C2	Loyalhanna Lake, RD 2, Saltsburg 15681	412-639-9013	na / na
33	B2	Mahoning Creek Lake, RFD 1, Box 229, New Bethlehem 16242	814-257-8811	na / na
34	C1	Maxwell Locks & Dam (Monongahela Ri, RD 1, Box 181-A, E Millsboro 15433	412-785-5027	na / na
35	B1	Montgomery Locks & Dam (Ohio River), 100 Montgomery Dam Rd, Monaca 15061	412-643-8400	na / na
36	B1	Point Marion Lock & Dam (Monongahel, RD 1, Box 56, Dilliner 15327	412-725-5289	na / na
37	B1	Shenango River Lake, 2442 Kelly Rd. Hermitage 16150	412-962-7746	na / na
38	A2	Tionesta Lake, Tionesta Lake, Tionesta 16353	814-755-3512	na / na
39	A1	Union City Dam, Woodcock Creek Lake, Saegertown 16433	814-763-4422	na / na
40	A1	Woodcock Creek Lake, PO Box 629, Saegertown 16433	814-763-4422	na / na
41	C2	Youghiogheny Rive' Lake, RD 1, Box 17, Confluence 15424	814-395-3242	na / na
1	A1	Erie NWR, Wood Duck Lane, RD #1, Guys Mills 16327 [at 4-way stop in town go E on SR 198 0.8 mi; turn R at sign]	814-789-3585	8,750 / na
2	C5	John Heinz NWR at Tinicum, Suite 104, Scott Plaza 2, Philadelphia 19113 [close to Philadelphia Int. Airport]	215-365-3118	1,200 / 0-50
1	C2	Allegheny Portage Railroad NHS, PO Box 189, Cresson 16630 [Gallitzin exit, Hwy. 22]	814-886-6100	1,247 / 2,300

Column headings for the symbol matrix (FACILITIES, SERVICES, RECREATION OPPORTUNITIES & CONVENIENCES): Info Office (IO) / Visitor Center (VC); IO / VC Open Saturday / Sunday; Entry Fee; Concessionaire Services Available; Free Literature or Education Services; Agency Guided Tours / Study Programs; Interpretive Literature; Nature Education; Wildflower Viewing Sites; Archaeological / Geological Sites; Historic Sites; Interpretive Services; Developed Picnic Sites; No-Charge Campgrounds / Campsites; Developed Campgrounds / Campsites; Wilderness Areas / Hiking Trails; Walking / Hiking Opportunities; Bicycling Opportunities; Swimming Permitted; Off-Road Motorized Vehicle Area; Fishing in Season; Boating in Season; Horseback Riding; Motorized Watercraft OK; Non-Motorized Watercraft OK; Park & Walk-In Only Area; Winter Sports; Hunting in Season; Day Use Only, no overnight; Drinking Water; Restrooms.

★ INFORMATION CHART ★

AGENCY/MAP LEGEND ... INITIALS, MAP SYMBOLS, COLOR CODES

U.S. Forest Service Supervisor & Ranger Dist. Offices	NFS	61
U.S. Army Corps of Engineers Rec. Areas & Offices	COE	31
USFWS National Wildlife Refuges & Offices	NWR	40
National Park Service Parks & other NPS Sites	NPS	7
Bureau of Land Management Rec. Areas & Offices	BLM	26
Pennsylvania Fish Commission Sites		16
State Parks (also see State Agency notes)	SPS	52
State Wildlife Areas (also see State Agency notes)	SWA	19
Private Preserves, Nature Centers & Tribal Lands		(15)
The Wild Rivers ~~~ and Wilderness Areas		

Note: Refer to yellow block on page 7 (top right) for location name and address abbreviations.

INFORMATION CHART LEGEND - SYMBOLS & LETTER CODES

■ means **YES** & □ means **Yes** with disability provisions
sp means spring, March through May
S means Summer, June through August
F means Fall, September through November
W means Winter, December through February
T means Two (2) or Three (3) Seasons
A means All Four (4) Seasons
na means Not Applicable or Not Available
Note: empty or blank spaces in the chart mean **NO**
★ that symbol is not shown on the map.

S#	MAP	LOCATION NAME (state initials if more than one) with ADDRESS and/or LOCATION DATA	TELEPHONE	ACRES / ELEVATION
2	B5	Delaware Water Gap NRA (NJ/PA), Delaware Nat'l. Scenic River, Bushkill 18324	717-588-2435	68,170 / na
3	C1	Fort Necessity NB, The National Pike, RD 2, Box 528, Farmington 15437	412-329-5512	903 / 2,000
4	C1	Friendship Hill NHS c/o Ft. Necessi, The Nat'l. Pike, RD #2, Box 528, Farmington 15437	412-725-9190	661 / 1,000
5	C3	Gettysburg National Military Park, PO Box 1080, Gettysburg 17325	717-334-1124	3,865 / 500-750
6	C4	Hopewell Furnace NHS, 2 Mark Bird Lane, Elverson 19520 [6 mi S of Birdsboro on PA Rt. 345]	215-582-8773	848 / 460-920
7	C2	Johnstown Flood Nat'l. Memorial, PO Box 355, St. Michael 16951	814-495-4643	163 / 2,200-2,400
8	C5	Valley Forge National Historical Pa, Rt. 23 & N. Gulf Road, Box 953, Valley Forge 19481	215-783-1077	3,468 / 100
1	C3	BLM - PA Wild Horse & Burro Adopt. Ctr., PO Box 178, Lewisberry 17339 [between York & Harrisburg]	717-938-2560	na / na
1	C3	**Pennsylvania Fish Commission**, 3532 Walnut St., PO Box 1673, Harrisburg 17105	717-657-4518	na / na
2	B1	Northwest Region, Box 349, Franklin 16323	814-437-5774	na / na
3	C2	Southwest Region, RD #2, Box 39, Somerset 15501	814-445-8974	na / na
4	B3	North Central Region, Box 187, Lamar 16848	717-726-6056	na / na
5	C3	South Central Region, 1704 Pine Road, Newville 17214	717-486-7087	na / na
6	B4	Northeast Region, Box 88, Sweet Valley 18656	717-477-5717	na / na
7	C4	Southeast Region, Box 8, Elm 17521	717-626-0228	na / na
8	B3	Bellefonte Fish Culture Station VC #4, Box 230, Bellefonte 16823	814-355-3371	na / na
9	A1	Corry Fish Culture Station VC, 13363 W. Smith Street Ext., Corry 16407	814-664-2122	na / na
10	C3	Huntsdale Fish Culture Station VC, 195 Lebo Road, Carlisle 17013	717-486-3419	na / na
11	A1	Linesville Fish Culture Station VC, Box 127, Linesville 16424	814-683-4451	na / na
12	B3	Pleasant Gap Fish Culture Sta. VC, 450 Robinson Lane, Bellefonte 16823	814-359-5132	na / na
13	C2	Reynoldsdale Fish Culture Sta. VC, RD #1, Box 50, New Paris 15554	814-839-2211	na / na
1	C3	**PA DER, Bur. of State Parks**, 2150 Harr St., PO Box 8551, Harrisburg 17105	800-637-2757	na / na
1	C4	**Pennsylvania Game Commission**, 2001 Elmerton Avenue, Harrisburg 17110	717-787-4250	na / na
2	B3	Northcentral Region, PO Box 5038, Jersey Shore 17740	800-422-7551	na / na
3	B4	Northeast Region, PO Box 220, Dallas 18612	800-228-0789	na / na
4	B2	Northwest Region, PO Box 31, Franklin 16323	800-533-6764	na / na
5	C4	Southcentral Region, PO Box 537, Huntingdon 16652	800-422-7554	na / na
6	C4	Southeast Region, RD #2, Box 2584, Reading 19605	800-228-0791	na / na
7	C2	Southwest Region, PO Box A, Ligonier 15658	800-243-8519	na / na
1	C5	**TNC Pennsylvania Field Office**, 1211 Chestnut St., 12th Floor, Philadelphia 19107	215-925-1065	na / na
2	C5	Bristol Marsh Preserve, contact Field Office, near Bristol	215-925-1065	20 / -10-10
3	C4	Goat Hill Serpentine Barrens, contact Field Office, near Nottingham	215-925-1065	803 / 180-450
4	B5	Long Pond Pre., c/o Monroe Co. CD, mail to: 8050 Running Valley Rd., Stroudsburg, PA. 18360, near Blakeslee	717-629-3061	453 / 1,820-1,970
5	C4	Periglacial Marsh Preserve, contact Field Office, N of Downingtown	215-925-1065	400 / na
6	B5	Tannersville Cranberry Bog & SM Stein Mem. Pre, c/o Monroe Co CD, 8050 Running Valley Rd., Stroudsburg 18360	717-629-3061	719 / 910-950
7	A5	Thompson Wetlands Preserve, contact Field Office, N of Thompson	215-925-1065	453 / 1,660-1,720
8	A4	Woodbourne Forest & Wildlife Sanct., RD #6, Box 6294, Montrose 18801	717-278-3384	648 / 1,300-1,650

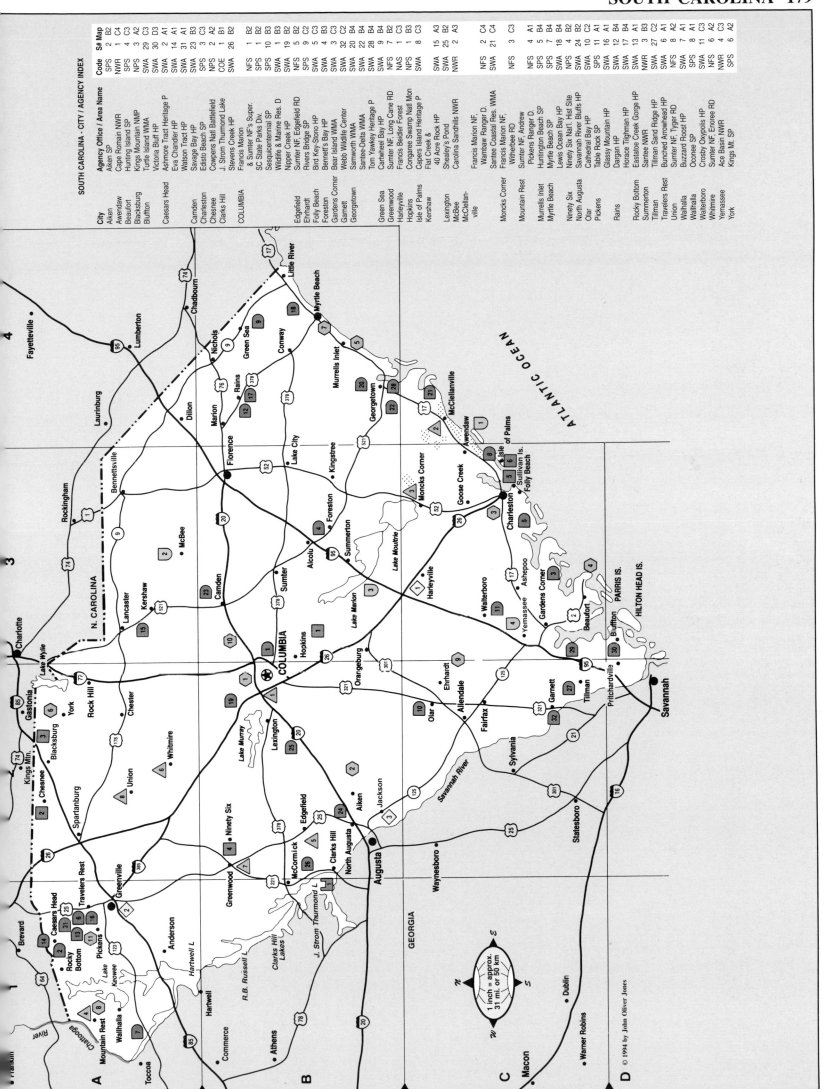

SOUTH CAROLINA NOTES

Summary

There are 19 federal, 45 state, and 4 private recreation areas or local administrative offices covered in this state chapter. Of these, 51 appear in the Information Chart and 17 are covered in the notes. The special indexes feature 7 federally designated wilderness areas and wild rivers, and 6 agency published outdoor maps.

U.S. Forest Service

South Carolina is in the Southern Region (see Georgia chapter - U.S. Forest Svc., Southern Region listing).

National Park Service

Kings Mountain Nat'l Military Park in South Carolina has a North Carolina post office address.

Additional NPS Locations in South Carolina

Charles Pinckney National Historic Site (25 acres)
(S# 5, map C3)
c/o Fort Sumter National Monument
1214 Middle Street
Sullivan Island, SC 29482
803-883-3123

Federal Agencies

U.S. Forest Service

National Park Service

Fort Sumter National Monument (194 acres)
(S# 6, map C3)
1214 Middle Street
Sullivan Island, SC 29482
803-883-3123

National Wildlife Refuges

The Savannah (GA) coastal refuges extend for 100 miles along the coast and include Pinckney Island in South Carolina. See the Georgia chapter for details.

Wilderness/Wild River Index

Wilderness Areas

Ellicott Rock Wilderness - 2,809 acres
Sumter NF, Andrew Pickens RD (S# 4, map A1)
Hell Hole Bay Wilderness - 1,980 acres
Francis Marion NF, Witherbee RD (S# 3, map C3)
Little Wambaw Swamp Wilderness - 5,000 acres
Wambaw Creek Wilderness - 1,640 acres
Wambaw Swamp Wilderness - 5,100 acres
Francis Marion NF, Wambaw RD (S# 2, map C2)
Cape Romain Wilderness - 29,000 acres
Cape Romain NWR (S# 1, map C4)

Wild River

Chattooga Wild River - also see GA and NC
Sumter NF, Andrew pickens RD (S# 4, map A1)

Outdoor Map Index

U.S. Forest Service Maps

Chattooga National Wild & Scenic River [1981]
Francis Marion National Forest [1981]
Sumter NF, Andrew Pickens Ranger D. [1981]
Sumter NF, Edgefield/Long Cane RDs [1985]
Sumter NF, Enoree & Tyger RDs [1985]
Trail Guide Andrew Pickens RD, Sumter NF [1985]

State Agencies

Department of Parks, Recreation, & Tourism

State Parks Division

A *South Carolina State Parks Guide* (33 state parks) is available free. The guide describes each area, contains a locator map, and includes information on facilities and activities. Selected parks are listed here and symbolized on the map.

state-owned and leased wildlife management areas open to the public.

Tourism Division

PO Box 71
Columbia, SC 29201

Private Organizations

ANCA Locations in South Carolina

Roper Mountain Science Center (S# 2, map A1)
504 Roper Mountain Road
Greenville, SC 29615   803-297-0232

Silver Bluff Sanctuary (S# 3, map B2)
RR #1, Box 391
Jackson, SC 29831   803-827-0781

S. Carolina Chamber of Commerce

1201 Main St., #1810   Phone 803-799-4601
Columbia, SC 29201-3254   Fax 803-799-6043

S#	MAP	PARK NAME & LOCATION
2	B2	Aiken SP, Aiken
3	C3	Edisto Beach SP, Charleston
4	C3	Hunting Island SP, Beaufort
5	B4	Huntington Beach SP, Murrells Inlet
6	A2	Kings Mt. SP, York
7	B4	Myrtle Beach SP, Myrtle Beach
8	A1	Oconee SP, Walhalla
9	C2	Rivers Bridge SP, Ehrhardt
10	B3	Sesquicentennial SP, Columbia
11	A1	Table Rock SP, Pickens

South Carolina Forestry Commission

PO Box 21707
Columbia, SC 29221   803-737-8800
There is no state forest recreation program in South Carolina.

Wildlife & Marine Resources Dept. (WMRD)

South Carolina Heritage Preserves and selected WMAs are covered on the Guide map and in the Information Chart. A twice-a-year publication, *The Resource*, is available free to residents and for $2 per issue to nonresidents. The hunting regulations contain a list of

★ INFORMATION CHART ★

INFORMATION CHART LEGEND - SYMBOLS & LETTER CODES

■ means **YES** & □ means **Yes with disability provisions**
sp means spring, March through May
S means Summer, June through August
F means Fall, September through November
W means Winter, December through February
T means Two (2) or Three (3) Seasons
A means All Four (4) Seasons
na means Not Applicable or Not Available
Note: empty or blank spaces in the chart mean **NO**

AGENCY/MAP LEGEND ... INITIALS, MAP SYMBOLS, COLOR CODES

U.S. Forest Service Supervisor & Ranger Dist. Offices NFS [61]
U.S. Army Corps of Engineers Rec. Areas & Offices . COE [31]
USFWS National Wildlife Refuges & Offices ...... NWR [40]
National Park Service Parks & other NPS Sites ..... NPS [7]
Bureau of Land Management Rec. Areas & Offices ... BLM [26]
Bureau of Reclamation Rec. Areas & Reg. Offices ... BOR [8]
State Parks (also see State Agency notes) .... SPS [52]
State Wildlife Areas (also see State Agency notes) . SWA [19]
Private Preserves, Nature Centers & Tribal Lands .. [15]
The Wild Rivers ～ and Wilderness Areas

Note: Refer to yellow block on page 7 (top right) for location name and address abbreviations. If a symbol number has a star ★ that symbol is not shown on the map.

FACILITIES, SERVICES, RECREATION OPPORTUNITIES & CONVENIENCES

S#	MAP	LOCATION NAME (state initials if more than one) with ADDRESS and/or LOCATION DATA	TELEPHONE	ACRES / ELEVATION
	B2	**Francis Marion & Sumter NF's**, 1835 Assembly St., Rm 333, Columbia 29201 [moving to Broad River Rd in 1994]	803-765-5222	560,000 / 20-2,000
2	C4	Francis Marion NF, Wambaw Ranger D., PO Box 788, McClellanville 29458	803-887-3311	120,000 / 10
3	C3	Francis Marion NF, Witherbee RD, HC 69, Box 1532, Moncks Corner 29461	803-336-3248	130,000 / 20
4	A1	Sumter NF, Andrew Pickens Ranger S., Sumphouse Ranger S., 112 Andrew Pickens Cir., Mountain Rest 29664	803-638-9568	80,000 / 2,000
5	B2	Sumter NF, Edgefield Ranger D., 321 Bacon Street, PO Box 30, Edgefield 29824	803-637-5396	55,000 / 350
6	A2	Sumter NF, Enoree Ranger D., Rt. #1, Box 179, Whitmire 29178	803-276-4810	60,000 / 350
7	B2	Sumter NF, Long Cane Ranger D., Room 201, Federal Bldg., PO Box 3168, Greenwood 29648	803-229-2406	60,000 / 350
8	B2	Sumter NF, Tyger Ranger D., Duncan By-Pass, Highway 176, Union 29379	803-427-9858	55,000 / 350
1	B1	**COE, Savannah District**, PO Box 889, Savannah, GA 31402	912-944-5997	na / na
1	B1	J. Strom Thurmond Lake, Rt. #1, Box 6, Clarks Hill 29821	706-722-3770	na / na
1	C4	**Cape Romain NWR**, 390 Bulls Island Rd., Awendaw 29429	803-928-3368	65,000 / 10
2	A3	Carolina Sandhills NWR, Rt. #2, Box 330, McBee 29101 [3.5 mi N of McBee on US 1]	803-335-8401	45,586 / 250-500
3	B3	Santee NWR, Rt. #2, Box 66, Summerton 29148	803-478-2217	15,095 / 76
4	C3	Ace Basin NWR, PO Box 840, Yemassee 29945	803-846-9110	na / na
1	B3	**Congaree Swamp Natl Monument**, 200 Caroline Sims Rd., Hopkins 29061 [20 mi SE of Columbia off SC-48]	803-776-4396	22,200 / 85-110
2	A2	Cowpens Natl Battlefield, PO Box 308, Chesnee 29323 [from I-85, W on SR 11 10 mi to N3, 0.2 mi E of int. w/SR 110]	803-461-2828	841 / 900
3	A2	Kings Mtn. NMP, mail to: PO Box 40, Kings Mtn., NC 28086 [take NC I-85 exit, go S on Hwy 216, near Blacksburg SC]	803-936-7921	3,945 / na
4	A2	Ninety Six Nat'l. Historic Site, 1103 Hwy, 248, PO Box 496, Ninety Six 29666	803-543-4068	989 / na
1		**SC State Parks Div.**, Dept. Parks, Rec. & Tourism, 1205 Pendleton St., Columbia 29201 [see notes]	803-734-0156	na / na

#	Code	Name/Location	Phone	Acres	1	2	3	4	5	6	7	8	9	10	11	#
3	C3	Bear Island WMA, Colleton Co., E of Gardens Corner	803-844-2952	11,055 / na	■	■			■				■	■ ■	■	3
4	B3	Bennett's Bay HP, Clarendon County, Foreston	803-734-3894	532 / na		■		■	■				■	■ ■		4
5	C3	Bird Key-Stono HP, Charleston County, Folly Beach	803-734-3894	20 / na		■		■	■				■	■ ■		5
6	A1	Bunched Arrowhead HP, Greenville County, Travelers Rest	803-734-3894	181 / 300		■		■	■					■ ■		6
7	A1	Buzzard Roost HP, Oconee County, Walhalla	803-734-3894	285 / 1,769		■		■	■			■		■ ■		7
8	C3	Capers Island Heritage Preserve, Charleston County, Isle of Palms	803-734-3894	2,100 / na		■			■	■	■ ■ ■ ■		■			8
9	B4	Cartwheel Bay HP, Horry County, Green Sea	803-734-3894	568 / na		■		■	■				■	■ ■		9
10	C2	Cathedral Bay HP, Bamberg County, Olar	803-734-3894	58 / na		■		■	■				■	■ ■		10
11	C3	Crosby Oxypolis HP, Colleton County, Walterboro	803-734-3894	32 / na		■		■	■				■	■ ■		11
12	B4	Dargan HP, Marion County, Rains	803-734-3894	1,624 / na		■		■	■		■	■	■ ■			12
13	A1	Eastatoe Creek Gorge HP, Pickens County, Rocky Bottom	803-734-3894	373 / 2,100		■	■	■					■			13
14	A1	Eva Chandler HP, Greenville County, Caesars Head	803-734-3894	251 / 1,600		■		■					■ ■			14
15	A3	Flat Creek/40 Acre Rock HP, Lancaster County, Kershaw	803-734-3894	1,436 / na		■	■	■					■ ■			15
16	A1	Glassy Mountain HP, Pickens County, Pickens	803-734-3894	65 / 2,000		■		■					■ ■			16
17	B4	Horace Tilghman HP, Marion County, Rains	803-734-3894	455 / na		■		■	■	■	■	■	■ ■			17
18	B4	Lewis Ocean Bay HP, Horry County, Myrtle Beach	803-734-3894	6,422 / na		■			■				■ ■			18
19	B2	Nipper Creek HP, Richland County, NW of Columbia	803-734-3894	68 / na		■	■ ■						■ ■			19
20	B4	Samworth WMA, N of Georgetown	803-546-9849	1,263 / na	■	■					■	■	■	■		20
21	C4	Santee Coastal Reserve WMA, Charleston/Georgetown Cos., McClellanville	803-546-8665	24,000 / na	■	■					■	■ ■	■			21
22	B4	Santee-Delta WMA, Georgetown County, S of Georgetown	803-546-9849	1,722 / na	■						■	■ ■				22
23	B3	Savage Bay HP, Kershaw County, Camden	803-734-3894	74 / na		■		■	■			■	■ ■			23
24	B2	Savannah River Bluffs HP, Aiken County, North Augusta	803-734-3894	70 / na		■			■				■ ■			24
25	B2	Shealey's Pond, Lexington County, Lexington	803-734-3894	62 / na		■			■				■ ■			25
26	B2	Stevens Creek HP, McCormick County, Clarks Hill	803-734-3894	220 / na		■		■	■				■ ■			26
27	C2	Tillman Sand Ridge HP, Jasper County, Tillman	803-734-3894	953 / na		■		■	■				■ ■			27
28	B4	Tom Yawkey Heritage Preserve, Georgetown County, SE of Georgetown	803-546-6814	17,700 / na	■	■			■				■ ■			28
29	C3	Turtle Island WMA, on coast in Jasper Co., N of Bluffton	803-734-3888	1,700 / na							■	■ ■	■ ■			29
30	D3	Victoria Bluff HP, Beaufort County, Bluffton	803-734-3894	1,111 / na		■		■					■ ■			30
31	A1	Watson Tract HP, Greenville County, Caesars Head	803-734-3894	1,660 / 3,000		■		■	■			■	■ ■			31
32	C2	Webb Wildlife Center, Hampton County, SW of Garnett	803-625-3569	5,866 / na	■	■			■	■	■		■	■		32
◇1	C3	**Francis Beidler Forest**, Rt. #1, Box 600, Harleyville 29448	803-462-2150	5,800 / na	■	■ ■ ■		■ ■		■			◇1	■ ■ ■		1

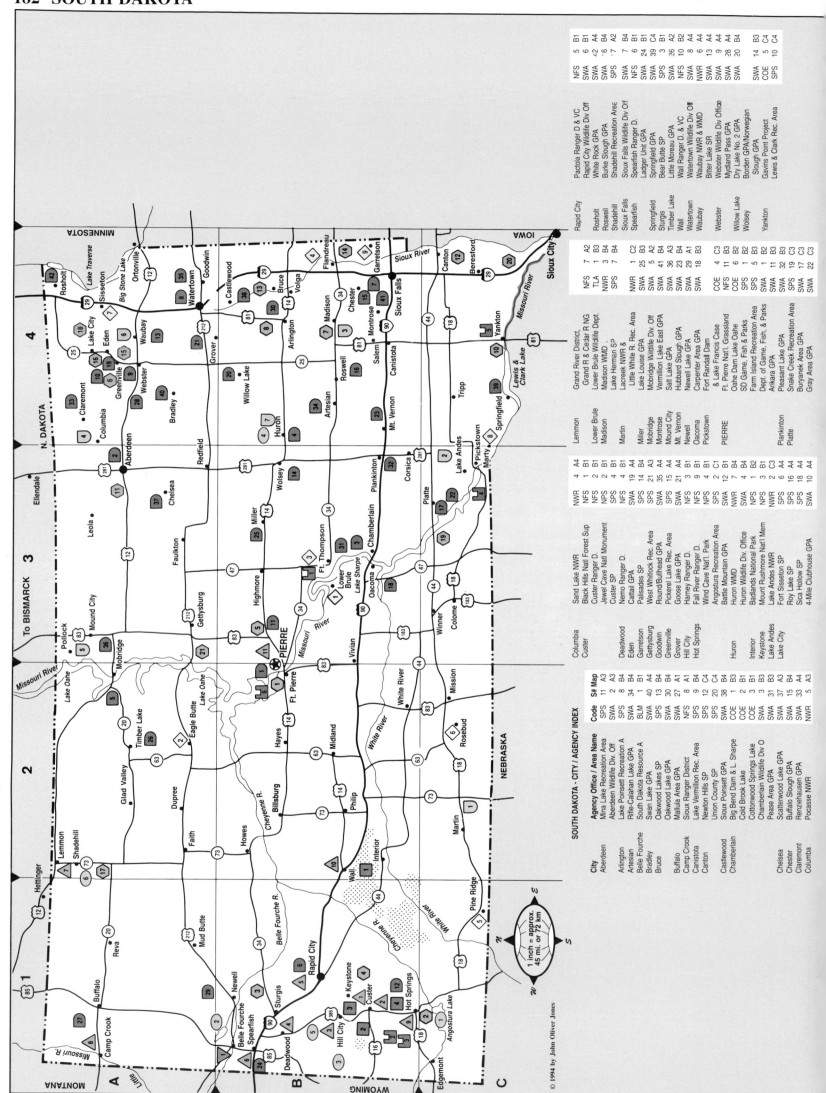

SOUTH DAKOTA - CITY / AGENCY INDEX

City	Agency Office / Area Name	Code	S#	Map
Aberdeen	Mina Lake Recreation Area	SPS	11	A3
	Aberdeen Wildlife Div. Off	SWA	2	A3
Arlington	Lake Poinsett Recreation A	SPS	8	B4
Artesian	Rifle-Calahan Lake GPA	SWA	34	B4
Belle Fourche	South Dakota Resource A	BLM	1	B1
Bradley	Swan Lake GPA	SWA	40	A4
Bruce	Oakwood Lakes SP	SPS	13	B4
	Oakwood Lakes GPA	SWA	30	B4
Buffalo	Mallula Area GPA	SWA	27	A1
Camp Crook	Sioux Ranger District	NFS	8	A1
Canistota	Lake Vermilion Rec. Area	SPS	9	B4
Canton	Newton Hills SP	SPS	12	C4
	Union County SP	SPS	20	C4
Castlewood	Sioux Poinsett GPA	SWA	38	B4
Chamberlain	Big Bend Dam & L. Sharpe	COE	1	B3
	Cold Brook Lake	COE	2	B1
	Cottonwood Springs Lake	COE	3	B1
	Chamberlain Wildlife Div O	SWA	31	B3
Chelsea	Scatterwood Lake GPA	SWA	37	A3
Chester	Buffalo Slough GPA	SWA	15	B4
Claremont	Renziehausen GPA	SWA	33	A4
Columbia	Pocasse NWR	NWR	5	A3

Columbia	Sand Lake NWR	NWR	4	A4
Custer	Black Hills Natl Forest Sup	NFS	1	B1
	Jewel Cave Natl Monument	NPS	2	B1
	Custer SP	SPS	4	B1
Deadwood	Nemo Ranger D.	NFS	3	B1
Eden	Cattail GPA	SWA	19	A4
Garretson	Palisades SP	SPS	14	B4
Gettysburg	West Whitlock Rec. Area	SPS	21	A3
Goodwin	Round/Bullhead GPA	SWA	5	A4
Greenville	Pickerel Lake Rec. Area	SPS	35	A4
Grover	Goose Lake GPA	SWA	21	A4
Hill City	Harney Ranger D.	NFS	3	B1
Hot Springs	Fall River Ranger D.	NFS	9	B1
	Wind Cave Nat'l. Park	NPS	4	B1
	Angostura Recreation Area	SPS	2	C1
Huron	Battle Mountain GPA	SWA	12	B1
	Huron WMD	NWR	7	B4
	Huron Wildlife Div. Office	SWA	4	B4
Interior	Badlands National Park	NPS	1	B2
Keystone	Mount Rushmore Nat'l Mem	NPS	2	C3
Lake Andes	Lake Andes NWR	NWR	2	C3
Lake City	Fort Sisseton SP	SPS	6	A4
	Roy Lake SP	SPS	16	A4
	Sica Hollow SP	SPS	18	A4
	4-Mile Clubhouse GPA	SWA	10	A4

Lemmon	Grand River District,	NFS	7	A2
	Grand R & Cedar R NG	TLA	1	B3
Lower Brule	Lower Brule Wildlife Dept.	NWR	3	B4
Madison	Madison WMD ,	SPS	7	B4
	Lake Herman SP			
Martin	Lacreek NWR &	NWR	1	C2
	Little White R. Rec. Area			
Miller	Lake Louise GPA	SWA	25	B3
Mobridge	Mobridge Wildlife Div. Off	SWA	5	A2
Montrose	Vermillion Lake East GPA	SWA	41	B4
Mound City	Salt Lake GPA	SWA	36	A3
Newell	Hubbard Slough GPA	SWA	23	B4
Oacoma	Newell Lake GPA	SWA	29	A1
Pickstown	Carpenter Lake GPA	SWA	18	A3
PIERRE	Fort Randall Dam	COE	4	C3
	& Lake Francis Case	NFS	11	B1
	Ft. Pierre Nat'l. Grassland	COE	6	B2
	Oahe Dam Lake Oahe	SPS	5	B3
	SD Game, Fish & Parks	SWA	1	B2
	Farm Island Recreation Area	SPS	11	B4
	Dept. of Game, Fish, & Parks	SWA	32	B3
Plankinton	Pleasant Lake GPA	SPS	19	C3
Platte	Snake Creek Recreation Area	SWA	17	C3
	Buryanek Area GPA	SWA	22	C3
	Gray Area GPA			

Rapid City	Pactola Ranger D & VC	NFS	5	B1
	Rapid City Wildlife Div Off	SWA	6	B1
Rosholt	White Rock GPA	SWA	-2	A4
Roswell	Burke Slough GPA	SPS	-7	A2
Shadehill	Shadehill Recreation Area	SWA	7	B4
Sioux Falls	Sioux Falls Wildlife Div Off	NFS	6	B1
Spearfish	Spearfish Ranger D.	SWA	24	B1
	Ladger Unit GPA	SPS	39	C4
Springfield	Springfield GPA	SPS	3	B1
Sturgis	Bear Butte SP	SWA	26	A2
Timber Lake	Little Moreau GPA	NFS	10	B2
Wall	Wall Ranger D. & VC	SWA	8	A1
Watertown	Watertown Wildlife Div Off	NWR	6	A4
Waubay	Waubay NWR & WMD	SWA	13	A4
	Biter Lake SR	SWA	28	A4
Webster	Webster Wildlife Div Office	SWA	20	B4
Willow Lake	Mydland Pass GPA			
Wolsey	Dry Lake No. 2 GPA	SWA	14	B3
	Borden GPA/Norwegian	COE	5	C4
Yankton	Gavins Point Project	SPS	10	C4
	Lewis & Clark Rec. Area			

SOUTH DAKOTA NOTES

Summary

There are 37 federal, 65 state and 10 private recreation areas or local administrative offices covered in this state chapter. Of these, 60 appear in the notes. The special indexes feature 3 federally designated wilderness areas and wild rivers, and 8 agency published outdoor maps. See North Dakota chapter for information on 56 BLM intermediate scale maps covering South Dakota.

Federal Agencies

U.S. Forest Service

South Dakota is in the Rocky Mountain Region (see Colorado chapter - U.S. Forest Svc., Rocky Mountain Region listing).

Pactola Visitor Center - Cultural and natural history orientation for the Black Hills.

(see S# 5, map B1, Pactola RD of the Black Hills NF)
Rapid City, SD   605-343-1567

Bureau of Reclamation Recreation Areas

Six recreation areas are listed here and symbolized on the South Dakota state map.

S#	MAP	RECREATION AREA
1	C1	Angostua Res.
2	B1	Belle Fourche Res.
3	B1	Deerfield Res.
4	B4	James Diversion Cam
5	B1	Pactola Res.
6	A2	Shadehill Res.

Wilderness/Wild River Index

Wilderness

Black Elk Wilderness - 9,824 acres
  Black Hills Natl. Forest (S# 1, map B1)
Badlands Wilderness - 64,250 acres
  Badlands National Park (S# 1, map B2)

Wild River

Missouri National Recreation River
  see Nebraska, Midwest Region, NPS (S# 1, map B5)

Outdoor Map Index

National Park Service (USGS Maps)

Badlands National Park [1981]
  Scale: 1 inch = 0.8 mile (1 cm = 0.5 km)
  Size: 54x26 inches (137x65 cm)
Wind Cave National Park [1957]
  Scale: 1 inch = 0.4 mile (1 cm = 0.3 km)
  Size: 37x41 inches (94x104 cm)

U.S. Forest Service Maps

Black Hills National Forest
  Scale: 1 inch = 0.5 mile (1 cm = 0.3 km)
Buffalo Gap National Grassland
  Scale: 1 inch = 0.5 mile (1 cm = 0.3 km)
Custer National Forest, Sioux Div [1982]
Custer NF, Little Missouri Natl. Grassland [1986]
Custer, Grand & Cedar River N. Grasslands [1981]
  Scale: 1 inch = 0.5 mile (1 cm = 0.3 km)
Fort Pierre National Grassland
  Scale: 1 inch = 0.5 mile (1 cm = 0.3 km)

Bureau of Land Management Maps

The BLM map grid for South Dakota is featured in the North Dakota chapter notes. Refer to the North Dakota chapter regards intermediate scale maps for both states.

USGS Earth Science Information Centers

USGS Sioux Falls-ESIC
EROS Data Center
Sioux Falls, SD 57198   605-594-6151

State Agencies

SD Game, Fish & Parks Department

Game & Fish Office

The *South Dakota Sportsman's Atlas* is a basic reference guide for all DGFP wildlife areas. A bi-monthly magazine, *South Dakota Conservation Digest*, is available by subscription for $5 per year.

The Information Chart lists agency Division Offices. There are more than 300 South Dakota Game Production, Refuge, Game Bird, Waterfowl, Lake Access, and Public Shooting Areas, and Federal Waterfowl Production Areas. Selected larger areas are listed here and are symbolized on the Guide map.

S#	MAP	NAME & LOCATION
10	A4	4-Mile Clubhouse GPA, Lake City
11	B3	Arikara GPA, Pierre
12	B1	Battle Mountain GPA, Hot Springs
13	A4	Bitter Lake SR, Waubay
14	A3	Borden/Norwegial Slough GPAs, Wolsey
15	B4	Buffalo Slough GPA, Chester
16	B4	Burke Slough GPA, Roswell
17	C3	Buyanek Area GPA, Platte
18	B3	Carpenter Area GPA, Oacoma
19	A4	Cattail GPA, Eden
20	B4	Dry Lake No. 2 GPA, Willow Lake
21	A4	Goose Lake GPA, Grover
22	C3	Gray Area GPA, Platte
23	A4	Hubbard Slough GPA, Mt. Vernon
24	B1	Ladger Unit GPA, Spearfish
25	B3	Lake Louise GPA, Miller
26	A2	Little Moreau GPA, Timber Lake
27	A1	Mallula Area GPA, Buffalo
28	A4	Mydland Pass GPA, Webster
29	A1	Newell Lake GPA, Newell
30	B4	Oakwood Lake GPA, Bruce
31	B3	Pease Area GPA, Chamberlain
32	B3	Pleasant Lake GPA, Plankinton
33	A4	Renziehausen GPA, Claremont
34	B4	Rifle-Calahan Lake GPA, Artesian
35	A4	Round/Bullhead GPA, Goodwin
36	A3	Salt Lake GPA, Mound City
37	A3	Scatterwood Lake GPA, Chelsea
38	B4	Sioux Poinsett GPA, Castlewood
39	C4	Springfield GPA, Springfield
40	A4	Swan Lake GPA, Bradley
41	B4	Vermillion Lake East GPA, Montrose
42	A4	White Rock GPA, Rosholt

SD Game, Fish & Parks Department

Office of State Parks

A *South Dakota State Park Guide* provides information on 13 state parks, 25 recreation areas, 40 lakeside use areas, and two nature areas. There are 14 park district

offices throughout the state. The guide contains a locator map and includes information on facilities and activities at each area. There is a daily entry fee at most of the parks, and camping fees.

Department of Agriculture

Division of Forestry

Sigurd Anderson Bldg.
445 E Capitol
Pierre SD 57501   605-773-3623

There is no state forest recreation program in South Dakota.

South Dakota Division of Tourism

PO Box 1000
Pierre, SD 57501   1-800-843-1930
in state   1-800-952-2217

Private Organizations

Tribal Land Areas in South Dakota

Cheyenne River Sioux Tribe of the Cheyenne River Indian Reservation - Fishing, hunting, camping, boating.
Cheyenne River Sioux Tribal Council (S# 2, map A2)
PO Box 590
Eagle Butte, SD 57625   605-964-4155

Crow Creek Sioux Tribe of the Crow Creek Indian Reservation - Fishing, hunting, camping, boating, hiking.
Crow Creek Sioux Tribal Council (S# 3, map B3)
PO Box 658
Fort Thompson, SD 57339   605-245-2221

Flandreau Santee Sioux Tribe of the Flandreau Santee Sioux Indian Reservation - Camping.
Flandreau Santee Sioux Executive Committee
(S# 4, map B4)
Flandreau Field Office
Box 283
Flandreau, SD 57028   605-997-3891

Oglala Sioux Tribe of the Pine Ridge Indian Reservation - Fishing, hunting, boating.
Oglala Sioux Tribal Council (South Dakota/Nebraska)
(S# 5, map C1)
Pine Ridge, SD 57770   605-867-5821

Rosebud Sioux Tribe of the Rosebud Indian Reservation - Fishing, hunting, camping, boating.
Rosebud Sioux Tribal Council (S# 6, map C2)
Rosebud, SD 57339   605-747-2381

Sissetcn-Wahpeton Sioux Tribe of the Lake Traverse Indian Reservation - Fishing, hunting, boating.
Sissetcn-Wahpeton Sioux Tribal Council (N. & S. Dakota) (S# 7, map A4)
Route 2, Agency Village
Sisseton, SD 57262   605-698-3911

Yankton Sioux Tribe of the Yankton Indian Reservation - Fishing, hunting, camping, boating.
Yankton Sioux Tribal Business and Claims Committee
(S# 8, map C4)
Box 243
Marty, SD 57361   605-384-3641

ANCA Locations in South Dakota

Beaver Creek Nature Area (S# 9, map B4)
Route 3, Box 70
Garretson, SD 57005   605-594-3824

Industry & Commerce Assn. of SD

(State Chamber of Commerce)
PO Box 190
Pierre, SD 57501-0190   605-224-6161

★ INFORMATION CHART ★

INFORMATION CHART LEGEND - SYMBOLS & LETTER CODES

- ■ means **YES** & □ means **Yes** with disability provisions
- **sp** means **spring**, March through May
- **S** means **Summer**, June through August
- **F** means **Fall**, September through November
- **W** means **Winter**, December through February
- **T** means **Two** (2) or **Three** (3) Seasons
- **A** means **All Four** (4) Seasons
- **na** means Not Applicable or Not Available
- Note: empty or blank spaces in the chart mean **NO**

★ that symbol is not shown on the map.

If a symbol number has a ★ (top right) for location name and address abbreviations.

AGENCY/MAP LEGEND ... INITIALS, MAP SYMBOLS, COLOR CODES

- U.S. Forest Service Supervisor & Ranger Dist. Offices . NFS [61]
- U.S. Army Corps of Engineers Rec. Areas & Offices . COE [H]
- USFWS National Wildlife Refuges & Offices .... NWR [9]
- National Park Service Parks & other NPS Sites ..... NPS [7]
- Bureau of Land Management Rec. Areas & Offices .. BLM [26]
- Bureau of Reclamation Rec. Areas & Reg. Offices .. BOR [8]
- State Parks (also see State Agency notes) .... SPS [52]
- State Wildlife Areas (also see State Agency notes) . SWA [19]
- Private Preserves, Nature Centers & Tribal Lands [15]
- The Wild Rivers ～～ and Wilderness Areas

Note: Refer to yellow block on page 7 (top right) for location name and address abbreviations.

S#	MAP	LOCATION NAME with ADDRESS and/or LOCATION DATA	TELEPHONE	ACRES / ELEVATION
		Black Hills National Forest Sup. (RR #2, Box 200, Custer 57730 [N of town on Hwy 16/385, top of hill]	605-673-2251	1,250,000 / 3,000-7,242
1	B1	Custer Ranger D., 330 Mt. Rushmore Rd., Custer 57730	605-673-4853	na / na
2	B1	Harney Ranger D., Hwy. 385, HCR, Box 571, Hill City 57745	605-574-2534	na / na
3	B1	Nemo Ranger D., 460 Main St., Deadwood 57732	605-578-2744	na / na
4	B1	Pactola Ranger D & Visitor Center, 803 Soo San Dr., Rapid City 57701	605-343-1567	na / na
5	B1	Spearfish Ranger D., 320 Ryan Rd., Spearfish 57783	605-642-4622	na / na
6	B1	**Custer National Forest** (MT-ND-SD), 2602 First Ave. N., PO Box 2556, Billings, MT 59103	406-657-6361	2,446,130 / 1,000-12,800
7	A2	Grand River District, Grand R & Ced. Nat'l. Grasslands (ND-SD), Box 390, Lemmon 57638	605-374-3360	162,000 / 2,000-3,000
8	A1	Sioux Ranger District (MT-SD), Hwy. 20, Box 37, Camp Crook 57724	605-797-4432	163,000 / 2,500-3,500
		Nebraska National Forest Sup., 111 North Main, Chadron, NE 69337	308-432-3367	1,000,000 / 3,000-4,700
9	B1	Fall River Ranger D., 209 N. River St., Hot Springs 57747 [manages west half Buffalo Gap Nat'l Grassland]	605-745-4107	330,000 / 3,200
10	B2	Wall Ranger D. & Visitor Center, Wall 57790 [manages east half Buffalo Gap Nat'l Grassland]	605-279-2125	265,000 / 2,900
11	B2	Ft. Pierre Nat'l. Grassland, 124 S. Euclid Ave., Box 147, Pierre 57501	605-224-5517	116,000 / 2,200
	B3	**COE, Omaha District,** 215 N. 17th St., Omaha, NE 68102	402-221-4137	na / na
1	B3	Big Bend Dam & Lake Sharpe, HC 69, Box 74, Chamberlain 57325	605-245-2255	na / na
2	B1	Cold Brook Lake, HC 69, Box 74, Chamberlain 57325 [W of Hot Springs]	605-245-2331	na / na
3	C3	Cottonwood Springs Lake, HC 69, Box74, Chamberlain 57325 [W of Hot Springs]	605-245-2255	na / na
4	C3	Fort Randall Dam & Lake Francis Cas, Lake Francis Case Project, Pickstown 57367	605-487-7847	na / na
5	C4	Gavins Point Project, PO Box 710, Yankton 57078	402-667-7873	na / na
6	C4	Oahe Dam Lake Oahe, PO Box 997, Pierre 57501 [NW of Pierre]	605-224-5862	2,540 / na
1	C2	**Lacreek NWR & Little White R. Rec. Area.** HWC 3, Box 14, Martin 57551 [office at refuge]	605-685-6508	16,500 / 3,000
2	C2	Lake Andes NWR, RR #1, Box 77, Lake Andes 57356 [1 mi N & 5 mi E of Lake Andes]	605-487-7603	5,840 / 1,450
3	B4	Madison WMD, PO Box 48, Madison 57042 [0.75 mi S., Jct. Hwys. 34 & 19]	605-256-2974	na / na
4	A4	Sand Lake NWR, RR #1, Box 25, Columbia 57433	605-885-6320	21,500 / 1,200-1,300
5	A3	Pocasse NWR, RR #1, Box 25, Columbia 57433 [located at Pollock]	605-885-6320	na / na
6	A4	Waubay NWR/WMD, RR #1, Box 79, Waubay 57273 [go 1 mi on Hwy. 12, 7 mi on CR 1, 1.5 mi W on gravel rd at sign]	605-947-4521	5,000 / 1,800
7	B4	Huron WMD, FOB, 200 4th St. SW, Rm. 113, Huron 57350	605-352-7014	11,000 / na
1	B2	**Badlands Nat'l Park,** PO Box 6, Interior 57750 [at Wall go S on SR 240 to Pinnacles Ent or exit 131 S 8.5 mi to VC]	605-433-5361	243,300 / 2,450-3,300
2	B1	Jewel Cave National Monument, RR #1, Box 60AA, Custer 57730	605-673-2288	1,274 / 4,900-5,700
3	B1	Mount Rushmore Nat'l. Memorial, PO Box 268, Keystone 57751	605-574-2523	1,278 / 4,420-5,725
4	A4	Wind Cave Nat'l. Park, RR #1, Box 190 - WCNP, Hot Springs 57747	605-745-4600	28,292 / na
		BLM - Miles City District, PO Box 940, Miles City, MT 59301 [W of Miles City]	406-232-4331	3,214,499 / 1,900-3,597
1	B2	South Dakota Resource A., 310 Roundup St., Belle Fourche 57717	605-892-2526	280,700 / 1,200-6,500
		SD Game, Fish & Parks (Parks), 523 E. Capitol, Pierre 57501	605-733-3485	na / na
2	C1	Angostura Recreation Area, HC 52, Box 131-A, off Hwy. 80, 10 mi. SE of Hot Springs 57747	605-745-6996	1,125 / na
3	B1	Bear Butte SP, Box 688, located 6 mi. NE of Sturgis 57785	605-347-5240	1,931 / na
4	B1	Custer SP May/Sep.ph. 255-4464), HC 83, Box 70, located 6 mi. E of Custer 57730	605-255-4515	73,000 / 3,200-6,200
5	B3	Farm Island Recreation Area, HCR 531, Box 111, off SD 34, 4 mi. E of Pierre 57501	605-224-5605	1,225 / na
6	A4	Fort Sisseton SP, c/o Roy Lake SP, RR #2, Box 51, 10 mi. SW of Lake City 57247	605-448-5701	125 / na
7	B4	Lake Herman SP, RR #3, Box 79, located 2 mi. W of Madison 57042	605-256-3613	176 / na
8	B4	Lake Poinsett Recreation Area, RR #3, Box 75, off Hwy. 81, 12 mi. N & 2 mi. E of Arlington 57212	605-983-5085	151 / na
9	B4	Lake Vermillion Recreation Area, RR #1, Box 193-A, 7 mi. S off I-90 at Montrose exit, Canistota 57012	605-296-3643	267 / na
10	C4	Lewis & Clark Recreation Area, RR #1, Box 240, off SD 52, 5 mi. W of Yankton 57078	605-668-3435	855 / na
11	A3	Mina Lake Recreation Area, c/o Richmond Lake RA, RR #2, Box 500, 11 mi. W of Aberdeen 57401	605-225-5325	300 / na
12	B4	Newton Hills SP, RR #1, Box 162, located 7 mi. S of Canton 57013	605-987-2263	948 / na
13	B4	Oakwood Lakes SP, RR #2, Box 10, 7 mi. N & 3 mi. W of Volga near Bruce 57220	605-627-5441	255 / na
14	B4	Palisades SP, RR #3, Box 70, Corson exit off I-90 & 10 mi. N, Garretson 57030	605-594-3824	155 / na
15	A4	Pickerel Lake Recreation Area, Box 113, off Hwy. 12, 10 mi. N of Waubay, Greenville 57239	605-486-4753	368 / na
16	A4	Roy Lake SP, RR #2, Box 51, located 3 mi. W of Lake City 57247	605-448-5701	509 / na

Column category headers (rotated): **FACILITIES, SERVICES, RECREATION OPPORTUNITIES & CONVENIENCES**

INFO OFFICE (IO) / VISITOR CENTER (VC); IO / VC OPEN SATURDAY / SUNDAY; VC OPEN SATURDAY / SUNDAY; ENTRY FEE not camping / permit fee; FREE LITERATURE or EDUCATIONAL DISPLAY; INTERPRETIVE SERVICES AVAILABLE; CONCESSIONAIRE SERVICES AVAILABLE; AGENCY GUIDED TOURS / STUDY PROGRAMS; WILDFLOWER VIEWING AREA or DRIVE; NATURE EDUCATION / STUDY PROGRAMS; ARCHAEOLOGICAL / GEOLOGICAL SITES; HISTORIC SITES; INTERPRETIVE TRAILS; WILDLIFE IS ABUNDANT OR COMMON; ENDANGERED SPECIES ARE COMMON; DEVELOPED VIEWING SITES, birds, etc.; WILDLIFE VIEWING SITES; NO-CHARGE PICNIC AREAS / PICNIC SITES; DEVELOPED CAMPGROUNDS / CAMPSITES; WILDERNESS AREAS / WILD RIVERS; WALKING PERMITTED, at one's own risk...areas, trails; HIKING TRAILS; HORSEBACK RIDING, / your own horse; OFF-ROAD Motorized Vehicle Area / Use OK; BICYCLING OPPORTUNITIES; SWIMMING PERMITTED, at one's own risk; FISHING OPPORTUNITIES; BOATING FACILITIES, ramps, marina, etc.; NON-MOTORIZED WATERCRAFT OK / Use OK; MOTORIZED WATERCRAFT OK, check limits; HUNTING IN SEASON, license / permit req'd.; WINTER SPORTS OPPORTUNITIES; PARK & SPORTS OPPORTUNITIES; DAY USE, WALK-IN ONLY AREA; DRINKING WATER; RESTROOMS

#	Map	Name / Location	Phone	Acres
18	A4	Sica Hollow SP, c/o Roy Lake SP, RR #2, Box 51, 15 mi. NW of Sisseto, Lake City 57247	605-448-5701	807 / na
19	C3	Snake Creek Recreation Area, RR #2, Box 113-A, located off SD 44, 14 mi. W of Platte 57369	605-337-2587	735 / na
20	C4	Union County SP, c/o Newton Hills SP, RR #1, Box 162 (11 mi. S Beresford), Canton 57013	605-987-2263	499 / na
21	A3	West Whitlock Recreation Area, HRC 3, Box 73-A, off Hwy. 212, 18 mi. W of Gettysburg 57442	605-765-9410	175 / na
1	B2	**SD Game, Fish & Parks** (Fish & Game), 523 E Capitol (Anderson Bldg), Pierre 57501 [see notes]	605-773-3485	na / na
2	A3	Aberdeen Wildlife Div. Office, 5850 E. Hwy. 12, Aberdeen 57401	605-622-2391	na / na
3	B3	Chamberlain Wildlife Div. Office, HC-69, Box 7, Chamberlain 57325	605-734-5622	na / na
4	B4	Huron Wildlife Div. Office, State Fairgrounds, Box 915, Huron 57350	605-353-7145	na / na
5	A2	Mobridge Wildlife Div. Office, 1019 E. Grand Crossing, Mobridge 57601	605-845-7814	na / na
6	B1	Rapid City Wildlife Div. Office, 3305 W. South St., Rapid City 57702	605-394-2391	na / na
7	B4	Sioux Falls Wildlife Div. Office, 517 W. Tenth, Sioux Falls 57104	605-339-6621	na / na
8	A4	Watertown Wildlife Div. Office, 400 W. Kemp, Watertown 57201	605-886-4769	na / na
9	A4	Webster Wildlife Div. Office, 603 E. 8th Ave., Box 637, Webster 57274	605-345-3381	na / na
1	B3	**Lower Brule Wildlife Dept.**, Lower Brule Wildlife Enterprise, PO Box 246, Lower Brule 57548	605-473-5666	133,000 / 1,400-2,000

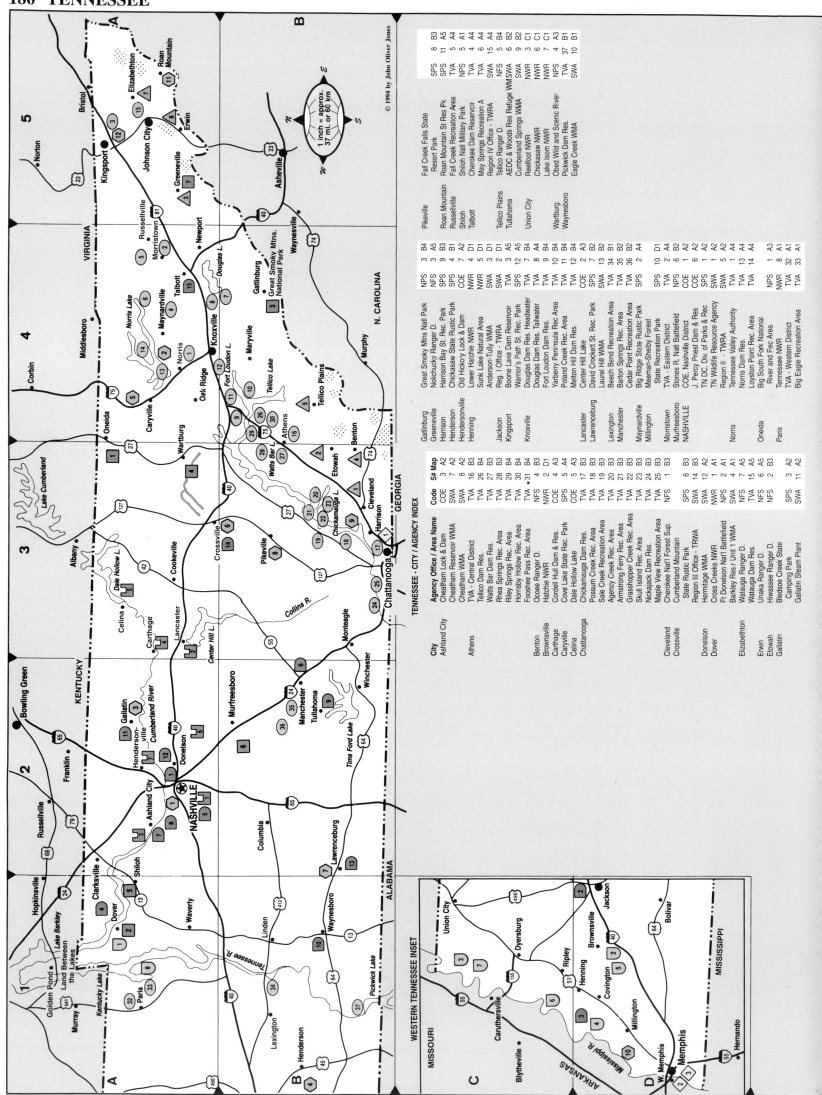

TENNESSEE NOTES

Summary

There are 68 federal, 30 state, and 4 private recreation areas or local administrative offices covered in this state chapter. Of these, 92 appear in the Information Chart and 10 are covered in the notes. The special indexes feature 12 federally designated wilderness areas and wild rivers, and 6 agency published outdoor maps.

Federal Agencies

U.S. Forest Service

Tennessee is in the Southern Region (see Georgia chapter - U.S. Forest Svc., Southern Region listing).

National Park Service

The 445 mile long **Natchez Trace Parkway** extends northeast from Natchez, Mississippi, through the northwest corner of Alabama and into central Tennessee where it ends just southwest of Nashville. See Mississippi chapter S# 2 for Parkway details.

Additional NPS Location in Tennessee

Andrew Johnson National Historic Site (17 acres)
(S# 7, map A5)
PO Box 1088
Greenville, TN 37744   615-638-3551

Tennessee Valley Authority (TVA)

There are four TVA district offices. The Eastern, Central, and Western district are in Tennessee. Another is located in Alabama (see Alabama chapter). TVA managed recreation areas are located in Alabama, Georgia, Kentucky, Mississippi, and Tennessee. The Information Charts have site and recreation details.

Probably the best known TVA recreation area is the Land Between the Lakes or LBL (map A1), 170,000 acres located between Kentucky Lake and Lake Barkley in western Tennessee and Kentucky. Daily programs, camping, a nature center, and one of the largest buffalo herds east of the Mississippi River are a few of the attractions. For information and literature, including the annually published LBL "Calendar of Events" contact:

TVA
Land Between the Lakes
100 Van Morgan Drive
Golden Pond, KY 42211-9000   502-924-1243

There are 15 recreation maps of TVA reservoirs (some are in the process of revision). These maps are described in the *TVA Maps Price Catalog*. The first page of the catalog has a map showing the department office location in downtown Chattanooga (map B3). The catalog and recreation maps are available from:

TVA Maps & Surveys Department
100 Haney Building
311 Broad St.
Chattanooga, TN 37402   615-751-MAPS

TVA lake elevation and stream flow information is available by calling (615) 632-6065 between 8:30 a.m. and 4:00 p.m. Monday through Friday. Reservoir elevation forecasts covering a nine-day period are available each Friday afternoon.

Wilderness/Wild River Index

Wilderness Areas

Cherokee National Forest, 11 areas (S# 1, map B3)
Bad River Gorge Wilderness - 3,887 acres
Big Frog Wilderness - 7,972 acres
Big Laurel Branch Wilderness - 6,251 acres
Citico Creek Wilderness - 16,000 acres
Cohutta Wilderness - 1,795 acres
Gee Creek Wilderness - 2,493 acres
Joyce Kilmer-Slickrock Wilderness - 3,832 acres
Little Frog Mountain Wilderness - 4,800 acres
Pond Mountain Wilderness - 6,665 acres
Sampson Mountain Wilderness - 8,319 acres
Unaka Mountain Wilderness - 4,700 acres

Wild River

Obed River
NPS, Obed Wild & Scenic River (S# 4, map A3)

Outdoor Map Index

National Park Service (USGS Maps)

Great Smoky Mountains NP East [1931]
  Scale: 1 inch = 1.0 mile (1 cm = 0.6 km)
Great Smoky Mountains NP (NC-TN) [1972]
  Scale: 1 inch = 2.0 miles (1 cm = 1.3 km)
Great Smoky Mountains NP West [1931]
  Scale: 1 inch = 1.0 mile (1 cm = 0.6 km)

U.S. Forest Service Maps

Cherokee NF, No. District [1986]
Cherokee NF, So. District [1986]
Trails of the Cherokee NF

State Agencies

Department of Conservation

701 Broadway
Customs House
Nashville, TN 37234-0435   615-742-6758

Parent agency for the Division of Parks and Recreation and the Division of Forestry.

Division of Parks & Recreation

A Tennessee State Parks Guide (51 state parks) is available free. The guide describes each area, contains a locator map, and includes information on facilities and activities.

Division of Forestry

701 Broadway
Nashville, TN 37219   615-742-6616
Contact the Division for state forest recreation literature.

Wildlife Resources Agency (WRA)

The Hunting and Trapping Guide lists 65 wildlife management areas. Selected WMAs within Regions I and II, and the WRA regional offices, are listed in the Guide. A bi-monthly magazine, *Tennessee Wildlife*, is available by subscription for $5 per year. Licensing and game harvest information is published annually.

Dept. of Tourist Development

PO Box 23170
Nashville, TN 37202   615-741-2158

A *Tennessee Vacation Guide* provides information on Tennessee's attractions and events. There are other publications on private accommodations, fishing, scenic parkways, campgrounds, and historic sites. An official road map is also available.

Private Organizations

ANCA Locations in Tennessee

Chattanooga Nature Center (S# 1, map B3)
400 Garden Road
Chattanooga, TN 37419   615-821-1160

Lichterman Nature Center (S# 2, map D1)
5992 Quincy Road
Memphis, TN 38119   901-767-7200

Memphis Zoological Garden & Aquarium (S# 3, map D1)
2000 Galloway Ave.
Memphis, TN, 38112   901-726-4787

No State Chamber of Commerce in Tennessee

There are local Chamber of Commerce offices throughout the state.

AGENCY/MAP LEGEND . . . INITIALS, MAP SYMBOLS, COLOR CODES

U.S. Forest Service Supervisor & Ranger Dist. Offices NFS
U.S. Army Corps of Engineers Rec. Areas & Offices . COE
USFWS National Wildlife Refuges & Offices . . . . NWR
National Park Service Parks & other NPS Sites . . . . . NPS
Bureau of Land Management Rec. Areas & Offices . . BLM
Tennessee Valley Authority Offices & Sites . . . . TVA
State Parks (also see State Agency notes) . . . . SPS
State Wildlife Areas (also see State Agency notes) . . SWA
Private Preserves, Nature Centers & Tribal Lands . .
The Wild Rivers and Wilderness Areas

★ INFORMATION CHART ★

INFORMATION CHART LEGEND - SYMBOLS & LETTER CODES

■ means **YES** & □ means **Yes with disability provisions**
sp means **sp**ring, March through May
S means **S**ummer, June through August
F means **F**all, September through November
W means **W**inter, December through February
T means **T**wo (2) or **T**hree (3) Seasons
A means **A**ll Four (4) Seasons
na means Not Applicable or Not Available
Note: empty or blank spaces in the chart mean **NO**

Note: Refer to yellow block on page 7 (top right) for location name and address abbreviations. If a symbol number has a star ★ that symbol is not shown on the map.

FACILITIES, SERVICES, RECREATION OPPORTUNITIES & CONVENIENCES

S#	MAP	LOCATION NAME (state initials if more than one) with ADDRESS and/or LOCATION DATA	TELEPHONE	ACRES / ELEVATION	INFO OFFICE (IO) / VISITOR CENTER (VC)	IO / VC OPEN SATURDAY / SUNDAY	ENTRY FEE, not camping or permit fee	CONCESSIONAIRE SERVICES AVAILABLE	INTERPRETIVE or EDUCATIONAL DISPLAY	FREE LITERATURE, brochures, maps, etc.	AGENCY GUIDED TOURS, scheduled / by res.	NATURE EDUCATION / STUDY PROGRAMS	WILDFLOWER VIEWING AREA or DRIVE	ARCHAEOLOGICAL / GEOLOGICAL SITES	HISTORIC SITES	INTERPRETIVE TRAILS	WILDLIFE IS ABUNDANT OR COMMON	ENDANGERED SPECIES ARE COMMON	WILDLIFE VIEWING SITES, blinds, signs, etc.	DEVELOPED PICNIC AREAS / PICNIC SITES	DEVELOPED CAMPGROUNDS / CAMPSITES	NO-CHARGE CAMPGROUNDS / CAMPSITES	WILDERNESS AREAS / WILD RIVERS	WALKING / HIKING TRAILS	SWIMMING PERMITTED, at one's own risk	BICYCLING OPPORTUNITIES...areas, trails	HORSEBACK RIDING, w/ your own horse	OFF-ROAD Motorized Vehicle Area / Use OK	FISHING IN SEASON, license / permit reqd.	BOATING FACILITIES, ramps, marinas, etc.	MOTORIZED WATERCRAFT OK, check limits	NON-MOTORIZED WATERCRAFT OK	HUNTING IN SEASON, license / permit reqd.	WINTER SPORTS OPPORTUNITIES	PARK & WALK-IN ONLY AREA	DAY USE ONLY, no overnight	DRINKING WATER	RESTROOMS	S#
1	B3	**Cherokee National Forest Sup.**, 2800 N. Ocoee St., PO Box 2010, Cleveland 37320	615-476-9700	627,405 / 1,000-6,000	□				■	■					■	■	A		■	□	□	A	■	■	■	■	■	■	□	□		■	■			■	□	□	1
2	B3	Hiwassee Ranger D., Mecca Pike, Drawer D, Etowah 37331 [1 mi E of Etowah on Mecca Pike]	615-263-5486	90,000 / 800-2,300	□	T				■							T			■	□		■	■		■	■	■	■	■		■	■				■	■	2
3	A5	Nolichucky Ranger D., 120 Austin Ave., Greeneville 37743 [corner of Austin and Tusculum]	615-638-4109	80,000 / na	□				■	■					■		A		■	□	□		■	■	■	■	■	■	□	■		■	■				□	□	3
4	B3	Ocoee Ranger D., Rt. #1, Parksville, Hwy. 64, Benton 37307	615-338-5201	87,000 / na	■					■					■	■			■	■	■		■	■	■	■	■	■	■	■		■	■				■	■	4
5	B4	Tellico Ranger D., 250 Ranger Station Road, Tellico Plains 37385	615-253-2520	123,000 / na	■					■									■	■	■	A	■	■	■	■	■	■	□	■		■	■				■	■	5
6	A5	Unaka Ranger D., 1205 N. Main Street, Rt. #1, Erwin 37650	615-743-4452	110,000 / na	□				■	■						■			■	□	□		■	■	■	■	■	■	■			■	■				□	□	6
7	A5	Watauga Ranger D., Rt. #9, Box 2235, Star Route 91, Elizabethton 37643 [1 mi E of town on Hwy 91]	615-542-2942	136,000 / 1,500-4,000	□					■						■	A		■	■	□		■	■	■	■	■	■	■	■	■	■	■			■	□	□	7
1	A2	**COE, Nashville District**, PO Box 1070, Nashville 37202	615-736-5115	na / na	■					■																										■	■	■	1
2	A3	Center Hill Lake, Rt. #1, Box 260, Lancaster 38569	615-858-3125	na / na	■					■						■				■	■	A		■	■		■		■	■	■	■					■	■	2
3	A2	Cheatham Lock & Dam, 1798 Cheatham Dam Road, Ashland City 37015	615-792-5697	na / na	■					■						■				■	■	A			■				■	■	■	■					■	■	3
4	A3	Cordell Hull Dam & Reservoir, Rt. #1, Box 62, Carthage 37030	615-735-1034	na / na	■					■						■				■	■	A		■	■	■	■		■	■	■	■					■	■	4
5	A3	Dale Hollow Lake, Rt. #1, Box 64, Celina 38551	615-243-3136	na / na	■					■										■	■	A		■	■	■	■		■	■	■	■					■	■	5
6	A2	J. Percy Priest Dam & Reservoir, J. Percy Priest Lake, Nashville 37214	615-889-1975	na / na	■					■						■				■	■	A		■	■	■	■		■	■	■	■					■	■	6
7	A2	Old Hickory Lock & Dam, No. 5 Power Plant Road, Hendersonville 37075	615-822-4846	na / na	■					■						■				■	■	A		■	■	■	■		■	■	■	■					■	■	7
1	A1	**Cross Creeks NWR**, 643 Wildlife Rd., Dover 37058 [2.5 mi S of Dover on TN Hwy. 49]	615-232-7477	8,862 / 350-550	□				■	■	□	■			■	■	T	W						■		■	■		□	■	■	■	■			■	■		1
2	D1	Hatchie NWR, PO Box 187, Brownsville 38012 [Hwy. 76 at I-40]	901-772-0501	11,556 / na	■					■							A										■		□	■		■	■			■			2
3	C1	Reelfoot NWR (KY-TN), 4343 Hwy. 157, Union City 38261 [office on NWR, 16 mi S of city & R on Hwy 157, follow signs]	901-538-2481	10,428 / 282	□	T			■	■	□	□	T	■		□	A	A	□					■	■	■			□	□	■	■	■		□	■			3
4	D1	Lower Hatchie NWR, Rt #2, Box 126A, Henning 38041 [4mi S Ripley on 51, R on 87 22mi, L on Prudhomme Rd0.25 mi]	901-738-2296	7,100 / na	■					■							A	T					■						■	■	■	■	■			■			4
5	D1	Sunk Lake Natural A, Rt. #2, Box 126 A, Henning 38041 [4mi S of Ripley on US 51, R on 87 15mi, R on Sunk L Rd 2mi]	901-738-2296	1,478 / na													A	W											■	■	■	■			■	■			5
6	C1	Chickasaw NWR, 4343 Hwy. 157, Union City 38261 [8 mi W of Ripley on Edith Central Rd, L 4mi on Sand Bluff Rd]	901-635-7621	21,940 / na	■					■							A	A			■	F							■	■	■	■	■						6
7	C1	Lake Isom NWR, 4343 Hwy. 157, Union City 38261 [5 mi E of Tiptonville, R on Greasy Lane, S 2 mi, follow signs]	901-538-2481	1,850 / 281						■		■					A	A							■				■	■	■	■	■			■			7
8	A1	Tennessee NWR, 810 E. Wood St., PO Box 849, Paris 38242	901-642-2091	51,358 / 468-571	■			■		■					■				■					■					■	■	■	■	■		■	■	■		8
1	A3	**Big South Fork Nat'l. River and Rec. Area**, Rt. #3, Box 401, Oneida 37841	615-879-3625	105,000 / 900-1,600	■					■				■	■					■	■		■	■	■	■	■		■	■	■								1
2	A1	Fort Donelson National Battlefield, PO Box 434, Dover 37058	615-232-5706	536 / na	□	A			■	■					□					□				■					■							■	□	□	2
3	B4	Great Smoky Mtns. Natl Park (NC/TN), 107 Park HQ Rd., Gatlinburg 37738 [three VCs, brochure has map/details]	615-436-1200	520,270 / 1,200-6,642	□	T		■	■	■		■	T		□	□	T	A		□	■		■	■	■	■	■		■								□	□	3
4	A3	Obed Wild and Scenic River, 208 Maiden St., PO Box 429, Wartburg 37887	615-346-6295	5,005 / 840-1,900	■					■				■						■			■		■			■	■	■		■	■						4
5	A1	Shiloh National Military Park, PO Box 67, Shiloh 38376 [on Hwy 22, 4 mi N of Shiloh and 50 mi S of I-40 Hwy. 22 exit]	901-689-5696	4,000 / na	■	A	A			■				■	■					■																■			5
6	B2	Stones R. Natl Battlefield, 3501 Old Nashville Hwy., Murfreesboro 37129 [27 mi SE Nashville, NW cor. Murfreesboro]	□ 615-893-9501	400 / 560	□	A			■	■					□	■				■				■					■							■			6
1	A4	**Tennessee Valley Authority**, 17 Ridgeway Road, Norris 37828	615-632-1805	na / na	□				■	■																													1
2	A4	TVA - Eastern District, 2611 W. Andrew Johnson Hwy., Morristown 37814	615-632-3791	na / na	□				■	■																													2
3	A5	Boone Lake Dam Reservoir, SE of Kingsport [TN Hwy. 75]	615-587-5600	na / na																□					■					■	■	■						□	3
4	A4	Cherokee Dam Reservoir, NW of Talbott [TN Hwy. 92]	615-587-5600	na / na																■	■				■					■	■	■					□	□	4
5	A4	Fall Creek Recreation Area, Russellville	615-587-5600	na / na																	■									■	■	■					□	□	5
6	A4	May Springs Recreation Area, N of Talbott [TN Hwy. 375]	615-587-5600	na / na																	■																□	□	6
7	B4	Douglas Dam Res. Headwater, E of Knoxville [TN Hwy. 338]	615-587-5600	na / na																■	■				■					■	■	■					□	□	7
8	A4	Douglas Dam Res. Tailwater, E of Knoxville [TN Hwy. 338]	615-587-5600	na / na																	■								□	■	■	■					□	□	8
9	B4	Fort Loudon Dam Res., SW of Knoxville [US Hwy. 321]	615-587-5600	na / na																■					■				■	■	■	■					■	■	9
10	B4	Yarberry Peninsula Recreation Area, SW of Knoxville [US Hwy. 321]	615-587-5600	na / na																■	■				■					■	■	■					□	□	10
11	B4	Poland Creek Recreation Area, SW of Knoxville [TN Hwy. 333]	615-587-5600	na / na																	■									■	■	■					□	□	11
12	B4	Melton Hill Dam Res., SW of Knoxville [TN Hwy. 95]	615-587-5600	na / na																□	■				■					■	■	■					□	□	12
13	A4	Norris Dam Res., near Norris [US Hwy. 441]	615-587-5600	na / na																■				■					□									□	13
14	A4	Loyston Point Recreation Area, near Norris [TN Hwy. 61]	615-587-5600	na / na																■	□			■	■					■	■	■					□	□	14
15	A5	Watauga Dam Res., Elizabethton	615-587-5600	na / na																■				■						■	■	■						□	15
16	B3	TVA - Central District, 1101 Congress Parkway, Athens 37303	615-632-2088	na / na	□				■	■																										■	■	■	16
17	B3	Chickamauga Dam Res., N of Chattanooga [TN Hwy. 153]	615-745-1783	na / na																□				■	■				□	■	■	■						□	17
18	B3	Possum Creek Recreation Area, N of Chattanooga [US Hwy. 27]	615-745-1783	na / na																□					■					■	■	■					□	□	18
19	B3	Sale Creek Recreation Area, N of Chattanooga [US Hwy. 27]	615-745-1783	na / na																■	■				■					■	■	■					□	□	19
20	B3	Agency Creek Recreation Area, N of Chattanooga [TN Hwy. 58]	615-745-1783	na / na																	■				■													■	20
21	B3	Armstrong Ferry Recreation Area, N of Chattanooga [TN Hwy. 58]	615-745-1783	na / na																	■				■					■	■	■						■	21
22	B3	Grasshopper Creek Recreation Area, N of Chattanooga [TN Hwy. 60]	615-745-1783	na / na																	■				■					■	■	■					□	□	22

No.	Grid	Name / Location	Phone	Acreage
23	B3	Skull Island Recreation Area, N of Chattanooga [TN Hwy. 312]	615-745-1783	na / na
24	B3	Nickajack Dam Res., W of Chattanooga [I-24 exit 158]	615-745-1783	na / na
25	B3	Maple View Recreation Area, W of Chattanooga [TN Hwy. 156]	615-745-1783	na / na
26	B4	Tellico Dam Res., NE of Athens [US Hwy. 321]	615-745-1783	na / na
27	B3	Watts Bar Dam Res., N of Athens [TN Hwy. 681]	615-745-1783	na / na
28	B3	Rhea Springs Recreation Area, N of Athens [at Spring City]	615-745-1783	na / na
29	B4	Riley Springs Recreation Area, N of Athens [TN Hwy. 58]	615-745-1783	na / na
30	B4	Hornsby Hollow Recreation Area, N of Athens [TN Hwy. 304]	615-745-1783	na / na
*31	B4	Fooshee Pass Recreation Area, N of Athens [TN Hwy. 304]	615-745-1783	na / na
32	A1	TVA - Western District, 202 West Blythe St., PO Box 280, Paris 38242	901-642-2041	na / na
33	A1	Big Eagle Recreation Area, near Paris [US Hwy. 79]	901-642-2041	na / na
34	B1	Beech Bend Recreation Area, E of Lexington [TN Hwy. 100]	901-642-2041	na / na
35	B2	Barton Springs Recreation Area, near Manchester [at Normandy]	205-386-2223	na / na
36	B2	Cedar Point Recreation Area, near Manchester [at Normandy]	205-386-2223	na / na
37	B1	Pickwick Dam Res., SW of Waynesboro [TN Hwy. 128]	205-386-2223	na / na
1	A2	TN DC, Div. of Parks & Recreation, 701 Broadway, Nashville 37243	615-742-6667	na / na
2	A4	Big Ridge State Rustic Park, Rt. #1 Maynardville 37807	615-992-5523	3,640 / na
3	A2	Bledsoe Creek St. Camping Park, Rt. #2, Box 60, Gallatin 37066	615-452-3706	160 / na
4	B1	Chickasaw State Rustic Park, State Hwy. 100, Henderson 38340	901-989-5141	1,280 / na
5	A4	Cove Lake State Recreational Park. Rt. #2, Caryville 37714	615-562-8355	670 / na
6	B3	Cumberland Mountain St. Rustic Park, Rt. #8, Box 330, Crossville 38555	615-484-6138	1,560 / na
7	B2	David Crockett St. Rec. Park, PO Box 398, Lawrenceburg 38464	615-762-9408	1,070 / na
8	B3	Fall Creek Falls St. Resort Park, Rt. #3, Pikeville 37367	615-881-3241	16,090 / na
9	B3	Harrison Bay St. Rec. Park, Rt. #2, Box 118, Harrison 37341	615-344-6214	1,200 / na
10	D1	Meeman-Shelby Forest St. Rec. Park, U.S. 51 & Rt. 3, Millington 38053	901-876-5201	12,470 / na
11	A5	Roan Mountain St. Resort Park, Rt. #1, Box 50, Roan Mountain 37687	615-772-3303	2,000 / na
12	A5	Warrior's Path St. Rec. Park, PO Box 5026, Kingsport 37663	615-239-8531	870 / na
1	A2	TN Wildlife Resource Agency (TWRA), Ellington Ag. Center, PO Box 40747, Nashville 37204	615-781-6500	na / na
2	D1	Reg. I Office - TWRA, 225 Martin Luther King Blvd., State Office Bldg., Box 55, Jackson 38301	901-423-5725	na / na
3	D1	Anderson-Tully WMA, Hwy. 19 W of Ripley and Hwy. 87 W of Henning	901-423-5725	11,000 / 200-300
4	A1	Barkley Reservoir Unit 1 WMA, Stewart County, Hwy. 79, Dover	901-423-5725	8,090 / 360
5	A2	Region II - TWRA, Ellington Agricultural Center, PO Box 40747, Nashville 37204	615-781-6622	na / na
6	B2	AEDC & Woods Reservoir Refuge WMA, in Coffee/Franklin Cos., near Tullahoma	901-781-6622	32,000 / 961-1,000
7	A2	Cheatham Reservoir WMA, in Cheatham County, W of Ashland City	615-781-6622	5,112 / 385-400
8	A2	Cheatham WMA, S of Cumberland River near Ashland City	615-781-6622	20,810 / 700-800
9	B2	Cumberland Springs WMA, near Tullahoma	615-781-6622	6,079 / 950-1,000
10	B1	Eagle Creek WMA, Wayne County, near Waynesboro	901-781-6622	22,000 / 600-850
11	A2	Gallatin Steam Plant, in Sumner County, near Gallatin	615-781-6622	2,200 / 330-400
12	A2	Hermitage WMA, in Davidson County, near Donelson	615-781-6622	460 / 600-650
13	B2	Laurel Hill WMA, off Hwy. 64, W of Lawrenceburg	901-762-2079	15,000 / 500-650
14	B3	Region III Office - TRWA, 216 E. Penfield St., Crossville 38555	615-484-9571	na / 1,600
15	A4	Region IV Office - TWRA, 6032 W. Andrew Johnson Hwy., Talbott 37877	615-587-4670	na / 800

TEXAS NOTES

Summary

There are 75 federal, 61 state, and 11 private recreation areas or local administrative offices covered in this state chapter. Of these, 100 appear in the Information Chart and 47 are covered in the notes. The special indexes feature 7 federally designated-wilderness areas and wild rivers, and 8 agency published outdoor maps.

Federal Agencies

U.S. Forest Service
Texas is in the Southern Region (see Georgia chapter - U.S. Forest Svc., Southern Region listing).

U.S. Army Corps of Engineers (COE)
Southwestern Division
1114 Commerce Street
Dallas, TX 75242-0216   214-767-2435

The Fort Worth and Galveston, Texas, and the Albuquerque, New Mexico, Little Rock, Arkansas, and Tulsa, Oklahoma District Offices manage COE projects in the Southwestern area (see information charts).

National Park Service

Additional NPS Locations in Texas
Albates Flint Quarries National Monument (1,371 acres)
c/o Lake Meredith Recreation Area (chart S# 8, map D2)
PO Box 1438
Fritch, TX 79036   806-857-3152

Chamizal National Memorial (55 acres) (S# 9, map B1)
800 S. San Marcial
El Paso, TX 79905   915-534-6668

Fort Davis National Historic Site (460 acres)
(S# 10, map D4)
PO Box 1456
Fort Davis, TX 79734   915-426-3224

Lyndon B. Johnson NHP (1,572 acres) (S# 11, map B4)
PO Box 329
Johnson City, TX 78636   512-868-7128

Palo Alto Battlefield NHS (50 acres) (S# 12, map D4)
9405 S. Padre Island National Seashore
c/o Padre Island National Seashore
Corpus Christi, TX 78418-5597

San Antonio Missions NHP (493 acres) (S# 13, map C4)
2202 Roosevelt Ave.
San Antonio, TX 78210   512-229-5701

Bureau of Reclamation Recreation Areas
Four recreation areas are listed here and symbolized on the Texas state map.

S#	MAP	LOCATION NAME
1	C4	Choke Canyon Dam and Res.
2	D2	Lake Meredith Natl. Recreation Area
3	C4	Lake Texana
4	B3	Twin Buttes Res.

USDC, Natl. Oceanic & Atmospheric Admin. (NOAA)
National Ocean Service

For information about the Flower Garden National Marine Sanctuary (LA & TX) which lies 120 miles south southwest of Galveston Texas, contact the following office.

NOAA, Sanctuaries and Reserves Division
1825 Connecticut Ave., NW
Washington, DC 20235   202-673-5122

Wilderness/Wild River Index

Wilderness Areas
Big Slough Wilderness - 3,000 acres
Davey Crockett NF, Trinity RD (S# 4, map B5)
Indian Mounds Wilderness - 10,033 acres
Sabine NF, Yellow Pine RD (S# 7, map B5)
Little lake Creek Wilderness - 4,083 acres
Sam Houston NF, San Jacinto RD (S# 9, map B5)
Turkey Hill Wilderness - 5,735 acres
Angelina NF & RD (S# 2, map B5)
Upland Island Wilderness - 12,562 acres
Angelina NF & RD (S# 2, map B5)
Guadalupe Mountains Wilderness - 46,850 acres
Guadalupe Mountains National Park (S# 5, map B1)

Wild River
Rio Grande
Big Bend National Park (S# 2, map C2)

Outdoor Map Index

National Park Service (USGS Maps)
Amistad Natl. Recreation Area [1985]
  Scale: 1 inch = 0.8 mile (1 cm = 0.5 km)
Big Bend National Park [1985]
  Scale: 1 inch = 1.6 miles (1 cm = 1.0 km)

U.S. Forest Service Maps
Angelina National Forest [1984]
Caddo, Lyndon B. Johnson Natl. Grassland [1983]
Davey Crockett National Forest [1983]
Sabine National Forest [1981]
Sam Houston National Forest [1984]
Turkey Hill-Upland Island Wilderness

State Agencies

Texas Parks & Wildlife Department
Park Operations
A Guide to the State Parks of Texas (96 parks) is available free. It describes facilities and activities at each park area. There is a telephone number and address for each park, and a park locator map. There are entry fees and fees for varying levels of accommodations. Thirty-four selected state parks are included in the Guide.

Texas Parks & Wildlife Department
Wildlife Division (WD)
Much of Texas is private land, with landowners charging a fee to hunt. Agency brochures describing two types of wildlife management areas are available. Type I areas are owned by the department; Type II areas are leased from private landowners. Hunters must draw a permit for some Type I areas. Access to Type II areas is by a permit that may be purchased.

There are a variety of other permits required. Seasons and bag limits can vary from county to county. The Texas Hunting Guide is a basic reference on permits and seasons. Licensing and harvest information is published annually. A monthly magazine, Texas Parks & Wildlife Magazine, is available by subscription for $8 per year.

The 28 Regional and Law Enforcement Managers in cities throughout Texas are the best source for current local recreation opportunity and rules and regulations information. They are listed in the Texas Hunting Regulations brochure. Selected larger WMAs are listed here and symbolized on the Guide map.

S#	MAP	NAME & LOCATION
2	B5	Bannister Wildlife MA, San Augustine
3	A4	Caddo WMA, Bonham
4	C3	Chaparral WMA, Carrizo Springs
5	C3	Daughtrey WMA, Pearsall
6	B5	Eastern WMA-Angelina-Neches Unit, Jasper
7	B4	Eastern WMA-Granger Unit, Austin
8	B5	E. WMA-N. Toledo Bend U., San Augustine
9	A5	Eastern WMA-Pat Mayse unit, Paris
10	C4	Eastern WMA-Somerville unit, San Antonio
11	C2	Elephant Mtn. WMA, Big Bend National Park
12	B4	Engeling WMA, Fairfield
13	D2	Gene Howe WMA, Canadian
14	C4	Guadalupe Delta WMA, Austwell
15	C4	Honey Creek WMA, San Antonio
16	B4	Keechi Creek WMA, Mexia
17	B3	Kerr WMA, Junction
18	D2	Matador WMA, Childress
19	C4	Matagorda Island WMA, Wharton
20	B5	Moore Plantation WMA, Hemphill
21	C5	Murphree WMA, Anahuac
22	C5	Peach Point WMA, Angleton
23	B1	Sierra Diablo WMA, Kent
24	B3	Walter Buck WMA, Junction

Texas Forest Service
College Station, TX 77843   409-845-2641
Contact the Service for state forest recreation literature.

Tourism Division, Dept. of Commerce
PO Box 12008
Austin, TX 78711   1-800-888-8839
in state   512-462-9191
Two publications, Texas, the Friendship State, and the Texas highway map, provide information on the state's attractions and events.

Private Organizations

Tribal Land Areas in Texas
Alabama and Coushatta Tribes of Texas - Fishing, camping, boating, touring.
Alabama-Coushatta Tribes of Texas (S# 2, map B5)
Route 3, Box 640
Livingston, TX 77351   409-563-4391

ANCA Locations in Texas
Armand Bayou Nature Center (S# 3, map C5)
PO Box 58828
Houston, TX 77024   713-474-2551

Austin Nature Center (S# 4, map B4)
301 Nature Center Drive
Austin, TX 78746   512-327-8180

Dallas Nature Center (S# 5, map A4)
7575 Wheatland Road
Dallas, TX 75249   214-296-1955

Fort Worth Nature Center (S# 6, map A4)
Route 10, Box 53
Fort Worth, TX 76135   817-237-1111

Fort Worth Zoological Park (S# 7, map A4)
2727 Zoological Park Drive
Fort Worth, TX 76110   817-870-7050

Houston Arboretum & Nature Center (S# 8, map C5)
4501 Woodway Drive
Houston, TX 77024   713-681-8433

Houston Zoological Gardens (S# 9, map C5)
1513 North MacGregor
Houston, TX 77030   713-525-3300

The Valley Nature Center (S# 10, map D4)
PO Box 8125
Weslaco, TX 78596-8125   512-969-2475

Texas Chamber of Commerce
900 Congress Ave., #501   Phone 512-472-1594
Austin, TX 78701   Fax 512-320-0280

Information Chart

Code	S#	Map	Location	City
NFS	3	B5	Davy Crockett NF, Neches Ranger D.	Crockett
SPS	13	A5	Daingerfield SP	Daingerfield
NFS	5	A4	Caddo & LBJ Nat'l Grasslands	Decatur
NPS	1	C3	Amistad Nat'l Recreation Area	Del Rio
SPS	16	A4	Eisenhower SP	Denison
NWR	5	C4	Attwater Prairie Chicken NWR	Eagle Lake
SPS	3	A4	Bardwell Lake	Ennis
SPS	17	B4	Fairfield Lake SP	Fairfield
SWA	12	B4	Engeling WMA	
COE	14	A4	Davis Mountains SP	Fort Davis
COE	1	A4	COE, Fort Worth District	Fort Worth
NPS	6	A4	Benbrook Lake	Fort Worth
COE	2	D2	Lake Meredith Rec. Area	Fritch
COE	26	C5	COE, Galveston District	Galveston
COE	12	B4	Lake Georgetown	Georgetown
COE	8	B4	Dinosaur Valley SP	Glen Rose
COE	9	A4	Granger Lake	Granger
NFS	7	B5	Grapevine Lake	Grapevine
SWA	20	B5	Sabine NF, Yellow Pine RD	Hemphill
COE	27	C5	Moore Plantation WMA	Houston
COE	28	C5	Addicks Dam	Houston
SPS	20	B5	Barker Dam	Houston
COE	19	B5	Huntsville SP	Huntsville
SPS	28	B5	Sam Rayburn Reservoir	Jasper
SWA	6	B5	Cassells Boykin SP	
			Martin Dies Jr SP	
			Eastern WMA-Angelina-Neches Unit	
SWA	6	B5	Ferrells Bridge Dam & Lake O' The Pines	Jefferson
COE	7	A5	South Llano River SP	Junction
SPS	34	B3	Walter Buck WMA	
SWA	24	B3	Caddo Lake SP	Karnack
SPS	7	A5	Sierra Diablo WMA	Kent
SWA	23	B1	Big Thicket Natl Preserve	Kountze
NPS	14	A4	Lewisville Lake	Lewisville
COE	*18	A4	Ray Roberts Lake	Livingston
NFS	1	B5	Lake Livingston SP	Lufkin
NFS	2	B5	National Forests In Texas	
SPS	29	B4	Angelina NF & Ranger D.	Meridian
SPS	18	A4	Meridian SP	Mexia
SWA	16	B4	Fort Parker SP	
SPS	25	A4	Keechi Creek WMA	Mineral Wells
SPS	30	B2	Lake Mineral Wells SP	Monahans
SPS	31	B4	Monahans Sandhills SP	Moody
NWR	11	D1	Mother Neff SP	Muleshoe
NFS	8	B5	Muleshoe NWR	
SWA	5	C3	Grulla NWR	New Waverly
SWA	7	B4	Sam Houston NF, Raven RD	Paris
COE	15	B4	Eastern WMA-Pat Mayse U	Pearsall
COE	5	B4	Pat Mayse Lake	Powderly
SPS	12	A3	Daughtrey WMA	Purdon
NWR	14	D4	Navarro Mills Lake	Quanah
SPS	33	C5	Copper Breaks SP	Quitaque
NWR	5	B1	Caprock Canyon SP	Rio Hondo
COE	16	B3	Laguna Atascosa NWF	Rusk
SWA	4	C3	Rusk-Palestine SP	Sabine Pass
SWA	15	C4	McFaddin/Texas Point WR	Salt Flat
NFS	6	B5	Guadalupe Mtns Natl Park	San Angelo
NFS	2	B5	O.C. Fisher Lake	San Antonio
SPS	2	B5	Eastern WMA-Somerville U	
			Honey Creek WMA	
			Sabine NF, Tenaha RD	San Augustine
			Bannister Wildlife MA	
SWA	8	B5	Eastern WMA-North Toledo Bend U	
NWR	13	A4	Hagerman NWR	Sherman
COE	4	A4	Somerville Lake	Somerville
SPS	27	B5	Martin Creek Lake SP	Tatum
COE	25	A5	Wright Patman Dam & Lake	Texarkana
NWR	15	C1	Rita Blanca Natl Grasslands	Texline
COE	10	C4	Balmorhea SP	Toyahvale
COE	31	A3	Truscott Brine L, Area VIII	Truscott
SPS	2	B3	Abilene SP	Tuscola
SPS	35	A5	Tyler SP	Tyler
NWR	23	C4	Buffalo Lake NWR	Umbarger
COE	23	B4	Waco Lake	Waco
SWA	19	C4	Matagorda Island WMA	Wharton
SPS	26	B4	Lake Whitney SP	Whitney
SPS	21	A4	Lake Arrowhead SP	Wichita Falls
COE	22	B5	Town Bluff Dam & B.A. Steinhagen Lake	Woodville
COE	13	A4	Lavon Lake	Wylie

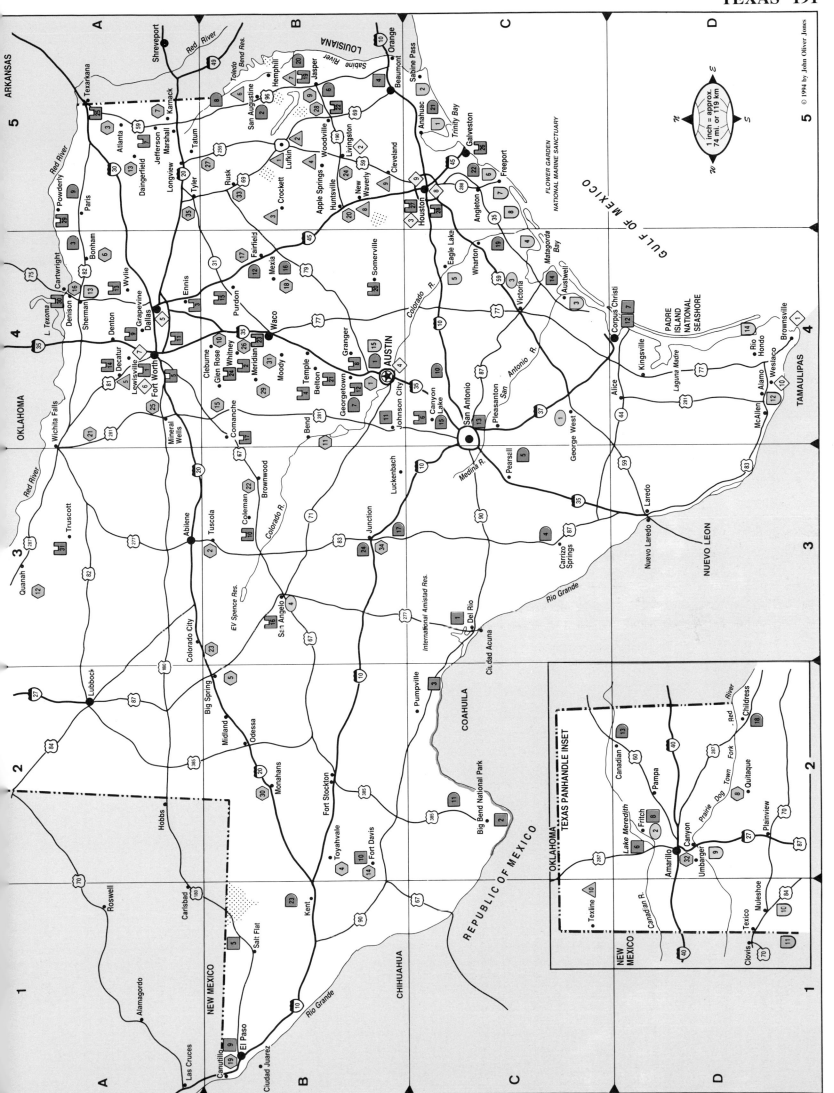

© 1994 by John Oliver Jones

1 inch = approx.
74 mi. or 119 km

FLOWER GARDEN
NATIONAL MARINE SANCTUARY

GULF OF MEXICO

PADRE
ISLAND
NATIONAL
SEASHORE

ARKANSAS

LOUISIANA

OKLAHOMA

NEW MEXICO

CHIHUAHUA

COAHUILA

REPUBLIC OF MEXICO

NUEVO LEON

TAMAULIPAS

TEXAS PANHANDLE INSET

NEW MEXICO

OKLAHOMA

★ INFORMATION CHART ★

AGENCY/MAP LEGEND . . . INITIALS, MAP SYMBOLS, COLOR CODES

U.S. Forest Service Supervisor & Ranger Dist. Offices . NFS
U.S. Army Corps of Engineers Rec. Areas & Offices . . COE
USFWS National Wildlife Refuges & Offices . . . . NWR
National Park Service Parks & other NPS Sites . . . . . . NPS
Bureau of Land Management Rec. Areas & Offices . . . BLM
Bureau of Reclamation Rec. Areas & Reg. Offices . . . BOR
State Parks (also see State Agency notes) . . . . SPS
State Wildlife Areas (also see State Agency notes) . . . SWA
Private Preserves, Nature Centers & Tribal Lands
The Wild Rivers — and Wilderness Areas
Note: Refer to yellow block on page 7 (top right) for location name and and address abbreviations.

INFORMATION CHART LEGEND - SYMBOLS & LETTER CODES

- ■ means YES and □ means **Yes with disability provisions**
- **sp** means spring, March through May
- **S** means Summer, June through August
- **F** means Fall, September through November
- **W** means Winter, December through February
- **T** means Two (2) or Three (3) Seasons
- **A** means All Four (4) Seasons
- **na** means Not Applicable or Not Available

Note: empty or blank spaces in the chart mean **NO**
★ that symbol is not shown on the map.

S#	MAP	LOCATION NAME (state initials if more than one) with ADDRESS and/or LOCATION DATA	TELEPHONE	ACRES / ELEVATION
1	B5	**National Forests In Texas** (Supervisor), Homer Garrison FOB, 701 N. 1st St., Lufkin 75901	409-639-8501	675,122 / 200-400
2	B5	Angelina NF & Ranger D., 1907 Atkinson Dr., PO Box 756, Lufkin 75901	409-639-8620	1,530,098 / na
3	B5	Davy Crockett NF, Neches Ranger D., East Loop 304, Crockett 75835	409-544-2046	94,262 / na
4	B5	Davy Crockett NF, Trinity RD, Highway 94, PO Box 130, Apple Springs 75926	409-831-2246	67,691 / na
5	A4	Caddo & LBJ Nat'l. Grasslands, FM Road 730 South, PO Box 507, Decatur 76234	817-627-5475	38,098 / na
6	B5	Sabine NF, Tenaha Ranger D., Sparks Bldg., 101 South Bolivar, San Augustine 75972	409-275-2632	63,354 / na
7	B5	Sabine NF, Yellow Pine Ranger D., Highway 83, PO Box F, Hemphill 75948	409-787-3870	98,010 / na
8	B5	Sam Houston NF, Raven Ranger D., FM 1375, PO Drawer 1000, New Waverly 77358	409-344-6205	101,681 / na
9	B5	Sam Houston NF, San Jacinto RD, 308 N. Belcher, Cleveland 77327	713-592-6462	59,683 / na
10	C1	Cibola Nat'l. Forest Sup., 2113 Osuna Rd. NE, #A, Albuquerque, NM 87113	505-761-4650	1,886,000 / 2,000-11,300
10	A4	Rita Blanca National Grasslands, PO Box 38, Texline 79087	806-362-4254	95,000 / 3,700-4,400
1	C1	**COE, Fort Worth District,** PO Box 17300, Fort Worth 76102	817-334-2705	na / na
2	A4	Aquilla Dam & Lake, PO Box 5038 L.P.S., Clifton 76634	817-694-3189	na / na
3	A4	Bardwell Lake, Rt. #4, Box 60, Ennis 75119	214-875-5711	na / na
4	B4	Belton Lake, 99 FM (Farm to Market) 2271, Belton 76513	817-939-1829	na / na
5	A4	Benbrook Lake, PO Box 26619, Fort Worth 76126	817-292-2400	na / na
6	C4	Canyon Lake, HC 4, Box 400, Canyon Lake 78133	210-964-3341	na / na
7	A5	Ferrells Bridge Dam & Lake O' The P, Drawer W, Jefferson 75657	903-665-2336	na / na
8	A4	Granger Lake, Rt. #1, Box 172, Granger 76530	512-859-2668	na / na
9	A4	Grapevine Lake, 110 Fairway Dr., Grapevine 76051	817-481-4541	na / na
10	B3	Hords Creek Lake, HCR 75, Box 33, Coleman 76834	915-625-2322	na / na
11	A4	Joe Pool Lake, PO Box 872, Cedar Hill 75104	214-299-2227	na / na
12	A4	Lake Georgetown, Rt. #5, Box 500, Georgetown 78626	512-863-2028	na / na
13	A4	Lavon Lake, Box 1560, Wylie 75098	214-442-3141	na / na
14	A4	Lewisville Lake, 1801 N. Mill Street, Lewisville 75057	214-434-1666	na / na
15	B4	Navarro Mills Lake, Rt. #1, Box 33D, Purdon 76679	817-578-1431	na / na
16	B3	O.C. Fisher Lake, 3900 Mercedes Avenue, San Angelo 76901	915-949-4757	na / na
17	B4	Proctor Lake, Rt. #1, Box 71A, Comanche 76442	817-879-2424	na / na
*18	A4	Ray Roberts Lake, 1801 N. Mill St., Lewisville 75067	214-434-1667	*18
19	B5	Sam Rayburn Reservoir, Rt. #3, Box 486, Jasper 75951	409-384-5716	na / na
20	B4	Somerville Lake, PO Box 549, Somerville 77879	409-596-1622	na / na
21	B4	Stillhouse Hollow Reservoir, 99 FM 2271, Belton 76513	817-939-1829	na / na
22	B5	Town Bluff Dam & B.A. Steinhagen La, 890 FM 92, Woodville 75979	409-429-3491	na / na
23	B4	Waco Lake, Rt. #10, Box 173 G, Waco 76708	817-756-5359	na / na
24	B4	Whitney Lake, PO Box 5038 L.P.S., Clifton 76634	817-694-3189	na / na
25	A5	Wright Patman Dam & Lake, PO Box 1817, Texarkana 75504	903-838-8781	na / na
26	C5	COE, Galveston District, PO Box 1229, Galveston 77553	409-766-3979	na / na
27	C5	Addicks Dam, PO Box 218747, Houston 77218	713-497-0740	na / na
28	C5	Barker Dam, PO Box 218747, Houston 77218	713-497-0740	na / na
29	A5	COE, Tulsa District, PO Box 61, Tulsa, OK 74121	918-581-7349	na / na
29	A5	Pat Mayse Lake, PO Box 129, Powderly 75473	903-732-3020	na / na
30	A4	Texoma Lake, PO Box 60, Cartwright 74731	903-465-4990	na / na
31	A3	Truscott Brine Lake, Area VIII, PO Box 696, Truscott 79260	817-474-3293	na / na
1	C5	**Anahuac NWR,** 509 Washington Ave., PO Box 278, Anahuac 77514 [across from County Courthouse]	409-267-3337	30,000 / 0-12
2	C5	McFaddin/Texas Point NWR, PO Box 609, Sabine Pass 77655	409-971-2909	51,000 / 3
3	C4	Aransas NWR, PC Box 100, Austwell 77950	512-286-3559	54,800 / 0-20
4	C4	Matagorda NWR, PO Box 100, Austwell 77950 [phone is Texas Parks & Wildlife #]	512-983-2215	55,000 / 0-10
5	C4	Attwater Prairie Chicken NWR, PO Box 518, Eagle Lake 77434 [6.5 mi NE of Eagle Lake on Farm Road 3013]	409-234-5940	7,980 / 170-220
6	C5	Brazoria NWR, 1212 N. Velasco, Angleton 77516	409-849-6062	40,000 / 0-15
7	C5	Big Boggy NWR, PO Box 1088, Angleton 77516 [near Wadsworth, waterfowl hunting only in season]	409-849-6062	4,300 / 0-8

Column headings (FACILITIES, SERVICES, RECREATION OPPORTUNITIES & CONVENIENCES): DRINKING WATER; RESTROOMS; DAY USE ONLY AREA, no overnight; PARK & WALK-IN SPORTS OPPORTUNITIES OK; NON-MOTORIZED WATERCRAFT OK; HUNTING IN SEASON, license / permit reqd.; Use of horse OK / check limits; MOTORIZED BOATING FACILITIES, ramps / permit reqd.; FISHING FACILITIES, ramps, marinas, etc.; OFF-ROAD MOTORIZED Vehicle Area; HORSEBACK RIDING w/ your own horse; BICYCLING OPPORTUNITIES; WALKING / HIKING TRAILS; SWIMMING AREAS / WILD RIVERS; WILDERNESS AREAS / TRAILS; NO-CHARGE CAMPGROUNDS / CAMPSITES; DEVELOPED CAMPGROUNDS / CAMPSITES; COMMON PICNIC AREAS / PICNIC SITES; WILDLIFE VIEWING AREA COMMON; ENDANGERED SPECIES ARE COMMON; WILDLIFE IS ABUNDANT OR COMMON; INTERPRETIVE TRAILS; HISTORIC SITES / GEOLOGICAL SITES; ARCHAEOLOGICAL SITES; WILDFLOWER VIEWING AREA / STUDY PROGRAMS; NATURE EDUCATION; AGENCY GUIDED TOURS, scheduled / by res.; INTERPRETIVE or EDUCATIONAL DISPLAY; FREE LITERATURE, brochures, maps, etc.; CONCESSIONAIRE SERVICES AVAILABLE; ENTRY FEE, not camping or permit fee; IO / VC OPEN SATURDAY / SUNDAY; INFO OFFICE (IO) / VISITOR CENTER (VC).

#	Map	Name / Address	acres / elev.	Phone
9	D2	Buffalo Lake NWR, PO Box 179, Umbarger 79091 [take Hwy 60 1.5 mi S of Umbarger to sign]	7,664 / 3,500	806-499-3382
10	D1	Muleshoe NWR, PO Box 549, Muleshoe 79347 [on Hwy. 214, 20 mi. S of Muleshoe]	5,809 / 3,200	806-946-3341
11	D1	Grulla NWR, PO Box 549, Muleshoe 79347 [located in NM, 20 mi. SE of Portales]	3,236 / 3,800	806-946-3341
12	D4	Santa Ana NWR, Rt. #2, Box 202A, Alamo 78516	2,088 / 80-100	512-787-3079
13	A4	Hageman NWR, Rt. #3, Box 123, Sherman 75090	11,320 / 650	903-786-2826
14	D4	Laguna Atascosa NWR, PO Box 450, Rio Hondo 78583	45,000 / 0-12	210-748-3607
15	B5	Balcones Canyonlands NWR, 611 E. 6th St., Room 403 C, Austin 78701 [not open to public, off SH 1431 NW of Austin]	11,000 / na	512-482-5700
1	C3	Amistad National Recreation Area, PO Box 420367, Del Rio 78842 [on I-90 just W of Del Rio]	57,292 / na	210-775-7491
2	C2	Big Bend National Park, Big Bend National Park 79834	801,163 / 1,800-7,835	915-477-2251
3	C2	Rio Grande Wild & Scenic River, c/o Big Bend Nat'l. Park, Big Bend Nat'l. Park 79834	9,600 / na	915-427-2251
4	D4	Big Thicket National Preserve, FM 420, Kountze 77625 [7 mi N of Kountze & 2.5 mi E on US 69]	86,000 / 0-350	409-246-2337
5	B1	Guadalupe Mountains National Park, HC 60, Box 400, Salt Flat 79847 [110 mi E of El Paso & 55 mi S of Carlsbad, NM]	86,000 / na	915-828-3251
6	D2	Lake Meredith Recreation Area, PO Box 1460, Fritch 79036	44,977 / 3,000	806-857-3151
7	D4	Padre Island Nat'l. Seashore, 9405 S. Padre Island Drive, Corpus Christi 78418	130,690 / na	512-949-8068
1	B4	Texas Parks & Wildlife, Park Operations, 4200 Smith School Road, Austin 78744	na / na	800-792-1112
2	B3	Abilene SP, Rt. #1 Tuscola 79562	507 / 1,950-2,050	915-572-3204
3	A5	Atlanta SP, Rt. #1, Box 116, Atlanta 75551	1,470 / 280	903-796-6476
4	B3	Balmorhea SP, Box 15, Toyahvale 79786	48 / 3,300	915-375-2370
5	B2	Big Spring SP, Box 1064, Big Spring 79720	382 / 3,000	915-263-4931
6	A4	Bonham SP, Rt. #¹, Box 337, Bonham 75418	300 / 600	903-583-5022
7	A5	Caddo Lake SP, Rt. #2, Box 15, Karrack 75661	480 / 320	903-679-3351
8	D2	Caprock Canyon SP, Ranch Road 1065, PO Box 204, Quitaque 79255	13,960 / 2,180-3,180	806-455-1492
9	B5	Cassells Boykin SP, Rt. #4, Box 274, Jasper 75951	200 / 120	409-384-5231
10	B4	Cleburne SP, Rt. #2, Box 90, Cleburne 76031	na / na	817-645-4215
11	B4	Colorado Bend SP Box 118, Bend 76824	5,328 / 1,115	915-628-3240
12	B3	Copper Breaks SP. Rt. #3, Box 480, Quanah 79252	1,933 / 1,345-1,563	817-839-4331
13	A5	Daingerfield SP. Rt. #1, Box 286-B, Daingerfield 75638	600 / 400	903-645-2921
14	B2	Davis Mountains SP, Box 786, Fort Davis 79734	2,300 / 5,100	915-426-3337
15	B4	Dinosaur Valley SP, Box 396, Glen Rose 76043	1,272 / 850	817-897-4588
16	A4	Eisenhower SP, Rt. #2, Box 50K, Denison 75020	460 / 670	903-465-1956
17	B4	Fairfield Lake SP, Rt. #2, Box 912, Fairfield 75840	1,460 / 310	903-389-4514
18	B4	Fort Parker SP, Rt. #3, Box 95, Mexia 76667	1,450 / 430	817-562-5751
19	B1	Franklin Mountains SP, PO Box 200, Canutillo 79835	27,000 / 5,250	915-877-1528
20	B5	Huntsville SP, I-45, Park Rd. 40 exit 109, PO Box 508, Huntsville 77340	2,083 / 300	409-295-5644
21	A4	Lake Arrowhead SP, Rt. #2, Box 260, Wichita Falls 76301	524 / 926	817-528-2211
22	B3	Lake Brownwood SP, Rt. #5, Box 160, Brownwood 76801	na / na	915-784-5223
23	B3	Lake Colorado City SP, Rt. #2, Box 232, Colorado City 79512	500 / 2,900	915-728-3931
24	B5	Lake Livingston SP, Rt. #9, Box 1300, Livingston 77351	634 / 132	409-365-2201
25	A4	Lake Mineral Wells SP, Rt. #4, Box 39C, Mineral Wells 76067	3,000 / 900	817-328-1171
26	B4	Lake Whitney SP, Box 1175, Whitney 76692	955 / 550	817-694-3793
27	B4	Martin Creek Lake SP, Rt. #2, Box 2C, Tatum 75691	250 / 340	903-214-5952
28	B5	Martin Dies Jr SP, Rt. #4, Box 274, Jasper 75951	800 / 100	409-384-5231
29	B4	Meridian SP, Box 188, Meridian 76665	502 / 1,200	817-435-2536
30	B2	Monahans Sandhills SP, Box 1738, Monahans 79756	3,840 / 2,500	915-943-2092
31	B4	Mother Neff SP, Rt. #1, Box 58, Moody 76557	259 / 1,365	817-853-2389
32	D2	Palo Duro Canyon SP, Rt. #2, Box 285, Canyon 79015	16,400 / 3,500	806-488-2227
33	B5	Rusk-Palestine SP, Hwy. 84 W, Rt. #4, Box 431, Rusk 75785	115 / 435	903-683-5126
34	B4	South Llano River SP, HC-15, Box 223, Junction 76849	507 / 1,800	915-446-3994
35	A5	Tyler SP, Rt. #29, Box 29030, Tyler 75706	995 / 575	903-214-5975
1	B4	Texas Parks & Wildlife, Wildlife Division, 4200 Smith School Rd., Austin 78744	na / na	512-389-4800
1	D4	Sabal Palm Grove Sanctuary, PO Box 5052, Brownsville 78523 [on FM 1419, 5 mi SE of Brownsville]	172 / 25	512-541-8034

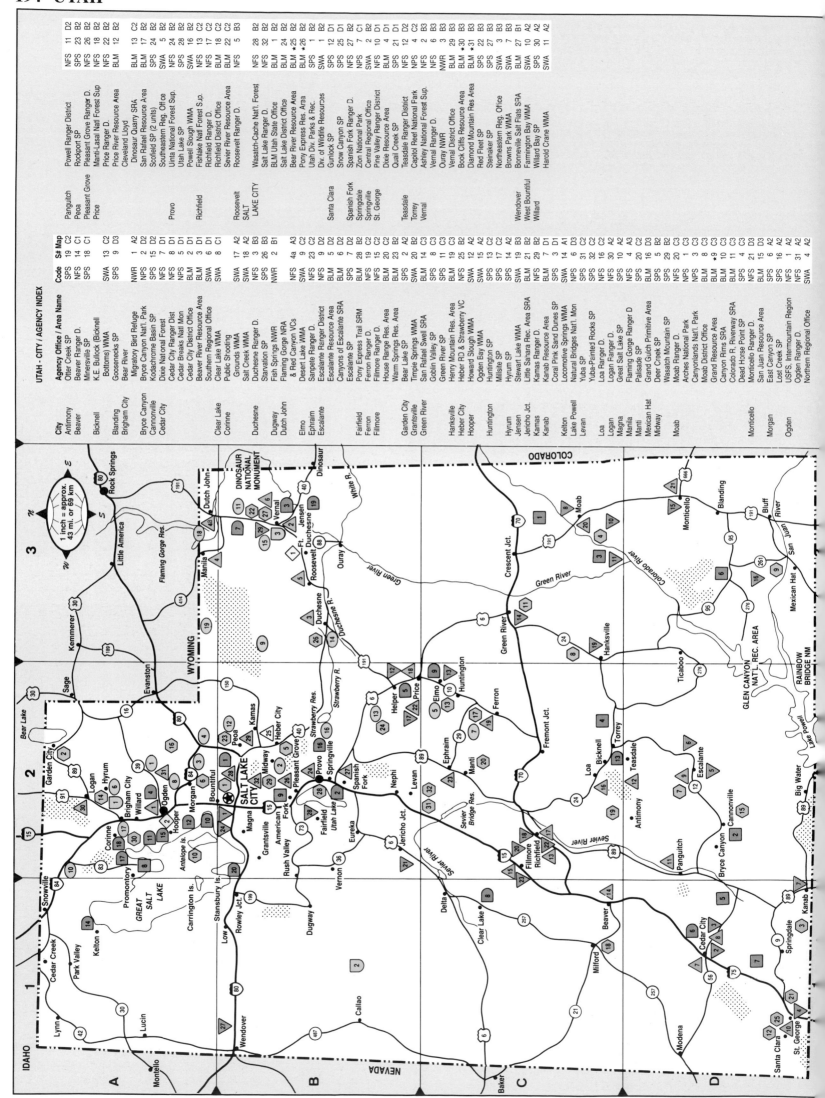

UTAH NOTES

Summary
There are 99 federal, 55 state, and 3 private recreation areas or local administrative offices covered in this state chapter. Of these, 112 appear in the Information Chart and 45 are covered in the notes. The special indexes feature 15 federally designated wilderness areas and wild rivers, and 60 agency published outdoor maps.

Federal Agencies

U.S. Forest Service
The Intermountain Regional Office visitor facility is located inside the Union Station (south end) in Ogden.

Flaming Gorge NRA Visitors Center is operated jointly by the Ashley NF Flaming Gorge Ranger District (S# 4, map A3) and the Bureau of Reclamation to provide recreation information about Flaming Gorge NRA and the Green River. The Red Canyon Visitors Center offers a fantastic view of the Red Canyon portion of the Flaming Gorge NRA and the High Uintas. Exhibits, photos, maps, books, and an audio-visual proram are featured.
Phone 801-784-3445 for details.

Strawberry Visitors Center is operated by the Uinta NF Heber Ranger District (S# 25, map B2). There are exhibits, a fish stripping station, and book sales. Inter-agency management of Strawberry River and Reservoir (bureau of Reclamation) resources are explained.

National Park Service Note:
The Natural Bridges National Monument (S# 6, map D3) city address, Lake Powell, is a post office address and is not shown as a city on typical Utah road maps.

Additional NPS Locations in Utah
Golden Spike National Historic Site (2,735 acres)
(S# 8, map A2)
PO Box W
Brigham City, UT 84302   801-471-2209

Timpanogos Cave National Monument (250 acres)
(S# 9, map B2)
RR 3, Box 200
American Fork, UT 84003   801-756-5238

Bureau of Land Management
The Arizona Strip District, and Shiwits and Vermillion Resource Area joint office is located in St. George, Utah. The lands they manage are in Arizona. See Arizona chapter for Information Chart details.

Bureau of Reclamation - USDI
Upper Colorado Region
125 S. State St.
PO Box 11568
Salt Lake City, UT 84147   801-524-5403

Bureau of Reclamation Recreation Areas
This office administers bureau recreation areas in Utah and portions of Arizona, Colorado, Idaho, New Mexico, West Texas, and Wyoming.
Nineteen recreation areas are listed here and symbolized on the Utah state map.

S#	MAP	LOCATION NAME
1	A2	Causey Res.
2	A2	Deer Creek Res.
3	A2	East Canyon Res.
4	A2	Echo Res.
5	C2	Huntington North Res.
6	A2	Hyrum Res.
7	A2	Joes Valley Res.
8	A2	Lost Creek Res.
9	B3	Moon Lake Res.
10	A2	Newton Res.
11	B3	Red Fleet Res.
12	B2	Rockport Lake
13	B2	Scofield Res.
14	B3	Starvation Res.
15	B3	Steinaker Res.
16	B2	Strawberry Res.
17	A2	Willard Res.
18	A3	Flaming Gorge natl. Recreation Area — Utah/Wyoming
19	A3	Meeks Cabin Res.

Wilderness Index
Ashdown Gorge Wilderness - 7,000 acres
Box-Death Hollow Wilderness - 26,000 acres
Pine Valley Mountain Wilderness - 50,000 acres
Dixie National Forest (S# 7, map D1)
Dark Canyon Wilderness - 45,000 acres
Manti-Lasal National Forest (S# 18, map B2)
Deseret Peak Wilderness - 25,500 acres
Mount Naomi Wilderness - 44,350 acres
Mount Olympus Wilderness - 16,000 acres
Twin Peaks Wilderness - 13,100 acres
Wellsville Mountain Wilderness - 28,350 acres
Wasatche-Cache National Forest Sup. (S# 28, map B2)
High Uintas Wilderness - 460,000 acres
Ashley National Forest (S# 2, map B3), and
Wasatche-Cache National Forest Sup. (S# 28, map B2)
Lone Peak Wilderness - 30,088 acres
Uinta National Forest (S# 24, map B2), and
Wasatche-Cache National Forest Sup. (S# 28, map B2)
Mount Nebo Wilderness - 28,000 acres
Mount Timpanogos Wilderness - 10,750 acres
Uinta National Forest (S# 24, map B2)
Beaver Dam Mountains Wilderness - 2,600 acres
Paria Canyon-Vermillion Cliffs Wilderness - 20,000 acres
BLM Cedar City District Office (S# 2, map D1)

Outdoor Map Index

National Park Service (USGS Maps)
Arches National Park [1974]
 Scale: 1 inch = 0.8 mile (1 cm = 0.5 km)
 Size: 24x34 inches (61x86 cm)
Bryce Canyon National Park [1939]
 Scale: 1 inch = 0.5 mile (1 cm = 0.3 km)
 Size: 32x44 inches (81x111 cm)
Canyonlands National Park [1968]
 Scale: 1 inch = 1.0 mile (1 cm = 0.6 km)
 Size: 46x61 inches (116x154 cm)
Cedar Breaks National Monument [1936]
 Scale: 1 inch = 0.2 mile (1 cm = 0.1 km)
 Size: 17x21 inches (43x53 cm)
Dinosaur National Park (CO-UT) [1971]
 Scale: 1 inch = 1.0 mile (1 cm = 0.6 km)
 Size: 30x51 inches (76x129 cm)
Glen Canyon Natl. Recreation Area [1969]
 Scale: 1 inch = 4.0 miles (1 cm = 2.5 km)
 Size: 32x36 inches (81x91 cm)

U.S. Forest Service Maps
The regional office offers Administrative and Secondary base Series maps as temporary Visitor Maps. Inquire about them at local USFS offices or at the regional office Visitor Center in Ogden.

Ashley National Forest [1982]
Dixie NF-Powell/Escalante/Teasdale RD [1982]
Dixie NF-Pine Valley/Cedar City RDs [1982]
Fish Lake National Forest [1982]
High Uinta's Wilderness, Wasatch/Ashley NFs [1987]
Manti-LaSal National Forest RDs
Uinta National Forest [1976]
Wasatch - Cache National Forest [1976]

Bureau of Land Management Maps
See the BLM Utah intermediate scale map grid. A few maps do not have topographic features and this is noted below the map name in the grid with the letters NT. Other maps are available such as the State of Utah - Area of Responsibility maps in 1:1,000,000 and 1:500,000 scale. They are also printed as Minerals Status Maps (same size and scale). There are two Land Status Quad Map series available. The state office Public Room n Salt Lake City hours are 9 a.m. to 4 p.m. Monday through Friday. Phone 801-539-4001.

USGS Earth Science Information Center
USGS Salt Lake City-ESIC
8105 Federal Bldg.
125 S. State St.
Salt Lake City, UT 84138   801-524-5652

State Agencies

Department of Natural Resources (DNR)
1636 West North Temple
Salt Lake City, UT 84116-3154   801-538-4700

The three Divisions that follow operate under the DNR.

Division of Parks & Recreation
A Utah State Parks Guide (47 state parks) is available free. The guide describes the facilities and activities available at each park, and contains a locator map. Individual brochures are available for many of the parks, as are brochures for other specific interests and activities.

Division of State Lands & Forestry
3 Triad Center, Suite 400
355 West North Temple
Sal: Lake City, UT 84180   801-538-5508

Contact the Division for state forest recreation literature.

Division of Wildlife Resources (DWR)
Various types of Wildlife Management Areas are listed in the Utah Hunting & Fishing Guide. Licensing and game harvest information is published annually. In this Guide, the agency offices are recorded in the Information Chart. Selected wildlife areas shown on the Guide map are listed here.

S#	MAP	NAME & LOCATION
7	B3	Browns Park WMA, Vernal
8	C1	Clear Lake WMA, Clear Lake
9	C2	Desert Lake WMA, Elmo
10	A2	Farmington Bay WMA, West Bountiful
11	A2	Harold Crane WMA, Willard
12	C3	Howard Slough WMA, Hooper
13	C2	K.E. Bullock (Bicknell Bottoms)WMA, Bicknell
14	A1	Locomotive Springs WMA, Kelton
15	A2	Ogden Bay WMA, Hooper
16	B2	Powell Slough WMA, Provo
17	A2	Public Shooting Grounds WMA, Corinne
18	B3	Salt Creek WMA, Corinne
19	B3	Stewart Lake WMA, Jensen
20	B2	Timpie Springs WMA, Grantsville

Utah Travel Council
Council Hall/Capitol Hill
Salt Lake City, UT 84114   801-538-1030

This office offers a set of five regional multi-purpose maps that contain a wealth of information for the recreationist. They show land ownership, topography, recreation areas, and the location of forests, parks, wildlife refuges, and fishing waters. Cost is $2 per map or $10 for the set. A Utah Tour Guide, Travel Guide and Dept. of Transportation map are also available.

Private Organizations

Tribal Land Area in Utah
Ute Tribe of the Uintah & Ouray Indian Reservation - Fishing, hunting, camping, boating.
Uintah and Ouray Tribal Business Committee
(S# 1, map B3)
Fort Duchesne, UT 84026   801-722-5141

ANCA Locations in Utah
Ogden Nature Center (S# 2, map A2)
966 West 12th
Ogden, UT 84404   801-621-7595

Utah Chamber of Commerce Assn.
97 East St. George Blvd.
St. George, UT 84770   801-628-1658

115°–114°	114°–113°	113°–112°	112°–111°	111°–110°	110°–109°
Jackpot	Grouse Creek NT	Tremonton	Logan	Kings Peak	Dutch John
Wells	Newfoundland Mountains NT	Promontory Peak NT	Ogden NT	Duschene NT	Vernal
Wendover	Bonneville	Tooele	Salt Lake City	Price	Seep Ridge
Currie	Wildcat Mountain	Rush Valley	Provo NT	Huntington	West Water
Kern Mountains	Fish Springs	Lynndyl	Nephi	San Rafael	Moab
Ely	Tule Valley	Delta	Manti	Hanksville	La Sal
Garrison	Wah Wah North	Richfield	Salina	Hite Crossing	Blanding
Wilson Creek	Wah Wah South	Beaver	Loa	Navajo Mountain	Bluff
Callente	Cedar City	Panguitch	Escalante		
Clover Mountains	Saint George	Kanab	Smokey Mountain		

BLM UTAH
1:100,000 INTERMEDIATE SCALE MAPS
SURFACE & SURFACE / MINERAL SERIES
NT (no topography)

AGENCY/MAP LEGEND . . . INITIALS, MAP SYMBOLS, COLOR CODES

U.S. Forest Service Supervisor & Ranger Dist. Offices NFS (61)
U.S. Army Corps of Engineers Rec. Areas & Offices . COE (31)
USFWS National Wildlife Refuges & Offices . . . . NWR (40)
National Park Service Parks & other NPS Sites . . . . . NPS (7)
Bureau of Land Management Rec. Areas & Offices . . BLM (26)
Bureau of Reclamation Rec. Areas & Reg. Offices . . . BOR (8)
State Parks (also see State Agency notes) . . . . SPS (52)
State Wildlife Areas (also see State Agency notes) . . SWA (19)
Private Preserves, Nature Centers & Tribal Lands . . (15)
The Wild Rivers and Wilderness Areas

★ INFORMATION CHART ★

INFORMATION CHART LEGEND - SYMBOLS & LETTER CODES

- ■ means **YES** & □ means **Yes with disability provisions**
- **sp** means **sp**ring, March through May
- **S** means **S**ummer, June through August
- **F** means **F**all, September through November
- **W** means **W**inter, December through February
- **T** means **T**wo (2) or **T**hree (3) Seasons
- **A** means **A**ll Four (4) Seasons
- **na** means Not Applicable or Not Available

Note: empty or blank spaces in the chart mean **NO**

Note: Refer to yellow block on page 7 (top right) for location name and address abbreviations. If a symbol number has a star ★ that symbol is not shown on the map.

FACILITIES, SERVICES, RECREATION OPPORTUNITIES & CONVENIENCES

S#	MAP	LOCATION NAME (state initials if more than one) with ADDRESS and/or LOCATION DATA	TELEPHONE	ACRES / ELEVATION	INFO OFFICE (IO) / VISITOR CENTER (VC)	IO / VC OPEN SATURDAY / SUNDAY	ENTRY FEE, not camping or permit fee	CONCESSIONAIRE SERVICES AVAILABLE	INTERPRETIVE or EDUCATIONAL DISPLAY	FREE LITERATURE, brochures, maps, etc.	AGENCY GUIDED TOURS, scheduled / by res.	NATURE EDUCATION / STUDY PROGRAMS	WILDFLOWER VIEWING AREA or DRIVE	ARCHAEOLOGICAL / GEOLOGICAL SITES	HISTORIC SITES	INTERPRETIVE TRAILS	WILDLIFE IS ABUNDANT OR COMMON	ENDANGERED SPECIES ARE COMMON	WILDLIFE VIEWING SITES, blinds, signs, etc.	DEVELOPED PICNIC AREAS / PICNIC SITES	DEVELOPED CAMPGROUNDS / CAMPSITES	NO-CHARGE CAMPGROUNDS / CAMPSITES	WILDERNESS AREAS / WILD RIVERS	WALKING / HIKING TRAILS	SWIMMING PERMITTED, at one's own risk	BICYCLING OPPORTUNITIES...areas, trails	HORSEBACK RIDING, w/ your own horse	OFF-ROAD Motorized Vehicle Area / Use OK	FISHING IN SEASON, license / permit reqd.	BOATING FACILITIES, ramps, marinas, etc.	MOTORIZED WATERCRAFT OK, check limits	NON-MOTORIZED WATERCRAFT OK	HUNTING IN SEASON, license / permit reqd.	WINTER SPORTS OPPORTUNITIES	PARK & WALK-IN ONLY AREA	DAY USE ONLY, no overnight	DRINKING WATER	RESTROOMS	S#
1	A2	**U.S. Forest Svc., Intermtn. Region**, FOB, 324 25th St., Ogden 84401 [Visitor Center at Union Station in Ogden]	801-625-5306	31,000,000 / na	■					■																													1
2	B3	Ashley National Forest Sup., 355 North Vernal Ave., Vernal 84078	801-789-1181	1,384,133 / 5,400-13,528	■					■				■	■					■	■		■	■	■	■	■	■	■	■	■	■	■	■			■		2
3	B3	Duchesne Ranger D., 85 West Main, PO Box I, Duchesne 84021	801-738-2482	359,000 / 6,000-11,800	■					■										■	■		■				■		■	■	■	■	■					■	3
4	A3	Flaming Gorge Ranger D (branch office in Dutch John), PO Box 278, Manila 84046	801-784-3445	369,123 / 6,000-11,500	■			■		■	■	■		■	■				■	■	■		■		■		■		■	■	■	■	■	■			■	■	4
4a	A3	Flaming Gorge NRA & Red Canyon VCs, PO Box 157, Dutch John 84023	801-885-3315	na / na																																	■		4a
5	B3	Roosevelt Ranger D., 244 West Hwy. 40 (333-6), Roosevelt 84066	801-722-5018	na / 5,000	■					■				■	■					■	■		■		■		■	■	■		■	■	■	■			■		5
6	B3	Vernal Ranger D., 353 N. Vernal Ave., Vernal 84078	801-789-1181	333,000 / 7,000-12,000	■					■					■					■	■		■	■		■	■	■	■		■	■	■	■				■	6
7	D1	Dixie National Forest, 82 North 100 East, PO Box 580, Cedar City 84720	801-865-3700	1,970,000 / 5,000-11,000	□	S		□	■	■					■	□	T			□	□		■	■	■	■	■	■	■	■	■	■	■	■			□	□	7
8	D1	Cedar City Ranger District, 82 North 100 East, PO Box 627, Cedar City 84720	801-865-3200	355,797 / 8,000-11,000	■	A		□	■	■			T			□	T			□	□		■	■	■	■	■	■	■	■	■	■	■	■			■	□	8
9	D2	Escalante Ranger District, 270 West Main, PO Box 246, Escalante 84726	801-826-4221	430,070 / 8,000-11,000	□	A			■	■			T				T			□	□		■	■	■	■	■	■	■	■		■	■				■	□	9
10	D1	Pine Valley Ranger District, 196 E. Tabernacle St., Room 40, PO Box 2288, St. George 84770	801-673-3431	461,477 / 5,000-10,000	□			■	■	■		■	T		■	■				□	□		■	■	■	■	■	■	■	■	■	■	■				□	□	10
11	D2	Powell Ranger District, 225 East Center, PO Box 80, Panguitch 84759	801-676-8815	385,222 / 8,000-10,000	■	S			■	■			T			■	T			□	□			■	■	■	■	■	■	■	■	■	■	■			■	□	11
12	D2	Teasdale Ranger District, 138 E. Main, PO Box 99, Teasdale 84773	801-425-3702	251,154 / 8,000-11,000	□	A			■	■			T				T			□	□			■	■	■	■	■	■			■	■				■	■	12
13	C2	Fishlake National Forest Sup., 115 East 900 North, Richfield 84701 [about 1 block E of Main on 900 North]	801-896-9233	1,500,000 / 5,200-12,000	□			■		■			T	■	■	■	T		■	■	□	T		■	■	■	■	■	■	■	■	■	■	■			■	□	13
14	C1	Beaver Ranger D., 190 North 100 East, PO Box E, Beaver 84713	801-438-2436	295,000 / 6,000-12,200	■					■			T	■	■		T		■	■	□	T		■	■	■	■	■	■		■	■	■	■			■	□	14
15	C2	Fillmore Ranger D., 390 South Main, PO Box 265, Fillmore 84631	801-743-5721	463,000 / 4,800-10,200	■					■			T	■		■	T			■	■	T		■	■	■	■	■	■			■	■				■	□	15
16	C2	Loa Ranger D., 150 South Main, PO Box 128, Loa 846317	801-836-2811	261,000 / 6,500-11,600	■			■		■		■	T	■			T		■	□	■	T		■	■	■	■	■	■	■	■	■	■	■			■	■	16
17	C2	Richfield Ranger D., 115 East 900 North, Richfield 84701	801-896-9233	416,000 / 5,400-11,500	■					■			T	■			T			■	■			■	■	■	■	■	■		■	■	■	■			■	■	17
18	B2	Manti-Lasal National Forest Sup., 599 W. Price River Dr., Price 84501	801-637-2817	na / na	■					■				■						■	■		■	■	■	■	■	■	■	■	■	■	■	■				■	18
19	C2	Ferron Ranger D., 98 South State, PO Box 310, Ferron 84523	801-384-2372	na / na	■			■		■										■	■			■	■	■	■	■	■	■	■	■	■	■				■	19
20	C3	Moab Ranger D., 125 West 200 South, Moab 84532	801-259-7155	na / na	■					■										■	■				■	■	■	■	■		■		■	■				■	20
21	D3	Monticello Ranger D., 496 East Central, PO Box 820, Monticello 84535	801-587-2041	na / na	■					■				■						■	■		■	■		■	■	■	■				■	■				■	21
22	B2	Price Ranger D., 599 West Price River Dr., Price 84501	801-637-2817	na / na	■					■										■	■			■	■	■	■	■	■				■	■				■	22
23	C2	Sanpete Ranger D., 150 South Main St., PO Box 692, Ephraim 84627	801-283-4151	na / na	■					■										■	■			■	■	■	■	■	■	■	■	■	■	■				■	23
24	B2	Uinta National Forest Sup., 88 West 100 North, PO Box 1428, Provo 84603	801-377-5780	979,247 / 6,100-11,877	□					■				■	■				■	■	■		■	■	■	■	■	■	□	□	■	■	■	■			□	□	24
25	B2	Heber RD & Strawberry VC, 125 East 100 North, PO Box 190, Heber City 84032	801-654-0470	347,925 / na	□	T			■	■	□	□	T	■	■	□	A	A	■	□	□	T		■		■	■	■	□	□	■	■	■	■			■	■	25
26	B2	Pleasant Grove Ranger D., 390 North 100 East, PO Box 228, Pleasant Grove 84062	801-785-3563	150,118 / na	□	S				■		■	T	■	■	■	A		■	■	■	T	■	■		■	■	■	□	□	■	■	■	■			□	□	26
27	B2	Spanish Fork Ranger D., 44 West 400 North, Spanish Fork 84660	801-798-3571	481,204 / na	■	S				■		■		■	■	□	A	T	■	□	□	T	■	■	■	■	■	■	□	□	■	■	■	■			□	□	27
28	B2	Wasatch-Cache Nat'l. Forest Sup., 8230 FOB, 125 S. State St., Salt Lake City 84138	□ 801-524-5030	1,219,800 / na	■					■		□	sp	■	□	□			□	□	□		■	■	■	■	■	■	□	■	■	■	■	■			□	□	28
29	B2	Kamas Ranger D., 50 East Center St., PO Box 68, Kamas 84036	801-783-4338	182,700 / na	□	S		■	■	■									■	■	■	T	■	■	■	■	■	■	■		■	■	■	■			■	■	29
30	A2	Logan Ranger D., 860 No. 1200 E., Logan 84321	801-753-2772	258,200 / na	■			■		■				■	■	■			■	■	■		■	■	■	■	■	■	■			■	■	■			■	■	30
31	A2	Ogden Ranger D., 507 25th Street, PO Box 1433, Ogden 84401	801-625-5112	157,000 / na	■	S		■		■				■	■	□			■	□	□		■	■	■	■	■	■	□	■	■	■	■	■			□	□	31
32	B2	Salt Lake Ranger D., 6944 South 3000 East, Salt Lake City 84121	801-524-5042	212,700 / na	■			■		■			sp	■	■				■	■	■		■	■		■	■		□				■	■		■	■	■	32
1	A2	**Bear River Migratory Bird Refuge**, 866 South Main, Brigham City 84302	801-723-5887	65,000 / 4,206						■							A	sp											□				■					□	1
2	B1	Fish Springs NWR, PO Box 568, Dugway 84022 [office at NWR 60 mi SW of Dugway & 15 mi E of Callao, follow signs]	801-831-5353	17,992 / 4,285-4,600	□				■	■					■	■	A		□	□												■	■		■	■	■	□	2
3	B3	Ouray NWR, 1680 W. Highway 40, Suite 112C, Vernal 84078	801-789-0351	11,827 / 4,660						■	■			■					■										■				■		■	■	■	■	3
1	C3	**Arches National Park**, PO Box 907, Moab 84532 [5 mi N of Moab on Hwy 191, 25 mi S of I-70 on Hwy 191]	□ 801-259-8161	73,379 / 4,000-5,650	□	A	A	□	■	■	■	■		□	■	■				□	□	W		■			■										■	□	1
2	D2	Bryce Canyon Nat'l. Park, Bryce Canyon 84717 [take Hwy 12 E off US 89 for 16 mi, then S on Hwy 163 for 8 mi.]	□ 801-834-5322	35,835 / 6,600-9,100	□	A	A	□	■	■			S	□	□	□	T	T		□	□			■		■	■							■			□	□	2
3	C3	Canyonlands Nat'l. Park, 125 West 200 South, Moab 84532 [three VCs, call for list/details]	801-259-7164	337,570 / 3,720-7,000	■	A				■				■	■					■	■		■	■	■		■		■	■	■	■							3
4	C2	Capitol Reef National Park, Torrey 84775	801-425-3791	241,900 / 3,960-9,280	□	A	A		■	■			T	■	■	□	T			■	□		■	■			■		■						■		■	□	4
5	D1	Cedar Breaks National Monument, PO Box 749, Cedar City 84720 [23 mi E of Cedar City via SRs 14 & 148]	801-586-9451	6,154 / 10,300	■	S	S		■	■		■	S	■		■	T			■	□			■										■			■	□	5
6	D3	Natural Bridges Nat'l. Monument, Box #1, Lake Powell 84533 [off Hwy. 95 W of Blanding]	801-259-5174	7,636 / 6,500	■					■				■						■	■																		6
7	C1	Zion National Park, Springdale 84767	801-772-3256	146,600 / 3,700-8,700	□	A	A	□	■	■				■		□	A	A		□	□	A	■	■	■		■		■					■			■	□	7
1	B2	**BLM Utah State Office**, 324 South State Street, Suite 301, Salt Lake City 84111	801-539-4001	22,000,000 / na	■					■														■												■	■		1
2	D1	Cedar City District Office, 176 East D.L. Sargent Drive, PO Box 724, Cedar City 84720	801-586-2401	na / na	■					■														■												■			2
3	D1	Beaver River Resource Area, 1st Interstate Bank Bldg., Suite 3C, 444 S. Main, Cedar City 84720	801-586-2458	na / na	■					■														■												■			3
4	D1	Dixie Resource Area, 225 North Bluff Street, PO Box 726, St. George 84770	801-673-4654	na / na	■					■														■												■			4
5	D2	Escalante Resource Area, PO Box 225, Escalante 84726	801-826-4291	na / na	■					■														■												■			5
6	D2	Canyons of Escalante SRA, near Escalante	801-826-4291	45,000 / 5,500						■										■	■		■	■			■						■						6

#	Grid	Location / Address	Phone	Acres / Elev.
*9	C3	Grand Resource Area, Sand Flats Road, PO Box M, Moab 84532	801-259-8193	na / na
10	C3	Canyon Rims SRA, near Moab	801-259-8193	285,000 / 4,520-6,500
11	C3	Colorado River, Riverway SRA, near Moab	801-259-8193	40,000 / 4,000
12	C3	Price River Resource Area, 900 North Seventh East, Price 84501	801-637-4584	na / na
13	C2	Cleveland Lloyc Dinosaur Quarry SRA, near Price	801-637-4584	160 / 5,000
14	C3	San Rafael Swell SRA, near Green River	801-637-4584	800,000 / 5,000-6,500
15	D3	San Juan Resource Area, 435 North Main Street, PO Box 7, Monticello 84535	801-587-2141	na / na
16	D3	Grand Gulch Primitive Area, N of Mexican Hat	801-587-2141	33,000 / 4,000-6,500
17	B2	San Rafael Resource Area, 900 North Seventh East, Price 84501	801-637-4584	na / na
18	C2	Richfield District Office, 150 East 900 North, Richfield 84701	801-896-8221	na / na
19	C3	Henry Mountain Resource Area, PC Box 99, Hanksville 84734	801-542-3461	na / na
20	C2	House Range Resource Area, PO Box 778, Fillmore 84631	801-743-6811	na / na
21	B2	Little Sahara Recreation Area SRA, near Jericho Jct.	801-743-6811	60,000 / 4,500
22	C2	Sevier River Resource Area, 180 North 100 East, Suite F, Richfield 84701	801-896-8221	na / na
23	B2	Warm Springs Resource Area, PO Box 778, Fillmore 84631	801-743-6811	na / na
24	B2	Salt Lake District Office, 2370 South 2300 West, Salt Lake City 84119	801-977-4300	na / na
*25	B2	Bear River Resource Area, 2370 South 2300 West, Salt Lake City 84119	801-977-4300	na / na
*26	B2	Pony Express Resource Area, 2370 South 2300 West, Salt Lake City 84119	801-977-4300	na / na
27	B1	Bonneville Salt Flats SRA, near Wendover	801-977-4300	30,100 / 4,200
28	B2	Pony Express Trail SRM, near Fairfield	801-977-4300	21,000 / 5,000-7,000
29	B3	Vernal District Office, 170 South 500 East, Vernal 84078	801-789-1362	na / na
*30	B3	Book Cliffs Resource Area, 170 South 500 East, Vernal 84078	801-789-1362	na / na
*31	B3	Diamond Mountain Resource Area, 170 South 500 East, Vernal 84078	801-789-1362	na / na

Utah Div. Parks & Recreation

#	Grid	Location / Address	Phone	Acres / Elev.
1	B2	Utah Div. Parks & Recreation, 1636 West North Temple, Salt Lake City 84116	801-538-7221	na / na
2	A2	Bear Lake SP, PO Box 184, Marina is 2 mi. N, & Rendezvous Beach 10 mi. S of Garden City 84028	801-946-3343	na / 5,900
3	D1	Coral Pink Sand Dunes SP, PO Box 95, 10 mi. W of Kanab 84741	801-874-2408	3,000 / 6,000
4	C3	Dead Horse Point SP, PO Box 609, 32 mi. SW of Moab 84532	801-259-6511	5,022 / 5,900
5	B2	Deer Creek SP, 8 mi. SW of Heber, PO Box 257, Midway 84049	801-654-0171	3,000 / 5,400
6	A2	East Canyon SP, 5535 S Hwy. 66, 10 mi. S of Morgan 84050	801-829-6866	950 / 5,700
7	D2	Escalante SP, PO 3ox 350, 1 mi. W of Escalante 84726	801-826-4466	1,640 / 5,800
8	C3	Goblin Valley SP, 35 mi. NW of Hanksville, PO Box 93, Green River 84525	801-564-3633	4,294 / 5,200
9	D3	Goosenecks SP, 8 mi. N of Mexican Hat, PO Box 788, Blanding 84511	801-678-2238	10 / 4,500
10	A2	Great Salt Lake SP, 16 mi. W of Salt Lake City, PO Box 323, Magna 84044	801-533-4080	na / 4,200
11	C3	Green River SP (Green River City Limits), PO Box 93, Green River 84525	801-564-3633	53 / 4,100
12	D1	Gunlock SP, 16 mi NW of St. George, PO Box 140, Santa Clara 84765	801-628-2255	6,600 / 3,600
13	C2	Huntington SP, PO Box 1343, 2 mi. N of Huntington 84528	801-687-2491	350 / 5,800
14	A2	Hyrum SP, 405 West 300 South, Hyrum 84319	801-245-6866	15 / 4,700
15	D2	Kodachrome Basin SP, PO Box 238, 9 mi. S of Cannonville 84718	801-679-8562	2,240 / 5,800
16	A2	Lost Creek SP, (for mail) 5535 S Hwy. 66, 10 mi. NE of Morgan 84050	801-829-6866	1,038 / 6,000
17	C2	Millsite SP, 4 mi. W of Ferron, PO Box 1343, Huntington 84528	801-687-2491	111 / 6,100
18	C1	Minersville SP, PO Box 1531, 12 mi. W of Beaver 84713	801-438-5472	207 / 5,500
19	D2	Otter Creek SP, PO Box 43, 4 mi. N of Antimony 84712	801-624-3268	80 / 6,400
20	D1	Palisade SP, 2 mi. E of Sterling, PO Box H, Manti 84642	801-835-7275	700 / 5,800
21	D1	Quail Creek SP, PO Box 1943, 14 mi. NE of St. George 84770	801-879-2378	na / 3,300
22	B3	Red Fleet SP, Steinaker Lake 4335, 10 mi. N of Vernal 84078	801-789-4432	1,200 / 5,500
23	B3	Rockport SP, 4 mi. S. of Wanship, 9040 North St. Hwy. 302, Peoa 84061	801-336-2241	770 / 6,000
24	B2	Scofield SP (2 units) 3 & 5 mi. N Scofield, PO Box 166 (winter ph: 637-8497), Price 84501	801-448-9449	476 / 7,600
25	D1	Snow Canyon SP, 11 mi. NW of St. George, PO Box 140, Santa Clara 84765	801-628-2255	6,500 / 3,400
26	B3	Starvation SP, PO Box 584, 4 mi. NW of Duchesne 84021	801-738-2326	3,520 / 5,700
27	B3	Steinaker SP, Steinaker Lake 4335, 7 mi. N of Vernal 84078	801-789-4432	500 / 5,500
28	B2	Utah Lake SP, 4400 West Center, 4 mi. W of Provo 84601	801-375-0731	296 / 4,500
29	B2	Wasatch Mountain SP, PO Box 10, 2 mi. NW of Midway 84049	801-654-1791	22,000 / 6,000
30	A2	Willard Bay SP, 2 marinas, located, 7 mi. S and 15 mi. N of Ogden, 650 North 900 West #A, Willard 84340	801-734-2402	na / 4,200
31	C2	Yuba SP, 30 mi. S of Nephi, PO Box 159, Levan 84639	801-758-2611	120 / 5,500
32	C2	Yuba-Painted Rocks SP, PO Box 159, 15 mi. S of Levan 84639	801-758-2611	na / 5,500

Utah Div. of Wildlife Resources

#	Grid	Location / Address	Phone	Acres / Elev.
1	B2	Utah Div. of Wildlife Resources, 1596 West North Temple St., Salt Lake City 84116	801-538-4700	na / na
2	B2	Central Regional Office, 1115 N. Main St., Springville 489567	801-489-5678	na / na
3	B3	Northeastern Regional Office, 152 East 100 North, Vernal 84078	801-789-3103	na / na
4	A2	Northern Regional Office, 515 East 5300 South, Ogden 84405	801-479-5143	na / na
5	B2	Southeastern Regional Office, 455 W. Railroad Ave., Price 84501	801-637-3310	na / na
6	D1	Southern Regional Office, 622 N. Main St., Cedar City 84720	801-586-2455	na / na

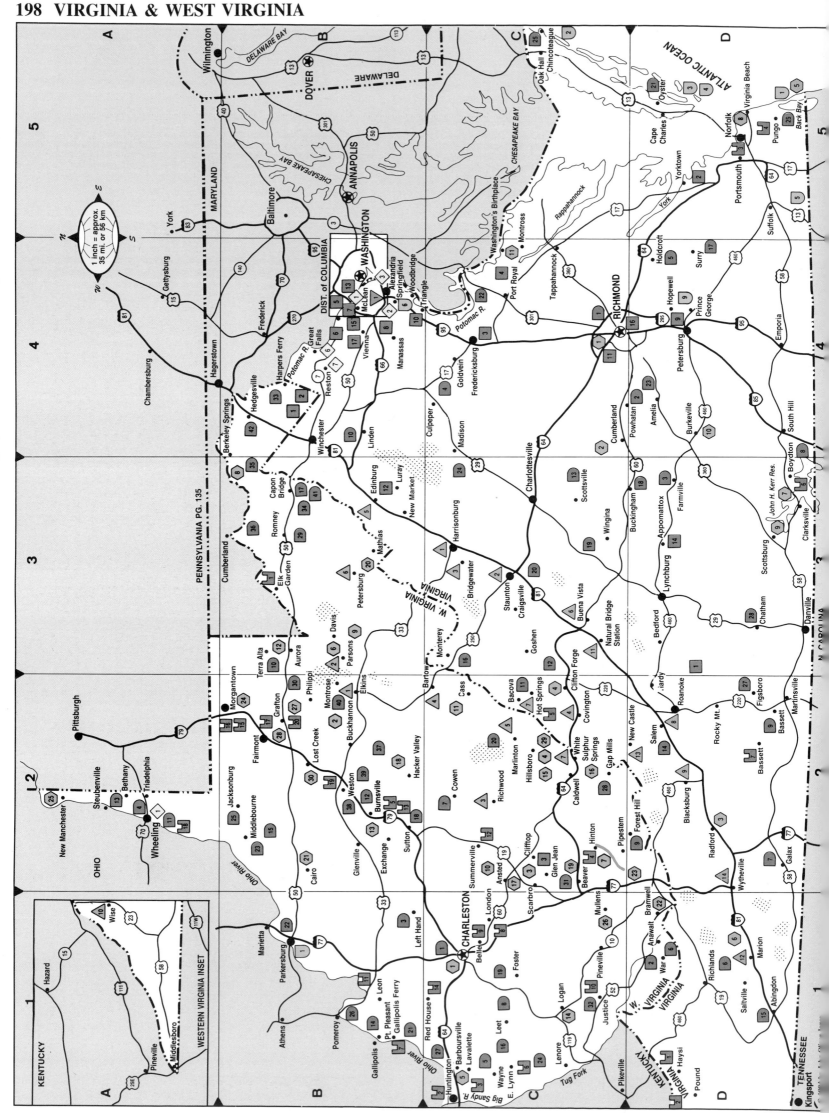

VIRGINIA - CITY / AGENCY INDEX

City	Agency Office / Area Name	Code	S#	Map
Abingdon	Hidden Valley WMA	SWA	15	D1
Amelia	Amelia WMA	SWA	2	D4
Bacova	Gathright WMA	SWA	11	C2
Bassett	Philpott Lake	COE	7	D2
	Fairystone Farms WMA	SWA	9	D2
Blacksburg	Blacksburg Ranger D.	NFS	9	D2
Boydton	John H. Kerr Dam & Res.	COE	6	D3
Bridgewater	Dry River Ranger D.	NFS	3	C3
Buckingham	Horsepen Lake WMA	SWA	18	D3
Buena Vista	Pedlar Ranger D.	NFS	6	C3
Burkeville	Twin Lakes SP	SPS	10	D4
Cape Charles	Eastern Shore of VA NWR	NWR	3	D5
	Fisherman Island NWR	NWR	4	D5
Chatham	White Oak Mtn. WMA	SWA	28	D3
Chincoteague	Chincoteague NWR	NWR	2	C5
Clarksville	Occoneechee SP	SPS	7	D3
Clifton Forge	Douthat SP	SPS	4	C2
Covington	James River Ranger D.	NFS	4	C2
	Gathright Dam & L Moomaw	COE	5	C2
Craigsville	Little North Mountain WMA	SWA	20	C3
Cumberland	Bear Creek Lake SP	SPS	2	C4
Edinburg	Lee Ranger District	NFS	5	B3
Farmville	Briery Creek WMA	SWA	3	D3
Figsboro	Turkeycock Mountain WMA	SWA	27	D2
Fredericksburg	Fredericksburg & Spotsylvania Co Battlefield Mem NMP	NPS	3	C4
Galax	Crooked Creek WMA	SWA	7	D2
Goldvein	C.F. Phelps WMA	SWA	4	C4
Goshen	Goshen WMA	SWA	12	C3
Great Falls	Great Falls Park	NPS	6	B4
Hardy	Booker T. Washington NM	NPS	1	D3
Harrisonburg	Geo. Washington NF Sup.	NFS	1	C3
Haysi	John W Flannagan Dam & Reservoir	COE	1	D1
Holdcroft	Chickahominy WMA	SWA	5	D4
Hot Springs	Warm Springs Ranger D.	NFS	7	C2
Linden	G. Richard Thompson WMA	SWA	10	B4
Luray	Shenandoah Nat'l. Park	NPS	12	B3
Madison	Rapidan WMA	SWA	24	C3
Manassas	Manassas Natl Battlefield P	NPS	8	B4
Marion	Mt. Rogers Nat'l. Rec Area	NFS	12	D1
	Hungry Mother SP	SPS	6	D1
McLean	Geo Washington Mem Parkway	NPS	5	B4
	LBJ Memorial Grove on the Potomac	NPS	7	B4
	Theodore Roosevelt Island	NPS	13	B4
Monterey	Highland WMA	SWA	16	C3
Montross	Westmoreland SP	SPS	11	C4
Natural Br. Station	Glenwood Ranger D.	NFS	11	C3
New Castle	New Castle Ranger D.	NFS	13	D2
Norfolk	COE, Norfolk District	COE	3	D5
	Aiww Albemarle & Chesapeake Canal	COE	4	D5
Oak Hall	Saxis WMA	SWA	25	C5
Oyster	Mockhorn Island WMA	SWA	21	D5
Petersburg	Petersburg Natl Battlefield	NPS	9	D4
Port Royal	Pettigrew WMA	SWA	22	C4
Pound	N Fork of Pound River Lake	COE	2	D1
Powhatan	Powhatan WMA	SWA	23	D4
Prince George	Presquile & James R NWRs	NWR	9	D4
Pungo	Trojan-Pocahontas WMA	SWA	26	D5
Radford	Claytor Lake SP	SPS	3	D2
RICHMOND	Richmond Natl Battlefield P	NPS	11	C4
	Dept. of Consv. & Rec.	SPS	1	C4
	Dept. of Game & Inland Fisheries	SWA	1	C4
Roanoke	Jefferson Nat'l Forest Sup	NFS	8	D2
Salem	Havens WMA	SWA	14	D2
Saltville	Clinch Mountain WMA	SWA	6	D1
Scottsburg	Staunton River SP	SPS	9	D3
Scottsville	Hardware River WMA	SWA	13	C3
South Hill	Dick Cross WMA	SWA	8	D4
Springfield	BLM Eastern States Office	BLM	1	B4
Staunton	Deerfield Ranger D.	NFS	2	C3
Suffolk	Great Dismal Swamp NWR	NWR	5	D5
Surry	Hog Island WMA	SWA	17	D4
Triangle	Prince William Forest Park	NPS	10	B4
Virginia Beach	Back Bay NWR	NWR	1	D5
	False Cape SP	SPS	5	D5
	Seashore SP	SPS	8	D5
Washington's Birthplace	George Washington Birthplace NM	NPS	4	C4
Wingina	James River WMA	SWA	19	C3
Wise	Clinch Ranger D.	NFS	10	A1
Woodbridge	Mason Neck NWR	NWR	6	B4
	Featherstone NWR (closed)	NWR	7	B4
	Marumsco NWR (closed)	NWR	★8	B4
Wytheville	Wythe Ranger D.	NFS	14	D2
Yorktown	Colonial Nat'l. Hist. Park	NPS	2	D5

WEST VIRGINIA - CITY / AGENCY INDEX

City	Agency Office / Area Name	Code	S#	Map
Anawalt	Anawalt Lake PH&FA	SWA	2	D1
Ansted	Hawks Nest SP	SPS	17	C2
Aurora	Cathedral SP	SPS	12	B3
Barboursville	Beech Fork SP	SPS	5	C1
Bartow	Greenbrier Ranger D.	NFS	4	C2
Beaver	Little Beaver SP	SPS	19	C2
Belle	Marmet Locks & Dam (Kanawha River)	COE	9	C1
Berkeley Springs	Cacapon RP	SPS	8	B3
Bramwell	Pinnacle Rock SP	SPS	22	D1
Buckhannon	Audra SP	SPS	2	B2
Burnsville	Burnsville Lake	COE	5	B2
Cairo	North Bend SP	SPS	21	B2
Caldwell	Greenbrier River Trail SP	SPS	16	C2
Capon Bridge	Edwards Run PH&FA	SWA	17	B3
Cass	Carnifex Ferry Battlefield SP	SPS	10	C2
	Cass Scenic Railroad SP	SPS	11	C2
CHARLESTON	State Parks & Rec Section	SPS	1	C1
	DNR, Wildlife Res Div.	SWA	1	C1
Clifftop	Babcock SP	SPS	3	C2
Cowen	Big Ditch Lake PH&FA	SWA	7	C2
Davis	Blackwater Falls SP	SPS	6	B3
	Canaan Valley RP	SPS	9	B3
East Lynn	East Lynn Lake	COE	6	C1
Elk Garden	Jennings Randolph Lake	COE	1	B3
Elkins	Monongahela Nat'l. Forest	NFS	1	B2
Exchange	Burnsville PH&FA	SWA	12	B2
	Stonecoal Lake PH&FA	SWA	37	B2
	Summersville Lake PH&FA	SWA	39	C2
Fairmont	Opekiska Lock & Dam (Monongahela R)	COE	17	B2
	Pricketts Fort SP	SPS	24	B2
Forest Hill	Bluestone PH&FA	SWA	9	D2
Foster	Fork Creek PH&FA	SWA	19	C1
Gallipolis Ferry	Gallipolis Locks & Dam (Ohio River)	COE	7	B1
Gap Mills	Moncove Lake PH&FA	SWA	28	C2
Glen Jean	New River Gorge Nat'l River/Gauley R NRA	NPS	3	C2
Glenville	Cedar Creek SP	SPS	13	B2
Grafton	Tygart Lake	COE	20	B2
	Tygart Lake SP	SPS	27	B2
	Valley Falls SP	SPS	28	B2
Hacker Valley	Holly River SP	SPS	18	B2
Harpers Ferry	Appalachian NS Trail, c/o Ap. Trail Conf	NPS	1	B4
	Harpers Ferry NH Park	NPS	2	B4
Hedgesville	Shannondale Springs PH&FA	SWA	33	B4
	Sleepy Creek PH&FA	SWA	35	B4
	Widmeyer PH&FA	SWA	42	B4
Hillsboro	Beartown SP	SPS	4	C2
	Droop Mtn Battlefield SP	SPS	15	C2
Hinton	Bluestone Lake	COE	4	C2
	Bluestone SP	SPS	7	C2
Huntington	COE, Huntington District	COE	2	C1
Jacksonburg	Lewis Wetzel PH&FA	SWA	25	B2
Justice	R.D. Bailey Lake	COE	10	C1
Lavalette	Beech Fork Lake	COE	3	C1
Leet	Big Ugly PH&FA	SWA	8	C1
Left Hand	B.J. Taylor PH&FA	SWA	3	B1
Lenore	Laurel Lake PH&FA	SWA	24	C1
Leon	Chief Cornstalk PH&FA	SWA	14	B1
Letart	Racine L & D (Ohio River)	COE	11	B1
Logan	Chief Logan SP	SPS	14	C1
London	London L & D (Kanawha R)	COE	8	C1
Lost Creek	Watters Smith Memorial SP	SPS	30	B2
Marlinton	Marlinton Ranger D.	NFS	5	C2
	Watoga SP	SPS	29	C2
	Handley PH&FA	SWA	20	C2
Mathias	Lost River SP	SPS	20	B3
Middlebourne	Conaway Lake PH&FA	SWA	15	B2
Montrose	Teter Creek Lake PH&FA	SWA	40	B2
Morgantown	Hildebrand Locks & Dam (Monongahela R)	COE	15	B2
	Morgantown Lock & Dam (Monongahela R)	COE	16	B2
Mullens	Twin Falls RP	SPS	26	C1
New Manchester	Tomlinson Run SP	SPS	25	A2
Parkersburg	Ohio River Islands NWR	NWR	1	B1
	Hughes River PH&FA	SWA	22	B1
	Jug PH&FA	SWA	23	B2
Parsons	Cheat Ranger D.	NFS	2	B3
Petersburg	Potomac RD & Seneca Rocks VC	NFS	6	B3
Philippi	Pleasants Creek PH&FA	SWA	30	B2
Pineville	R.D. Bailey PH&FA	SWA	32	C1
Pipestem	Pipestem RP	SPS	23	D2
Pt. Pleasant	Hilbert PH&FA	SWA	21	B1
	McClintic PH&FA	SWA	26	B1
	Mill Creek PH&FA	SWA	27	C1
Red House	Winfield Lock & Dam (Kanawha River)	COE	14	C1
Richwood	Gauley RD & Cranberry Mtn. VC	NFS	3	C2
Romney	Nathaniel Mountain PH&FA	SWA	29	B3
	Short Mountain PH&FA	SWA	34	B3
	Springfield PH&FA	SWA	36	B3
	Warden Lake PH&FA	SWA	41	B3
Scarboro	Plum Orchard Lake PH&FA	SWA	31	C2
Summersville	Summersville Lake	COE	12	C2
Sutton	Sutton Lake	COE	13	B2
	Elk River PH&FA	SWA	18	B2
Terra Alta	Briary Mountain PH&FA	SWA	10	B3
War	Berwind Lake PH&FA	SWA	6	D1
Wayne	Beech Fork PH&FA	SWA	5	C1
	East Lynn PH&FA	SWA	16	C1
Weston	Stonewall Jackson Lake	COE	19	B2
	Stonewall Jackson PH&FA	SWA	38	B2
Wheeling	Pike Island Locks & Dam (Ohio River)	COE	18	A2
	Bear Rock Lake PH&FA	SWA	4	A2
	Burches Run Lake PH&FA	SWA	11	A2
	Castleman Run PH&FA	SWA	13	A2
White Sulphur Springs	White Sulphur Ranger D.	NFS	7	C2

VIRGINIA NOTES

Summary

There are 54 federal, 42 state, and 8 private recreation areas or local administrative offices covered in this state chapter. Of these, 73 appear in the Information Chart and 31 are covered in the notes. The special indexes feature 12 federally designated wilderness areas and wild rivers, and 11 agency published outdoor maps.

Federal Agencies

U.S. Forest Service

Virginia is in the Southern Region (see Georgia chapter - U.S. Forest Svc., Southern Region listing).

The Massanuttan Visitor Center near New Market (see map B3), provides orientation to the Massanuttan area of the George Washington National Forest (S# 1, map C3). Learn about the geographic significance of Massanuttan during the Civil War, and prehistoric populations of the Shenandoah Valley. The VC address is:
Rt. 1, Box 100
New Market, VA 22844.

Located near Marion, Virginia, the Mount Rogers NRA (S# 12, map D1) Visitor Center, in the Jefferson National Forest (S# 8, map D2), introduces visitors to special cultural and natural features of the NRA.

The new Gateway Center VC is located at the Factory Merchant's Outlet Mall near Wytheville. Contact the Wythe Ranger District Office (S# 14, map D2) for details.

The Glenwood Ranger District (S# 11, map C3) operates the Natural Bridge Visitor Center from May through September. Educational exhibits introduce the concept of a working forest and inform visitors about recreation and cultural opportunities in the area.

National Park Service
Additional NPS Locations in Virginia

Appomattox Court House NHP (1,325 acres)
(S# 14, map D3)
PO Box 218
Appomattox, VA 24522 — 804-352-8782

Arlington House, The Robert E. Lee Memorial (28 acres)
(S# 15, map B4)
c/o G. Washington Memorial Pkwy., Turkey Run Park
McLean, VA 22101 — 703-557-0663

Maggie L. Walker National Historic Site (1.29 acres)
(S# 16, map C4)
c/o Richmond NBP
3215 East Broad Street
Richmond, VA 23223 — 804-226-1981

Wolf Trap Farm Park for the Performing Arts (130 acres)
1551 Trap Road (S# 17, map B4)
Vienna, VA 22182 — 703-255-1800

Bureau of Land Management

The Eastern States office listed in the Information Chart schedules weekend wild horse and burro adoption center activities in 31 eastern states. Contact them for schedule and location information.

Natl. Oceanic & Atmospheric Administration, USDC

National Ocean Service

The Monitor National Marine Sanctuary (USS Monitor site) is located about 16 miles south-southeast of Cape Hatteras (see North Carolina chapter). For information contact:
Monitor National Marine Sanctuary
NOAA Atlantic Marine Center
439 West York St.
Norfolk, VA 23510 — 804-441-6469

Wilderness Index

Jefferson Natinal Forest, 9 areas (S# 8, map D2)
- Beartown Wilderness - 6,375 acres
- James River Face Wilderness - 8,903 acres
- Kimberling Creek Wilderness - 5,580 acres
- Lewis Fork Wilderness - 5,730 acres
- Little Dry Run Wilderness - 3,400 acres
- Little Wilson Creek Wilderness - 3,855 acres
- Mountain Lake Wilderness - 8,253 acres
- Peters Mountain Wilderness - 3,326 acres
- Thunder Ridge Wilderness - 2,450 acres

George Washington National Forest (S# 1, map C3)
- Ramseys Draft Wilderness - 6,725 acres
- Saint Marys Wilderness - 10,090 acres

Shenandoah National Park (S# 12, map B3)
- Shenandoah Wilderness - 79,579 acres

Outdoor Map Index

National Park Service (USGS Maps)

Colonial National Historical Park [1981]
Scale: 1 inch = 0.4 mile (1 cm = 0.3 km)
Size: 28x48 inches (71x121 cm)
Shenandoah National Park [1969]
Scale: 1 inch = 1.0 mile (1 cm = 0.6 km)
Size: 21x38 inches (53x96 cm)

U.S. Forest Service Maps

Appalachian Tr., Blacksburg RD, Jeff. NF [1983]
Appalachian Tr., Glenwood/New Castle RD's-Jeff. NF [1986]
Appalachian Tr., Mt. Rogers NRA, Jeff. NF [1986]
Appalachian Tr., Pedlar RD, Geo. W. NF [1986]
Appalachian Tr., Wythe RD, Jefferson NF [1986]
George Washington National Forest [1985]
Jefferson National Forest [1983]
Jefferson NF, Clinch Ranger District [1983]
Ramsey's Draft Wilderness, Geo. Washington NF

Unites States Geological Survey USGS

Earth Sciences Information Center
12201 Sunrise Valley Drive
Reston, VA 22092 — 703-860-6045
The Center is open from 8 a.m. to 4 p.m. weekdays. Call for information and directions.

State Agencies

Department of Conservation and Recreation
Division of State Parks

A *Virginia State Parks Guide* (35 state parks) is available free. The guide describes the facilities and activities available at each area and contains a locator map. There is a parking fee from Memorial Day through Labor Day weekends, an admission fee to some parks, and additional fees for specific activities. Many of the parks are closed during the winter.

Selected parks are listed here and their locations symbolized on the Guide map.

S#	MAP	NAME & LOCATION
2	C4	Bear Creek Lake SP, Cumberland
3	D2	Claytor Lake SP, Radford
4	C2	Douthat SP, Clifton Forge
5	D5	False Cape SP (NO veh. access), VA Beach
6	D1	Hungry Mother SP, Marion
7	D3	Occoneechee SP, Clarksville
8	D5	Seashore SP, Virginia Beach
9	D3	Staunton River SP, Scottsburg
10	D4	Twin Lakes SP, Burkeville
11	C4	Westmoreland SP, Montross

Department of Game & Inland Fisheries

A free catalog of publications is available. The DGIF has publications about hunting, fishing, boating, natural history, and how to help wildlife. The Hunters Guide lists and descriibes agency managed wildlife and hunting areas. A monthly magazine, *Virginia Wildlife*, is available by subscription for $10 per year. There is also a film library of more than 70 titles. Licensing and harvest information is published annually.

Marine Resources Commission
PO Box 756
Newport News, VA 23607   804-247-2200
Has jurisdiction over commercial and sport fishing.
Contact the Commission Office for literature, rules and regulations.

Division of Forestry
Dept. of Forestry
PO Box 3758
Charlottesville, VA 22903   804-977-6555
There is no state forest recreation program in Virginia.

Division of Tourism
Dept. of Economic Development
Ninth Street Office Bldg.
Richmond, VA 23219   804-786-4484
A *Virginia Vacation Guide* provides information on Virginia attractions and events. An official road map is also available.

Private Organizations
ANCA Locations in Virginia
Gulf Branch Nature Center (S# 1, map B4)
3608 North Military Road
Arlington, VA 22207   703-558-2340

Hidden Pond Nature Center (S# 2, map B4)
8511 Greeley Blvd.
Springfield, VA 22152   703-451-9588

Huntley Meadows Nature Center (S# 3, map B4)
3701 Lockheed Blvd.
Alexandria, VA 22306   703-768-2525

Long Branch Nature Center (S# 4, map B4)
625 South Carlin Springs Road
Arlington, VA 22204   703-358-6535

Potomac Overlook Nature Center (S# *5, map B4)
2845 Marcey Road
Arlington, VA 22207   703-528-5406

Riverbend Nature Center (S# 6, map B4)
8814 Jeffrey Road
Great Falls, VA 22066   703-759-3211

Vernon J. Walker Nature Center (S# 7, map B4)
1930 Isaac Newton Square
Reston, VA 22090   703-437-9580

Virginia Chamber of Commerce
9 S. Fifth St.
Richmond, VA 23219   Phone 804-644-1607
                            Fax 804-783-6112

WEST VIRGINIA NOTES
Summary
There are 32 federal, 74 state, and 2 private recreation areas or local administrative offices covered in this state chapter. Of these, 61 appear in the Information Chart and 47 are covered in the notes. The special indexes feature 6 federally designated wilderness areas and wild rivers, and one agency published outdoor map.

Federal Agencies
U.S. Forest Service
West Virginia is in the Eastern Region (see Wisconsin chapter - U.S. Forest Svc., Eastern Region listing).

The Cranberry Mountain Visitor Center features exhibits including a diorama of the water cycle, a model of a coal mining operation, wildlife of the area, forest products, and a model of the forest area. Check with the Gauley Ranger District (S# 3, map C2) in Richwood about visitor hours.

The Seneca Rocks-Spruce Knob National Recreation Area (NRA) Visitor Center southwest of Petersburg (see Potomac Ranger District S# 6, map B3) burned in 1992. Contact the Ranger District Office for current information about the VC and NRA opportunities.

Wilderness/Wild River Index
Wilderness Areas
Monongahela National Forest, 5 areas (S# 1, map B2)
Cranberry Wilderness - 35,864 acres
Dolly Sods Wilderness - 10,215 acres
Laurel Fork North Wilderness - 6,055 acres
Laurel Fork South Wilderness - 5,997 acres
Otter Creek Wilderness - 20,000 acres

Wild Rivers
Bluestone River
New River Gorge Natl. River (S# 3, map C2)

Outdoor Map Index
U.S. Forest Service Map
Monongahela National Forest [1987]
Scale: 1 inch = 4.0 miles (1 cm = 2.5 km)
Size: 33x47 inches (83x119 cm)

State Agencies
State Parks & Recreation Section
A West Virginia State Parks & Forests brochure is available from this agency and the Tourism Division.
There is information on resort parks, vacation parks, day use and natural areas, historical parks, and nine forests. A facilities and activities chart is included.

Dept. of Commerce Labor Environmental Resources
Forestry Division
State Capitol
Charleston, WV 25305   304-348-2788
Contact the Division for state forest recreation literature.

Department of Natural Resources
Wildlife Division
The magazine, *Wonderful West Virginia*, is published twice each year. Licensing and harvest information is published annually. The current location and telephone numbers of 8 major local Wildlife Division offices is available.

The *Official State Highway Map* shades and names West Virginia wildlife management areas. Note: Most are identified as "Public Hunting & Fishing Areas" (PH&FA) although the Wildlife Division defines them as "Wildlife Management Areas." Selected areas are symbolized on the Guide Virginia/West Virginia map and are listed here using the area name used on the official highway map.

S#	MAP	PH&FA NAME & LOCATION
2	D1	Anawalt Lake PH&FA, Anawalt
3	B1	B.J. Taylor PH&FA, Left Hand
3	B1	Bear Rock Lake PH&FA, Wheeling
4	B1	Beech Fork PH&FA, Wayne
5	C1	Berwind Lake PH&FA, War
6	D1	Big Ditch Lake PH&FA, Cowen
7	C2	Big Ugly PH&FA, Leet
8	C1	Bluestone PH&FA, Forest Hill
9	D2	Briary Mountain PH&FA, Terra Alta
10	B3	Burches Run Lake PH&FA, Wheeling
11	A2	Burnsville PH&FA, Exchange
12	B2	Castleman Run PH&FA, Wheeling
13	A2	Chief Cornstalk PH&FA, Leon
14	B1	Conaway Lake PH&FA, Middlebourne
15	B2	East Lynn PH&FA, Wayne
16	C1	Edwards Run PH&FA, Capon Bridge
17	B3	Elk River PH&FA, Sutton
18	B2	Fork Creek PH&FA, Foster
19	C1	Handley PH&FA, Marlinton
20	C2	Hilbert PH&FA, Pt. Pleasant
21	B1	Hughes River PH&FA, Parkersburg
22	B1	Jug PH&FA, Parkersburg
23	B2	Laurel Lake PH&FA, Lenore
24	C1	Lewis Wetzel PH&FA, Jacksonburg
25	B1	McClintic PH&FA, Pt. Pleasant
26	B1	Mill Creek PH&FA, Pt. Pleasant
27	C1	Moncove Lake PH&FA, Gap Mills
28	C2	Nathaniel Mountain PH&FA, Romney
29	B3	Pleasants Creek PH&FA, Philippi
30	B2	Plum Orchard Lake PH&FA, Scarboro
31	C2	R.D. Bailey PH&FA, Pineville
32	C1	Shannondale Springs PH&FA, Hedgesville
33	B4	Short Mountain PH&FA, Romney
34	B3	Sleepy Creek PH&FA, Hedgesville
35	B4	Springfield PH&FA, Romney
36	B3	Stonecoal Lake PH&FA, Exchange
37	B2	Stonewall Jackson PH&FA, Weston
38	B2	Summersville Lake PH&FA, Exchange
39	C2	Teter Creek Lake PH&FA, Montrose
40	B2	Warden Lake PH&FA, Romney
41	B3	Widmeyer PH&FA, Hedgesville
42	B4	

Tourism Division
Dept. of Commerce
2101 Washington St., E.
Charleston, WV 25305   1-800-225-5982

In addition to the State Parks & Forests brochure, this agency can provide highway maps, a calendar of events, information on camping and lodging, state travel guides, and other information.

Private Organizations
ANCA Location in West Virginia
A. B. Brooks Nature Center (S# 1, map A2)
Wheeling, WV 26003   304-242-6855

West Virginia Chamber of Commerce
300 Capitol St.
PO Box 2789
Charleston, WV 25330   Phone 304-342-1115
                              Fax 304-342-1130

★ INFORMATION CHART ★

INFORMATION CHART LEGEND - SYMBOLS & LETTER CODES

- ■ means YES & □ means Yes with disability provisions
- **sp** means spring, March through May
- **S** means Summer, June through August
- **F** means Fall, September through November
- **W** means Winter, December through February
- **T** means Two (2) or Three (3) Seasons
- **A** means All Four (4) Seasons
- **na** means Not Applicable or Not Available

Note: empty or blank spaces in the chart mean NO

AGENCY/MAP LEGEND ... INITIALS, MAP SYMBOLS, COLOR CODES

- U.S. Forest Service Supervisor & Ranger Dist. Offices ... NFS [61]
- U.S. Army Corps of Engineers Rec. Areas & Offices ... COE [31]
- USFWS National Wildlife Refuges & Offices ... NWR [40]
- National Park Service Parks & other NPS Sites ... NPS [7]
- Bureau of Land Management Rec. Areas & Offices ... BLM [26]
- Bureau of Reclamation Rec. Areas & Reg. Offices ... BOR [8]
- State Parks (also see State Agency notes) ... SPS [52]
- State Wildlife Areas (also see State Agency notes) ... SWA [19]
- Private Preserves, Nature Centers & Tribal Lands ... [15]
- The Wild Rivers ~~~ and Wilderness Areas

Note: Refer to yellow block on page 7 (top right) for location name and address abbreviations. If a symbol number has a star ★ that symbol is not shown on the map.

FACILITIES, SERVICES, RECREATION OPPORTUNITIES & CONVENIENCES

S#	MAP	LOCATION NAME (state initials if more than one) with ADDRESS and/or LOCATION DATA	TELEPHONE	ACRES / ELEVATION
		VIRGINIA		
1	C3	**Geo. Washington Nat'l. Forest Sup.**, Harrison Plaza, 101 North Main St., PO Box 233, Harrisonburg 22801	703-433-2491	1,010,922 / 544-4,465
2	C3	Deerfield Ranger D., 2314 West Beverley St., Staunton 24401	703-885-8028	164,823 / 1,500-4,500
3	C3	Dry River Ranger D., 112 North River Road, Bridgewater 22812	703-828-2591	228,279 / 1,625-4,397
4	C2	James River Ranger D., 313 South Monroe Ave., Covington 24426	703-962-2214	164,500 / 1,000-4,072
5	B3	Lee Ranger District (VA-WV), Windsor Knit Road, Rt. #4, Box 515, Edinburg 22824 [ask about Massanutten VC]	703-984-4101	186,327 / 200-3,400
6	C3	Pedlar Ranger D., 2424 Magnolia Ave., Buena Vista 24416	703-261-6105	160,000 / 800-4,000
7	C2	Warm Springs Ranger D., Rt. #2 Box 30, Hot Springs 24445	703-839-2521	165,000 / 1,000-4,470
8	D2	Jefferson Nat'l. Forest Sup., 210 Franklin Road, SW, Roanoke 24001	703-982-6270	700,000 / 500-5,730
9	D2	Blacksburg Ranger D., 3089 Pandapas Pond Rd., Blacksburg 24060	703-552-4641	111,800 / 500-3,000
10	A1	Clinch Ranger D., Rt. #3, Box 820, Wise 24293	703-328-2931	90,000 / 500-3,000
11	C3	Glenwood Ranger D., PO Box 10, Natural Bridge Station 24579	703-291-2188	74,000 / 500-2,500
12	D1	Mt. Rogers Nat'l. Recreation Area, Rt. #1, Box 303, Marion 24354	703-783-5196	115,000 / 1,000-5,730
13	D2	New Castle Ranger D., PO Box 246, New Castle 24127	703-864-5195	138,000 / 500-2,500
14	D2	Wythe Ranger D., 1625 West Lee Highway, Wytheville 24382	703-228-5551	170,000 / 500-3,000
1	D1	**COE, Huntington District**, 502 8th St., Huntington, WV 25701	304-529-5607	na / na
2	D1	John W Flannagan Dam & Reservoir, Rt. #1, Box 268, Haysi 24256	703-835-9544	na / na
3	D1	North Fork of Pound River Lake, Rt. #1, Box 369, Pound 24279	703-796-5775	na / na
4	D5	COE, Norfolk District, 803 Front St., Norfolk 23510	804-441-7641	na / na
5	D5	Aiww Albemarle & Chesapeake Canal, 803 Front Street, Norfolk	804-441-7641	na / na
5	C2	Gathright Dam & Lake Moomaw, PO Box 432, Covington	703-962-1138	na / na
	C2	COE, Wilmington District, PO Box 1890, Wilmington, NC 28402	919-251-4827	na / na
6	D3	John H. Kerr Dam & Reservoir, Rt. #1, Box 76, Boydton 23917	804-738-6143	na / na
7	D2	Philpott Lake, Rt. #6, Box 140, Bassett 24055	703-629-2703	na / na
1	D5	**Back Bay NWR**, 4005 Sandpiper Road, PO Box 6286, Virginia Beach 23456 [S of Virginia Beach]	804-721-2412	7,700 / 5
2	C5	Chincoteague NWR, PO Box 62, Chincoteague 23336 [office on refuge]	804-336-6122	13,680 / 0
3	D5	Eastern Shore of Virginia NWR, 5003 Hallett Circle, Cape Charles 23310 [at the tip of Delmarva Peninsula]	804-331-2760	653 / 0-25
4	D5	Fisherman Island NWR, 5003 Hallett Circle, Cape Charles 23310	804-331-2760	1,000 / 0-20
5	D5	Gr Dismal Swamp NWR (NC-VA), 3100 Desert Rd, PO Box 349, Suffolk 23439 [Rt 32 S of town for 4.5 mi, follow signs]	804-986-3705	107,000 / na
6	B4	Mason Neck NWR, 14416 Jefferson Davis Hwy., Suite 20A, Woodbridge 22191	703-690-1297	2,277 / 50
7	B4	Featherstone NWR (closed), 14416 Jefferson Davis Hwy., Suite 20A, Woodbridge 22191	703-690-1297	322 / 10
*8	B4	Marumsco NWR (closed), 14416 Jefferson Davis Hwy., Suite 20A, Woodbridge 22191	703-690-1297	63 / 10
9	B4	Presquile & James River (closed) NW, 6610 Commons Dr., PO Box 189, Prince George 23875 [ferry access only]	703-458-7541	4,867 / 0-20
1	D3	**Booker T. Washington National Monument**, Rt. #3, Box 310, Hardy 24101 [on SR 122 bet. Bedford & Rocky Mount]	703-721-2094	224 / na
2	D5	Colonial Nat'l. Historical Park, PO Box 210, Yorktown 23690	804-898-3400	9,316 / 10-100
3	C4	Fredericksburg and Spotsylvania Cou, Battlefields Mem. NMP, 120 Chatham Lane, Fredericksburg 22405	703-373-4461	5,909 / na
4	C4	George Washington Birthplace NM, RR #1, Box 717, Washington's Birthplace 22443 [E of Port Royal]	804-224-1732	538 / na
5	B4	George Washington Memorial Parkway, Turkey Run Park (13 areas), McLean 22101	703-285-2598	7,145 / 0-200
6	B4	Great Falls Park, PO Box 66, Great Falls 22066 [off Georgetown Pike-Rt. #193]	703-285-2966	800 / na
7	B4	LBJ Memorial Grove on the Potomac, c/o Geo. Washington Mem. Pkwy., Turkey Run Park, McLean 22101	703-285-2598	17 / 20
8	B4	Manassas National Battlefield Park, 12521 Lee Highway, Manassas 22110	703-361-1339	4,513 / 250-325
9	B4	Petersburg National Battlefield, Rt. #36 E, PO Box 549, Petersburg 23803	804-732-3531	2,484 / 50
10	B4	Prince William Forest Pk, PO Box 209, Triangle 22172 [from I-95 exit 150 B, W 0.25 mi on SR 619 to entrance]	703-221-7181	17,000 / 20-400
11	C4	Richmond National Battlefield Park, 3215 E. Broad Street, Richmond 23223	804-226-1981	771 / na
12	B3	Shenandoah Nat'l. Park, Rt. #4, Box 348, Luray 22835	703-999-3483	195,347 / 1,000-3,500
13	B4	**Theodore Roosevelt Island**, c/o George Washington Mem. Pkwy., Turkey Run Park, McLean 22101	703-285-2598	88 / 40
1	B4	**BLM Eastern States Office**, 7450 Boston Blvd., Springfield 22153	703-444-1200	na / na
1	C4	**Dept. of Consv. & Recreation**, Div. of State Parks, 203 Governor St. - Suite 306, Richmond 23219	804-786-1712	na / na
1	C4	**Dept. of Game & Inland Fisheries**, 4010 W. Broad St., PO Box 11104, Richmond 23230	804-367-1000	na / na
2	D4	Amelia WMA, Amelia County, N of Amelia	804-367-1000	2,217 / na

★ INFORMATION CHART ★

AGENCY/MAP LEGEND ... INITIALS, MAP SYMBOLS, COLOR CODES

- U.S. Forest Service Supervisor & Ranger Dist. Offices ... NFS
- U.S. Army Corps of Engineers Rec. Areas & Offices ... COE
- USFWS National Wildlife Refuges & Offices .... NWR
- National Park Service Parks & other NPS Sites .... NPS
- Bureau of Land Management Rec. Areas & Offices ... BLM
- Bureau of Reclamation Rec. Areas & Reg. Offices ... BOR
- State Parks (also see State Agency notes) .... SPS
- State Wildlife Areas (also see State Agency notes) .... SWA
- Private Preserves, Nature Centers & Tribal Lands
- The Wild Rivers ...... and Wilderness Areas

Note: Refer to yellow block on page 7 (top right) for location name and address abbreviations.

INFORMATION CHART LEGEND - SYMBOLS & LETTER CODES

- ■ means YES & □ means Yes with disability provisions
- **sp** means spring, March through May
- **S** means Summer, June through August
- **F** means Fall, September through November
- **W** means Winter, December through February
- **T** means Two (2) or Three (3) Seasons
- **A** means All Four (4) Seasons
- **na** means Not Applicable or Not Available

Note: empty or blank spaces in the chart mean NO. If a symbol number is shown in location name and/or location data, that symbol is not shown on the map.

Column categories (FACILITIES, SERVICES, RECREATION OPPORTUNITIES & CONVENIENCES): INFO OFFICE (IO) / VISITOR CENTER (VC); IO / VC NOT OPEN SATURDAY / SUNDAY; IO / VC ENTRY FEE or PERMIT REQUIRED; CONCESSIONAIRE SERVICES AVAILABLE; FREE LITERATURE or PERMIT DISPLAY; INTERPRETIVE or EDUCATIONAL DISPLAY; AGENCY GUIDED TOURS, brochures, maps, etc.; NATURE PROGRAMS scheduled / by res.; WILDFLOWER VIEWING AREA or DRIVE; INTERPRETIVE TRAILS / GEOLOGICAL SITES; HISTORIC SITES / ARCHAEOLOGICAL SITES; WILDLIFE VIEWING SITES, birds, signs, etc.; ENDANGERED SPECIES ARE COMMON; WILDLIFE IS ABUNDANT OR COMMON; DEVELOPED PICNIC AREAS / PICNIC SITES; NO-CHARGE CAMPGROUNDS / CAMPSITES; WILDERNESS AREAS / WILD TRAILS; WALKING PERMITTED, at one's own risk; HIKING TRAILS / NATURE TRAILS; BICYCLING OPPORTUNITIES; SWIMMING PERMITTED, w/ your own risk; HORSEBACK RIDING, w/ your own horse; OFF-ROAD Motorized Vehicle Area, trails; FISHING OPPORTUNITIES; BOATING FACILITIES, ramps, marinas, etc.; MOTORIZED WATERCRAFT OK, check limits; NON-MOTORIZED WATERCRAFT OK; HUNTING IN SEASON, license, permit req'd.; WINTER SPORTS OPPORTUNITIES; PARK & WALK-IN AREA, Use ONLY, no overnight; DAY USE ONLY AREA; DRINKING WATER; RESTROOMS

S#	MAP	LOCATION NAME (state initials if more than one) with ADDRESS and/or LOCATION DATA	TELEPHONE	ACRES / ELEVATION
3	D3	Briery Creek WMA, Prince Edward County, near Farmville	804-367-1000	2,775 / na
4	C4	C.F. Phelps WMA, Fauquier County, W of Goldvein	804-367-1000	4,540 / na
5	D4	Chickahominy WMA, Charles City Co., S of Holdcroft	804-367-1000	5,111 / na
6	D1	Clinch Mountain WMA, Smyth, Russel & Tazewell Cos., NE of Saltville	804-367-1000	25,477 / na
7	D2	Crooked Creek WMA, Carroll County, near Galax	804-367-1000	na / na
8	D4	Dick Cross WMA, Mecklenburg County, SW of South Hill	804-367-1000	13,727 / na
9	D2	Fairystone Farms WMA, Patrick & Henry Cos., W of Bassett	804-367-1000	5,286 / na
10	B4	G. Richard Thompson WMA, Fauquier County, N of Linden	804-367-1000	4,160 / na
11	C2	Gathright WMA (adjacent Nat'l Forest, Bath & Alleghany Cos.), SW of Bacova	804-367-1000	13,428 / na
12	C3	Goshen WMA, Rockbridge County, SW of Goshen	804-367-1000	16,128 / na
13	C3	Hardware River WMA, Fluvanna County, E of Scottsville	804-367-1000	880 / na
14	D2	Havens WMA, Roanoke County, W of Salem	804-367-1000	7,158 / na
15	D1	Hidden Valley WMA, Washington County, N of Abingdon	804-367-1000	6,400 / na
16	C2	Highland WMA, Highland County, S of Monterey	804-367-1000	13,978 / na
17	D4	Hog Island WMA, Surry County, SE of Surry	804-367-1000	3,908 / na
18	D3	Horsepen Lake WMA, Buckingham County, S of Buckingham	804-367-1000	2,688 / na
19	C3	James River WMA, Nelson County, N of Wingina	804-367-1000	671 / na
20	C3	Little North Mountain WMA, Augusta & Rockbridge Cos., E of Craigsville	804-367-1000	17,538 / na
21	D5	Mockhorn Island WMA (boat access only), Northampton County, E of Oyster	804-367-1000	9,452 / na
22	C4	Pettigrew WMA, Caroline County, NW of Port Royal	804-367-1000	934 / na
23	D4	Powhatan WMA, Powhatan County, S of Powhatan	804-367-1000	4,171 / na
24	C3	Rapidan WMA, Madison & Green Cos., W of Madison	804-367-1000	9,373 / na
25	C5	Saxis WMA, Accomack County, E of Oak Hall	804-367-1000	5,775 / na
26	D5	Trojan-Pocahontas WMA, Virginia Beach City, S of Pungo	804-367-1000	1,143 / na
27	D2	Turkeycock Mountain WMA, Franklin County, NE of Figsboro	804-367-1000	1,789 / na
28	D3	White Oak Mtn. WMA, Pittsylvania County, E of Chatham	804-367-1000	2,711 / na
WEST VIRGINIA				
1	B2	**Monongahela Nat'l. Forest Sup.**. 200 Sycamore St., Elkins 26241	304-636-1800	900,000 / 2,000-4,861
2	B3	Cheat Ranger D.., off Hwy. 219, PO Box 368, Parsons 26287	304-478-3251	na / na
3	C2	Gauley RD & Cranberry Mtn. Visitor . Hwys. 39 & 55, PO Box 110, Richwood 26261	304-846-2695	159,000 / na
4	C2	Greenbrier Ranger D.., Hwy. 250, PO Box 67, Bartow 24920	304-456-3335	na / na
5	C2	Marlinton Ranger D.., off SR 39, PO Box 210, Marlinton 24954 (also Spruce Knob/Seneca Rocks NRA)	304-799-4334	na / na
6	B3	Potomac RD & Seneca Rocks VC, HC 59, Box 240, Petersburg 26847 [Seneca Rocks VC on SR 33 at SR 28]	304-567-2827	200,000 / 900-5,000
7	B3	White Sulphur Ranger D.., 410 E. Main St., PO Box 520, White Sulphur Springs 24986	304-536-2144	na / na
		COE, Baltimore District, PO Box 1715, Baltimore, MD 21203	410-962-3693	na / na
1	B3	Jennings Randolph Lake, PO Box 247, Elk Garden 26717	304-355-2346	na / na
2	C1	COE, Huntington District, 502 8th St., Huntington 25701	304-529-5607	na / na
3	C2	Beech Fork Lake, 5441 Beech Fork Road, Lavalette 25535	304-525-4831	na / na
4	C2	Bluestone Lake, 701 Miller Ave., Hinton 25951	304-466-1234	na / na
5	B2	Burnsville Lake, PO Box 347, Burnsville 26335	304-853-2371	na / na
6	C1	East Lynn Lake, Star Route Box 35-C, East Lynn 25512	304-849-2355	na / na
7	B1	Gallipolis Locks & Dam (Ohio River), Gallopolis Ferry 25515	304-576-2272	na / na
8	C1	London Locks & Dam (Kanawha River), London 25126	304-442-8422	na / na
9	C1	Marmet Locks & Dam (Kanawha River), 2007 W. Riverview Drive, Belle 25015	304-949-1175	na / na
10	C1	R.D. Bailey Lake, Drawer 70, Justice 24851	304-664-3229	na / na
11	B1	Racine Locks & Dam (Ohio River), Rt. 2, Box 380, Letart 25253	304-882-2118	na / na
12	C2	Summersville Lake, Rt. #2, Box 470, Summersville 26651	304-872-3412	na / na
13	B2	Sutton Lake, PO Box 426, Sutton 26601	304-765-2816	na / na
14	C1	Winfield Lock & Dam (Kanawha River), RFD 1, Box 530, Red House 25168	304-586-2501	na / na
		COE, Pittsburgh District, 1000 Liberty Ave., Pittsburgh, PA 15222	412-644-4191	na / na

#	Grid	Name / Address	Phone	Acres / Elev.
15	B2	Hildebrand Lock & Dam (Monongahela R), RD 2, Box 89-B, Morgantown 26505	304-983-2300	na / na
16	B2	Morgantown Lock & Dam (Monongahela R), RD 2, Box 3, Morgantown 26505	304-292-1885	na / na
17	B2	Opekiska Lock & Dam (Monongahela R), RD 8, Box 294, Fairmont 26554	304-366-4224	na / na
18	A2	Pike Island Locks & Dam (Ohio River), RD 1, Box 33, Wheeling 26003	304-277-2240	na / na
19	B2	Stonewall Jackson Lake, Rt. #3, Box 370, Weston 26452	304-269-4588	na / na
20	B2	Tygart Lake, Rt. #1, Box 63, Grafton 26354	304-265-1760	na / na
1	B1	Ohio River Islands NWR, 3004 E. 7th St., PO Box 1811, Parkersburg 26102 [extends from Cincinnati to Pittsburgh]	304-422-0752	na / na
1	B4	Appalachian NS Trail, c/o Ap. Trail Washington & Jackson Sts., PO Box 807, Harpers Ferry 25425	304-535-6331	250,000 / 124-6,643
2	B4	Harpers Ferry NH Park (MD/VA/WV), PO Box 65, Harpers Ferry 25425	304-535-6029	2,238 / 280
3	C2	New River Gorge Nat'l River/Gauley, PO Box 246, Glen Jean 25846	304-465-0508	62,024 / 800-1,400

State Parks & Recreation Section, Bldg. 6, Room B 451, State Capitol Complex, Charleston 25305

#	Grid	Name / Address	Phone	Acres / Elev.
1	C1		800-225-5982	na / na
2	B2	Audra SP, Rt. #4, Box 564, Buckhannon 26201	304-457-1162	355 / na
3	C2	Babcock SP, Rt. #1, Box 150, Clifftop 25831	304-438-6205	4,127 / na
4	C2	Beartown SP, HC 64, Box 189, Hillsboro 24946	800-225-5982	110 / 3,400
5	C1	Beech Fork SP, Rt. #2, Box 333, Barboursville 25504	504-522-0303	3,981 / na
6	B3	Blackwater Falls SP, Drawer 490, Davis 26260	800-225-5982	1,688 / 2,500-3,400
7	C2	Bluestone SP, Box 3, Athens Star Route, Hinton 25951	304-466-1922	2,146 / na
8	B3	Cacapon RP, Berkeley Springs 25411	304-258-1022	6,115 / 900-2,200
9	B3	Canaan Valley RP, Rt. #1, Box 39, Davis 26260	304-258-1022	6,015 / 3,200
10	C2	Carnifex Ferry Battlefield SP, Rt. #2, Box 435, Cass 24927 [near Ansted]	304-872-3773	156 / 1,500
11	C2	Cass Scenic Railroad SP, Box 75, Cass 24927	304-456-4300	1,080 / na
12	B3	Cathedral SP, Aurora 26705	304-735-3771	132 / 2,600
13	B2	Cedar Creek SP, Rt. #1, Box 9, Glenville 26351	304-462-7158	2,443 / na
14	C1	Chief Logan SP, Logan 25601	304-792-7125	3,303 / na
15	C2	Droop Mountain Battlefield SP, HC 64, Box 189, Hillsboro 24946	304-752-8558	287 / 3,500
16	C2	Greenbrier River Trail SP, Star Route, Box 125, Caldwell 24925	304-799-4087	950 / na
17	C2	Hawks Nest SP, PO Box 857, Ansted 25812	304-658-5212	276 / 1,200
18	B2	Holly River SP, PO Box 8, Hacker Valley 26222	304-493-6353	8,292 / na
19	C2	Little Beaver SP, Rt. #9, Box 179, Beaver 25813	304-763-2494	562 / 2,300
20	B3	Lost River SP, Rt. #2, Box 24, Mathias 26812	304-897-5372	3,712 / na
21	B2	North Bend SP, Cairo 26337	304-643-2931	1,405 / 950-1,100
22	D1	Pinnacle Rock SP, Box 342, Bramwell 27415	304-248-8362	300 / 2,500
23	D2	Pipestem RP, Pipestem 25979	304-466-1800	4,023 / 3,000
24	B2	Picketts Fort SP, Rt. #3, Box 403, Fairmont 26554	304-363-3030	188 / 1,000
25	A2	Tomlinson Run SP, PO Box 97, New Manchester 26056	304-564-3651	1,398 / na
26	C1	Twin Falls RP, PO Box 1023, Mullens 25882	304-294-4000	3,776 / 2,450-2,600
27	B2	Tygart Lake SP, Rt. #1, Box 260, Grafton 26354	304-294-4000	2,134 / 1,800-2,100
28	B2	Valley Falls SP, Rt. #6, Box 244, Grafton 26354	304-363-3319	1,145 / 1,000
29	C2	Watoga SP, Star Rt. #1, Box 252, Marlinton 24954	304-799-4087	10,100 / na
30	B2	Watters Smith Memorial SP, PO Box 296, Lost Creek 26385	304-745-3081	532 / 800
1	C1	**DNR, Wildlife Resources Div.**, Capitol Complex, Bldg. 3, Charleston 25305 [at 1900 Kanawha Blvd. E]	304-348-2754	na / na

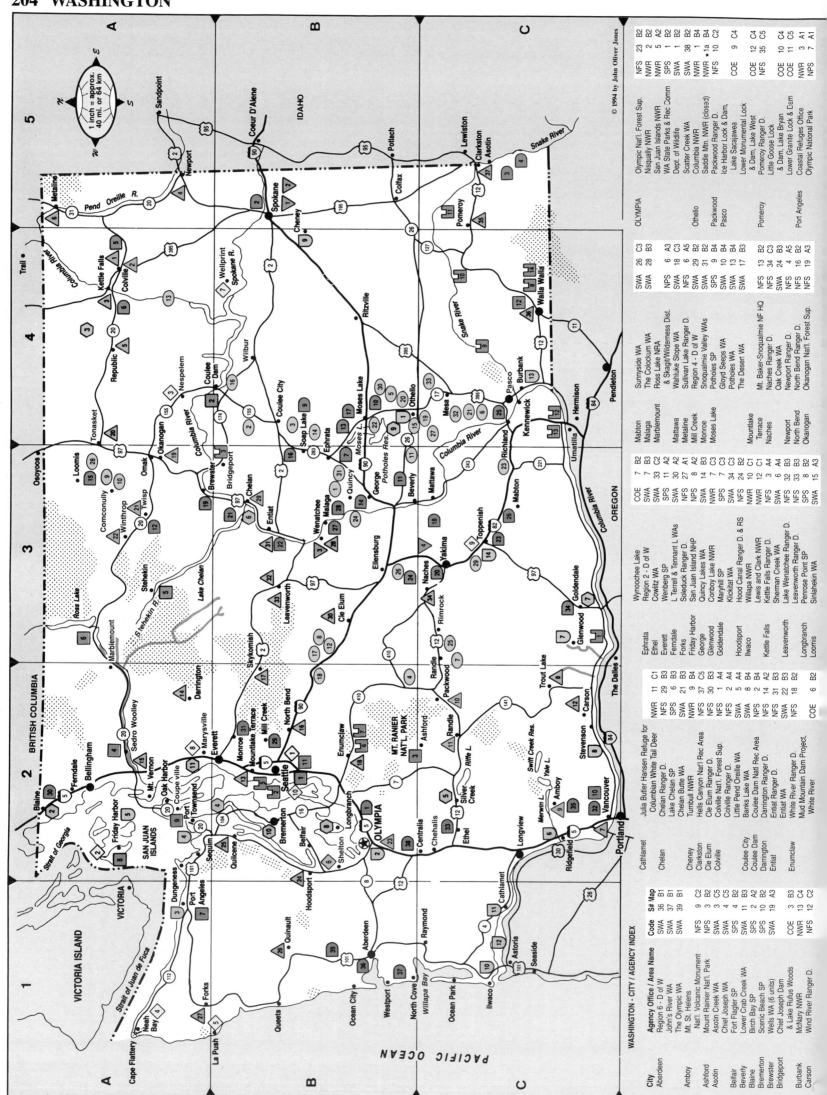

Office & Area Directory

City	Office / Area	Agency	S#	Map
Quilcene	Quilcene Ranger D.	NFS	25	B2
Quinault	Quinault Ranger D.	NFS	26	B1
Randle	Randle Ranger D.	NFS	5	A4
Republic	Republic Ranger D.	NFS	5	A4
	Curlew Lake SP	SPS	3	A4
Richland	Rattlesnake Slope WA	SWA	25	C4
Ridgefield	Ridgefield NWR	NWF	6	C2
	Pierce NWR (closed)	NWF	8	C2
San Juan Islands	Yellow Island Preserve	TNC	2	A2

City	Office / Area	Agency	S#	Map
Seattle	COE, Seattle District	COE	2	B2
	Lake Crockett/Keystone Harbor/Ft Casey	COE	*4	B2
	L Washington Ship Canal	COE	5	B2
	NPS, Pacific NW Reg.	NPS	1	B2
	TNC Washington Field Off	TNC	1	B2
Sedro Woolley	Mt. Baker Ranger D. & NRA	NFS	15	A2
	North Cascades Natl Park & Park Complex	NPS	4	A2
Sequim	Dungeness NWR	NWR	4	A2

City	Office / Area	Agency	S#	Map
Silver Creek	Ike Kinswa SP	SPS	5	C2
Skykomish	Skykomish Ranger D.	NFS	17	B2
Soap Lake	Sun Lakes WA	SWA	16	B3
Spokane	Spokane District Office	BLM	1	B5
	Border Resource Area	BLM	8	B5
	Region 1 - D of W	SWA	2	B5
Stehekin	Lake Chelan NRA & Stehekin Dist.	NPS	5	A3

City	Office / Area	Agency	S#	Map
The Dalles	The Dalles Lock & Dam, Lake Celilo	COE	1	C3
Tonasket	Tonasket Ranger D.	NFS	20	A4
Toppenish	Toppenish NWR	NWR	14	C3
Trout Lake	L.T. Murray WA	SWA	23	C3
	Mt. Adams Ranger D.	NFS	8	C2
Twisp	Twisp Ranger D.	NFS	21	A3
Umatilla	Mcnary L & D, Lake Wallula	COE	13	C4
Vancouver	Gifford Pinchot NF Sup.	NFS	7	C2
	Region 5 - D of W	SWA	32	C2
	Shillapoo-Vancouver L WA	SWA	35	C2

City	Office / Area	Agency	S#	Map
Walla Walla	Walla Walla Ranger D.	NFS	36	C4
	COE, Walla Walla Dist.	COE	8	C4
	Mill Creek Lake	COE	14	C4
Wenatchee	Wenatchee Natl Forest Sup	NFS	28	B3
	Wenatchee Resource Area	BLM	3	B3
	Swakane WA	SWA	27	B3
Winthrop	Winthrop Ranger D.	NFS	22	A3
	Methow WA	SWA	12	A3
Yakima	Yakima River Canyon SRA	BLM	4	C3
	Region 3 - D of W	SWA	20	C3

WASHINGTON NOTES

Summary

There are 120 federal, 53 state, and 11 private recreation areas or local administrative offices covered in this state chapter. Of these, 130 appear in the Information Chart and 54 are covered in the notes. The special indexes and special feature 29 federally designated wilderness areas and wild rivers, and 58 agency published outdoor maps.

Outdoor Recreation Information Center

A Joint Agency Visitor Center
915 Second Ave., Rm. 442   206-553-0170
Seattle, WA 98174   TDD number 206-220-7450

This one-of-a-kind information center in downtown Seattle is jointly operated by the USDA Forest Service, National Park Service, and Washington State Parks to provide information on trails, camping, winter activities, horse trails, firewood, safety, weather reports, and avalanche potential in Washington. Also available are educational materials, maps, books and brochures.

Federal Agencies

U.S. Forest Service

Washington is in the Pacific Northwest Region (see Oregon chapter - U.S. Forest Svc., Pacific Northwest listing).

The Mt. Saint Helens National Volcanic Monument (S# 9, map C2) Visitor Center is located on Silver lake, 5 miles from I-5, in the Gifford Pinchot National Forest (S# 7, map C2). This VC features a walk-in volcano model, exhibits, a multi-media slide show, and affords a beautiful view of the mountains.

The Early Winters Visitor Center is located in the early historic Twisp Ranger Station. Contact the Twisp Ranger District Office (S# 21, A3) for visitor hours information. The early human history and natural resources of the area are featured in exhibits at the Station.

The Hells Canyon National Recreation Area main Visitor Center (S# 37, map C5) is located in Clarkston. Other VCs are located in Idaho and Oregon. See those state chapters for details.

National Park Service

Additional NPS Locations in Washington

Ebby's Landing National Historic Reserve (8,000 acres) (S# 9, map B2)
23 Front Street
Coupeville, WA 98239   206-553-5565

Fort Vancouver National Historic Site (209 acres)
(S# 10, map C2)
612 E. Reserve Street
Vancouver, WA 98661-3897   206-696-7655

Klondike Gold Rush NHP Visitor Center (S# 11, map B2)
Note: A 3,716,000 acre NHP, see Alaska chapter and NPS S# 11, map C4
117 South Main Street
Seattle, WA 98104   206-553-7220

Whitman Mission National Historic Site (98 acres)
(S# 12, map C4)
Route 2, Box 247
Walla Walla, WA 99362   509-552-6360

Bureau of Reclamation Recreation Areas

Thirty-three recreation areas are listed here and symbolized on the Washington state map.

S#	MAP	LOCATION NAME
1	B3	Babcock Ridge Lake
2	B3	Banks Lake
3	B4	Billy Clapp Lake
4	B2	Bumping Lake
5	B4	Canal, Heart, Windmill, Virgin, and Susan Lakes
6	C4	Clark Lake
7	B2	Clear Lake
8	B3	Cle Elum Lake
9	A3	Conconully Lake
10	A3	Conconully Res.
11	B3	Crab Creek, Wanapum, and Corfu Areas
12	B3	Easton Diversion Dam
13	A4	Franklin D. Roosevelt L. (Coulee Cam NRA)
14	B4	Gloyd Seeps Wildlife Recreation Area
15	B4	Goose Lake Area
16	B4	Grand Coulee Dam
17	B3	Kachess Lake
18	B2	Keechelus Lake
19	C4	Lake Linda
20	B4	Lyle Lake
21	C4	Mesa Lake
22	B4	Potholes Res.
23	C3	Prosser Diversion Dam
24	B4	Quincy Wildlife Recreation Area
25	C3	Rimrock
26	B3	Rosa Diversion Dam
27	C4	Scooteney Res.
28	A3	Spectacle Lake
29	C3	Sunnyside Diversion Dam
30	B4	Warden Lake
31	B3	Winchester Wasteway Res.
32	C4	Worth Lake
33	C4	Esquatzel Wasteway

Wilderness/Wild River Index

Wilderness Areas

Alpine Lakes Wilderness - 305,407 acres
Glacier Peak Wilderness - 576,648 acres
Henry M. Jackson Wilderness - 102,671 acres
Norse Peak Wilderness - 50,902 acres
Mt. Baker-Snoqualmie NF Sup. (S# 13, map B2), and Wenatchee National Forest (S# 28, map B3)
Boulder River Wilderness - 49,000 acres
Clearwater Wilderness - 14,300 acres
Mount Baker Wilderness - 117,580 acres
Noisy-Diobsud Wilderness - 14,300 acres
Mt. Baker-Snoqualmie NF Sup. (S# 13, map B2)
Buckhorn Wilderness - 45,601 acres
Colonel Bob Wilderness - 12,120 acres
Mount Skokamish Wilderness - 15,686 acres
The Erothers Wilderness - 17,239 acres
Wonder Mountain Wilderness - 2,320 acres
Olympic National Forest (S# 23, map B2)
Glacier View Wilcerness - 3,050 acres
Indiar Heaven Wilderness - 20,650 acres
Moun: Adams Wilderness - 46,776 acres
Tatoosh Wilderness - 15,720 acres
Trapper Creek Wilderness - 6,050 acres
Gifford Pinchot NF Sup. (S# 7, map C2)
Goat Rocks Wilderness - 105,023 acres
Giffcrd Pinchot National Forest (S# 7, map C2), also Mt. Baker-Snoqualmie NF Sup. (S# 13, map B2)
William O. Douglas Wilderness - 166,603 acres
Gifford Pinchot National Forest (S# 7, map C2), also Wenatchee National Forest (S# 28, map B3)
Lake Chelan-Sawtooth Wilderness - 151,435 acres
Okanogan National Forest (S# 19, map A3), also Wenatchee National Forest (S# 28, map B3)
Pasayten Wilderness - 530,031 acres
Mt. Baker-Snoqualmie NF Sup. (S# 13, map B2), also Okanogan National Forest (S# 19, map A3)
Salmc-Priest Wilderness - 41,335 acres
Colville National Forest (S# 1, map A4)
Wena'na-Tucannon Wilderness - 111,048 acres
Umatilla NF, Walla Walla RD (S# 36, map C4), also Umatilla National Forest (see Oregon S# 50, map A4)
Washington Islands Wilderness areas:
Copalis - 60 acres
Flattery Rocks - 125 acres
Quillaytel Wasteway - 300 acres

Coastal Refuges Office (see USFWS S# 3, map A2)
San Juan Islands Wilderness - 353 acres
San Juan Islands NWR (S# 5, map A2)

Juniper Dunes Wilderness - 7,140 acres
BLM Spokane District (S# 1, map B5)

Wild Rivers

Klickitat River and
White Salmon River
Columbia River Gorge National Scenic Area, for information about access see Oregon Chapter, USFS
Columbia River Gorge NSA (S# 22, map A2)
Skagit River

Outdoor Map Index

National Park Service (USGS Maps)

Mount Rainier National Park [1971]
Scale: 1 inch = 0.8 mile (1 cm = 0.5 km)
Size: 33x34 inches (83x86 cm)
Mount Saint Helens & Vicinity [1981]
Scale: 1 inch = 1.6 miles (1 cm = 1.0 km)
Size: 36x40 inches (91x101 cm)
North Cascades National Park [1974]
Scale: 1 inch = 1.6 miles (1 cm = 1.0 km)
Size: 39x40 inches (99x101 cm)

Olympic National Park [1957]
Scale: 1 inch = 2.0 miles (1 cm = 1.3 km)
Size: 33x47 inches (83x119 cm)

Bureau of Land Management Maps

See BLM Map Index in Oregon for information on special maps. The Oregon/Washington state office and public room is located in Portland, Oregon. The BLM Washington map grid features the intermediate series maps available covering portions of the state.

U.S. Forest Service Maps

Colville National Forest [1985]
Scale: 1 inch = 2.0 miles (1 cm = 1.3 km)
Gifford Pinchot National Forest [1984]
Scale: 1 inch = 2.0 miles (1 cm = 1.3 km)
Glacier Peak Wilderness [1979]
Scale: 1 inch = 2.0 miles (1 cm = 1.3 km)
Goat Rocks Wilderness [1987]
Scale: 1 inch = 1.0 mile (1 cm = 0.6 km)
Mount Adams Wilderness [1976]
Scale: 1 inch = 0.5 mile (1 cm = 0.3 km)
Mount Baker - Snoqualmie NF [1985]
Scale: 1 inch = 2.0 miles (1 cm = 1.3 km)
Mount Saint Helens National Volcanic Monument [1986]
Scale: 1 inch = 0.5 mile (1 cm = 0.3 km)
Okanogan National Forest [1987]
Scale: 1 inch = 2.0 miles (1 cm = 1.3 km)
Mount Baker-Snoqualmie Natl Forest (S# 12, map B2)

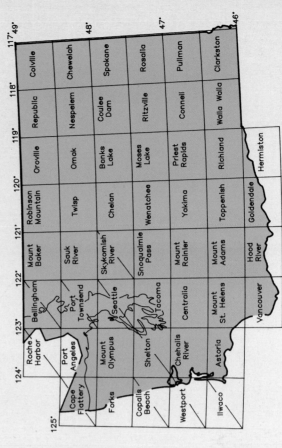

BLM WASHINGTON
1:100,000 INTERMEDIATE SCALE MAPS
SURFACE & SURFACE / MINERAL SERIES
/ Unpublished

Olympic National Forest [1987]
Scale: 1 inch = 2.0 miles (1 cm = 1.3 km)
Pacific Crest Trail, North Portion [1987]
Scale: 1 inch = 1.0 mile (1 cm = 0.6 km)
Pacific Crest Trail, South Portion [1987]
Scale: 1 inch = 1.0 mile (1 cm = 0.6 km)
Wenatchee National Forest [1986]
Scale: 1 inch = 2.0 miles (1 cm = 1.3 km)

USGS Earth Science Information Center
USGS Spokane-ESIC
678 U.S. Courthouse
W. 920 Riverside Ave.
Spokane, WA 99201
509-353-2524

State Agencies

State Parks & Recreation Commission (S# 1, map B2)
A Washington State Parks Guide (128 state parks) is available free. The guide describes each area, contains a locator map, and includes information on facilities and activities. Individual brochures are available for a number of parks and for specific activities. A small pamphlet, How to Find Information about Washington State's Resources, contains an extensive list of information sources.

Department of Natural Resources
201 John A. Cherberg Bldg.
Mail Stop QW-21
Olympia, WA 98504   206-753-5331
Contact the Department for state forest recreation literature.

Department of Wildlife
manage fish and wildlife resources. Information and maps on individual wildlife management areas are available. Drawings are held for a variety of special hunting permits. Licensing, permit, and harvest information is published annually.

Department of Fisheries
115 General Administration Bldg.
Olympia, WA 98504   206-753-6600
Manage and protect marine food fish, shellfish, and anadromous fish resources. Contact this office for literature, rules and regulations.

Department of Trade & Economic Development
Tourism Development Division
101 General Administration Bldg., AX-13
Olympia, WA 98504   206-586-2088

A Washington Vacation Guide provides information on Washington's attractions and events. There are other publications on travel and tours. An official road map is also available. It has symbols for state parks, camping, ski areas, wildlife areas, and ranger stations.

Private Organizations

Tribal Land Areas in Washington

Confederated Tribes of the Colville Indian Reservation - Fishing, hunting, camping, boating, touring.
Colville Business Committee (S# 3, map A4)
PO Box 150
Nespelem, WA 99155   509-634-4711

Makah Tribe of the Makah Indian Reservation - Fishing, camping, boating, hiking, touring.
Makah Tribal Council (S# 4, map A1)
PO Box 115
Neah Bay, WA 98357   206-645-2205

Quileute Tribe of the Quileute Indian Reservation - Fishing, camping, boating, hiking.
Quileute Tribal Council (S# 5, map B1)
PO Box 279
La Push, WA 98350   206-374-6163

Skokomish Tribe of the Skokomish Indian Reservation - Camping, boating, hiking.
Skokomish Tribal Council (S# 6, map B2)
Number 80 Tribal Center Road
Shelton, WA 98584   206-426-4232

Spokane Tribe of the Spokane Indian Reservation - Fishing, camping, boating.
Spokane Business Council (S# 7, map B4)
PO Box 100
Wellpinit, WA 99040   509-258-4581

Tulalip Tribes of the Tulalip Indian Reservation - Fishing, boating.
Tulalip Board of Directors (S# 8, map A2)
6700 Totem Beach Road
Marysville, WA 98270   206-653-4585

Confederated Tribes and Bands of the Yakima Indian Nation, Yakima Indian Reservation - Fishing, hunting, camping, boating, hiking, touring.
Yakima Tribal Council (S# 9, map C3)
PO Box 151
Toppenish, WA 98948   509-865-5121

ANCA Locations in Washington
The Seattle Aquarium (S# 10, map B2)
Pier 59, Waterfront Park
Seattle, WA 98101   206-386-4300

Association of Washington Business
(State Chamber of Commerce)
1414 South Cherry
PO Box 658
Olympia, WA 98507
Phone 206-943-1600
Fax 206-943-5811

★ INFORMATION CHART ★

INFORMATION CHART LEGEND - SYMBOLS & LETTER CODES

■ means **YES** & □ means **Yes with disability provisions**
sp means **spring**, March through May
S means **Summer**, June through August
F means **Fall**, September through November
W means **Winter**, December through February
T means **Two** (2) or **Three** (3) Seasons
A means **All Four** (4) Seasons
na means **Not Applicable or Not Available**

Note: empty or blank spaces in the chart mean **NO** ★ that symbol is not shown on the map.

AGENCY/MAP LEGEND ... INITIALS, MAP SYMBOLS, COLOR CODES
U.S. Forest Service Supervisor & Ranger Dist. Offices NFS (61)
U.S. Army Corps of Engineers Rec. Areas & Offices . COE (31)
USFWS National Wildlife Refuges & Offices .... NWR (40)
National Park Service Parks & other NPS Sites ...... NPS (7)
Bureau of Land Management Rec. Areas & Offices . BLM (26)
Bureau of Reclamation Rec. Areas & Reg. Offices . BOR (8)
State Parks (also see State Agency notes) .... SPS (52)
State Wildlife Areas (also see State Agency notes) . SWA (19)
Private Preserves, Nature Centers & Tribal Lands .. (15)
The Wild Rivers ~~~ and Wilderness Areas

Note: Refer to yellow block on page 7 (top right) for location name and address abbreviations. If a symbol number has a star ★ that symbol is not shown on the map.

Column headings (rotated) for the facilities matrix:
INFO OFFICE (IO) / VISITOR CENTER (VC); IO / VC OPEN SATURDAY / SUNDAY; ENTRY FEE not camping or permit fee; CONCESSIONAIRE SERVICES AVAILABLE; FREE LITERATURE brochures, maps, etc.; INTERPRETIVE or EDUCATIONAL DISPLAY; AGENCY GUIDED TOURS / SUNDAY; NATURE EDUCATION / STUDY PROGRAMS; WILDFLOWER VIEWING / STUDY PROGRAMS; INTERPRETIVE TRAILS; HISTORIC SITES; ARCHAEOLOGICAL / GEOLOGICAL SITES; WILDLIFE VIEWING SITES, blinds, signs, etc.; WILDLIFE IS ABUNDANT OR COMMON; ENDANGERED SPECIES ARE COMMON; DEVELOPED PICNIC AREAS; NO-CHARGE CAMPGROUNDS / PICNIC SITES; DEVELOPED CAMPGROUNDS / CAMPSITES; WILDERNESS AREAS / WILD RIVERS; WALKING PERMITTED / HIKING TRAILS; BICYCLING OPPORTUNITIES; SWIMMING OPPORTUNITIES / by res.; BOATING IN FACILITIES; FISHING OPPORTUNITIES, at one's own risk; OFF-ROAD Motorized RIDING... w/ your own horse; NON-MOTORIZED WATERCRAFT OK; MOTORIZED WATERCRAFT OK, check limits; HUNTING IN SEASON, license/permit req'd; WINTER SPORTS OPPORTUNITIES OK; PARK & WALK-IN ONLY AREA; DAY USE ONLY, no overnight; DRINKING WATER; RESTROOMS

S#	MAP	LOCATION NAME (state initials if more than one) with ADDRESS and/or LOCATION DATA	TELEPHONE	ACRES / ELEVATION
1	A4	Colville National Forest Sup., 765 S. Main, Colville 99114	509-684-3711	1,960,097 / 3,500-7,300
2	A4	Colville Ranger D., 755 South Main St., Colville 99114	509-684-4557	na / na
3	A4	Kettle Falls Ranger D., 255 West 11th, Kettle Falls 99141	509-738-6111	na / 1,600-6,000
4	A5	Newport Ranger D., PO Box 770, Newport 99156	509-447-3129	na / na
5	A4	Republic Ranger D., PO Box 468, Republic 99166	509-775-3305	na / na
6	A5	Sullivan Lake Ranger D., 12641 Sullivan Lake Road, Metaline 99153	509-446-7500	na / 2,000-7,000
7	C2	Gifford Pinchot Nat'l. Forest Sup., 6926 E. Fourth Plain Blvd., Vancouver 98661	206-696-7500	1,371,720 / 100-12,326
8	C2	Mt. Adams Ranger D., 2455 Hwy. 141, Trout Lake 98650	509-395-2501	na / na
9	C2	Mt. St. Helens Nat'l. Volcanic Monu., 42218 NE Yale Bridge Rd., Amboy 98601	206-247-5800	110,000 / 1,000-8,365
10	C2	Packwood Ranger D., Hwy. 12, Packwood 98361	206-494-5515	290,000 / 1,000-8,200
11	C2	Randle Ranger D., 10024 US Hwy. 12, Randle 98377	206-497-7565	na / na
12	C2	Wind River Ranger D., M.P. 0.23 Hemlock Rd., Carson 98610	509-427-5645	251,050 / 1,800
13	B2	Mt. Baker-Snoqualmie NF Headquarters, 21905 64th Ave. W., Mountlake Terrace 98043	206-775-9702	1,709,700 / 100-10,778
14	A2	Darrington Ranger D., Darrington 98241	206-436-1155	561,906 / 680-10,568
15	A2	Mt. Baker Ranger D. & NRA, 2105 Highway 20, Sedro Woolley 98284 [joint office w/Nat'l. Park Service]	206-856-5700	524,719 / 100-10,778
16	B2	North Bend Ranger D., 42404 SE North Bend Way, North Bend 98045	206-888-1421	181,657 / 950-7,432
17	B2	Skykomish Ranger D., 74920 NE Stevens Pass Hwy., PO Box 305, Skykomish 98288	206-677-2414	315,985 / 420-7,899
18	B2	White River Ranger D., 857 Roosevelt Ave. East, Enumclaw 98022	206-825-6585	125,441 / 1,600-6,859
19	A3	Okanogan Nat'l. Forest Sup., 1240 Second Ave. South, Okanogan 98840	509-826-3275	1,745,000 / 900-8,795
20	A4	Tonasket Ranger D., 1 West Winesap, PO Box 466, Tonasket 98855	509-486-2186	420,000 / 900

No.	Grid	Name / Address	Phone	Acres / Elev.
21	A3	Twisp Ranger D., 502 Glover, PO Box 188, Twisp 98856	509-997-2131	375,000 / 1,200-8,795
22	A3	Winthrop Ranger D., West Chewuch Rd., PO Box 579, Winthrop 98862	509-996-2266	928,000 / 1,760
23	B2	Olympic Nat'l. Forest Sup., 1835 Black Lake Blvd. SW, Olympia 98512 [off Hwy. 101]	206-956-2400	631,514 / na
24	B2	Hood Canal Ranger D. & Ranger S., 150 N. Lake Cushman Rd., PO Box 68, Hoodsport 98548	206-877-5254	210,000 / 0-6,950
25	B2	Quilcene Ranger D., PO Box 280, Quilcene 98376 [on Hwy. 101, o.25 mi S of Quilcene]	206-765-3368	160,000 / 0-6,200
26	B1	Quinault Range' D., South Shore Rd., PO Box 9, Quinault 98575	206-288-2525	138,286 / 200-4,500
27	A1	Soleduck Ranger D., RR #1, Box 5750, Forks 98331	206-374-6522	129,000 / 300-4,000
28	B3	Wenatchee Nat'l. Forest Sup., 301 'Yakima Street, PO Box 811, Wenatchee 98807	509-662-4335	2,100,000 / 700-8,000
29	B3	Chelan Ranger D., 428 Woodin Ave., PO Box 189, Chelan 98816	509-682-2576	na / na
30	B3	Cle Elum Ranger D., 803 W. 2nd Street, Cle Elum 98922	509-674-4411	na / na
31	B3	Entiat Ranger D., 2108 Entiat Way, PO Box 476, Entiat 98822	509-784-1511	na / na
32	B3	Lake Wenatchee Ranger D., 22976 Highway 207, Star Rt., Box 109, Leavenworth 98826	509-763-3103	na / na
33	B3	Leavenworth Ranger D., 600 Sherbourne Street, Leavenworth 98826	509-782-1413	na / na
34	B3	Naches Ranger D., 10061 Highway 12, Naches 98937	509-653-2205	na / na
35	C3	Pomeroy Ranger D., Rt. #1, Box 53-F, Pomeroy 99347	509-843-1891	358,741 / 2,200-5,900
36	C4	Walla Walla Ranger D., 1415 West Rose, Walla Walla 99362	509-522-6290	366,116 / 1,900-5,800
37	C5	Hells Canyon Nat'l Recreation Area, 2535 Riverside Dr., PO Box 699, Clarkston 99403 [offices in ID & OF]	509-758-0616	652,488 / 1,000-9,393

COE, Portland District, PO Box 2945, Portland, OR 97208

No.	Grid	Name / Address	Phone	Acres / Elev.
1	C3	The Dalles Lock & Dam, Lake Celilo, PO Box 564, The Dalles 97058	503-326-6075	na / na
2	B2	COE, Seattle District, PO Box 3755, Seattle 98124	503-296-1181 / 206-764-3442	na / na
3	B3	Chief Joseph Dam & Lake Rufus Woods, PO Box 1120, Bridgeport 98813	509-686-5501	na / na
*4	B2	Lake Crockett/Keystone Harbor/Ft Casey, 3015 NW 54th St., Seattle 98107	206-764-3402	na / na
5	B2	Lake Washington Ship Canal, 3015 NW 54th St., Seattle 98107	206-783-7001	na / na
6	C3	Mud Mountain Dam Project, White Riv, 30525 SE Mud Mountain Rd., Enumclaw 98022	206-825-3211	na / na
7	C3	Wynoochee Lake, 30525 Mud Mountain Rd., Enumclaw 98022	206-825-3211	na / na
8	C4	COE, Walla Walla District, City County Airport, Walla Walla 99362	509-522-6714	na / na
9	C4	Ice Harbor Lock & Dam, Lake Sacajaw, RR 6, Box 693, Pasco 99301	509-547-7781	na / na
10	C4	Little Goose Lock & Dam, Lake Bryan, RR 3, Box 54, Pomeroy 99347	509-843-1494	na / na
11	C5	Lower Granite Lock & Dam, RR 3, Box 54, Pomeroy 99347	509-843-1494	na / na
12	C4	Lower Monumental Lock & Dam, Lake W, RR 6, Box 693, Pasco 99301	509-547-7781	na / na
13	C4	Mcnary Lock & Dam, Lake Wallula, PO Box 1441, Umatilla 97882	503-922-3211	na / na
14	C4	Mill Creek Lake, 3200 Reservoir Road, Walla Walla 99362	509-522-6863	na / na

No.	Grid	Name / Address	Phone	Acres / Elev.
(1)	B4	**Columbia NWR**, 735 E. Main St., PO Drawer F, Othello 99344 [refuge is 6 mi NW of Othello]	509-488-2668	23,200 / 1,000
*1a	B4	Saddle Mtn. NWR (closed to public), 735 E. Main St., PO Drawer F, Othello 99344	509-488-2668	na / na
2	B2	Nisqually NWR, 100 Brown Farm Road, Olympia 98516	206-753-9467	2,800 / 0-250
3	A1	Coastal Refuges Office, 33 South Barr Rd., Port Angeles 98382 [refuge 5 mi from this office]	206-457-8451	na / na
4	A2	Dungeness NWR, Voice of America Rd., Sequim	206-457-8451	671 / 0-100
5	B2	San Juan Islands NWR, 100 Brown Farm Road, Olympia 98516 [NWR is 83 islands, 2 are open to the public]	206-753-9467	450 / 0-100
6	C2	Ridgefield NWR, 301 N. Third St., PO Box 457, Ridgefield 98642 [3 mi W of I-5 exit 14]	206-887-4106	5,150 / 0-50
7	C3	Conboy Lake NWR, 100 Wildlife Refuge Rd., Box 5, Glenwood 98619 [office at NWR, 5 mi W of Glenwood]	509-364-3410	5,814 / 1,800
8	C2	Pierce NWR (closed, access by permit), 301 N. Third St., PO Box 457, Ridgefield 98642 [near Stevenson]	206-887-4106	337 / 70-150
9	B4	Turnbull NWR, S. 26010 Smith Road, Cheney 99004	509-235-4723	15,470 / 2,350
10	C1	Willapa NWR, HC 01, Box 910, Ilwaco 98624	206-484-3482	11,000 / 0-250
11	C1	Julia Butler Hansen Refuge for the Columbian White-tailed Deer, PO Box 566, Cathlamet 98612 [2 mi W on Hwy 4]	206-795-3915	4,400 / 1
12	C1	Lewis and Clark NWR, HC 01, Box 910, Ilwaco 98624	206-484-3482	38,000 / 0-10
13	C4	Umatilla NWR (OR/WA), PO Bldg., 6th & I Sts., PO Box 239, Umatilla, OR 97882 [4 mi. W of Irrigon]	503-922-3232	22,857 / 30
14	C4	McNary NWR, P.O Box 544, Burbank 99323 [in town at corner of maple & S Lake Sts.]	509-547-4942	3,600 / 340-560
		Toppenish NWR, 1671 Pumphouse Rd., Toppenish 98948 [10 mi S of Toppenish on Hwy. 97]	509-865-2405	2,009 / 1,200

Nat'l. Park Svc., Pacific NW Reg., NPS/USFS Outdoor Rec. Info. Center, FOB, 915 2nd Ave., Rm. 442, Seattle 98714

No.	Grid	Name / Address	Phone	Acres / Elev.
(1)	B4	Coulee Dam National Recreation Area, 1008 Crest Drive, Coulee Dam 99116	206-220-7450	100,390 / 1,290
2	B4		509-633-9441	
3	B2	Mount Rainier Nat'l. Park, Tanoma Woods, Star Route, Ashford 98304	206-569-2211	235,400 / 1,880-14,410
4	A2	North Cascades NP & Park Complex, 2105 Hwy. 20, Sedro Woolley 98284 [joint office w/US Forest Svc. S# 15]	206-856-5700	684,237 / 400-9,200
5	A3	Lake Chelan NRA & Stehekin Dist., PO Box 7, Stehekin 98852 [access by plane, boat or foot]	206-856-5700	61,890 / na
6	A3	Ross Lake NRA & Skagit/Wilderness D, 728 Ranger Station Rd., Marblemount 98267	206-873-4590	117,580 / na
7	A1	Olympic National Park, 600 East Park Ave., Port Angeles 98362	206-452-0330	922,000 / 0-7,965
8		San Juan Island NHP, 125 Spring St., PO Box 429, Friday Harbor 98250	206-378-2240	1,752 / 0-650

BLM Oregon/Washington States Office, 1300 NE 44th St., PO Box 2965, Portland, OR 97208

No.	Grid	Name / Address	Phone	Acres / Elev.
1		Spokane District Office, East 4217 Main Avenue, Spokane 99202	503-280-7001	16,000,000 / na
2	B5	Border Resource Area, East 4217 Main Avenue, Spokane 99202	509-353-2570	320,000 / 0-8,000
3	B3	Wenatchee Resource Area, 1133 North Western Avenue, Wenatchee 98801	509-353-2570	105,000 / 400-6,000
			509-662-4223	215,000 / 8,000

WA State Parks & Recreation Comm., 7150 Clearwater Lane, Olympia 98504

No.	Grid	Name / Address	Phone	Acres / Elev.
4	C3	Yakima River Canyon SRA, US Hwy. 821, between Ellensburg and Yakima	509-662-4223	na / 1,200-3,200
1	B2	Birch Bay SP, 5105 Helwig Rd., 8 mi. S of Blaine 98230	206-753-2027	193 / C
2	A2	Curlew Lake SP, 10 mi. NE of Republic	206-371-2800	123 / na
3	A4	Fort Flagler SP, beolw Port Townsend, NE 410 Beck Road, Belfair 98528	206-478-4625	783 / C

AGENCY/MAP LEGEND . . . INITIALS, MAP SYMBOLS, COLOR CODES

U.S. Forest Service Supervisor & Ranger Dist. Offices . NFS [61]
U.S. Army Corps of Engineers Rec. Areas & Offices . COE [40]
USFWS National Wildlife Refuges & Offices . . . . . NWR [7]
National Park Service Parks & other NPS Sites . . . . NPS [26]
Bureau of Land Management Rec. Areas & Offices . . . BLM [8]
Bureau of Reclamation Rec. Areas & Reg. Offices . . . BOR [52]
State Parks (also see State Agency notes) . . . . . . SPS [19]
State Wildlife Areas (also see State Agency notes) . . SWA [15]
Private Preserves, Nature Centers & Tribal Lands . .
The Wild Rivers 〰️ and Wilderness Areas
Note: Refer to yellow block on page 7 (top right) for location name and address abbreviations.

★ INFORMATION CHART ★

INFORMATION CHART LEGEND - SYMBOLS & LETTER CODES

■ means YES & □ means Yes with disability provisions
sp means spring, March through May
S means Summer, June through August
F means Fall, September through November
W means Winter, December through February
T means Two (2) or Three (3) Seasons
A means All Four (4) Seasons
na means Not Applicable or Not Available
Note: empty or blank spaces in the chart mean NO   *that symbol is not shown on the map.

If a symbol number has a star ★ (top right) for location name and address abbreviations.

FACILITIES, SERVICES, RECREATION OPPORTUNITIES & CONVENIENCES

S#	MAP	LOCATION NAME (state initials if more than one) with ADDRESS and/or LOCATION DATA	TELEPHONE	ACRES / ELEVATION
5	C2	Ike Kinswa SP, on Mayfield Lake, N of Hwy. 12, 873 Harmony Rd, Silver Creek 98585	206-983-3402	454 / na
6	B3	Lake Chelan SP, Rt. #1, Box 90, 9 mi. W of Chelan 98816	509-687-3710	127 / na
7	C3	Maryhill SP, 12 mi. S of Goldendale	206-753-2027	98 / na
8	B4	Penrose Point SP, 3 mi. N of Longbranch	206-753-2027	152 / na
9	B4	Potholes SP, 25 mi. SW of Moses Lake	206-752-2027	640 / na
10	B2	Scenic Beach SP, 12 mi. NW of Bremerton	206-753-2027	88 / na
11	A2	Wenberg SP, 18 mi. NW of Everett	206-753-2027	46 / na
1	B2	WA Dept. of Wildlife (D of W), 600 Capitol Way North, Olympia 98501	206-753-5700	na / na
2	B5	Region 1 - D of W, N. 8702 Division St., Spokane 99218	509-456-4082	na / na
3	C5	Asotin Creek WA, 13 mi. SW of Asotin	509-456-4082	11,800 / na
4	C5	Chief Joseph WA, 30 mi. S of Asotin	509-456-4082	9,176 / 860-5,000
5	A4	Little Pend Oreille WA, 1310 Bear Creek Rd., 13 mi. E of Colville 99114	509-684-5343	40,379 / 2,000-5,572
6	A4	Sherman Creek WA, 4 mi. W of Kettle Falls	509-684-5343	7,508 / 1,400-4,600
7	B4	Region 2 - D of W, 1540 Alder St. NW, Ephrata 98823	509-754-4624	na / na
8	B4	Banks Lake WA, near Coulee City	509-754-4624	44,662 / 1,570
9	B4	Billy Clap Lake WA, 12 mi. E of Soap Lake	509-754-4624	4,639 / 1,400
10	B4	Gloyd Seeps WA, Rt. #2, Box 333-6, Moses Lake 98837	509-754-4624	9,640 / 1,150
11	B3	Lower Crab Creek WA, 7 mi. E of Beverly	509-754-4624	24,968 / 530
12	A3	Methow WA, near Twisp, Rt. #1, Box 295, Winthrop 98862	509-996-2559	20,437 / 2,000-5,000
13	B4	Potholes WA (3 units), Rt. #2, Box 333-6, Moses Lake	509-754-4624	33,490 / 1,040
14	B3	Quincy Lakes WA, W of Quincy-George Hwy., near George	509-754-4624	15,330 / 1,200
15	A3	Sinlahekin WA, 3 mi. S of Loomis	509-754-4624	14,035 / 1,500-2,500
16	A3	Sun Lakes WA, 5 mi. N of Soap Lake	509-754-4624	9,140 / 1,200
17	B3	The Desert WA, Rt. #2, Box 333-6, Moses Lake 98837	509-754-4624	35,100 / 1,150
18	C3	Wahluke Slope WA, runs along crest of Saddle Mtns., 14 mi. W of Mattawa	509-754-4624	59,000 / 450-2,200
19	A3	Wells WA (6 units), near Brewster	509-754-4624	9,292 / 780-3,050
20	C3	Region 3 - D of W, 2802 Fruitvale Blvd., Yakima 98902	509-575-2740	na / na
21	B3	Chelan Butte WA, near Chelan	509-663-6260	9,424 / 700-3,500
22	B3	Entiat WA (upstream from Wenatchee), near Entiat	509-663-6260	9,675 / 700-4,000
23	C3	L.T. Murray WA (3 units), Yakima & Kittitas Cos., near Toppenish	509-575-2740	106,119 / 500-5,000
24	B3	Oak Creek WA (4 units), 23205 Hwy. 12, along Naches River, Naches 98937	509-575-2740	142,400 / 1,700-5,100
25	C4	Rattlesnake Slope WA, near Richland	509-575-2740	3,662 / 0-3,000
26	B3	Sunnyside WA, 35 mi. SE of Yakima, 2030 Holiday Rd., Mabton 98935	509-575-2740	7,604 / 0-500
27	B3	Swakane WA, near Wenatchee	509-663-6260	11,199 / 5,500-7,000
28	C3	The Colockum WA, 9000 Tarpiscan Rd., SE of Colockum Pass Rd., Malaga 98828	509-663-6260	92,108 / 560-6,900
29	B2	Region 4 - D of W, 16018 Mill Creek Blvd., Mill Creek 98012	206-775-1311	na / na
30	A2	Lake Terrell & Tennant Lake WAs, N of Ferndale	206-775-1311	1,320 / na
31	B2	Snoqualmie Valley WAs (3 units), off Hwy. 203 & 3 mi. N of Carnation, 1 mi N of Duval, & 3 mi S of Monroe	206-775-1311	1,201 / 25
32	C2	Region 5 - D of W, 5405 NE Hazel Dell Ave., Vancouver 98663	206-696-6211	na / na
33	C2	Cowlitz WA, 36 mi. along Cowlitz R. & Hwy. 12, between Glenoma & Ethel	206-496-6223	6,000 / 350-1,500
34	C3	Klickitat WA, 495 Glenwood Hwy., Goldendale 98620	509-773-4459	14,000 / 600-2,200
35	B1	Shillapoo-Vancouver Lake WA, 12 mi. N of Vancouver	206-696-6211	432 / 30
36	B1	Region 6 - D of W, 905 E. Heron St., Aberdeen 98520	206-533-9335	na / na
37	B1	John's River WA, 12 mi. SW of Aberdeen	206-533-9335	1,528 / na
38	B2	Scatter Creek WA, 18 mi. S of Olympia	206-533-9335	1,269 / na
39	B1	The Olympic WA (numerous areas), 15 mi. N of Aberdeen	206-533-9335	6,361 / 500-1,500
1	B2	TNC Washington Field Office, 1601 Second Ave. Suite 910, Seattle 98101	206-728-9696	na / na
2	A2	Yellow Island Preserve, contact Field Office, San Juan Islannds	206-343-4344	na / na

Column categories (diagonal headers, left to right): DRINKING WATER; RESTROOMS; DAY USE ONLY, no overnight; PARK & WALK-IN ONLY AREA; WINTER SPORTS OPPORTUNITIES; HUNTING IN SEASON / license, check limits; MOTORIZED WATERCRAFT OK; NON-MOTORIZED WATERCRAFT OK; BOATING FACILITIES / ramps, marinas, etc.; FISHING IN SEASON / license / permit reqd.; OFF-ROAD MOTORIZED VEHICLE USE OK; HORSEBACK RIDING, w/ your horse / Use OK; BICYCLING OPPORTUNITIES; WALKING / HIKING TRAILS; SWIMMING AREAS / WILD RIVERS; WILDERNESS AREAS / TRAILS; NO-CHARGE CAMPGROUNDS / CAMPSITES; DEVELOPED CAMPGROUNDS / CAMPSITES; DEVELOPED PICNIC SITES; WILDLIFE VIEWING SITES / blinds, signs, etc.; ENDANGERED SPECIES ARE COMMON; WILDLIFE IS ABUNDANT OR COMMON; HISTORIC SITES; ARCHAEOLOGICAL / GEOLOGICAL SITES; WILDFLOWER VIEWING AREA or DRIVE; NATURE STUDY PROGRAMS; NATURE GUIDED TOURS, scheduled / by res.; AGENCY LITERATURE, brochures, maps, etc.; FREE LITERATURE or EDUCATIONAL DISPLAY; INTERPRETIVE or EDUCATIONAL SERVICES AVAILABLE; CONCESSIONAIRE SERVICES AVAILABLE; ENTRY FEE, not camping or permit fee; INFO OFFICE (IO) / VISITOR CENTER (VC); IO / VC OPEN SATURDAY / SUNDAY.

WISCONSIN NOTES

Summary

There are 32 federal, 80 state, and 41 private recreation areas or local administrative offices covered in this state chapter. Of these, 66 appear in the Information Chart and 87 are covered in the notes. The special indexes feature 7 federally designated wilderness areas and wild rivers, and 2 agency published outdoor maps.

Federal Agencies

USFWS National Wildlife Refuges

The Upper Mississippi River Wildlife & Fish Refuge headquarters office is in Winona, Minnesota. This 195,000-acre refuge extends for 260 miles along the Mississippi River from Wabasha, Minnesota, to Rock Island, Illinois. Ask about the special USFWS-published "Pool Maps" covering sections of the refuge and recreation information.

National Trail

Ice Age National Scenic Trail covers 1,000 miles (1,610 km) in Wisconsin and extends from Lake Michigan to the St. Croix River. The approximate trail route is shown on the map. It follows the southern edge of glaciers and the moraine hills left behind when the glaciers melted 10,000 years ago. Today about half the trail is open to public use and some sections are used for marathons, ski races, and ultra-running. For details about access contact:

Ice Age Park and Trail Foundation
PO Box 422
Sheboygan, WI 53082
or
National Park Service
Ice Age National Scenic Trail (S# 2, map D3)
700 Rayovac Drive, Suite 100
Madison, WI 53711   608-264-5610

Wilderness/Wild River Index

Wilderness Areas

Nicolet National Forest (S# 8, map B3)
Blackjack Springs Wilderness - 5,886 acres
Headwaters Wilderness - 19,950 acres
Whisker Lake Wilderness - 7,345 acres
Chequamegon National Forest (S# 2, map B2)
Porcupine Lake Wilderness - 4,195 acres
Rainbow Lake Wilderness - 6,583 acres

Wild Rivers

St. Croix River
St. Croix and Lower St. Croix National Scenic Rivers
(S# 5, Wisconsin map B1)
Wolf River
Menominee Tribe of the Menominee Indian Reservation
(see below, Tribal Land Areas in Wisconsin)

Outdoor Map Index

U.S. Forest Service Maps

There is a free Forest Visitor Guide (Mini-map) series. Mini-maps (1 inch = 11 miles) have basic information but do not include the recreation detail found on Visitor Maps.

Two other map series available a: the eastern regional office in Milwaukee, and some of the local offices, are

Primary and Secondary base series maps. Primary map scale is 2.64 inches = 1 mile. Topography is indicated with a 10-foot contour interval. They are essentially special 7.5-minute quad maps. The secondary map scale is 1/2 inch = 1 mile. They have more detail but do not contain a recreation site index and the reverse-side description information included on Visitor Maps.

Chequamegon NF-Glidden, Hayward, Washburn RD's [1981]
Scale: 1 inch = 2.7 miles (1 cm = 1.7 km)
Size: 32x47 inches (81x119 cm)
Nicolet National Forest [1984]
Scale: 1 inch = 2.0 miles (1 cm = 1.3 km)
Size: 33x47 inches (83x119 cm)

State Agencies

Department of Natural Resources (DNR)

101 S. Webster St.
Madison, WI 53702   608-266-2277

Parent agency for parks, wildlife, forests and natural areas in Wisconsin.

DNR, Bureau of Parks & Recreation

A Wisconsin State Parks Guide (52 state parks) is available free. The guide describes each area, contains a locator map, and includes information on facilities and activities. There is an entry fee.

Department of Natural Resources

State Forester
PO Box 7921
Madison, WI 53707   608-266-0842
Contact the State Forester for recreation literature.

Wisconsin Bureau of Wildlife Management

A bi-monthly magazine, *Wisconsin Natural Resources*, is available by subscription for $6.97 per year. A fold-out map/brochure, *Public Lands Open to Hunting*, lists 287 State Public Hunting Grounds (wildlife areas) open to hunting in season. The area size, habitat, and principal game species present are listed. They are open at least part of the year to all - hikers, picnickers, birdwatchers, and others looking for quiet places to enjoy nature. Selected larger areas are listed here.

S#	MAP	WA NAME & LOCATION
2	B3	Ackley WA, Antigo
3	D3	Albany WA, Albany
4	B1	Amsterdam Sloughs WA, Webster
5	C2	Augusta WA, Augusta
6	C2	Bangor WA, Bangor
7	D3	Bong WA, Burlington
8	C3	Brillion WA, Brillion
9	D3	Brooklyn WA, Belleville
10	C3	Chaffee Creek WA, Westfield
11	C3	Colburn WA, Friendship
12	C4	Collins Marsh WA, Reedsville
13	B1	Crex Meadows WA, Grantsburg
14	D3	Deansville WA, Sun Prairie
15	C2	Dell Creek WA, Reedsburg
16	C3	Dewey Marsh WA, Stevens Point
17	C2	Dike 17 WA, Black River Falls
18	A1	Douglas County WA, Solon Springs
19	B3	Dunbar WA, Dunbar
20	C*	Dunnville WA, Downsville
21	C3	Eldorado WA, Fond du Lac
22	B*	Fish Lake WA, Grantsburg
23	D3	Footville WA, Footville
24	C3	French Creek WA, Portage
25	C3	Germania Marsh WA, Montello
26	C3	Grand River Marsh WA, Kingston
27	A2	Hay Creek-Hoffman Lake WA, Park Falls
28	D3	Horicon Marsh WA, Horicon
29	B2	Jim Falls WA, Jim Falls
30	C3	Killsnake WA, Valders
31	B2	Kimberly-Clark WA, Phillips
32	C2	LaFarge Reservoir WA, LaFarge
33	D3	Lima Marsh WA, SE of Madison
34	B1	Loon Lake WA, Turtle Lake
35	B1	McKenzie Creek WA, Clam Falls
36	B2	McMillan Marsh WA, Spencer
37	C3	Mead WA, Mosinee
38	C2	Meadow Valley WA, Necedah
39	D3	Mud Lake WA, Reeseville
40	B1	Muddy Creek WA, Elk Mound
41	A1	Namekagon Barrens WA, Webb Lake
42	C3	Navarino Marsh WA, Shawano
43	D3	New Glarus WA, New Glarus
44	B2	Pershing WA, Gilman
45	B3	Peshtigo Brook WA, Suring
46	C3	Pine Island WA, Portage
47	A2	Powell Marsh WA, Lac du Flambeau
48	C3	Poygan Marsh WA, Poy Sippi
49	C3	Rat River WA, Menasha
50	B1	Rice Beds Creek WA, Milltown
51	C2	Sandhill WA, Babcock
52	B3	Spread Eagle WA, Florence
53	C3	Springvale WA, Pardeeville
54	C3	St. Cloud WA, St. Cloud
55	C3	Theresa WA, Kewaskum
56	B3	Thunder Lake WA, Three Lakes
57	C1	Tiffany WA, Nelson
58	A1	Totagatic River WA, Hayward
59	C2	Van Loon WA, Holmen
60	D3	Vernon WA, Mukwonago
61	D2	Waterloo WA, Waterloo
62	B2	Weirgor Springs WA, Exeland
63	C3	White River Marsh WA, Princeton
64	A2	White River WA, Drummond
65	D2	Witwen WA, Sauk City
66	B3	Wolf River WA, Langlade
67	C2	Wood County WA, Babcock

Division of Tourism

PO Box 7970
Madison, WI 53707   1-800-432-8747
in state   608-266-2161
A Vacation Guide provides information on Wisconsin's attractions and events. Other free publications cover private accommodations, fishing, campgrounds, and historic s'es. An official road map is available.

Private Organizations

TNC Wisconsin Chapter

333 W. Mifflin St., Suite 107
Madison, WI 53703   608-251-8140

Jordan Park Nature Center (S# 35, map C3)
1516 Church Street
Stevens Point, WI 54481   715-346-1433

Marsh Haven Nature Center (S# 36, map D3)
West 6431 Sunset Road
Juneau, WI 53039   414-386-2182

Mosquito Hill Nature Center (S# 37, map C3)
Rogers Road
New London, WI 54961   414-779-6433

Riveredge Nature Center (S# 38, map D3)
4438 West Hawthorne Drive
Newberg, WI 53060   414-931-8095

Wehr Nature Center (S# 39, map D3)
9701 West College Ave.
Franklin, WI 53129   414-425-8550

West Shores Interpretive Center (S# 40, map C3)
2024 Lakeview Drive
Suamico, WI 54173   414-434-2824

Wisconsin Mfgrs. & Commerce

(State Chamber of Commerce)
501 E. Washington Ave.
PO Box 352   Phone 608-258-3400
Madison, WI 53701   Fax 608-258-3413

Places We Save is a guide-book to 35 conservancy areas in Wisconsin. The guide includes a description of the biological communities protected. Most areas are open for public hiking, bird watching, nature study, and photography.

Tribal Land Areas in Wisconsin

Lac Courte Oreilles Band of Lake Superior Chippewa Indians of the Lac Courte Oreilles Indian Reservation - Fishing, camping.
Lac Courte Oreilles Tribal Council (S# 26, map A2)
Route 2, Box 2700
Hayward, WI 54843   715-634-8934

Lac du Flambeau Band of the Lac du Flambeau Indian Reservation - Fishing, hunting, camping, boating, touring.
Lac du Flambeau Tribal Council (S# 27, map A2)
PO Box 67
Lac du Flambeau, WI 54538   715-588-3303

Menominee Tribe of the Menominee Indian Reservation - Fishing, hunting, boating.
Menominee Tribal Council (S# 28, map B3)
PO Box 397
Keshena, WI 54135   715-799-3341

Sokaogon Chippewa Community of the Mole Lake Band of the Chippewa Indians of Wisconsin - Camping, boating.
Sokaogon Chippewa Tribal Council (S# 29, map B3)
Route 1, Box 625
Crandon, WI 54520   715-478-2604

Oneida Tribe of the Oneida Indian Reservation - Fishing, hunting, hiking.
Oneida Executive Committee (S# 30, map C3)
PO Box 365
Oneida, WI 54155   414-869-2772

Red Cliff Band of Lake Superior Chippewa Indians of the Red Cliff Indian Reservation - Fishing, hunting, camping, boating.
Red Cliff Tribal Council (S# 31, map A2)
PO Box 529
Bayfield, WI 54814   715-779-5805

St. Croix Chippewa Indians of the St. Croix Indian Reservation - Boating.
St. Croix Council (S# 32, map B1)
PO Box 287
Hertel, WI 54845   715-349-2195

Stockbridge-Munsee Community of Mohican Indians of the Stockbridge-Munsee Indian Reservation - Fishing, hunting, hiking.
Stockbridge-Munsee Tribal Council (S# 33, map B3)
Route 1
Bowler, WI 54416   715-793-4111

ANCA Locations in Wisconsin

Hixson Forest Nature Center (S# 34, map C2)
2702 Quarry Road
Lacrosse, WI 54601   608-784-0303

City / Agency Index continues on page 210 -

WISCONSIN - CITY / AGENCY INDEX

City	Agency Office / Area Name	Code	S#	Map
Albany	Albany WA	SWA	3	D3
Antigo	Ackley WA	SWA	2	B3
Augusta	Augusta WA	SWA	5	C2
Babcock	Sandhill WA	SWA	51	C2
	Wood County WA	SWA	67	C2
Bangor	Bangor WA	SWA	6	C2
Bayfield	Apostle Is Nat'l Lakeshore	NPS	1	A2
Belleville	Brooklyn WA	SWA	9	D3
Black Earth	Rettenmund Prairie	TNC	5	D3
Black River Falls	Dike 17 WA	SWA	17	C2
	Thousand's Rock Pt. Prairies	TNC	24	D2
Blue Mounds	Nelson Oak Woods Preserve	TNC	16	D3
Brillion	Brillion WA	SWA	7	D3
Burlington	Bong WA	SWA	10	D3
Chippewa Falls	Hoganson Preserve	TNC		B1
Clam Falls	McKenzie Creek WA	SWA	35	B1
Denzer	Pan Hollow Preserve	TNC	18	D2
	Pine Hollow Preserve	TNC	★19	D2
Dodgeville	Governor Dodge SP	SPS	22	D2
Dousman				
Downsville	Dunnville WA	SWA	20	C1
Drummond	White River WA	SWA		A2
Dunbar	Dunbar WA	SWA	19	B3
Eagle River	Eagle River Ranger D.	NFS		B3
Elk Mound	Muddy Creek WA	SWA	40	B1
Elkhart Lake	Muehl Springs Preserve	TNC	15	C3
Ellison Bay	Newport SP	SPS	6	B4
	Mink River Estuary	TNC	14	B4
Exeland	Weirgor Springs WA	SWA	62	B2
Fish Creek	Peninsula SP	SPS	8	B4
Florence	Florence Ranger D.	NFS	10	B3
	Spread Eagle WA	SWA	52	B3
Fond du Lac	Eldorado WA	SWA	21	C3
Footville	Footville WA	SWA	23	C3
Friendship	Colburn WA	SWA	11	C3
Galesville	Decorah Mounds Preserve	TNC	7	C2
	Sacia Mem Ridge Preserve	TNC	20	C2

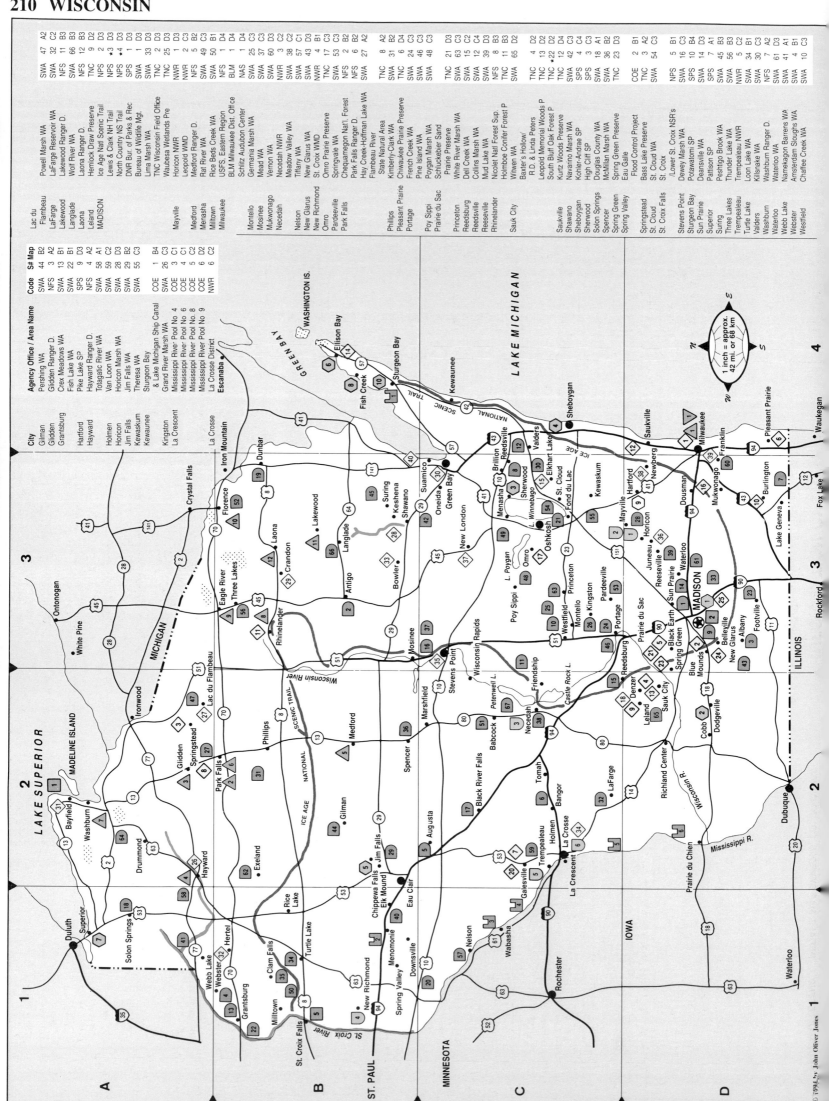

★ INFORMATION CHART ★

INFORMATION CHART LEGEND - SYMBOLS & LETTER CODES

- ■ means **YES** & □ means **Yes** with disability provisions
- **sp** means spring, March through May
- **S** means Summer, June through August
- **F** means Fall, September through November
- **W** means Winter, December through February
- **T** means Two (2) or Three (3) Seasons
- **A** means All Four (4) Seasons
- **na** means Not Applicable or Not Available

Note: empty or blank spaces in the chart mean **NO**

Note: *Refer to yellow block on page 7 (top right) for location name and address abbreviations. If a symbol number has a star ★ that symbol is not shown on the map.*

AGENCY/MAP LEGEND . . . INITIALS, MAP SYMBOLS, COLOR CODES

- U.S. Forest Service Supervisor & Ranger Dist. Offices .. NFS
- U.S. Army Corps of Engineers Rec. Areas & Offices .. COE
- USFWS National Wildlife Refuges & Offices .... NWR
- National Park Service Parks & other NPS Sites .... NPS
- Bureau of Land Management Rec. Areas & Offices ...... BLM
- Bureau of Reclamation Rec. Areas & Reg. Offices ...... BOR
- State Parks (also see State Agency notes) .... SPS
- State Wildlife Areas (also see State Agency notes) .... SWA
- Private Preserves, Nature Centers & Tribal Lands
- The Wild Rivers ━━━━ and Wilderness Areas

S#	MAP	LOCATION NAME (state initials if more than one) with ADDRESS and/or LOCATION DATA	TELEPHONE	ACRES / ELEVATION
	D4	**U.S. Forest Svc., Eastern Region.** 310 W. Wisconsin Ave., Rm. 500, Milwaukee 53203	414-297-3693	na / na
1	D4	Chequamegon Natl. Forest Sup., 1170 South 4th Ave., Park Falls 54552	715-762-2461	850,000 / na
2	B2	Glidden Ranger D., Hwy. 13, PO Box 126, Glidden 54527	715-264-2511	na / na
3	A2	Hayward Ranger D., 604 Hwy. 27 N., PO Box 232, Hayward 54843	715-634-4821	na / na
4	A2	Medford Ranger D., 850 N. Hwy. 13, PO Box 150, Medford 54451	715-748-4875	na / na
5	B2	Park Falls Ranger D., 1170 South 4th Ave., Park Falls 54552	715-762-2461	na / na
6	B2	Washburn Ranger D., 113 E. Bayfield St., PO Box 578, Washburn 54891 [in town, cor. of First Ave & Bayfield]	715-373-2667	220,000 / 1,100-1,500
7	A2	Nicolet National Forest Sup., FOB, 68 S. Stevens, Rhinelander 54501	715-362-3415	661,000 / 1,100-1,800
8	B3	Eagle River Ranger D., PO Box 1809, Eagle River 54521	715-479-2827	171,000 / 1,800
9	B3	Florence Ranger D., Rt. #1, Box 161, Florence 54121	715-528-4464	144,000 / 1,500
10	B3			
11	B3	Lakewood Ranger D., Lakewood 54138 [on Hwy 32, 0.5 mi S of Lakewood]	715-276-6333	173,000 / 1,100
12	B3	Laona Ranger D., Rt. 1, Box 11 B, Laona 54541 [on Hwy 8]	715-674-4481	173,000 / 1,500
1	B4	**COE, Detroit District.** PO Box 1027, Detroit, MI 48231	313-226-6809	na / na
		Sturgeon Bay & Lake Michigan Ship C, Kewaunee Project Office, Kewaunee 54216	414-388-3720	na / na
		COE, St. Paul District, 180 E. Kellog Blvd., Rm. 1421, St. Paul, MN 55101	612-220-0325	na / na
2	B1	Eau Galle Flood Control Project, PO Box 190, Spring Valley 54767	715-778-5562	na / na
3	C1	Mississippi River Pool No. 4, 300 S. 1st St., La Crescent 55947 [SE of Nelson]	507-895-6341	na / na
4	C1	Mississippi River Pool No. 6, 300 S. 1st St., La Crescent 55947	507-895-6341	na / na
5	C2	Mississippi River Pool No. 8, 300 S. 1st St., La Crescent 55947 [S of La Crosse]	507-895-6341	na / na
6	D2	Mississippi River Pool No. 9, 300 S. 1st St., La Crescent 55947 [S of La Crosse]	507-895-6341	na / na
1	D3	**Horicon NWR.** W. 4279 Headquarters Rd., Mayville 53050	414-387-2658	20,976 / 850
2	C3	Leopold WMD, W. 4279 Headquarters Rd., Mayville 53050	414-387-2658	6,500 / na
3	C2	Necedah NWR, Star Route West, Box 386, Necedah 54646	608-565-2551	43,000 / 925
4	B1	St. Croix WMD, 146 W. 2nd St., New Richmond 54017 [W off Main St/Hwy 65 in town]	715-246-7784	5,000 / na
		Upper Miss. River NW & Fish Refuge, 51 East 4th St., Room 101, Winona, MN 55987	507-452-4232	200,000 / na
5	C2	Trempealeau NWR, Rt. #1, Box 1602, Trempealeau 54661 [office at refuge, 3 mi SW of Centerville, on W Prairie Rd]	608-539-2311	5,617 / 680
6	C2	La Crosse District, 425 State St., PO Box 415, La Crosse 54601 [Post Office Bldg, at 4th & State]	608-784-3910	40,000 / 635
1	A2	**Apostle Islands National Lakeshore.** Rt. #1, Box 4, Bayfield 54814 [Old Co Courthouse, cor. Washington & 4th Sts.]	715-779-3397	68,084 / na
2	D3	Ice Age National Scenic Trail, 700 Rayovac Drive, Suite 100, Madison 53711	608-264-5610	na / na
3	D3	Lewis & Clark Natl Historic Tra., 700 Rayovac Dr. Suite 100, Madison 53711	608-264-5610	na / na
4	D3	North Country Natl Scenic Trail, 700 Rayovac Dr. Suite 100, Madison 53711	608-264-5410	na / na
5	B1	St. Croix/Lower St. Croix NSR's (MN PO Box 708, St. Croix Falls 54024	715-483-3284	78,263 / 700-900
		BLM Eastern States Office. 7450 Boston Blvd., Springfield, VA 22153	703-444-1200	na / na
1	D3	BLM Milwaukee D strict Office, 310 W. Wisconsin Ave., Suite 225, Milwaukee 53203	414-297-4400	na / na
		DNR Bur. of Parks & Recreation. 101 S. Webster St., PO Box 7921, Madison 53707	608-266-2181	na / na
2	D3	Governor Dodge SP, near Dodgeville	608-935-2315	5,029 / na
3	C3	High Cliff SP, near Sherwood	414-989-1106	1,145 / na
4	C4	Kohler-Andrae SP, near Sheboygan	414-452-3457	842 / na
5	B2	Lake Wissota SP, near Chippewa Falls	414-382-4574	1,062 / na
6	B4	Newport SP, near Ellison Bay	414-854-2500	2,371 / na
7	A1	Pattison SP, near Superior	715-399-8073	1,374 / na
8	B4	Peninsula SP, Fish Creek	414-868-3258	3,763 / na
9	D3	Pike Lake SP, near Hartford	414-644-5248	678 / na
10	B4	Potawatomi SP, near Sturgeon Bay	414-743-8869	1,223 / na
1	D3	**DNR Bur. of Wildlife Management.** 101 S. Webster St., PO Box 7921, Madison 53707	608-266-1877	na / na
1	D4	**Schlitz Audubon Center,** 1111 E. Brown Deer Rd., Milwaukee 53217 [need reservations for guided tours]	414-352-2880	225 / na
	D3	**TNC Wisconsin Field Office.** 333 W. Mifflin St., Suite 107, Madison 53703	608-251-8140	na
2	D3	Bass Lake Preserve, contact Field Office, near Springstead	608-251-8140	840 / na
3	A2	Baxter's Hollow/R.D. & Linda Peters, contact Field Office, near Sauk City	608-251-8140	3,279 / na
4	D2	Black Earth Rettenmund Prairie, contact Field Office, W of Black Earth	608-251-8140	16 / na
5	D3			

FACILITIES, SERVICES, RECREATION OPPORTUNITIES & CONVENIENCES

★ INFORMATION CHART ★

AGENCY/MAP LEGEND ... INITIALS, MAP SYMBOLS, COLOR CODES

U.S. Forest Service Supervisor & Ranger Dist. Offices . NFS
U.S. Army Corps of Engineers Rec. Areas & Offices . COE
USFWS National Wildlife Refuges & Offices .... NWR
National Park Service Parks & other NPS Sites ...... NPS
Bureau of Land Management Rec. Areas & Offices ... BLM
Bureau of Reclamation Rec. Areas & Reg. Offices ... BOR
State Parks (also see State Agency notes) .... SPS
State Wildlife Areas (also see State Agency notes) .. SWA
Private Preserves, Nature Centers & Tribal Lands . .
The Wild Rivers —— and Wilderness Areas

Note: Refer to yellow block on page 7 (top right) for location name and address abbreviations.

INFORMATION CHART LEGEND - SYMBOLS & LETTER CODES

■ means **YES** & □ means **Yes with disability provisions**
sp means **spring**, March through May
S means **Summer**, June through August
F means **Fall**, September through November
W means **Winter**, December through February
T means **Two (2) or Three (3) Seasons**
A means **All Four (4) Seasons**
na means **Not Applicable or Not Available**
Note: empty or blank spaces in the chart mean **NO**
Note: If a symbol number has a star ★ that symbol is not shown on the map.

S#	MAP	LOCATION NAME (state initials if more than one) with ADDRESS and/or LOCATION DATA	TELEPHONE	ACRES / ELEVATION
6	D4	Chiwaukee Prairie Preserve, contact Field Office, in, Pleasant Prairie	608-251-8140	226 / na
7	C2	Decorah Mounds Preserve, contact Field Office, E of Galesville	608-251-8140	40 / na
8	A2	Flambeau River State Natural Area, contact Wisconsin DNR, N of Park Falls	608-251-8140	1,214 / na
9	D2	Hemlock Draw Preserve, contact Field Office, N of Leland	608-251-8140	630 / na
10	D3	Hoganson Preserve, contact Field Office, NW of Burlington	608-251-8140	219 / na
11	B3	Holmboe Conifer Forest Preserve, contact Field Office, near Rhinelander	608-251-8140	32 / na
12	D4	Kurtz Woods Preserve, contact Field Office, near Saukville	608-251-8140	31 / na
13	D2	Leopold Memorial Woods Preserve, contact Field Office, NW of Sauk City	608-251-8140	80 / na
14	B4	Mink River Estuary, contact Field Office, SE of Ellison Bay	608-251-8140	1,116 / na
15	C3	Muehl Springs Preserve, contact Field Office, N of Elkhart Lake	608-251-8140	75 / na
16	D3	Nelson Oak Woods Preserve, contact Field Office, S of Dousman	608-251-8140	114 / na
17	C3	Omro Prairie Preserve, contact Field Office, S of Omro	608-251-8140	5 / na
18	D2	Pan Hollow Preserve, contact Field Office, N of Denzer	608-251-8140	65 / na
*19	D2	Pine Hollow Preserve, contact Field Office, N of Denzer	608-251-8140	204 / na
20	C2	Sacia Memorial Ridge Preserve, contact Field Office, NW of Galesville	608-251-8140	30 / na
21	D3	Schluckebier Sand Prairie Preserve, contact Field Office, W of Prairie du Sac	608-251-8140	23 / na
*22	D2	South Bluff Oak Forest Preserve, contact Field Office, N of Sauk City	608-251-8140	140 / na
23	D2	Spring Green Preserve, contact Field Office, N of Spring Green	608-251-8140	260 / na
24	D3	Thousand's Rock Point Prairies, contact Field Office, S of Blue Mounds	608-251-8140	11 / na
25	D3	Waubesa Wetlands Preserve, contact Field Office, SE of Madison	608-251-8140	191 / na

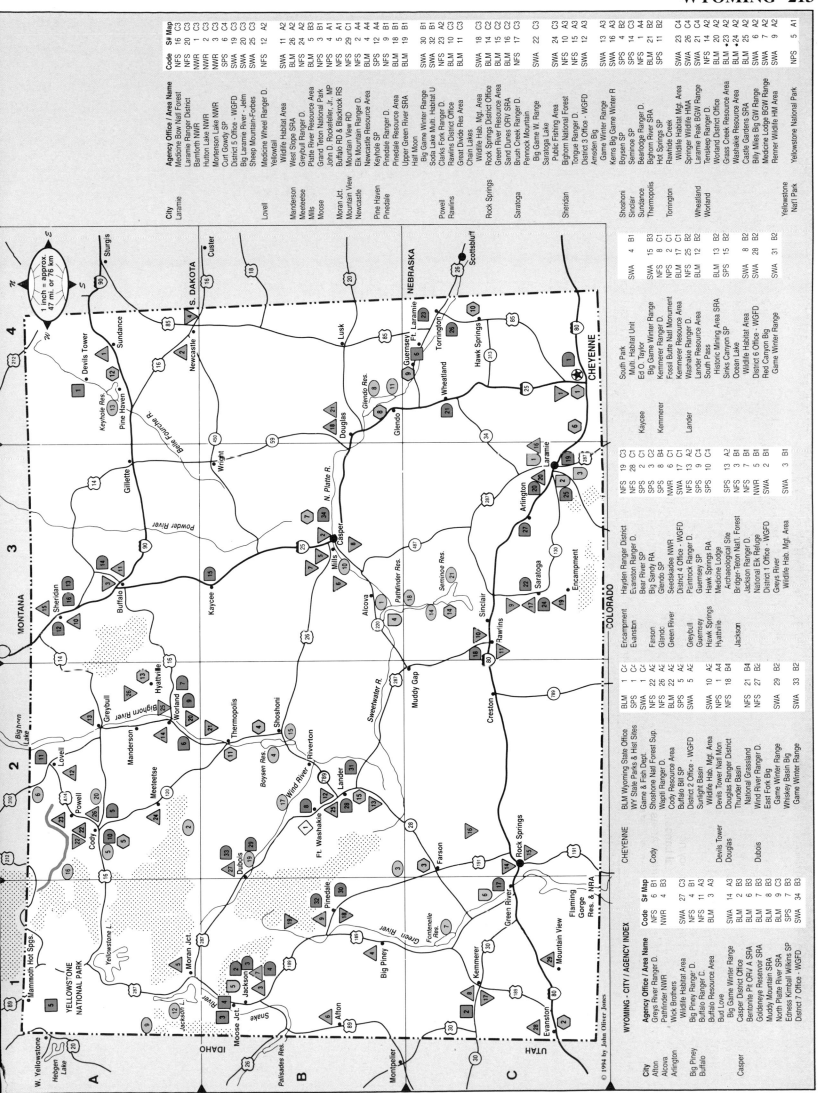

© 1984 by John Oliver Jones

WYOMING NOTES

Summary

There are 88 federal, 51 state, and 2 private recreation areas or local administrative offices covered in this state chapter. Of these, 101 appear in the Information Chart and 40 are covered in the notes. The special indexes feature 16 federally designated wilderness areas and wild rivers, and 68 agency published outdoor maps.

Federal Agencies

U.S. Forest Service

The Bridger-Teton National Forest is in the Intermountain Region (see Utah chapter - U.S. Forest Svc., Northern Region listing). The other national forests in Wyoming are in the Rocky Mountain Region (see Colorado chapter - U.S. Forest Svc., Rocky Mountain Region listing).

National Park Service

Additional NPS Location in Wyoming

Fort Laramie National Historic Site (833 acres)
(S# 6, map C4)
Fort Laramie, WY 82212   307-837-2221

Bureau of Reclamation Recreation Areas

Twenty-one recreation areas are listed here and symbolized on the Wyoming state map.

S#	MAP	LOCATION NAME
1	B3	Alcova Res.
2	A2	Anchor Res.
3	B2	Big Sandy Res.
4	B2	Boysen Res.
5	A2	Buffalo Bill Res.
6	A2	Deaver Res.
7	C1	Fontenelle Res.
8	B4	Glendo Res.
9	A1	Grassy Lake
10	B3	Gray Reef Res.
11	B4	Guernsey Res.
12	A1	Jackson Lake
13	A4	Keyhole Res.
14	C3	Kortes Res./Miracle Mile
15	A2	Lake Cameahwait
16	A1	Newton Lakes
17	B2	Ocean Lake
18	C3	Pathfinder Res.
19	B2	Pilot Butte Res.
20	A2	Ralston Res.
21	C3	Seminoe Res.

Wilderness/Wild River Index

Wilderness Areas

Absaroka-Beartooth Wilderness - 23,750 acres
Fitzpatrick Wilderness - 198,838 acres
North Absaroka Wilderness - 350,538 acres
Popo Agie Wilderness - 22,230 acres
Washakie Wilderness - 704,274 acres
Shoshone National Forest (S# 22, map A2)

Bridger Wilderness - 428,169 acres
Gros Ventre Wilderness - 287,000 acres
Teton Wilderness - 585,468 acres
Bridger-Teton National Forest Sup. (S# 3, map B1)

Cloud Peak Wilderness - 195,500 acres
Bighorn National Forest (S# 10, map A3)

Encampment River Wilderness - 10,400 acres
Huston Park Wilderness - 31,300 acres
Platte River Wilderness - 22,230 acres
Savage Run Wilderness - 14,940 acres
Medicine Bow National Forest (S# 16, map C3)

Jedediah Smith Wilderness - 116,535 acres
Winegar Hole Wilderness - 14,000 acres
Targhee National Forest (see Idaho S# 57, map D3).
also inquire at
Bridger-Teton National Forest Sup. (S# 3, map B1)

Wild Rivers

Clarks Fork of the Yellowstone River
Shoshone National Forest (S# 22, map A2)

Outdoor Map Index

National Park Service (USGS Maps)

Devils Tower National Monument [1949]
Scale: 1 inch = 0.1 mile (1 cm = 0.1 km)
Size: 22x23 inches (56x58 cm)

Grand Teton National Park [1968]
Scale: 1 inch = 1.0 mile (1 cm = 0.6 km)
Size: 34x50 inches (86x127 cm)

Yellowstone National Park (ID-MT-WY) [1961]
Scale: 1 inch = 2.0 miles (1 cm = 1.3 km)
Size: 38x41 inches (96x104 cm)

U.S. Forest Service Maps

See the Outdoor Map Index in Colorado for information on travel maps.

Bighorn National Forest

Scale: 1 inch = 0.5 mile (1 cm = 0.3 km)
Bridger-Teton NF-Kemmerr/B. Piney/Greys RDs [1966]
Bridger-Teton NF, Pinedale RD-Bridger Wilderness [1988]

Medicine Bow National Forest

Scale: 1 inch = 0.5 mile (1 cm = 0.3 km)
Shoshone National Forest, South Half
Scale: 1 inch = 0.5 mile (1 cm = 0.3 km)
Shoshone National Forest, North Half
Scale: 1 inch = 0.5 mile (1 cm = 0.3 km)
Thunder Basin National Grassland
Scale: 1 inch = 0.5 mile (1 cm = 0.3 km)

Bureau of Land Management Maps

In addition to the 1:100,000 series surface and surface/mineral maps featured on the Wyoming grid, a free fold-out BLM Recreation Guide of Wyoming is available at the state office in Cheyenne, and at local BLM offices in the state.

State of Wyoming Land Status and Mineral Status Maps are available in two sizes, 26x22-inch 1:1,000,000 scale and 54x44-inch 1:500,000 scale.

State Agencies

Wyoming State Parks & Historic Sites

A Wyoming State Parks Guide covering 11 parks and two recreation areas is available free. The guide describes each area, contains a locator map, and includes information on state parks and other areas, facilities, and activities. Wyoming parks, a recreation area, and an archaeological site are listed here and the symbols appear on the Guide map.

S#	MAP	AREA & LOCATION
2	C1	Bear River SP, Evanston
3	C2	Big Sandy RA, Farson
4	B2	Boysen SP, Shoshoni
5	A2	Buffalo Bill SP, Cody
6	C4	Curt Gowdy SP, Laramie
7	B3	Edness Kimball Wilkins SP, Casper
8	B4	Glendo SP, Glendo
9	C4	Guernsey SP, Guernsey
10	C4	Hawk Springs RA, Hawk Springs
11	B2	Hot Springs SP, Thermopolis
12	A4	Keyhole SP, Pine Haven
13	A2	Medicine Lodge Archaeo. Site, Hyattville

---

includes a vacation guide, official state road map, Wyoming facts, and travel tips: An accommodations directory lists camping and RV parks, hotels and motels, dude ranches, lodges and resorts, and bed-and-breakfast facilities. There is also a *Find Yourself in Wyoming* brochure available.

Private Organizations

Tribal Land Area in Wyoming

Shoshone and Arapahoe Tribes of the Wind River Indian Reservation - Fishing, camping, boating, hiking.
Arapahoe Business Council (S# 1, map B2)
PO Box 396
Fort Washakie, WY 82514   307-255-8394
or
Shoshone Tribal Council (same symbol as above)
PO Box 538
Fort Washakie, WY 82514   307-332-3532

No State Chamber of Commerce in Wyoming

There are local Chamber of Commerce offices throughout the state.

Wyoming State Forestry Division

1100 W. 22nd St.
Cheyenne, WY 82002   307-777-7586

There is no state forest recreation program in Wyoming.

Wyoming Game & Fish Dept. (GFD)

The department is developing a publication listing GFD properties. A monthly magazine, *Wyoming Wildlife*, is available by subscription for $8 per year. There is a quota on nonresident hunting licenses. Licensing, permit and harvest statistics are published annually.

Travel Commission

I-25 at College Dr.
Cheyenne, WY 82002-0660
1-800-225-5996
307-777-7777

A Wyoming Vacation Kit is available from this office. It

S#	MAP	NAME & LOCATION
14	C3	Seminoe SP, Sinclair
15	B2	Sinks Canyon SP, Lander

	111°	110°	109°	108°	107°	106°	105°	104° 45°
44°	Yellowstone National Park North	Cody	Powell	Burgess Junction	Sheridan	Recluse	Devil's Tower	Sundance
	Yellowstone National Park South	Carter Mountain	Basin	Worland	Buffalo	Gillette		
43°	Jackson Lake	The Ramshorn	Thermopolis	Nowater Creek	Kaycee	Reno Junction	Newcastle	
	Jackson	Gannett Peak	Riverton	Lysite	Midwest	Bill	Lance Creek	
	Afton	Pinedale	Lander	Rattlesnake Hills	Casper	Douglas	Lusk	
42°	Fontenelle Reservoir	Farson	South Pass	Bairoil	Shirley Basin	Laramie Peak	Torrington	
	Kemmerer	Rock Springs	Red Desert Basin	Rawlins	Medicine Bow	Rock River	Chugwater	
41°	Evanston	Firehole Canyon	Kinney Rim	Baggs	Saratoga	Laramie	Cheyenne	

BLM WYOMING

1:100,000 INTERMEDIATE SCALE MAPS
SURFACE & SURFACE / MINERAL SERIES

AGENCY/MAP LEGEND . . . INITIALS, MAP SYMBOLS, COLOR CODES

U.S. Forest Service Supervisor & Ranger Dist. Offices   NFS   61
U.S. Army Corps of Engineers Rec. Areas & Offices . . COE   31
USFWS National Wildlife Refuges & Offices . . . . . . NWR   40
National Park Service Parks & other NPS Sites . . . . . NPS   7
Bureau of Land Management Rec. Areas & Offices . . . BLM   26
Bureau of Reclamation Rec. Areas & Reg. Offices . . BOR   8
State Parks (also see State Agency notes) . . . . SPS   52
State Wildlife Areas (also see State Agency notes) . . . SWA   19
Private Preserves, Nature Centers & Tribal Lands . . . — 15
The Wild Rivers ⌒ and Wilderness Areas ░░░

Note: Refer to yellow block on page 7 (top right) for location name and address abbreviations.